...and China in the
north are disputed.

120°   140°   160°

Lena

SERIA

Sea of Okhotsk

Bering Sea

KAMCHATKA
PENINSULA

KURILES

Amur

HOKKAIDO

Lake Baikal   •Sapporo

Irkutsk•   •Harbin   •Vladivostok

Ulan Bator   Sea of Japan

MONGOLIAN   DEMOCRATIC
PEOPLE'S   PEOPLE'S
REPUBLIC   Shenyang•   REPUBLIC   HONSHU JAPAN
            (Mukden)   OF KOREA   •Tokyo

o b i   •P'yŏngyang   •Kyoto
            Beijing• Dalian• •Seoul   •Osaka   20°
            Tianjin• REPUBLIC OF   Pusan SHIKOKU
Huang   Qingdao• KOREA   •Kitakyushu
•Taiyuan   He   CHEJU   KYUSHU
         (Yellow River) Yellow Sea
N   •Xi'an A •Nanjing
I   Yangtze •Shanghai   East China Sea

•Chengdu   •OKINAWA   P a c i f i c
•Chongqing •Wuhan   RYŪKYŪ ISLANDS

                                    •Taipei   O c e a n
Irrawaddy Salween   TAIWAN

•Mandalay Guangzhou•
BURMA LAOS (Canton)   LUZON
            Hanoi• Hong Kong   Philippine Sea
•Vientiane   (Brit.)
Chiang Mai• Gulf of HAINAN
•Rangoon   Tonkin   South China   •Manila PHILIPPINES
THAILAND Mekong VIETNAM Sea   SAMAR
•Bangkok KAMPUCHEA   MINDORO
Andaman   (CAMBODIA)   PALAWAN
Sea   Phnom Penh• Ho Chi Minh City   Sula Sea MINDANAO
          Gulf of   (Saigon)
          Thailand
                    M A L A Y S I A SABAH   HALMAHERA
          MALAYA   BRUNEI
Kuala Lumpur•   Sibu• SARAWAK Sulawesi Sea
          SINGAPORE KALIMANTAN
                     BORNEO   SULAWESI   Banda Sea   Arafura Sea
SUMATRA   •Banjarmasin (CELEBES)
                  Java Sea   AUSTRALIA
         •Jakarta Surabaya• I N D O N E S I A Timor Sea
              Bandung• JAVA BALI LOMBOK   TIMOR
                              SUMBA FLORES

100°   120°   140°

0°

ENCYCLOPEDIA
OF
ASIAN
HISTORY

ENCYCLOPEDIA OF ASIAN HISTORY

Prepared under the auspices of
The Asia Society

Ainslie T. Embree

EDITOR IN CHIEF

Volume 4

Charles Scribner's Sons

New York

Collier Macmillan Publishers

London

Charles Scribner's Sons
Macmillan Publishing Company
866 Third Avenue, New York, N.Y. 10022

Collier Macmillan Canada, Inc.

Library of Congress Catalog Card Number: 87–9891

Library of Congress Cataloging-in-Publication Data

Encyclopedia of Asian History

Includes bibliographies and index
1. Asia—History—Dictionaries I. Embree, Ainslie Thomas
DS31.E53 1988   950   87-9891
ISBN 0–684–18619–5 (set)
ISBN 0–684–18901–1 (v. 4)

Acknowledgments of permissions to reproduce photographs
are gratefully made in a special listing in volume 4.

Printed in the United States of America

printing number

2 3 4 5 6 7 8 9 10

ENCYCLOPEDIA
OF
ASIAN
HISTORY

S

(CONTINUED)

SRI INDRADITYA (reigned c. 1240–1270), founder and first king of Sukhothai in Thailand. As Bang Klang Hao, chief of the small town of Bang Yang near Sukhothai, he joined with Pha Muang, lord of Rat, near Uttaradit, in conquering the main Cambodian garrison at Sukhothai and declaring Thai independence of Angkor's rule. He then took Pha Muang's Sanskrit title and ruled, slowly expanding his new kingdom. His sons Ban Muang (reigned c. 1270) and Ramkhamhaeng (reigned c. 1279–1298) succeeded him.

[See also Sukhothai and Angkor.]

A. B. Griswold and Prasert na Nagara, "The Inscription of Ramkamhaeng of Sukhodaya (1292 A. D.)," *Journal of the Siam Society* 59.2 (1971): 179–228. David K. Wyatt, *Thailand: A Short History* (1984).

DAVID K. WYATT

SRI KSETRA. *See* Prome.

SRI LANKA, a teardrop-shaped island of twenty-five thousand square miles, is separated from the southern tip of peninsular India by a narrow sea, which at its narrowest point is less than twenty-five miles wide. The island has a recorded history of over two thousand years, during which time Indian influences have had a considerable impact on its development. In religion, culture, and language it has nevertheless retained a distinct identity. From earliest times Sri Lanka has had a multiethnic society, with its main components, the one North Indian and "Indo-Aryan," the other South Indian and "Dravidian," sharing a common Indian origin. The majority group in ancient times (as today) were the Sinhalese, a people of Indo-Aryan origin who first came to the island from northern India about 500 BCE. The exact location of their original home in

India is still a matter of debate. We know little about the first Tamil settlements in the island. From about the third century BCE there appear to have been trade relations between Sri Lanka and South India and possibly also settlements of Tamils who came as traders and subsequently as invaders.

Anuradhapura and Polonnaruva Kingdoms. The ancient civilizations of Sri Lanka emerged and flourished in its dry zone, the extensive plain covering the northern half of the island and stretching southward along the east coast to a smaller southern plain. The earliest settlements were on the banks of the rivers of this region. Rice was the staple crop and its cultivation was dependent on the vagaries of the northeast monsoon. As the settlements spread there was need to insure against drought. By the first century BCE a solution had been devised—a highly sophisticated irrigation system remarkably attuned to the geological and geographical peculiarities of the island's dry zone.

The first five centuries of the common era form the most creative and dynamic phase in the development of this irrigation system. The construction of canals and channels exhibited an amazing knowledge of trigonometry, and the design of the tanks, a thorough grasp of hydraulic principles. By the third century BCE Sri Lankan engineers had discovered the principle of the valve tower or valve pit to regulate the escape of water from the "tanks," as these artificial lakes are called. Some of these tanks were manmade lakes of prodigious dimensions. Thus, the Kantalai tank attributed to King Mahasena (274–302 CE) covered an area of 4,560 acres. It was served by a canal 25 miles long and had a dam 40 to 50 feet high. [*See also* Mahasena.] The Kalavava tank constructed by King Dhatusena (460–478) was more sophisticated technologically: it covered an area of 7 square miles, had a dam 3.5 miles long and 36 to 58 feet high with a spill of

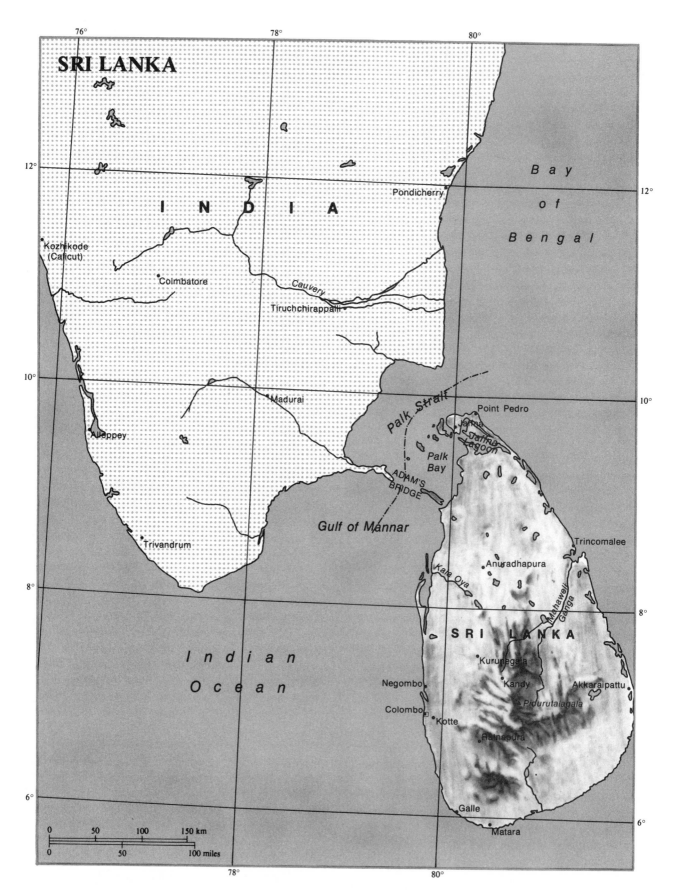

hammered granite. A canal that was 54 miles long and 40 feet wide linked it with the capital city of Anuradhapura. This canal was a marvelous engineering feat; the gradient in its first 17 miles was a mere 6 inches to a mile. [See also Anuradhapura.]

Two important cores of Sinhalese civilization developed in the north-central regions, and control of these gave the Sinhalese rulers the resources to extend their sway over the whole island. There was a third core in Rohana, the dry zone of the south and southeast, which was settled almost simultaneously with the north-central plain. [See Rohana.]

In the early years of the island's history the main centers of agricultural settlement were under the control of independent or semi-independent rulers. With the expansion of population an aspiration to an all-island sovereignty emerged. A fifteen-year campaign waged in the first century BCE by Dutthagamani, a Sinhalese prince from Rohana, against Elara, a Chola general from South India who had established himself at Anuradhapura in the north-central plains, dominates the later chapters of the *Mahavamsa*, a historical chronicle written about the sixth century CE, and is dramatized there as a decisive confrontation between the champion of the Sinhalese cause and a Dravidian invader. The campaign culminated in Dutthagamani's victory. His triumph over Elara was significant for being the first notable success of centripetalism over centrifugalism in Sri Lanka's history. Despite the growing increase in the power of the ruler at Anuradhapura, however, the problem of control over the outer provinces from the capital was just as intractable in Sri Lanka as it was in the Indian subcontinent. Periodically Rohana asserted its independence or served as a refuge for defeated Sinhalese kings or aspirants to the throne, but it was as frequently controlled by the former and seems never to have rivaled it in economic power or population resources. [See also Dutthagamani; Elara; and Mahavamsa.]

With its celebrated mastery of irrigation technology, Sri Lanka ranked, along with China and the Fertile Crescent of West Asia, among the greatest of the hydraulic civilizations of the ancient world. Its political system, however, was altogether less authoritarian and bureaucratic, and demonstrated much greater tolerance, if not acceptance, of local autonomy than in the other Asian hydraulic societies. Ancient Sri Lanka had many features of a feudal society. One such feature was the importance of land in social and economic relationships, although we have no evidence of a contractual bond between lord and vassal, or any evidence of peasants working

as serfs on the manor of the lord. These relationships were also determined by consideration of caste, which became in time the basis of social stratification. Castes had a service or occupational role as their primary distinguishing function, but in the Sinhalese system—in contrast to the Indian prototype—there was no religious sanction for caste, which therefore softened its impact considerably. [See also Slavery and Serfdom: Slavery and Serfdom in South Asia and Caste.]

The introduction of Buddhism to the island around the third century BCE in the reign of Devanampiya Tissa, a contemporary of the Indian ruler Ashoka, was as significant a landmark in the island's history as the development of irrigation technology. Buddhism became in time the state religion and the bedrock of Sinhalese culture and civilization. The intermingling of religion and national identity has always had a profound influence on the Sinhalese, a belief in a divine mission, as it were, of a "chosen" people destined to protect and preserve Buddhism in their island home. [See also Devanampiya Tissa and Buddhism: An Overview.]

The most striking feature of Buddhist Sri Lanka was the stupa, or *chetiya*, which came to the island from northern India. These usually enshrined relics of the Buddha and the more celebrated *illuminati* of early Buddhism. Generally solid hemispherical domes, these stupas dominated the skyline of Anuradhapura and were awe-inspiring evidence of the state's commitment to Buddhism and to the wealth at its command. The scale of comparison is with the largest similar monuments in other parts of the world. The Abhayagiri, and the Jethavana, taller than the third pyramid at Giza in Egypt, were the wonders of their time. The Jethavana was, very likely, the largest monument in the Buddhist world. [See also Stupa.]

The two cities of Anuradhapura and Polonnaruva are testimony to the wealth and refinement of Sri Lanka's rulers of old. Anuradhapura was a sprawling city, and at the height of its glory was one of the great cities of ancient South Asia. Polonnaruva, the capital in the eleventh century, was more compact but contained within its boundaries all the characteristic features of a capital of ancient Sri Lanka: tanks, stupas, palaces, and parks, along with their architectural and sculptural embellishments. It too was a gracious cosmopolitan city.

The flourishing irrigation civilization of Sri Lanka's northern plain was vulnerable to invasions from South India. These began as early as the third century BCE but increased in frequency and intensity after the sixth century CE. The Sinhalese contributed to their own discomfiture by calling in Tamil assistance in settling disputed successions and dynastic squabbles. The Kasyapa episode of the fifth century CE is the first and most memorable illustration of this. Having killed his father, Dhatusena, the builder of the Kalavava, Kasyapa usurped the throne and ruled for eighteen years. Kasyapa was a most remarkable man. He chose a rock fortress—Sigiriya—as his capital, and converted this forbidding granite outcrop into a royal residence of exquisite taste, a palace perched on top of the rock, with ornamental gardens at the base, and large areas of the rock covered with frescoes. [*See also* Sigiriya.] His brother Mugallan, Dhatusena's rightful heir, returned from India with an avenging army of Indian mercenaries. This latter act proved to be more significant, historically, than his victory over Kasyapa, for in time South Indian auxiliaries became a vitally important element in the armies of Sinhalese rulers and an unpredictable, turbulent group that was often a threat to political stability. They were also the nucleus of a powerful Tamil influence in the court.

In the fifth and sixth centuries CE a new factor of instability was introduced into the politics of Sri Lanka with the rise of three Hindu states in South India, the Pandyas, the Pallavas, and the Cholas. Sri Lanka was drawn into conflicts among them and became an integral element in the power politics of South India while Tamil settlements in the island became sources of support for South Indian invaders. [*See also* Pandya Dynasty *and* Pallava Dynasty.]

In the middle of the ninth century the Sinhalese intervened in South India with disastrous consequences for themselves in provoking the hostility of the rising power of the Cholas. Under Rajaraja (985–1018) the Cholas, having conquered all of South India, extended their control to Sri Lanka. For seventy-five years Sri Lanka was ruled as a province of the Chola empire. [*See also* Chola Dynasty.]

The Cholas established their capital at Polonnaruva in the northeastern part of the dry zone, nearer the Mahavali River, a shift determined by reasons of security. They were eventually driven out of Sri Lanka in 1070 by Vijayabahu I, with Rohana serving as his base of operations. [*See* Vijayabahu I.] Vijayabahu regained control of Anuradhapura and followed the Cholas in retaining Polonnaruva as the capital. During his reign of forty years the country recovered from the ravages of the Chola occupation. But he left a disputed succession, and another period of extensive civil war followed until stability was restored by Parakramabahu I, who ruled at Polonnaruva from 1153 to 1186. He unified Sri Lanka

and built a remarkable series of irrigation works and public and religious monuments. [*See* Parakramabahu I.] The Parakrama Samudra ("Sea of Parakrama"), with a bund nearly nine miles long at an average height of forty feet, was the greatest of the irrigation works of ancient Sri Lanka.

Parakramabahu's reign, despite its revival of ancient grandeur, was the Indian summer of Sinhalese greatness. After him there was a brief decade of order and stability under Nissanka Malla (r. 1187–1196) during which Polonnaruva reached the peak of its development as a capital city. Its architectural features rivalled those of Anuradhapura. But renewed dissension and dynastic disputes among the Sinhalese attracted South Indian invasions, which culminated in a devastating campaign of pillage under Magha of Kalinga. These invasions from India, and the apocalyptic destruction they wrought, have contributed greatly to creating an image of the Tamils as the implacable historical foe of Sri Lanka and the Sinhalese. [*See also* Tamil Nadu.]

The Drift to the Southwest. The collapse of the irrigation civilizations of Sri Lanka's dry zone is one of the great landmarks in its history. The four centuries from about 1200 to 1600 constitute a period of decline in which we see three main trends: first and most important, the drift of the Sinhalese kingdoms to the southwest; the establishment of a Tamil kingdom in the north; and the emergence of a separate political entity in the central hills, the Kandyan kingdom. There was also a fundamental change in the economic organization and basis of state revenues, from an overwhelming dependence on irrigation-based rice cultivation to rain-fed agriculture, while in the scale of the rulers' priorities, trade rose higher than ever before, with cinnamon as one of the main export commodities. This was especially so in the principal Sinhalese kingdom.

Muslim settlers in the island largely controlled its export trade. As this trade grew in importance they settled in larger numbers in the coastal areas and in the ports. Gradually they penetrated to the interior.

In the thirteenth century a Tamil kingdom was established with the Jaffna Peninsula as its core. [*See also* Jaffna.] As Sinhalese power declined, the Tamils advanced southward and by the middle of the fourteenth century they seemed poised for the conquest of the rest of the island. They were thwarted in this when the Sinhalese kingdom, with its capital at Kotte near Colombo, at last claimed a ruler resourceful and dynamic enough to resist their pressure. This was Parakramabahu VI (r. 1412–1467), the last Sinhalese ruler to bring the whole island under his rule. He overran Jaffna in 1450.

But Sinhalese control over the north was not maintained for long after his death, and Jaffna reasserted its independence when the politics of Kotte returned to its usual state of turmoil, instability, and dissension. [See also Kotte.]

Sri Lanka under Western Rule. Western influence on the island began in the sixteenth century with the Portugese intrusion into the affairs of its littoral. They met with prolonged opposition from Sinhalese and, to a lesser extent, Tamil rulers. By 1600 the Portuguese were well in control in parts of the coastal regions. Within sixty years, however, they were displaced, with the assistance of the Sinhalese, by the Dutch, who in turn were dislodged by the British at the end of the eighteenth century.

While the Portuguese and, later, the Dutch controlled parts of the littoral, the interior and parts of the coast remained under the Kandyan kings who defeated several invading armies despatched by the Portuguese and the Dutch. The survival of this independent Sinhalese kingdom was an important factor in the emergence of a distinction among the Sinhalese themselves between those of the southwest littoral—the low-country Sinhalese—and the Kandyans of the interior. The Portuguese conquered the Jaffna kingdom. This northern region never recovered its independence but became a unit of a colonial administrative structure under the Portuguese and under the Dutch and British thereafter.

The Portuguese ruled Sri Lanka's maritime regions for a much shorter period than the Dutch, but with a more enduring influence. Christianity was introduced in all its sectarian variety by or under the aegis of these Western powers. Roman Catholicism, Calvinism, and Anglicanism, in turn, held a special relationship with the ruling power, with converts to the orthodox version of Christianity in vogue enjoying a privileged status, especially under the Portuguese and the Dutch. Conversions to Roman Catholicism under Portuguese rule stood the test of harassment under the Dutch and the indifference of the British. From the 1830s onward Roman Catholics have constituted nine-tenths of the Christian community in the island.

The impact of the Portuguese and Dutch on the island's economy was just as significant. They monopolized the export trade in cinnamon, and the profits from it became the mainstay of their revenues. This marked the beginning of a fundamental change in the island's economy, the dominance of the export sector over the traditional sources of state revenue.

The first phase in the British conquest of Sri Lanka began in 1795–1796, when they captured the Dutch possessions there. By 1815 they controlled the Kandyan kingdom as well, and their hold on Sri Lanka was consolidated when they crushed the great Kandyan rebellion of 1817–1818.

Within a generation there was a remarkable transformation of Sri Lanka's economy with the success of coffee as a plantation crop. The coffee industry reached its peak in the 1870s and then succumbed to a virulent leaf disease. Nevertheless, plantation agriculture demonstrated an extraordinary resilience over the three decades from 1880 to 1910 when a still-prevailing pattern in the island's economy was established: an overwhelming dominance of three crops—tea, rubber, and coconuts. [See also Tea in India and Sri Lanka.] At that time—and until independence and for some time thereafter—British interests were dominant in tea and strong in rubber but much less so in regard to coconuts. Shipping, banks, insurance, and the import-export trade were mainly if not entirely controlled by British commercial interests. Labor on the coffee plantations was provided mainly by immigrant Indians. A significant change in the pattern of immigration occurred when tea and rubber replaced coffee, for unlike coffee these required a permanent and resident labor force. South India provided the labor, once more, no longer as seasonal migrants but as permanent or semipermanent residents. From this change emerged Sri Lanka's Indian problem in its modern form.

One far-reaching effect of the development of a capitalist economy on the foundation of plantation agriculture and trade was the growth of a new elite, largely an indigenous capitalist class. The traditional elite, especially in the low country, was absorbed into this expanding new elite but was soon left far behind in the two most important channels of social mobility: the acquisition of a Western education and participation in capitalist enterprise.

The growth of plantations was accompanied by a neglect of traditional agriculture. This was despite the sustained, if not unbroken, effort made in the second half of the nineteenth century to rehabilitate the dry zone through a revival of the ancient irrigation works there.

The British initially encouraged change and reform in Sri Lankan society. But by the last quarter of the nineteenth century they became much more sympathetic to the forces of tradition and conservatism in the island. There was, for instance, a notable reversal of policy on Buddhism, from neglect and studied indifference to judicious patronage, and an emphasis on the state's neutrality in religious affairs. The attitude to the traditional elite changed too, from suspicion and mistrust to a policy of aristocratic resuscitation, which continued into the first two decades of the twentieth century. Both changes stemmed from an effort to check the more vocal and assertive sections of the elite who were seeking a share of political power in the colony.

Incipient nationalist sentiment was religious (in the main, Buddhist) in outlook and content. Political overtones in it were perceptible from the beginning in the appeal to the glories of the past in contrast to the contemporary reality of foreign domination. Nevertheless, even among the most ardent nationalists a belief in the permanence of British rule remained unshaken.

In the first two decades of the twentieth century the colonial administration purposefully resisted pressure from a growing reform movement whose keynotes were restraint and moderation. The 1920s, on the other hand, were characterized by bolder initiatives in politics, not the least significant of which was a heightening of working class activity and trade unionism, particularly in Colombo and its suburbs. A more intractable problem was the breakdown of the comparative harmony of interests and outlook that had characterized relations between the Sinhalese and Tamil politicians in the first two decades of the twentieth century, with minority groups led by the Tamils increasingly anxious to protect their interests against the dominant Sinhalese Buddhist majority.

The constitutional reforms introduced in 1931 on the recommendations of the Donoughmore Commission marked the first phase in self-government. But more far-reaching in its impact was the introduction, on the initiative of the Donoughmore commissioners, of universal suffrage. [See also Donoughmore Constitution.] Sri Lanka was the first Asian colony of the British empire to enjoy that privilege. The first general election under universal suffrage was held in 1931, only two years later than Britain's own. In Britain, extension of the franchise followed upon the expansion of educational opportunities and the growth of political awareness; in Sri Lanka the process was reversed.

Universal suffrage had an immediate impact on the electorate in the resurgence of nationalism linked with Buddhist revivalism and its associated cultural heritage. Again, although the massive rural vote swamped the working class vote, universal suffrage strengthened working class movements and opened the way for them to play an independent role in politics. By the early 1930s Marxists had established themselves in the leadership of the indigenous working class movement. (The Indian plantation workers, by far the larger segment of the working class, had their own leadership.) Universal suffrage also stimulated a broad impulse toward social welfare, especially in the period 1936 to 1947. These included a program of restoring the irrigation works of the dry zone and the settlement of peasant "colonists" there. This return to the heartland of the irrigation civilizations of old is associated with the dynamism and vision of Don Stephen Senanayake as Minister of Agriculture and Lands. There were three other areas of importance in this trend towards social welfare: increased expenditure on education, health, and food subsidies. Together, these formed the basis of Sri Lanka's mini-welfare state. [See also Senanayake, Don Stephen.]

The final phase in the transfer of power began under the leadership of Senanayake, who was to become the country's first prime minister. In response to the agitation in Sri Lanka the British government appointed the Soulbury Commission in 1944 to examine the constitutional problem. [See also Soulbury Commission.] The constitution that emerged from their deliberations was based substantially on one drafted for Senanayake in 1944 by his advisers. It gave the island internal self-government while retaining some imperial safeguards in defense and external affairs, but Sri Lanka's leaders pressed, successfully, for the removal of these restrictions, and the island was granted independence on 4 February 1948. The transfer of power was smooth and peaceful in contrast to the cognate process in the Indian subcontinent and Burma.

Sri Lanka since Independence. Sri Lanka provides an unusual example of a thriving democracy in a Third World situation. The electorate is largely literate and its level of politicization is exceptionally high. These factors, in combination with a natural political establishment, have ensured the survival of a modern democratic system whose origins go back to the Donoughmore Constitution. The continuation and strengthening of the social welfare measures discussed earlier have had a great deal to do with it. This welfare policy to which all Sri Lankan governments since independence have been committed, has narrowed the gap between rich and poor much more effectively than in most Asian and African states.

Sri Lankan democracy has confronted and surmounted some of the most difficult problems imaginable: ethnic and religious tensions; inflationary pressures; massive unemployment in a society where education is much more widespread and the rate of literacy higher than in almost every other Third World country; and for much of the 1970s and 1980s, a stagnant economy.

The country owes much to the impressive start in nation-building and national regeneration given by its first prime minister, D. S. Senanayake. The guiding principles of his mature statecraft were a deliberate attempt to soften the dominance of the Sinhalese Buddhist majority (the Sinhalese were then over 70 percent of the population, and the Buddhists over 67 percent) in the Sri Lanka polity by establishing a consensus of moderate political forces, a respect for pluralism, and a refusal to mix state power and politics with religion.

These policies bore immediate fruit in enabling his party, the United National Party (UNP) to stabilize its position in country, and its hold on Parliament. [See also United National Party.] Moreover, the national coffers had quite adequate resources to sustain the welfare measures to which the country had grown accustomed. The achievement of self-sufficiency in rice and subsidiary foodstuffs became a major objective. The principal means of achieving this was the rapid development of the dry zone. One of the noteworthy achievements of his government was the massive Gal-Oya multipurpose irrigation scheme. The tank constructed there was larger than the Parakrama Samudra, and appropriately enough it was named the Senanayake Samudra. One discerns in this a search for inspiration from the past and from the traditional sources of legitimacy for Sri Lanka's rulers. But there was no great stress on far-reaching changes in the economic structure inherited from the British. The result was that in economic affairs as in the political realm there was an affirmation of the status quo.

The main opposition to Senanayake's regime came from the Marxist left, which, however, was too sharply divided ideologically as well as on personal issues to offer an effective challenge. Senanayake died in March 1952 and was succeeded by his son Dudley, who at age forty-one won a massive electoral victory in May of the same year. This victory appeared to stabilize the political forces and the political establishment his father had nurtured. [See also Senanayake, Dudley Shelton.] Over the next two years, however, factionalism within the government and a faltering economy precipitated a change of leadership within the government. The Marxist left skillfully exploited these difficulties of the new government, but a more formidable threat came from S. W. R. D. Bandaranaike, a potential

successor to the elder Senanayake, who had resigned his cabinet posts and crossed over to the opposition in July 1951. Although defeated soundly in 1952, Bandaranaike's Sri Lanka Freedom Party (SLFP) was much better equipped than the Marxists to exploit the transformation of the political scene in the mid-1950s, which occurred through a combination of religious, cultural, and linguistic issues. Bandaranaike successfully channelled the discontent that these issues signified into a campaign that swept the UNP out of office at the general election held in 1956. [See Bandaranaike, Solomon West Ridgeway Dias and Sri Lanka Freedom Party.]

Bandaranaike's victory represented the triumph of a more democratic and populist nationalism than that associated with the elder Senanayake, but one that was also fundamentally divisive because it was unabashedly Sinhalese and Buddhist in content. The 2,500th anniversary of the death of the Buddha was marked in 1956, and an intense religious fervor became the catalyst of political change and social and economic reform. The years 1955 and 1956 also marked the beginning of three decades of ethnic and linguistic tensions, not to mention religious strife, which erupted occasionally into fearsome race riots.

Bandaranaike's brief administration (1956–1959) saw the initiation of several social and economic reforms, but while the effects of these were not always beneficial to the poor and disadvantaged, they served the purpose of giving the common people a sense of dignity and fortifying their self-respect. Like most governments of reform and reconstruction, Bandaranaike's attracted much opposition, both within his administration and outside it. Eventually, tensions within his own party culminated in his assassination in September 1959. After a few months of drift and regrouping his party emerged more powerful than before under his widow Sirimavo Bandaranaike, who was to dominate the island's politics for nearly two decades. The Bandaranaikes established a new equilibrium of forces within the country, to which their supporters and associates as well as their opponents had to accommodate themselves. The chief feature of the new balance of forces was the acceptance of the predominance of the Sinhalese Buddhists within the Sri Lanka polity, and a sharp decline in status of the ethnic and religious minorities. [See also Bandaranaike, Sirimavo Ratwatte Dias.]

The dominance of the SLFP in national politics up to 1977 resulted in a corresponding decline in the electoral fortunes of the Marxist groups. In joining the SLFP in an electoral alliance (in 1956 and in 1960) and later in a coalition (1964–1975 and 1976), the Marxists sought to protect what was left of the mass support they had once enjoyed. They were compelled, by the very nature of their alliance with the SLFP, to accept the latter's stand on language and religion, and eventually on minority rights. But they had the satisfaction of seeing large and important sectors of the economy brought under state control to the point where, after the nationalization of the plantations in 1972 and 1975, the state sector had achieved a position of overwhelming dominance in the economy. [See also Communism: Communist Parties in South Asia.]

The strength of these forces and the narrowness of the limits within which changes could be effected in the new system were demonstrated most starkly in the years 1965–1970, when Dudley Senanayake's UNP-dominated coalition was in power. The expansion of state control over the economy was checked but not reversed. Nor was it possible to implement some of the key legislative and administrative measures that would have made his policy of ethnic and religious reconciliation effective. While its economic policies, especially with respect to food production, achieved substantial success, the government's popularity was eroded by inflation and its failure to solve the problems imposed by unemployment and especially the rising expectations of educated youth.

In 1970 Mrs. Bandaranaike led a center-left coalition of forces to another electoral triumph. A few months after their victory this coalition faced a serious political threat, an insurrection led by the youthful and ultraleft Janatha Vimukti Peramuna (JVP). The insurrection jolted the government but failed to dislodge it. Nevertheless, it had a marked influence on future developments, hastening proceedings begun in 1970 for an autochthonous constitution for Sri Lanka and giving impetus to radical economic and social reforms, the most far-reaching of which was the nationalization of the plantations. From 1972 to 1975 state control over trade and industry was accelerated and reached its high watermark.

The adoption of the new constitution gave rise to a new phase of communal antagonism in the island, in an increasing alienation of the Tamils and a transformation of their political aspirations from federalism to separatism. This separatist agitation, in combination with terrorism, has bedeviled ethnic relations in the island since the mid-1970s, and has led to serious ethnic disturbances on several occasions: 1977, 1981, and 1983.

The United Front coalition forged in the early 1970s broke up in stages; 1975 proved decisive to its fate and the process was completed by early 1977. The purportedly socialist measures of this "united front" did little to improve the position of the poor, while its attempted restructuring of the economy did nothing to stimulate economic growth or check inflationary pressures. Inevitably, this resulted in a sharp and consistent decline in public support for the government.

The election of 1977 was as significant an electoral landmark as that of 1956, marking as it did not merely a change of government but a change of regime. Under the leadership of J. R. Jayawardene a revitalized UNP government set about introducing far-reaching changes in every sphere of activity. [See Jayawardene, Junius Richard.] It included a presidential form of government under a new constitution that offered the minorities a more secure position in the Sri Lanka polity than any previous one. Far-reaching economic reforms have been introduced, reducing state controls and restrictions in the economy and providing greater incentives to the private sector. The rate of economic growth has improved substantially since 1977 and has remained at a uniformly high level. The key features of its policies include an Export Processing Zone to the north of Colombo and an acceleration of the massive multipurpose irrigation project based on the water resources of the Mahaveli River, the greatest and most complex irrigation enterprise in the country's history. Improved economic conditions explain to a large extent the government's successive political triumphs: a victory at every election held since it came to power, culminating in the victory of President Jayawardene at the first presidential elections of October 1982; the first head of government in Sri Lanka to win two consecutive terms of office; and the first time since 1952 that a government was returned to power at a general election. Jayawardene then held a referendum on 22 December 1982 to ask the people to extend the life of the Parliament elected in 1977 by a period of six years, beginning in August 1983. The electorate voted in support of this by a large majority, thus effectively guaranteeing the UNP its huge majority in Parliament until 1990.

By the middle of 1983 the UNP had consolidated its hold on the electorate; its opponents had been defeated in four sets of elections held at a national level between October 1982 and June 1983. But it confronted the problems posed by separatism and terrorism in the north of the island, and for the moment a solution to these had eluded even the ingenuity of J. R. Jayawardene.

[See also Sinhala; Tamils in Sri Lanka; Muslims in Sri Lanka; Kandy; and Colebrooke-Cameron Reforms.]

S. Arasaratnam, Ceylon (1964). R. L. Brohier, Ancient Irrigation Works in Ceylon, 3 vols. (1933). Colvin R. de Silva, Ceylon Under the British Occupation, 1795–1932, 2 vols. (1941–1942). K. M. de Silva, ed., History of Ceylon, vol. 3 (1973). K. M. de Silva, Sri Lanka, A Survey (1976) and A History of Sri Lanka (1981). T. Fernando and R. N. Kearney, Modern Sri Lanka: A Society in Transition (1978). Wilhelm Geiger, Culture of Ceylon in Medieval Times, edited by Heinz Bechert (1964). J. Jupp, Sri Lanka, Third World Democracy (1978). R. N. Kearney, The Politics of Sri Lanka (1973). E. F. C. Ludowyk, The Story of Ceylon (1962) and The Modern History of Ceylon (1966). G. C. Mendis, Early History of Ceylon (1932). S. Paranavitana, ed., History of Ceylon, vol. 1, parts 1 and 2 (1959–1960). Walpola Rahula, The History of Buddhism in Ceylon (1956). A. J. Wilson, Politics of Sri Lanka, 1947–1979 (1979). W. H. Wriggins, Ceylon: The Dilemmas of a New Nation (1960).   K. M. DE SILVA

SRI LANKA FREEDOM PARTY. Formed in 1951 by S. W. R. D. Bandaranaike, the party has alternated with the United National Party as the governing party of Sri Lanka, forming the government between July 1960 and 1965 and the ruling majority of the Mahajana Eksath Peramuna and the United Front, which came into power in 1956 and 1970, respectively. Sinhalese Buddhist populism has formed the core of its support, but its programs have incorporated socialist goals, giving it a center-left image. Its ability to enter into electoral agreements with the Marxists, with whom it competed for the anti-United National Party vote, has been decisive in its electoral fortunes.

[See also Bandaranaike, Solomon West Ridgeway Dias and United National Party.]

A. J. Wilson, Politics of Sri Lanka, 1947–1979 (1979).
VIJAYA SAMARAWEERA

SRINAGAR. For centuries, the cultural and political center of Kashmir has been the city of Srinagar. Some scholars maintain that the city was laid by Ashoka (third century BCE), while others date it to the time of the king Pravarasena, late in the sixth century. Built on the banks of the Jhelum River, Srinagar is linked by ten (for a long time and until recently seven) bridges, and bears witness to the long and checkered history of Kashmir. Prehistoric Neolithic sites and the remains of Buddhist monasteries have been excavated near the city, which is overlooked by a Shiva temple atop one hill and a Mughal fort atop another. A mosque in the heart of the city commemorates Sayyid Ali Hamdani, and nearby is the tomb of the mother of Zain ud-Abidin, who ruled Kashmir from 1423 to 1473. There are Hindu temples, Sikh gurdwaras, and Christian churches in the city. The most famous of the city's Mughal gardens are the Shalimar, Nishat, and Chashma-Shahi, all three overlooking the Dal lake. Shawl and carpet weaving, needlework, embroidery, papier-mâché work, wood carving—all traditional arts and crafts—are carried on mostly inside homes, which have a distinctive architecture. Modern buildings include a university, medical and engineering colleges, hospitals, and hotels. Srinagar also has one of the holiest Muslim shrines of the world at Hazratbal, on the bank of Nagin Lake. Recently rebuilt in white marble, this shrine boasts a holy relic of the prophet Muhammad (a hair from his face). A short distance from it is the tomb of Sheikh Abdullah, considered the creator of modern Kashmir.

[See also Kashmir and Abdullah, Muhammad.]
T. N. MADAN

SRIVIJAYA. Under the Srivijaya maritime state, which dominated Strait of Melaka (Malacca) commerce from the late seventh until the early eleventh century, a pattern of riverine system statecraft emerged, built on alliances with Malay coastal populations and balanced by an expanding inland power base. In the eyes of the Chinese, Srivijaya was the perfect trade partner. It was able to keep goods moving into South China ports by servicing vessels voyaging through the Southeast Asian archipelago. Srivijaya's ports were used as centers of exchange for those ships traveling over but one segment of the international maritime route or as a port of call for ships awaiting the appropriate monsoon winds to take them to their destination. Srivijaya also successfully protected the Southeast Asian zone of the international commercial route from piracy. In recognition of Srivijaya's power, the Chinese granted the maritime state preferred trade status, suggesting that those who used Srivijaya's ports were given preferential treatment when entering Chinese ports. O. W. Wolters has argued that this Chinese connection was critical to Srivijaya's prosperity and that Srivijaya's power was dependent upon the fluctuations of the Chinese economy. When trade with

China's ports was prosperous, Srivijaya thrived. But when China's ports periodically closed, the economic repercussions were disastrous to Srivijaya's political authority. With declining trade revenues, Srivijaya was unable to maintain the loyalty of its seafarers, who shifted their energies to open piracy.

The political center of the Srivijaya state was at Palembang, a downriver port on the edge of the southeastern Sumatra hinterland, which served as a locus for economic redistributions, fulfilling roles both as a trade entrepôt and as the central treasury for a series of ports. The capital's political and economic authority depended on physical force or alliance relationships, symbolized by an oath administered to state subordinates, to establish and maintain its political and economic hegemony over its subject populations—upriver tribesmen and coastal sea nomads. While a royal navy of sea nomads maintained the capital's position as the dominant port on the Sumatra coast, a network of alliances with its hinterland tribesmen allowed a flow of goods from the interior to the ports, giving Srivijaya its economic and political strength.

There are three primary sources for the study of Srivijaya. Ninth- through eleventh-century Arab geographers provide extremely generalized accounts of the Srivijaya realm, which they knew as the domain of the Lord of the Mountain and Maharaja of the Isles, a land of immense wealth. Chinese dynastic records report diplomatic and economic contact between China and Srivijaya and provide the majority of the surviving evidence of Srivijaya's history after the seventh century. Buddhist pilgrims who traveled from China to Buddhism's Indian homeland often stopped to study in Srivijaya monasteries, and they have left accounts of their experiences.

The inscriptions left by the Srivijaya state, most of which have come from the seventh-century period, are the third major source. The majority of these have been recovered in the Palembang area. The earliest of the dated Old Malay inscriptions (683–684) report the establishment of Srivijaya's sovereignty by the military conquest of the neighboring Batang Hari River system and its urban center at Jambi. In these inscriptions the sovereign expressed his desire that the merit gained by his victory and all his other good works should be shared with all his subjects and should bring them closer to enlightenment. Another seventh-century inscription collected at Telaga Batu, on the northern edge of present-day Palembang, records a water oath of service that was sworn by the ruler's subordinates over a ceremonial stone protected by seven carved serpent heads, representing the seven-headed *naga* that protected the Lord Buddha in Indian tradition. Edited versions of this inscription have been found at Kotakapur on the island of Bangka off the east coast of Sumatra, Karangbrahi on the Batang Hari river system (upriver from present-day Jambi), and Palas Pasemah on the southeast Sumatra cost adjacent to the Sunda Strait, all areas that were linked to the Srivijaya center by the inscriptions' oath.

In addition to these other late seventh-century records, there are two inscriptions from Nakhon Si Thammarat on the east coast of the Malay Peninsula. One, dated 775, records the dedication of a Buddhist monastery by the Srivijaya monarch. On the reverse side of this dated inscription is a reference to the Sailendra line of kings, who ruled Srivijaya during the late ninth century, after they had lost their authority in Java.

The Srivijaya monarch drew upon the local belief that chiefs possessed magical qualities. Traditionally a chief's use of magic influenced his followers' prosperity in this lifetime as well as in the next. The Telaga Batu inscription stresses this locally defined power and also associates the Srivijaya monarch with a higher level of magic—that derived from Buddhism—to further reinforce his stature. Buddhism gave the king not only new magic but also international prestige. The royal capital of Srivijaya became a major pilgrimage center and the Srivijaya ruler and his representatives became participants in Buddhism's international intellectual dialogue of the seventh- through tenth-century era. His prowess was well publicized (e.g., in the Srivijaya inscriptions noted above) and was intended to impress his followers—to awe them into submission. The emphasis on magically derived legitimacy was critical to ensure that the king could maintain his authority during periods marked by drops in port activity caused by regular fluctuations in the volume of international trade, often the consequence of disorders on either end of the trade route.

The Srivijayan era of economic hegemony came to an abrupt close in 1025, when the South Indian Chola dynasty successfully attacked the Melaka region's ports and shattered Srivijaya's authority over the strait. This raid began a two-century restructuring of the patterns of Southeast Asian maritime trade. Srivijaya never regained its old prosperity and control after the Chola raid. By 1079–1082, its capital had moved from Palembang to the central Sumatra port of Jambi. Java had become a dominant port area, and the ports of northern Sumatra and the Malay Peninsula were beginning to function independently as alternative centers. Yet in its description of the rise of Melaka in the fourteenth and fifteenth centuries, the seventeenth-century *Sejarah Melayu,* the court chronicle of Melaka's history, purposely connects Melaka genealogies to Srivijaya-Palembang and not to Srivijaya-Jambi. This substantiates the legacy of Srivijaya in Malay history—and the success of the Palembang monarchs in establishing a political network within the context of Malay-Sumatran culture. Despite its political demise, Srivijaya-Palembang remained a viable symbol of Malay unity and common prosperity and was the standard for all Malay riverine states that followed.

[*See also* Palembang; Sumatra; *and* Jambi.]

Kenneth R. Hall, *Maritime Trade and State Development in Early Southeast Asia* (1985). O. W. Wolters, *Early Indonesian Commerce: The Origins of Srivijaya* (1967) and *The Fall of Srivijaya in Malay History* (1970).

KENNETH R. HALL

SSU-MA CH'IEN. *See* Sima Qian.

SSU-MA KUANG. *See* Sima Guang.

STILWELL, JOSEPH W. (1883–1947), American army general in command of all American forces in the China-Burma-India theater from 1942 to 1944. Stilwell's confrontation with Chiang Kai-shek in Chongqing in 1944 set the course of US-China relations for the next twenty-eight years.

Stilwell saw China for the first time in November 1911, as a touring West Point graduate and US Army officer, and witnessed the relatively bloodless Republican revolution that saw the Qing dynasty overthrown and a parliamentary democracy established. By the time he returned to China in 1920 for three years of language training, the Republic had collapsed into warlordism. During these years Stilwell made a point of taking long solitary trips into the countryside and was appalled at the misery of the Chinese peasantry.

Stilwell was one of the US Army's few China experts when he returned to live in Tianjin in 1927, at the height of the Northern Expedition and antiforeign riots. In addition to interpreting the chaotic Chinese scene in military terms for Washington he cemented a relationship with World War II giant and Roosevelt confidant, George Marshall. His relationship with Marshall would later be the key to Stilwell's influence on US policy toward China. Stilwell spent most of the years from 1935 to 1944 in China, first as a military attaché to the American embassy between 1935 and 1939 and then, after 1941, as theater commander for Allied operations in China during World War II. In the first period Stilwell was upset by US unwillingness to confront Japanese imperialism in China. More importantly, Stilwell developed a deep antipathy for Generalissimo Chiang Kai-shek and his regime, especially after it settled in the wartime capital of Chongqing in 1939.

Stilwell's personal difficulties with Chiang Kai-shek came to a head in September of 1944 as a result of Stilwell's growing irritation at the corruption of Chiang's regime and its reluctance to fight the Japanese, particularly at a time when Stilwell's troops were pressing ahead with his plans to reopen the Burma Road, which had fallen to the Japanese in 1941. By the summer of 1944 the war in East Asia had reached a critical point and the military situation in China itself appeared to be worsening. Impressed by the anti-Japanese efforts of the Communists in the northwest, Stilwell arranged, over Chiang's protests, to send a special US military observer mission (known as the Dixie Mission) to Yan'an, the Communist headquarters. Stilwell also obtained President Roosevelt's initial approval to be made supreme commander of all troops, Chinese and Allied, in the China theater. This meant that ultimate control over Nationalist and Communist Chinese troops would pass to Stilwell. Begrudgingly, Chiang Kai-shek seemed to agree. Then in September, after an especially sharp cable from Roosevelt, Chiang became adamant, refusing to work with Stilwell any longer under any circumstances.

Suddenly, Roosevelt was forced to choose between Chiang and Stilwell. An election was approaching and Roosevelt wanted China to play a major role in the new United Nations. The result was a decision to remove Stilwell in support of Chiang Kai-shek, a decision that turned out to have far-reaching effects. Thereafter, US policy moved basically in a pro-Chiang direction that was to last for more than twenty-seven years. Stilwell returned to the United States in October 1944, stunned and profoundly upset by what had happened. In a sense he never recovered. Not wishing to fan the fires of a China policy debate in Congress, the Army forbade him to speak out publicly on China. Stilwell died suddenly in 1947 on the eve of his retirement from the Army.

[*See also* Burma Road; World War II in China; Chiang Kai-shek; *and* Marshall, George C.]

Barbara Tuchman, *Stilwell and the American Experience in China, 1911–1945* (1971).

STEPHEN R. MACKINNON

STRACHEY, SIR JOHN (1823–1907), younger brother of Richard Strachey and distinguished civil servant under three viceroys of India. Strachey was lieutenant-governor of the Northwest Provinces from 1874 to 1876, member of the Viceroy's Council from 1868 to 1872, and finance minister from 1876 to 1879, when he also served on the secretary of state's Council of India.

USHA SANYAL

STRACHEY, SIR RICHARD (1817–1908), served in the Royal Engineers in India from 1836 to 1875. Strachey superintended numerous construction works, including the Ganges Canal. He headed the public works department (1862–1865) and was inspector-general of irrigation. In 1889 he became chairman of the East India Railway Company, which ran the Indian railways under government control.

USHA SANYAL

STRAITS SETTLEMENTS. The Straits Settlements consist of Penang, Melaka (Malacca), and Singapore. The British acquired Penang in 1786, when the sultan of Kedah, seeking assistance against oppressive Siamese suzerainty, asked the East India Company for protection. The company (and the British government) wished to extend trading links and to check the French in the Indian Ocean. A treaty was therefore signed, providing for British occupation of Penang Island, later extending to territory on the mainland (Province Wellesley). The British paid an annual sum in exchange, but, shamefully, they failed to provide the promised protection.

British acquisition of Melaka resulted from the wars conducted by the French after the 1789 revolution. France occupied Holland in 1794, and in 1795 the British took over Melaka from the Dutch, at their request, to save it from French occupation. In 1818 it was restored to the Dutch, but in 1824 the British and the Dutch tidied up their boundaries, and Melaka was exchanged for the island of Bencoolen in Sumatra.

Sir Thomas Stamford Raffles, who had governed Java during the wartime occupation of the Dutch East Indies, was seeking a new British port, better situated geographically as an entrepôt for the China trade than Penang or Melaka. He found it in Singapore, then virtually unpopulated. Taking advantage of dynastic quarrels among local rulers, he founded Singapore in 1819. It expanded more rapidly than Penang or Melaka and replaced the former as capital of the Straits Settlements in 1832.

[*See also* Java, British Occupation of; Anglo-Dutch Treaty; Penang; Melaka; *and* Singapore.]

R. Bonney, *Kedah, 1771–1821: The Search for Security and Independence* (1971). C. E. Wurtzburg, *Raffles of the Eastern Isles* (1954).

R. S. MILNE

STRONG, ANNA LOUISE (1885–1970), American author who wrote about the Chinese revolution for more than forty-five years. Strong also served as the American confidant of the Chinese Communist leaders before and after they came to power in 1949. A brilliant woman from a long line of midwestern preachers, missionaries, and abolitionists, she was the first woman to receive a doctorate from the University of Chicago. By the 1920s Strong had become a communist and was living in Moscow. She first visited China in 1925; from that time until her death in Beijing in 1970, she lived alternately in Moscow, the United States, and China. During the 1940s she became closer to the Chinese leaders and more estranged from the Soviets, who symbolically expelled her from Moscow over the China issue in 1947. By the late 1950s Strong was again living in Beijing and writing her famous series, *Letter from China*, which at that time provided the West with one of the few sources of information about life in China. Altogether, Strong wrote thirty-seven books and pamphlets, twelve of which are about China.

STEPHEN R. MACKINNON

STUART, J. LEIGHTON (1876–1962), the last American ambassador to China before the Communists came to power in 1949. An American missionary and for years president of Yenching (Yanjing) University in Beijing, Stuart brought to his post in the summer of 1946 unusual qualifications. The task he inherited after the failure of the Marshall mission to establish a coalition was an impossible one: mediate peace between the Communists and Nationalists. Through former Yenching students like Huang Hua and others who were close to Zhou Enlai, Stuart tried to open a dialogue with the Communists. By 1948 he also tried to persuade Chiang Kai-shek to step down and make way for a new regional government system. The result was failure, with Stuart earning the distrust of both sides. Stuart left China in August 1949, recommending nonrecognition of the new government in Beijing for the time being.

[*See also* Marshall, George C.]

STEPHEN R. MACKINNON

STUPA, circular dome, surmounted by an umbrella (*chattra*), intended to enshrine a Buddhist saint's remains or appurtenances. Stupas can be portable works of fine metal or ceramic art, or massive monuments made from stone, brick, and/or earth. Identifying the teachings as part of the Buddha's remains, devotees in later eras enshrined texts (*sutra*) or spells (*dharani, mantra*) in stupas. Some later schools conceived the stupa form to be a cosmological archetype, and thus they arranged Buddhas, bodhisattvas, and their consorts according to a directional orientation. Worshipers make offerings to stupas and circumambulate them in a clockwise direction (*pra-*

FIGURE 1. *Svayambhunath Stupa, Kathmandu Valley, Nepal.*

dakshina). Stupas have been built according to local style wherever Buddhism has spread and represent one of the great continuities in the religious architecture of Asia.

[*See also* Buddhism: An Overview *and* Architecture: South Asian Architecture.]

Anne Libera Dallapiccola, ed., *The Stupa: Its Religious, Historical, and Architectural Significance* (1980). Dietrich Seckel, *The Art of Buddhism* (1964).

TODD THORNTON LEWIS

SUBANDRIO (b. 1914), Indonesian politican and diplomat. After medical training and a brief career in the Partai Sosialis Indonesia (PSI), Dr. Subandrio was posted to London in 1947 as Indonesian official representative and later ambassador. He joined the Partai Nasional Indonesia (PNI) in 1957 and served as foreign minister from 1957 to 1966. He was an architect of the so-called Jakarta-Beijing Axis. From 1963 he was first deputy prime minister and was associated with the shift to the left that occurred during the later years of Sukarno's Guided Democracy. Arrested in March 1966, Subandrio was tried in October, convicted of participation in the 1965 Gestapu coup, and sentenced to death. He remains, however, in detention in Jakarta.

[*See also* Partai Sosialis Indonesia; Partai Nasional Indonesia; *and* Gestapu.]

Harold Crouch, *The Army and Politics in Indonesia* (1978).

ROBERT B. CRIBB

SU DONGPO (Su Shi; 1037–1101), leading literatus of the Northern Song period in China. Su gained fame as a protégé of Ouyang Xiu (1007–1072) in the 1050s and achieved further prominence as a critic of Wang Anshi (1021–1086) and his so-called New Policies in the 1070s. This stance led to his arrest and subsequent exile in Hangzhou from 1080 to 1084, where he wrote many of his most famous works. From 1085 to 1093 he held important central and local positions in a government led by opponents of the New Policies but was exiled to the far south when that government fell.

In politics Su was critical of both the New Policies and the attempt to abolish them in their entirety, arguing instead for compromises that could restore political consensus. He approached the ideological debates of the day in a similar manner, opposing dogmatic attempts to replace the influence of Buddhist and Daoist ideas with a narrowly defined Confucian morality. He had his greatest influence among those who believed in the importance of literature and art in the education of literati, claiming that they taught the individual literatus to master tradition while developing his own creativity. He is recognized as one of China's greatest poets, prose stylists, and calligraphers, and as one of the first to promote painting as a literati art form.

[See also Ouyang Xiu; Neo-Confucianism; Song Dynasty; and Wang Anshi.]

George Hatch, "Su Shih," in Sung Biographies (1976). Lin Yu-tang, The Gay Genius: The Life and Times of Su Tungpo (1947). Burton Watson, Su Tung-p'o: Selections from a Sung Dynasty Poet (1965).   PETER K. BOL

SUEZ CANAL, man-made, sea-level navigational waterway traversing the Isthmus of Suez in northeastern Africa and linking the eastern Mediterranean with the Red Sea; extends 108 miles from the city of Port Said in the north to the city of Suez in the south. Constructed between 1859 and 1869 under the supervision of the French engineer Ferdinand de Lesseps and subsequently operated by the Compagnie Universelle du Canal Maritime de Suez (Suez Canal Company), the Suez Canal enormously shortened the sailing route from Europe to Asia, which had previously extended around Africa, around the Cape of Good Hope. Although Great Britain originally opposed construction, seeing in the canal a threat to its maritime supremacy, in 1875 it became the largest shareholder in the Suez Canal Company. For Britain, France, the Netherlands, and Spain, the canal served as a vital strategic and economic link to their Asian colonial possessions. Although the Convention of Constantinople (1888), ultimately signed by all major European states, guaranteed in principle free passage to all ships, Spanish naval vessels were denied transit during the Spanish-American War of 1898, as were Axis ships during World War II.

By greatly reducing the cost, duration, and hazards of the Europe–Asia route, the canal greatly stimulated international trade and passenger traffic. The easier passage to Asia for women and dependents significantly affected the nature of colonial society, especially for India. Egyptian nationalization of the canal in 1956 precipitated a brief war with Israel, Britain, and France. For six months thereafter and again from the Israeli occupation of the Sinai in 1967 until 1975 the canal was closed. The development during this period of supertankers, the increased importance of air travel, the loss by

European powers of their colonial possessions, and the strategic withdrawal of Great Britain from the Indian Ocean basin all contributed to a decline in the relative importance of the canal.

[See also Indian Ocean.]

D. A. Farnie, East and West of Suez: The Suez Canal in History, 1854–1956 (1969). Charles W. Hallberg, The Suez Canal: Its History and Diplomatic Importance (1936).   JOSEPH E. SCHWARTZBERG

SUFISM, Muslim mysticism. The term is believed to derive from the Arabic suf ("wool"), which refers to the coarse garments of wool worn by early Muslim ascetics.

The earliest manifestations of a burgeoning mystical tradition in Islam date from the eighth and ninth centuries. This ascetical movement centered primarily in the province of Khurasan, especially the city of Balkh; in Iraq, especially the cities of Baghdad, Basra, and Kufa; and in Egypt.

Literature. While our knowledge of the lives and teachings of many of the early ascetics is restricted to hagiographic sources, some early Sufis did write religious poetry, prayers, and treatises on the spiritual life. These texts were very influential in shaping the classical Sufi tradition. Hasan al-Basri (d. 728) and Rabi'a al-Adawiyya (d. 801) are two pivotal figures of this period; Rabi'a is credited with introducing love mysticism into Islam.

The late tenth and eleventh centuries saw the production of important manuals of the Sufi life written as guides to novices newly embarked on the Path. Prominent examples are the *Qut al-qulub* of Abu Talib al-Makki (d. 996) and the *Kashf al-mahjub* of Ali ibn Uthman al-Jullabi al-Hujwiri (d. 1071). A didactic genre of a different sort, the biographical dictionary, attained prominence during the same period. These collections of the lives of Sufis provide a wealth of practical guidance in the form of the preserved teachings of Sufi masters and edifying stories, both historical and mythical, about their lives. Well known are the *Tabaqat al-sufiyya* of Abu Abd al-Rahman al-Sulami (d. 1021), which was expanded and revised first by Abd Allah Ansari (d. 1089) and later by Abd al-Rahman Jami (d. 1492). The most comprehensive biographical dictionary is the multivolume *Hilyat al-awliya* of Abu Nu'aim al-Isfahani (d. 1037).

Theoretical speculation about the nature of mysticism developed in tandem with expressions of mystical ecstasy, exemplified by the ecstatic utterances of Abu Yazid al-Bistami (d. 874) and Husain ibn Mansur al-Hallaj (d. 922). Al-Hallaj's "Ana al-Haqq" ("I am the Divine Truth") and his other mystical paradoxes could not help but shock the uninitiated and raise questions about the nature of mystical experience in Islam. For al-Hallaj and other prominent Sufis, paradox was the means to express the suprarational quality of mysticism. None of the traditional religious sciences was believed capable of encompassing in rational discourse what mystics experience in ecstasy.

The science of paradox had serious ramifications: in certain Sufis' understanding of ethics, good and evil are seen to have no objective basis in reality; rather, whatever God wills for the individual is good, no matter how it appears to the common folk. For the Sufi ecstatic, God's will is mediated by the mystical relationship of loving union, not by the synthesis of Qur'an, *hadith,* and *shari'a* that mediates for the rest of the Muslim faithful. This did not necessarily lead to antinomianism or to the rejection of the religious structures of the Islamic community. The more common result was a two-tiered ethical system, the primary tier for the mass of believers, the secondary and more elitist for the Sufi adepts.

The tension in Sufism between sober and ecstatic, or "drunken," mysticism reached a unique point of resolution in the life of Abu Hamid al-Ghazali (d. 1111), who strove to integrate the life of the scholar-theologian with that of the enraptured mystic. The blueprint of his spiritual quest, his autobiography, *Al-munqidh min al-dalal,* and his classic theological treatise *The Revivification of the Religious Sciences (Ihya ulum al-din)* remain, with his numerous other writings, major sources of inspiration and learning in the Islamic world.

In the twelfth and thirteenth centuries the *mathnavi* literary form, familiar in secular Persian literature principally through Firdausi's *Shahnama (The Epic of the Kings),* became popular among a number of Sufi writers. Several of these mystical *mathnavis* have become classics of Muslim spirituality, chief among them the *mathnavis* of Farid al-Din Attar (d. 1221) and Jalal al-Din Rumi (d. 1273).

The literary developments of twelfth and thirteenth century Sufism must share center stage with the theoretical advances sparked by the work of one of the most creative minds of Islam, Muhyi al-Din ibn Arabi (d. 1240). Ibn Arabi was born at Murcia in Muslim Spain in 1165; he traveled widely, finally settling in Damascus in 1230. The volume of his literary output was enormous, matched only by the complexity and density of his ideas.

Sufism before Ibn Arabi focused primarily on the experience of loving union between the soul and God. The arduous Sufi path was the means by which the initiate prepared himself or herself for this unique experience of intimacy. The mystical encounter could not be induced, only prepared for. The success or failure of the quest depended primarily on the desire of the Beloved to enter into union with the Lover.

Ibn Arabi's understanding of the mystical relationship was radically different. At the heart of his synthesis is the metaphysical principle of *wahdat al-wujud,* the unity of being. It would be an oversimplification to conclude that Ibn Arabi's system is but another form of monism, for God is not identified substantially with his creation. God transcends all categories, even that of substance.

Creation results from God's longing to be known and loved; the world of plurality is, therefore, the mirror of the Ultimate. Existents are not identical with God but reflections of his attributes. An analogy to breathing would be most apt: as breath is exhaled and inhaled so too does God continue to create and annihilate until all is eventually reunited in the One.

Because of creation's illusory quality, God is identified as the only true existent. All created realities by their very nature yearn to be restored to the source from which they have sprung. Abd al-Karim Jili (d. 1428) describes in detail how the Perfect Man, al-Insan al-Kamil, acts as the ultimate mediator between God and creation, for the Perfect Man is the reality in which God is most perfectly manifest. When the process of return reaches its culmination, all the paradoxes and tensions of opposites that characterize the experience of the Sufi mystic will be resolved. Good and evil, reward and punishment, union and separation—all become empty concepts, for nothing exists but the One.

Sufi Fraternities. Sufism after Ibn Arabi bears his indelible imprint. There is perhaps no other Sufi whose influence has been so pervasive. The evolution of Sufism during the thirteenth century should not, however, be restricted to theoretical issues. One extremely significant social phenomenon was the growth and development of Sufi orders or fraternities *(tariqas).*

Signs of Sufi social groupings date back as far as the eighth century, but these early organizations remained fluid in character through the eleventh century. Individual charismatic Sufi masters (known as shaikhs or pirs) attracted a number of disciples who would settle around the master, but the group would often disband after the death of the charismatic guide. Some disciples would seek another master; others might have begun to attract their own followers. There were no codes, however, to regulate the structure of the group.

The support of Sufi convents through the *waqf* system and the increased involvement of the civil authorities in funding and regulating Sufi convents during the Seljuk period contributed to the growing trend toward stabilization among Sufi groups. By the thirteenth century, self-perpetuating *tariqas* became more the norm. Rather than disband after the death of the founder, the Sufis would select a new leader from among the members of the group; in some *tariqas* the transmission of authority was hereditary. The new shaikh would be entrusted with preserving and promulgating the teachings of the deceased master. Consequently, each order began to take on a unique personality, molded by the spirit and writings of the original shaikhs as well as by the contributions of renowned later members.

The success of the *tariqas* cannot be attributed solely to their charisma and social stability. Many of them provided the wider community with a vibrant and easily accessible form of devotional piety. Whereas the abstruse and highly sophisticated mystical theory of Ibn Arabi appealed to the Sufi intellectual elite, the rituals of *dhikr* and *sama* opened important avenues of religious experience to the majority of the faithful.

Dhikr ("remembrance") is an exercise that can be performed alone or with a group, silently or aloud; it consists of the rhythmic repetition or chanting of phrases that often contain one or more of the ninety-nine names of God. The performance of *dhikr* may also entail rhythmic body movements, breath control, and other practices usually associated with meditation techniques. The goal of the *dhikr* ceremony is to foster interior states and an exterior environment conducive to an intense and intimate experience of God; for one or more of the participants this involves the attainment of mystical ecstasy.

A devotional exercise similar to *dhikr* is that of *sama* (lit., "audition"). *Sama* involves the musical recital of religious poetry and is often accompanied by the chanting of verses from the Qur'an. The music acts as the stimulus for various forms of Sufi dance. The types of poetry, music, and ritual movement are as varied as the Sufi groups themselves. The Mevlevis, for example, founded in Turkey by Jalal al-Din Rumi, are noted for the aesthetic refinement of their *sama* ceremony. The mystical dance of the Mevlevis (known popularly as the Whirling Dervishes) is the consummate example of the wedding of interior religious states to the external forms of ritual movement.

Not all performances of *sama* are as aesthetically refined as that of the Mevlevis. Nevertheless, *sama* possesses a power that is independent of aesthetics, whether the performance be encountered in a rural village or modern city in the Islamic world, whether its music and poetry be artistically sophisticated or the popular music and poetry inspired by local Sufi saints. The *sama* invariably creates an environment charged with religious fervor that provides men and women with an important outlet through which to express their pent-up religious and emotional feelings.

The immediacy of the experiences of *dhikr* and *sama* contrasts dramatically with the traditional Sufi path, which demands years of dedication and training. Yet it is the easy accessibility of these experiences that facilitated the integration of the *tariqas* into the religious life of the general Muslim population.

To the power of *dhikr* and *sama* must be added the widespread acknowledgment by both Sufi and layperson of the potent spiritual force known as *baraka* ("blessing"). The great shaikhs of the *tariqas* as well as individual Sufis of spiritual renown were believed to possess a unique spiritual power that could be transmitted to their disciples or devotees. *Baraka* even survived the death of the holy person; thus visits to tombs and shrines are considered particularly efficacious.

The attribution of *baraka* to the great Sufi shaikhs is closely related to the sophisticated theory of the Perfect Man (al-Insan al-Kamil) elaborated by Jili: the charismatic Sufi saint who possesses extraordinary *baraka* serves as the *qutb* ("pole"), that is, the unique manifestation of spiritual authority in the universe and the mediator of all religious experience.

The pervasive influence of the *tariqas* is evident throughout the Muslim world, from the Middle East and Central Asia through Africa, the Indian subcontinent, Malaysia, Indonesia, and other Islamic lands. In addition to responding to the religious needs of the populace, the *tariqas* played an important missionary role. A prime example is the Indian subcontinent, which first encountered Islam in 711–712 with the conquest of Sind by a representative of the Umayyad caliph. A more extensive empire was established by Mahmud of Ghazna (d. 1030), from which Lahore emerged as an important political and intellectual center. It is here that al-Hujwiri, the author of the *Kashf al-mahjub*, died in 1071; he is still revered as the city's patron saint under the name of Data Ganj Bakhsh.

The Chishti was the first major Sufi order in the subcontinent, established there in the late twelfth and early thirteenth centuries by Muinuddin Chishti (d. 1236). The Chishtis attracted many followers through their *dhikr* ceremonies and through their devotion to music and poetry. The Chishti convent (*jama'at-khana* or *khangah*) functioned as a center not only for Sufis but for the wider community as well, since the Chishtis were devoted to the care of the poor and needy. Life in the convent centered around the pir, who closely directed the lives of his followers and managed the secular affairs of the convent.

The second great order was the Suhrawardi, whose first master was Bahauddin Zakariya of Multan (d. about 1267). In contrast to the Chishtis, the Suhrawardis placed a greater emphasis on material well-being and family life. They accepted government support and were more intimately involved with the ruling powers.

By no means were these the only Sufi groups to have a significant impact on Islamic life in the region. Many other Sufi communities—ranging from the strict, reform-minded Naqshbandis (whose center of power was in Central Asia and Afghanistan) to the antinomian Qalandars—were integral elements in the evolving religious life of South Asia.

While it is true that the classical period of Sufism (ninth to fifteenth century) was a time of enormous religious, literary, and social creativity, the modern period possesses its own vibrancy. Sufism remains an extremely influential force throughout the Islamic world and will continue to contribute to the evolution of Muslim religious life in the future.

[*See also* Ghazali, al-; Malamati; *and* Safavi.]

Farīd al-Dīn 'Aṭṭār, *The Conference of the Birds*, translated by Afkham Darbandi and Dick Davis (1984). Peter J. Awn, *Satan's Tragedy and Redemption: Iblīs in Sufi Psychology* (1983). Richard M. Eaton, *Sufis of Bijapur 1300–1700* (1978). Ibn 'Aṭā' Allāh and 'Abd Allāh Anṣārī, *The Book of Wisdom and Intimate Conversations*, translated by Victor Danner and Wheeler M. Thackston (1978). Reynold A. Nicholson, *Studies in Islamic Mysticism* (1921; reprint, 1978). Annemarie Schimmel, *Mystical Dimensions of Islam* (1975) and *As Through a Veil: Mystical Poetry in Islam* (1982). J. Spencer Trimingham, *The Sufi Orders in Islam* (1971; reprint, 1973).

PETER J. AWN

SUGAR. Sugarcane originated in Melanesia, from which it spread both eastward and westward into Southeast Asia via Sulawesi (Celebes), Borneo, Java, and Sumatra and on to the Southeast Asian mainland, India, and China. Despite its deep roots in the region, however, one cannot speak of a sugar industry in Southeast Asia until at least the seventeenth century.

Throughout the eighteenth century sugar was either used as ballast in homeward-bound ships in the East Indies trade or as a commodity in the inter-Asian trade in which Japan, Surat, Malabar, and Persia accounted for the bulk of consumption. Only in the nineteenth and twentieth centuries did it make an impact. Thailand's sugar production increased at the beginning of the period only to dwindle after mid-century, becoming by the nineteenth century's close a net import. In contrast the Philippine sugar industry developed rapidly during the latter half of the nineteenth century and was integrated into the American tariff system in the early twentieth century. Java, the greatest sugar-producing area in Southeast Asia, showed a similar development. The difference was that it started from higher levels and the profits of its production were to benefit the Dutch colonial regime.

More important than its effects on the region's commercial structure was the sugar industry's impact on agricultural patterns. In the New World sugar was cultivated on land cleared for that purpose by foreign, unfree (slave or indentured) labor; in Southeast Asia it was cultivated on arable lands by the resident population. Thus, the commercial export crop not only competed with food crops for limited land and water resources but also for manpower, as the agricultural community was often the sole source of the labor force required both to grow the cane and subsequently to extract the sugar from it for export to the refineries in Europe or America. A particularly onerous variant, the Kultuurstelsel (Dutch, "cultivation system"), was applied to Java during the middle of the nineteenth century. Under this system the colonial government commandeered land and labor to produce, among other things, commercial sugar for sale abroad.

[*See also* Kultuurstelsel.]

Noel Deerr, *The History of Sugar* (1949). Clifford Geertz, *Agricultural Involution: The Process of Ecological Change in Indonesia* (1963).

M. C. HOADLEY

SUGAWARA NO MICHIZANE (845–903), Japanese scholar-bureaucrat of the early Heian period. Born into an erudite family with a short pedigree, Sugawara no Michizane passed the state examinations for entrance into the bureaucracy at a young age. He was appointed to a governorship in Shikoku in 886. While writing poetry and pining for life in Kyoto, he came face-to-face with the difficulties of local administration in the late ninth century, such as decreasing revenues and crime.

In 890 Michizane returned to Kyoto, where he became a confidant of the emperor Uda. For the next ten years, Michizane and his rival Fujiwara no Tokihira guided the government. [See Fujiwara Lineage.] Michizane advocated the cancellation of the government mission to the Chinese Tang dynasty, to which he had been appointed head, because of its drain on the treasury and the decline of the Tang. In 896 he championed the cause of provincial governors, but found his position undermined when tax supervisors were dispatched to prod governors into increasing revenues.

In 899 the former emperor Uda died. Tokihira promptly had Michizane appointed to a post in Kyushu, effectively banishing him from court politics. Two years later Michizane died. However, he had his revenge, not merely because his policies proved correct, but also because his reputation as a scholar spread. He is credited with compiling several Chinese-style court histories and poetry collections.

[See also Heian Period.]

Robert Borgen, *Sugawara no Michizane* (1984).

WAYNE FARRIS

SUGITA GEMPAKU (1733–1817), Japanese physician, an early disseminator of Western medical knowledge. Sugita Gempaku was born in Edo, the son of a daimyo's physician. He helped establish the Dutch studies (rangaku) movement, focusing particularly on Western medical knowledge and techniques. He is best known as a translator, from 1771 to 1774, of a Dutch medical text into Japanese. Sugita and his translator-colleagues undertook this historic task after noting that "actual dissections performed on human bodies confirmed the accuracy of Dutch anatomical diagrams and disproved Chinese and Japanese theories." This episode is important in two respects. First, it reveals that Tokugawa thinkers existed who recognized value in experimental proofs: this was essential for Western empirical science to establish itself against indigenous traditional medical methods based on custom or faith. Second, this was the first direct translation from a Western language by Japanese nationals. (Similar attempts in China would not take place for another century.) It initiated Japan's systematic and sustained assimilation of advanced Western culture through written accounts.

[See also Rangaku.]

Donald Keene, *The Japanese Discovery of Europe* (1969).

BOB TADASHI WAKABAYASHI

SUHARTO (b. 1921), second president of Indonesia. The son of a minor village official in Central Java, Suharto pursued a professional military career, joining the Dutch colonial army in 1940 and the Japanese-sponsored PETA in 1943. During the Indonesian Revolution (1945–1950), he became a prominent army commander in the Yogyakarta region (Central Java). He commanded the Central Java Diponegoro Divison (1956–1959) but was removed following allegations of involvement in smuggling. In 1960, however, Suharto was appointed first deputy army chief of staff and in 1961 head of the army's strategic reserve (Kostrad). In 1962 he commanded the Mandala military campaign to capture West Irian from the Dutch. He was still Kostrad commander at the time of the Gestapu (also known as the 30th September Affair), an attempted coup d'état, and as one of the most senior surviving generals he played a major role in defeating the coup.

During the following months, Suharto gradually consolidated his power at the expense of President Sukarno. On 11 March 1966 he obtained from Sukarno the Supersemar (Surat Perintah Sebelas Maret, Executive Order of 11 March), vesting him with authority "to take all measures considered necessary to guarantee security, calm and stability of the government and the revolution." He was sworn in as acting president in March 1967, was elected by Parliament as full president in March 1968, and was subsequently reelected in 1973, 1978, and 1983.

Suharto's New Order has been characterized by an emphasis on economic development and a relatively low profile in international affairs. Internally, Suharto has stressed political stability and considerably restricted political party activity. He has also sought to remove the basis for political conflict by insisting that all political organizations take the official national ideology, Pancasila, as their basic principle. In recent years accusations of corruption and abuse of position have been leveled against members of Suharto's immediate family, especially his wife Hartinah (Tien).

[See also Indonesia, Republic of; PETA; Gestapu; Sukarno; and Pancasila.]

Harold Crouch, *The Army and Politics in Indonesia* (1978). Hamish McDonald, *Suharto's Indonesia* (1980).

ROBERT B. CRIBB

SUHRAWARDY, HUSSAIN SHAHID (1892–1963), talented and controversial leader of Bengal's Muslims who played an important role in both pre- and post-partition South Asia. He hailed from a distinguished Muslim family, was educated in Calcutta and Britain, where he was called to the bar, and returned to enter Bengal politics. Elected to the Bengal Legislative Council in 1921, he actively participated in its work and was also deputy mayor of Calcutta under the Swarajist leader Chittaranjan Das. After Das's death in 1925, Bengal politics moved in a more communal direction. Suhrawardy worked at labor organizing and also within the legislative council. With the 1935 reforms, he was elected to the Bengal Legislative Assembly and became secretary of the Bengal Provincial Muslim League. A minister in Muslim League-dominated ministries from 1937 to 1941 and 1943 to 1945, he became chief minister of Bengal during 1946. Although he was against the partition of Bengal, he eventually moved to Pakistan in 1949 and founded the Awami Muslim League (later Awami League), a constituent of the United Front, which overwhelmed the Muslim League in 1954. In 1956 he became prime minister of Pakistan and served for more than a year until brought down by the turbulence of the nation's politics.

[See also Awami League; All-India Muslim League; and Das, Chittaranjan.]

Shila Sen, *Muslim Politics in Bengal 1937–1947* (1976). Rounaq Jahan, *Pakistan: Failure in National Integration* (1972). Khalid B. Sayeed, *Pakistan, The Formative Phase 1857–1948* (2d ed., 1968).

LEONARD A. GORDON

SUI DYNASTY. The contributions to Chinese history of the short-lived Sui dynasty (581–618) are vastly out of proportion to its length. The Sui ended more than three centuries of splintered political authority and the growth of regional cultures, known as the Period of Disunion, and reunited all of China. It laid the foundations for the second great empire, the Tang (618–906), and for many of the institutions that operated in China all during the imperial period until 1912. The Sui served many of the same functions and experienced much the same fate as the Qin dynasty (221–207 BCE) had some eight hundred years earlier: both established strongly centralized regimes and greatly expanded China's borders, but both disintegrated within two generations, to be succeeded by more resilient and mightier dynasties—the Han and Tang, respectively.

The Sui came to power in 581, after a palace coup that toppled the Northern Zhou but represented no social revolution: the Sui founder, Yang Jian (541–604), known as Emperor Wen (Wendi; r. 581–604), was of essentially the same northwestern "Sino-barbarian" aristocratic background as his Northern Zhou predecessors. In 557 Wendi had married into the Dugu, a high-ranking non-Chinese clan. His eldest daughter later married the Northern Zhou heir, Yuwen Bin, who succeeded to the throne in 578. Wendi's son-in-law, a harsh and pathological ruler, threatened to set aside his legitimate wife in favor of another woman, and to kill the entire Yang clan if necessary. In the summer of 580, when Yuwen Bin fell ill and died, Wendi took advantage of the situation to found his own regime, putting down loyalist resistance with an iron hand.

Wendi's sudden rise to eminence left him prey to grave insecurities. He was hypersensitive to criticism, suspicious of everyone, and easily provoked, to the point of personally beating to death some of his officials. Wendi was a strong and hardworking ruler, however, and his reign was eminently successful. In 587 he succeeded in conquering the dynasty of Later Liang centered in modern Hubei Province; two years later, with little bloodshed, he overran the southern dynasty of Chen, with its capital at modern Nanjing, thus reuniting all of China for the first time in centuries.

The policies Wendi pursued during his reign did much to consolidate Sui power and also provided a powerful legacy for the Tang. In a series of reforms and reorganizations, he recentralized civil and military power and destroyed claims to hereditary privilege that had helped to keep China fragmented all during the Period of Disunion. With the conquest of the South, the southern ruling class was incorporated into the Sui bureaucracy, which he strengthened and rationalized. Wendi revived the civil service system, applying merit standards to appointments and promotions in order to reverse centuries of entrenched aristocratic privilege. Local officials were subjected to a degree of central control unknown even in the Han; the *fubing* militia was similarly placed under central supervision. Wendi's central administrative apparatus, the Three Department (*sansheng*) system, with its Six Boards (*liubu*), provided a model for the Tang. Wendi reimposed the Northern Dynasties' state-controlled system of land tenure, the "equal field" (*juntian*) system, and raised the efficiency of tax collection, thereby increasing dynastic wealth.

This wealth was expended on various public

works projects and military adventures. In 583 the Sui founder took up residence in his new capital, aptly named "Great Revival City" (Daxingcheng), modern Xi'an in Shaanxi Province, which had been the site of royal capitals in China for fifteen hundred years. Daxingcheng, the largest city for its time anywhere in the world, was a colossal undertaking that remained unfinished all during the Sui. A second major project was the construction, between 684 and 689, of a canal leading from the capital eastward to the Tong Pass, the gateway to the eastern plain, a more productive agricultural region than the northwest. Between 586 and 587 Wendi repaired the frontier barrier known as the Great Wall, which since Qin times had served to check invasions by the northern "barbarians." The most powerful of these were the Eastern and Western Turks, called Tujue by the Chinese, descendants of the old Xiongnu, who controlled the region stretching all the way from modern Liaoning Province to the borders of Persia. It was fortunate for the Sui that at the moment of its founding the Turks, whose livelihood partially depended on raiding sedentary agricultural populations like the Chinese, were disintegrating as a result of fierce political rivalries: the Western Turks broke free of the Eastern, and internal dissension further weakened the Eastern Turks. Wendi exploited these rivalries, supporting khans and anti-khans to China's advantage and forcing some tribes to acknowledge Sui suzerainty. By the end of Wendi's reign only the Eastern Turks posed a serious threat to the Sui.

Finally, Wendi successfully began the process of overcoming centuries of division between North and South China. His extensive ideological use of Confucianism and Buddhism, and to a lesser extent of Daoism, not only helped him to legitimate and consolidate his authority but also to transcend divisions of race, class, region, and religion in order to bind up the wounds of centuries and reforge China's political and cultural unity. One symbol of this unity was a new, streamlined five-hundred-article law code, drafted in 581 and revised in 583, which represented a synthesis of northern and southern legal traditions and served as a model for the code of the Tang dynasty as well as for those of later imperial ages.

By Wendi's death in 604 the Sui had become an empire unrivalled in prosperity since the Han. This legacy was rapidly squandered by Wendi's successor and second son, Yang Guang (569–618), canonized Yangdi (r. 605–617), whom Chinese historians have depicted as a traditional political stereotype—the profligate and licentious "bad-last" emperor. At the age of thirteen Yangdi was married into the royal house of the southern dynasty of Later Liang. In 591, following the Sui conquest of Chen, he became viceroy of the South, with headquarters at Jiangdu (modern Yangzhou), on the Yangtze River, where he spent the next nine years. Although Yangdi was not the Sui heir, he began to have imperial ambitions after his elder brother, the crown prince, became estranged from his mother, the empress. Yangdi's long-distance plotting soon bore fruit; in 600 the crown prince was demoted to commoner status and Yangdi proclaimed heir apparent in his place. There is speculation that Yangdi may have had a role in hastening the death of his father after the latter grew ill, fearing that Wendi might one day restore the former crown prince.

Inheriting a registered population of about 50 million, Yangdi sought further to solidify and extend the Sui empire; in this effort he proved to be creative but overly ambitious. Yangdi expanded the use of civil service examinations for bureaucratic recruitment, introducing the famous *jinshi* examination degree, which later became the most important badge of scholarly attainment in China. He continued the vigorous foreign policy of his father, succeeding in filling out much of the old Han empire. Sui suzerainty was extended over some of the Silk Road oases of modern Xinjiang Province, and briefly over the Eastern Turks. He reconquered northern Vietnam and sent expeditions against the Cham farther south.

In the end, Yangdi's love of extravagance and pomp and his pursuit of costly military adventures proved to be his undoing. While retaining Daxingcheng as his administrative capital, from 605 to 610 he rebuilt the city of Luoyang (northern Henan Province), designating it his eastern capital. In 607, in a frenzy of construction, he reinforced the Great Wall, causing the death of many of the one million labor conscripts. Reconstruction of the Grand Canal between 605 and 607 extended the Sui water transport network from Luoyang to Jiangdu and then as far north as modern Beijing, assuring the Sui the fruits of some of the richest land in the empire. Granaries, roads, and pleasure palaces were also built in great number. All these projects, while designed to consolidate Sui power and weld together North and South, stretched Sui resources to the breaking point and placed heavy burdens, monetary and physical, on an already downtrodden peasantry.

Adding to peasant unrest were three unsuccessful land and sea expeditions from 611 to 614 against the northern Korean kingdom of Koguryŏ, which had once been part of the Han empire. Peasant conscription for these campaigns was largely centered on the northeastern plain, a region that recently had been plagued by massive flooding from the Yellow River. Soon the region was engulfed in large-scale revolt, which spread to the rest of China. In the autumn of 616 Yangdi set sail along his newly built canal for Jiangdu, where he lived in increasing isolation from news of a disintegrating empire. There, early in 618, less than forty years after the founding of the Sui, Yangdi was murdered by one of his officials. Within a few short months, after having placed a Sui child-emperor, Gongdi (r. 617–618), on the throne, Li Yuan, one of the many rebel contenders for power, would found his dynasty of Tang in the former Sui capital.

[*See also* Tang Dynasty.]

Arthur F. Wright, "The Formation of Sui Ideology, 581–604," in *Chinese Thought and Institutions*, edited by John K. Fairbank (1957); "Sui Yang-ti: Personality and Stereotype," in *The Confucian Persuasion*, edited by Arthur F. Wright (1960), pp. 47–76; *The Sui Dynasty: The Unification of China, A.D. 581–617* (1978); and "The Sui Dynasty (581–617)," in *The Cambridge History of China*, vol. 3, *Sui and Tang China, 589–906, Part 1*, edited by Denis Twitchett (1979), pp. 48–149.

HOWARD J. WECHSLER

SUIKA SHINTO, a sect of the Shinto religion of Japan. Yamazaki Ansai (1618–1682), founder of Suika Shinto, was originally a Buddhist priest who left the order to study Neo-Confucian and Shinto thought. Ansai held that *kami* (divinities, numinous forces) is the heart-mind of the universe, activated by the principles of *ki* (vital breath) and *ri* (reason). The supreme god of the universe is Ame no Minakanushi no Kami, and Shinto is the "Way" of Amaterasu (the sun goddess) and Sarutahiko (the god of learning).

Ansai proclaimed the unity of Heaven and humanity, a doctrine that became the hallmark of the system. Influenced by Daoist conceptions, Ansai taught that all fulfillment stems from the attitude of reverent exactitude *(tsutsushimi),* a word that he derived etymologically from the graphs meaning "earth" and "metal." When expounded at a popular level, this doctrine took the form of a promise that metal (i.e., money) would surely result from cultivating reverent exactitude.

Ansai upheld reverence for the emperor as an absolute and wrote extensively on the mystic significance of the imperial regalia as sacred symbols. His followers, such as Wakabayashi Kyōsai (1679–1732), further elaborated doctrines of loyalty and reverence toward the emperor. It was in Ansai's doctrines concerning the imperial institution that his school had its greatest influence.

[*See also* Shinto.]

HELEN HARDACRE

SUKARNO (1901–1970), first president of the Republic of Indonesia, a position he held from 17 August 1945, the day on which he proclaimed Indonesia's independence, until his formal deposition on 27 March 1968. Sukarno was one of the charismatic leaders of Afro-Asian nationalism. He could claim, with some justice, to be the founder of the Indonesian Republic, but his closing years were marked by controversy and, ultimately, rejection.

Born in Surabaya, the son of a Javanese schoolteacher and a Balinese mother, Sukarno was educated in his father's school in Mojokerto (East Java), the Dutch elementary school at Mojokerto, and the Dutch secondary school (HBS) in Surabaya. As a secondary student he boarded in the house of Umar Said Cokroaminoto, chairman of the mass Islamic organization Sarekat Islam, and he met many of the nationalist leaders of the time there. On graduation from HBS, Sukarno, unlike others of his generation who proceeded to tertiary education in the Netherlands, studied engineering and architecture at the Bandung Technical College.

In Bandung he became involved in nationalist activity. He was chairman of the local branch of Jong Java and one of the founders of the General Study Club in 1926. His article "Nationalism, Islam and Marxism," in the Study Club's journal, *Indonesia Muda*, urged the unity of the major streams of nationalist thought in the interests of the common goal of independence. He also developed the idea of the Marhaen, the "little people" of Indonesia who were poor but who were not a proletariat.

In 1927 he assisted in the formation of the Indonesian Nationalist Party (PNI) and became its first chairman. Following the decline of Sarekat Islam and the destruction of the Indies Communist Party after the revolts of 1926–1927, the PNI became the main voice of Indonesian secular nationalism, and Sukarno's skills of oratory drew large crowds to its meetings. Its success led, in December 1929, to Sukarno's arrest, trial, and conviction for behavior calculated to disturb public order. His defense speech became a classic of nationalist literature. After his release from prison in December 1931, Sukarno joined Partindo (the PNI's successor) and was arrested again in 1933. In spite of his resignation from Partindo and his promise to the authorities to abstain from political activity in the future, he was exiled first to Flores and then to Bengkulu.

With the Japanese invasion of the Indies in 1942, Sukarno returned to Jakarta where, within the Occupation regime, he served as chairman of its mass organizations and of a Central Advisory Committee. In those positions he was able to soften some Japanese demands, and through access to the radio provided in all villages he became the most widely known Indonesian leader. He claimed that his speeches, though necessarily supporting the Japanese, kept alive the idea of nationalism. In June 1945 he expounded his Pancasila: nationalism, internationalism, democracy, social prosperity, and belief in God.

In August 1945, Sukarno was accepted as the only person who could proclaim Indonesia's independence and assume office as president. During the independence struggle that followed, he agreed to demands for a parliamentary, rather than a presidential, convention in forming governments. Giving up executive authority strengthened his independence and enabled him to be a symbol of unity against the Dutch, a mediator between rival Indonesian factions and the focus of resistance to such internal challenges to the republic as the Communist-led Madiun Affair in 1948.

After the transfer of sovereignty, the provisional constitution of 1950 provided for a parliamentary system and encouraged the emergence of a large number of political parties. Sukarno, irked by the constitutional checks on his authority, did, on occasion, interfere in politics. Growing political instability and regional resistance to the central government eventually gave him an opportunity to intervene more directly. In 1957, after attacking the selfishness of political parties, he called for the replacement of "50 percent plus one" democracy by a system of Guided Democracy more suited to Indonesian methods of deliberation and consensus. In 1959, following the defeat of rebellion in Sumatra and Sulawesi, and with the support of the army, he reintroduced by decree the 1945, presidential-type constitution and assumed executive authority.

Guided Democracy depended initially on a delicate balance between Sukarno and the army but with the Indonesian Communist Party (PKI) becoming more visible and powerful. Sukarno's style had echoes of court politics, government by access, impulse, and display. Against a background of economic crisis and spiraling inflation, Sukarno, "President for Life," expropriated Dutch property, embarked on grand building projects, played host to the Asian Games, and pursued an adventurist foreign policy. Dividing the world ideologically into "new emerging" and "old established" forces, he campaigned successfully for the recovery of West Irian; opposed, by "confrontation," the formation of Malaysia; and withdrew from the United Nations. The frenetic character of his regime reflected, perhaps, an increasingly desperate attempt to balance opposing domestic forces, and it ended in October 1965 with an attempted coup involving PKI leaders. Swift military action under General Suharto suppressed the coup and led to the destruction of the PKI and of the balance on which Sukarno's power had depended. In 1967 Suharto became acting president, and in 1968 Sukarno was formally deposed in his favor. He died two years later.

Sukarno was a complex figure, combining elements of Javanese tradition and modernity in his leadership. To some he was a catastrophic president, wasting resources on grandiose policies. To others he remained the father of the nation. Politically resourceful, he was skilled in balancing rival factions, but with his mercurial style and his external appearance of confidence went signs of an inner vulnerability. At times he could act decisively, as in forming the PNI in 1927, handling the Japanese in 1942–1945, and introducing Guided Democracy in 1957–1959. At other times he appeared hesitant and uncertain. He posed as a revolutionary but recognized the fragility of the republic, and it could be argued that his revolutionary rhetoric disguised a desire to preserve the social status quo. Perhaps his greatest achievement was his projection of a vision of a unified Indonesian nation in an archipelago of great ethnic, religious, and geographical diversity.

[See also Indonesia, Republic of; Sarekat Islam; Partai Nasional Indonesia; Pancasila; Madiun; Marhaen; Partai Komunis Indonesia; Gestapu; and Suharto.]

Bernhard Dahm, *Sukarno and the Struggle for Indonesian Independence,* translated by Mary F. Somers Heidhues (1969). Herbert Feith, *The Decline of Constitutional Democracy in Indonesia* (1962) and "The Dynamics of Guided Democracy," in *Indonesia,* edited by Ruth T. McVey (1963). George McT. Kahin, *Nationalism and Revolution in Indonesia* (1952). J. D. Legge, *Sukarno: A Political Biography* (1972). Sukarno, *Autobiography as Told to Cindy Adams* (1965) and *Nationalism, Islam and Marxism* (1969).   JOHN D. LEGGE

SUKHOTHAI, the first Siamese kingdom in what is now Thailand, founded in the thirteenth century.

By the 1240s, the northern fringe of the great Central Plain of Thailand had been under the loose administration and influence of the Cambodian empire of Angkor for a century or more. Its local chiefs had been given Khmer titles and regalia and its towns had Hindu and Buddhist monuments. Local Tai chiefs and their people had been moving from northern Laos into the region for a century or two, and in the 1240s two chiefs joined together to evict the Angkorian governor and establish their own regime at Sukhothai. One became king, assuming the Khmer title of his comrade, and as King Sri Indraditya he maintained power in the region between the Ping and Nan rivers for the next three decades. Following the short reign of his elder brother, Ban Muang, King Ramkhamhaeng (r. circa 1279–1298) greatly expanded the kingdom using a combination of diplomacy and warfare and gaining vassals as far away as Luang Prabang and Nakhon Si Thammarat. His expansion, however, was squeezed between the Tai kingdoms of Lan Na (Chiang Mai) and Phayao to the north and the remnants of Angkorian power centered on Lopburi to the south. Whether his successes should be credited to the genial, patriarchal style of his rule and his undoubted military prowess or to the slowness of his rivals to respond to the political opportunities of the era is moot. By the end of the century, however, there was now, for the first time, a major Tai state on the political landscape of mainland Southeast Asia (see map 1 on the following page).

Ramkhamhaeng's successors were not nearly as successful as he was, and they increasingly found themselves challenged by newer Tai states, especially those to the south, where the kingdom of Ayudhya

FIGURE 1. *Phra Achana*. Wat Si-chum, Sukhothai. Brick, 11.3 m. from knee to knee.

was founded in 1351. Especially from the reign of Ayudhya's King Borommaracha I (r. 1370–1388), who made it his policy to eliminate his Tai rivals, Sukhothai was on the defensive. It had lost its influence in Laos following the creation of the kingdom of Lan Sang (1353), and now Ayudhya captured most of its southern dependencies, forcing Sukhothai into vassal status by 1378. King Mahathammaracha III (r. 1398–1419) declared Sukhothai's independence in 1400, but by 1412 Ayudhya had regained the upper hand and, by 1419, had even manipulated the accession of the last king of Sukhothai, Mahathammaracha IV. He moved his capital to Phitsanulok, more convenient to Ayudhya. On his death, the now small region was incorporated into Ayudhya as a province, though for the next century or two it was often ruled by a prince with blood ties to the old Sukhothai house.

Save for its extraordinary bronze sculptures, Sukhothai was almost forgotten in subsequent centuries until the 1830s when Mongkut, then prince, rediscovered Ramkhamhaeng's celebrated inscription from 1292. This discovery promoted interest in Sukhothai, and Thai in particular became attracted to the ideal of the patriarchal monarch exemplified in the inscription. The city has been restored as a national historical park.

[*See also* Ayudhya; Angkor; Borommaracha I; Lan Na; Lo Thai; Mahathammaracha I; Mahathammaracha II; Mahathammaracha III; Mahathammaracha IV; Mangrai; Nakhon Si Thammarat; Ngam Muang; Phayao; Ramkhamhaeng; *and* Tai Peoples.]

David K. Wyatt, *Thailand: A Short History* (1984).

DAVID K. WYATT

TABLE 1.   *Kings of Sukhothai*

KING	REIGN DATES
Sri Indraditya	c. 1240–1270
Ban Muang	c. 1270–1279
Ramkhamhaeng	1279?–1298
Lo Thai	1298–1346/47
Ngua Nam Thom	1346/47
Mahathammaracha I (Luthai)	1346/47–1368/74?
Mahathammaracha II	1368/74?–1398
Mahathammaracha III (Sai Luthai)	1398–1419
Mahathammaracha IV	1419–1438

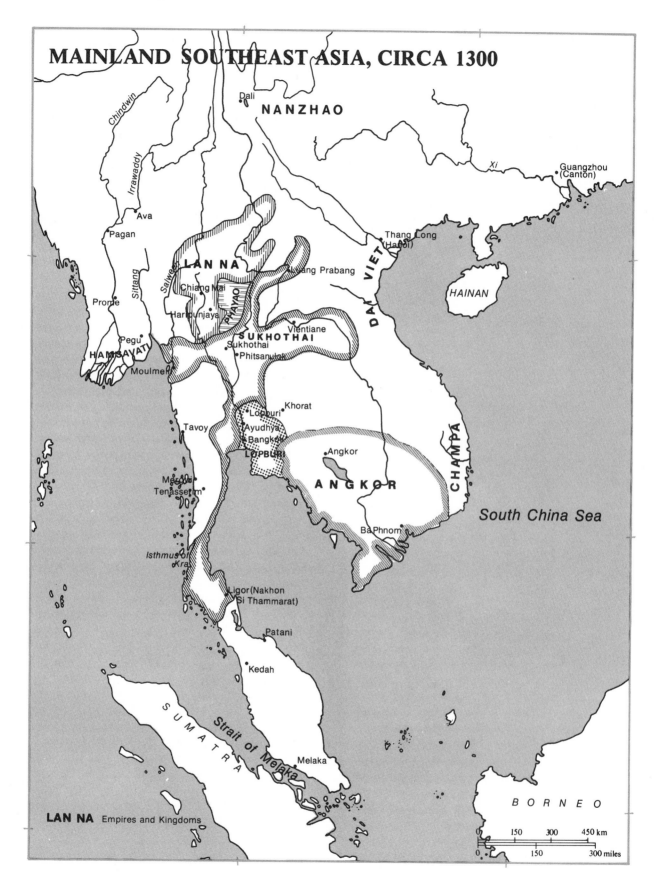

MAINLAND SOUTHEAST ASIA, CIRCA 1300

LAN NA Empires and Kingdoms

SUKIMAN WIRJOSANDJOJO (born c. 1898), Indonesian politician and modernist Islamic leader. Briefly chairman of the nationalist party Perhimpunan Indonesia in Holland, Sukiman was active in the Partai Sarekat Islam Indonesia and later in his own Partai Islam Indonesia. He chaired the Masjumi on its formation in October 1945 and headed the group of modernists within the party who inclined toward radical nationalism rather than Islamic socialism. He was interior minister in the Hatta cabinet (January 1948–August 1949), and as prime minister from April 1951 to February 1952 he attempted unsuccessfully to suppress the Partai Komunis Indonesia. His cabinet fell over a secret aid agreement with the United States that committed Indonesia to defending the "free world."

[See also Sarekat Islam; Masjumi; Hatta, Mohammad; and Partai Komunis Indonesia.]

Herbert Feith, *The Decline of Constitutional Democracy in Indonesia* (1962). Deliar Noer, *The Modernist Muslim Movement in Indonesia 1900–1942* (1973).

ROBERT B. CRIBB

SULAWESI, also known as Celebes, is one of the four Greater Sunda Islands of Indonesia. Sulawesi is located east of Borneo and west of the Maluku (Molucca) Islands; its area encompasses 69,225 square miles and its population exceeds eight million people.

The earliest evidence of human habitation on Sulawesi are stone implements of the Toalian culture. Historically, the Muslim sultanates in southern Sulawesi preceded the arrival of the Europeans. The Portuguese arrived in 1512 in search of a spice-trade monopoly, and the Dutch built a settlement at Makassar in 1607. Dutch control gradually spread from Makassar until the states of Bone and Gowa lost their independence in 1905 and 1911, respectively. Sulawesi was occupied by Japan during World War II. In 1950 the island joined the Republic of Indonesia. Although political disturbances and communist uprisings continue, the central government has maintained control over the port towns and adjacent areas since 1950.   DAVID R. CLAUSSENIUS

SULU. The Sulu sultanate, located in what is now the Philippines, lay at a most strategic point for the maritime trade of the nineteenth century: China, the Philippines, and Mindanao were situated to the north, Borneo to the southwest, and Sulawesi and the Moluccas (Maluku) to the southeast. The geo-political and economic advantages inherent in the sultanate's location were both enviable and unique.

By fitting into the patterns of European trade with China in the late eighteenth century, the Sulu sultanate established itself as a powerful commercial center. Its geographical position in relation to Asian routes of trade and exchange and its abundant natural resources attracted the attention of the West. The maritime and jungle products—*tripang* (sea slug), bird's nest, wax, camphor, and mother of pearl—found within the Sulu zone and in the area of its trading partners were new products for redressing the British East India Company's adverse trade balance on the Canton tea market with China. The trade that Sulu established with Bengal, Manila, Macao, and Canton (and later Labuan and Singapore) initiated large-scale importation of weapons, luxury goods, and foodstuffs. On the coast, Taosug (Sulu) merchants and their descendants developed an extensive redistributive trade with the Bugis of Samarinda and Berau to the south, enabling the Sulu sultanate to consolidate its dominance over the outlying areas of the zone.

Slave raiding became fundamental to the Sulu sultanate as its economy expanded, and in the period from 1768 to 1848 it contributed significantly toward making Sulu one of the most powerful states in Southeast Asia. As the sultanate organized its economy around the collection and distribution of marine and jungle produce, the Sulu economy had a greater need for large-scale recruitment of workers to do the labor-intensive work of procurement. Slaving activity, carried out by the Iranun and Balangingi, developed to meet the accentuated demands of external trade. Jolo, the seat of the Sulu sultante, became the nerve center for the coordination of long-distance slave raiding. From the end of the eighteenth century to the middle of the nineteenth, Southeast Asia felt the full force of the Sulu zone slave raiders, who earned a reputation as daring and fierce marauders who threatened Southeast Asia's maritime trade routes, subsistence agriculture, and settlement patterns and dominated the capture and transport of slaves to the Sulu sultanate. Trade created the material and social conditions for the large-scale recruitment of slaves and the exploitation of dependent communities. At the same time, the labor of captive and tributary peoples provided the raw materials for expanding trade. More than anything else, it was this source and application of labor that was to give Sulu its distinctive predatory character in the eyes of Europeans—past and present—as a pirate and slave state.

The Spanish naval campaign of the 1870s, including the blockading of Jolo and the establishment of a garrison there in 1878, and the large-scale emigration of Straits Chinese traders from Singapore provided the formula for the economic and political collapse of the Sulu trading zone on the eve of the twentieth century.

[See also Moro Wars and Jolo.]

Thomas M. Kiefer, *The Taosug: Violence and Law in a Philippine Moslem Society* (1972). Cesar A. Majul, *Muslims in the Philippines* (1973). James Francis Warren, *The Sulu Zone 1768–1898: The Dynamics of External Trade, Slavery, and Ethnicity in the Transformation of a Southeast Asian Maritime State* (1981).

JAMES FRANCIS WARREN

SUMATRA, westernmost and third largest island in the Indonesian archipelago (180,380 square miles). Sumatra had a population of more than twenty-three million in 1975. Its largest ethnic groups are Acehnese, Bataks, Minangkabau, and Malays, with smaller groups (Gayo, Alas, Rejang, and Lebang) inhabiting upland areas, and large immigrant populations of Javanese Sundanese and Bugis.

Sumatrans traded with India at least from the early common era, and merchants, particularly from southeastern regions, had links with China from the early fifth century. Srivijaya (with its capital near present-day Palembang) became the most important trading empire and center of Buddhist scholarship from the late seventh until the eleventh century. With its decline, other kingdoms arose in Jambi (thirteenth century) and Minangkabau (mid-fourteenth) to compete for Sumatra's trade. By 1292 Islamic sultanates were forming on Sumatra's north coast. In the sixteenth century Aceh emerged as the main power on the island (particularly under Iskandar Muda, r. 1607–1636), monopolizing the pepper trade and challenging Portuguese and later Dutch attempts to control the Malacca (Melaka) Straits.

The Dutch East India Company (VOC) established footholds on the island as individual coastal principalities (Jambi, 1615; Palembang, 1616; and Indrapura, Tiku, and Padang, 1662) asked its protection against the Acehnese. Meanwhile the British established their major factory in Bengkulu in 1685, ceding it to the Dutch only in 1824, together with their other possessions on Sumatra, under the Treaty of London.

For some time thereafter the Dutch colonial government's authority extended over only limited regions of the island. In 1837 the Dutch defeated the religious-led Padri movement to gain control of upland central Sumatra; private Dutch companies established tobacco plantations in Deli from 1863, and the Batak highlands were opened to missionary activity in the late 1800s. Only in the early twentieth century, after a thirty-year war, did the Dutch succeed in extending their government to Aceh. Under their colonial administration Sumatra was divided into ten residencies.

Under the Japanese (1942–1945) Sumatra was governed by the Twenty-fifth Army. In the Indonesian Revolution (1945–1949) the Dutch were able to reestablish control only over limited areas of the island, particularly in some lowland and coastal regions, but nowhere in Aceh. After the Dutch transfer of sovereignty (1949) to the Republic of Indonesia, Sumatra was first divided into three provinces (North, Central, and South Sumatra). Dissatisfaction with the policies of the central government sparked a revolt in Aceh (1953–1957) that led to granting of considerable autonomy to the region. Regional movements led by local military commanders in Padang, Medan, and Palembang, also demanding greater local autonomy, developed into open rebellion against the Sukarno government in February 1958, when, in cooperation with some prominent national Islamic leaders, a revolutionary government (PRRI) was proclaimed. Jakarta's forces soon crushed the major military challenge posed by the rebels, but guerrilla war continued in the hills until 1961. Since the suppression of the rebellion, military forces located on the island have been largely under Javanese leadership. Sumatra is currently made up of seven provinces and the special region of Aceh.

[See also Srivijaya; Aceh; Iskandar Muda; Dutch East India Company; Anglo-Dutch Treaty; Padri War; Indonesian Revolution; Sukarno; and Pemerintah Revolusioner Republik Indonesia/Perdjuangan Semesta.]

Edwin Loeb, *Sumatra: Its History and People* (1935). Anthony Reid, *The Blood of the People* (1979). O. W. Wolters, *The Fall of Srivijaya in Malay History* (1970).

AUDREY R. KAHIN

SUMITOMO, the third largest of Japan's *zaibatsu*, or conglomerates. By the early seventeenth century it was already operating a vertically integrated enterprise by mining, smelting, and exporting copper, the profits from which enabled it to establish a money-exchange business.

By the Meiji Restoration of 1868, however, its fortunes had reached a low ebb because of a prolonged decline in the copper market and the possible loss of its Besshi copper mine. Sumitomo's head manager, Hirose Saihei, succeeded in retaining the Besshi mine and modernized it through the use of highly paid foreign technical advisers. Hirose's heavy investments in the mine and his reluctance to utilize salaried managers in positions of authority, however, undercut his attempts at diversification. Following his resignation in 1894, Bank of Japan personnel were hired to reform Sumitomo's banking, while salaried managers were given authority over a long-term diversification program. This led Sumitomo into steel, chemicals, electronics, and various copper-related ventures. Sumitomo put such high priority on heavy industry prior to World War II that it decided against diverting resources to trading. After the war, however, it built a major trading firm by recruiting outside businessmen, an unusual practice for Japanese management.

[See also Zaibatsu.]

Johannes Hirschmeier and Tsunehiko Yui, *The Development of Japanese Business* (2d ed., 1981).

WILLIAM D. WRAY

SUMO, Japan's national sport, a form of wrestling, possibly of continental origin, that is mentioned in the earliest national chronicles. Matches were held before the aristocrats of the Nara and Heian eras, and interest and participation increased in the period of warrior ascendancy. The sport developed its modern structure and organization in the seventeenth century, and the ritual and hierarchical aspects of present procedure can be seen in woodblock prints of the Tokugawa period (1600–1868). The shogunate staged a sumo match as part of its entertainment for Commodore Perry in 1854, as noted in the official chronicle of the mission by Francis L. Hawkes, who wrote that "attention of all was suddenly riveted upon a body of monstrous fellows, who tramped down the beach like so many huge elephants."

In tournaments pairs of enormous wrestlers, the product of years of hardening, training, and diet, stamp, squat, and glower at each other, throwing salt in the air, and finally charge, meeting in the middle of a cement-hard ring approximately 15 feet in diameter. Victory goes to the wrestler who forces his opponent out of this circle or forces him to touch the surface with any part of his body other than the soles of his feet. The wrestlers, who numbered about seven hundred in the 1980s, weigh between 250 and 500 pounds, are trained and produced by "stables" headed by former professionals, ranked with meticulous care on the basis of tournaments, and listed on rolls called *banzuke,* which divide them into east and west groups for tournament purposes. "Warm-up" flexing and intimidation aside, the match seldom requires more than a few seconds, and tournaments find successive lists of wrestlers halved until the final bout between the east and west champions. Elaborate processions of entry of the wrestlers, Shinto rites of purification, and elaborately garbed referees and judges retain the ritual of feudal society. The balance, grace, agility, and power of the leading wrestlers make them national figures. Television has brought the sport into every home.

P. L. Cuyler, *Sumo: From Rite to Sport* (1979). John E. Thayer III, "Sumō," in *Encyclopedia of Japan*, vol. 7 (1983).   MARIUS B. JANSEN

SUMULONG, JUAN (1874–1942), Filipino politician. From a Tagalog *principalia* family of Rizal Province, Sumulong was educated in Manila (LL. B., Santo Tomas, 1900) and became one of the first Filipinos to pass the bar exam while the country was under American rule. As a central figure in the Federal Party, he led the movement against its US statehood policy, advocating eventual independence under American tutelage. Having lost in the 1907 Assembly elections, he was rewarded by his American admirers with major appointments, becoming a member of the Philippine Commission in 1909. After retiring from the commission (1913), he practiced law and remained a leading force in the political opposition to the Nacionalista Party leaders. Although he lost more elections than he won, he was always a respected political figure.

[See also Principalia; Philippine Commissions; and Nacionalista Party.]

MICHAEL CULLINANE

SUNNI, short form of the Arabic phrase *ahl al-sunna wa-al-jama'a* ("the people of custom and community"). The term was gradually adopted during the Abbasid caliphate by those factions of Muslims who, in opposition to the Shi'a, had accepted the religious authority of Muhammad's early associates (Abu Bakr, 632–634; Umar, 634–644; Uthman, 644–656; and Ali, 656–661) without distinction, despite the schism that had taken place among them following Muhammad's death in 632.

What prompted the adoption of the term *Sunni* was the emphasis laid on the continuity of the Muslim community consciousness with the Umayyad past and the growing interest in the religious practice derived from the *sunna* (understood as "model pattern of behavior"), as expressed in the prophetic communications, the *hadith*. The Sunnis represented the idea of a community bound by the principle of *jama'a*, which upheld the early caliphate and the *sunna*, in contrast to the Shi'a, who had rejected the religious authority of those who had not recognized Ali's sole right to the caliphate; they had instead developed their own version of the *sunna* that included the elaborations of their imams.

The eighth and ninth centuries were a time of political turmoil for the Muslim community, and Muslim scholars were bent on establishing the *jama'a* principle that would provide much-needed solidarity. They were soon convinced that the *sunna* of the Prophet could provide detailed directives and that these were deducible from the Qur'anic religious-legal expressions and their presuppositions. Thus the *shari'a*, the system of Islamic religious-moral law, was evolved by the community of scholars. Adherence to the detailed prescriptions of the *shari'a* as defined by scholars held the Muslims together as the *jama'a* of Sunni Islam.

Four schools of Sunni *shari'a* subsequently came to be acknowledged as valid interpretations of Islamic revelation; their attitude toward the *sunna* as a source equally as authoritative as the Qur'an differed, however. Abu Hanifa (d. 767), the founder of the Hanafi school, which became accepted in Turkey, the Fertile Crescent, Afghanistan, and the Indian subcontinent, did not consider the *sunna* to be sufficient in deriving a decision based on the *shari'a*; he sought a rational method based on *ra'y* (independent judgment) and *qiyas* (argument by analogy with known cases to secure direction for new situations). Both of these principles were regarded by other scholars as undermining the authority of the Qur'an and the *sunna*. On the other hand, Malik ibn Anas (d. 795), founder of the Maliki school of law, whose adherents are dominant in Upper Egypt, North Africa, and much of West Africa, regarded the *sunna* of Medina, where Malik lived, as normative and as the basis for organization within the community. But, like Abu Hanifa, he was aware of the notoriously untrustworthy manner in which the *sunna* was being produced. Malik, therefore, admitted the principle of *istislah* (seeking of public welfare), which could override deduction from the Qur'an and the *sunna*.

It was not until the time of the most systematic and influential legal theorist, al-Shafi'i (d. 820) that principles for the derivation of law from the two sacred sources were laid down firmly. Al-Shafi'i, the founder of the Shafi'i school of Sunni law, whose followers are in northern Egypt, East Africa, southern Arabia, and the Asian archipelago, ironically paved the way for the most effective means of subordinating independent reasoning in deriving the *sunna* by insisting that decisions be made on the analogy with decisions found in the *sunna* or the Qur'an. Such a requirement gave rise to the collection and compilation of authentic *sunna;* this resulted in six major collections of *hadith,* recognized as canonical among the Sunnis. Al-Shafi'i's emphasis upon carefully chosen *hadith* gave rise to the fourth school of Sunni law, the Hanbali. Ahmad ibn Hanbal (d. 855), whose followers are dominant only in parts of the Arabian Peninsula and the Fertile Crescent, preferred even a weak *hadith* over a strong analogy in his derivation of legal decision.

The Shi'ite-Sunni distinction has its genesis in the dispute over the succession to the leadership of the Muslim community. The Shi'ites believed that the Prophet had designated Ali, his cousin and intimate associate, as his successor. The legitimate caliphs thus descended from Ali and his wife Fatima, the Prophet's daughter. The Umayyads, who represented the later Sunni view, claimed a nomination by the choice of the Muslims themselves. This difference still distinguishes Shi'ite political theory from Sunni. For the Sunnis, the caliph is essentially a political authority; whereas for the Shi'ites, the Prophet's successor is a political-religious leader whom they prefer to designate as the imam of the Muslims. So construed, the imam was regarded as endowed with prophetic wisdom and divine grace. No such assumption was held by the Sunnis. The caliph was to be chosen from among the believers and could claim no such endowments. The attitude of the Sunnis to their caliphs has, consequently, been determined by the respect shown him by the community; whereas the Shi'ite attitude is determined by the office of the imamate, which hallows the imam, who is regarded with the deepest religious veneration.

In ritual practices the Sunni and the Shi'ite differ only in nonessential points. However, the Sunnis do not accord to the Prophet's family (*ahl al-bait,* i.e., the descendants of Ali and Fatima) the degree of veneration shown by the Shi'ites, especially in the Muharram ceremonies held to commemorate the martrydom of Husain, the Prophet's grandson.

The authority of the *ulama* (the Muslim jurist-theologians) among the Sunnis is very great, although as a class they do not exercise the same level of influence and/or are not as venerated as the Shi'ite *mujtahids*. The *ulama* are responsible for modification in the religious requirements of the Sunnis. In the absence of any effective link between the ruler and the community at large, it is the *ulama* and the *shari'a* they represent that have maintained the *jama'a* principle of cohesive community among the Sunnis.

[*See also* Hadith; Hanafi; Hanbali; Maliki; Mujtahid; Shafi'i; Shari'a; *and* Shi'a.]

Ignácz Goldziher, *Muslim Studies,* vol. 2 (1971). Marshall G. S. Hodgson, *The Venture of Islam,* 3 vols. (1974). Fazlur Rahman, *Islam* (2d ed., 1979). Joseph Schacht, *An Introduction to Islamic Law* (1979). W. Montgomery Watt, *The Formative Period of Islamic Thought* (1973). A. J. Wensinck, *The Muslim Creed* (1965).

ABDELAZIZ SACHEDINA

SUN QUAN (182–252), founder of the Wu dynasty during the Three Kingdoms period in China. With his brother Sun Ce (175–200), Sun Quan opposed the rise to power in North China of Cao Cao during the long years of decline of the Latter Han dynasty. He allied himself with Liu Bei, the last defender of Han legitimacy. Sun was defeated by Cao Cao in 219, submitted, and was ennobled as marquis of Wu, with a fief encompassing the central and lower Yangtze River valley and the provinces to the south. When Cao Cao died in 220, Sun Quan proclaimed his independence as emperor of Wu. His Wu dynasty, one of the Three Kingdoms (along with Shu Han and Wei) endured until 265.

[*See also* Cao Cao; Han Dynasty; Liu Bei; *and* Three Kingdoms.]

Rafe de Crespigny, *The Last of the Han* (1969). Achilles Fang, *The Chronicle of the Three Kingdoms (220–265)* (1952).   JOHN S. MAJOR

SUNTHON PHU (1782–1855), poet who is considered one of Thailand's great literary figures. Of modest background, Phu led an unconventional life, in and out of favor with the court, and was twice imprisoned. Rama II employed him as a court poet, honoring him with the title Khun Sunthon Wohan. Neglected by royal circles during the third reign, he spent several years in various monasteries. Phu's frequent travels throughout the country provided the setting for such poems as the popular romance *Phra*

Aphaimani and several *nirat* (travelogues). His works offer vivid descriptions of everyday Thai life.

M. R. Seni Pramoj, *Interpretative Translations of Thai Poets* (1978).   CONSTANCE M. WILSON

SUN YAT-SEN (Sun Yixian, also known as Sun Zhongshan; 1866–1925), leader of the 1911 Chinese republican revolution and the Guomindang, (Kuomintang, or Nationalist Party). Sun has been called "the father of the republic."

Sun came from a farming family in Guangdong Province. When he was fourteen years old he joined an older brother in Hawaii, where he attended school. Subsequently he became a Christian, and received a degree from the Hong Kong College of Medicine in 1892. Exposure to foreign practices, the influence of Christian principles, and anger over the Manchu Qing dynasty's failure to defend China during the Sino-French War (1884–1885) pushed Sun toward revolutionary ideas. His first political acts came during the Sino-Japanese War (1894–1895), when he organized the Revive China Society (Xingzhonghui) in Honolulu and plotted a rising in Canton (Guangzhou) with revolutionary friends and secret society leaders. Discovery of this plot forced Sun to flee to Japan, and thereafter the Qing government considered him a dangerous enemy.

Sun became internationally famous in 1896 because of the publicity surrounding an unsuccessful Qing attempt to kidnap him in London in order to bring him back to China for trial and presumably execution. Subsequently, he spent several years in Japan. Although his early contacts had been mainly with secret societies and Overseas Chinese, he now made the acquaintance of liberal, pan-Asianist, Japanese adventurers. More important, he met Chinese students, who were coming to Japan in increasing numbers after 1902. Radical students formed the basis for the Revolutionary Alliance (Tongmenghui) established in Tokyo during 1905. Sun was director, and the party adopted his "Three Principles of the People" (nationalism, democracy, and the people's livelihood—a gradualist conception of socialism) as its platform.

Sun was involved in establishing party branches in Southeast Asia and in preparing for uprisings in South China between 1907 and 1908. When these failed, his leadership was challenged within the party. Moreover, the Qing persuaded other Asian governments to expel him. Most of the following years were spent raising funds and recruiting in the United States and Europe, and Sun did not return to China until more than two months after the 1911 Revolution had begun. He was elected president of the provisional republican government, but he soon resigned in favor of Yuan Shikai to break the stalemate between revolutionary and imperial armies and to facilitate the Manchu abdication. [*See* Xinhai Revolution *and* Yuan Shikai.]

With Yuan's encouragement, Sun then concentrated on plans for railway development, although he was nominal director of the new parliamentary party, the Guomindang. However, he angrily returned to politics after the assassination of the Guomindang's parliamentary leader and took part in the unsuccessful "Second Revolution" in 1913. Thereafter, Sun consistently sought to overthrow Yuan until the latter's death in 1916, and then worked to defeat militarist contenders to control the national government in Beijing.

Sun failed to reorganize revolutionaries effectively into a conspiratorial Revolutionary Party (Gemingdang), personally loyal to him, and also did not succeed in rallying opposition to northern militarists in the name of restoring the 1912 constitution. The governments he formed with unreliable militarist allies in Canton were short lived. When forced to retire to Shanghai, he wrote articles later published as *Principles of National Reconstruction (Jianguo fanglüe)* and began work on *The Three Principles of the People (Sanmin zhuyi)*. Repeated frustrations pushed him toward new tactics: in 1919 he revived the Guomindang, and in 1921 decided to establish a rival national government at Canton. Sun, as president, launched a "northern expedition" to unify China, but southern army commanders refused to move far from home and ousted Sun as president.

After this failure Sun adopted an entirely new approach of alliance with the newly formed Chinese Communist Party and cooperation with the Soviet Union. With the help of Soviet advisers, the Guomindang was reorganized into a disciplined, centralized, pyramidal structure, and the Whampoa Military Academy was established to train a loyal, revolutionary officers corps. [*See also* Comintern *and* Whampoa Military Academy.] The First National Congress in January 1924 elected Sun party leader for life, and Sun's Three Principles were expanded to stress anti-imperialism and party unity, and the "Three Policies" of alliances with the Soviet Union, the Chinese Communist Party, and the workers and peasants were added to party doctrine. Unable to begin another northern expedition immediately, Sun went to Beijing for negotiations with northern warlords. There he died of cancer, leaving

behind a political testament enjoining his followers to complete the revolution that he had begun.

Sun's leadership of the republican revolution has been widely recognized. The Nationalist government made him the object of a cult, and the Communists have included him among their revolutionary heroes. On the other hand, he has been criticized for vanity, rashness, and impatience, and for the shallowness of much of his writing. He has also been called a poor organizer, out of touch with events before 1911, who made excessive promises in endless quests for foreign support and naively trusted the southern warlords who repeatedly betrayed him.

The movement toward revolution in China was far too broad to have had only one leader. Within the narrower circles of the professional revolutionaries, Sun was more hampered than his colleagues by the enmity of the Qing government before 1911. Unable to operate freely in Asia, he was pushed toward the peripheral position of international spokesman and fund raiser. He was, however, also able to transcend, to some extent, the divisions among revolutionaries, and his dedication, optimism, and personal magnetism inspired strong loyalty.

As a contender for power after 1912 Sun repeatedly demonstrated organizational and military weakness. His perseverance in revolution and unwavering idealism, however, made him a symbol of national unity, social equity, and political participation during a discouraging period of disunity and warfare. The contribution that, more than any other, assured Sun's place in history was the reorganization of the Guomindang between 1923 and 1924. This step enabled the party to overcome its organizational and military difficulties to became a broader revolutionary force and a serious contender for national power. Thus, Sun laid the groundwork for the successful Northern Expedition after his death, and different aspects of this new revolutionary phase would be carried on by competing Nationalists and Communists after the alliance had dissolved.

[*See also* China, Republic Period; Guomindang; Northern Expedition; Chen Qimei; Chiang Kai-shek; Huang Xing; *and* Song Qingling.]

Edward Friedman, *Backward toward Revolution: The Chinese Revolutionary Party* (1974). Marius Jansen, *The Japanese and Sun Yat-sen* (1954). Paul Linebarger, *Sun Yatsen and the Chinese Republic* (1925). Harold Z. Schiffrin, *Sun Yat-sen and the Origins of the Chinese Revolution* (1968). Lyon Sharmon, *Sun Yat-sen, His Life and Meaning: A Critical Bibliography* (1934). Sun Yat-sen,

San min chu i, the Three Principles of the People, translated by Frank W. Price (1928). Martin C. Wilbur, *Sun Yat-sen: Frustrated Patriot* (1976). Martin C. Wilbur and Julie Lien-ying How, *Documents on Communism, Nationalism, and Soviet Advisors in China, 1918–1927* (1956).
MARY BACKUS RANKIN

SUPAYALAT, the last queen of Burma, consort of King Thibaw (r. 1878–1885).

Supayalat was one of the three daughters of Queen Hsinbyumashin by King Mindon, whom she married to their half brother, the Thibaw prince, as a key element in her machinations to control the throne on the death of Mindon in 1878. Her plans, supported by such influential figures at court as Kinwun Mingyi, went awry, and she found she could control neither her daughter nor her son-in-law. As chief queen, Supayalat became the real power behind the throne in the chaotic last days of the Mandalay monarchy. On the fall of Burma to Britain in 1885, Supayalat and Thibaw were taken off to exile in western India. On the death of Thibaw in 1916, she returned to Rangoon, where she died.

[See also Thibaw; Mindon; and Kinwun Mingyi.]

J. F. Cady, *A History of Modern Burma* (1958). W. S. Desai, *A Pageant of Burmese History* (1961). E. C. V. Foucar, *Mandalay the Golden* (1963). F. Tennyson Jesse, *The Lacquer Lady* (1929).   DAVID K. WYATT

SURABAYA (Surabaja), major city located at the mouth of the Kali River on the northeastern coast of the island of Java, Indonesia. Historically, the city was the site of the Dutch fort Prins Hendrik. Occupied by Japan during World War II, it was heavily bombed by the Allies and damaged again during Indonesia's war for independence (1945–1949).

Surabaya's port, Tandjungperak, lies just north of the city and next to Udjung, Indonesia's principal naval station. Surabaya is Indonesia's second largest port after Jakarta, and most of Java's chief products are shipped from Surabaya, including sugar, coffee, tobacco, teak, tapioca, rubber, spices, and petroleum products. The surrounding area is a flat, rich agricultural region. As of 1980 the population of Surabaya stood at 2,027,913.

[See also Java.]

DAVID R. CLAUSSENIUS

SURAJ MAL (c. 1706–1763), ruler of the small kingdom of Bharatpur in India, south of Delhi, was an important figure in the political history of his time. The state had been founded in the early eighteenth century when the chieftains of the Jat castes or tribes in the area between Delhi and Mathura had asserted their authority as that of the Mughal emperor decayed. He was the adopted son of Badan Singh, who through conquest and marriage alliances had secured his authority over the areas around Agra and Mathura. While his father was still alive he superintended the building of the magnificent fort at Bharatpur, one of the most impregnable in India. In 1756 he succeeded to power on the death of Badan Singh. The following year he was attacked by Ahmed Shah Abdali, the Afghan ruler who had invaded India, but he managed to survive the onslaught through diplomacy and the strength of his fortifications. In 1761 he captured the city of Agra, the former capital of the Mughal empire, and then moved north to attempt the conquest of the Haryana region, which had a large Jat population. He was opposed by Najib ud-Daulah, the commander whom Abdali had left in charge of Delhi, and he died in battle in 1763 outside the capital. Suraj Mal's simultaneous troubles with the Marathas and the Rajputs are an indication of the complexity of the power struggle taking place in North India in the late eighteenth century.

[See also Jats; Haryana; Marathas; and Mughal Empire.]

K. Natwar-Singh, *Maharaja Suraj Mal, 1707–1763* (1981).   AINSLIE T. EMBREE

SURAKARTA. *See* Sala.

SURAT, at the mouth of the Tapti River on the eastern shore of the Gulf of Cambay, was for centuries a major port for the export of the many products of the fertile interior of Gujarat, India. Among these products cotton cloth was most important, but saltpeter, indigo, and a host of other goods were also produced. The port was also the gateway through which North Indian Muslim pilgrims passed on their way to the Red Sea and Mecca. During the sixteenth century Surat rose to be India's greatest port, especially after the Mughal conquest of Gujarat in 1572 facilitated the export of products from the Ganges River valley through Surat. Seventeenth-century European travelers spoke in awe of the wealth of the town and the variety among its merchant inhabitants.

Despite several disasters in the seventeenth century, such as the great famine of 1630–1632 and two sacks by the Maratha leader Shivaji in 1664 and 1670, Surat was an important port throughout the century; indeed even in the 1730s its trade was greater than that of the new British port of Bombay. After a period of conflict between the Mughal government and the invading Marathas, the town government was taken over by the British in 1759. It was by then eclipsed by Bombay, and remains today a medium-sized port.

[*See also* Maharashtra.]

Ashin Das Gupta, *Indian Merchants and the Decline of Surat, c. 1700–1750* (1979). G. B. Gokhale, *Surat in the Seventeenth Century* (1979).

MICHAEL N. PEARSON

SURI DYNASTY. The Suri dynasty (1538–1545) represents the resurgence of Indian Afghan authority over North India during a brief (1540–1555) caesura of Mughal power. Sher Shah (c. 1486–1545), the first Suri sultan, was a brilliant general and administrator who consolidated much of North India with the unified support of divergent Afghan tribes. His son and successor, Islam Shah (r. 1545–1554), a skilled general, overcentralized the administration; moreover, he distrusted his father's nobles, thus splintering the Afghans. His successors, Firoz Shah (r. 1554) and Muhammad Adil Shah (r. 1554–1556), were ineffectual, allowing for the Mughal Humayun's return to power in 1555. Until about 1570 Suri claimants continued to assert power in eastern India.

[*See also* Sher Shah *and* Humayun.]

Muhammad Abdur Rahim, *History of the Afghans in India, A.D. 1545–1631* (1961). I. H. Siddiqi, *Afghan Despotism in India, 1451–1555* (1966).

CATHERINE B. ASHER

SURINYAVONGSA (Soulignavongsa), king of Lan Sang in Laos. Perhaps the most powerful Lao king, he welcomed Western visitors to Vientiane in the seventeenth century.

Apparently the grandson of Setthathirat, Surinyavongsa was born about 1613 and defeated brothers and cousins to take the throne in Vientiane in 1637. He was fortunate to reign in the aftermath of a violent period, surrounded by neighbors who wanted warfare no more than he did. He reached agreements with Siam and Vietnam concerning their frontiers, in the last case demarcating the border at the point where people living in houses raised on piles above the ground (the Lao) gave way to those whose houses were built directly on the earth (Vietnamese). He entered into marriage alliances with the rulers of Vietnam, Siang Khwang, and Chiang (or Keng) Hung in Yunnan.

Dutch merchants and Iberian Jesuits reached his kingdom in the 1640s and wrote very favorable accounts of the quality of the king's administration and the prosperity of the kingdom. It was during this period that Lao were most intensely settling the Khorat Plateau of northeastern Thailand and the lower valley of the Mekong, and Nakhon Phanom in particular rose to prominence. Despite the king's great apparent strength, the administration must have been fairly loosely structured, with considerable autonomy allowed to provincial ruling families. These families' internal squabbles tore the kingdom apart after the king's death about 1694. Surinyavongsa had had his only son executed for adultery, so there was no clear successor to the throne. His death marked the real end of the kingdom of Lan Sang and the beginning of a long period of division, during which many looked back to his reign as a golden age.

[*See also* Lan Sang; Setthathirat; Luang Prabang; Vientiane; and Champassak.]

René de Berval, ed., *Kingdom of Laos* (1959). David K. Wyatt, *Thailand: A Short History* (1984).

DAVID K. WYATT

SURIYA MAL CAMPAIGN. Originating in 1926 as a means to retain funds from the sale of flowers on Armistice Day for Sri Lankan veterans, the Suriya Mal ("flowers of the tulip tree") campaign was adopted by leftists in Sri Lanka as an anti-British protest. From 1935 to 1939 the Lanka Sama Samaja Paksa (Ceylon Socialist Peace Party, or LSSP) sold the flowers as an explicitly antiwar, antifascist, and anti-imperialist measure. The campaign was a propaganda tactic to mobilize the urban poor, and the LSSP used the proceeds for propaganda and education. It also brought women such as Doreen Young Wickramasinghe, who married state councillor S. A. Wickramasinghe, into Marxist politics.

[*See also* Lanka Sama Samaja Party.]

PATRICK PEEBLES

SURMAN'S EMBASSY, embassy of representatives of the (British) East India Company, led by John Surman, to the court of Emperor Farrukiyar in Delhi to obtain a set of *farmans,* or imperial grants, for the company. On 30 December 1716 the embassy obtained from the emperor three *farmans* addressed to the Mughal governors of Bengal, Ahmadabad, and Hyderabad. The right of the company to duty-free trade in Bengal, subject to an annual payment of three thousand rupees, was conferred. The company was also allowed to purchase thirty-eight villages around Calcutta. This right, however, could not be exercised fully until 1757, owing to the opposition of the nawab of Bengal. The success of the mission was an important step toward the consolidation of the British position in Bengal, especially in the region of Calcutta.

[*See also* East India Company.]

Sukumar Bhattacharya, *The East India Company and the Economy of Bengal* (1954).   PRADIP SINHA

SURYAVARMAN I, ruler of the Cambodian kingdom of Angkor (1002–1050). After the death of Jayavarman V in 1001, there was a decade of division and conflict. Prince Suryavarman, who had important connections in the northeast of the kingdom and in Thailand, gained power through diplomacy, marriage, and warfare. By 1011 he had taken possession of the capital district and had a famous oath of allegiance sworn to him by four thousand officials. His empire annexed the Theravada Buddhist kingdom of Louvo (modern Lopburi). Irrigation expanded, trade increased, and urbanization accelerated. His rule was centralized and bureaucratic, with royal sponsorship of many religious foundations; untypically for a ruler of Angkor, he patronized Buddhism.

[*See also* Angkor.]

David P. Chandler, *A History of Cambodia* (1983). G. Coedès, *The Indianized States of Southeast Asia,* translated by Susan B. Cowing (1968).   IAN W. MABBETT

SURYAVARMAN II, twelfth-century ruler of the Cambodian kingdom of Angkor who acceded to the throne in 1113. He reunited the country after a period of division and embarked upon an expansionist military career, leading ambitious campaigns to the east against Champa and the Vietnamese. He formed diplomatic links with China. Untypically for rulers of Angkor, Suryavarman was a devotee of the Hindu god Vishnu, to whom he dedicated Angkor Wat. This great cult shrine, the most impressive and famous monument of Angkor, was not completed

until after Suryavarman's death, which occurred sometime after 1150.

[*See also* Angkor *and* Angkor Wat.]

David P. Chandler, *A History of Cambodia* (1983). G. Coedès, *The Indianized States of Southeast Asia,* translated by Susan B. Cowing (1968).   IAN W. MABBETT

SU SHI. *See* Su Dongpo.

SUVARNABHUMI (Suvarnadvipa), ancient and vague name applied to western portions of Southeast Asia from Lower Burma to Sumatra by those approaching from the west. The Indian emperor Ashoka is said to have sent Buddhist missionaries to Suvarnabhumi, the "land of gold," in the third century BCE, and early Greek authors such as Ptolemy refer to Chryse, or the Golden Khersonese, as early as the second century CE. The term seems to have been geographical, rather than political, and to have referred to the Malay Peninsula in general.

[*See also* Golden Khersonese.]

G. Coedès, *The Indianized States of Southeast Asia,* translated by Susan B. Cowing (1968). Paul Wheatley, *The Golden Khersonese* (1961).   DAVID K. WYATT

SUZHOU, a city of many canals and gardens in southern Jiangsu Province, is one of China's oldest centers of commerce. The city was founded in the fifth century BCE, but its present name dates only from the Sui dynasty (589–618). By the thirteenth century Suzhou had become a city famous for its educated elite, wealth, and silk trade. Suzhou was first opened to large-scale foreign trade in 1896. Since 1949 the city has been partially industrialized. Silk remains the mainstay of Suzhou's economy and the industry has been greatly expanded. The city of 670,000 (1982) has also developed the production of chemicals, paper, ceramics, metallurgy, cotton textiles, machine tools, and electronics.

ANITA M. ANDREW

SUZUKI DAISETSU (1870–1960), known in the West as D. T. Suzuki, author of many books on Buddhism, mysticism, and Japanese culture. Suzuki was one of the first and most effective Japanese interpreters of Zen Buddhism to the West.

Suzuki began to practice Zen as a university student, under the Rinzai Zen master Shaku Sōen of Engakuji in Kamakura. Sōen encouraged his brilliant young student to make Zen better known in the West, and Suzuki accepted the challenge. Working at first in a publishing house for Buddhist texts, Suzuki perfected his English and began to write and lecture prolifically in Japanese and English. Suzuki married an American woman, Beatrice Lane, who was herself extremely well versed in Buddhism, and settled in the West. His public and university lectures in America and Europe attracted large audiences and his many books reached a wide international readership.

Using some of the psychological categories of William James, whose *Varieties of Religious Experience* exerted a strong influence on him, Suzuki stressed the centrality of the experience of spiritual enlightenment, *satori*, in Zen. He also placed great emphasis on meditation and the resolution of *kōan*, or problem "cases," as leading most directly to *satori*. Although Suzuki may have overemphasized certain elements—the differences between Rinzai and Sōtō Zen, which he rarely mentioned, the mystical aspect of Zen, its identification with Japanese culture, the suprarational element in *satori*, and the paradoxical qualities of *kōan*—his contribution to the Western understanding of Zen has been, and continues to be, enormous. Toward the end of his life Suzuki wrote and lectured not only about Zen but also about Pure Land Buddhism, with its promise of salvation for all through faith in the compassion of the Buddha Amida.

[*See also* Zen.]

D. T. Suzuki, *An Introduction to Zen Buddhism* (1934; rev. ed., 1960), *The Training of the Zen Buddhist Monk* (1934; rev. ed., 1965), *A Manual of Zen Buddhism* (1935; rev. ed., 1960), and *Essays in Zen Buddhism* (3d ser., 1953).

MARTIN COLLCUTT

SUZUKI KANTARŌ (1868–1948), Japanese navy admiral and statesman. Suzuki commanded a torpedo boat in the Sino-Japanese War of 1894 to 1895, and in the Russo-Japanese War of 1904 to 1905 he saw action at the Battle of Tsushima Straits as the commander of a destroyer flotilla. Suzuki developed his reputation as a torpedo specialist while an instructor at the Naval Staff College (1905–1908). In the 1920s, after several important sea and base commands, he was named commander of the Combined Fleet and ended his career as chief of the Naval General Staff (1925–1929). He was grand chamberlain and privy councillor (1929–1936) and was wounded by assassins during the Young Officers' Rebellion (1936). During World War II Suzuki was president of the Privy Council (1944) and then Japan's last wartime prime minister (1945); in this last capacity he worked quietly to bring about surrender. Suzuki's apparently flat rejection in July 1945 (through the use of an ambiguous Japanese phrase) of the Allied demand at Potsdam for Japan's unconditional surrender was a major factor in the decision by the United States to use atomic weapons to end the war.

MARK R. PEATTIE

SWABHASA CAMPAIGN. The Swabhasa ("own language") campaign was a movement designed to replace English with Sinhalese and Tamil as the languages of government in Sri Lanka. Although by the 1940s English had been the primary language of Sri Lanka's political elite for almost 150 years, this elite was itself only a small fraction of the English-literate 8 percent of the population. Elected politicians began to call for making Sinhalese and Tamil the languages of government, culminating in a state council resolution to that effect in 1944. In 1951 Soloman Bandaranaike agitated for an immediate adoption of Sinhalese as the official language. This policy was enacted soon after his victory in 1956, and extended in 1961 by Sirimavo Bandaranaike. Since then the relative place of Sinhalese and Tamil has displaced Swabhasa as a political issue.

[*See also* Bandaranaike, Sirimavo Ratwatte Dias *and* Bandaranaike, Solomon West Ridgeway Dias.]

PATRICK PEEBLES

SWADESHI. The Swadeshi ("own country") movement, involving a boycott of British goods, began in Bengal in 1905 as a response to the partition of the Bengali-speaking region into two new provinces. Many varieties of Indian nationalists, mostly Hindu, joined the movement, which continued for almost three years. This movement gave impetus in the early part of the century to the development of the extremist wing of the Indian National Congress and later to bands of revolutionaries, particularly in Bengal, who assassinated officials of the Raj. The boycott was only briefly effective, but was closer to a mass movement than almost anything hitherto seen in Indian nationalism. The idea of the boycott and of producing one's own goods within India became especially important to Mohandas Gandhi.

[*See also* Gandhi, Mohandas Karamchand *and* Indian National Congress.]

Aurobindo Ghose, *The Doctrine of Passive Resistance* (2d ed., 1952). Sumit Sarkar, *The Swadeshi Movement in Bengal 1903–1908* (1973).   LEONARD A. GORDON

SWAT is a fertile, beautiful, and densely populated district in Pakistan's Northwest Frontier Province. The Yusufzai Pathans and their retainers farm the lowlands and dominate the Gujar nomads and Kohistani "mountain men" who also live in the district. Swat is of particular interest for its ecological and social complexity, and it is one of the few places in the world where a political system based on opposition between patrilineal relatives coincides with intensive cultivation.

Traditionally, Swat had no permanent central leadership. Instead, Muslim religious figures were used as mediators and temporary war leaders. Following such leaders, the Swatis were able to unite and expel invaders. The dynasty of the *wali* of Swat, Miangul Abdul Wadud, arose from a religious leader of this type. Wadud's family ruled Swat from 1915 until Swat was fully integrated into Pakistan in 1969.

[*See also* Pakhtun.]

F. Barth, *Political Leadership among Swat Pathans* (1959). Charles Lindholm. *Generosity and Jealousy: The Swat Pukhtun of Northern Pakistan* (1982).

CHARLES LINDHOLM

SWATANTRA PARTY. The Indian Swatantra (Freedom) Party was founded in 1959 by a group of prominent public figures representing rich peasants, industrialists, and former princes opposed to government policies of socialism, planning, agricultural collectivization, and statism. The candidates of this conservative, secular party were very successful in the 1960s in both federal and state elections. The party, however, suffered a massive defeat in the 1971–1972 elections and was never able to recover. It became defunct in 1974.

H. L. Erdman, *The Swatantra Party and Indian Conservatism* (1967).   STANLEY A. KOCHANEK

SWATOW. *See* Shantou.

SWETTENHAM, SIR FRANK (1850–1946), British colonial administrator. He entered colonial service in the Straits Settlements in 1870 and was prominent in British expansion in Perak and Selangor (1874–1876). After working as assistant colonial secretary in Singapore, Swettenham returned to the Malay States as resident of Selangor (1882) and Perak (1889) and as first resident-general of the Federated Malay States (1896–1900). He ended his Malayan career as governor and high commissioner (1901–1904). In retirement he served as director of several rubber companies, chaired the Royal Commission to the Mauritius (1909), and opposed the Malayan Union scheme (1946). He is author of *Malay Sketches* (1895) and *The Real Malay* (1899), among other works.   A. J. STOCKWELL

SYAHBANDAR. The *syahbandar (shahbandar, sjahbandar;* from Persian, "lord of the port") was the official responsible for matters relating to the port and trade in a Malay principality. His duties were wider than those of the harbormaster of a European port. Malay Melaka had four *syahbandars,* chosen from among the many groups of foreign merchants. Their primary task was to look after merchants of their particular nation and manage the warehouses and marketplaces.

M. A. P. Meilink-Roelofsz, *Asian Trade and European Influence* (1962). R. J. Wilkinson, *A Dictionary of Malay* (1959).   DIANNE LEWIS

SYKES, SIR PERCY MOLESWORTH (1867–1945), British official of the colonial government of India who served for several years in Iran. Sykes established Britain's consulates in Kerman and Zabol in the 1890s. From 1916 to 1918, during World War I, he was the commander of the South Persia Rifles, a military force of Iranian recruits and British officers. Under Sykes the South Persia Rifles captured and held the main towns of eastern and southern Iran, which had been occupied by armed tribes hostile to British interests in Iran. Sykes also was a student of Iranian history and wrote several books and articles about Iran, including the classic two-volume *History of Persia.*

[*See also* South Persia Rifles.]

William J. Olson, *Anglo-Iranian Relations during World War I* (1984), pp. 153–213.   ERIC HOOGLUND

SYLHET, district located in northeastern Bangladesh, except for a small territory that remained with the Indian state of Assam following partition in 1947. Until the creation of Bangladesh in 1971, Syl-

het provided a large portion of the foreign exchange resources of Pakistan, including 90 percent of tea production, of which 80 percent was exported. Immensely fertile, the Surma River valley yields three rice crops per year. Sylhet is also a source of natural gas, used primarily in the production of fertilizers. The 1961 census counted 3.49 million people; by 1986 that number had grown by at least two million.
[See also Bangladesh and Assam.]

Kazi Ahmed, The Geography of Pakistan (1972).

DAVID LELYVELD

SYMES, MICHAEL, British East India Company emissary to Burma, 1795 and 1802. The primary concern of both missions by Captain Symes was the prevention of French use of Burmese ports to attack British commerce. The secondary concern was the problem of refugees and dissidents crossing the common border between British India and turbulent Burmese-ruled Arakan. Although never granted an audience by the Burmese ruler Bodawhpaya (1782–1819), Symes considered his 1795 mission well treated and returned with a favorable report and some minor commercial concessions. After the fiasco of Hiram Cox's attempted residence in Burma (1796–1798), Symes (by then a colonel) was sent on a second mission in 1802. His experience this time was closer to that of Cox; Symes' mission was unsuccessful. Severely disillusioned by this failure, he retired from the service a few years later.
[See also Bodawhpaya and Cox, Hiram.]

D. G. E. Hall, ed., Michael Symes: Journal of His Second Embassy to the Court of Ava in 1802 (1955). Michael Symes, An Account of an Embassy to the Kingdom of Ava . . . in the Year of 1795 (1800).

WILLIAM J. KOENIG

SYR DARYA. See Jaxartes River.

SYRIAM functioned as Burma's chief port for almost two centuries. Although omitted from commercial itineraries of 1512–1515, by the last part of the sixteenth century Italian reports suggest that Syriam had come into greater prominence. It served as the center of an abortive Portuguese-Burman empire in the early 1600s and thereafter was generally recognized as Burma's premier provincial city. Syriam specialized in the exchange of Indian textiles for Burmese raw materials and luxury goods and also supplied Indian Ocean traders with ships built from excellent local teak. The accumulation of sandbanks outside the port and bitter civil wars led to the eclipse of Syriam by Rangoon after 1756.

D. G. E. Hall, Early English Intercourse with Burma, 1587–1743 (reprint, 1968). B. R. Pearn, A History of Rangoon (reprint, 1971).   VICTOR B. LIEBERMAN

T

TABARISTAN. Arab geographers of the Middle Ages applied the name *Tabaristan* to the Persian province situated between the Caspian coast and the Elburz Mountains, in the area of present-day Mazandaran. The name is derived from the Pahlavi *Tapuristan*, "land of the Tapurs." The province of Gilan or Dailam bordered it in the west; the province of Gorgan lay on its eastern border. In 650 the caliph Uthman sent the first Arab expeditions against the Sasanid army commanders who ruled the area. Although Mu'awiya I also tried unsuccessfully to subdue Tabaristan, it was only during the time of the Abbasid caliph al-Mansur that the Muslim armies made long-term gains. Amol was the first residence of the Arab governors. By the mid-ninth century Islam had won many converts; in the next century Tabaristan was to become the scene of significant Shi'ite activism.

[*See also* Gilan *and* Mazandaran.]

Wilhelm Barthold, *An Historical Geography of Iran* (1984), pp. 230–233. Claude Huart, "Tabaristān," in *The Encyclopaedia of Islam* (new ed., 1960–). Guy Le Strange, *The Lands of the Eastern Caliphate* (1905), pp. 368 and 376.　　　　　　　　　　　　　ARIEL SALZMANN

TABATABA'I, MUHAMMAD (b. 1841), Iranian religious scholar and one of the main leaders of the Constitutional Revolution of 1905. It appears that he had a clearer concept of constitutionalism than many of his colleagues in the revolutionary movement, possibly because of his early contacts with liberals such as Shaikh Hadi Najmabadi and his own masonic connections inherited from his father, Sadiq Tabataba'i. He even claimed that he had first begun to work for the goal of a constitutional government in 1894, more than a decade before the revolution. From 1905 onward he shared the leadership of the revolution with Abd Allah Bihbahani,

showing always an acute sense of strategy, and was widely respected for his consistency of purpose. After the bombardment of the Majles in July 1908, he was arrested and banished to Mashhad, but with the restoration of the constitution he was able to return in triumph to Tehran the following year.

[*See also* Bihbahani, Abd Allah; *and* Constitutional Revolution.]

Abdul-Hadi Hairi, *Shi'ism and Constitutionalism in Iran* (1977), pp. 81–87.　　　　　HAMID ALGAR

TABINSHWEIHTI (r. 1531–1550), founder of the First Toungoo empire of Burma. In 1531 he inherited the throne of Toungoo, a principality in the southeastern sector of the Irrawaddy River basin. Despite, or perhaps because of, Toungoo's interior location and agrarian economy, he determined to employ the workers under his control in systematic attacks on coastal ports, then prospering from the development of trade with India and Melaka (Malacca). Throughout his career, Tabinshweihti envisioned not a north-south polity based on the Irrawaddy axis but an empire extending east and west along the Southeast Asian littoral. In 1537–1538, combining conventional military levies with firearms probably obtained from the western Irrawaddy Delta, he captured Pegu, the traditional capital of Lower Burma, which became his imperial seat in preference to ancestral Toungoo. Three years later he seized the eastern port city of Martaban. This was followed by ambitious but ultimately unsuccessful campaigns against other maritime states to the west and east: Arakan, on the Bay of Bengal, in 1546–1547 and Siam, controlling the transpeninsular trade between the Gulf of Siam and the Bay of Bengal, in 1547–1548.

Tabinshweihti's ethnic and cultural policy was a logical counterpart to his strategic vision. Although himself of Burman origin, while he was at Pegu he sought to conciliate the Mon population of the coast through well-publicized acts of political and cultural patronage. His forces, moreover, included numerous Indian Ocean mercenaries, among whom the Portuguese, by virtue of their advanced ships, harquebuses, and artillery, were most prominent. Indeed, Tabinshweihti was one of the earliest mainland rulers to appreciate the offensive value of Portuguese technology. Despite the failure of his final campaigns, his policy of combining conventional forces and Indian Ocean mercenaries was elaborated by his successors to extend the Toungoo empire over Upper Burma and Siam.

[*See also* Bayinnaung *and* Toungoo Dynasties.]

G. E. Harvey, *History of Burma from the Earliest Times* (1925; reprint, 1967). Arthur Phayre, *History of Burma* (reprint, 1969). Victor B. Lieberman, *Burmese Administrative Cycles: Anarchy and Conquest, c. 1580–1760* (1984).   VICTOR B. LIEBERMAN

TABLIGH MOVEMENT. In India, conversion to Islam was often a slow process. Individuals and groups adopted some Muslim beliefs or practices while retaining many of their pre-Islamic religious and social customs. In the late nineteenth century groups such as the Arya Samaj began reclaiming the half-islamicized for Hinduism, often by writing insulting pamphlets about the Prophet. Muslims opposed those efforts, and by the 1920s the conflict was acute. Local groups sponsored preachers to do *tabligh* ("message") work and a national Tabligh organization was founded in 1923. During the 1920s competitive missionizing sparked riots in a dozen cities. The movement also contributed to the breakdown of the Hindu-Muslim unity displayed during the Khilafat and Non-Cooperation campaigns.

[*See also* Arya Samaj *and* Khilafat Movement.]

P. Hardy, "Modern European and Muslim Explanations of Conversion to Islam in South Asia," *Journal of the Royal Asiatic Society* 2 (1977):177–208. Y. B. Mathur, *Muslims and Changing India* (1972).

GREGORY C. KOZLOWSKI

TABRIZ, administrative center and provincial capital of the Iranian province of Azerbaijan; imperial capital under successive dynastic rulers of Iran from the Ilkhanid period (mid-thirteenth century) to the establishment of control by the Safavids (early sixteenth century). During this period of 250 years, Tabriz grew to become a wealthy city of more than 100,000 inhabitants; this growth was due primarily to the city's role as an important terminus and place of exchange on the trans-Asiatic caravan route and as a major textile center in its own right: from Tabriz large quantities of raw silk and finished woven products were exported to Anatolian and Syrian market centers such as Bursa and Aleppo.

According to the Castilian envoy Clavijo, who visited Tabriz on his way to the Timurid court at Samarkand in the early years of the fifteenth century, the city was a bustling commercial metropolis of some 200,000 souls that rivaled contemporary European cities in its architectural splendors and general air of prosperity. Because of its importance as a market for textile products, it was frequently visited by Western merchants, and several of the important Italian commercial houses maintained offices there.

Throughout the period corresponding to its imperial stature, Tabriz flourished as a center of learning and of artistic and architectural activity. Tabriz was situated close to the point of convergence of the competing cultures of Christian Byzantium, Arabo-Islamic Iraq, and the Turco-Islamic world east of the Caspian; thus, the city benefited from the rich combination of talents offered by a variety of craftsmen representing a mixture of traditions, and this mixture gave a characteristic stamp to the intellectual, artistic, and architectural achievements of Tabriz in the late medieval period. Earthquakes and a succession of military conquests have destroyed much of the architectural evidence of these achievements, but from miniaturistic depiction by court painters, eulogistic description by historians and poets, and the accounts of fourteenth- and fifteenth-century travelers to Iran, it is possible to recapture some feeling for the grandeur of the age.

During the sixteenth and seventeenth centuries, Tabriz, in the heart of the region bitterly contested by the Ottomans and Safavids, suffered the ravages of persistent military conflict; the city changed hands repeatedly as the frontier shifted from the east to the west of the city and back again. As a consequence of its strategic and administrative importance to the Ottomans, however, the city was the focus of considerable building activity during the periods of Ottoman occupation. On the Iranian side its importance had long since been eclipsed by the development of Isfahan as the Safavids' new imperial capital from the time of Shah Abbas I (r. 1587–1629; at Isfahan from 1596 onward). As described by a mid-seventeenth-century Ottoman traveler and author of a ten-volume descriptive and statistical compendium of Ottoman provincial cities, towns, and their hinterlands, Tabriz seems still to have retained much of its earlier economic vitality and prosperity.

[See also Azerbaijan and Safavid Dynasty.]

L. Lockhart, Persian Cities (1960).

RHOADS MURPHEY, JR.

TAEWŎN'GUN ("grand prince"), title by which Yi Ha-ŭng (1821–1898), the effective ruler of Korea from 1864 to 1873, was known.

In his youth Yi, a member of an obscure branch of Korea's royal Yi clan, was schooled in Confucianism and the Chinese classics and also acquired a reputation for his calligraphy and painting. His wife was a member of the Yŏhŭng branch of the Min clan. When King Ch'ŏlchong (r. 1849–1864) died without a male heir, the Taewŏn'gun's second son, Myŏng-bok (1852–1919), was chosen as his successor. Because Myŏng-bok, posthumously known as King Kojong (r. 1864–1907), was then only twelve years old, his father was given the title of Hŭngsŏn Taewŏn'gun (Grand Prince Hŭngsŏn) and made to "assist the king" in conducting government affairs. Until March 1866, however, the regency was de jure in the hands of the eldest living dowager, a member of the Cho clan of P'ungyang.

From behind the scenes and without official legitimation the Taewŏn'gun determined domestic and foreign policies to such a degree that the years 1864 to 1873 became known as "the decade of the Taewŏn'gun." He was a strong-willed, forceful, but at times erratic man who did not hesitate to go against established interests and to defy traditional relationships. In modern historiography he is depicted either as an early modernizer or a social revolutionary, as a benevolent despot or an idealistic Confucian. In fact, his approach to reform was tradition-oriented and conservative. He was not an innovator, but a restorer. This quality is particularly evident in his efforts to revitalize the royal house after decades of interference by the royal in-law clans and to strengthen the central government apparatus. He tried to do this within the framework of the traditional social and economic order. Although he espoused Confucian ideals, he was a pragmatist, little interested in philosophical debate.

Faced with unprecedented peasant unrest and rebellion and chronically empty state coffers, the Taewŏn'gun crusaded against such endemic economic evils as local corruption, unequal distribution of taxes, and untaxed and unregistered land. He ordered new land surveys and introduced some new taxes. He reformed the military tax system and the grain loan system and minted a new coin. He tried to extend state control over land and people held by royal estates and private academies and shrines, many of which he abolished. He abated corruption and inefficiency in government and recruited new officials on the basis of merit. He revived the National Academy (Sŏnggyun'gwan) and compiled some legal and ritual works. At great expense, he rebuilt Kyŏngbok Palace to bolster royal prestige.

In foreign affairs the Taewŏn'gun intensified Korea's traditional seclusion policy. With military force he repelled the French in 1866 and the Americans in 1871. Formal relations with foreign "barbarians" were as unthinkable as a modification of the relationship with Japan. He believed the Catholics to be in contact with foreign powers and therefore mercilessly persecuted them from 1866. His military successes convinced the Taewŏn'gun of the moral superiority of the Confucian state. Thus, the country's isolation was preserved and Korea's response to the outside world postponed until after 1874.

In December 1873 the Taewŏn'gun was forced to retire. Kojong increasingly stood on his royal prerogatives in decision making, perhaps encouraged by his queen and her relatives, the Min. While the Taewŏn'gun's foreign policy was applauded by the conservative officialdom, his domestic measures were often attacked as being in violation of Confucian principles. The first signs of dissent appeared as early as 1866. In 1873 the demands for his retirement presented by vociferous Confucian literati could no longer be overlooked. These demands may in addition have motivated Kojong finally to assert his independence.

Although the Taewŏn'gun retired to the countryside, he remained a political figure. During subsequent years several requests for his recall were submitted. In 1882, at the height of the antigovernment riots, he was reinstated as the head of government, but was abducted by the Chinese to exile in Tianjin. He did not return to Korea until 1885. As the greatest enemy of the Min, the Taewŏn'gun was briefly restored to power by the Japanese in 1894, and in 1895 he facilitated Queen Min's murder. He died in 1898.

[See also Yi Dynasty; Kojong; Min, Queen; and 1882 Uprising.]

Ching Young Choe, The Rule of the Taewŏn'gun, 1864–1873 (1972). C. I. Eugene Kim and Han-Kyo Kim, Korea and the Politics of Imperialism, 1876–1910 (1967). James B. Palais, Politics and Policy in Traditional Korea (1975).

MARTINA DEUCHLER

TAFT, WILLIAM HOWARD (1857–1930), twenty-seventh president of the United States. Taft also served as president of the Philippine Commission (1900–1901), first civilian governor of the Philippines under US control (1901–1904), secretary of war (1904–1908), and chief justice of the Supreme Court (1921–1930).

Taft was a judge before going to the Philippine Islands at the request of President William McKinley, who directed Taft to take the administration of the islands away from the US Army. As governor of the islands, Taft moved quickly to establish relations with members of the Filipino elite who had abandoned the government of Emilio Aguinaldo. He also worked to undercut the power of the Philippine Independent Church (PIC), a nationalist church led by Father Gregorio Aglipay y Labayan. He went to Rome to ask that land held by Roman Catholic religious orders be sold to the state, and he refused to allow the PIC to retain church property it had seized. Taft also set the standards to be met by Filipino civil servants aspiring to promotion.

As secretary of war, Taft opened the first session of the Philippine Assembly in 1907. He accepted Filipino participation in government as necessary for maintaining good relations between the United States and the Philippines, and in this post as well as in the presidency he worked to forge economic links between Filipinos and Americans by making proposals for mutual free trade. He believed that once the Philippine economy was integrated into the American one, Filipinos would be tied forever to the United States. The Underwood-Simmons Tariff, passed in 1913, provided for such free trade.

The growth of political parties in the Philippines led Taft to believe that what he considered a lesser breed of Filipinos would inherit the leadership positions that had once been held by those he considered loyal to the United States. He was enraged by President Woodrow Wilson's appointment of Francis Burton Harrison as governor-general of the Philippines (1913) and by the passage of the Jones Act (1916), which made provisions for the independence of the Philippines in the future. In general his feelings about, and interest in, the Philippines cooled during the Wilson administration, and he would not be reconciled to the new policies until he was approached by Filipino leaders Sergio Osmeña and Manuel L. Quezon shortly after the sudden death of the incumbent governor-general, Leonard Wood (7 August 1927). They appealed personally to Taft to request that President Calvin Coolidge appoint Henry L. Stimson as chief executive of the Philippines.

Taft did not live to see the independence legislation passed by the US Congress in 1935. It is safe to assume, however, that he would have opposed independence and instead favored extended autonomy, whereby Filipinos controlled their domestic affairs but left foreign policy and defense to the United States.

[See also Philippines; Philippine Commissions; Aguinaldo, Emilio; Aglipay y Labayan, Gregorio; Philippine Independent Church; Harrison, Francis Burton; Jones Act; Osmeña, Sergio; Quezon, Manuel Luis; and Wood, Leonard.]

Michael Paul Onorato, *Leonard Wood as Governor General (1969)*. Henry F. Pringle, *The Life and Times of William Howard Taft (1939)*. Bonifacio S. Salamanca, *The Filipino Reaction to American Rule, 1901–1913* (1968). Peter W. Stanley, *A Nation in the Making* (1974).

MICHAEL PAUL ONORATO

TAFT-KATSURA AGREEMENT. Neither a formal intergovernmental arrangement nor a secret treaty, the Taft-Katsura Agreement of 1905 was simply an "agreed memorandum" of a conversation between Prime Minister Katsura Tarō of Japan and Secretary of War William Howard Taft of the United States.

Taft was in Tokyo en route to the Philippines, which had become an American colony in 1899 as a result of the Spanish-American War. He and Katsura took advantage of the occasion to discuss matters of mutual concern in East Asia. The Russo-Japanese War was about to end with a Japanese victory, a circumstance that focused attention on three topics: the Philippines, Korea, and general peace in East Asia.

The Philippines were a problem in US-Japanese relations because "malicious and clumsy slanders" were circulating that Japan had "aggressive designs" on the Philippines. Taft and Katsura agreed that it was to Japan's interest to have the Philippines under the control of a friendly US, not under the "misrule" of either a Filipino people allegedly unprepared for self-government or an unfriendly European power. Katsura declared that Japan harbored no aggressive intentions toward the islands. He also emphasized Japan's great interest in preventing Korea from becoming the cause of another war, as had happened in the Russo-Japanese War. Taft replied that it was his opinion that Japan would be justified in controlling Korea militarily to the extent that Korea could enter into no foreign treaty without Japanese consent.

The prime minister asserted that the maintenance

of general peace in East Asia was the fundamental principle of Japan's foreign policy and that the best means of achieving this was cooperation between the US, Great Britain, and Japan. Taft agreed and said that the US would take any appropriate action with the others to maintain the peace, even without a formal agreement among the three.

Although the memorandum had no binding force on the two governments, it was significant because it stated the position of each party toward a territory of vital concern to both. The US acceptance of Japan's dominant position toward Korea was another step toward Japanese annexation of Korea in 1910.

[See also Taft, William Howard.]

Tyler Dennett, *Roosevelt and the Russo-Japanese War* (1925). Raymond A. Esthus, *Theodore Roosevelt and Japan* (1966).   JOHN M. MAKI

TAGALOG, a member of the Malayo-Polynesian family of languages, is one of eight major Philippine language groups. It is spoken in Manila and the neighboring provinces on the island of Luzon. Records in Tagalog predate the arrival of the Spaniards in the sixteenth century. The term *Tagalog* also denotes those people residing in areas where the language is spoken.

Tagalog first came into view as a potential official national language with the nationalist movement that arose prior to the islands' independence from Spain in 1898. With the imposition of American rule and the consequent introduction of English, however, the chance for Tagalog to become the national language was delayed for thirty-seven years. Tagalog received its greatest impetus in 1934, when the Institute of National Language was created "to choose the native tongue that is to be used as a basis for the evolution and adoption of the Philippine national language" (Gonzalez, 1978). In 1940 President Manuel Quezon proclaimed Tagalog the official language of the Philippines. Its actual promulgation as the new lingua franca can be credited largely to the influence of the mass media; film, television, radio drama, and comic books helped spread the language into the further reaches of the archipelago.

As a result of resurgent nationalism, Tagalog overtook English in the 1960 census as the language most widely spoken. Another factor enhancing the role of Tagalog was the development of Manila as the center of both higher education and economic opportunity, resulting in a steady influx of people from the rural provinces. The new generation absorbed the rising nationalism and adopted Tagalog as their common language of choice.

At the third constitutional convention in 1973, President Ferdinand Marcos called for the formation of a new national language, to be called Pilipino. This language was to be based not on one but on all the existing languages in the Philippines. Although Pilipino attempted to incorporate the major language groups, it remains a basically Tagalog-derived language with some words borrowed from the other Philippine languages and from English and Spanish.

Andrew B. Gonzalez, *Language and Nationalism: The Philippine Experience Thus Far* (1978).

DAVID R. CLAUSSENIUS

TAGORE, DEBENDRANATH (1817–1905), endearingly known as Maharshi ("great sage"), established the Brahmo Samaj in 1843, dedicating himself to the Hindu Reformation. His Hindu modernism not only drew the wrath of orthodox countrymen and Christian missionaries but also of his own father, Dwarkanath, who had groomed his son as successor to vast holdings of land and commercial property.

Debendranath Tagore was esteemed for his ability to attract into Brahmo ranks the most progressive members of the Bengali intelligentsia, including deists, agnostics, and atheists. He also codified the Brahmo Dharma, or "this-worldly ethic," for Hindu modernizers to use as an alternative to the Protestant ethic. His son Rabindranath became one of India's foremost poets.

[See also Brahmo Samaj.]

Debendranath Tagore, *The Autobiography of Maharshi Debendranath Tagore*, translated by S. Tagore and I. Devi (1914); *Brahmo Religion and Ethics*, translated by H. C. Sarkar (1928).   DAVID KOPF

TAGORE, DWARKANATH (1794–1846), Bengali entrepreneur and social reformer. Tagore headed coal, tea, and steamboat businesses and banking companies, and he owned or managed silk, indigo, and sugar factories, landed estates, and a fleet of ocean-going ships. With his friend Rammohan Roy he worked for social and religious reform. Although he lavishly entertained British officials and businessmen in his magnificent homes and traveled twice to Europe to meet with leading authorities, he failed to achieve his goal of mutual friendship with the British. The financial crises of the 1840s, too casual management of his companies, and his own death led to the collapse of his enterprises. His descendants, including the poet Rabindranath Tagore, were his real legacy—perhaps the most distinguished family in modern Bengal.

[*See also* Tagore, Debendranath; Tagore, Rabindranath; *and* Roy, Rammohan.]

Blair B. Kling, *Partner in Empire: Dwarkanath Tagore and the Age of Enterprise in Eastern India* (1976).

WARREN GUNDERSON

TAGORE, RABINDRANATH (1861–1941), major nineteenth-century Bengali poet and writer, winner of the 1913 Nobel Prize in literature. Grandson of the wealthy merchant Dwarkanath Tagore and youngest child in the large family of Brahmo Samaj leader Debendranath Tagore, Rabindranath Tagore published his first Bengali poem at the age of twelve and went on to a prolific career writing not only poetry but also songs, short stories, drama, novels, and philosophic and literary essays. Some of Tagore's best-known poetry (*Chitra,* 1896) and short stories ("The Post Office," 1891) record the natural world and the people of rural East Bengal, where he managed his family's estates in the 1890s. In 1901 Tagore established a school at Shantiniketan where classes were held in the open air and students were encouraged to do craft work and study nature. Seventeen years later this school became Visvabharati (International University). In 1912, with the help of William Rothenstein and William Butler Yeats, a collection of Tagore's poems was published in English under the title *Gitanjali.* On the basis of this volume Tagore was awarded the Nobel Prize in literature in 1913, the first time the prize was awarded to an Asian.

Tagore had protested the partition of Bengal in 1905 and was in favor of Indian self-government. In 1919 he resigned his knighthood to protest the massacre at Jallianwala Bagh. [*See also* Jallianwala Bagh Massacre.] But as a humanist and an internationalist Tagore often found himself out of sympathy with the narrow perspective of nationalism, feelings he had expressed in two novels, *Gora* (1911) and *Gharer Baire* (*The Home and the World,* 1915). During the 1920s and 1930s, although he maintained a friendship with Mohandas Gandhi, Tagore frequently found himself opposed to Gandhi's nationalist tactics. Today, Tagore's poems and songs are well known throughout Bengal. Many critics consider him the finest writer the Bengali language has ever known.

[*See also* Tagore, Dwarkanath; Tagore, Debendranath; *and* Gandhi, Mohandas Karamchand.]

Krishna Kripalani, *Rabindranath Tagore* (1962). Sukumar Sen, *History of Bengali Literature* (1960). Rabindranath Tagore, *My Reminiscences* (1917).

JUDITH E. WALSH

TAHIRID DYNASTY. The Tahirids, a dynasty of semiautonomous governors, ruled Khurasan from 821 to 873. Since several of the ancestors and relatives of these governors also played prominent roles in early Islamic history, *Tahirid* is often used to refer to the entire family.

Recent research suggests that the Tahirid family was not Khurasani in origin. Asad, the earliest known member of the family, may have lived in Basra, where he converted to Islam and, as was customary, attached himself as "client" (*maula*) to an Arab tribe (in this case, Khuza'a). Asad and/or his son Ruzaiq accompanied Khuza'i warriors to Khurasan and eventually settled in the area of Herat and Pushang. Ruzaiq is definitely known to have been under the patronage of Talha al-Khuza'i, governor of Sistan, in the late seventh century. The political fortunes of the family began to rise at the time of the Abbasid revolution (mid-eighth century). Ruzaiq's sons, Talha and Mus'ab, both served in the Abbasid conspiratorial organization in Khurasan. Talha was detained for suspected political subversion as early as 735; he later became one of the twelve chiefs (*nuqaba*) of the Abbasid mission in Khurasan and served as the organization's official secretary. When the revolt was imminent, he was instrumental in winning support for the new leader, Abu Muslim, over the bitter opposition of some of the veteran local chieftains. Thereafter, Talha was one of Abu Muslim's most trusted lieutenants and advisers.

After the success of the revolt, Talha seems to have been rewarded with the governorship of the district of Herat; his brother Mus'ab was similarly made governor of Pushang. Talha then disappears from history, but Mus'ab is known to have still been in possession of Pushang (and perhaps Herat) as late as 767. His son Husain and his grandson Tahir (eponym of the dynasty) also held office at Pushang. Husain was among the Khurasani dignitaries who opposed the unpopular governor of Khurasan, Ali ibn Isa ibn Mahan, and who persuaded Harun al-Rashid (r. 786–809) to depose Ali. Subsequently, Husain and Tahir played leading roles in encouraging Harun's son Ma'mun to resist subordination to the new caliph, his brother Amin. When Amin attempted to reinstall Ali as governor of Khurasan, civil war between the two brothers erupted. Ma'mun chose Tahir as one of his commanding generals. Tahir's troops defeated Ali's and Amin's forces, captured Baghdad, and executed Amin, thus paving the way for the caliphate of Ma'mun (813–833). From 813 to 821, Tahir served Ma'mun as governor of Syria and the Jazira, as administrator of taxation in the Sawad, as head of state security forces (shurta) in Baghdad. He acquired vast estates in Iraq that yielded him revenues said to have totaled some thirteen million dirhams. He retained possession of these lucrative properties even after his return to Khurasan, and in fact members of his family held land and offices in Iraq as late as the tenth century.

In 821, Ma'mun appointed Tahir governor of the eastern part of the Abbasid empire, including Khurasan. Although it appears understandable in view of Tahir's services to Ma'mun, the appointment was and is surrounded by mystery and controversy. Some reports allege that Tahir coveted the office and conspired to bring about the fall of Ma'mun's first appointee in an unscrupulous manner. However, there is also evidence of political chaos in Khurasan during these years; Ma'mun, faced with considerable problems of his own in the western part of the empire, probably needed someone of Tahir's stature to restore order. Stranger still was Tahir's behavior once he was established in Khurasan: he had the customary mention of the caliph omitted from the Friday prayer services and minted some coins that did not include the caliph's name.

Normally, these would be taken as signs of revolt, and it was rumored that Tahir's death by poison in 822 had consequently been arranged by Ma'mun. Yet there is no convincing explanation of what prompted Tahir to revolt (if that was his intent) or why, having disposed of Tahir, Ma'mun would then have proceeded to recognize Tahir's son as the new governor. It is possible that there had been a fundamental change in the political relationship between the caliph and the provincial government that compelled Ma'mun to rely on governors with solid bases of local support. Neither the caliph nor the governor may have known quite what to make of this; confusion about their respective legal positions may have inspired stories about the mutual intrigues. In any event, Tahir's family continued to hold the office in hereditary succession for half a century: Talha from 822 to 828, Abd Allah from 828 to 845, Tahir II from 845 to 862, and Muhammad from 862 to 873. All theoretically derived their authority from the caliph and continued to pay tribute, but their power was real enough. Some of the Abbasid caliphs reportedly feared and resented the Tahirids, but none could or would displace them.

The Tahirids won considerable praise for bringing a period of political order and social stability to Khurasan. This stability was due in part to their cultivation of the Sunni religious establishment in the cities and the military landholding elite in the countryside; it was also, however, due to the genuine concern they showed for the peasantry and the agricultural base of the economy. The Tahirids were admired for their fair taxation, supervision of the irrigation system, and close scrutiny of the conduct of administrative officials, all ideals of Perso-Islamic statecraft. At the same time, they were patrons of the literary arts and learning; many were famous as scholars in their own right.

The Tahirids were less successful in their expansionist efforts in areas on the periphery of Khurasan. Abd Allah invaded Tabaristan and brought much of the Caspian littoral under Tahirid control. Members of the Tahirid family ruled there for some time but were gradually displaced by revolts led by Zaidi Shi'ites. In Sistan, Talha struggled inconclusively with the leader of a Kharijite socioreligious revolt until his death in 828. In 854 a local military leader in Sistan ousted the Tahirid governor. Apparently exhausted, the Tahirid dynasty collapsed without a fight when Ya'qub ibn Laith, founder of the Saffarid dynasty (ninth to fifteenth century) invaded Khurasan (873). The last Tahirid ruler was captured by Ya'qub; he escaped but could never restore Tahirid rule.

[See also Abbasid Dynasty and the map accompanying Samanid Dynasty.]

C. E. Bosworth, "The Tahirids and Saffarids," in The Cambridge History of Iran, vol. 4, The Period from the Arab Invasion to the Saljuqs, edited by Richard N. Frye (1975).

E. L. DANIEL

TAIBEI. See Taipei.

TAIHEIKI (c. 1370), the last of the great Japanese military tales. The Taiheiki deals with events from 1318 to 1333, during which time the emperor Go-Daigo attempted to revive direct imperial rule. Why this romanticized military history was called Taiheiki, which means "chronicle of great peace" is unknown; "great pacification" may be what was meant, or perhaps in view of the carnage that accompanied these events the title is ironic. The outlines of the plot are simple: Go-Daigo schemes against the Kamakura shogunate, hoping to overthrow it with the help of disaffected warriors and warrior-monks; he fails to raise enough support, is banished, and finally returns and restores imperial rule, only to find himself subject to another military man, Ashikaga Takauji. Hōjō Takatoki, titular head of the Kamakura forces, is cast in the role of chief villain; Kusunoki Masashige, who sacrificed himself in the imperial cause, is the loyalist hero. The tale maintains a rhythm through the set battle pieces, which are interspersed with lengthy excursions into examples drawn from Chinese history and legend. It is also famous for some lengthy *michiyuki,* or "travel passages," that draw upon the sacred nature of names and naming. Like many tales of this kind, the rhetoric of classical allusion, incantation of names, and hyperbole are used to elevate a description of chaos to the level of the heroic. In great contrast to the earlier *Tale of the Heike (Heike monogatari),* where war was still seen from a partly Buddhist perspective, the *Taiheiki* is more openly wedded to the glorification and justification of the warrior ethic.

[*See also* Kemmu Restoration.]

H. C. McCullough, trans., *The Taiheiki* (1959).

RICHARD BOWRING

TAIKA REFORMS. The years between 645 (the first year of the Taika era) and 710 (the year when the Japanese capital was moved to the city that was later called Nara) are referred to as the period of Taika reforms. During these years aristocratic leaders were constantly striving, under the influence of Chinese political ideas and techniques, to strengthen state control.

The men who engineered the successful coup of 645 were painfully aware of political disunity within Japan. From scholars who had lived and studied for years in China, they had learned much about the power and splendor of early Tang China (618–907) and that empire's expansion in the direction of Japan. They were therefore firmly convinced, from the outset, that special efforts were needed to make the court strong enough to prevent factional upheavals and to defend Japan against a possible invasion from abroad. They were also certain that a Japanese *tennō* (emperor) and his court could be made really strong only if Chinese forms of governance were adopted.

The disturbed internal situation in which the re-

formers were personally involved, and from which the impulse for reform arose, had become quite serious after the death of Jomei Tennō in 641. Court factions then backed three different princes as Jomei's successor: the son of the famous Prince Shōtoku; the son of Jomei; and the grandson of the powerful Soga no Emishi. Because the conflict between these factions could not be resolved, a compromise was struck: Jomei's consort ascended the throne as Kōgyoku Tennō. By 643 Soga no Emishi was replaced, because of illness, by his son Soga no Iruka, who was so determined to have a Soga prince enthroned that he had a rival claimant (the son of Prince Shōtoku) attacked and murdered. This aroused bitter opposition among those who had supported the candidacy of Jomei's son, a group that included Fujiwara no Kamatari (614–669) and Prince Nake no Ōe (later enthroned as Tenchi Tennō). On the occasion of a welcoming ceremony for Korean envoys in 645, Kamatari and his followers had Soga no Iruka assassinated. Kōgyoku Tennō then passed the throne to her brother, who reigned as Kōtoku Tennō. Fujiwara no Kamatari immediately replaced Soga no Iruka as the most influential person at court and—with the advice and assistance of experts on China—initiated the changes that are known as the Taika Reforms.

While court factions were engaged in the murder of men in high places, the great Tang empire of China was gaining influence on the Korean peninsula. The Tang emperor decided to send military forces against the Korean state of Koguryŏ in 641, the year of Jomei Tennō's death. By 645—about the time Fujiwara no Kamatari had seized control of the court from Soga no Iruka—Chinese troops had moved into the state of Koguryŏ and seized several fortified positions. Tang troops met such strong resistance, however, that they were withdrawn from Koguryŏ the following year. Meanwhile, the Korean state of Silla, plagued by pressures from neighboring states, was seeking Tang military assistance; in 647 a Silla nobleman, planning to accept Chinese terms for intervention, rebelled. The revolt was put down, but the Japanese leaders continued to be nervous about the possibility that the great Chinese empire would continue, with the support of Silla, to expand its influence over Korean states and eventually engulf Japan. The nervousness was aggravated by reports of how strong and large the empire was becoming.

As early as the reign of Suiko Tennō (593 to 628), steps had been taken to make local and court officials responsible to the throne, not to one of the many *uji* (lineages). Chinese ranks were also adopted, and students were sent abroad to learn more about conditions in and around the Tang court. Reportedly in 604—it may have been later—Prince Shōtoku issued a Seventeen Article Statement (usually referred to as a "constitution") of Confucian and Buddhist principles that, if followed, would have made Japan's *tennō* more like a Chinese emperor.

After the coup of 645, and in the face of troubles both at home and abroad, however, the new government adopted far broader reform measures. The very first moves were harbingers of what was to come. First, on the fourteenth day of the sixth month, Retired Emperor Kogyoku, Crown Prince Naka no Ōe, and other nobles gathered at the Asuka Temple to swear an oath of allegiance to the *tennō*, an oath that included the words of a principle incorporated into Prince Shōtoku's earlier statement. Second, a Chinese-type era name, Taika, was adopted in Japan for the first time. Third, the new regime sent envoys to all three Korean states in the following seventh month: to Koguryŏ (then under pressure from China), expressing the hope that good relations would be continued; to Paekche (which had traditionally sent tribute to Japan for that portion of the state of Mimana that had been removed from Japanese control), asking that Paekche continue to submit tribute; and to Silla (involved in military conflict with Paekche), asking for hostages. In analyzing Japan's relations with Korean states at the time, historians have concluded that, in the face of Tang advances on the Korean peninsula, the new Taika administration was attempting to improve its position with each of the three states while attempting to maintain its independence.

One month later the new government sent representatives to local regions of Japan with instructions to set up districts responsible to the court, have surveys made of local resources, establish arrangements for adjudicating conflicting claims between members of the local gentry, and seize weapons for storage in government warehouses. In that same month a "law of men and women" introduced the Chinese custom of separating free citizens (*ryōmin*) from slaves (*nuhi*), not permitting marriages between these two classes, and making it clear that the children of *ryōmin* belonged to their father's household. By such measures, legal foundations for accurate and reliable household registers (*koseki*) were established. Another order issued in that historic eighth month placed Buddhist temples and priests, including those who had studied in China, under a

court-created bureaucracy and established guidelines for court grants to Buddhist temples. Thus, during this eighth month of 645 the leaders of the new regime had moved to bring all parts of the country under *tennō* control, had set the stage for using the Chinese household (*koseki*) and rice-land allotment (*handen*) systems to control all people and land, and had made clan temples (*ujidera*) into state temples. A Chinese legal (*ritsuryō*) state was gradually being formed.

Considerable attention was given in the last months of 645 to obtaining accurate surveys of Japan's population and cultivated land, as well as to implementing orders that had been issued in the eighth month. Internal strife continued, however, as is revealed in chronicle reports of plots against the new government, first in the ninth month and again in the eleventh. A particularly important reform edict was issued by Kōtoku Tennō during the first month of 646. Postwar studies of this long and detailed document show that certain terms in it did not come into existence until the Taihō Code was promulgated in 702, forty-six years later. Thus, the authenticity of the *Nihon shoki* version of the 646 edict is suspect. Historians are generally agreed, however, that arrangements were made then for (1) implementing the Chinese principle that all land and people should be controlled by the *tennō* state; (2) appointing officials in the capital, as well as the provinces and counties, who would be responsible to the *tennō* state; (3) enforcing laws that required the keeping of household registers (*koseki*) and tax records (*keichō*), and allotting rice land (*handen*) to registered householders; and (4) fixing the responsibilities of public officials for collecting produce assessments (*chō*) and service levies (*yō*). Detailed studies of actions taken in each of these four areas leave no doubt but that the edict was meant to create a new administrative structure (the *ritsuryō* state) manned by officials responsible to the *tennō*, rather than to the various *uji* that had traditionally possessed and controlled the country's land and people.

Another order was handed down in the second month of 646 regulating the size of burial mounds. Ever since the third century, the rise of increasingly powerful *uji* (and federations of *uji*) had been associated with building and equipping burial mounds for deceased *uji* leaders. As certain *uji* (notably the *tennō uji*) came to dominate *uji* federations, mounds became larger and more impressive. As Sadao Nishijima and other historians have pointed out, burial mounds were essentially power symbols for the old *uji*-oriented state. After the beginning of the Suiko reign in 593, however, the strongest *uji* started building exotic Buddhist temples that, along with capital cities modeled after the great capitals of China, were beginning to replace burial mounds as impressive power symbols. The progressive decline in mound-building was further accelerated, however, by the 646 order that regulated their size, permitting only the strongest *uji* (those associated with the new Taika regime) to build the largest mounds. Inoue Mitsusada concluded that there were three reasons for issuing the new regulations: the desire to adopt Chinese practices, to make certain that the size of a burial mound was in accord with the status assigned to that particular *uji* by the new regime, and to reduce taxes and services levied for the construction of burial mounds. [*See* Tumuli.]

Throughout the remainder of the Kōtoku reign, which ended in 654, reformers continued to work at strengthening and adjusting the new order. Historians are inclined to think, however, that status relationships between court aristocracy and local gentry were largely unchanged and that the *uji* continued to be socially and politically important. Nevertheless, acts of reform apparently had already produced a stronger and more centralized state, elevated court aristocrats (as well as the *tennō*) to positions superior to those of local gentry, and given the entire ruling class (court aristocrats and local gentry) greater control over commoners. Even so, another fifty years passed before the task of building Japan's ancient despotic *tennō*-state was finished—before the reformers' objectives were fully realized.

Until the close of the Kōtoku reign these changes were causing discontent in high places, as is revealed in the 649 plot of Minister of the Left Soga no Ishikawamaro to assassinate Crown Prince Naka no Ōe. After the plot was put down, and the leaders were ruthlessly executed or exiled, the reform faction of Fujiwara no Kamatari and Crown Prince Naka no Ōe seems to have felt that their positions were, at long last, secure. At the beginning of the next year some white pheasants were fortuitously presented at court, and Kōtoku Tennō announced the start of a new era: the Hakuchi ("white pheasants") era. Kamatari and his fellow reformers must have thought of the new era as bringing the five-year period of reform to a close and as portending the eventual completion of a Chinese-style despotic state in Japan. Further optimism may also have been generated by Kōtoku Tennō's moving into his new palace at Naniwa in 652, and by the first use of household registers for the allocation of rice land, as stipulated in an edict that Kōtoku had handed down at the beginning of his reign.

Before many months of the new Hakuchi era had passed, however, there was a split between Kōtoku Tennō and his crown prince. Kōtoku refused to move from his new palace at Naniwa when the crown prince and other members of the royal family (including Retired Emperor Kōgyoku) moved to a temporary palace in Asuka. While relations between the two were still strained, Kōtoku took ill and died, whereupon Retired Emperor Kōgyoku, not the crown prince, reoccupied the throne as Saimei Tennō. Moreover, the situation in Korea was becoming serious as Silla appeared to be strengthening its ties with the Tang empire, and the emerging Tang-Silla alliance seemed as if it was planning to seize control of the entire Korean peninsula. Some people at the Japanese court had proposed an attack on Silla as early as 651, but instead students and Buddhist priests had been sent to China to learn as much as possible about the latest techniques and cultural developments of the Tang empire.

At this point a Tang-Silla joint military force did attack the Korean state of Paekche and captured its capital in 660. Paekche leaders then asked Japan for military assistance. In the face of the likelihood that the Tang-Silla combination would soon subjugate other areas of the Korean peninsula, and in view of previous close associations with Paekche, Japanese leaders readily complied with the request. Saimei Tennō, Crown Prince Naka no Ōe, and Fujiwara no Kamatari all went to Kyushu to oversee the establishment of a base for dispatching expeditionary forces to the support of Paekche. Three such forces were sent within the next three years. In the fifth month of 663, however, after Saimei Tennō had died and been replaced by Tenchi Tennō (the former Crown Prince Naka no Ōe), a Japanese naval force of 170 ships was soundly defeated. Japan's remaining forces were then withdrawn; and before another five years had passed Tang and Silla had seized control of the Korean peninsula.

For some time after the naval defeat of 663 much of the government's attention and resources seems to have been devoted to preparations for a Tang-Silla invasion of Japan. Fortresses were soon built at strategic points in Kyushu. The removal of Tenchi Tennō's capital to Ōtsu in the province of Omi— further inland than Naniwa and in a strategic position for easy contact with other regions of Japan— is thought to have been motivated by the threat that Japan would be invaded. When it was reported that a large militay force had in fact invaded the northern state of Koguryǒ, the Japanese ordered the construction of a fort on the island of Tsushima and strengthened its defenses in Kyushu.

Attention was also given to shoring up the re-formed and sinicized bureaucracy. Some sources suggest that, at the very beginning of the Tenchi reign—even before the fighting in Korea had ended—the new *tennō* followed the Chinese practice of having a new code of law compiled during each reign, resulting in an Omi Administrative Code that has been lost. Tenchi also issued three edicts in 663 that required that (1) the title system be revised; (2) the heads of *uji* be permitted to wear swords and bear bows and arrows appropriate to their rank and position; and (3) distinctions between free com-moners *(kakibe)* and other commoners *(yakabe)* be made clear.

After the conquest of Paekche and Koguryŏ hundreds of refugees (including members of the no-bility) fled to Japan, where they were often given positions of responsibility in artistic and technical fields. References in contemporary chronicles sug-gest that these refugees rendered particularly valu-able service in two important areas of reform: in law, where at least one refugee was appointed to the law-compilation office (in which the Omi Ad-ministrative Code was compiled); and in education, where a refugee occupied a position that was later held by the president of the university *(daigaku)*, founded in the Tenchi reign. Still other refugees were prominent in the teaching of the Confucian classics and the founding, early in the next reign, of an office for the study and practice of yin-yang divination. So while the reform endeavors may have been weak-ened by the heavy burden of military costs, the new state structure must have been substantially strengthened by the technical and cultural contri-butions of refugees from Koguryŏ and Paekche.

The government itself, not merely its reform pro-gram, was threatened by civil war in 672. Like the coup by which the new regime had seized power in 645, this short war (the *Jinshin no ran*) resulted from a clash between factions that favored one or the other of two candidates for enthronement: Prince Ō-ama (later Temmu Tennō), who was Tenchi's younger brother and had been named crown prince; and Prince Ōtomo, who was Tenchi's favorite son and had been appointed chancellor in 671 (a posi-tion that made him, by law, the next *tennō*). Al-though the court was divided over which prince to support, the backing of the former included many nobles and commoners who had become disgruntled over the results of one or more reform measures. On his deathbed Tenchi entrusted Crown Prince Ōtomo (his favorite son and successor) to the care of Prince Ō-ama, but the latter refused to assume this responsibility and instead secluded himself in

the Yoshino mountains as a Buddhist priest. Other court nobles—including members of the hapless Ōtomo *uji*—followed him. Soon after Tenchi's death, envoys were sent to outlying provinces to mobilize troops for a war that, lasting less than a month, ended in victory for Prince Ō-ama, who then ascended the throne as Temmu Tennō and reigned at the Kiyomira no Miya in Asuka. [*See* Jinshin War.]

Rather than rejecting the Taika reform program, Temmu Tennō strengthened and expanded it. He greatly increased *tennō* power and authority by in-corporating many local *uji* into the control structure and by subjecting commoners to even more restraint and exploitation than had existed in previous reigns. He made a number of revisions of, and additions to, earlier laws and regulations, and even had an-other law code (the Asuka Kiyomihara Penal and Administrative Code) compiled. Probably Temmu's most important contributions to *tennō* control, however, were made by underpinning *tennō* au-thority with a system for worshiping native *kami* and by ordering the compilation of chronicles that would provide genealogical support for such au-thority.

Temmu Tennō gave more attention to the func-tions of the Department of Shrines than any pre-decessor. In the second year of his reign he instructed an imperial princess to "purify herself" and worship the sun goddess at Ise in his behalf. One month later, according to an item in the *Nihon shoki*, he had offerings made to every *kami* of the land. Next, he initiated the practice of sending *tennō* messengers at rice-planting time to two shrines for the worship of agricultural *kami*: the Hirose Shrine, located at the confluence of three rivers where a *kami* was worshiped for its divine power to supply rice fields with water; and the Tatsuta Shrine, situated on a shore frequently hit by typhoons and where a wind *kami* was worshiped for its power to prevent such wind-connected disasters as droughts and typhoons. Whenever there was a serious drought, Temmu sent messengers to all shrines with instructions to offer up prayers in his behalf. Thus, he seems to have been intent on making the point, in meaningful ways, that he was not simply the high priest of sun-goddess worship but the high priest of *kami* worship all over Japan.

Temmu's purpose in having chronicles compiled is revealed in his 681 edict that led to the compi-lation of the *Kojiki*: "If errors are not corrected now, the meaning of the records and accounts—the warp and woof of the Japanese state and the foundations of *tennō* rule—will be lost before many years have passed." Thus, the *Kojiki* (thought to have been completed in 712, and still extant) provides a genealogy of *kami* and *tennō* descent from the sun goddess, and of *tennō* descent from the first *tennō*. Although the *Kojiki* shows the influence of Chinese thought, the Japanese compilers were obviously not much affected by the Chinese assumption that a dynasty would eventually fall and be replaced by a new one. Instead, the compilers were piecing together, under instructions handed down by Temmu Tennō, a chronicle that would make the *tennō* line long and clear (in a Chinese way) and include ancient myths about divine origins, largely ignoring Chinese ideas about the rise and fall of dynasties.

One year before his death Temmu Tennō restored the old title *(kabane)* system in ways that would give the highest titles to *uji* heads who had risen to the highest posts in his government. Temmu's consort, who reigned as Jitō Tennō from 686 to 697, was a faithful follower of Temmu's policies, apparently adding further touches to his system. It was under Mommu Tennō (Temmu's grandson), however, that the Taihō Penal and Administrative Code was completed and promulgated; it provided a full legal definition to the sinified state structure that had been produced by the Taika Reforms. Surely the most significant representation of that structure, however, was the magnficent new capital erected at Heijō (the present city of Nara) at the beginning of the Nara period, a period when the *ritsuryō* state reached its highest point of development and then lost strength and coherence.

[*See also* Tang Dynasty; Koguryŏ; Paekche; Silla; Nara Period; Ritsuryō State; Temmu; *and* Uji.]

DELMER M. BROWN

TAINAN, important agricultural and commercial center of southwest Taiwan and the island's oldest city. The first Chinese settlements date from 1599. In the early seventeenth century the Dutch conquered the island and established a colonial government at Tainan. The city also served as the stronghold of the Ming loyalist Koxinga (Zheng Chenggong), who expelled the Dutch in 1661. When the island was finally conquered by Qing dynasty forces in 1683, Tainan (then named Taiwan City) was designated its capital and remained so until the late nineteenth century. In the mid-1980s Tainan is a thriving city with a population of 609,934 (1982). It is a major processing center for rice, sugar cane, peanuts, salt, and fish, and also produces textiles, machinery, ice, and soy products.

ANITA M. ANDREW

TAIPEI (Taibei), Chinese city and capital of Taiwan, situated in the northern part of the island near the Tan-shui (Danshui) River. Founded in 1708, Taipei was a minor city until 1875 when it became a walled prefectural center. After 1886, when Taiwan became a separate province of China, Taipei eventually replaced Tainan as the provincial capital. The city quickly developed under the direction of Taiwan's first governor, Liu Mingquan, who transformed Taipei into a modern center with paved streets, electric lights, and a railway system connecting it with the port of Keelung (Jilong) to the east and Hsin-chu (Xinzhu) to the south. Taipei remained the provincial capital following China's defeat in the Sino-Japanese War (1894–1895), when the island was ceded to the Japanese, who occupied it from 1895 to 1945.

Taipei has been the provisional capital of the Nationalists since 1949, when they fled to the island after their defeat by the Communists on mainland China. The city was designated as a special municipality in 1967. In recent years Taipei has become a cosmopolitan, highly industrialized city with a population of 2,327,641 (1982). Its chief products include textiles, fertilizers, chemicals, cement, paper, and electronics.

ANITA M. ANDREW

TAI PEOPLES, major ethnic and linguistic family of Southeast Asia. The relationship of the Tai languages with other Asian tongues has not been established, although a few scholars have suggested an affinity with Austronesian languages. In general, Tai languages are monosyllabic and tonal, but because of their spread from southeastern China to northeastern India, they have borrowed from a wide variety of other languages. Culturally, Tai (variously, Thai, T'ai) peoples are characterized by bilateral kinship systems, domestic architecture featuring houses raised on piles above the ground, and the cultivation of rice. Women traditionally enjoyed high status, and traditional religion included animistic practices.

Of the seventy to eighty million speakers of Tai languages, about half are Thai (Siamese), inhabitants of the central region of Thailand. The next largest group is the Lao, comprising more than twenty million people, most of whom live in northeastern Thailand and the rest in Laos. The Shan of northeastern Burma number approximately three million. The remainder fall into two broad groups. The first, including the Lu of southern Yunnan Province (China) and various upland Tai of northern Vietnam and Laos (Black Tai, White Tai, Red Tai, etc.), numbers nearly three million. The second, including especially the Chuang people of southeastern China, as well as the Nung of Vietnam and a few smaller groups, comes to nearly twenty million. Except for the Chuang and their immediate neighbors, most Tai peoples have maintained some contact over more than two thousand years; their languages have grown apart, but they retain some degree of mutual intelligibility, although they employ a wide variety of different writing systems. The Tai from Laos and Yunnan westward all adopted Buddhism, and their culture, values, and arts were profoundly influenced by the religion and by Indian civilization, while their cousins to the northeast were more influenced by China.

[See also Austronesian Languages; Lao; Shan; and Nung.]

David K. Wyatt, *Thailand: A Short History* (1984). Erik Seidenfaden, *The Thai Peoples* (1967).

DAVID K. WYATT

TAIPING REBELLION. Between the time Buddhism was assimilated and communism arose in China, no movement challenged the Confucian orthodoxy more seriously than did the Taiping Rebellion (1851–1864), an uprising inspired by the efforts of Hong Xiuquan to create a universal, theocratic "Heavenly Kingdom of Great Peace" *(taiping tianguo)*. This kingdom was to be based on Hong's religious vision of a new China redeemed by a synthesis of Biblical monotheism, morality, and universalism with the Chinese notion of filial devotion. It was to be administered by God himself ruling through Hong's vice-regency.

The rebellion grew out of Hong's moral crusade to improve the spiritual and material conditions of his fellow Hakka in the southwestern province of Guangxi during the late 1840s. In the wake of the First Anglo-Chinese War of 1839 to 1842 (the Opium War), Guangxi experienced a stagnating economy and the concentration of land ownership. For the Hakka, this resulted in widespread unemployment, escalating rents, and conflict with earlier settlers and ethnic minorities over land. Banditry, administrative decline, and government corruption were endemic.

By 1847 Feng Yunshan (1822–1852), one of Hong's disciples, organized some three thousand Hakka throughout southeastern Guangxi into the God Worshipers Association. This was a multivillage network of mutual-assistance congregations devoted to Hong's salvationist doctrines. Hong taught that the Chinese should seek spiritual salvation by worshiping God—whom he called the Heavenly Father—and by rejecting Confucian ethics and the polytheistic worship that reinforced it. Moral purity was to be achieved through adherence to the Ten Commandments, which Hong adapted to the conditions in Guangxi. In particular, he prohibited the use of alcohol and opium, gambling, promiscuity, banditry, violence, and feuding over land. Spiritual anxiety was engendered by the Old Testament image of a watchful and exacting Heavenly Father who rewarded the virtuous with Heaven and punished the wicked with Hell—ideas that were also prominent in Chinese religion.

Initiation into the God Worshipers was through the Protestant rite of baptism. Individually, the God Worshipers venerated the Heavenly Father through the traditional Chinese practice of burning incense and gold paper before a tablet on which the characters for Heavenly Father were written. Congregational worship consisted of prayers for spiritual and social salvation, Christian hymns, and sermons exhorting social betterment.

Material salvation came from the "Sacred Treasury," into which all God Worshipers (who called themselves "brothers" and "sisters") pooled their possessions and from which all were given equal shares. These congregations also provided for the defense of the Hakka. Sexual equality was strictly enforced. The God Worshipers dramatized their opposition to the established order by desecrating holy places and religious objects.

By 1848 the God Worshipers entered a second, more militant phase as Hong's theology was linked with a traditional shamanism provided by Yang Xiuqing (d. 1856) and Xiao Chaogui (d. 1852). Amid the onset of famine, typhus, and growing violence over land, Yang and Xiao claimed to speak for the Heavenly Father, to heal in the name of Jesus Christ, and to have the "omniscience" of the Holy Spirit. The enthusiasm this generated, along with the generosity of the Sacred Treasury to relieve hunger, quickly expanded God Worshiper numbers from about three thousand in 1847 to more than one million by 1850.

In 1850 the Qing government decided to suppress the God Worshipers. For this, Hong denounced the Manchus as agents of the "devil," usurpers of the Heavenly Father's role as China's ruler. In January 1851 Hong declared the Taipings' intention to overthrow the Manchu "demons" and to inaugurate the Taiping Heavenly Kingdom throughout China. Hong's moral crusade thus became a political movement.

Hong used the Ten Commandments and the image of an immediate and wrathful Heavenly Father to forge Taiping men and women into an impressive fighting force that won important victories against the Qing. Hong also developed an effective form of theocratic government. This system provided for the reconstruction of state and society in far more revolutionary terms than had been proposed by previous rebel movements. Following the ancient text the *Rites of Zhou,* Taiping officials combined political, military, social, economic, and religious authority and extended state power from the Heavenly Father directly to the individual troops.

In March 1853 the Taipings captured Nanjing, where they established their "New Jerusalem." From here Hong claimed to reign as Heavenly King over a new universal order in which all people—Chinese and non-Chinese alike—were to be treated as brothers and sisters. Integration into this new international community demanded that a "new China" be created, beginning with the ouster of the Manchus. All Chinese in Taiping-held territory were to declare their Han ethnicity by cutting the queue and by wearing Ming-dynasty dress. A cultural revolution was initiated to abolish such "decadent" customs as opium-smoking, gambling, and lewdness. A combination solar and lunar calendar was developed to abolish "superstitious" practices connected with the traditional lunar calendar. The destruction of temples and religious art continued. The scholar's monopoly of learning and bureaucratic power was to be broken with the development of a simplified written vernacular.

Compliance with theocratic rule was reinforced through constant worship. Every Sabbath, Hong, as Heavenly King, publicly venerated the Heavenly Father at the Grand Palace of Glory and Light, in the center of Nanjing. He ordered every government office and private residence to convert a room into a chapel, where a Taiping official was to lead public worship and explain the Bible. Beginning in 1854, every basic administrative unit of twenty-five families, called a "congregation," was to be under the supervision of a "sergeant." This official was responsible for leading worship and supervising the daily lessons for children, who were taught literacy through the Bible and Hong's writings. These also became the basis of the Taiping examination systems.

Every Sabbath the Taiping faithful recited Christian prayers and sang hymns and the doxology to the accompaniment of gongs, drums, and firecrackers. Patriotic sermons preached loyalty to the Heavenly Father and the Taiping leadership and exhorted

victory against the Manchus. Every fourth Sabbath the eucharist was celebrated. The Ten Commandments were read to assembled crowds weekly and were to be committed to memory. Adherence to them was ruthlessly enforced, most infractions resulting in summary execution. The Lord's Prayer was to be posted in every home, and grace was to be said before each meal.

The Taipings raised the status of women by educating them, admitting them into civil and military service, and by abolishing prostitution, concubinage, and footbinding. The Taipings' land system offered a revolutionary view of ownership and social welfare, based on the notion that the Heavenly Father himself owned the land. Men and women were to be granted equal units of similarly productive land. Rents were to be abolished, and taxes were to be drastically modified. Each family was to keep as much produce from its own labors as it needed for food and seed. The surplus was to be stored in public granaries in order to provide for the people's livelihood and to relieve suffering in hard times.

Although the Taipings failed to capture northern China, they did occupy much of the rich lower Yangtze Valley. Problems soon arose, however; Hong Xiuquan withdrew into mental instability, leaving the daily civil and military administration to Yang Xiuqing and his shamanistic antics. By 1856 competition among the competing kings weakened theocratic control. Hong Ren'gan (1822–1864), a cousin of Hong Xiuquan, tried to reverse this downward trend by introducing orthodox Christianity and by offering reform proposals for democracy and economic modernization, but these measures were not taken seriously. [*See also* Hong Ren'gan.]

The Taipings' anti-Confucian ideology failed to win the support of China's gentry. By 1864 the Taipings were eradicated by militia forces loyal to Confucianism and the Manchus under such regional leaders as Zeng Guofan (1811–1872). Imperial forces were assisted by mercenaries from Europe and America, whose governments opposed Taiping notions of international equality and whose missionaries were scandalized by the rebels' unorthodox brand of Christianity. In the end, the Taiping conflict cost twenty million lives and ravaged seventeen provinces. [*See also* Zeng Guofan.]

Beyond the confines of Nanjing and a few experimental areas, the Taipings could not implement much of their revolutionary vision. There were two ways, however, in which they went beyond traditional rebellions to make way for China's modern history of revolution. First, Taiping social radicalism anticipated certain programs championed by the Communists. Second, the Taipings initiated the first phase of China's attempt to restore its lost international prestige. They hoped to achieve China's equality with the West by making China the site of the Heavenly Father's latest revelation. To this end, they sought to abolish Confucianism and destroy the imperial institution by divine means. The Taipings' religiously inspired ideology and organization proved unable to accomplish this goal, yet their efforts anticipated future revolutionary efforts based on strictly secular ideas and methods.

[See also Hong Xiuquan; Hakka; Rebellions in China; and Qing Dynasty.]

Prescott Clarke and J. S. Gregory, eds., *Western Reports on the Taiping* (1982). C. A. Curwen, trans. and ed., *Taiping Rebellion: The Deposition of Li Hsiu-ch'eng* (1977). History of Modern China Series, comp., *The Taiping Revolution* (1976). Jen Yu-wen, *The Taiping Revolutionary Movement* (1973). Franz Michael, in collaboration with Chung-li Chang, *The Taiping Rebellion: History and Documents*, 3 vols. (1966–1971). Vincent Y. C. Shih, *The Taiping Ideology: Its Sources, Interpretations, and Influences* (1967). S. Y. Teng, *The Taiping Rebellion and the Western Powers: A Comprehensive Survey* (1971).   P. RICHARD BOHR

TAIRA NO KIYOMORI (1118–1181), Japanese military leader and the country's foremost politician of the last decades of the Heian period. Taira no Kiyomori was born the eldest son of the chief of the Taira clan, Tadamori, although some sources report he was really the offspring of the emperor Go-Shirakawa. Kiyomori advanced rapidly in his early career, reaching the fourth court rank at age twenty-eight. He assumed the post of chief of the Taira clan upon his father's death in 1153. In 1156 he sided with Go-Shirakawa against the Sūtoku faction in the Hōgen War. He succeeded in eliminating most of the rivalrous Minamoto clan in the Heiji War of 1159. [See Hōgen and Heiji Wars.]

As a favorite of the retired emperor Go-Shirakawa, Kiyomori was named grand chancellor (*dajō daijin*) and elevated to the top court rank, both of which positions he resigned a year later to take the tonsure. Despite his religious vows, Kiyomori bolstered his position by having his nephew (later the emperor Takakura) named heir apparent, marrying a daughter into the Fujiwara clan to obtain their property, and striking an alliance with the temple abbot Meiun of Enryakuji. His economic base included over five hundred *shōen* (feudal estates) and many proprietary provinces; from his villa at

Fukuhara (modern Kobe) he built military power by forming vassal (*gokenin*) ties throughout Japan and even through investing some followers with the newly devised position of steward (*jitō*).

As Kiyomori's power increased so did the number of courtiers who were jealous of him. In 1177 he foiled a scheme against the Taira known as the Shigatani Plot. In 1179, Kiyomori assumed dictatorial power by firing thirty-nine envious officials and imprisoning Go-Shirakawa. However, Kiyomori's coup provoked Minamoto no Yorimasa and his kinsman Yoritomo to open warfare against the Taira. Before he could oversee a successful campaign, Kiyomori caught a fever and died early in 1181.

[See also Heian Period.]

G. Cameron Hurst III, *Insei: Abdicated Sovereigns in the Politics of Late Heian Japan, 1086–1185* (1976). George B. Sansom, *A History of Japan to 1334* (1958). Bruce Tsuchida, trans., *The Tale of the Heike* (1960).

WAYNE FARRIS

TAISHŌ EMPEROR. See Yoshihito.

TAISHŌ POLITICAL CHANGE, term applied to a shift in the balance between rival concepts of administration in Japan (nonpartisan versus party-led cabinets); the change resulted from a political crisis in the first year of the reign of the Taishō emperor (Yoshihito, r. 1912–1926). The crisis began in early December 1912 with the resignation of Saionji Kimmochi's cabinet after the army refused to replace the army minister. The minister had withdrawn because the cabinet disapproved expenditures for two new divisions. Criticism of the army's action escalated when the veteran Chōshū soldier-politician Katsura Tarō, who only four months earlier had retired from political life to serve the inexperienced emperor as lord of the privy seal and grand chamberlain, was designated prime minister by the *genrō* (elder statesmen).

The appointment was denounced as a brazen use of imperial authority, an accusation that gained strength when Katsura employed an imperial edict to force the navy, antagonized by the army's conduct, to provide a minister to complete his cabinet. The major Diet parties joined to form a League for the Protection of the Constitution, which burgeoned into a mass protest movement attracting nationwide support. Katsura countered in two ways: by acting independently of his *genrō* mentor, Yamagata Aritomo, and by organizing a new political party (Dō-shikai). When a resolution of no-confidence was introduced in the House of Representatives, however, he prorogued the body and resorted to an imperial rescript to force its withdrawal. This infuriated and emboldened the opposition. The unprecedented refusal of the Seiyūkai to heed the imperial order to recall the no-confidence resolution, combined with spreading antigovernment riots, caused Katsura to resign only 53 days after taking office.

The crisis passed with the appointment of a cabinet headed by the Satsuma admiral Yamamoto Gonnohyoei, with Seiyūkai members comprising a majority of cabinet members. The crisis illustrated the decline of the bureaucratic old guard and witnessed the first instance in Japan of a political party, combined with popular opinion, toppling a cabinet; it was also the last time a prime minister would use an imperial rescript to intimidate a Diet party. In the end, the crisis represented a political change from conservative bureaucratic dominance to the ascendance of political parties in a period of contending elites.

[See also Saionji Kimmochi; Yamagata Aritomo; and Seiyūkai.]

ROGER F. HACKETT

TAIWAN. Lying in the South China Sea, Taiwan consists of the major island of Taiwan plus two minor island groups—the Penghu Islands (Pescadores) and several uninhabited islands. Taiwan's size is 13,807 square miles, nearly equivalent to the area of Massachusetts. Shaped like a tobacco leaf, it is 244 miles long and 97 miles wide at its broadest point. The island lies 80 miles from the China mainland; the Penghus lie halfway between Taiwan and the mainland in the Taiwan Straits. Three-fourths of the land area of Taiwan is not arable. A high and jagged mountain range with forty peaks over 9,800 feet dominates the eastern spine of the island. Home to 18.9 million people, Taiwan is one of the most densely populated regions in the world, with more than 1,181 persons per square mile. Taiwan today is recognized as a province of China, currently under the rule of the Republic of China. Ninety-seven percent of the people speak Han Chinese. The dialects include Mandarin, Taiwanese, and Hakka. [See also Pescadores and the map accompanying China.]

Early History. Until the Pleistocene epoch Taiwan was attached to the Asian mainland. The discovery of cord-marked pottery shards dated to about 3000 BCE has led to speculations about similarities with Japanese and especially Chinese cord-ware cultures. The earliest inhabitants of Taiwan originated from southern or oceanic stock and are identified linguistically by Malayo-Polynesian language characteristics. These indigenous groups practiced slash-and-burn agriculture, tatooed their bodies, and engaged in headhunting. Prior to the migration of the Chinese to the island, this indigenous population lived in the plains. The Chinese immigrants, primarily from Fujian and Guangdong provinces, drove them up into the mountains, where they were called Gaoshan ("high mountain"). Today they number about 220,000 people.

Not until the seventeenth century did the Chinese finally refer to the island as Taiwan. The name means "terraced bay" and may have referred to the harbor of Tainan. Significant settlement by Chinese occurred under the Dutch colonists (1642–1661). Owing to their colonization policies, the Dutch required the services of migrant laborers, skilled farmers, and traders, and thus promoted immigration. Consequently, the Chinese population of the island increased from 25,000 in 1624 to 100,000 in 1650. The Manchu conquest of China in the early seventeenth century also drove many refugees from South China to Taiwan. Among these refugees were Ming-dynasty loyalists.

One famous loyalist was Zheng Chenggong (Koxinga), who in 1662 expelled the Dutch. After his short-lived reign on the island, internal turmoil led to the island's surrender to the Manchu government of China in 1683. [See also Zheng Chenggong.] For the first time Taiwan became a formal administrative district under the authority of China's Fujian Province. Taiwan received separate provincial status in 1885, and under the leadership of Governor Liu Mingquan (from 1885 to 1891) produced the first railway system in China. Liu's reforms in education, transportation, communications, and industry made Taiwan the most modernized province in China. In 1895 Taiwan, with a population of 3.2 million, was ceded to Japan as a prize of the Sino-Japanese War of 1894 to 1895. [See also Sino-Japanese War.]

Formosa and Japanese Rule. Article II of the Treaty of Shimonoseki (1895) gave Japan full sovereignty over "the island of Formosa." This name, *Formosa*, which is still in use today, is what the Portuguese named the island in 1590. Impressed by its beauty, they called it Ilha Formosa, or "beautiful island." Japanese colonialization of Taiwan was hampered by strong Taiwanese political and military resistance. On 25 May 1895, the Taiwanese proclaimed the establishment of a short-lived democratic Republic of Taiwan. Although brief in duration, this was the first "republic" in Asia. After five months of "pacification," the Japanese crushed the new republic.

Japan's first overseas possession, Taiwan was intensively developed and rigorously administered by the Japanese colonial bureaucracy. Japanese colonial policies were in large part shaped by the needs and interests of the home islands rather than those of the Taiwanese, who were permitted little voice in the management of the Colony. This colonial relationship was reflected in the Japanese policy slogan "Agricultural Taiwan—Industrial Japan." Nevertheless, Japanese colonialism yielded substantial benefits to the Taiwanese. Under Kodama Gentarō, the fourth governor-general, and his energetic and talented civil administrator, Gotō Shimpei, a series of administrative and economic reforms were carried out in the early 1900s, marking the initial stage of the remarkable modernization and economic growth that the island enjoyed under Japanese rule over the next forty years.

Through the 1920s Taiwan played an important role in satisfying Japan's growing demands for agricultural products and raw materials. In the 1930s, as Japan began to prepare for war, Taiwan was intensively developed as an industrial base. Early in the Pacific War the island was a staging area for Japanese offensives into Southeast Asia, but by 1944 Taiwan came under heavy American aerial attack.

The Republic of China. On 25 October 1945 Japan surrendered Taiwan to the government of China in accordance with the Cairo Declaration of 1943. Misrule and oppression by rapacious Chinese troops resulted in the bloody Taiwanese uprising of 1947 and the brief formation of an autonomous republic. This was quickly suppressed by Chinese troops.

In 1949, as the Chinese Communists took power on the mainland, the Nationalist regime of Chiang Kai-shek and the remnants of his army escaped to Taiwan. Initially, the US government refused to provide military protection, but two days after the outbreak of the Korean War on 27 June 1950, President Truman ordered the Seventh Fleet to protect Taiwan from Communist attack. This presidential directive prevented the Communists from uniting Taiwan with the mainland. As a result, the governments in both Beijing and Taipei (Taibei) continue to claim to be the legitimate authority for all of China.

Retreating from the Communist victory on the mainland in 1949, Chiang Kai-shek established the seat of government of the Republic of China (ROC) in Taipei. As president, he was responsible for per-petuating the policy of mainland recovery and rejecting all compromises with the People's Republic of China (PRC). In maintaining his claim to represent all of China, Chiang reorganized the government to place more control in the hands of the mainlanders. This policy created tensions between the mainlander refugees (about two million) and the Taiwanese (about nine million). Security controls were increased and martial law was employed against both Communist and Taiwanese "rebels." Since Chiang concentrated on military and political preparations for retaking the Chinese mainland, he delegated the economic policies to a pragmatic group of technocrats. As military reconquest became an improbable dream and Chiang aged, he withdrew into an austere and ascetic life. He died on 5 April 1975 at the age of eighty-seven. His body is temporarily interred near Taipei, awaiting a final resting place in China.

Following Chiang Kai-shek's death, power was turned over to his son Chiang Ching-kuo. He has not abandoned his father's ultimate goal of mainland recovery, but has actively concentrated on economic reforms, reindustrialization, and modernization. Under Chiang Ching-kuo Taiwan has become more than just a province of China supporting a hostile competitor to Beijing. Reelected in 1984 to another six-year term, Chiang Ching-kuo chose the Taiwanese-born technocrat Lee Deng-hui to be vice president. The "taiwanization" of the political regime is a major issue for the leaders of the Republic of China.

Politically, the government of the ROC is based on a national legislative body that includes representatives initially elected or appointed in 1948 from each of the provinces of China. The national capital is Taipei. The provincial capital of Taiwan is Taichung (Taizhong). The government is basically run by the Guomindang (Kuomintang), but recently a small opposition has emerged. The governor and the mayors of Taipei and Kao-hsiung (Gaoxiong) are appointed by the national government. Other local officials are elected. Full expression of human rights is hampered by martial law, one-party rule, the banning of journals, and the arrest of opposition leaders. Labor unions are tightly controlled.

Economically, the island has shown spectacular growth. Success has been made possible by the strong Japanese legacy, substantial US aid, an energetic land reform program, state intervention, and a growing class of technocrats. In 1981 Taiwan boasted a per capita income of US $2,570, one of the highest in Asia. Its income distribution pattern is very narrow. The top twentieth percentile earned only 4.4 times as much as the lowest twentieth percentile in 1979. This places Taiwan in the low inequality range with Korea, Canada, and Japan.

Taiwan's main crops are rice, sugar cane, sweet potatoes, and tropical fruits. Sugar is the second most important cash crop. Industrially, Taiwan's heavy industry is well developed in iron, steel, and petroleum. The Export Processing Zones produce computers, textiles, and other consumer goods for export. Owing to poor sources for hydroelectric power and the pollution from burning coal, Taiwan is pursuing a large-scale expansion of the use of nuclear power.

Taiwan has retained many cultural and religious traditions. Confucianism, Daoism, and Buddhism are still widespread. Folk religions and shamanistic practices enjoy great popularity, especially in the countryside. Christianity is a minor religion but is important because many adherents are political and intellectual leaders and because the church receives support from abroad. The Presbyterian church is the oldest Christian establishment, founded by George Leslie Mackay in 1871. It is the largest single Christian denomination in Taiwan, with more than two hundred thousand members, a seminary, a medical school, and many outreach activities.

A new vernacular literature dealing with everyday social, political, and economic problems has gained popularity. Taiwan's intellectual climate promotes modern expressions in the arts, music, and literature.

International Status. In 1955, by a mutual assistance treaty, the United States pledged to defend the island from attacks from the mainland. It also led a political and economic boycott of China. In 1972 the Nixon visit to China initiated a process that led to the erosion of formal diplomatic ties with Taiwan. The Shanghai Communiqué, signed by President Nixon and Premier Zhou Enlai in February 1972, has become the basis for relations between the US and China. It confirms that there is but one China and that Taiwan is part of that China. It led to US withdrawal of troops from Taiwan and the gradual reduction of military sales. The United States dropped its boycott of China, and the representative of China replaced Taiwan's representative in the United Nations. In 1978 President Carter's normalization of relations with China was followed by the suspension of embassy status in Taiwan. Through the Congressional Taiwan Relations Act of 1979, a private-government institute known

as the American Institute in Taiwan took over all diplomatic responsibilities. This is a unique development in American foreign relations. [*See also* Shanghai Communiqué.]

The future of Taiwan remains a thorny issue. The People's Republic of China has mounted an intensive campaign to reclaim Taiwan, warning that full US relations cannot be realized until incorporation of the island is accomplished. The Republic of China shows no willingness to compromise its sovereignty, although it does allow for third-party commercial trade. The Taiwanese, with the support of the native Presbyterian church, have supported a movement for an independent republic.

Ironically, Taiwan's unclear future has not harmed its economic development or its international activities. As an island, it is more strategically positioned to develop its own course than if it were on the Chinese mainland. However, its political status is still questioned by Beijing, resulting in a continual sense of crisis on the island in international affairs.

[*See also* China, Republic of; Guomindang; Chiang Kai-shek; *and* Chiang Ching-kuo.]

Ralph Clough, *Island China* (1978). Frederick J. Foley, *The Great Formosan Imposter* (1968). George H. Kerr, *Formosa: Licensed Revolution and the Home Rule Movement, 1895–1945* (1974). E. Patricia Tsurumi, *Japanese Colonial Education in Taiwan, 1895–1945* (1977).

RICHARD C. KAGAN

TAIYUAN, the capital of Shanxi Province, China, is a city of 1,750,000 inhabitants (1982). For centuries Taiyuan has been the economic, political, and cultural center of the province. It has also been of great strategic importance as the guardian of the central Shanxi plain. As a result of its location, Taiyuan has experienced great violence in its long history of invasion and rebellion. Taiyuan was first known by the name Jinyang during the Western Zhou dynasty (1122–771 BCE) and flourished as a frontier trading post for many centuries. Taiyuan and the entire province were among the earliest regions to rebel against the Qing dynasty in the 1911 Revolution. In 1912 the warlord Yan Xishan established a local military government in the region and ruled with great power until 1949. In recent years Taiyuan has been an important iron and steel center, in addition to producing aluminum, tractors, agricultural machinery, heavy machinery, cement, chemicals, and ceramics.   ANITA M. ANDREW

TAIZHOU SCHOOL, Chinese Neo-Confucian philosophical school that represents the activist-oriented branch of the School of Mind. While members of the Taizhou school followed Wang Yangming's (1472–1529) lead in seeking to break out of the rigid philosophical orthodoxy of Zhu Xi (1130–1200), they went beyond Wang's identification of knowledge with action to make action the key to the sagely mind. This school of thought derives its name from the native district of its founding philosopher, Wan Gen (1483–1540). Exerting a wide influence on the intellectual climate of sixteenth-century China, Taizhou adherents represented a diversity of socioeconomic groups and intellectual ideas and spread the teachings of Wang Yangming as never before.

[See also Ming Dynasty; Neo-Confucianism; Wang Gen; Wang Yangming; and Zhu Xi.]

Judith Berling, *The Syncretic Religion of Lin Chao-en* (1980). Wm. Theodore de Bary, "Individualism and Humanitarianism in Late Ming Thought," in *Self and Society in Ming Thought* (1970), pp. 145–247.

ANITA M. ANDREW

TAJIKISTAN. The Tajik Soviet Socialist Republic, commonly referred to as Tajikistan (Tadzhikistan), is a republic of the Soviet Union located in southeastern Central Asia. Its capital is the city of Dushanbe. Bordered by Afghanistan in the south and the People's Republic of China in the east, its Soviet neighbors are the Uzbek and Kirghiz republics.

Tajikistan is traversed from east to west by a number of mountain ranges. Its generally mountainous terrain has two of the Soviet Union's highest mountains, Communism Peak and Lenin Peak. To the north flows the Syr Darya River and to the south, the Amu Darya. In the mountains, the average yearly temperature is below freezing, while a hot and dry climate prevails in the lowlands, with temperatures ranging from 3 degrees centigrade in January to 40 degrees centigrade in July. Rain falls heavily in the foothills.

In the fifteenth century the Uzbeks, Turkic nomads who were part of the Golden Horde, swept through Central Asia. It was the last major invasion before the Russians came. One could distinguish Tajiks from Uzbeks by their use of the Persian language. Persian was accepted as the court language by the different khans.

The British, established in India, attempted to extend their influence to Afghanistan from the southeast, while the Russians expanded from the north-west. In the 1860s the Russian conquest of Central Asia began. It was motivated in part by their need for cotton. In 1867 the Russian province of Turkestan was formed, and by 1868 the Russians had forced Bukhara to become their protectorate, as they had forced Khiva in 1873. In 1876 Khokand was incorporated into Russian Turkestan. The region of modern Tajikistan was divided between the khanate of Bukhara and the Samarkand and Ferghana provinces of Russian Turkestan at the beginning of the twentieth century. Turkestan was governed by military governors under Russian colonial rule.

Much of Tajikistan was included in the Turkestan Autonomous Soviet Socialist Republic established in 1918. The Bukharan People's Soviet Republic was declared in 1920, and in 1921 the Soviets took Dushanbe and Kulyab. There was a Basmachi revolt in Tajikistan from 1922 to 1923. On 5 December 1929 the area was renamed Tajik Soviet Socialist Republic. According to the 1970 census, Tajikistan has a population of 2.9 million. Its principal cities are Dushanbe, Leninabad, Ura-Tyube, Kulyab, and Kurgan-Tyube.

The culture of the Tajik people is Iranian and their language is a Persian dialect, although it has been written in the Cyrillic script since 1940. About 27 percent of the population of Tajikistan is of Turkic descent, mainly Uzbeks who resist iranization. For that reason there are several newspapers published in Uzbek as well as Uzbek schools. Radio and television broadcasts are in the Tajik, Russian, and Uzbek languages.

The economy of Tajikistan is based on the cultivation of cotton. Food processing is the main industry. Although cotton is the main agricultural crop large quantities of fruit are also grown. Tajikistan has a considerable cattle-breeding industry as well.

Edward Allworth, ed., *Central Asia: A Century of Russian Life* (1967). Teresa Rakowska-Harmstone, *Russia and Nationalism in Central Asia: The Case of Tadzhikistan* (1970).   ISABELLA IBRAHIMOV

TAJ MAHAL. Shah Jahan, the fifth Mughal emperor, built the Taj Mahal in Agra as a mausoleum for his favorite wife, Mumtaz Mahal (d. 1631). The single-domed white marble structure, flanked by four towering minarets, is evolved from Timurid tombs and more immediately from Humayun's tomb in Delhi. Located in a walled garden divided by four watercourses, the Taj Mahal's setting is inspired by Qur'anic descriptions of paradise. Para-

FIGURE 1. *View of the Taj Mahal, Agra.*

disical symbolism here is more complex than in earlier Mughal tombs, for the Taj Mahal likely represents the Throne of God on the Day of Judgment, which, according to Islamic thought, is situated just above paradise. The program of the tomb's Qur'anic verses reveals a preoccupation with this final day. Moreover, the layout of the entire complex closely resembles Ibn al-Arabi's diagram of the assembled on the Day of Judgment, where the Throne of God is located at the far end, corresponding to the position of the Taj Mahal within its walled garden.

[*See also* Agra *and* Shah Jahan.]

Wayne E. Begley, "The Myth of the Taj Mahal and a New Theory of its Symbolic Meaning," *Art Bulletin* 56 (1979). John D. Hoag, *Islamic Architecture* (1977). R. Nath, *The Immortal Taj Mahal: The Evolution of the Tomb in Mughal Architecture* (1972).

CATHERINE B. ASHER

TAKAHASHI KOREKIYO (1854–1936), prime minister of Japan from 1921 to 1922; better remembered for his skillful service as minister of finance in the cabinets of Tanaka Giichi (1917–1929), Inukai Tsuyoshi, Saitō Makoto, and Okada Keisuke (1931–1936), after which his service was cut short by assassination in the army rebellion of 26 February 1936 (known as the February Twenty-sixth Incident).

Takahashi was born in Edo (modern Tokyo) in the closing years of the Tokugawa shogunate to an artist in government service. He was adopted by a samurai family of Sendai and sent by Sendai authorities to the United States for study in 1867. On his return he served as student assistant to Mori

Arinori and filled a number of low-ranking bureaucratic posts thereafter. A post in the Patent Office was followed by jobs in the Bank of Japan and the Yokohama Specie Bank, after which alternating service in the latter two found him heading each in turn and becoming nationally and internationally known.

After 1913 Takahashi entered politics as finance minister under Yamamoto Gonnohyōei and again under Hara Takashi. Known for sound finance in Meiji times, he achieved even greater success in his efforts to reflate the economy through public spending after depression struck Japan in 1927. His tenure as prime minister was brief and undistinguished, but his contributions as a financial expert were widely praised. By the mid-1930s he was resisting further spending on arms as irresponsible, however, and this helped bring on the attack that cost him his life. His death marked the beginning of the military's increasing influence on Japan's fiscal policies in the prewar years.

[*See also* February Twenty-sixth Incident.]

MICHIO UMEGAKI

TAKAMAGAHARA, "Heaven" in Japanese myth. The word *Takamagahara* literally means "the high fields of Heaven." In the *Kojiki* (712) and *Nihon shoki* (720) Takamagahara is the uppermost plane of a three-tiered cosmology. Beneath it is the world of human beings (*ashihara,* "land of the reed fields"), and beneath that is a shadowy underworld of the dead (*ne no kuni* and other terms). In Japanese myth the deities (*kami*) living in Takamagahara eat, sleep, and perform other mundane activities, much as in the human world. Takamagahara is a pure place, and to defile it, as the deity Susano-o does, is evil. Life in Takamagahara is not a reward for past good deeds. Some of the Shinto sects, however, hold that after death people become *kami* and dwell in Takamagahara.

In addition to the literal interpretation of Takamagahara as an actual place, it is regarded also as a state of mind or an ideal state of affairs in which a person is in perfect harmony with his environment and other people, and in which his heart and mind are at peace. This interpretation is found among the Shinto sects and more generally in popular culture.

HELEN HARDACRE

TAKANO CHŌEI. *See* Watanabe Kazan and Takano Chōei.

TAKEDA SHINGEN (1521–1573), a powerful daimyo of northern Japan during the late Sengoku period. The Takeda family had been *shugo* (feudal lords) of Kai province from the medieval period. Family fortunes waned during the first half of the sixteenth century, but in 1541 Takeda Shingen assumed family headship and over the course of the next two decades fought his way to domination of the provinces of Kai and Shinano. Although Shingen was never able to defeat his neighbor and rival Uesugi Kenshin, he did battle his way into Hida and the northern Kantō, and by the 1570s he had extended his authority over Suruga, becoming one of the most powerful daimyo in the Chūbu region. In the early 1570s Shingen moved his troops deeper into central Japan. Historians are divided about the purpose of this campaign, some seeing it as merely a foray to add more regional power, others as the first step in a drive toward Kyoto and a try for national conquest. Shingen fought brilliantly in the opening battle at Mikatagahara, along the lower reaches of the Tenryū River, dealing a sharp defeat to the allied forces of Tokugawa Ieyasu and Oda Nobunaga in January 1573. But a month later Takeda Shingen fell ill and died in the field.

Shingen was succeeded by Katsuyori, who was defeated by the combined armies of Tokugawa Ieyasu and Oda Nobunaga at the Battle of Nagashino in 1575. Takeda family fortunes never recovered, and Katsuyori committed suicide after being attacked again by Nobunaga in 1582, bringing an end to the Takeda line of daimyo.

In addition to their battlefield exploits, the Takeda family is remembered for the techniques they employed to enhance their authority over the people and resources of their domain. They encouraged the development of new paddy and the opening of mines. In the early sixteenth century, the Takeda were among the first damiyo families to compile a detailed set of house laws covering weights and measures, coinage, trade, commerce, taxation, and jurisdiction over the affairs of their vassals. Such codes represented the beginnings of a new legal and administrative structure, institutionalized during the early modern period, by which daimyo claimed powers that were tantamount to sovereign authority over their domains.

[*See also* Sengoku Period.]

JAMES L. MCCLAIN

TAKIZAWA BAKIN (1767–1848), Japanese writer of historical romances. Takizawa Bakin was born to a samurai family that had come down in the world, and he was determined to restore the family's fortunes. He turned to fiction out of financial necessity and eventually became successful as a professional author. His writings played a great part in the commercialization of literature in the late Tokugawa period. His two most famous works are *Crescent Moon* (*Chinzetsu yumiharizuki*, 1806–1810), a transformation of the twelfth-century hero Minamoto no Tametomo into an exemplar of the samurai ideal, and *Biographies of Eight "Dogs"* (*Nansō Satomi hakkenden*, 1814–1841), which deals with the restoration of a samurai family's fortunes by a band of eight men, each of whom personifies one of the Confucian virtues. Both of these are modeled partly on Chinese colloquial fiction. Bakin's plots are invariably set in pre-Tokugawa times and their intent is didactic. They represent an attempt to shift the arena of the heroic away from the pleasure quarters and the world of the townsman and back to that of the warrior. The inevitable result was not a romanticized history of Kamakura times but rather full-blown historical romances, a sure sign that the samurai himself had already passed into the realm of fiction.

[*See also* Tokugawa Period.]

Leon M. Zolbrod, *Takizawa Bakin* (1967).

RICHARD BOWRING

TAKLAMAKAN, one of the world's largest sand deserts (c. 105,000 square miles). Located in the central Tarim Basin, the Taklamakan is bounded by Lop Nur in the east and by high mountains on the other three sides. Its few Turkic inhabitants farm along the Tarim River and its tributaries, among great dunes and scanty wildlife.

CHRISTOPHER I. BECKWITH

TAKSIN, king of Siam (r. 1768–1781), was a military hero who reunited the Siamese kingdom after it had shattered into several rival camps when its capital, Ayudhya, was captured and sacked by a Burmese army in 1767. Taksin was born in 1734 to a Teochiu Chinese father, a petty merchant and gambling-tax concessionaire, and a Thai mother. As a boy he received the patronage of an aristocratic Thai family and was given the education a young Thai male of good birth would have received. He entered government service and rose to the rank of governor of the frontier province of Tak. (The name by which he is remembered is a combination of his gubernatorial title, Phraya Tak, and his personal name, Sin.)

During the defense of Ayudhya, he distinguished himself in battle, but when a Burmese victory seemed inevitable, he took several hundred followers and broke out of the encirclement, establishing a base on the coast near the Cambodian border. After the victorious Burmese army withdrew, he recaptured the central Thai plain from the remaining Burmese garrison, distributed food to the starving populace, and began reestablishing orderly government. Within three years, he had defeated all rival pretenders to the throne, incorporating their territories into his kingdom. Abandoning plans to rebuild the ruined capital, he began constructing a new capital at Thonburi, across the river from modern Bangkok, but it remained uncompleted at his death. He also began a program of cultural reconstruction, sponsoring, for example, recopyings of the Tripitaka and the *Thai Three Worlds Cosmology,* to replace the treasures lost in the sack of Ayudhya. Meanwhile, he—and, after he quit active campaigning, his generals—repulsed new Burmese invasion attempts while also leading Thai armies into Cambodia and the Lao states, forcing these kingdoms to send tribute to Thonburi.

Taksin appears to have been deeply committed to Buddhism and seems to have been particularly interested in esoteric meditation techniques. Millennial and esoteric forms of Buddhism appear to have been particularly strong in the Theravada Buddhist world during this period, and perhaps Taksin was merely responding to his times. Toward the end of his reign he became convinced he had entered the fourth-highest stage of consciousness leading to ultimate arahatship, and he demanded that monks venerate him as a living Buddha image when he was sitting in *samadhi* (meditative) pose. Schism in the Thai *sangha* (monastic order) followed, and this, together with other policies of his that appear to have threatened the existing social and economic order, led to accusations that he was mad and to loss of the elite support he had gained earlier. When a rebellion of low-ranking officials broke out against him, no one of higher standing intervened until it was too late, and he was forced to relinquish his throne. The crown was offered to and accepted by his most famous and brilliant general, and Taksin was executed.

Lorraine Gesick, "The Rise and Fall of King Taksin," in *Centers, Symbols, and Hierarchies,* edited by Lorraine Gesick (1983). David K. Wyatt, *Thailand: A Short History* (1984).

LORRAINE M. GESICK

TALEGHANI, MAHMUD (1911–1979), Iranian religious scholar who devoted his life to struggle against the Pahlavi regime. He was born in the village of Gilird in the Talaqan (Taleghan) district of northern Iran to Abu al-Hasan Taleghani, himself a religious scholar and activist of note, but he grew up and received his early education in Tehran, where the elder Taleghani had settled in 1899. In the early 1930s he went to Qom for his further religious education; there he studied under such luminaries as Shaikh Abd al-Karim Ha'eri and the ayatollahs Muhammad Taqi Khwansari, Hujjat Kuhkamari, and Muhammad Taqi Yazdi. But for all the erudition he acquired during his years in Qom, Taleghani never identified fully with the religious institution and its hierarchy (in marked contrast to, for example, Ayatollah Khomeini); it was rather in bringing the message of Islam to society at large and in collaborating with persons and parties outside the hierarchy that he acquired his great standing and influence.

Taleghani completed his training in Qom in 1939 and, returning to Tehran, he began teaching at the Sipahsalar *madrasa.* At the same time, he embarked on the teaching of Qur'anic exegesis to the secularly educated—which was to remain a lifelong concern—under the auspices of an organization he founded, the Kanun-i Islam. This led to a period of banishment from Tehran that ended in 1941. He then began to preach and lecture at the Hidayat Mosque in central Tehran, which soon became a gathering place for the religiously inclined youth of the capital and remained inseparably linked with him to the end of his life. In addition, he gave frequent lectures to the Islamic societies that were springing up at the time, both in the universities and among professionals.

Although Taleghani accompanied the government troops that entered Azerbaijan in 1946 to overthrow the remnants of a separatist regime in that province, his political activity in the 1940s and 1950s was more typically in collaboration with personalities opposed to the Pahlavis. Among these were Navvab Safavi, founder and leader of the Fida'iyan-i Islam, who took shelter in Taleghani's house on more than one occasion when being hunted by the police; and Ayatollah Kashani, the celebrated religious scholar and militant who played a crucial role in organizing mass support for the nationalization of the Iranian oil industry. Taleghani also broadcast on behalf of Mohammed Mossadegh, the prime minister under whose auspices the nationalization was carried out, and he did his utmost to avert the split between Kashani and Mossadegh that came on the eve of the foreign-sponsored royalist coup d'état of August 1953 that restored the Pahlavis to power.

Four years after the coup, Taleghani organized the National Resistance Movement, the first broad-based movement of opposition to the resurgent Pahlavi dictatorship. This earned him a period of imprisonment that lasted for more than a year. Undaunted, in 1960 he addressed a mass protest meeting at the Maidan-i Arg in Tehran and was accordingly rearrested. Released anew, he established the Iran Freedom Movement in collaboration with his lifelong colleague and friend, Mehdi Bazargan, a political organization that has survived into the postrevolutionary period. This led to a new spell in prison, which came to an end shortly before the uprising of June 1963. The speeches Taleghani delivered in support of this uprising caused him to be rearrested and, after a lengthy public trial in which he conducted himself with great dignity, to be condemned to ten years' imprisonment. He was released after serving half of this sentence. In 1971 he helped to establish the Sazman-i Mujahidin-i Khalq (Organization of People's Mujahidin), a guerrilla group initially of Islamic inspiration. As a consequence he was banished from Tehran for three years. When he returned he found the leadership of the group about to make an ideological transition to Marxism. Taleghani kept his links with the still-Islamic rump of the Mujahidin, and this earned him a new sentence of ten years' imprisonment.

This final incarceration was brought to an end on 30 October 1978, when the Pahlavi state was crumbling under the onslaught of revolution. Released from prison, Taleghani immersed himself in the revolutionary movement, and it was he who marched at the head of the historic mass demonstration of 10 December 1978. He was appointed to the Council of the Islamic Revolution established by Ayatollah Khomeini, and after the triumph of the revolution he traveled in its service to Kurdistan and the Turkmen-inhabited areas of the northeast to negotiate with autonomist groups. In August 1979, Taleghani was elected to the Assembly of Experts, which was to elaborate a constitution, with over two million votes, more than any other candidate, a clear measure of his wide popularity. Later the same month, Khomeini appointed him *imam jum'a* (Friday prayer leader) of Tehran, and his weekly sermons, delivered at Tehran University, drew millions.

A dominant concern of Taleghani in 1979 was maintaining the unity of the revolutionary and Islamic forces, and this led to a frequent misperception of him as "an ayatollah of the left." Although willing to engage in ideological debate with Marxists and, for a time, inclined to regard them as sincere, if misled, he was always firmly opposed to Marxism. In the last sermon of his life he bitterly denounced "those infantile communists" who were working against the Islamic Republic.

Ayatollah Taleghani died of a heart attack on 10 September 1979 and was buried in the Bihisht-i Zahra cemetery to the south of Tehran, next to the martyrs of the revolution whose advent he had done so much to foster.

[*See also* Bazargan, Mehdi; Khomeini, Ruhollah Musavi; *and* Mossadegh, Mohammed.]

Sayyid Mahmud Taleghani, *Society and Economics in Islam*, translated by R. Campbell (1983).

HAMID ALGAR

TALI. *See* Dali.

TALUQDAR. Derived from the Arabic *ta'aluq* (dependence upon or connection with a superior), the term *taluqdar* was applied in India from late Mughal times onward to landholders possessed of substantial estates for whose revenue they were responsible either to a superior landholder (in Bengal, the *zamindar*) or directly to the government. After the 1857 revolt the British awarded the title as a specially privileged mark of membership in a landed elite, to some three hundred individuals in Awadh (Oudh).

[*See also* Awadh *and* Land Tenure and Reform: Land Tenure, Revenue, and Reform in South Asia.]

THOMAS R. METCALF

TAMANG, a Mongoloid people inhabiting the highlands of central and eastern Nepal and Darjeeling, where they are known as Murmi. Tamang language and culture suggest Tibetan origins; their name has been translated from the Tibetan to mean "horsemen" or "cavalry," but their major means of livelihood today is subsistence agriculture supplemented with migrant wage labor, especially in Kathmandu, where they work as porters and rickshaw drivers. Tamangs are nominal Buddhists, employing both Tantric lamas and spirit mediums to propitiate local deities. The Tamang constitute Nepal's largest ethnic minority.

[*See also* Nepal: History of Nepal.]

A. MacDonald, *The Ethnology of Nepal and South Asia* (1975).

RICHARD ENGLISH

TAMAN SISWA, nationalist education movement in the Netherlands East Indies (Indonesia).

The movement was founded at Yogyakarta in 1921 by Suwardi Suryaningrat (Ki Hadyar Dewantoro), a leading nationalist intellectual of the previous decade, upon his return from exile in the Netherlands. It aimed to establish an educational system synthesizing the best of Western and Indonesian culture. Many of the graduates of the more than two hundred Taman Siswa schools became leading nationalist politicians.

Ruth McVey, "Taman Siswa and the Indonesian National Awakening," *Indonesia* (1967).

DAVID K. WYATT

TAMBRALINGA, ancient state on the Malay Peninsula, centered on the region of Nakhon Si Thammarat. It is referred to in Indian texts from the second century CE and later in Chinese records. Connected at various times with the empires of Srivijaya (Sumatra), Angkor (Cambodia), and Pagan (Burma), it owed its strength to its access to forest products of the peninsula and its ability to control transpeninsula trade routes, and it was an early important center of Buddhism. The apogee of its power was reached under Chandrabhanu in the thirteenth century. The Thai state of Nakhon Si Thammarat then succeeded to its fortunes.

[*See also* Nakhon Si Thammarat; Srivijaya; Angkor; Pagan; Chandrabhanu; *and* Langkasuka.]

G. Coedès, *The Indianized States of Southeast Asia,* translated by Susan B. Cowing (1968). O. W. Wolters, "Tambralinga," *Bulletin of the School of Oriental and African Studies* 21 (1958): 587–607. DAVID K. WYATT

TAMERLANE. *See* Timur.

TAMIL LANGUAGE AND LITERATURE. *See* Dravidian Languages and Literatures.

TAMIL NADU is the historic land of speakers of the Dravidian language, Tamil; it also denotes a state in the Republic of India, and like other states (e.g., Bengal, Gujarat), it takes its name from the language of most of its people.

The contemporary state of Tamil Nadu occupies an area of about 81,000 square miles in the southernmost portion of the Indian subcontinent; its population was 41 million in 1971. Of the states of the Indian Republic, Tamil Nadu ranks eleventh in area and seventh in population. It has a long sea frontier (over 600 miles) and a history of commercial, cultural, and social contacts with the world beyond India proper. With 30 percent of its population designated as "urban" (i.e., living in "municipal" settlements of 5,000 or more persons), Tamil Nadu is reckoned as highly urbanized in a nation that counts 18 percent of its people as town-dwellers. Corresponding with this degree of urbanism are other characteristics: literacy in the state in 1971 was 39 percent, ranking second in a nation whose overall literacy was 29 percent; in economic terms, Tamil Nadu is considered one of the most advanced states, comparing favorably with the states of Punjab and Maharashtra.

Tamil Nadu is culturally homogeneous. Ninety percent of its people are Hindus, 5 percent are Muslims, and 5 percent are Christians. Linguistically, over 90 percent of the most populous districts of the state are Tamil speakers; this declines to between 75 and 90 percent in interior districts where substantial minorities speak Telugu, Kannada, or Malayalam. As of 1961 Urdu was spoken by about one-half million Muslims in the state; a little over 2 percent spoke Hindi (the lowest of any Indian state); and almost 4 percent of the people of Tamil Nadu spoke English (along with Delhi territory, the highest proportion in India).

The relative cultural homogeneity of Tamil Nadu is the product of modern political processes as well as those of great antiquity. *Tamil Nadu* replaced *Madras* as the name of the state in 1969 following the election, in 1967, of the Dravida Munnetra Kazhagam, a movement and party dedicated to the preservation of Tamil culture and the displacement of brahman dominance in public affairs. This victory had followed a dismemberment of the Madras state that had succeeded to control of the British-ruled Madras Presidency at the time of independence in 1947. Between 1953 and 1956 the large Madras state had been halved in extent by the creation of the state of Andhra Pradesh to its north, which received the districts in northern Madras where Telugu was the dominant language, and by the transfer of speakers of Kannada to the state of Mysore (renamed Karnataka in 1973) and speakers of Malayalam to the state of Kerala. It was within this now diminished Madras, consisting of speakers of Tamil, that the Dravida Munnetra Kazhagam won power from the Congress Party and capped a struggle of over a generation for its cultural and social objectives. The central element in this struggle was the Tamil language and its historic role.

Tamil is the oldest of the Dravidian family of languages in India; it is also distinctive among the Dravidian languages by the fact that the technical apparatus of the language—its standardized forms and its grammars—was created much earlier than those in other Dravidian languages and in the Tamil language itself, not in the Sanskrit, as was the case with Kannada, Telugu, and Malayalam. The term *Tamil Nadu* occurs in the *Kural*, a text thought to date from the late fifth century CE, where it designates the region in which Tamil was then spoken. But long before then we have Tamil texts. The earliest are brief cave inscriptions of Jains and Buddhists, dated from between the third and first centuries BCE. Within the next two centuries the first of a bardic corpus was composed; in the form of later anthologies, these poems came to be known as "Sangam poetry." In its full development by the sixth century, Tamil Sangam poetry comprised 26,000 lines of verse fully deserving of its title "classical."

From the very earliest times for which there are historical records of any sort until the seventh century, Tamil country was open to and influenced by the Sanskrit language and its learning; in the South generally, this influence was borne more by Jains and Buddhists than by proponents of the Vedic religion. Between the seventh and the ninth centuries two important processes changed the course of cultural development in Tamil country. One, political, was the establishment of the Pallava kingdom in the central part of Tamil Nadu. The Pallavas were unrelated to any of the Tamil kingships that had existed before. These latter—the Cholas, Cheras, and Pandyas—are mentioned in rock edicts of the Maurya king Ashoka in the third century BCE, and their competition and heroes are celebrated in the Sangam poems. Jain and Buddhist institutions were ruthlessly swept aside by the Pallava kings, and Sanskrit and Vedic gods were established by them over their Tamil subjects. [*See also* Pallava Dynasty.]

The other process supported the displacement of Jain and Buddhist influences and the political order of the Pallavas, but simultaneously maintained the vigor of the Tamil language and much of its earlier values. This was the devotional (*bhakti*) worship of the god Shiva. Singers of the praises of Shiva in Tamil, called Nayanars, associated all manner of ancient sacred places in Tamil Nadu with that god. In the same way that the country of the Tamils—Tamil Nadu—had been defined by the itinerant bards, or *panar,* from about the second century BCE to the sixth century CE, now a group of Tamil poets and devotees of Shiva marked out that part of India that was Tamil.

Political and religious processes continued to configure Tamil society and culture for the next three centuries. The era of the tenth to the thirteenth century is conventionally delineated by the term *Chola,* the name of the kingdom that succeeded the Pallavas. This new Tamil kingdom took its name from and located its capital in the Kaveri River territory of the ancient Tamil kings of that name, but these later Chola constructed a wholly different state, one that became an empire over other Dravidian peoples, and perhaps the greatest Indian kingdom of its day. Greatness then, as earlier and later, was achieved by conquest, but enduring sovereignty was maintained by the Cholas through ritual means. Temples of a royal Shiva cult, gifts to brahmans—including the establishment of great settlements of them throughout the realm—and the setting of Tamil and Sanskrit inscriptions together constituted the media of lordship of the Cholas. Their conquests in Sri Lanka and Malaysia carried Tamil inscriptions to these places, thus deepening the imprint of Tamil culture, which had already spread to neighboring mainland Southeast Asian societies in what is now Burma, Thailand, and Vietnam during the Pallava period. With the power of the Chola kingdom, Tamils moved in substantial numbers to Sri Lanka. [*See also* Chola Dynasty.]

For most of the period from 1300 to 1947 Tamil country was appended to two great empires, that of Vijayanagara and that of the British. Under the Vijayanagara kingdom (early fourteenth to the early seventeenth century) Tamils were ruled first by warriors from Karnataka and later by Telugus. It was during the later and most glorious phase of Vijayanagara, the sixteenth century, that descendants of the present Telugu-speaking minority in Tamil Nadu made their way south into lands not then densely settled by Tamils. In the late days of Vijayanagara, as that kingdom weakened under the onslaught of expanding Muslim power in the peninsula, successor states were set up by Telugus among Tamils, the so-called Nayaka kingdoms of Madurai, Gingee, and Tanjavur in the seventeenth century. These in turn were swept away by eighteenth-century powers from Karnataka (the Muslim state of Haidar Ali and his son Tipu Sultan) and from Maharashtra (the Marathas). It was by the conquest of these last that British hegemony was established around 1800, and Tamils were now a part of the vast Madras Presidency of the English East India Company to 1858 and after that of the British Crown. The Madras Presidency covered most of the southern peninsula and included, beside Tamils, speakers of Telugu and Kannada; Tamils were a minority with only a slight edge over Telugus in the population. Between 1896 and 1928, one-half million Tamils left Tamil Nadu to become laborers in Ceylon and another third of a million went to Malaya and elsewhere in the British empire, including Natal in South Africa; in all of these places, Tamils have constituted a minority and, often, a beleaguered, population.

[*See also* Dravidian Languages and Literatures; Dravidian Movement; *and* Tamils in Sri Lanka.]

C. J. Baker, *The Politics of South India* (1976). K. A. Nilakanta Sastri, *A History of South India from Prehistoric Times to the Fall of Vijayanagar* (1958). B. Stein, *Peasant State and Society in Medieval South India* (1980). R. Suntharalingam, *Politics and Nationalist Awakening in South India* (1974). D. A. Washbrook, *The Emergence of Provincial Politics: The Madras Presidency, 1870–1920* (1976). K. Zvelebil, *The Smile of Murugan: On Tamil Literature of South India* (1973).

BURTON STEIN

TAMILS IN SRI LANKA. Tamil-speaking peoples constitute a large ethnic minority in Sri Lanka. They consist of two principal groups: Sri Lanka (or Jaffna) Tamils (population in 1981, 1.8 million, or 12.6 percent of the national population) and Indian Tamils (population in 1981, 825,000, or 5.5 percent of the national population). Sri Lankan Tamils are descendants of South Indian migrants who settled in northern Sri Lanka many centuries ago. About one-half of these Tamils still live in the north, in and around the Jaffna and northeast areas. The balance have moved, primarily into urban centers elsewhere in the island. Northern and eastern Tamils include many agricultural workers, while most other Sri Lankan Tamils are professional or white collar workers. They speak Tamil (a Dravidian language), are predominantly Hindu (some are Christian), are socially divided into caste groups, and have a rich historical tradition. Since the mid-1950s recurrent problems have arisen between the Sinhala majority of Sri Lanka and the Tamil minority concerning political separatism, the status of Tamil language, and employment and education quotas. The Sri Lanka Tamils have largely preserved their cultural identity and no significant assimilation has taken place with the Sinhala majority in the past twenty centuries.

Indian Tamils are of recent origin, having been brought to work on the tea plantations of the central highlands by the British since the nineteenth century. They remain mostly plantation workers with low literacy and education levels. Caste is an important social element of these Tamil-speaking, Hindu people. Many of them have retained affinities with their kinship groups in South India and there is no significant intermingling with the Sri Lankan Tamils. After Sri Lankan independence in 1947, disputes arose over the citizenship of the Indian Tamils. Under Indo-Lankan governmental agreements of 1964 and 1974, about 600,000 were to be repatriated to India and the balance given Sri Lankan citizenship.

[*See also* Sri Lanka *and* Tamil Nadu.]

K. M. de Silva, ed., *Sri Lanka: A Survey* (1977). E. F. C. Ludowyk, *A Short History of Ceylon* (1967). N. D. Wijesekera, *The People of Ceylon* (1965). S. J. Wilson, *Politics in Sri Lanka* (1976).   RALPH BUULTJENS

TANAKA GIICHI (1863–1929), modern Japanese military leader who was president of the Seiyūkai political party from 1925 to 1929 and served as prime minister and foreign minister from 1927 to 1929. Born in Chōshū (now Yamaguchi Prefecture) in 1863, he excelled in his military education, studied in Russia (1898–1902), and rose rapidly in the army hierarchy. The comprehensive military program he drafted in 1906, calling for an increase in the armed forces, became national defense policy. He strengthened popular support for the military by organizing the Imperial Military Reserve Association (1910) and the Greater Japan Youth Association (1915).

Tanaka's political career blossomed while he served, as a lieutenant general and baron, in two cabinets as army minister (1918–1921, 1923–1924) and when he became leader of the Chōshū clique after the death of his mentor, Yamagata Aritomo. He retired from active duty in 1925 and accepted the presidency of the Seiyūkai. In 1927 he formed a cabinet, serving as both prime minister and foreign minister. His government restored some order to the economy, curbed unrest by the mass arrest of communists, and pursued an aggressive continental policy. To protect Japanese residents in China caught in the dislocations of the nationalist revolution, he dispatched troops on three occasions. Anti-Japanese reactions and fear of the loss of influence in China caused Japanese officers in Manchuria to assassinate local warlord Zhang Zuolin in 1928. Tanaka disapproved of this reckless act, but the disgrace he suffered when the army blocked his pledge to satisfy the emperor's demand that the guilty be punished, and growing criticism of his domestic policies, led to his resignation in July 1929. He died two months later.

[See also Seiyūkai and Yamagata Aritomo.]

ROGER F. HACKETT

TANAKA KAKUEI (b. 1918), prime minister of Japan from 1972 to 1974. Tanaka's premiership began with the dramatic opening of diplomatic relations with the People's Republic of China in 1972. Yet his domestic policy, the remodeling of the Japanese islands for further industrial efficiency, cost him his credibility among business leaders as it spurred an inflation in land prices. Many Japanese, who once loved Tanaka's down-to-earth style, had also grown wary of the continuation of the "growth first" policy that Tanaka was about to renew. In 1974 Tanaka resigned in the middle of financial scandals that eventually led to his arrest in 1976 in connection with the so-called Lockheed Scandal. A protracted trial finally declared him guilty in 1983.

Tanaka was born in rural Niigata Prefecture. Unlike the majority of the Conservative (Liberal-Democratic) Party politicians, Tanaka's formal education ended with middle school. An apprenticeship to a contractor, however, allowed him eventually to form his own construction firm, which in turn brought him financial success during World War II. First elected to the House of Representatives in 1947, Tanaka managed to align himself with established party politicians, who usually had distinguished family backgrounds or bureaucratic careers. His cabinet posts included minister of finance, minister of postal services and communications, and minister of international trade and industry.

Tanaka was a skillful political infighter. With his wealth he began to gain an increasing number of followers within his party. His apprenticeship to Ikeda Hayato and to Satō Eisaku eventually made him heir apparent to them as party president. Even after financial scandals cost him his office, Tanaka continued to exercise formidable influence over the internal politics of the Liberal-Democratic Party. Nakasone Yasuhiro, Suzuki Zenkō, and Ōhira Masayoshi, three of those who have served as premier since Tanaka's resignation, could not have reached power without the support of the Tanaka faction in the Diet.   MICHIO UMEGAKI

TAN CHENG LOCK (1883–1960), Malayan Chinese political leader. He was born into a rich Baba family in Melaka whose wealth derived from plantations. Prior to the Japanese occupation he campaigned for the entry of Asians into the Malayan civil service and for their greater participation in the legislative councils. After the occupation he briefly adopted a radical stance in the campaigns against the Malayan Union and the federation agreement. In 1949 he became president of the Malayan Chinese Association and pressed for citizenship to be given to all Malayan Chinese. Essentially an Anglophile, he pursued a paternalistic philanthropy with a belief in state activism in social welfare. His English education and Straits background frequently divided him from the Chinese-educated masses.

[See also Malayan Union; Malaya, Federation of; and Malayan Chinese Association.]

Soh Eng Lim, "Tan Cheng Lock: His Leadership of the Malayan Chinese," *Journal of Southeast Asian History* 1, (1960): 29–55. Tjoa Hock Guan, "The Social and Political Ideas of Tun Datuk Sir Tan Cheng Lock," in *Melaka: The Transformation of Malay Capital c. 1400–1980*, edited by K. S. Sandhu and Paul Wheatley.

RAJESWARY AMPALAVANAR

TANEGASHIMA, the island off the coast of southern Kyushu, Japan, where a storm-tossed boat carrying three Portuguese accidently came ashore in 1543, marking the arrival of the first Europeans in Japan. These men carried with them several short muskets, a weapon that attracted the immediate attention of their rescuers. Some daimyo soon began to produce their own versions of this firearm, popularly known as the Tanegashima rod, and all came to realize the full military significance of the weapon after the Battle of Nagashino in 1575, when Oda Nobunaga deployed a corps of musketeers to turn back the more numerous mounted troops of Takeda Katsuyori. The nature of Japanese warfare was changed. Within a generation, nearly all daimyo had organized similar rifle corps and integrated them into large-scale battalions of foot soldiers (ashigaru), a tactical departure from the medieval battle style of one-on-one combat between mounted men.

Another important consequence of the landing of the Portuguese castaways was the subsequent arrival of traders and missionaries. Japanese daimyo soon recognized that foreign trade generated new wealth that could enable them to increase their military strength. The pace of foreign trade quickened at the end of the sixteenth century, and such trade furthered the growth of domestic trade and commerce that changed the character of economic life in Japan during the following century. The spread of Christianity in Japan was largely a result of a prodigious effort by Catholic missionaries, who claimed to have made nearly 150,000 converts by 1582.

Christianity was interdicted in 1587 and suppressed by 1640, while foreign trade was limited and brought under a strict set of controls during the seventeenth century.

[*See also* Ashigaru *and* Nagashino, Battle of.]

JAMES L. McCLAIN

TANG DYNASTY. The Chinese Tang dynasty (618–907) so brilliantly capitalized on and extended the institutional, cultural, and territorial contributions of its ill-fated predecessor, the Sui, that within a few generations of its founding it had exceeded even the great Han dynasty in material splendor and international power. Chang'an, the Tang capital, became the diplomatic, commercial, and cultural center of East Asia, attracting scholars, diplomats, missionaries, and merchants from surrounding lands and as far away as Persia and Arabia. Foreign influences entering China over the Silk Road and other arteries helped to create a sophisticated and lively pan-Asian culture. At the same time, the Tang furnished the models by which neighboring states were permanently able to transform their own civilizations. From the middle of the eighth century the dynasty was weakened by institutional strains and internal rebellion. Central authority collapsed for a time. The Tang permanently lost direct control over some of its richest and most productive areas, and much of its empire fell away. Even the far-reaching political and economic changes that the dynasty now implemented failed to stem its ultimate decline and collapse. Nevertheless, so powerful was the self-image fashioned by the Tang at its height that from this time forward, all during the imperial period, those Chinese who emigrated overseas proudly called themselves "men of Tang."

Founding. The Tang founder, Li Yuan (566–635), known by his imperial epithet Gaozu (r. 618–626), came from essentially the same northwestern "semibarbarian" aristocracy as his Sui predecessors: his mother, née Dugu, was a sister of the first Sui empress, and his ancestors had served successive northern regimes from the time of the Northern Wei (386–533). Taking advantage of his relationship to the imperial family, Gaozu first served in the Sui provincial bureaucracy and then as a military officer in the modern provinces of Gansu and Shanxi, bat-

tling the widespread banditry that helped bring down the Sui. In the fifth lunar month of 617, realizing that Sui authority had already been effectively destroyed, he rose in rebellion, marching from Taiyuan in central Shanxi southwestward through the Tong Pass to take the Sui capital, which fell in the eleventh month. In the fifth month of 618 he ascended the throne, naming his dynasty after his patrimony in Shanxi. Daxingcheng, the Sui capital, was retained as the center of Tang government and renamed Chang'an, "Enduring Peace." Although traditional Chinese sources have given much of the credit for the establishment of the Tang to Gaozu's son and successor, Li Shimin, it appears that after becoming emperor Shimin had the historical records emended in his favor, and that his father had a far greater role in launching the Tang revolt and bringing it to a successful conclusion than previously believed.

Because the short-lived Sui had established such firm foundations for its successor, initially the Tang did not need to undertake any basic governmental reforms, expending its energies instead on institutional adaptation and improvement. It is during the Tang that the outline of many Chinese political institutions that endured until modern times began to take shape. The core of the Tang central administration consisted of the Three Departments (*sansheng,* a holdover from Sui administration)—a Secretariat, Chancellery, and Department of State Affairs—whose functions and powers were carefully divided and balanced. The Secretariat and Chancellery were charged with policy formulation and review, while the Department of State Affairs was an executive organ, controlling the Six Boards (*liubu*) of civil appointments, finance, rites, war, punishments, and public works. For local government, Gaozu established prefectures (*zhou*) and under them counties (*xian*), the chief officials of which were, continuing Sui practice, centrally appointed and controlled. To help staff his bureaucracy Gaozu reintroduced the Sui system of state examinations, which gave men of relatively humble background an opportunity for official recruitment and promotion on the basis of talent. But Gaozu's highest-ranking officials were mostly holdovers from the Sui administration or else belonged to families that had served that dynasty or other northern regimes, especially the Northern Zhou.

Military needs were largely served by an institution of Sui and earlier times, the *fubing,* or militia, consisting of units of self-sufficient farmer-soldiers serving periodic tours of duty in and around the capital and on the frontiers. The state was financed by the *zuyongdiao,* a fixed tax levied in grain, labor service, and cloth, paid by adult cultivators on the basis of theoretically equitable land allotments distributed to them under the "equal field" *(juntian)* system. Both of these systems, holdovers from the Northern Dynasties and Sui, were relatively inflexible, demanding a uniformity of administrative practice without regard to variations in local conditions. [*See also* Fubing System.]

Lending legal force to early Tang government and institutions was a five-hundred article code of laws that Gaozu issued in 624 and that was revised frequently during the reign of his successors. Indeed, the Tang is famed as a great period for the codification of law. Tang law and institutions provided the models for neighboring states that now began to organize themselves along lines similar to those of the Tang, among them, Japan, Korea, and Vietnam. [*See also* Law: Law in China.]

The Reign of Tang Taizong. Gaozu's second son, Shimin (600–649), canonized Taizong (r. 627–649), presided over one of the most successful reigns in all Chinese history. Largely by means of Taizong's personal efforts, serious military opposition to Tang

FIGURE 1. *Tang-dynasty Horse.* Three-color *(sancai)* ware, white earthenware with variegated lead glaze, c. eighth century. Height 58.4 cm.

rule throughout the country was eliminated by 624. Although Taizong achieved power by assassinating his elder brother, the crown prince, in the sixth month of 626 and forcing his father from the throne a short while afterward, as a reigning monarch he more than redeemed himself. A heroic warrior, Taizong nevertheless also personified a Confucian paragon: the wise, conscientious, frugal, and benevolent ruler who is willing to be guided on matters of state by the counsel of his ministers.

Domestically, Taizong fine-tuned the central governmental machinery. He divided all of China proper into ten *dao,* or "circuits," periodically visited by commissioners of inspection; these were later to develop into full-fledged provincial administrations. He reduced and rationalized the units of prefectural and county government and improved the quality of their officials. He increased the Tang reliance on the examination system; by this means, a higher proportion of Taizong's officials than his father's was recruited outside the old northwestern aristocracy. Taizong expanded the *fubing* to approximately 630 units, called the Intrepid Militia *(zhechongfu),* stationing about one-third to one-half in the capital region. In order to insure against crop failure and reduce grain prices, Taizong reestablished the Sui system of relief granaries. Good weather also eased the plight of the peasants, who experienced their most prosperous period since before the chaotic last years of the Sui.

In foreign policy, in 630 Taizong destroyed the great nemesis of the Chinese, the Eastern Turks north of the Great Wall, whose leader was captured and brought to Chang'an as a political hostage. By playing one khan against the other, by the mid-630s Taizong was able to reduce the Western Turks to vassalage and reassert Chinese suzerainty over the Silk Road oasis kingdoms of modern Xinjiang Province, stretching westward all the way to the Pamirs. Only in the last years of his reign was Taizong's image tarnished somewhat by disastrous military reversals against the northern Korean kingdom of Koguryŏ.

With the creation of a pan-Asian empire China's gates were thrown open to foreign peoples. Chang'an and other major cities became thronged with traders from many lands: Arabs, Jews, Persians, and Uighurs, all of whom brought their own customs, cuisine, and entertainments, as well as their religions—Islam, Judaism, Manichaeism, Zoroastrianism, and Nestorian Christianity. Such foreign influences created a greater degree of cosmopolitanism in China than at any other time before or since,

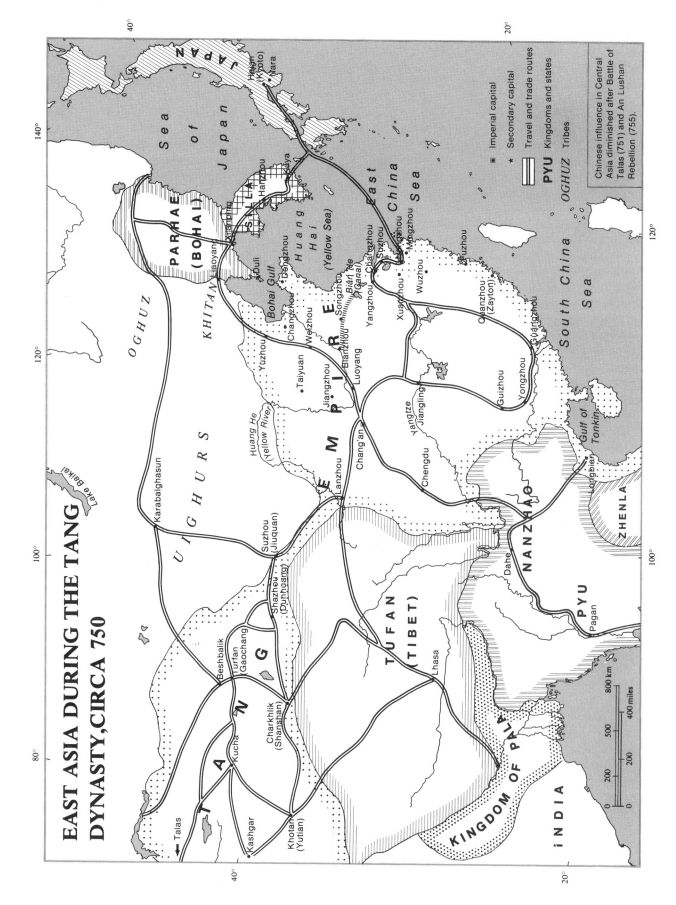

EAST ASIA DURING THE TANG DYNASTY, CIRCA 750

- ■ Imperial capital
- ★ Secondary capital
- ▨ Travel and trade routes
- **PYU** Kingdoms and states
- *OGHUZ* Tribes

Chinese influence in Central Asia diminished after Battle of Talas (751) and An Lushan Rebellion (755).

Lake Baikal

OGHUZ

UIGHURS

Karabalghasun

Beshbalik

TANG

Talas

Kashgar

Kucha

Khotan (Yutian)

Turfan Gaochang

Charkhlik (Shanshan)

Suzhou (Jiuquan)

Shazhou (Dunhuang)

Lanzhou

TUFAN (TIBET)

Lhasa

KINGDOM OF PAL

INDIA

PYU

Pagan

Dahe

NANZHAO

ZHENLA

Longbian

Gulf of Tonkin

Yongzhou

Guizhou

Guangzhou

Quanzhou (Zayton)

Jiangling

Yangtze

Chengdu

Chang'an

Huang He (Yellow River)

Taiyuan

Jiangzhou

Yuzhou

KHITAN

PARHAE (BOHAI)

Xianzhou

Liaoyang

Duli

Dengzhou

Changzhou

Weizhou

Bohai Gulf

Huang Hai (Yellow Sea)

Bianzhou Songzhou

Bian He (Canal)

Luoyang

Yangzhou

Changzhou

Suzhou

Xuezhou

Wuzhou

Mingzhou

East China Sea

Guazhou

South China Sea

SILLA

Hanzhou

Kaya

Nara

Heian (Kyoto)

Sea of Japan

JAPAN

0   200   500   800 km

0   200   400   miles

and helped to transform Chinese music, fashion, poetry, and art. [See also Chang'an.]

The strongest of all foreign influences was Buddhism, which pervaded all levels of Tang society from the educated class down to the peasantry. During the Tang, Buddhism became a thoroughly Chinese religion, with its own traditions and practices. Perhaps the best-known development of the time was the growth of the Chan (Japanese, Zen) school, which maintained that enlightenment can be achieved instantaneously by means of intuition rather than through time-consuming scriptural study. Taizong's philosophical inclinations were essentially Confucian, and officially the Tang owed a special debt to the highest Daoist deity, Laozi, who had been declared the ancestor of the Tang dynasts (they shared the surname Li) during his father's reign. Because of its large following, and largely for political ends, however, Taizong also paid lip service to Buddhism. His post facto patronage of the Buddhist pilgrim Xuanzang (602–664), who made the arduous journey to India and back between 629 and 645 and spent the rest of his life translating the Buddhist texts he had brought with him, can be seen in this light. [See also Xuanzang and Buddhism: Buddhism in China.]

The Reign of the Empress Wu. Gaozong (628–683; r. 650–683), Taizong's successor, was not his father's first choice as heir but was catapulted to prominence after personal scandal and political intrigue had eliminated two of his brothers from the succession. A well-meaning but weak ruler, he was incapacitated for much of his reign by poor health, probably the result of strokes. Filling the resulting political vacuum was the ruthless Empress Wu (627?–705), who had first served Taizong as a concubine before entering his son's harem. As the mother of one and possibly two of Gaozong's sons by the early 650s, Wu incessantly schemed to have the emperor set aside his legitimate wife, the childless Empress Wang, and install herself in Wang's place. This she succeeded in doing in 655, after which Wang suffered a horrible death at the hands of her unforgiving successor. From 660 onward Wu largely dominated court politics, relying on and rewarding a series of favorites and brutally eliminating anyone who opposed her. Still, Wu was a capable ruler with a natural genius for politics, and she and Gaozong took care to not entirely squander the legacy of Gaozu and Taizong. Modest improvements were made in administration. The *jinshi* examination degree for the first time in Chinese history began to confer more prestige than any other, and the first

palace examinations were inaugurated. For a time, Chinese military power and prestige surpassed those of any other period of Tang history. In the late 650s and 660s China controlled land stretching all the way from the Sea of China to the borders of Persia. In the 660s Gaozong and his consort were able to achieve a goal that had eluded Sui Yangdi and even the great Taizong: with the help of the southern Korean kingdom of Silla, the Tang was able to bring Koguryŏ to its knees and briefly establish a Chinese protectorate over it.

By the end of Gaozong's reign, however, China was in crisis. Early Tang government had been simple and economical, utilizing a small bureaucracy and a self-supporting militia to manage a population of perhaps fifty to sixty million. But recent conquests had made it necessary to establish large, permanent frontier garrisons manned by professional soldiers. The bureaucracy had increased in size and complexity. A permanent eastern capital had been designated at Luoyang in 657, and branches of every government department and agency set up there; periodically the court would move en masse to Luoyang to conduct its business. The costs associated with these developments placed new and heavy burdens on the registered peasantry, who were driven to escape the tax rolls in ever greater numbers. Moreover, great pressure was placed on the Tang frontiers by the revivified Turks and a newly aggressive Tibetan kingdom to China's west. The dynasty proved to be militarily overextended, losing much of its recently acquired territory, including northern Korea.

None of these problems daunted the empress, who in 690, after deposing two of her reigning sons, Zhongzong (r. 684, 705–710) and Ruizong (r. 684–690, 710–712) following the death of her husband, established her own dynasty, which she named Zhou, at Luoyang and became the first and only woman "emperor" in Chinese history. During a tyrannical and repressive regime she liquidated most of the Tang imperial clan and destroyed the spirit of bureaucratic independence that officialdom had enjoyed since Taizong's time. One effect of Wu's administration was to accelerate the reduction of the old northwestern aristocracy's power by relying far more than her predecessors on the examination system. By such means she recruited a larger number of officials from the great and lesser clans of the eastern plain and the South, who were not closely aligned with the imperial house or the northwestern aristocracy and were therefore more amenable to her will. Still, it is difficult to detect a simple polarization in early Tang government between the examination graduates and the aristocrats who achieved their offices by hereditary privilege. Bureaucratic tensions seem to have been more a result of a competition for power between the "ins" and the "outs" than between men of different classes or regional backgrounds. Moreover, the number of examination graduates in Wu's time and afterward during the Tang was still relatively small, comprising probably no more than 10 percent of officialdom. [See also Wu Zhao.]

Wu's legacy of female interference in politics proved costly to her son and successor, Zhongzong, who was first dominated, then poisoned, by his own Empress Wei. Empress Wei and her allies sold bureaucratic offices, greatly swelling the central government bureaucracy and ushering in an unprecedented era of corruption, and few problems of the preceding period were attended to. In 710 the future Xuanzong moved against Empress Wei and placed his own father, Ruizong, back on the throne. Ruizong's short reign was dominated by a struggle for power between Xuanzong, his third son, and Xuanzong's aunt, the Taiping princess, a daughter of Empress Wu. Although Ruizong abdicated in favor of Xuanzong in 712, the father continued to control real power in government. Causing Xuanzong further difficulty was the fact that most of the ministers he inherited from his father were adherents of the Taiping princess. Thus, in 713 he led another coup that removed the princess from power and established his own undisputed authority.

The Reign of Tang Xuanzong. Xuanzong (685–761; r. 712–756), the Tang monarch who reigned longest, presided over one of the most glorious epochs in all Chinese history, a second high point of the Tang. It is not without justification that he was commonly known by the name Minghuang, "the Brilliant Emperor." But by the end of his reign great calamity had befallen both him and his dynasty, and he had been reduced to a pitiful tragic hero.

Xuanzong's reign began promisingly enough with a series of reforms designed to strengthen the regime and to restore a healthier balance of power between the throne and the court. After a long decline in bureaucratic vigor and esprit de corps, there was an attempt to return to the halcyon days of Taizong: the massive corruption of the preceding decade was ended, political decision making became more open to official scrutiny, and the efficiency of local government was improved and the quality of its officialdom upgraded. In 733 the empire was redivided into fifteen circuits *(dao),* and the following year

each was assigned a permanent commissioner of inspection for the first time. The perennial problem of famine was addressed by reviving a coordinated system of granaries, the stocks of which cushioned the impact of natural disaster.

Military power was also strengthened. In 710–711 permanent military governors *(jiedu shi)* had begun to be appointed to areas of frontier defense. Under Xuanzong ten such military governors were appointed, each controlling between twelve and ninety thousand troops. This new military power allowed the Tang to defeat its most powerful neighbors, the Tibetans and the Khitan, while the Turks suffered internal collapse. But military power was now concentrated in the hands of the military governors, a potentially dangerous situation for the central government.

The expanded military establishment was funded by increased state revenues provided under policies generated by a group of financial experts, notable among whom was Yuwen Rong. Yuwen's most successful policy resulted in the addition of eight hundred thousand new households to the tax registers, providing a windfall for the government. Moreover, a reorganization of the canal and grain transport system ended the very costly expense of periodically moving the capital from food-poor Chang'an to the better-supplied city of Luoyang.

Xuanzong's court duly reflected, in its elegance and pageantry, China's restored prosperity and territorial expanse. The emperor was himself a lively patron of poetry, music, dance, and the arts. Attracted to his glittering court were some of the greatest cultural lights of the age, among them the poets Li Bai (701–762) and Du Fu (712–770), and the painters Wang Wei (699–759) and Wu Daozi (c. 700–760). Xuanzong's reign witnessed the high tide of Tang musical development, in which a new kind of entertainment music was created by combining the old Chinese ritual and popular music with foreign tunes from India, Iran, and Central Asia. So popular did this music become that by the mid-ninth century the old Chinese music had entirely disappeared. The new music was in turn exported to Korea, Japan, and the southern kingdom of Nanzhao. [See also Li Bai; Du Fu; and Music: Music in China.]

The An Lushan Rebellion. The success of many of Xuanzong's policies belonged to his chief minister, Li Linfu (d. 752), whose rise symbolized the renewed ascendancy of the old northwestern aristocracy during this period. As Xuanzong became increasingly preoccupied by a pursuit of mystical Daoism and Tantric Buddhism and paid less attention to matters of state, Li became a virtual dictator. One of Li's protégés was the non-Chinese military governor An Lushan, who controlled enormous military power along the northern and northeastern frontiers. Upon the death of Li Linfu in 752 the chief ministership was transferred to Yang Guozhong, who had skyrocketed to eminence because of his relationship to Yang Guifei, a beautiful and accomplished imperial concubine who had become Xuanzong's favorite. Yang Guozhong and An Lushan soon became political rivals, and Yang began building a base in the capital region and in the Yang clan's home province of Sichuan to counter An's military advantage on the frontier. In 755 An rebelled, taking Luoyang early in the next year, and his armies conquered Chang'an a few months later, forcing the emperor to flee the capital for Sichuan, along with the two Yangs. En route to their destination their military escorts mutinied, killing Yang Guozhong and demanding the death of Guifei, whom they also blamed for the Tang debacle. Seeing no choice in the matter, Xuanzong ordered his beloved strangled, a tragic denouement to an affair that was immortalized by countless generations of Chinese poets, painters, and dramatists. Late in 756 Xuanzong was deposed by his son, canonized Suzong (711–762; r. 756–762), and he died a few years later, a broken man. [See also An Lushan.]

Post-Rebellion Reorganization of Authority. Although An Lushan was killed by one of his own sons in 757, his rebellion was continued by other leaders until finally quelled in 763. Even so, the glorious era of the dynasty had ended and a period of far-reaching change was ushered in. Most significant was that, as a result of the rebellion, the central government had lost direct control over a large part of the country. In order to survive, the government had surrendered much of its power to the military governors. After the rebellion these military governors came to enjoy varying degrees of autonomy; some in the northeast were virtually independent of central control, even claiming hereditary succession for their sons. For its basic revenue the government now could depend only on taxes remitted from the more tightly controlled southern provinces and Sichuan. A further source of revenue was a monopoly on salt production and distribution, by which it was able to collect taxes, if only indirectly through merchants, even in those regions where it enjoyed only a tenuous authority. Government monopolies were later extended to wine, tea, and lacquer, among other commodities, and became an important new source of funds.

In an effort to increase revenues and lay the foundations for a recentralization of authority, in 780 a new emperor, Dezong (r. 779–805), replaced the old *zuyongdiao* tax with the "two tax system" (*liangshui fa*), named for the two periods when taxes fell due—summer and autumn. The two tax system was basedonly on the actual cultivated acreage and household wealth, and was therefore more equitable than the previous system in which taxes were calculated on a theoretically uniform grant of land. Each province was at the same time given wide latitude as to how the tax was to be collected and was to send to the capital a predetermined quota of revenue, with the surplus to be disposed of as it wished. With this new system, the government relinquished the principle of uniform taxes based on equal land allotments that had been in effect since the beginning of the dynasty.

Dezong's initial attempt to recentralize authority proved to be a failure—the military governors of the northeast revolted from 781 to 785, and the government was forced to recognize the status quo. But gradually Dezong and his successor, Xianzong (778–820; r. 805–820), whittled away at provincial autonomy, reducing the size of the most rebellious provinces and restoring the court's right to control appointments there, until only the Hebei region remained beyond its control.

In one respect the court paid dearly for its program of recentralization: an enhanced role for eunuchs. Until the mid-eighth century eunuchs had played only a minor role in Tang government. However, because the government desired to insulate from politics the powerful new palace armies that had been created to back up its recentralization policies, it appointed eunuch generals to command them. The eunuchs soon used their new posts to gain control of other levels of the central government. The political history of the ninth century is to a large extent a sordid account of eunuch meddling in politics, to the point where they and their henchmen enthroned and dethroned emperors, even murdering them with impunity.

Tang China changed in other fundamental ways in the late eighth and ninth centuries. With the abandonment by the central government of the equal field land allocation system and the revival of a free market in land, the powerful were able to build up large estates (*zhuangyuan*), which now became a common facet of rural life. Tenantry became more common, as economic pressures forced poor peasants to leave their lands and assume a status of serflike dependency on the estates of the great landowners. The center of population shifted to the Yangtze River valley region, which now replaced the northeastern plain as China's grain basket, and the central government became increasingly dependent on the South for both food and tax revenue. The South was also the center of China's most rapid urbanization, as regional metropolises arose to handle the expanded volume of trade made possible by a weakened central authority. Some merchants grew immensely wealthy, and gradually some of the traditional social discrimination against their class began to wane. The old aristocratic elite, whose status had been dependent on a strong and effective central power, finally disappeared, replaced by a far more broadly recruited provincial elite that was tied to the new provincial administrations.

In the field of religion, after centuries of Buddhist dominance, there were the beginnings of a Confucian philosophical revival led by the scholar and essayist Han Yu (768–824). A government-led suppression of Buddhism from 841 to 845 led to the wholesale closing of temples and monasteries and the return of hundreds of thousands of monks and nuns to lay life. The campaign, designed to restore Buddhist-controlled estates to the government and the Buddhist clergy to the tax rolls, dealt Chinese Buddhism a crippling blow from which it never recovered. All these trends created a vastly changed China in the post-Tang era. [See also Han Yu.]

Decline. During its final eighty years the Tang was only a specter of its former self. Beginning in the 830s natural disasters in the Yangtze Valley added greatly to the misery of the peasants. Social disorder became endemic in the 860s and 870s as banditry and rebellion engulfed much of south and central China. The climax of these disorders was reached in the decade from 875 to 884 with the rebellion of Huang Chao, a salt smuggler and embittered failed examination candidate. Huang's forces first swept south to Guangzhou (Canton), then north to the capital, Chang'an, causing appalling physical destruction and loss of life wherever they went. Although Huang's fall was as rapid as his rise, his rebellion caused such economic and social dislocation that the Tang could no longer be restored. [See also Huang Chao.] Thereafter, the government ruled in name only, and real power drifted to regional regimes, the most important of which were led by Li Keyong, a Shato Turk who had aided the dynasty in putting down the rebellion, and Zhu Wen, one of Huang's former followers. Eventually, Zhu Wen emerged supreme. In 903 he took control of Chang'an and slaughtered hundreds of eunuchs, who were casualties of the bitter factional politics of the time. Four years later he established his own regime over a large portion of North China, thus bringing an official close to a dynasty that had effectively ended several decades earlier.

[See also Sui Dynasty.]

Wallace Johnson, trans., *The T'ang Code,* vol. 1, *General Principles* (1979). Edwin O. Reischauer, *Ennin's Travels in T'ang China* (1955). Edward H. Schafer, *The Golden Peaches of Samarkand: A Study of T'ang Exotics* (1963). Denis Twitchett, *Financial Administration under the T'ang Dynasty* (2d ed., 1970). Denis Twitchett, ed., *Sui and T'ang China, 589–906, Part 1,* vol. 3 of *The Cambridge History of China* (1979). Arthur Waley, *The Poetry and Career of Li Po, 701–762 A.D.* (1950). Howard J. Wechsler, *Mirror to the Son of Heaven: Wei Cheng at the Court of T'ang T'ai-tsung* (1974). Arthur F. Wright and Denis Twitchett, eds., *Perspectives on the T'ang* (1973).
HOWARD J. WECHSLER

TANGSHAN, Chinese city, the coal mining center of eastern Hebei Province; population, 1.3 million (1982). Tangshan was almost totally leveled on 28 July 1976 by one of the most severe earthquakes in history, causing a great loss of life and extensive damage. Since 1976 the city has undergone extensive reconstruction. The development of the Tangshan mining industry began in 1912 with the establishment of the British-owned Kailuan Mining Administration. The mines quickly became Tangshan's most important industry. Tangshan is also known for its large-scale cement industry, iron and steel foundries, textiles, porcelain, paper-making, food processing, and a sizable thermal-generating power plant that serves both Tianjin and Beijing.

ANITA M. ANDREW

TAN'GUN, the legendary founder of Korea. According to myth, a bear prayed to become human; after eating a wormwood stalk and twenty cloves of garlic and staying in a cave out of sunlight for one hundred days as instructed, the bear was transformed into a woman. The woman mated with a divine being and gave birth to Tan'gun Wanggŏm, who in 2333 BCE founded a state called Chosŏn in the area of modern P'yŏngyang in North Korea.

The first written version of the Tan'gun myth is found in the *Samguk yusa (Memorabilia of the Three Kingdoms)* by the Buddhist monk Iryŏn (1206–1289). Modern historians associate it with Old Chosŏn, a walled-town state of the fourth century BCE, and speculate that the rulers of this state bore the title *tan'gun-wanggŏm;* linguistic analysis seems to indicate that *tan'gun* has to do with sacerdotal powers and *wanggŏm* has to do with political leadership.

Wanne J. Joe, *Traditional Korea: A Cultural History* (1972). Ki-baik Lee, *A New History of Korea,* translated by Edward W. Wagner (1984). Nam-young Lee, "Tan'gun Myth and the Korean Thought," *Korea Journal* 16.4 (1976): 35–44.   MICHAEL C. KALTON

TANGUTS. The Tanguts are known chiefly as founders, in the year 1038, of the Buddhist empire of Da Xia (or Xixia), which ruled the Ordos and Gansu Corridor (Hexi) until 1227, when it succumbed to Mongol armies. Xia coexisted with the Song, Liao, and Jin empires. It also had political and commercial dealings with the Kokonor (Qinghai) Tibetans, Uighurs, Khotanese, Kucheans, Tatars, and others. Straddling the traditional trade routes between China and Central Asia, the Tanguts hoped to profit as middlemen in the lucrative east-west commerce. But transcontinental trade slackened between the tenth and twelfth century partly owing to bad relations between the Xia and Song, and partly to Chinese encouragement of maritime commerce along its southeastern coast. Moreover, trade between China and the Tarim Basin largely avoided the Tanguts, passing southward to Qingtang (Xining), capital of the Kokonor Tibetans and target of intense rivalry between the Chinese, Tanguts, Tibetans, and Khitan toward the end of the eleventh century.

Studies of extant Tangut documents show that the Tangut language is an ancient member of the Tibeto-Burman family. The Tanguts called themselves Mi or Mi-niah (Mi-nag). Tangut, a name of uncertain Inner Asian origin, has been attached to peoples inhabiting the Sino-Tibetan borderland from the eighth to the twentieth century. It first appeared in the Orkhon Turkic runic inscription of 735, in reference to Ordos tribes called Dangxiang in Chinese sources. Dangxiang territory originally lay southeast of Qinghai at the headwaters of the Yellow River. During the early Tang period many Dangxiang clans abandoned their homeland and moved eastward into Hexi and the Ordos, in consequence of expanding Tibetan hegemony and other shifts in the Central Asian balance of power. Numerous steppe peoples thus settled along China's northwest frontier from the seventh to ninth century. By the end of the ninth century, following the collapse of the Tibetan and Uighur empires in the 840s, the Tanguts had emerged as the dominant group in the Ordos, and contended successfully with the Uighurs for control over the livestock trade with China.

The leading Tangut clan called itself Tuoba, a royal Xianbei surname. Some scholars have argued that the Tuoba Tanguts were a tibetanized Xianbei elite; others consider the Tanguts' claim to descent from the Tuoba Wei as a political expedient. The issue defies resolution. After emigrating into the Ordos, the Tuoba Tanguts cultivated the favor of the Tang court and built a power base around Xiazhou (Yulin), the ancient citadel of which had been the capital of the ephemeral fifth-century Xia dynasty of the Xianbei prince Helian Bobo. In reward for military assistance during the Huang Chao rebellion, in 881 the Tang court appointed the senior Tuoba chieftain as military governor of Dingnan Commandery, headquartered at Xiazhou. This office became hereditary, passing by "election" from brother to brother, uncle to nephew, or father to son, sometimes between competing lineages. [*See also* Xianbei.]

During the tenth century the Ordos enjoyed comparative isolation from the power struggles waged to reconstitute a central government in North China. At Xiazhou, the flourishing Tangut regime withstood attempts by Tang successor states to weaken or dismantle its power structure. When the Song dynasty (960–1279) endured longer than its predecessors, however, evincing a serious intention to assert centralized, civilian control over outlying regions, trouble began brewing at Xiazhou. Typically, discord emerged in disputes over succession to the military governorship. In the succession crisis of 981 one faction chose to surrender to the Song court, turning over the five prefectures under the jurisdiction of the Dingnan Commandery, regarded locally as the Tuoba patrimony. Another faction, led by the young Tangut chieftain Li (Tuoba) Jiqian (963–1004), favored autonomy and fled northward into the steppe to rally support for an independent Ordos state.

Li Jiqian and his followers (including Chinese) fashioned a tribal federation sufficiently cohesive to frustrate Song efforts to neutralize their movement. He recovered the five prefectures surrendered by his kinsmen, contracted a marital alliance with the mighty Khitan Liao, and in 1002 captured from Song its strategic Yellow River outpost of Lingzhou (Lingwu). The fertile farmland and irrigation canals around Lingwu ensured a viable economic base for the nascent Tangut state. Its capture, moreover, heralded the Tangut drive westward into Hexi, to displace the Uighur kingdom at Ganzhou and the Tibetan regime at Liangzhou (Wuwei). After an unsuccessful bid to seize Liangzhou, Li Jiqian died of battle wounds early in 1004. His son Li Deming (984?–1032) succeeded him.

Unquestionably, the Tangut cause benefited from Song preoccupation with and eventual discomfiture by the Khitan. In 1005 Song and Liao concluded a treaty as equal powers, whereby the Chinese nonetheless paid a handsome tribute ("annual gifts") to their northern neighbor. Determined to end hostilities with Song in order to concentrate his resources on the conquest of Hexi, Li Deming shortly thereafter extracted tolerable tributary terms from the Chinese court. The Song perforce recognized Tangut autonomy and de facto rule in the Ordos.

The contest for Hexi fitfully occupied Li Deming's long and otherwise peaceful reign. During a ten-year lull in the fighting, the Tangut ruler amassed considerable wealth from border trade and embassies to China and built a new capital east of Alashan, called Xingqing or Zhongxin (Yinchuan). In 1032 he was succeeded by his famed warrior son, Li (Tuoba) Yuanhao (r. 1032–1048).

An accomplished, forceful, and ambitious ruler, Li Yuanhao embarked on a series of bold governmental and cultural reforms. A native script and a new royal surname, Weiming, were formally adopted. After completing the conquest of Hexi, in 1038 Li (Weiming) Yuanhao proclaimed the independence of the imperial state of Da Xia, with himself as its third emperor. His demand that the Song court recognize him as a sovereign, if lesser, emperor led to the outbreak of war in 1039 to 1040. The fighting went badly for the Chinese and ended with a treaty of compromise late in 1044. Meanwhile, Tangut relations with Liao had soured, resulting in two inconclusive Khitan invasions of Xia. Relations between the two allies remained cool until the 1070s.

Under Weiming Yuanhao the Tangut state assumed its characteristic shape and orientation, combining native practices with institutions adapted from Tang, Song, Liao, Tibetan, and Uighur models. One of its features was a perennial tension between the throne on the one hand and the ministerial-consort clans on the other, that is, between the borrowed ideal of autocratic monarchy and native traditions of joint decision making.

Two powerful consort clans consecutively dominated the Tangut court for the remainder of the eleventh century. A gradual polarization between Weiming loyalists and adherents of the consort faction coincided with a menacing shift in Song policy from restraint to aggressive expansion into Qinghai. From 1094 to 1099, under bitter assault by Song armies, the Weiming clan reasserted control over the government. It strove to conciliate the Song, placed tribal armies under tighter central control, and curtailed the prerogatives of the great clans. The long reigns of Weiming Qianshun (1086–1139) and his son Weiming Renxiao (1139–1193) encouraged unprecedented stability. Nevertheless, a protracted contest between the throne and a powerful minister again nearly sundered the Xia state in the mid-twelfth century.

Following the regularization of relations with the Jurchen Jin state in 1124, relative peace and prosperity prevailed until the early thirteenth century. Confucian statecraft ideology achieved a certain influence in ruling circles and Confucian classical texts were translated into Tangut. Buddhism was firmly entrenched as the state religion and arena of zealous literary (translation) and devotional activity by the imperial family and urban classes. Increased tax receipts from farming, animal husbandry, and trade led to gradual monetization of certain fiscal practices. A cultural flourishing left its traces in numerous manuscript and block-printed books, paintings, artifacts, and architectural monuments that survived owing to the arid climate.

Beginning in the late twelfth century events attending the formation of the Mongol empire profoundly touched Tangut political life. Cordial relations with Jin ended as the Tanguts came under growing Mongol pressure. Hostilities between Xia and Jin from 1213 to 1223 spoiled hopes of an alliance against the Mongols. In 1209 the Tangut king submitted reluctantly as a vassal to Genghis Khan, but later the Xia court reneged on promises made under duress. An unstable throne and defections to the enemy reflect a state divided in its attitude toward the new steppe power. Finally, unable to compromise their sovereignty, the Tanguts lost their state in 1227. The death of Genghis during the last campaign ensured its thorough and sanguine conclusion. Many Tanguts had already joined the Mongol camp; many more followed suit. Others retreated southward, into western Sichuan and beyond, establishing local dynasties along the way.

Past and ongoing archaeological excavations of Tangut literary and artistic relics furnish new material for a fuller reconstruction of the history of the Tangut empire and its complex social, economic, and cultural life. A proper assessment of the Tanguts' contributions to Asian history poses formidable tasks to interested scholars.

[*See also* Song Dynasty; Liao Dynasty; Jurchen Jin Dynasty; *and* Mongol Empire: An Overview.]

Luc Kwanten and Susan Hesse, *Tangut (Hsi Hsia) Studies: A Bibliography* (1980). E. I. Kychanov, "Monuments of Tangut Legislation (Twelfth–Thirteenth Centuries)," in *Études tibétaines* (1976), pp. 29–42.

RUTH W. DUNNELL

TANIZAKI JUN'ICHIRŌ

TANIZAKI JUN'ICHIRŌ (1886–1965), Japanese novelist. Tanizaki first came to public attention in 1910 with a story of sexual possession entitled "The Tatooer" ("Shisei") and made an early reputation as an aesthete. After the Tokyo earthquake of 1923 he moved to the Osaka-Kobe region, and his best works date from this later period. His major theme, the fate of weak men in thrall to *femmes fatales,* remained constant, but such is the dazzling array of his narrative styles that the theme always appears fresh. His work manages to transmute fetishism, masochism, and intense longing for a lost mother figure into fiction by means of irony and the liberal use of impersonal narrators. Style mirrors content in that the narrator's relationship to his story is often voyeuristic, and the sensuality of his work is paralleled by a delight in the texture of his prose. Tanizaki discovered the significant role that traditional cultural norms might play in the composition of the modern Japanese sexual psyche. His most important works include *The Makioka Sisters (Sasameyuki), The Diary of a Mad Old Man (Fūten rōjin nikki),* and "In Praise of Shadows" ("In'ei raisan"). He is also known for three different modern versions of the classical *Tale of Genji.*

Howard Hibbett, trans., *Seven Japanese Tales* (1963). Donald Keene, *Landscapes and Portraits: Appreciations of Japanese Culture* (1971). Edward Seidensticker, "Tanizaki Jun'ichirō," *Monumenta Nipponica* 21.3–4 (1966): 249–265.

RICHARD BOWRING

TANJORE

TANJORE. The town of Tanjore (Tamil, Thanjavur) is located in a district of Tamil Nadu that bears the same name, long known as the "rice bowl" of South India. This core region has long sustained dense peasant settlements and intensive irrigated agriculture based on water from the Kaveri River. In spite of its celebrated and pristine Chola temple dedicated to Brihatisvarasvami, Tanjore was not successful as either a political or a pilgrimage center under the Chola kings. It was not until the arrival

FIGURE 1. *Shiva Temple near Tanjore.* The temple is notable for its large *gopuram,* an ornamental tower characteristic of South Indian temple architecture.

of the Nayakas, in the late sixteenth century, and the Marathas, in the late seventeenth century, that Tanjore became a political capital.

[*See also* Nayakas *and* Marathas.]

J. M. Somasundaram Pillai, *The Great Temple at Tanjore* (1935).   CAROL APPADURAI BRECKENRIDGE

TAN MALAKA

TAN MALAKA (1897–1947), Indonesian revolutionary figure. Born in Suliki, West Sumatra, his full name was Sutan Ibrahim Gelar Datuk Tan Melaka. He was educated first at the Sekolah Radja in Fort de Kock (now Bukittinggi) and in 1913 left for Holland, with local funding, to continue his education. Returning to Sumatra in 1919, he first taught on a rubber plantation in Siak, then went to Java, where he joined the newly established Indonesian Communist Party, or Partai Komunis Indonesia (PKI), and was elected party chairman in 1921.

The following year he went back to Holland, and

in the 1922 Dutch elections he won a seat in Parliament on the ticket of the Netherlands Communist Party but was found to be underage and denied the seat. He represented the PKI at the fourth Comintern Congress in Moscow in 1922, where he stressed the need for communist parties in colonized territories to cooperate with radical Islamic groups. He was appointed Comintern representative in Southeast Asia. His active opposition to the PKI's decision to launch the 1926–1927 insurrection in Indonesia led other communists to brand him a Trotskyist. He formed his own independent revolutionary party, Pari (Partai Republik Indonesia), in Bangkok in 1927. After a brief stay in the Philippines, from which he was expelled, he spent most of his long exile, teaching and writing, in China and later in Singapore.

After the Japanese invasion Tan Malaka returned secretly to Indonesia in 1942. When independence was proclaimed, he advocated a national front, nationalization of all Dutch properties, and an uncompromising policy of unconditional independence to expel the Dutch from Indonesia. In January 1946 he formed a revolutionary opposition (PP, Persatuan Perjuangan, or Struggle Union) to the Sukarno/Hatta government. Arrested in March 1946 together with other PP leaders, he was not released until September 1948, when Republican leaders hoped he would help crush the Madiun rebellion, an orthodox communist uprising. After the second Dutch attack of December 1948, he withdrew to East Java, where he was captured and executed by an Indonesian army unit in February 1949.

[See also Indonesia, Republic of; Partai Komunis Indonesia; Gestapu; Madiun; and Communism: Communism in Southeast Asia.]

B. R. Anderson, *Java in a Time of Revolution* (1972). Ruth T. McVey, *The Rise of Indonesian Communism* (1965). R. Mrazek, "Tan Malaka: A Political Personality's Structure of Experience," *Indonesia* 14 (1972): 1–48.

AUDREY R. KAHIN

TAN SITONG (1865–1898), Chinese philosopher and political activist of the late Qing dynasty, known principally as a martyr of the 1898 reform movement. In his best-known essay, *Ren xue (An Exposition of Benevolence,* alternately translated *On Universal Principles),* he attempted to syncretize Buddhist, Confucian, Christian, and Western scientific ideas in an effort to discover the ultimate meaning of the major religions.

A member of a transitional generation, Tan crit-

ically examined the traditional values surrounding him in light of the realities evident in the 1890s, yet was never free of those values himself. His sharpest comments focused on the traditional examination system and he promoted educational reform ideas, arguing "to reform to promote learning." Despite these opinions, Tan purchased an official title in 1895 and received appointment to a minor office in Hunan. While serving in this post he edited the province's first newspaper and chaired a reform association of South China provinces. It was during this period that he wrote *Ren xue.*

As one of the major reform thinkers of the period, along with Kang Youwei and Liang Qichao, Tan was summoned to Beijing in June 1898 to be interviewed by the Guangxu emperor. Tan received an appointment as an assistant grand councillor to handle documents of the reform movement. On 21 September Empress Dowager Cixi returned to power in a coup d'état. Tan, refusing to flee, was beheaded a week later.

[See also Kang Youwei; Liang Qichao; and Empress Dowager.]

Chan Sin-wai, trans., *An Exposition of Benevolence: The Jen-hsüeh of T'an Ssu-t'ung* (1984). Luke S. K. Kwong, *A Mosaic of the Hundred Days* (1984).

ADRIAN A. BENNETT

TANTRA. The term *tantra* (from the Sanskrit root *tan,* "to stretch, extend"; cognate with Latin *tendere, tensio*) brackets a number of radically different though overlapping South and Central Asian notions about a complex of rituals and beliefs, depending on whether it is applied in a popular or a learned sense. In popular Indian and Tibetan religion, the term denotes occult powers, including sorcery, witchcraft, curing, and soothsaying that are derived from esoteric and partly erotic practices and disciplines. Practitioners of Tantra, called tantrics, are therefore suspect and feared, and in most Indian vernaculars, Tantrism is virtually synonymous with antisocial ritual. The learned meaning of Tantra as understood by doxologically informed tantrics and their sophisticated sympathizers is radically different: the large number of Tantric texts (Agama and Nigama) provide instruction in an intensive salvific quest that, if successful, confers *moksha* (liberation from the karmic cycle of life and death and rebirth) considerably faster than the more traditional yogic techniques. Tantric meditation is, however, potentially dangerous to the practitioner, both physically and psychologically, and these dangers are seen as a trade-off for speedier success.

Tantric contemplative techniques are elaborate and exacting, but they eschew the orthoprax strictures of caste, sex, and ritual purity accepted by the exoteric majority. For these reasons modern Tantric apologists see Tantrism as socially revolutionary.

Basically, Tantric techniques consist of the simultaneous control of speech (vak), mind (citta), and body (kaya) through a graded visualization of divine images or mandalas in conjunction with the retention of breath as well as of semen during the sacralized sexual union with a female initiate (shakti or "power" in Hindu Tantrism; prajna, or "wisdom" in Buddhist Tantrism). These activities are accompanied by the ritualized ingestion of such otherwise forbidden ingredients as meat, fish, liquor, and Cannabis sativa.

To the Tantrics, the Agamas and Nigamas have the same canonical status as the Vedas for orthodox Hindus. The dominant philosophy propounded in the Tantric texts is monistic and absolutistic; there is a strong emphasis on female symbolism and on the identity of the male and female in the Absolute. Rather than complete innovation, Tantrism is a set of modifications of preexisting doctrine and practice aligned with the Shaivite and Shakta mythological complexes, which emphasize the union of female and male deities. In Hindu Tantrism the male deity is seen as passive, sapiential, and cognitive, the female as energetic and dynamic. In Buddhist Tantrism (Vajrayana) the reverse notion obtains, the male Buddha principle being active and dynamic, the female quiescent and gnostic.

[See also Buddhism: An Overview and Shaivism.]

Agehananda Bharati, *The Tantric Tradition* (1977). Sanjukta Gupta, Dirk Jan Hoens, and Teun Goudriaan, *Hindu Tantrism* (1979). Herbert V. Guenther, *The Tantric View of Life* (1977).   AGEHANANDA BHARATI

TANTRISM, CHINESE. *See* Zhenyan.

TANUMA OKITSUGU (1719–1788), Japanese political administrator of the Tokugawa period. Tanuma Okitsugu's spectacular rise from modest samurai origins to a position of great power and wealth, together with the unorthodox nature of his reform policies, surrounded him with controversy.

Okitsugu's father was in the service of Tokugawa Yoshimune, the daimyo of Kii (modern Wakayama Prefecture), and he moved with his son to Edo when Yoshimune became the eighth Tokugawa shogun in 1716. Under the patronage of Tokugawa Ieshige (the ninth shogun) and Tokugawa Ieharu (the tenth shogun), Okitsugu amassed substantial income from land. With his appointments as grand chamberlain (sobayōnin) in 1767 and councillor of state (rōjū) in 1772, he reached the pinnacle of his political power, concurrently holding two of the highest political offices in the shogunate.

As a reformer, Okitsugu directed his attention to the shogunate's chronic fiscal problems, launching an ambitious effort to increase revenues. Land reclamation projects followed the traditional pattern of attempting to create additional taxable lands. More unorthodox were his advocacy of (1) a colonization and development plan for Ezo (Hokkaido); (2) establishment of a system of monopolies for such commodities as copper and iron; (3) an attempt to rationalize the chaotic fiscal system by creating a standardized currency that could be controlled by the government; and (4) his support of a plan to profit from an expanded foreign trade.

The traditional view of Tanuma condemns him as an autocrat whose unwise reforms and control over a weak shogun resulted in political corruption, social and economic chaos, and immense personal profit. Recent revisionist interpretations, however, view Tanuma's reforms as "progressive" attempts to rectify fundamental structural flaws in the Tokugawa system and absolve him of sole responsibility by stressing the involvement of other officials desirous of institutionalizing a greater degree of shogunal autonomy. Tanuma became the target of bitter abuse from daimyo who perceived the reforms as direct threats to their political autonomy, and their collective action effected Tanuma's precipitious fall from power upon the death of Ieharu in 1786.

[See also Tokugawa Period.]

John Hall, *Tanuma Okitsugu, 1719-1788: Forerunner of Modern Japan* (1955).   RONALD J. DICENZO

TAN VIEN MOUNTAIN, located on the northwest edge of the Red River delta, about forty-five kilometers northwest of Hanoi, was the spiritual heart of the Lac Viet kingdom of Van Lang. It was there that the legendary fairy Au Co gave birth to a hundred sons, one of whom became the spirit of the mountain. This spirit was one of the most powerful in the ancient Viet pantheon and is the focus of several legends. Many later Viet rulers made sacrifices to this spirit. The mountain is approximately 1,250 meters in elevation.

[*See also* Lac Viet; Van Lang; *and* Au Co.]

Keith W. Taylor, *The Birth of Vietnam* (1983).

JAMES M. COYLE

TAOISM. *See* Daoism *and* Laozi.

TARAI, a narrow strip of alluvial lowlands marking the northern perimeter of India's Ganges Plain. From its westernmost limit in Uttar Pradesh, the Tarai stretches over one thousand miles along the southern borders of Nepal and Bhutan into Arunachal Pradesh, seldom rising more than six hundred feet above sea level nor exceeding thirty-three miles in width. Rich soils deposited by the snow-fed rivers of the Himalayas support a thick forest cover of sturdy hardwoods that was initially exploited by the British as a source of fuel and of ties for the Indian railway system in the 1900s. In 1954 a successful malaria-eradication program sponsored by the World Health Organization eliminated the most significant check against population expansion into the region. Since then the jungles of the Tarai have been rapidly reclaimed and settled by cultivators from the Himalayan foothills and from neighboring Indian states.

F. Gaige, *Regionalism and National Unity in Nepal* (1975).

RICHARD ENGLISH

TARAKI, NOOR MOHAMMED (1917–1979), a Ghilzai Pakhtun, born in Soor, a village in Ghazna, Afghanistan. Taraki was a founding member and the secretary-general of the People's Democratic Party of Afghanistan (PDPA), the country's pro-Soviet communist party. He was also the publisher of the party newspaper, *Khalq.* The PDPA split into several factions in 1967, and Taraki became the leader of one of these groups, called Khalq. When the officers sympathetic to his group carried out a coup in 1978, Taraki was named the country's president. He held this post until September 1979, when he was killed in a power struggle with Hafizollah Amin.

[*See also* Amin; Hafizollah *and* Khalq.]

ZALMAY KHALILZAD

TARIM BASIN, an arid plain (average elevation, c. 3,700 feet) dominated by the Taklamakan desert, drained partly by the Tarim River, and nearly sur-

rounded by high mountains. In antiquity the basin was populated by Buddhist Indo-Europeans speaking mainly Tocharian and Khotanese. Their flourishing cities on the Silk Route were conquered by China in the first century BCE, but Chinese control ended in the fifth century CE. From the late sixth to mid-ninth century the region was fought over by Turks, Chinese, and Tibetans. Subsequently, under the Uighurs, Karluks, and Karakhanids, the population became almost completely turkicized and, by the end of the fourteenth century, Muslim. With the collapse of the Manchu empire, Chinese gradually took over the region, and ethnic Chinese now predominate there.

[*See also* Taklamakan.]

G. Hambly, *Central Asia* (1969). Marc Aurel Stein, *Serindia* (1921).   CHRISTOPHER I. BECKWITH

TARUC, LUIS (b. 1913), Filipino peasant leader. Son of sharecroppers in central Luzon, Luis Taruc became a spokesperson in the 1930s for the region's peasants, demanding tenancy reforms in rice and sugarcane areas and decent wages for laborers. He was also active in the Socialist and Communist parties. During World War II he led the Hukbalahap, which resisted the Japanese-Filipino regime and in 1945 assisted returning American troops.

In 1946, Taruc was one of central Luzon's six congressmen elected on the new Democratic Alliance ticket. But by alleging illegal campaigning, the major parties (Liberal and Nacionalista) refused to seat them, probably because the Democratic Alliance ticket opposed the ratification of the controversial parity treaty with the United States on grounds that it compromised Philippine independence. The denial helped provoke the Huk rebellion, of which Taruc was a leader until he quit as the uprising diminished in 1954. He was arrested, convicted, and imprisoned until 1968.

Subsequently, as a newspaper columnist, adviser to President Ferdinand Marcos, and member of the National Assembly (1978–1984), he advocated agrarian reforms and official recognition of the Huk.

[*See also* Huk; Nacionalista Party; *and* Marcos, Ferdinand E.]

Luis Taruc, *Born of the People* (1953).

BENEDICT J. TRIA KERKVLIET

TASHKENT, capital of the Uzbek SSR, 1985 population approximately 1.5 million. The city lies in an oasis watered by two small upstream tributaries of the Jaxartes (Syr Darya), the Chirchik, and the Keles. As in other Central Asian oases, irrigated agriculture is almost certainly older than urbanization, but Chinese accounts of the second century BCE mention a stone-built town there. Better-detailed accounts of the third century CE show clearly that by this time it was a Turkish city, although the name *Tashkent* first appears on coins only in the Mongol period (thirteenth century).

The Tang Chinese briefly ruled the area in the eighth century but were defeated by combined Arab and Turkish forces in the Battle of the Talas River in 751, which permanently ended Chinese rule and established the supremacy of Islam in Central Asia. The Abbasid caliphate and then the Samanids ruled Tashkent successively from the late eighth to the end of the tenth century, after which it was reclaimed by the Turks, only then to fall to the Mongols, who, for reasons that are unclear, treated the city and its people far more generously than was their usual mode. Timur later incorporated Tashkent in his empire, but after it too faded, Uzbeks, Kazakhs, and Kalmuks succeeded one another as the city's rulers; their rule was punctuated by frequent fighting.

In 1865 Tashkent fell to the expansionist Russians, who later made it the chief administrative center of Russian Turkestan. The city progressively overshadowed Samarkand, becoming the largest city in Central Asia, for which it is also the chief commercial, educational, industrial, and cultural center. The new Russian town has grown beside the old Turkish city but has now greatly outstripped it in size.

[*See also* Turkestan.]

Wilhelm Barthold, *Turkestan down to the Mongol Invasion* (2d ed., 1958).   RHOADS MURPHEY, JR.

TASHKENT AGREEMENT

TASHKENT AGREEMENT, signed 10 January 1966 by President Mohammad Ayub Khan of Pakistan and Prime Minister Lal Bahadur Shastri of India, ending their 1965 border war. The two countries agreed to withdraw their forces to prewar positions, to reestablish diplomatic relations, and to settle future disputes peacefully. The agreement was forged in Tashkent in Uzbekistan, with Soviet Premier Aleksei Kosygin playing a vital mediating role. The drama of negotiations was heightened by Shastri's sudden death a few hours after he signed the agreement.

[*See also* Shastri, Lal Bahadur *and* Ayub Khan, Mohammad.]

FRANKLIN A. PRESLER

TATA FAMILY

TATA FAMILY, an outstanding Indian entrepreneurial family in industry, trade, and philanthropy. A descendant of Parsi priests and the son of a merchant, Jamshedji Nasarwanji Tata (1839–1904) organized cotton mills and pioneered India's first steel mill, the Tata Iron and Steel Company, in a new town in Bihar bearing his name, Jamshedpur, later Tatanagar. Other enterprises included laying the foundation for the use of hydroelectric power, the introduction of sericulture, and the construction of the Taj Mahal hotel in Bombay. For scientific research he founded the Tata (later, Indian) Institute of Science in Bangalore and financed the training of Indians overseas. Succeeding him, his sons and close relatives diversified and expanded the family enterprises to make the Tatas one of the premier industrial houses of India, and they continued its patronage of educational and health institutions.

F. R. Harris, *Jamsetji Nusserwanji Tata: A Chronicle of His Life*, 2d ed. (1958). *Times of India Directory and Yearbook, Including Who's Who*, 1914– (annual).

HOWARD SPODEK

TATARS

TATARS. The term *Tatar* refers today to a Turkic population of 6,317,468 (1979 census) made up of the Volga, Siberian (Ural), Crimean, and Polish/Lithuanian Tatars of the USSR. Until the first decades of the twentieth century, however, *Tatar* was applied even more broadly to almost all Muslim Turkic peoples living in the Russian empire.

The Volga and Siberian (Ural) Tatars are the focus of these remarks. Despite the fact that the 1979 census figures make no distinction between the four groups, the Volga and Siberian Tatars' share of the total population can be estimated at approximately 5.6 million. Of these, some 2.7 million live in the Middle Volga area, 2.4 million in Siberia, and more than half a million in various parts of Central Asia.

The Volga and Siberian Tatars are the descendants of the populations of the Golden Horde and the White Horde (the western and northern wings of the Mongol empire, respectively). The rulers of both hordes were direct descendants of Genghis Khan, but their population was overwhelmingly Turkic—the result of the biological and cultural assimilation between the Mongol conquerors and the local population. When Batu Khan and his brother Orda established their control over the western and northern *ulus* (lands) at the beginning of the thirteenth century, not only was the bulk of their army made up of a Turkic Kipchak contingent, but the population that the army encountered throughout the Volga-Ural area was also Turkic.

At the time of the Mongol conquest Islam had become such an important factor throughout the region that less than a century later the Golden Horde under Uzbek Khan and the White Horde under Toktamish Khan both became Muslim states. Islam contributed significantly to the cultural unity of the area but could prevent neither the emergence of centrifugal political forces nor political fragmentation. By the middle of the fifteenth century, the khanates of Kazan, Astrakhan, and Sibir had emerged after the disintegration of the Golden and White hordes. These khanates existed as independent entities, however, for only approximately one century; the armies of Ivan the Terrible conquered Kazan in 1552, Astrakhan in 1556, and Sibir in 1851.

Russian policies toward the Muslim Tatars of the conquered khanates were aimed at assimilation; between the sixteenth and nineteenth centuries policies ranged from forced conversion to economic coercion and cultural assimilation through education. Russification policies were particularly harsh in the Volga area, triggering deep resentment and prompting the Tatars more than once to join peasant rebellions such as those of Razin (1667–1671) and Pugachev (1773–1775).

By the end of the nineteenth century the Volga Tatars were articulating new responses to the russification policies of their government: they had embarked upon a multifaceted movement of cultural reform and renewal (Jedidism) aimed at achieving a harmonious balance between secularism and religion and between isolation and integration as imperatives of progress and modernization. Volga Tatars not only emerged as regional leaders but acquired a position of leadership among all Muslims of Russia. Their position was enhanced by the prestige of their culture, which was deeply rooted in the Kazan khanate; by the existence of a dynamic and enlightened merchant class capable of providing financial support to the reform movement; and by the existence of a progressive intellectual and professional elite capable of assuming the leadership of the Union of Russian Muslims—the Muslim party that emerged in 1706.

The revolutions of 1917 brought about dramatic changes in the life of the Volga-Ural Tatars. Their attempt to set up an independent Idil-Ural (Volga-Ural) state as a federation of the Turkic peoples living in the area failed. Instead, on 27 May 1920, the territory at the confluence of the Volga and Kama rivers, where only approximately 40 percent (1,164,342) of the Volga-Ural Tatars lived, was organized as the Tatar Soviet Socialist Republic, an autonomous unit of the Russian federation. The bulk of the remaining population was relegated to the Bashkir republic (organized 23 March 1919), the adjoining Siberian territories beyond the Urals, Central Asia, and small enclaves in Moscow and Leningrad.

The demise of the plans for a Volga-Ural federation, together with the renewal of russification policies under the guise of proletarian internationalism, contributed to the emergence of national communism. The theoretician of national communism was M. Sultan Galiev (purged in 1928), and one of its most remarkable manifestations was the defense of Tatar national culture (e.g., religion, Arabic script, traditions). The purges of the 1930s eliminated national communism as a political issue among the Tatars, but its cultural manifestations have become increasingly noticeable in the past two decades.

Today, the Volga-Ural Tatars are active participants in the economic life of their region, which is rich in natural resources (especially oil and gas) and is a leader in the heavy machinery and chemical industries. Thus, they approach the issue of their relationship with the Russian state with renewed confidence. As in the past, they respond to russification efforts with cultural resilience and dynamism, as reflected in the recent upsurge of interest in Islam and in the Tatar past.

[*See also* Gasprinskii, Ismail.]

A. Bennigsen and C. Lemercier-Quelquejay, *Islam in the Soviet Union* (1967).   AYSE-AZADE RORLICH

TAXILA (Takshashila), about twenty miles northwest of Rawalpindi, capital of Gandhara, was a flourishing city from at least the sixth century BCE. Situated at the western end of the Indian highway from Pataliputra and at the crossroads linking western and central Asia, it was a meeting place of indigenous and foreign cultures. Taxila was known as a famous center of learning; its political, cultural, and material prosperity and its artistic wealth during the Achaemenid, Mauryan, Indo-Greek, Saka-Pahlava, and Kushan times are amply vouchsafed by archaeological excavations. Some of the finest examples of the Gandhara art were produced here.

With the arrival of the Hunas early in the fifth century its fortune declined, but its monasteries and monuments continued to attract visitors, notably the seventh-century Chinese pigrim Xuanzang.

[See also Gandhara.]

J. H. Marshall, *Taxila*, 3 vols. (1951).

A. K. NARAIN

TAY DO ("western capital"), capital of Dai Viet/Dai Ngu (1397–1407) in Vietnam. Located near Vinh Loc, about 115 kilometers south of Hanoi, Tay Do was the largest stone structure in Viet history. It was hastily constructed at the order of Chief Minister Ho Quy Ly, who moved the Tran court there shortly before his deposition of the last Tran ruler. (The Vinh Loc region was Ho Quy Ly's regional power base.)

When the Ho were overthrown by the armies of the Ming in 1407, Thang Long became the capital once again. Tay Do later served as the ceremonial capital of the Restored Le dynasty in the 1540s.

[See also Tran Dynasty; Ho Dynasty; *and* Le Dynasties.]

E. Gaspardone, "Le Qui Ly," in *Dictionary of Ming Biography*, edited by L. Carrington Goodrich (1976). Thomas Hodgkin, *Vietnam: The Revolutionary Path* (1981).

JAMES M. COYLE

TAY SON REBELLION (1771–1802). Greatest of the numerous peasant uprisings of eighteenth-century Dai Viet, the Tay Son Rebellion destroyed the autonomous courts of north and south and overthrew the Restored Le dynasty.

Tay Son, the home village of the uprising's three leaders, Ho Nhac, Lu, and Hue, is located near An Khe in present-day Nghia Binh Province. This region was the most prosperous, but also the most heavily taxed, of the provinces of the Nguyen domain. The rebellion was a generalized reaction on the part of all social classes to conditions of uncontrolled inflation and incipient famine, exacerbated by the confiscatory tax policies of the Nguyen regent, Truong Phuoc Loan. These concerns are reflected in the two-point program proclaimed by the Tay Son brothers at the onset of the uprising in the spring of 1771: the restoration of the legitimate Nguyen line (symbolized by the brothers' adoption of the surname Nguyen) and the redistribution of the goods of the rich.

In the spring of 1773 the Tay Son forces burst onto the coastal plain, captured Qui Nhon, and defeated the armies sent against them by the Nguyen. Trinh Sam sought to take advantage of the confusion of his erstwhile enemies by launching his own invasion of the south in late 1774. The Trinh army captured the Nguyen capital Phu Xuan (Hue) in early 1775, then made a truce with the Tay Son, who proceeded to eliminate the vestiges of Nguyen power in the Mekong Delta (1777). By 1778 the Tay Son were masters of the center and south of Dai Viet, and Nguyen Nhac was proclaimed emperor at the former Cham capital of Xa Ban (Vijaya).

In 1782, 1783, and 1785 Nguyen Hue frustrated the efforts of the new Nguyen *chua*, Nguyen Phuc Anh, and his Siamese allies to reestablish themselves in the Mekong Delta, and in 1786, taking advantage of a succession struggle in the north, they attacked the Trinh. Trinh resistance collapsed, and Nguyen Hue entered the capital, Thang Long (Ha Noi), on 21 July.

Two years later the new Le emperor, Chieu Thong, in an effort to become more than a ceremonial figure, fled the capital and sought aid from the Qing. A Chinese army returned him to Thang Long on 19 December 1788, investing him as king of Annam. Nguyen Hue then proclaimed himself Quang Trung emperor (21 December), gathered his forces, and in a surprise attack on the capital during the lunar new year's holiday (30 January 1789) completely routed the Chinese.

The regime instituted by the Quang Trung emperor, in contrast to those of the Le and, later, the Nguyen dynasty, was self-consciously Viet in character. Construction was begun on a new capital in Nghe An Province, and new bronze drums were cast. *Chu nom* (Viet characters) replaced classical Chinese as the official language of the court, and translations of the Chinese classics into *nom* were begun. Military officials were given precedence over their civilian counterparts from the provincial level downward. A system of identity cards was introduced to facilitate conscription. There is evidence that Quang Trung wished to reconstitute the ancient kingdom of Nam Viet (Nanyue) by annexing part of southern China from the Qing.

The sudden death of the Quang Trung emperor on 16 September 1792 deprived the Tay Son house of both its paramount military leader and the driving force behind its program. During the reign of the small son of Nguyen Hue (Quang Toan, r. 1792–1802) the Tay Son movement became progressively weaker as its leadership dissolved in factional strife. The methodical conquest of Dai Viet by Nguyen

Anh, culminating in his entry into Thang Long on 20 July 1802, ended the Tay Son dynasty.

[*See also* Gia Long; Nguyen Dynasty; Nguyen Lords; Trinh Khai; Trinh Lords; *and* Trinh Sam.]

Thomas Hodgkin, *Vietnam: The Revolutionary Path* (1981). Alexander B. Woodside, *Vietnam and the Chinese Model* (1971).   JAMES M. COYLE

TEA CEREMONY, known in Japanese as *cha no yu* (literally, "hot water for tea") and *chadō*, or *sadō* ("the way of tea"), the formal service of tea to guests as a performing art. The study of the tea ceremony involves such arts as ceramics, calligraphy, poetry, and architecture, as well as historical, philosophical, and religious dimensions.

The ceremonial preparation of tea began in China and is described by the Tang encyclopedist Lu Yu in *Chajing (The Classic of Tea)*. Tea probably came to Japan during the Tang era, and the first reliable mention, in the *Nihon kōki (Latter Chronicle of Japan)*, dates its use to 815. It was not until the late twelfth century, however, that it began to enjoy widespread use, after its introduction by the Zen monk Eisai, who wrote *Kissa yōjōki (A Record of Tea Drinking for the Promotion of Health)*, which he presented to the shogun in 1214. [*See* Eisai.]

The use of tea in Zen ritual is a major source of *cha no yu*. A second source is tea contests, in which competitors vied to identify tea by the locale of production, often gambling on the outcome, with Chinese art objects as stakes. The first person generally believed to have combined these two strands was Murata Shukō (or Jukō) of Nara, who studied Zen at Daitokuji with Ikkyū and the arts with Nōami at Yoshimasa's court. He stressed the aesthetic principle of *wabi* ("poverty"), which caused him to incorporate simple, intimate forms of tea service and utensils.

The sixteenth-century Sakai teaman Takeno Jōō and his disciple Sen no Rikyū heightened the *wabi* taste in tea. Particularly in the hands of the latter, *cha no yu* reached its simplest and most classical form. Sen no Rikyū served the tea directly on the tatami, without a shelf, in an intimate, mud-walled tearoom smaller than two mats. Guests entered through an aperture that obliged them to crawl. He designed and used domestic ceramics of rough texture and subdued hue, as well as bamboo flower vases and wooden water containers.

Most modern tea traditions spring from Rikyū. Initially prominent was daimyo tea. Rikyū served both Oda Nobunaga and Toyotomi Hideyoshi as tea master and taught many others, including Furuta Oribe and Hosokawa Sansai. Oribe, especially, was influential as a designer and a patron of artisans. Kobori Enshū and Kanamori Sōwa continued that tradition and sharpened a courtly taste. A second, and today more significant, tradition was cultivated among townsmen such as Yabunouchi Jōchi (or Shōchi) and the Sen families. Sen Sōtan, the third generation after Rikyū, reaffirmed the *wabi* taste and also established three of his sons as *iemoto* heading the major schools of *cha no yu*: Omotesenke, Urasenke, and Mushanokōjisenke. They most successfully adapted to modern realities after the Meiji period by admitting women to study, by the establishment of local branches, and through public demonstrations; as a result, they claim the largest following today.

[*See also* Sen no Rikyū.]

Rand Castile, *The Way of Tea* (1971). Okakura Kakuzo, *The Book of Tea* (1906). Urasenke Foundation, *Chanoyu Quarterly* (1970–).   V. DIXON MORRIS

TEA IN INDIA AND SRI LANKA. Tea plants suitable for cultivation on the Indian subcontinent were successfully propagated from Chinese seeds by British botanists simultaneously in Assam and the Kumaon during the 1820s. Within a few decades officials of the Indian civil service were cultivating tea bushes in experimental gardens throughout the sub-Himalayan districts held by the British. The government's subsequent annexation of the Assam Valley, combined with the abolition of the East India Company's trade monopoly, opened northeast India to unlimited speculation by European merchants, planters, and entrepreneurs. The plantation economy was slow to develop, however, because of the lack of sufficient local labor to clear and terrace sites suitable for cultivation. Nevertheless, government incentives such as the Assam Clearance Act of 1854, which awarded up to three thousand acres of prime tea land to any European planter willing to grow the crop for export, spurred the reclamation of the northeastern jungles. By the 1870s nearly three hundred tea estates had been established in Darjeeling and Assam, producing more than six million pounds of Pekoe and Souchong tea annually.

The demand for plantation labor was alleviated by a system of bonded labor that stretched across eastern Nepal and southward to the tribal areas of Bihar and Orissa. By the turn of the century nearly a half-million "coolies" were indentured to some 764 tea gardens in Assam alone.

The European planters who opened Sri Lanka to the cultivation of coffee for export in the 1820s and 1830s were similarly hampered by the unwillingness of the local population to work their plantations and were forced to contract labor from southern India. Coffee dominated Sri Lanka's economy, eventually claiming over 200,000 acres of agricultural land, until the 1870s, when much of the island's crop was devastated by disease. The plantation economy was salvaged, however, as planters changed to tea cultivation, which proved extremely successful. By the turn of the century nearly 400,000 acres were given over to tea production, yielding 150 million pounds annually. By the time of independence, India and Sri Lanka together produced nearly three-quarters of the world's tea exports.

[See also Assam and Darjeeling.]

P. Griffiths, The History of the Indian Teas Industry (1967). M. Weiner, Sons of the Soil (1978).

RICHARD ENGLISH

TEHRAN CONFERENCE, meeting of Allied leaders in Iran on 1 December 1943. At this meeting Winston Churchill, prime minister of Great Britain, Franklin Roosevelt, president of the United States, and Joseph Stalin, premier of the Soviet Union, discussed overall strategy in their war with Germany and Japan. Their declaration included an expression of the three countries' desire for the maintenance of the independence, sovereignty, and territorial integrity of Iran, then under the occupation of armed forces of all three countries, once the war had ended. The declaration also recognized the assistance Iran had given to the overall war effort and promised to provide the country with economic aid.

Harry N. Howard, "Historical Backgrounds," in The Middle East in World Politics: A Study in Contemporary International Relations, edited by Tareq Ismael (1974), pp. 11–14. J. C. Hurewitz, Diplomacy in the Near and Middle East: A Documentary Record, 1914–1956 (1956), p. 238.   ERIC HOOGLUND

TELENGANA MOVEMENT, a peasant struggle in India from 1946 to 1951. When the movement began, Telengana was a region in the former princely state of Hyderabad, with dry, only moderately productive farming and feudal-like agrarian relations. In July 1946 a peasant was murdered by a landlord, and villagers retaliated by attacking large landholders and government offices. The movement soon coalesced, under Communist leadership, into an organized rural revolt, especially in Nalgonda and Warangal districts. Independent systems of law and order were set up in over one thousand villages, and large amounts of land were redistributed. The movement lost much of its force after 1948, when Hyderabad became part of India and the government asserted a strong administrative and military presence. The rebellion continued for another three years, however, until the Communist Party called it off in 1951.

[See also Communism: Communist Parties in South Asia and Hyderabad.]

Carolyn Elliott, "Decline of a Patrimonial Regime: The Telengana Rebellion in India 1946–51," Journal of Asian Studies 34 (1974): 27–47. Hugh Gray, "Andhra Pradesh," in State Politics in India, edited by Myron Wiener (1968). Mohan Ram, "The Telengana Peasant Armed Struggle 1946–51," Economic and Political Weekly 8 (1973): 1025–1032.   FRANKLIN A. PRESLER

TELUGU. See Dravidian Languages and Literatures.

TEMENGGONG, Melakan/Malay court title, now archaic. Originally the temenggong was the third-ranking chief of the Melakan state. Functionally, the temenggong controlled the police, the urban population, and the markets of the entrepôt and could be considered a mayor. The status of the office changed over time.

At times the office was held by the bendahara (chief minister) designate, who sometimes was the younger brother of the bendahara. When the Bugis moved into Riau in the 1740s, the office became associated with the descendants of Tun Abdul Jamal (d. circa 1765) and with the territory of Johor (which at the time included Singapore, Bulang, Galang, and several other nearby islands, as well as the mainland). Temenggong Abdul Rahman (d. 1825) signed the first treaty granting Singapore to the East India Company in 1819. His descendants founded the current ruling house of Johor. The title became defunct in Johor in 1865 when Temenggong Abu Bakar adopted the title of maharaja.

[See also Abu Baker; Ibrahim; and Abdul Rahman.]

Carl A. Trocki, Prince of Pirates: The Temenggongs and the Development of Johor and Singapore 1784–1885 (1979).   CARL A. TROCKI

TEMMU (631?–686, r. 672–686), Japan's fortieth emperor, according to the historical chronicle the *Nihon shoki*. As a youth, Prince Ōama (Temmu's name prior to accession) learned of the political and military advantages of the imperial system of Tang China. He also witnessed the painfully slow progress made by his elder brother, the emperor Tenji (r. 668–671), toward creating a similar system in Japan. Upon Tenji's death, Prince Ōama wrested the throne from Tenji's son, Prince Ōtomo, in the Jinshin War of 673.

The new emperor devoted his entire energies to remodeling the Japanese state. He prohibited aristocrats from acquiring private economic bases beyond the reach of the system of feudal obligations to the imperial court, and he undercut the independence of many local magnates. A central bureaucracy with objective criteria for hiring, promotion, and dismissal of officials was established. Systems of land tenure, population registration, and taxation were spelled out in the 681 Kiyomihara Civil Codes.

Temmu's greatest legacy may have been the formulation of an imperial mythology that declared Japan's rulers divine descendants of a line unbroken for ages eternal *(bansei ikkei)*. Emperor Temmu died before completing the task of centralization, but his consort (Empress Jitō, r. 686–697) and son (Emperor Mommu, r. 697–707) eventually fulfilled his dream.

[*See also* Jinshin War *and* Yamato.]

W. G. Aston, trans., *Nihongi* (1896). John W. Hall, *Government and Local Power in Japan, 500 to 1700* (1966).
                                                    WAYNE FARRIS

TEMPLER, SIR GERALD (1898–1979), British general and field marshal. Templer was appointed high commissioner and director of operations in Malaya (1952–1954) when British fortunes in the Emergency (1948–1960) seemed at their lowest after the assassination of High Commissioner Gurney. He set out to win "the hearts and minds of the people," vigorously hounding the insurgents while advancing toward Malayan independence. Most give him credit for ensuring eventual victory against the Communists, though some accuse him of vindictiveness; others note that he built on his predecessors' work.

[*See also* Emergency in Malaysia, The.]

Anthony Short, *The Communist Insurrection in Malaya, 1948–1960* (1975).   A. J. STOCKWELL

TEMPŌ REFORMS. The Tempō reform program, brainchild of Mizuno Tadakuni, has been ranked with the Kyōhō and Kansei reforms as one of the three great reforms of the Tokugawa period in Japan. Like its predecessors, it was strongly colored by traditional Confucian morality, with considerable emphasis on personal frugality and restraint, and with attacks on gambling, pornography, theater, and unlicensed prostitution. Much attention was also given to the economy, with the customary attempt (as usual unsuccessful) at price control.

In other respects, however, Mizuno's reforms, begun in 1841, decisively broke away from the traditional mold, because he had to take into account two new factors. One was the fear of foreign encroachment, heightened by reports of the Opium War in China; the other was a shift in the power relations between *bakufu* and daimyo domains in which the latter—some of which had initiated successful reforms of their own—were growing more overtly independent. The *bakufu* therefore, as coordinator of national defense, was obliged to reassert its authority and did so in these reforms, making new demands of daimyo, or reviving old ones, and abolishing domain monopolies. So unpalatable were such measures to many daimyo, including some in *bakufu* office, that in 1843 these particular reforms were abandoned, and Mizuno and his collaborators were dismissed and punished.

[*See also* Mizuno Tadakuni; Kyōhō Reforms; Kansei Reforms; *and* Tokugawa Period.]

                                              HAROLD BOLITHO

TEMPYŌ ERA, a regnal designation for the years 729 to 749 in Japanese history. *Tempyō*, meaning "heavenly peace," is also used by art historians in a broader sense to designate the period from 710 to 784, when Japan's capital was at Heijō, the present-day city of Nara. "Tempyō era" is often used interchangeably with "Late Nara period."

The Tempyō era is regarded as the golden age of Japanese Buddhist art. Under the patronage of the pious Emperor Shōmu (701–756) and his family, many temples filled with magnificent images were established in and around the capital. Both the pictorial and sculptural styles of this era were much influenced by continental prototypes, yet they have a distinctly indigenous flavor. The idealistic naturalism of the arts of the Tempyō era inspired artists for generations.

The vast complex of Tōdaiji ("great eastern temple"), designed to serve as the center of a vast network of monasteries and nunneries, is the most representative monument of the era. Its colossal, fifty-three-foot gilt bronze statue of the Buddha Dainichi (Sanskrit, Vairocana) remains a powerful emblem of both the Buddhist faith and the technical achievements of the time. Also on the Tōdaiji compound is the Shōsōin, a storehouse containing Emperor Shōmu's personal belongings, ranging from herbal medicines and musical instruments to screen paintings. These provide vivid testimony of the cosmopolitan, aristocratic culture of the era, when Japan was the easternmost terminus of the Silk Route.

[See also Tōdaiji.]

Kobayashi Takeshi, *Nara Buddhist Art: Tōdaiji* (1975). Sugiyama Jiro, *Classic Buddhist Sculpture* (1982). Langdon Warner, *Japanese Sculpture of the Tempyō Period* (1964).   CHRISTINE M. E. GUTH

TENASSERIM, narrow strip of land between Thailand (on the east) and the Andaman Sea (on the west). Extending approximately six hundred miles, Tenasserim makes up the southern extreme of Burma. Its population, consisting of Burmans and Karen, is in excess of 1.3 million. The main towns are Moulmein, Tavoy, and Mergui. Resources include teak, tin, rice, rubber, coconuts, and wolfram.

Tenasserim has been contested by Burma and Siam (later Thailand). It was reacquired by the Burmese king Alaungpaya in 1760 and successfully defended by Bodawhpaya in 1790. It was ceded to the British by the Treaty of Yandabo at the close of the First Anglo-Burmese War in 1826. A revolt against the British during the early period of their rule was unsuccessful. Britain considered returning Tenasserim to the Burmese for a ransom but ultimately decided to keep it.

The Japanese and the Burma Independence Army started their conquest of Burma in late December 1941 via the Myawaddy Pass, directly east of Moulmein. Some British opposition took place at Moulmein. The province has been a haven for rebels against the Rangoon government. Insurgents have frequently taken over the mines.

"The Tenasserim Provinces—Their Statistics and Government," *Calcutta Review* 8 (1847): 72–145.

OLIVER B. POLLAK

TENDAI (Chinese, Tiantai), has been one of the most influential schools of Chinese and Japanese Buddhism. The school takes its name from Mount Tiantai in China, where the teachings of the school were first formulated. It is also known as the Lotus school, Hokkeshū, because it bases itself on the *Lotus Sutra* (Sanskrit, *Saddharmapundarika Sutra*; Japanese, *Hokekyō*). Japanese Tendai Buddhism traces its ancestry back via the Japanese monk Saichō (767–822) to the Chinese master Zhiyi of the late sixth century.

Zhiyi (538–597), a scholarly monk who resided on Mount Tiantai in Zhejiang Province, emphasized devotion to the *Lotus Sutra* as the supreme expression of the Buddha's teaching. He elaborated a powerful philosophical and encyclopedic synthesis, referred to in Tendai thought as the teaching of the "five periods and eight teachings," in which the *Lotus Sutra* was presented as the epitome of the Buddha's life and teachings. Tiantai's openness to Hinayana as well as Mahayana teachings, its receptiveness to the new currents of Pure Land, Zen, and Tantric Buddhism, its affirmation of everyday life, and its promise of salvation for all through the efficacy of the *Lotus Sutra* made it one of the most powerful currents of Chinese Buddhism in the Sui and Tang dynasties.

The *Lotus Sutra* was probably introduced to Japan at, or shortly after, the introduction of Buddhism in the mid-sixth century. Prince Shōtoku is widely believed to have written a commentary on it, the *Hokke gisho*. Although this is almost certainly a later composition, it may date from as early as the seventh century. Tiantai teachings as articulated by Zhiyi were probably first made known in the Nara period by immigrant Chinese monks like Ganjin (688–763).

Tendai doctrines and the Tendai school were firmly established in Japan by the monk Saichō, who went to China in 804 and studied Tendai with the monks Zhanran and Daosui, as well as Zen and Tantrism. When Saichō returned to Japan he brought with him many Tiantai texts. Under imperial patronage he built a monastery, Enryakuji, on Mount Hiei to the northeast of the Heian capital and began to train monks who would serve as spiritual leaders and "treasurers of the nation." The Tendai school finally established its independence of the older Nara schools of Buddhism when it was permitted, shortly after Saichō's death, to maintain its own ordination platform.

Infused with the Tantric practices derived from China and from the Japanese monk Kūkai, and enjoying the patronage of the imperial court and the Fujiwara family, Tendai grew rapidly to become the dominant school of Heian-period Buddhism. Tendai monks were the religious leaders of their age and from their ranks in the twelfth and thirteenth centuries came the reform-minded founders of the Pure Land, True Pure Land, Zen, and Nichiren schools of Buddhism. In this sense Tendai can be said to have served as the womb for Japanese popular Buddhism in succeeding centuries.

[*See also* Saichō; Enryakuji; *and* Kūkai.]

Ryusaku Tsunoda, Wm. Theodore de Bary, and Donald Keene, comps., *Sources of Japanese Tradition* (1958).

MARTIN COLLCUTT

TEN KINGDOMS, a conventional term for the short-lived Chinese states in the period 907 to 960, following the fall of the Tang dynasty. Nine of the states were in South China, while the contemporary non-Chinese states known as the Five Dynasties were in the North. In the lower Yangtze region were the Wu dynasty (902–937), with its capital at Yangzhou, and the Southern Tang dynasty (937–975), with its capital at Nanjing. In the mid-Yangtze region was the small state of Jingnan (906–936); south of it was the state of Chu (927–951), in Hunan, with its capital at Changsha. As their names imply, the states of Former Shu (907–925) and Later Shu (934–965) successively occupied Sichuan, with capitals at Chengdu. Wu-Yue (907–978) was based at Hangzhou in Zhejiang, while the state of Min had its capital at Fuzhou in Fujian. The Guangdong-Guangxi region was ruled from Guangzhou (Canton) by the Southern Han (907–971). The only northern state in the group was the Northern Han (951–979) in northern Shanxi. [*See also* Five Dynasties.]

EDWARD L. FARMER

TENNENT, SIR JAMES EMERSON (1804–1869), author and colonial secretary of Sri Lanka (1845–1850). Tennent sought to make his mark as an administrator with his path-breaking *Report on the Finances and Commerce of Ceylon* (1848), which advocated a drastic revision of the colony's revenue system, but the severe depression made his proposals impracticable. His participation in the harsh repression of those who rebelled in 1848 against the tax measures of the new governor, Viscount Torrington, cut short his promising career. When he returned to England he produced his classic two-volume study, *Ceylon* (1859). His *Christianity in Ceylon* (1850) remains a perceptive scholarly work.

Dictionary of National Biography 56 (1898): 65–66.

VIJAYA SAMARAWEERA

TENRIKYŌ. *See* New Religions in Japan.

TEPE HISSAR, "citadel mound," a major archaeological site six kilometers southeast of Damghan, in northern Iran, excavated by E. F. Schmidt in 1932–1933 and reinvestigated by R. H. Dyson, Jr., in 1971. Extensive settlements have been revealed. The earliest, from the fourth millennium BCE, produced painted black-on-buff conical bowls and goblets with stylized decorations. The main phase, Hissar III, is indicated by the "Burnt Building," a fortified manor, where charred victims and their arrowheads, technically advanced metal utensils, and ornaments have been recovered. A little to the south of the main mound lie the remains of a fifth-century Sasanid palace, with its great *iwan* and walls ornamented originally with stucco decorations.

Sylvia A. Matheson, *Persia: An Archaeological Guide* (2d ed., 1976), pp. 196–197, 297–298. E. F. Schmidt, *Excavations at Tepe Hissar* (1940).

A. SHAHPUR SHAHBAZI

FIGURE 1. *Ceramic Cup.* Tepe Hissar, fourth millennium BCE. Unevenly fired, patchy red and greenish gray earthenware with a brownish-black painted design of bearded ibex and striations.

TEPE YAHYA, site 350 kilometers southeast of the city of Kerman, Iran, where excavations by

C. C. Lamberg-Karlovsky and P. L. Kohl (Peabody Museum, Harvard University) revealed evidence of long prehistoric cultural occupation from about 4500 to 2700 BCE. Its finds included clay tablets inscribed with Proto-Elamite inscriptions (c. 2900 BCE), a copper-bronze dagger evidencing very early copper-tin alloying in southwestern Asia, and many steatite vessels and beveled-rim bowls. These objects document direct trade and cultural links among Mesopotamia, north and central Iran, and the Indus Valley. Remains of Achaemenid, Parthian, and Sasanid settlements were also uncovered from the site, which after a gap of uncertain duration was reoccupied from the first millennium BCE to 500 CE.

Sylvia A. Matheson, *Persia: An Archaeological Guide* (2d ed., 1976), pp. 268–270 and 304.

A. SHAHPUR SHAHBAZI

TERAI. *See* Tarai.

TERAKOYA. *See* Education: Education in Japan.

TERAUCHI MASATAKE (1852–1919), Japanese army leader of the Meiji period and prime minister during World War I. Terauchi was a member of the army faction from Chōshū (now Yamaguchi Prefecture), where he was born. Trained at the Osaka military academy, he was wounded in action suppressing Satsuma rebels in 1877. Despite the loss of his right hand, he remained on active duty and rose in rank and assumed various posts: attaché in Paris, principal of the Officer's Academy (1886), bureau chief in the general staff, in charge of transportation and communications during the Sino-Japanese War (1894–1895), and first inspector-general of military education (1898). Terauchi served as army minister for ten years after 1902. Concurrently, he became the first governor-general in Korea in 1910, after presiding at its annexation as resident-general.

With the rank of field marshal and the title of count, Terauchi became prime minister in 1916. He pursued an aggressive foreign policy toward China, giving loans to friendly warlords and gaining recognition for Japan's expanded rights through agreements with Western powers (including the Lansing-Ishii Agreement with the United States in 1917). His government resigned in 1918 following widespread domestic riots caused by inflation and economic dislocation. He died the next year.

ROGER F. HACKETT

TET OFFENSIVE, a major offensive launched by Communist forces in South Vietnam in February 1968. The attack combined military assaults on provincial and district capitals with an attempt to provoke a general uprising through agitation and terrorist activities in major cities like Hue and Saigon. The Communists suffered severe casualties in the offensive, and although their forces held the center of Hue for several weeks, their territorial gains were short lived. But the offensive had a considerable psychological impact on public opinion in the United States and was a decisive factor in provoking the Johnson administration to seek a negotiated settlement of the war.

[*See also* Vietnam *and* Indochina War.]

Donald Oberdorfer, *Tet!* (1971). WILLIAM J. DUIKER

TEUGNGU DYNASTY. *See* Toungoo Dynasties.

TEUKU OEMAR (1854–1899), a traditional war chief (*uleebalang*), active in the Aceh War. As head of the village of Datar, he fought the Dutch at the outbreak of the war in 1873. After the Dutch destroyed Datar in 1878, he continued his struggle, but in 1883 he surrendered and offered his services to the Dutch. He defected the following year. In 1893 he was pardoned and appointed *panglima prang besar* by the Dutch. On that occasion he changed his name to Teuku Djohan Pahlawan. For a time he and his men assisted in the "pacification" of Greater Aceh. He changed sides again in March 1896 and was killed by Dutch troops near Meulaboh in 1899. [*See also* Aceh.]

C. VAN DIJK

THADOMINBYA (r. 1364–1367 CE), warrior-king who is virtually unknown although he founded Ava, which became the site of other Burmese dynasties. Struggling to establish legitimacy, he traced his lineage to the mythical founders of Tagaung and married a queen with some royal credentials, but to no avail. His rule was unstable and although he quelled several rebellions—the account of one is still available on stone—his reign ended when Minkyiswasawke (1367–1400), his brother-in-law, ascended the throne.

[*See also* Ava.]

Paul J. Bennett, *Conference under the Tamarind Tree: Three Essays in Burmese History* (1971). G. E. Harvey, *A History of Burma from the Earliest Times* (1925; reprint, 1967). Than Tun, "History of Burma: A.D. 1300–1400," *Journal of the British Royal Society* 42 (1959): 119–133. MICHAEL AUNG-THWIN

THAGI *(thugee)*, the killing of travelers by groups known as Thags or Thugs (literally, "deceivers"), probably an ancient institution in India, was allegedly based on worship of the Hindu goddess Kali. Thugs followed strict rituals and were distinct from the Pindaris or dacoits, who were essentially bandits. They used a *rumal*, a white or yellow handkerchief weighted on one end with a silver rupee, to strangle the victim and employed a pickaxe, said to symbolize Kali's tooth, to facilitate burial.

Virtually unknown except by villagers and local magnates who gave them protection, the Thugs were first seriously studied by William Sleeman (1788–1856) in the 1820s and 1830s. Sleeman found that Thug groups included both Hindus and Muslims, and were governed by their own moral code and complex internal organization. Despite their remarkable qualities of solidarity and leadership, by the late 1830s Sleeman, with government help, had virtually ended *thagi*.

[*See also* Pindaris.]

George Bruce, *The Stranglers: The Cult of Thugee and Its Overthrow in British India* (1969). William H. Sleeman, *Ramaseeana, or A Vocabulary of the Peculiar Language Used by the Thugs, with an Introduction and Appendix, Descriptive of the System Pursued by that Fraternity . . .* (1836).   USHA SANYAL

THAILAND, Southeast Asian state formerly known as Siam, was one of the few Asian countries to escape colonial rule. It has an area of 198,455 square miles and a population, as of 1984, of fifty million.

Widespread finds from the Stone Age attest to the antiquity of human settlement in Thailand, and the extraordinary Ban Chiang excavations have recently revealed the presence of an early advanced civilization, with knowledge of metallurgy and urban settlements, four thousand years ago on the Khorat Plateau in the northeast. The earliest populations in the region appear to have been of Austroasiatic (Mon-Khmer) linguistic stock. [*See* Ban Chiang *and* Austroasiatic Languages.]

Throughout the first millennium CE, two cultural complexes dominated the region. The Dvaravati civilization, characterized by oval-shaped walled cities, Mon-language inscriptions, and Buddhist monumental remains, lasted from the sixth to the ninth century and brought Buddhism to the countryside. The spread into the region of the control and influence of Cambodian Angkor toward the end of the period brought elements of Hindu religion, bu-

reaucratized administration, and the Indic arts and sciences. Some overland trade extending inland from the Gulf of Siam to the north and northeast began the patterns of interregional interaction that were to knit the region together. About the end of this period, during the tenth through the twelfth century, the Tai peoples began moving into what is now Thailand, perhaps even as far to the south as Nakhon Si Thammarat on the Malay Peninsula. Already, the people were referred to as Syam (i.e., "Siamese") in Cham, Khmer, and Mon inscriptions. [*See* Dvaravati; Angkor; Tai Peoples; Mon; Cham; *and* Nakhon Si Thammarat.]

In the thirteenth century, local Tai and other chiefs who had survived as vassals of the Angkor rulers began to establish independent principalities, notably at Sukhothai in the 1240s and at Chiang Mai in 1296. Older principalities to the south simply broke away from Angkor. The earlier Tai attempts at state building were fragile, for they featured personal political relationships—characteristic of the Tai peoples in narrow upland valleys—and the early Tai states were not durable. [*See* Sukhothai.]

A major turning point in Tai history comes in 1351, when a new kingdom was founded at Ayudhya. It combined traditional Tai forms of labor control through personalized, informal, patron-client relations with the more formal, impersonal, and legalistic relationships characteristic of bureaucracies. The latter forms were derived from the lower Chaophraya River basin under Angkorian rule and were established in such centers as Lopburi. Within a century the early kings of Ayudhya had developed a very powerful, bureaucratic state, most notably during the reign of King Borommatrailokanat (r. 1448–1488). [*See* Ayudhya; Lopburi; *and* Borommatrailokanat.]

From the beginning, Ayudhya's rulers had been acutely aware of events in the world beyond their horizons, and they welcomed foreign traders (at first, Chinese and Persians) to their capital. Compared with their country cousins in the interior, Ayudhya's rulers tended to be much more worldly and sophisticated, always up-to-date on the latest techniques of ruling and on fashionable currents of thought in the Asian maritime world.

Ayudhya was not, however, sufficiently well integrated as a state to be able to resist effectively the fierce aggression mounted against it by the kings of Burma in the middle of the sixteenth century, and the kingdom fell to Burmese armies in 1569. Its recovery under King Naresuan (r. 1590–1605), however, was dramatic, and the Siamese met the

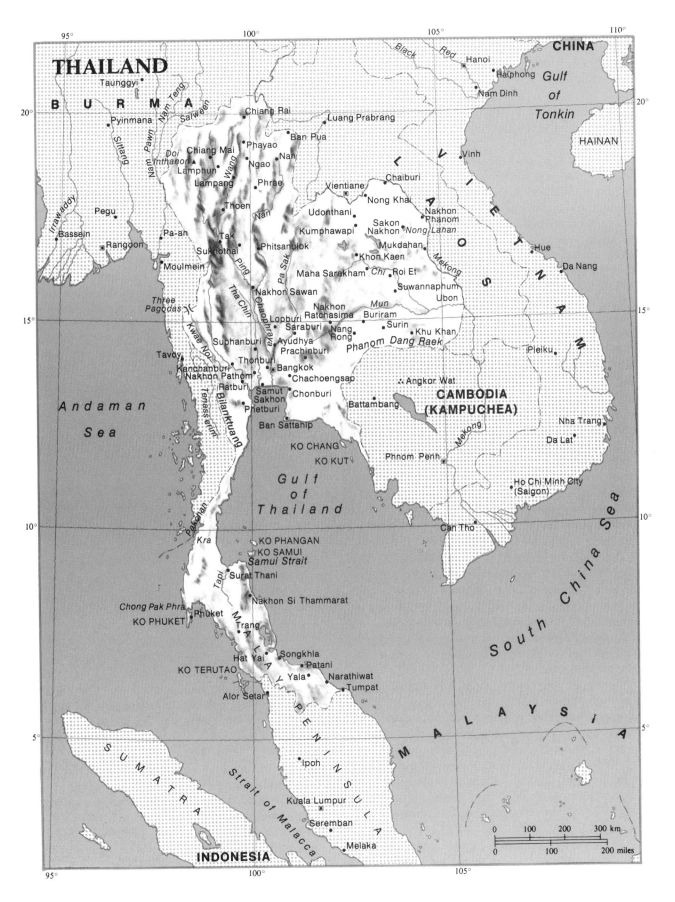

THAILAND

BURMA

CHINA

Taunggyi

Pyinmana

Nam Teng

Salween

Irrawaddy

Sittang

Pawn

Pegu

Bassein

Rangoon

Pa-an

Moulmein

Three Pagodas

Tavoy

Tenasserim

Kanchanburi
Nakhon Pathom
Ratburi

Kwae Noi

Bilanktuang

Chiang Rai

Luang Prabrang

Chiang Mai
Phayao
Nan
Ngao

Doi Inthanon
Lamphun
Lampang
Phrae

Thoen

Nan

Tak

Sukhothai

Phitsanulok

Nakhon Sawan

Lopburi
Saraburi

Nakhon Ratchasima

Nang Rong

Ayudhya
Prachinburi

Thonburi
Bangkok

Chachoengsap

Samut Sakhon
Phetburi

Chonburi

Ban Sattahip

Suphanburi

Pa Sak

Chao Phraya

Ping

Wang

Yom

Tha Chin

Vientiane

Nong Khai

Udonthani

Kumphawapi

Khon Kaen

Maha Sarakham

Sakon Nakhon

Nong Lahan

Nakhon Phanom

Mukdahan

Chi
Roi Et

Suwannaphum

Ubon

Surin

Khu Khan

Phanom Dang Raek

Mun

Buriram

Chaiburi

Vinh

Hue

Da Nang

Pleiku

Nha Trang

Da Lat

Ho Chi Minh City (Saigon)

Can Tho

Mekong

CAMBODIA (KAMPUCHEA)

Battambang

Angkor Wat

Phnom Penh

L A O S

V I E T N A M

Hanoi
Haiphong
Nam Dinh

Black
Red

Gulf of Tonkin

HAINAN

Andaman Sea

Chong Pak Phra
KO PHUKET

Phuket

Trang

Hat Yai

KO TERUTAO

Alor Setar

Pakchan

Kra

Tapi

Surat Thani

Nakhon Si Thammarat

Songkhla
Patani
Yala
Narathiwat
Tumpat

Ipoh

Kuala Lumpur

Seremban

Melaka

KO CHANG
KO KUT

KO PHANGAN
KO SAMUI
Samui Strait

Gulf of Thailand

South China Sea

M A L A Y

P E N I N S U L A

M A L A Y S I A

S U M A T R A

Strait of Malacca

INDONESIA

0   100   200   300 km

0   100   200 miles

95°   100°   105°   110°

20°

15°

10°

5°

Dutch and English trading expeditions that reached Ayudhya in the early seventeenth century full of self-confidence in their power. Nothing was to occur during the next century to shake that self-confidence, not even an abortive French bid to establish an outpost of Louis XIV in Bangkok during the reign of King Narai (r. 1657–1688). [See Naresuan and Narai.]

Throughout much of the eighteenth century, Siam, like many of its neighbors, was unsettled by major economic changes; these are still imperfectly understood, but they have to do with a major upswing in the inter-Asian trade and considerable movements of silver. Sources suggest a diffusion of power away from kings and courts toward lower officials and the provinces, a shift resulting in political tensions. Whatever the reasons, Siam was weak and divided when a revived Burma again began attacking the kingdom in 1760, and the country was completely devastated when the capital fell in 1767.

King Taksin (r. 1767–1782) provided a quick military solution to Siam's crisis. He not only reunified the kingdom but also added considerable territory—in Laos, Cambodia, and the Malay states on the peninsula—to it. But by ignoring the political and religious sensitivities of his officials, he provoked a palace coup that deposed and killed him and installed one of his generals, the Chaophraya Chakri, on the throne as King Rama I (Phra Phutthayotfa Chulalok; r. 1782–1809). [See Taksin and Phra Phutthayotfa Chulalok.]

Rama I's reign established a new style of politics, in which the old noble families had a real share of power and a new intellectual style. He and his officers genuinely believed that their country's future depended upon their thoughtful use of their powers of reason, even, if necessary, at the expense of tradition. Over the next century, this intellectual stance enabled Rama I's heirs to deal successfully with the mounting pressures against the kingdom from the Western powers.

During the reign of King Mongkut (1851–1868), Siam accepted unequal treaties imposed by the West, judging it better to yield on economic matters than to be forced to give up its independence. This pattern of accommodation was continued by Mongkut's son Chulalongkorn (1868–1910), whose forty-two-year reign brought about the complete overhaul of traditional institutions. By 1910 Siam was well on the way to becoming a modern state. [See Mongkut and Chulalongkorn.]

The successes of Chulalongkorn ultimately encouraged internal political pressures that led to the revolution of 1932, which ended the absolute monarchy. It was also, however, the incompleteness of Chulalongkorn's modernization that made political development so difficult. The society as a whole was still too factionalized, too underschooled, to be able to participate fully and effectively in the political process, and for the next half-century Siam alternated between harsher and softer forms of rule by the one strong, united, and modern segment of the society: the military, most notably under Luang Phibunsongkhram, Sarit Thanarat, and Thanom Kittikachorn. [See Phibunsongkhram, Luang; Sarit Thanarat; and Thanom Kittikachorn.]

Modernization finally caught up with military rule in 1973, when student demonstrations escalated to a revolution that toppled the military government and initiated a democratic, civilian government. It lasted only three years before the military stepped back in and imposed an uneasy and, at times, experimental process of trying to find a compromise between authority and participation. By the mid-1980s a limited civilian democracy was showing signs of some vigor and stability, abortive military coups notwithstanding.

[See also Patani; Langkasuka; Lan Na; Lan Sang; Bunnag Family; Franco-Siamese War; Emerald Buddha; Ramakian; Sunthon Phu; Phra Pathom Chedi; Preah Vihear; Bangkok; and Chakri Dynasty.]

David K. Wyatt, *Thailand: A Short History* (1984).

DAVID K. WYATT

THAKIN MOVEMENT. *See* Dobama Asiayon.

THAKIN NU. *See* Nu, U.

THAMMAYUTTIKA (or Dhammayutika), reform order of the Buddhist monkhood in Thailand. It originated with Prince Mongkut (later to rule as King Rama IV), who as a monk in the late 1820s grew dissatisfied with traditional Buddhism and led a return to fundamentals based on scholarship in the canonical texts. The monks around him, distinctively robed with both shoulders covered instead of one, grew in numbers and eminence, their reputation enhanced by their strict adherence to monastic discipline, high scholarship, and their active public preaching and education. From the time of the tenure of Mongkut's son Prince Wachirayan, first a patriarch of the order (1893–1910) and then as supreme patriarch of Siamese Buddhism (1910–1921), the Thammayut order wielded great influence, taking the leading role in organizing the national Buddhist monkhood and monopolizing leadership positions in the church. It became an important proponent of modernization, education, and public morality and retains that role to the present.

[*See also* Wachirayan Warorot.]

Donald K. Swearer, *Buddhism in Transition* (1970).
DAVID K. WYATT

THANESWAR, city in present-day Haryana state, India, home of King Harsha (r. 606–647). Thaneswar also witnessed historical battles, in 1192 and 1759, between Muslim invaders and local rulers.

[*See also* Harsha.]

USHA SANYAL

THANOM KITTIKACHORN (b. 1911), Thai military and political leader. Born in Tak Province, Thanom entered the Military Academy when he was eight. After receiving his commission in 1929 he was assigned to a regiment in Chiang Mai. Thanom saw brief action in the Franco-Siamese War of 1941, in which he distinguished himself as a good soldier. In 1946 he joined the faculty of the Military Academy. The following year, a group of cadets staged an army coup d'état against the Pridi Phanomyong and Luang Thamrong government. As a member of the 1947 coup group, Thanom was given command of strategic infantry regiments in Bangkok.

In 1949, under the command of Sarit Thanarat, Thanom and Praphas Charusathian led an assault on the Royal Palace to defeat pro-Pridi Seri Thai (Free Thai) rebels. Thanom quickly became Sarit's right-hand man and succeeded Sarit as commander of the First Army after the latter became army chief.

Thanom's first political post was deputy minister of cooperatives under the 1955 Luang Phibunsongkhram cabinet. Two years later, as Sarit's assistant commander in chief of the army, Thanom was appointed deputy minister of defense. Following the Sarit coup of 1957, Thanom became Sarit's surrogate while the latter was in the United States receiving medical attention. He resigned as prime minister when Sarit returned in 1958. In the subsequent Sarit government, Thanom assumed the posts of deputy prime minister and minister of defense.

After the death of Sarit in 1963, Thanom became prime minister for the second time. The following

year, he was elevated to the rank of field marshal. For the next decade, the Thanom regime continued to carry out Sarit's policy of encouraging trade and investment, anticommunism, a pro–United States stance, infrastructure building, and repression of local dissidents.

Thailand's involvement in the Vietnam War brought economic advantages to the business and service sectors, but few of these gains trickled down to the other strata of society. The war also raised fundamental moral issues that were openly discussed and debated. In 1971 Thanom reacted to the openness by staging a coup and attempting to reinstate a repressive Sarit-type regime. His authoritarian government was opposed by intellectuals and students, who led large public demonstrations that culminated in the 14 October 1973 uprising. Through the intervention of the king, Thanom, Praphas, and Narong Kittikachorn (Thanom's son, Praphas's son-in-law, and the duo's heir apparent) were allowed to leave the country. What followed in Thailand was a three-year civilian, democratic government marred by labor strikes, political intimidation from both left and right, and vacillating leadership. In 1976 Thanom secretly returned to Bangkok to visit his ailing father. He then joined the monkhood. His refusal to leave Thailand led to further student protests and demonstrations, which precipitated the storming of Thammasat University by units of the Border Police and the coup d'état of 6 October 1976. Praphas and Narong returned to Thailand shortly thereafter.

[*See also* Pridi Phanomyong; Sarit Thanarat; Free Thai; Phibunsongkhram, Luang; *and* Thailand.]

Thak Chaloemtiarana, *Thailand* (1979). John Girling, *Thailand* (1981).
THAK CHALOEMTIARANA

THAN TUN, THAKIN (1911–1967), secretary-general of Burma's Anti-Fascist People's Freedom League, or AFPFL (1945–1947), and chairman of the Burma Communist Party (1945–1967). Than Tun had been an organizer and Marxist author in the Dobama Asiayon in the 1930s. After serving as minister for agriculture in the Ba Maw cabinet (1942–1945), he led in the negotiations on the independence of Burma from Britain in 1945–1946. Then losing leadership of the AFPFL to General Aung San, Than Tun remained in open politics until the independent government of Burma ordered his arrest in March 1948. From then until his death in an internal party purge he remained in underground rebellion against the government, although he entered into negotiations several times in an attempt to be brought back into legal politics.

[*See also* Anti-Fascist People's Freedom League; Dobama Asiayon; Ba Maw; Aung San; *and* Burma.]

Frank N. Trager, *Burma: From Kingdom to Republic* (1966).   ROBERT H. TAYLOR

THAPA, BHIM SEN, prime minister of Nepal from 1807 to 1837. Under his leadership the kingdom of Gorkha reached its height, incorporating the Himalayan foothills lying between the Tista and Sutlej rivers. Thapa's success at rebuilding Nepal's army after its defeat in the Anglo-Nepali War and his repeated attempts to ally regional powers against the British proved serious obstacles to the expansion of British power in northern India in the early nineteenth century.

[*See also* Nepal: History of Nepal.]

RICHARD ENGLISH

THARRAWADDY (1786–1846), king of Burma (r. 1837–1845). A grandson of Bodawhpaya, Tharrawaddy deposed his brother Bagyidaw in a coup. Shortly after ascending to the throne, he rejected the provisions of the Treaty of Yandabo, which permitted a British Resident in Burma. Tharrawaddy's acts were measured to avoid war. He opposed the presence of Christian missionaries. By mid-1839 the resident withdrew, claiming ill health, but in reality he was harassed out of the kingdom. Tharrawaddy moved the capital from Ava to Amarapura.

Tharrawaddy was active in building pagodas, monasteries, canals, and dams. He had almost one hundred wives, and by 1842 a succession conflict existed among his sons. He was supplanted by his son Pagan in 1845 and was also the father of the future King Mindon.

[*See also* Bagyidaw; Yandabo, Treaty of; *and* Pagan Min.]

Walter Sadgun Desai, "The Rebellion of Prince Tharrawaddy and the Deposition of Bagyidaw as King of Burma, 1837," *Journal of the Burma Research Society* 25 (1935): 109–120. Oliver B. Pollak, "Dynasticism and Revolt: Crisis of Kingship in Burma, 1837–1851," *Journal of Southeast Asian Studies* 7 (1976): 187–196.

OLIVER B. POLLAK

THAT LUANG, chief Buddhist monument and shrine of Vientiane, Laos. On moving the capital of Lan Sang from Luang Prabang to Vientiane, King Setthathirat in 1566 ordered the erection of this towering Buddhist reliquary that served as the focus of the capital. It was destroyed by the Ho invaders in 1873 and restored under the direction of Prince Souvannaphouma in 1931–1935. [*See also* Setthathirat; Vientiane; Ho; Lan Sang; *and* Souvannaphouma.]

DAVID K. WYATT

FIGURE 1. *That Luang, Vientiane.* The largest national shrine in Laos, That Luang is said to be the repository of the Buddha's breastbone. The monument was restored in the early 1930s.

THATON. According to Burmese tradition, which has been supported in part by recent excavations, Thaton was the oldest urban Mon site in Burma. It was the seat of the Mon region known as Ramannadesa, located in Lower Burma near the coast. To the Mon of Burma, Thaton probably has the same political and cultural significance as Pagan has to Burmans. Partly because of this significance, and partly for more economic and strategic reasons, the Pagan king Anawrahta sacked Thaton in the mid-eleventh century, taking back with him the entire court. To justify his attack in the context of Buddhism, he also took the thirty-two sets of the Tipitaka, the Theravada Buddhist scriptures. Thaton remained under Upper Burma hegemony until about the end of the thirteenth century when Pagan began its political decline. But by that time, other Lower Burma cities had preempted Thaton's role as the center of Mon political power. Today it seems likely that sites close to Thaton will yield artifacts from the second century BCE.

[See also Mon and Ramannadesa.]

U Aung Thaw, Historical Sites in Burma (1972).

MICHAEL AUNG-THWIN

THAT PHANOM, Buddhist monument and shrine near Nakhon Phanom, northeastern Thailand. Religious monuments on this site may date back to the late first millennium CE, but the historical Buddhist reliquary dates with certainty only from the seventeenth century, when numerous inscriptions attested to its reconstruction between 1614 and 1693. It served as one of the holiest shrines for the Lao of the central Mekong River valley for many centuries. It collapsed to rubble in 1975, to be reconstructed yet again.

[See also Angkor.]

J. B. Pruess, The That Phanom Chronicle (1976).

DAVID K. WYATT

THERAVADA BUDDHISM. See Buddhism: An Overview.

THIBAW, king of Burma (r. 1878–1885), the last king of the Konbaung dynasty.

When his crown prince was killed in a rebellion in 1866, King Mindon (r. 1852–1878) feared to name his successor and so left the succession question unresolved at his death. An ambitious faction at court led by ex-queen Hsinbyumashin, the Kin-

wun Mingyi, and a Hluttaw minister placed a junior prince, Thibaw, on the throne, expecting they might be able to control him. Hsinbyumashin married three of her daughters to the new king; one of them, Supayalat, was his chief queen. The conspirators also succeeded in murdering more than seventy other princes and princesses who might challenge their power, an act of barbarism that poisoned relations with the British, who now ruled more than half of Burma and were threatening to seize the rest.

Thibaw and Supayalat were by no means as pliant as their sponsors had hoped. Faced with isolation and increasing British hostility, Thibaw desperately tried to establish his own foreign policy. When relations with Britain faltered over Thibaw's insistence on direct access to the British home government (instead of having to work through the government of British India), he began quiet negotiations with other European powers, notably France and Italy. Alarmed at the intrusion of their European rivals, Britain used a trumped-up economic grievance, involving the timber operations of the Bombay-Burmah Trading Corporation, to issue an ultimatum to the Mandalay government. Britain then invaded Upper Burma at the end of 1885. The annexation to British India of Upper Burma was proclaimed on 1 January 1886. Thibaw and Supayalat were led off to exile in western India, where Thibaw died in 1916.

[See also Konbaung Dynasty; Mindon; Supayalat; Kinwun Mingyi; Anglo-Burmese Wars; Bombay-Burmah Trading Corporation; and Hluttaw.]

J. F. Cady, A History of Modern Burma (1958). C. L. Keeton, King Thebaw and the Ecological Rape of Burma (1974). D. P. Singhal, The Annexation of Upper Burma (1960).

DAVID K. WYATT

THIEU TRI (1806–1847), third Nguyen emperor of Vietnam (r. 1841–1847). Although Thieu Tri's reign brought little change in domestic policies, there were important developments in foreign relations, including Cambodia's recognition of joint Vietnamese-Siamese sovereignty. Thieu Tri's major concern was the growing French threat in the region. While maintaining his father Minh Mang's anti-Christian laws, he initially enforced them less strictly. However, French naval actions on behalf of imprisoned missionaries in 1842 and 1845, followed by an actual skirmish at Tourane in 1847, caused him to promulgate more severe laws. These edicts were carried out after his death by Tu Duc.

[See also Minh Mang and Tu Duc.]

John Cady, *The Roots of French Imperialism in Eastern Asia* (1954). Nguyen Phut Tan, *Modern History of Vietnam (1802–1954)* (1964).   BRUCE M. LOCKHART

THIPHAKORAWONG KHAM BUNNAG

(1813–1870), Thai scholar and government official. A son of Dit Bunnag, Kham was appointed deputy *phrakhlang* in 1851 and *phrakhlang* in 1855. In addition to his diplomatic responsibilities—he handled all of Siam's negotiations with foreign powers until his retirement in 1868—he was also an engineer who supervised the reconstruction of Phra Pathom Chedi and who built several canals. He is best known, however, as a historian and as the first Thai scholar to move away from the strict form of the chronicle toward a more interpretive historiography. His two most important books were his multivolume history of the first four Chakri reigns and *Kitchanukit*, a survey of modern science.

[*See also* Phrakhlang.]

CONSTANCE M. WILSON

THIRTY COMRADES, label given to Aung San

and twenty-nine other young Burmese nationalists who received training from the Japanese military in 1940–1941. They formed the nucleus of the Burma Independence Army. [*See also* Aung San; Minami Kikan; *and* Burma Defense Army.]

ROBERT H. TAYLOR

THOMAS. Aside from biblical references, records

of the apostle Thomas's ministry from Parthia to India are preserved in unauthenticated Greek, Aramaic, and Syriac apocrypha. The *Acts of Thomas* (third century) traces Thomas's missionary labors to Baluchistan and Punjab in the kingdom of Gondophernes, a king whose reign in 46 CE is corroborated in the Takht-i-Bahai inscription. Mention of Thomas's work in the kingdom of Mazdai, thought by some to be in southern India, is hazy, but references in patristic literature are corroborated in Pahlavi inscriptions, Arabic travel chronicles, and the traditions of Indian coastal communities. Indigenous tradition holds that the Melankara Church was founded by Saint Thomas. Critical church historians, however, ascribe the Melankara Church to the Edessan bishop Thomas Cannaneus in 325. Similarly, Indian traditions hold that Thomas was martyred and buried near the city of Madras, whereas

Western sources have traced his remains to Edessa and later to Chios and Ortona.

[*See also* Christianity: An Overview.]

Adolphus E. Medlycott, *India and the Apostle Thomas* (1905). A. C. Perumalil, *The Apostles in India* (1971).

PATRICK ROCHE

THONBURI. *See* Taksin.

THREE FEUDATORIES REBELLION. The

sanfan, or Three Feudatories, were large sections of South China granted by the Qing dynasty to Wu Sangui, Shang Kexi, and Geng Jimao as a reward for their assistance in the Manchu conquest of China. The Kangxi emperor (r. 1661–1722) acted to abolish the feudatories because of the potential threat their independent power bases posed to the dynasty. The rebellion began in December 1673 when Wu Sangui proclaimed himself the first "emperor" of the rebel Zhou dynasty. During the next eight years the Qing government and the rebels were embroiled in a fierce struggle that produced heavy casualties on both sides and tremendous economic disruption. By 1676 the strength of the rebels began to erode with the surrender of Geng Jimao to imperial forces. Shang Kexi's son followed suit in 1677. Wu Sangui continued his resistance until his death in 1678. The rebel cause was continued under the leadership of Wu's grandson, Wu Shifan, until 1681.

[*See also* Ming Dynasty; Qing Dynasty; Shang Kexi; *and* Wu Sangui.]

Arthur W. Hummel, ed., *Eminent Chinese of the Ch'ing Period (1644–1912)* (1943–1944), p. 678. Lawrence D. Kessler, *K'ang-hsi and the Consolidation of Ch'ing Rule, 1661–1684* (1976). Jonathan D. Spence, *Emperor of China: Self-Portrait of K'ang-hsi* (1975).

ANITA M. ANDREW

THREE HANS (Korean, Samhan), three political

groups that formed in southern Korea between the first century BCE and the third century CE.

In the third and second centuries BCE, the area south of the Han River was referred to as Chin'guk. During this period the practice of rice cultivation became widespread and iron implements began to be introduced from the north. The northern part of the Korean peninsula was politically unsettled and many people fled to the south to escape the unrest in that region. With the advances in agriculture and the rapid influx of new people who bore the technology of a more sophisticated society, Chin'guk was transformed. Three political entities gradually emerged in the area formerly known as Chin'guk: Mahan, Pyŏnhan, and Chinhan, commonly referred to as the Three Hans.

Of the Three Hans, Mahan was the largest, occupying the area that today is part of Kyŏnggi, Ch'ungch'ŏng, and Chŏlla provinces in central and southwestern Korea. According to early sources, it comprised fifty-four small "states," varying in size from ten to one hundred thousand households. Although these figures are exceptionally high, they do indicate the comparatively large population of the Mahan area. Pyŏnhan, situated in modern Kyŏngsang Province in the western part of the Naktong River basin, was considerably smaller than Mahan. There were twelve Mahan "states," each with five or six hundred households. Chinhan occupied the area east of the Naktong River in Kyŏngsang and, like Pyŏnhan, had twelve "states" with a similar population.

The pattern of state development for the Three Hans was not uniform. Mahan was heavily influenced by outside forces, while Chinhan experienced more gradual political changes resulting from internal development. In the third and fourth centuries CE the Three Hans developed into more mature and distinct political states as Mahan became Paekche, Pyŏnhan became Kaya (Mimana), and Chinhan became Silla.

In the first century of the common era the Three Hans were made up of numerous small "states" referred to by some as "walled-town states." From these walled towns ruling elites dominated the surrounding region, providing security and guidance to a largely agricultural population. Paekche eventually emerged as the major state in southwestern Korea. Out of Saro developed the city of Kyŏngju, which became the center of the Silla kingdom. The rulers of these walled-town states were often from the most prominent clan or lineage in the region or represented a union of several lineages. Some scholars believe these states to have been tribal unions. The political leaders took charge of administration and warfare and by the third century some had established regular diplomatic ties with China.

In the Three Hans secular authority separated itself from the spiritual realm. Nevertheless, religion played an important part in the lives of the people. The religious leaders of the Three Hans were not just shamans but practiced ritual to supplicate the gods. Their religious services revealed a deep concern for the afterlife. Many ceremonies were also concerned with agriculture, particularly including prayers for a rich harvest. One unique tradition of the Three Hans was the *sodo*, or "asylum," a specially designated area that was considered sacred. If someone who committed a crime safely reached a *sodo* he was exonerated.

In order to maintain their cultivation of rice, the people of the Three Hans constructed reservoirs to assure an ample supply of irrigation water. A number of animals were domesticated and, as seen from artifacts discovered in the ancient shell mounds dating from this era, the people of the Three Hans consumed fish, deer, and boar. They also raised a special long-tailed chicken, cattle, and horses. Private land was common, and the peasants also joined together to cultivate specified parcels of community land.

As the various "states" within each of the Three Hans became more developed, they started to vie with each other for increased authority. With internal changes came added pressures from the northern part of the peninsula, the result of the breakup of the Chinese Han empire and the tensions caused by encroaching northern nomadic tribes. In the second and third centuries, the Three Han region witnessed increasing strife; by the fourth century most of the "walled-town states" had been destroyed by more sophisticated "confederated kingdoms" that were ruled by a king. Paekche, under King Kŭn Ch'ogo (r. 346–375), completely subjugated Mahan in 369, and at about the same time Kaya and Silla emerged.

[See also Paekche; Mimana; and Silla.]

EDWARD J. SHULTZ

THREE KINGDOMS. Founded after the collapse of the Han dynasty in China, the Three Kingdoms—Wei (220–265), Shu-Han (221–263), and Wu (222–280)—mark the beginning of 350 years of divided rule in China. Wei, the largest and most populous of the three, had its capital first at Xu and later in the rebuilt Han capital at Luoyang. It occupied all of North China from northern Korea in the northeast to the Gansu corridor in the northwest (excluding the Ordos region in the loop of the Yellow River), southward to a line below the Huai River; its population numbered around thirty million. Shu-Han, with its capital in Chengdu (Sichuan), occupied the land west of the Yangtze Gorges from the Qinling Range in the north to what is now Yunnan in the south, and claimed scarcely eight million inhabitants. Wu, with its capital first at Wuchang and

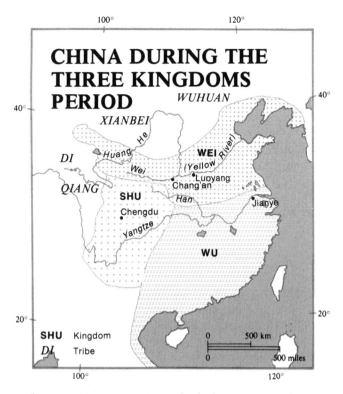

CHINA DURING THE THREE KINGDOMS PERIOD

SHU Kingdom
DI Tribe

[See also Cao Cao; Liu Bei; Sun Quan; Zhang Fei; Zhuge Liang; Six Dynasties; and Jin Dynasty.]

Wolfram Eberhard, A History of China (rev. ed., 1960). Achilles Fang, trans., The Chronicle of the Three Kingdoms (220–265), edited by Glen Baxter (1952). L. Carrington Goodrich, A Short History of the Chinese People (3d ed., 1959).

RICHARD MATHER

THUC DYNASTY, the name given by premodern Viet historians to the reign of An Duong Vuong (Thuc Phan) over the kingdom of Au Lac. These historians dated the reign of An Duong Vuong as 258–207 BCE; recent scholarship indicates that An Duong Vuong actually reigned from about 210 to about 179 BCE. [See also An Duong Vuong and Au Lac.]

JAMES M. COYLE

THUGS. See Thagi.

THUNBERG, CARL PETER (1743–1828), Swedish botanist attached to the Netherlands East India Company who was in Japan with the Dutch trading mission at Deshima in Nagasaki harbor from 1776 to 1777. A student of Linnaeus at the University of Uppsala, he introduced Linnaeus's methods of classification to studies of Japanese flora. He collected more than eight hundred specimens and influenced several leading Japanese students of Dutch Learning (rangaku). Upon his return to Sweden Thunberg taught at Uppsala, publishing his Flora Japonica (1784; translated and published by the scholar Itō Keisuke in Japan in 1828), as well as his Travels in Europe, Africa, and Asia (1794–1805).

[See also Rangaku and Deshima.]

MARIUS B. JANSEN

later at Jianye (Nanjing), laid claim to everything east of the Yangtze Gorges from the Huai River to Hanoi, and boasted a population of about twelve million, including aboriginal tribes in the mountainous areas. Most of the Han people—descendants of the old Chu population, with more recent immigrants from the north—were concentrated in the valleys of the Yangtze River and its tributaries.

The de facto founder of Wei, Cao Cao (155–220), had been an able general under the Han who had won power through his suppression of the Yellow Turban rebels in 184 and 192. He and his son, Cao Pei (r. 220–226), unsuccessfully attempted to curb the growing independence of the large landholding families, whose rise during the last decades of Han rule had broken the power of the central court and caused its downfall. Wei, in its turn, also fell victim to a coup by one of these families. The founder of Shu-Han, Liu Bei (r. 221–223), was a distant relative of the Han royal family who died in the third year of his reign. The founder of Wu, Sun Quan (r. 222–252) was a member of a powerful southern family who seized the opportunity to declare the independence of his area. Although all three founders claimed legitimate succession to the Han mandate and each fought to maintain that claim against the others, Wei finally subdued Shu-Han in 263. Wei was then overthrown by one of its own generals, who established the Jin in 265 and eventually absorbed Wu in 280.

TIANJIN, Chinese city located approximately seventy-four miles southeast of Beijing in Hebei Province; one of China's leading transportation and industrial centers. Reporting a population of 7,764,141 (1982), it is the third largest city of China. Together with Beijing and Shanghai, Tianjin is one of three centrally administered municipalities in the People's Republic.

Historical records show that during the Ming dynasty (1368–1644), Tianjin became a frontier garrison town and transshipment station for grain between the Grand Canal and Beijing. The city remained a small port until 1860, when Tianjin was forcibly opened to foreign trade as a treaty port following China's defeat by Britain and France in the Arrow War. By the turn of the century, nine foreign powers maintained concession areas in Tianjin: Britain, France, Japan, Germany, Belgium, Russia, Italy, Austro-Hungary, and the United States. During the Sino-Japanese War (1937–1945), Tianjin was again occupied by the Japanese, who developed the city as a important communications and transportation center.

Since 1949 Tianjin has been named a key economic zone, an area deemed essential for China's future development. Tianjin's industrial complex produces iron and steel, engineering equipment, heavy machinery, tractors, diesel engines, electronics, chemicals, paper, and rubber.

ANITA M. ANDREW

TIANJIN, TREATY OF. *See* Arrow War.

TIAN SHAN RANGE (Chinese, *tian shan;* "heavenly mountains"), an extensive highland system (about 386,000 square miles) with several peaks higher than 20,000 feet, branching east-northeast from the Pamirs for about 1,800 miles. From the appearance of the Turks there in the mid-sixth century until the mid-twentieth century, the population has been predominantly Turkic and Mongolian.

CHRISTOPHER I. BECKWITH

TIBET. Formerly an independent Buddhist state north of the Himalayas, Tibet is now an autonomous region of the People's Republic of China. Its population in 1982 was estimated at 1.89 million.

Geography. The Tibetan highlands cover an enormous area, almost one million square miles, about one-fourth the size of the United States, averaging an altitude of ten thousand feet in the south to fifteen thousand feet in the north. The plateau is rimmed with high mountain ranges: the Himalayas in the south, the Karakoram Mountains in the west, the Kunlun and Altyn Tagh ranges in the north, and the Bayankara and Amne Machin ranges in the east. The region is mostly dry, as the ocean's moisture cannot often get over the mountains, and the climate, at least in the central area, is much more mild than the snow-covered mountain peaks and high passes indicate. The great northern steppe can be bitterly cold in winter, causing the herdsmen to head

for shelter in the southern valleys. The northern reaches of that steppe are an extremely rich area for pastoralism, and the domestication of that hardy bovine creature, the yak, assured considerable wealth for seminomadic Tibetan husbandmen. The southern and eastern river valleys have a milder climate and enough space for a reliable irrigated agriculture, and additionally the dry climate and pure air make it possible to store surplus grains for many years without spoilage. As a whole, Tibet has not been barren or poverty stricken, and, while living tended to be simple and austere, there has never been famine in recorded Tibetan history except during the brief times when occupation armies have been present.

Most of the major rivers of Asia originate in the Tibetan highlands, including the Indus and its tributaries, the Ganges, the Brahmaputra, the Salween, the Mekong, the Yangtze, and the Yellow rivers. Part of the mythic dimensions of Tibet's image among outsiders may come from this pivotal position it occupies; the Chinese "Immortals," the *devas* of the Hindu pantheon, and important mountain deities of the Central Asian peoples are thought to live in the heavens above its peaks. The Tibetans themselves have a myth that the land is a great, fierce mother goddess lying on her back, supporting the land on her torso. Ethnic Tibet is much larger than the province China calls "Tibet Autonomous Region," which is actually only about one-third of traditional Tibet.

People. Tibet is a fringe area of the great nomadic belt that runs from Siberia to Kenya and is mentioned by anthropologists as the source of many Eurasian nations. It also lies on the fringe of the great civilizations of India and China. Yet it remains distinct from both steppe and sown lands, integrating the cultural patterns of both. There are nomads in the north, but the southern valleys are agricultural. The type of agriculture practiced is similar to that of the Iranian Plateau, dependent on sophisticated irrigation, conservative patterns of land tenure, careful crop rotation, and maintenance of a balanced population. The inhabitants of these high southern valleys appear to be related racially to the peoples on the other side of the high passes, to the Tai, Burmans, and Yunnanese in the east, to the Nepalis and North Indians in the middle, and to the Dards (Greco-Indo-Scythians) in the west. The northern seminomads appear to be related to the Turco-Mongols, and even to the Indo-European Yuezhi. All these highly varied Tibetan types seem to have arisen from groups of outside peoples who removed themselves from the main migration routes or civilization areas to a higher and less easily traveled terrain.

The beginning of the nation of Tibet, therefore, lies in the meeting of all these various peoples in the central valleys, where the nomads provided the meat and military strength, and the agriculturalists the food surplus and stable organizational patterns. The Tibetan stock is thus an extremely diverse genetic pool, as is amply evidenced upon acquaintance with any community of Tibetans. Tibet seems always to have been a place of spiritual refugees, who went up farther and farther away from steppe and river valley to escape the struggles for traditional territories, people who turned away from the cities and hordes, willing to live with the wind and altitude and sparseness of the high country in order to avoid the problems posed by violent humanity. The Tibetans have one legend that their first king escaped from the dreadful genocidal wars recorded in the *Mahabharata*, indicating refugees from the south, and another legend of descent from the sky, which might indicate refugees from the great steppes to the north. In any case, the present Tibetans are a hardy breed, strongly individualistic and self-reliant, inclined to think for themselves, tolerant of diversity, and open to new ideas and objects. From the nomadic component of their background comes a warrior toughness, and from the sedentary component comes a fun-loving, erotic tendency that makes them among the most relaxed of cultures about hierarchy and sexuality (they had no castes, and both polyandry and polygamy existed in Tibet). The two sides of their national character are well expressed in one of their cherished myths, that they are descended from the union of a divine monkey and a cannibal woman.

Language. The Tibetan language is variously considered to belong to the Tibeto-Burman or the Sino-Tibetan language family; it has strong connections with ancient Chinese, modern Daic, and Burmese, while modern Chinese has diverged markedly. Written Tibetan was not based on Chinese characters but was developed from the Sanskrit alphabet and grammar expressly to translate precisely the Buddhist literature of India. This resulted in a unique language, which fitted the monosyllabic, uninflected Sino-Tibetan vocabulary into the polysyllabic, fully inflected Indo-European grammatical pattern. This process of combination is a typical example of the complex hybridization involved in the formation of the Tibetan culture. [*See also* Sino-Tibetan Languages.]

History. As far back as the Chinese Shang dynasty (c. eighteenth–twelfth century BCE), there are references to the Qiang peoples of Inner Asia, ancestors of the Tibetans (as also perhaps of the Zhou conquerors of the Shang). In the Tibetan records, the first Tibetan king was Nyatri Dzenpo, dating anywhere from the second century BCE to the fifth century CE. The first Tibetan emperor was Songzen Gampo (ruled c. 620–649). He defeated the previous power of the region, the Zhang-zhung empire, unified all Inner Asia, held his own against the Tang emperor Taizong, and put up columns as far away as Bihar in India, Yunnan in China, and the Tarim basin in Inner Asia. He married princesses from the Tang empire and Nepal, built the capital in Lhasa, constructed a Buddhist cathedral, had a new alphabet created, and promulgated the Buddhist "law of ten virtues" in Tibet. For the duration of his dynasty Buddhism was the state religion, steadily opposed by the regional nobles in the name of the previous religion, Bon, a mix of animism and the religion of the Zhang-zhung. The first Tibetan Buddhist monastery, Samye, was constructed in about 775, and a great work of translation and cultural development was begun. Around 840 Lang Darma usurped the throne and began a persecution of Buddhism that demoralized the nation and led to the disintegration of the dynasty and the loss of imperial power.

From the tenth to the thirteenth century regional rulers sponsored the return of Buddhism and culture to Tibet. Monastic foundations assumed political responsibilities in the vacuum left by the lack of a central authority. From 1209 to 1260 the hierarchs of the Sakyapa order, Sakya Pandita and Phags-pa, represented Tibet to the Mongol emperors and were eventually given official rulership by Kublai Khan. [*See also* Phags-pa.] With the fall of the Mongols, the secular Tibetan dynasty was reestablished by Jangchub Janzen; it was to last, with some changes of families, until the early seventeenth century.

In the 1630s and 1640s, parallel with the rise of Manchu banners over China, the Mongolian chieftain Gushri Khan quelled factional struggles emerging from the decline of the secular dynasty and then gave the rule over Tibet to the leader of the Gelugpa order, the fifth Dalai Lama (1617–1682). His religious and secular rule of Tibet was respected and supported by the Manchu emperors of China, who looked to the spiritual authority of the Dalai Lamas to keep the Mongol nations peaceful. The fifth and seventh Dalai Lamas created a unique form of government by monastic bureaucracy, creating a cabinet and parliament arrangement in the early eighteenth century, demilitarizing Tibet and using the monastic institutions to mediate between noble and commoner. This government kept the peace within Tibet for three hundred years and served an important diplomatic role in avoiding conflicts throughout Inner Asia. In the nineteenth century, with the Mongol nations fully pacified, the Manchus encroached on Tibet's traditional independence after being called upon to defend against the Gurkhas. After the 1911 fall of the Manchu Qing dynasty, however, the thirteenth Dalai Lama expelled all Chinese representatives and, with British help, set about trying to modernize his people with only limited success.

Upon coming to power in China in 1949, Mao Zedong set the conquest of Tibet as a major priority. The Red Army invaded Khams through Dajian Lu in 1950, simultaneously entering Amdo via Lanzhou. Tibetan opposition was ineffective, and in 1953 the young fourteenth Dalai Lama's government was forced to accept a seventeen-point agreement with China that dictated terms of "modernization" under China's control. Guerrilla movements developed at once in the eastern areas where the impact of "class struggle," "thought-reform," and communization was most heavily felt. In 1959 the Dalai Lama gave up the attempt to cooperate with the Chinese military rulers and escaped into exile in India, along with more than one hundred thousand of his countrymen. Once he had left, the Chinese dropped all pretense of respecting Tibetan culture and human rights and began a systematic attempt at permanent assimilation of geographical Tibet into the Chinese "motherland." Recently, as the direction within China has changed with the death of Mao and the repudiation of the Gang of Four, Chinese policy in Tibet has been moderated, and the Chinese government has entered into serious negotiations with exiled Tibetan leaders about a new, more realistic status for Tibet.

[See also Buddhism: An Overview; Lamaism; and Dalai Lama.]

John F. Avedon, *In Exile from the Land of Snows* (1984). Helmut Hoffmann, *Tibet: A Handbook* (1976). N. N. Jigmei, *Tibet* (1981). Hugh Richardson and David Snellgrove, *A Cultural History of Tibet* (1968). Tsepon W. D. Shakabpa, *Tibet: A Political History* (1967). R. A. Stein, *Tibetan Civilization* (1972).

ROBERT A. F. THURMAN

TIBETO-BURMAN LANGUAGES. *See* Sino-Tibetan Languages *and* Language Families.

TICH QUANG (Chinese, Xi Guang) was responsible for governing the former Nam Viet Prefecture of Jiaozhi under Han emperor Ping (r. 1–6 CE). It is recorded that he carried out educational and administrative measures aimed at breaking down indigenous customs and replacing them with Chinese practices and regulations. The rites laid down in the Confucian classics were imposed on Jiaozhi's inhabitants, particularly in the areas of familial and marital relations. Tich Quang's reforms were later carried out in neighboring Cuu Chan Prefecture by his counterpart Nhiem Dien (Chinese, Ren Yan).

[See also Jiaozhi.]

Keith W. Taylor, *The Birth of Vietnam* (1983).

BRUCE M. LOCKHART

TILAK, BAL GANGADHAR (1856–1920), Indian nationalist popularly known as Lokamanya ("beloved of the people"). Born into a middle-class Chitpavan brahman family, he took B.A. and L.L.B. degrees at Deccan College, Pune. Also a Sanskrit scholar, his books include *Gita Rahasya*, a study of the *Bhagavad Gita*.

In Pune he taught at the New English School and helped found the Deccan Education Society and Fergusson College. After disputes, he resigned (1890) and took over the *Kesari* and *Mahratta*, newspapers in Marathi and English, respectively. Through writings and speeches he developed political consciousness and opposition to British rule. He politicized the local religious Ganapati festival (from 1894) and established (1896) annual commemorations of Shivaji, the seventeenth-century founder of the Maratha state. [See Shivaji.] In 1891 and 1892 he opposed the Age of Consent Bill, going against social reformers and politicians, and replaced them with his own followers in Pune's political body, the Sarvajanik Sabha (1895). [See also Age of Consent Act.] As joint secretary of the 1895 Indian National Congress Poona session, he opposed its link with the National Social Conference. He championed famine-affected peasants. He attacked British plague prevention measures (1896–1897) on the grounds that they interfered with private lives. After a British official's assassination in 1897, Tilak was jailed for eighteen months for sedition. Following the 1905 Bengal partition, he advocated boycott and the *swadeshi* ("own country") movement with his famous statement, "*Swaraj* ["self-rule"] is my birthright and I will have it." With other extremists he formed a new party that led to a split in the Congress in 1907. In 1908 he was sentenced to six years' imprisonment for sedition in the Andaman Islands.

Released in 1914, he formed a Home Rule League in his Marathi-speaking region (1916) and allied himself with Annie Besant's movement. Unity moves brought him back into Congress in 1915. He urged responsive cooperation to the Montagu-Chelmsford Reforms of 1919 (i.e., opposition from within the legislative councils). [*See* Montagu-Chelmsford Reforms.] His strategy was not implemented and he died on the day that Gandhi inaugurated his first Non-Cooperation campaign.

[*See also* Home Rule League; Indian National Congress; Swadeshi; Gandhi, Mohandas Karamchand; *and* Besant, Annie.]

R. I. Cashman, *The Myth of the Lokamanya: Tilak and Mass Politics in Maharashtra* (1975). D. Keer, *Lokamanya Tilak: Father of the Indian Freedom Struggle* (1969). I. M. Reisner and N. M. Goldberg, eds., *Tilak and the Struggle for Indian Freedom* (1966). S. A. Wolpert, *Tilak and Gokhale: Revolution and Reform in the Making of Modern India* (1962).   JIM MASSELOS

TILEWORK refers to the use of glazed bricks or inserts covering the surface of a building, mainly to decorate wall space but also as a protection against humidity. The development of tilework is connected with that of pottery and baked brick, and like them it has ancient origins. The ziggurat at Chogha Zambil in Khuzistan (thirteenth century BCE) had several types of dappled tiles; Achaemenid palaces of the fifth century BCE had friezes in multicolored relief brick showing winged bulls, lions, and the imperial guard.

Tilework seems to have given way to mosaic decoration in the first millennium CE, but it reemerged by the eleventh century. At first it was used tentatively on either single epigraphic bands framing architectural units or in pieces inset between the brick joints. Gradually, both its palette and its use expanded so that by the beginning of the fourteenth century artisans were on the threshhold of complete mosaic faience, in which small pieces of tile were cut and fitted together to form a uniform, glazed surface. By the middle of the century, dark blue, white, black, purple, yellow, and green had been added to the original turquoise.

Such brilliantly colored mosaic faience was widespread under the Timurids in Central Asia during the fifteenth century. In order rapidly to cover the buildings in their new capital at Isfahan, the Safavids turned to a cheaper technique of polychrome glaz-

FIGURE 1. *Wall Tiles.* Iranian, dating from the thirteenth century. Brown luster on opaque glaze, buff body. Width (each tile) 20.3 cm.

ing, in which individual tiles were painted in seven colors (known in Persian as *haft rang*) and fired a single time.

The most important center for the production of tiles in medieval Iran was the city of Kashan; the abbreviated form *kashi* is the Persian word for tiles. Kashan seemingly had a monopoly on the production of lusterware, in which glazed tiles were painted in metallic oxides and refired in a sophisticated reducing oven. These tiles were so expensive that they were applied only to the interior of important buildings such as palaces and shrines.

[*See also* Painting: Iranian and Central Asian Painting.]

C. Adle, "Kāshī," in *The Encyclopaedia of Islam* (new ed., 1960–). Donald Wilber, "The Development of Mosaic Faience in Islamic Architecture in Iran," *Ars Islamica* 6 (1939): 16–47; reprinted in *The Garland Library of the History of Art*, vol. 13, *Islamic Art and Architecture* (1976), pp. 121–161.   SHEILA S. BLAIR

TILOKARACHA (or Tilokaraja), king of Lan Na in northern Thailand in the fifteenth century, a great warrior who established Lan Na as a major state.

Tilok was the sixth son of King Sam Fang Kaen (r. 1401–1441) and initially was put on the throne by a scheming official who had overthrown his father. It took the young prince nearly a decade to establish his independence and stabilize his power. He was aided in doing so by frequent wars with the kingdom of Ayudhya. By 1450, he was aggressively expanding his state to the north and east and was enticed into moving southward by the opportunity presented by Ayudhya's extinguishing of the venerable old kingdom of Sukhothai. For a quarter of a century, Lan Na was almost constantly at war with King Borommatrailokanat of Ayudhya, a war memorialized in the famous Siamese poem "Yuan phai" ("The Defeat of the Northerners").

In the 1470s, as the war waned, Tilok constructed the imposing Maha Chedi Luang, the great Buddhist spire of Chiang Mai, his capital. He died on 24 May 1487, only a year before the death of his great rival, Trailok of Ayudhya. The century that followed his death was perhaps the most glorious in Lan Na's history, made possible by his accomplishments in strengthening and securing the kingdom.

[*See also* Lan Na; Sam Fang Kaen; *and* Borommatrailokanat.]

A. B. Griswold and Prasert na Nagara, "A Fifteenth-Century Siamese Historical Poem," in *Southeast Asian History and Historiography*, edited by C. D. Cowan and O. W. Wolters (1976). N. A. Jayawickrama, trans., *The Sheaf of Garlands and the Epochs of the Conqueror* (1968). David K. Wyatt, *Thailand: A Short History* (1984).   DAVID K. WYATT

TIMOR, island in eastern Indonesia, formerly divided into Dutch and Portuguese colonial administrations. The island was traditionally divided between two loosely structured kingdoms, Serviao in the west, controlling predominantly Melanesian Atoni, and Belu in the east, controlling areas of slightly later Malay settlement. Effective rule was generally by regional chiefs.

In the seventeenth and eighteenth centuries the island was subject to a prolonged struggle for religious and political dominance between Muslim Makassarese, Portuguese Dominican friars, Dutch East India Company (VOC) officers, and a powerful Portuguese-Timorese mestizo community known as Topasses. All these contending powers made shifting alliances with the regional chiefs in an effort to control the trade in sandalwood and slaves. By the mid-eighteenth century, the Dutch were firmly established in the coastal regions of West Timor and the Portuguese in the east, but it was not until the late nineteenth century that either of these two powers began to establish effective control of the rugged interior. The border between the two zones was laid down in 1904, and in 1930 East Timor formally became an overseas province of Portugal.

Despite a significant cattle industry in West Timor and coffee plantations in the east, Timor was not a major part of either colonial empire, and there were persistent rumors in the early twentieth century that either or both zones might be transferred or sold to Germany. Australian troops on the island fought a guerrilla war against Japanese occupation forces in 1942–1943, but despite Australian hopes of obtaining a sphere of influence on the island, Australian troops reoccupied West Timor on behalf of the Dutch in September 1945. East Timor was returned to the Portuguese. In 1946 West Timor became part of the Dutch-sponsored federal state of East Indonesia, and in May 1950 it was incorporated into the Indonesian Republic as part of the province of the Lesser Sundas.

Indonesia made no claim to East Timor, but at times Indonesian elements attempted to promote a nationalist revolution in the colony; a major nationalist rebellion was crushed in 1959. Portugal also resisted pressure from the United Nations to decolonize. From the late 1960s onward unrest grew, but there was no organized nationalist movement when the Armed Forces Movement took power in Portugal in April 1974.

In the absence of a clear Portuguese policy, tension developed between three groups favoring different political futures for the colony: União Democrática Timorense (UDT) advocated autonomy in association with Portugal, Associação Social Democrática Timor (ASDT) favored immediate independence, and Associação Popular Democrática Timorense (Apodeti) preferred integration with Indonesia. In August-September 1975 UDT was defeated by ASDT (now Frente Revolucionária de Timor Leste Independente, or Fretilin) in a brief civil war, during which the Portuguese administration abandoned the colony. Indonesia, alleging that Fretilin was communist, invaded East Timor in October, capturing the capital, Dili, in December. Fretilin declared independence on 28 November 1975, with Francisco Xavier do Amaral as president. Fretilin troops were soon driven into the interior, and East Timor was declared Indonesia's twenty-seventh province on 17 July 1976. A guerrilla struggle against incorporation continues.

C. R. Boxer, *The Topasses of Timor* (1947). F. J. Ormeling, *The Timor Problem* (1956). Jill Joliffe, *East Timor: Nationalism and Colonialism* (1978).

ROBERT B. CRIBB

TIMUR (1336–1405), known in the West as Tamerlane, the last of the great nomad conquerors. From his birthplace in Central Asia he overran an enormous territory stretching from Moscow to Delhi—the largest area ever conquered by a single ruler. The Timurid dynasty that he founded ruled over Iran and Central Asia until 1507, presiding over a period of exceptional cultural brilliance.

The official histories give the date of Timur's birth as 8 April 1336, but this is probably an approximation. He rose to power in Transoxiana, in present-day Soviet Uzbekistan and Tajikistan, within the Ulus Chagatai, the nomadic tribal confederation named after the second son of Genghis (more properly, Chinggis) Khan. Although Timur was a descendant of a Mongolian tribe, he and his followers, like the other members of the Mongol ruling class in western Asia, spoke Turkic.

As a junior member of his tribe, the Barlas, Timur began his career leading a sheep-stealing band; in 1361–1362 he seized the leadership of his tribe. Although he had no inherited claim to rule over the Ulus Chagatai, he succeeded in gaining power over it in 1370, after years of clever maneuvering. During the next ten years Timur fought to maintain and strengthen his position. He also pushed back the Mughal (eastern Chagatai) confederation on his eastern border and in about 1380 incorporated Khwarazm, east of the Caspian Sea. To further his influence in the Russian steppe he installed his protégé Tokhtamish over the White Horde, a Mongol confederation north of the Caspian.

According to Turco-Mongolian tradition only descendants of Genghis Khan could assume the sovereign title *khan*. As Timur was not a member of this dynasty, he used the title *amir* (commander) and ruled through a Chinggisid puppet khan; he also took a wife from the Chinggisid line, adopting the additional title *guregen* (royal son-in-law).

To retain power Timur needed to maintain and increase his personal charisma, and this he did through military activity. He began a course of ambitious conquests that continued almost without interruption to his death. Between 1381 and 1385 he campaigned in Iran, taking Khurasan (eastern Iran), Sistan (now southern Afghanistan), and northern Iran. In 1386 he began a three-year campaign to the west in which he conquered Azerbaijan, Georgia, Armenia, and southern central Iran. In the winter of 1387–1388 Timur learned that Tokhtamish, now also khan of the Golden Horde, had attacked Transoxiana; he thus returned and from 1388 through 1390 fought in Central Asia; in 1391 he led his army into the Russian steppe, where he defeated Tokhtamish. In 1392 Timur embarked on a five-year campaign in which he consolidated his rule in Iran and extended it into Iraq. He also campaigned in the Russian steppe, administering a crushing defeat to Tokhtamish in 1395 and burning the main cities of the Golden Horde, a blow from which it never recovered.

During the spring of 1398 Timur set off for India; he quickly conquered and sacked Delhi and returned home. In 1399 he began a longer campaign. He overran both Syria and Anatolia, where in 1402 he defeated and captured the Ottoman sultan Bayezid, an event that most scholars believe significantly delayed the Turkish conquest of Constantinople. In the summer of 1404 Timur began to prepare for the conquest of China, the most ambitious project of his life. He set out at the end of 1404, but on 18 February 1405 he died at the city of Utrar, and his army returned to Transoxiana.

Timur carried out his campaigns with a ferocity at once selective and deliberate. He usually kept his army well under control and pillaged only cities that either refused to submit or later rebelled; these were subjected to deliberate massacre and destruction. Cities that submitted received immunity but had to pay a ransom, often ruinously heavy.

Timur did not usually impose full control over an area during his first campaign there. In the Russian steppe, northern India, Syria, and Anatolia, for example, he established no permanent administration. The lands geographically and culturally close to his own did become part of his dominions; these included Khwarazm and most of what are now Afghanistan and Iran.

Timur's system of control was not highly organized, but for the space of his lifetime it was very successful. He installed his sons and grandsons as provincial governors, assigning part of his army to each. With the exception of a few insubordinate dynasties, he left local rulers in place, subservient to him and to his governors; any insubordination brought swift punishment.

Timur's government had two distinct spheres. One was based on the Arabo-Persian tradition and dealt with financial and local affairs; the other was founded on the tradition of the Mongol empire and dealt with court and military matters. The Turco-Mongolian administration was much the stronger, but even here Timur delegated little authority; he led all his major campaigns in person and interfered freely in the affairs of his governors.

In addition to his extraordinary political and mil-

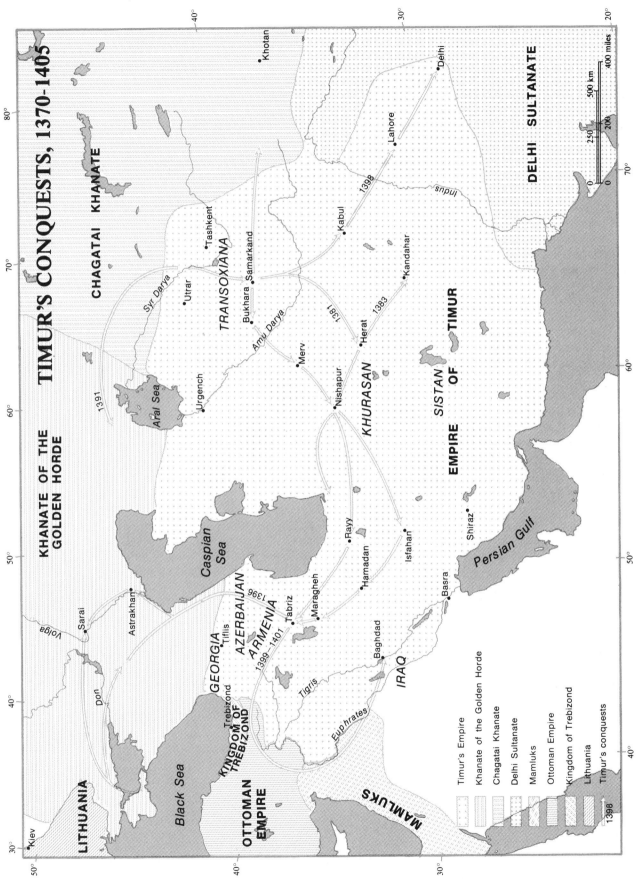

TIMUR'S CONQUESTS, 1370–1405

itary acumen, Timur had wide intellectual interests; he spoke Persian and Turkish, and although he was illiterate he had reciters read him scholarly works, particularly histories. He promoted Islamic culture and religion, patronizing the religious classes and protecting them during his conquests, and he delighted in debating with scholars from the regions he conquered. Timur also appreciated the needs of the settled economy; he soon restored agriculture in the regions he conquered, and he took measures to expand and safeguard trade. By collecting craftsmen in the regions he conquered and transporting them to work in Samarkand, Timur transformed the capital into an imperial city boasting magnificent buildings and lovely gardens.

Perhaps the most striking aspect of Timur's personality was his jealousy of power. This prevented an orderly succession to his rule, since he did not allow any of his descendants a secure power base or position of superiority. Timur's death, therefore, was followed by a lengthy succession struggle, which weakened the rule of his successors.

In the West little memory of Timur remains, except as he is immortalized in Christopher Marlowe's play *Tamburlaine the Great*. In the lands that Timur conquered, however, his memory is vivid, and to the Turks of Central Asia he remains a hero, both as a conqueror and as the initiator of a golden age in Central Asian history.

[See Chagatai *and* Timurid Dynasty.]

Wilhelm Barthold, *Four Studies on the History of Central Asia,* translated by V. and T. Minorsky (1956–1962), vol. 2. Ruy Gonzales de Clavijo, *Narrative of the Spanish Embassy to the Court of Timur at Samarkand in the Years 1403–1406,* translated by Guy Le Strange (1928). Hilda Hookham, *Tamburlaine, the Conqueror* (1962). Ibn 'Arabshāh, *Tamerlane or Timur the Great Amir,* translated by J. H. Sanders (1936; reprint, 1976).

BEATRICE FORBES MANZ

TIMURID DYNASTY. The Timurids, who controlled most of Iran and Central Asia from about 1385 to 1507, were the last Turco-Mongolian conquest dynasty to rule in the Middle East. Their reign was politically fragmented but rich in cultural achievement, and the synthesis of Turco-Mongolian and Islamic traditions that developed under their rule strongly influenced the dynasties that followed them.

The dynasty's founder was Timur (known in the West as Tamerlane), who rose to power about 1370 in Transoxiana among the Turkish tribes of the part of the former Mongol empire known as the Ulus Chagatai. From 1380 to his death in 1405 Timur conquered much of the Middle East. The succession struggle that followed his death severely depleted the dynasty's military and economic power. His youngest son, Shahrukh, emerged as victor; in 1409 he took his father's capital Samarkand, appointed his son Ulug Beg its governor, and then made his own capital in the eastern Iranian city of Herat. By 1421 he had established his rule throughout the Timurid realm.

The western Timurid provinces, however, were threatened by the nomadic Turkmen confederations of the Karakoyunlu and the Akkoyunlu. Shahrukh managed with some difficulty to maintain control over them, but later Timurid rulers were less successful. The Timurids also had to protect their realm from the threats of two Mongol successor states, the Uzbek horde north of the Aral Sea and the Mughal confederation on their eastern border.

Shahrukh's death in 1447 brought another power struggle, complicated by Ulug Beg's murder at the hands of his own son in 1449. The Timurid realm now broke up. Abu Sa'id, descended from Timur's son Amiranshah, ruled Transoxiana; Shahrukh's grandson Abu al-Qasim Babur controlled Khurasan; and another of his grandsons, Sultan Muhammad, held southern central Iran. In 1458 Abu Sa'id repulsed an invasion by the Karakoyunlu and then took over Khurasan, briefly reuniting most of the Timurid territories. In 1469 Abu Sa'id was killed campaigning against the Akkoyunlu; the realm now lost both its territories west of Khurasan and its internal unity. Transoxiana passed to Abu Sa'id's sons, and Khurasan fell to Sultan Husain Baiqara, a descendant of Timur's second son, Umar Shaikh, who ruled in Herat from 1470 to 1506.

Timurid and Turkmen rule ended in the early sixteenth century when the Safavids conquered Iran; the Uzbeks, who had become increasingly involved in Timurid affairs, took Samarkand in 1501 and Herat in 1507. The Timurid dynasty, however, continued; in 1526 Abu Sa'id's grandson Zahiruddin Muhammad Babur conquered India and founded the Indian Timurid, or Mughal, dynasty.

The Timurids inherited two political and cultural traditions, the Turco-Mongolian heritage of their ancestors and the Islamic tradition of the lands they controlled; they used both of these to legitimate their rule. They carefully established their connection to the charismatic dynasty of Genghis (more properly, Chinggis) Khan; in the Mongol tradition only Genghis Khan's descendants were entitled to the sovereign title *khan*. Both Timur and his grandson Ulug Beg maintained Chinggisid puppet khans. Many

Timurid rulers married Chinggisid princesses, and most added Turco-Mongolian titles to their names. At the same time the Timurids sought legitimacy within the Islamic tradition through patronage of culture and religion. They treated religious leaders with marked respect and turned their courts into centers of literary and artistic activity.

The political power of religious leaders now grew markedly, especially that of the Sufi Naqshbandi order, which rapidly became a major force in eastern Iran and Transoxiana. The Central Asian head of the Naqshbandi, Khwaja Ahrar (d. 1490), held great wealth and decisive influence over Abu Sa'id and his sons.

The dynasty and its Turkish followers also took an active interest in art and literature, which they both patronized and practiced. The numerous Timurid courts in Fars, Khurasan, and Central Asia provided support for a rich cultural and scientific life. Ulug Beg made Samarkand a center for astronomy and the exact sciences; he built an observatory there and with his scientists developed a well-known set of astronomical tables.

The greatest cultural center was Herat. Here Shahrukh patronized literature and historical writing in both Persian and Turkish, and his son Baysonghur founded a library and atelier for the creation of manuscripts. Under Sultan Husain Baiqara, Herat attracted the finest talents of the age in literature, calligraphy, miniature painting, and music. The Persian poet and mystic Abd al-Rahman Jami and the Chagatai poet Ali Shir Neva'i, both men of outstanding talent, flourished at Sultan Husain's court; it was there also that Chagatai (eastern Turkish) first became fully established as a language of high culture. The Timurids were also active builders; they left behind them many remarkable monuments distinguished for their imposing size and rich decoration.

The regional empires that followed the Timurids—the Ottomans, Safavids, Uzbeks, and Mughals—were ruled largely by Turks whose own heritage, like that of the Timurids, combined the Turco-Mongolian and Islamic traditions. Artists and writers who had served the Timurids received a ready welcome among their successors, and the Timurid courts, particularly Husain Baiqara's, long remained symbols of cultural brilliance throughout the Turco-Iranian world.

[See also Baiqara, Husain; Herat; Jami; Neva'i; Samarkand; Shahrukh; Timur; and Ulug Beg.]

Zahir al-Din Babur, *The Bābur-nāma in English* (1922; reprint, 1969). Wilhelm Barthold, *Four Studies on the History of Central Asia*, translated by V. and T. Minorsky (1956–1962), vols. 2 and 3. E. G. Browne, *A Literary History of Persia* (1928), vol. 3, pp. 159–549. Roger M. Savory, "The Struggle for Supremacy in Persia after the Death of Timur," *Der Islam* 40.1 (1964): 35–65.

BEATRICE FORBES MANZ

TIN is found abundantly in the Malay Peninsula, in rich deposits from southern Thailand down through Kedah, Perak, Selangor, and Negri Sembilan, continuing in the islands of Banka and Billiton to Sumatra. For centuries the Malays mined and smelted the mineral where it lay in alluvial deposits close to the surface, then floated it to the coast for sale to foreign merchants. Until the discovery of large deposits in Banka in 1710, Perak was the chief tin producer. Melaka ruled this and other "tin places" of the peninsula, but the Portuguese lost them, mostly to Aceh, in the sixteenth and seventeenth centuries. When the Dutch captured Melaka in 1641 they hoped to regain control of the peninsula's tin. They succeeded in ousting Aceh, but Johor, Kedah, and Perak benefited more than Melaka, which could not match the high prices paid by independent buyers. From 1722 onward the Dutch received large amounts of tin from Banka, and the 1746 Dutch alliance with Perak protected that state's independence of Johor and provided Melaka with adequate supplies of tin.

The growing market for tin in China in the thirteenth century stimulated demand and helped attract both Bugis and Minangkabau settlers to the Malay Peninsula, where they founded Selangor and Negri Sembilan. To increase production, the rulers of Palembang and Perak imported Chinese labor, for mining was not a full-time occupation of the Malays. The nineteenth century saw increasing Chinese involvement in the mines, bringing great Chinese immigration. After Dutch and English colonial rule was established, European capital was employed to mechanize and expand mining operations, which still supply a large proportion of the income of modern Indonesia and Malaysia.

Barbara Watson Andaya, *Perak, the Abode of Grace* (1979). Dianne Lewis, "The Tin Trade in the Malay Peninsula during the 18th Century," *The New Zealand Journal of History* 3.1 (1969): 52–69. Wong Lin Ken, *The Malayan Tin Industry to 1914* (1962).   DIANNE LEWIS

TIPU SULTAN (1750–1799), innovative son and successor of Haidar Ali Khan and an even more resolute rival of the English than his father. Born at

Devanhalli in Karnataka, Tipu was well versed in warfare and administration. He vigorously prosecuted the ongoing war with the British and forced them to sue for peace. The Treaty of Mangalore that was concluded in 1784 disappointed the British so much that Warren Hastings called it "a humiliating pacification." This treaty excited the jealousy of the Marathas and the *nizam* of Hyderabad, who declared a war against Tipu Sultan in 1786. Tipu Sultan emerged unscathed in this war, but felt that it was difficult to unite the Indian powers against the British. He therefore turned to the external powers of France and the Ottoman empire, whose help he sought by sending embassies, but was disappointed in these ventures as well. His efforts to promote commercial relations with the Ottoman empire, China, Muscat, Pegu, Armenia, and Hormuz bore some fruit.

Such hectic activity hostile to the interests of the British strained Tipu's relations with them. In 1790 Charles Cornwallis formed a triple confederacy of the British, the Marathas, and the *nizam*, who joined in the Third Mysore War to reduce Tipu Sultan's kingdom by half. This war intensified his hostility against the British, and he again sought French support. Napoleon was willing to come to India, but his defeat in Syria resulted in his return to France. Tipu invited Zaman Shah of Afghanistan to invade India, but the British frustrated this attempt as well. Arthur Wellesley declared war on Tipu, who was defeated and killed in the Fourth Mysore War on 4 May 1799. He preferred death to dishonor, in accordance with his maxim, "To live like a lion for a day is far better than to live like a jackal for a hundred years." His promotion of the well-being of his people through trade, commerce, industry, and agriculture, his reforms of coinage and the calendar, banking and finance, revenue and the judiciary, the army and navy, and several other innovative measures make him a fascinating historical figure.

[*See also* Haidar Ali Khan.]

M. H. Khan, *History of Tipu Sultan* (1951). B. Sheik Ali, *Tipu Sultan: A Study in Diplomacy and Confrontation* (1982). M. Wilks, *History of Mysore*, 2 vols. (1930).

B. SHEIK ALI

TIRMIDH, or Termez, an ancient town on the right bank of the Oxus River (Amu Darya) near the confluence of the Surkhan in present-day Soviet Uzbekistan. Its site has moved somewhat over time, but it has remained one of the main crossing points of the river.

Legend has it that Alexander himself founded Tirmidh. The town flourished under the Kushans (second century BCE–second century CE) and archaeological finds place it in the center of Greco-Bactrian culture. In the centuries before the Arab-Muslim conquests in the early eighth century, Tirmidh was a Buddhist center. Under Islamic dominion, the town became known for its scholars, including Abu Isa Muhammad al-Tirmidhi (d. 892), compiler of one of the canonical collections of *hadith*.

ROBERT MCCHESNEY

TIRTHANKARA ("ford maker"), also called Jina ("victor"); in Jainism, spiritually perfected beings. Twenty-four appear in each age of the world. The first Tirthankara of the present age was Rishibha, father of Bharata. Only Parshva (eighth century BCE), the twenty-third Tirthankara, and Vardhamana (sixth century BCE), also known as Mahavira, the twenty-fourth and final Tirthankara and the founder of Jainism, are considered to be historical figures.

[*See also* Jainism.]

Padmanabh S. Jaini, *The Jaina Path of Purification* (1979).

RANDOLPH M. THORNTON

TIRUCHCHIRAPPALLI. Located in the South Indian state of Tamil Nadu, Tiruchchirappalli (alternate form, Trichinopoly) is the administrative headquarters of a district that bears the same name. Hindu pilgrims and kings on annual pilgrimages and processionals traditionally halted there to worship at the neighboring Sri Vaishnava shrine of Sri Ranganathasvami.

[*See also* Tamil Nadu *and* Vaishnavism.]

J. Nelson, *The Madura Country* (1860).

CAROL APPADURAI BRECKENRIDGE

TIWANA, MALIK SIR KHIZR HAYAT KHAN (1900–1975), Unionist premier of the Punjab from 1943 to 1946 and again from 1946 to 1947. He joined the first cabinet under provincial autonomy in 1937 and succeeded Sikandar Hayat Khan as premier after the latter's death in December 1942. In 1946, following the election in which the Muslim League became the plurality party but was unable to form a ministry, Khizr headed a Unionist-Congress-Akali Dal ministry until April 1947. He was not directly active in politics after India's independence later that year.

[*See also* Unionist Party; Indian National Congress; Akali Dal; and Khan, Sir Sikandar Hayat.]

Khizr Hayat Khan Tiwana, "The 1937 Elections and the Sikandar-Jinnah Pact," *Panjab Past and Present* 10.2 (October 1976), edited by Craig Baxter.   CRAIG BAXTER

TJOKROAMINOTO (1882–1934), Indonesian political leader. Raden Mas Haji Umar Said Tjokroaminoto was born in the village of Bakur, Madiun. After completing his education he was employed as secretary to the *patih* of Ngawi. In 1906 he moved to Surabaya, where he became chairman of the local Budi Utomo branch. In May 1912 he entered Sarekat Islam, where he soon rose to prominence. He became its deputy chairman and later its president and represented it in the Volksraad (1918–1921). In 1927 he refused a seat in the Volksraad. His charismatic personality and oratory skills made him the most popular Sarekat Islam leader. He attracted large crowds. In their youth a number of nationalist leaders, among them Sukarno, were influenced by him. In 1926 he represented the Sarekat Islam at a world Islamic conference in Mecca. He served as an editor of several periodicals, such as *Utusan Hindia*, *Al-Islam*, *Fadjar Asia*, and *Al-Djihad*.

[*See also* Budi Utomo *and* Sarekat Islam.]
                                                C. VAN DIJK

TOBACCO MONOPOLY, the system of government administration, introduced by the Spaniards into Luzon at the beginning of the 1780s, ruling the internal trade in tobacco leaf and its products. Although the precise nature of the monopoly's operations varied considerably, both between each province of Luzon and over time, in essence they involved the purchase of tobacco leaf from contracted farmers, the manufacture of cigars and cigarettes, and the sale of those manufactures through government retail shops.

Until the 1830s the authorities restricted the cultivation of tobacco in the interests of maintaining the domestic monopoly. Beginning with that decade, however, cultivation was encouraged, particularly in Cagayan, to meet a growing foreign demand for Philippine tobacco. From its earliest years the tobacco monopoly not only ensured the solvency of the Spanish administration in the islands but also made possible the remittance of substantial payments to Spain herself. In the mid-nineteenth century, however, the bureaucratic and financial burden of administering and policing the monopoly (there were continually severe problems in curbing the illicit cultivation of tobacco leaf and the illegal trade in tobacco products), coupled with increasing criticism of its oppressive, corrupt, and inefficient character, led to the dismantling of the system at the beginning of the 1880s.

[*See also* Spain and the Philippines.]

Ed C. de Jesus, ed., *The Tobacco Monopoly in the Philippines: Bureaucratic Enterprise and Social Change, 1766–1880* (1980).   IAN BROWN

TOBACCO REBELLION (1891–1892), the first successful Iranian national protest against Western incursions. Sir Henry Drummond Wolff, as minister to Iran from 1888 to 1890, attained a number of concessions for the British, including one (to a Major Talbot) of a monopoly on the purchase, sale, and export of all Iranian tobacco, granted in March 1890 in return for bribes and small payments. The concession was at first secret, but late in 1890 the Istanbul Persian newspaper *Akhtar* ran articles condemning it. In January 1891 leaflets in Tehran condemned it and other concessions (these brought the expulsion of Jamal al-Din al-Afghani from Iran), and new hostile leaflets circulated in the spring. This concession elicited more protest than others because it was the only one to cover a product already exploited by, and profitable to, many Iranians.

A rebellion then began in Tabriz, where the government had to suspend the concession. Bazaar and other merchants were most active in planning protests, but they enlisted prestigious *ulama* (religious scholars), who took on the formal leadership positions in protests that spread to Mashhad, Isfahan, Tehran, and other towns. In December 1891 the movement culminated in a boycott of all smoking and dealings in tobacco, based on an order probably drafted in Iran but attributed to Shirazi, the leader of the Shi'i *ulama* then living in Iraq, who confirmed it. The government tried to end only the company's internal monopoly, leaving its export monopoly, but this attempt aroused much protest. A mass Tehran demonstration culminated in the opening of fire on an unarmed crowd, an attack that resulted in several deaths and brought on more massive protests. The government was forced to cancel the entire concession early in 1892.

The affair left the Iranians with their first foreign debt—£500,000 from the British-owned Imperial

Bank for exorbitant compensation to the company. The movement combined the bazaar classes, the *ulama,* and the intellectuals in a coordinated and successful movement against the government's subservience to the West and was a "dress rehearsal" for the Constitutional Revolution of 1905 to 1911.

[*See also* Constitutional Revolution *and* Qajar Dynasty.]

Nikki Keddie, *Religion and Rebellion in Iran: The Tobacco Protest of 1891–1892* (1966).   NIKKI KEDDIE

TOBA-FUSHIMI. *See* Meiji Restoration.

TŌDAIJI, a temple in Nara, Japan, one of the main temples of the Kegon, or Flower Garland (Sanskrit, Avatamsaka), school of Japanese Buddhism. *Tōdaiji* means "great eastern temple," and the structure is also known by names meaning "great Kegon temple" and "temple of the four heavenly kings of the golden light, protectors of the nation." The Tōdaiji is one of the largest and most important temple complexes in Japan and a major repository of Japanese art.

Tōdaiji was established in 743 by decree of Emperor Shōmu (701–756). Its principal image was a vast gilt bronze statue, over fifty feet high, of Lochana Buddha, Vairocana, the central figure in the Kegon cosmology of universal interdependence. The

great Buddha Hall in which it was housed was completed in 751. The eye-opening ceremony, to give life to the Great Buddha, was held the following year. It was an international event attended by reigning empress Kōken, the cloistered emperor Shōmu and his consort, hundreds of officials, and thousands of monks, some from China, Korea, and India.

With so much invested in its establishment, Tōdaiji quickly became the largest and most influential temple in Nara. It was one of only three temples where monks could be officially ordained. It was also designated the central monastery in the nationwide network of provincial monasteries and nunneries, *kokubunji* and *kokubunniji*, established for spiritual protection of the country and to further the centralization of Buddhism and the state.

Tōdaiji was a very wealthy temple. No expense was spared in the provision of sculptures and paintings. Treasures from the Silk Road collected by Shōmu at the time of the foundation of Tōdaiji were stored in a specially constructed treasure house, the Shōsōin. By the early ninth century Tōdaiji had acquired some ninety titles to estate holdings, *shōen*, in twenty-three provinces.

The Great Buddha and Buddha Hall were badly damaged when the Nara temples were razed by Taira warriors in 1180. The monastery was restored through the fund-raising efforts of the monk Chōgen (1121–1206) and the patronage of the shogun Minamoto Yoritomo. Tōdaiji was badly burned

FIGURE 1. *Buddha Hall, Tōdaiji, Nara.* The hall, the largest building under a single roof in the world, houses the Daibutsu, a monumental sculpture of the Buddha.

again and the Great Buddha destroyed in 1567 during the revolt of Matsunaga Hisahide. The statue and damaged buildings were restored in the early Edo period, when Tōdaiji enjoyed the protection of the Tokugawa shoguns. Of the earliest buildings, only the Sangatsudō and the Shōsōin still survive. The Great Southern Gate and Bell Tower date from the Kamakura period restoration. The Tōdaiji, however, houses national treasures of sculpture from the Nara period and many documents from the Heian period.

[See also Nara Period.]

M. W. de Visser, *Ancient Buddhism in Japan* (1935). Joan R. Piggot, "Hierarchy and Economics in Early Medieval Tōdaiji," in *Court and Bakufu in Japan*, edited by Jeffrey P. Mass (1982), pp. 45–91.

MARTIN COLLCUTT

TODAR MAL (d. 1589), administrator of the Mughal empire in India. A Khatri (Punjabi merchant and clerical caste), Todar Mal started his career with Sher Shah and rose to the highest office during the reign of Emperor Akbar. Akbar also conferred the title raja on him. Todar Mal had wide-ranging administrative and military experience, from supervising the construction of forts in hostile territory to several military campaigns. His lasting contribution lay in developing a system of revenue administration under Akbar. He had made several experiments first in Gujarat and later in the central domain of the empire. Ultimately, the "Ten-Year Settlement" was established; it maximized revenue collection while creating checks and balances that kept the system from complete breakdown. [See also Sher Shah; Akbar; *and* Mughal Empire.]

HARBANS MUKHIA

TODAS, one of four traditionally interdependent tribal groups inhabiting the cool Nilgiri Hills of South India. Toda culture is noted for its focus on sacred buffalo and dairying as well as for the practice of fraternal polyandry. By 1941 the Todas numbered only 630; since then their population has gradually increased.

[See also Adivasis.]

David G. Mandelbaum, "Nilgiri Peoples of India: An End to Old Ties," in *Vanishing Peoples of the Earth*, edited by the National Geographic Society (1968), pp. 76–91. W. H. R. Rivers, *The Todas* (1906).

DORANNE JACOBSON

TOGHRIL BEG (d. 1063), the leading member of the Seljuk family during the period of its transition from a band of refugees on Islam's eastern frontier to rulers over all of Iran and Iraq.

Active in Khurasan from the early 1030s, Toghril had begun negotiating with the area's major cities even before the Seljuks' decisive defeat of the Ghaznavids at Dandanqan in 1040. From his initial base at Nishapur (1038), Toghril moved quickly to Rayy (1042) and finally Baghdad (1055). There the caliph al-Qa'im received him as "king of the east and the west" in 1058, thereby recognizing his and his family's dominance over the Islamic heartlands and the effective end of the Buyid dynasty.

Toghril achieved status for Turkish rule in Islam, however, beyond that which accompanied military power; a certain legitimation was realized through his willingness to employ Iranian advisers and adapt to traditional Iranian expectations. It was also during Toghril's reign that the policy of using the most warlike and troublesome of the Seljuks' nomadic followers for expansion into Anatolia was initiated.

Toghril left no adult male heir; thus, at his death leadership of the family and empire transferred to the line of his brother and coregent Chaghri.

[See also Seljuk Dynasty.]

C. E. Bosworth, "The Political and Dynastic History of the Iranian World (A.D. 1000–1217)," in *The Saljuq and Mongol Periods*, edited by J. A. Boyle (1968), vol. 5 of the *Cambridge History of Iran*.

RUSSELL G. KEMPINERS, JR.

TŌGŌ HEIHACHIRŌ (1848–1934), Japanese admiral and national hero. As a youth Tōgō took part in the fighting by the Satsuma domain against the British at Kagoshima (1863) and saw action in the civil war that ended the rule of the Tokugawa shoguns (1868). Entering the new Imperial Navy, Tōgō was sent to Britain for naval training from 1871 to 1878. After a period of extended sea duty (1878–1894) he commanded a cruiser in the Sino-Japanese War (1894–1895). Tōgō was appointed commander of the Combined Fleet just before the Russo-Japanese War (1904–1905), and as such he directed the naval attacks against Port Arthur and commanded the fleet at the Battle of the Yellow Sea (1904) and the Battle of Tsushima Straits (1905). The last-named encounter, in which the Russian Baltic Fleet was utterly destroyed, became Japan's most famous naval victory and made Tōgō a national hero. He ended his active career as chief of the Naval

General Staff, was named a count, and attained the rank of admiral of the fleet.

[*See also* Tsushima Straits, Battle of.]

Edwin A. Falk, *Togo and the Rise of Japanese Sea Power* (1936).   MARK R. PEATTIE

TŌJŌ HIDEKI

TŌJŌ HIDEKI (1884–1948), Japanese general and statesman, most closely associated with the Japanese war effort from 1941 to 1945. His rapid rise in the army was largely the result of his aggressive bureaucratic efficiency, which earned him the nickname of "The Razor." As army vice-minister (1938–1941) Tōjō was in the forefront of the pro-Axis, aggressively expansionist elements in the army. His accession as prime minister in October, 1941 marked the final triumph of those in the army who advocated war with the United States. As wartime prime minister, Tōjō simultaneously held the post of army minister and several other cabinet positions and, for a time, that of chief of the Army General Staff. With the fall of Saipan in the Marianas (July 1944) and the worsening of Japan's military situation, Japan's elder statesmen forced his retirement. He attempted suicide at the war's end, but recovered and was arrested, tried, and executed—some historians believe unjustly—as a war criminal.

[*See also* World War II in Asia.]

Courtney Browne, *The Last Banzai* (1967). Robert Butow, *Tojo and the Coming of the War* (1961). Alvin Coox, *Tojo* (1975).   MARK R. PEATTIE

TŌKAIDŌ

TŌKAIDŌ ("eastern sea road"), historically, the major land artery along the Pacific coast of central Honshu, Japan, connecting Edo (Tokyo) with the Kyoto-Osaka region. Three hundred twenty-three miles in length, the Tōkaidō was and still is the most heavily traveled route in Japan. During its heyday in the Tokugawa period (1600–1868) it was maintained by the shogunate because of its strategic and political significance, which had been established in previous centuries. It was heavily used by daimyo on *sankin kōtai* (alternate attendance) duty: in 1821, of 198 daimyo leaving Edo to return to their domains, 116 used the Tōkaidō.

Apparently eighteen feet in width, the roadbed consisted of a thick layer of crushed gravel covered by sand; steep stretches were paved with stone. Gutters, guideposts, shade trees, and mileage markers facilitated travel, but *sekisho* (barrier-inspection stations) and rivers posed problems. The fifty-three post towns provided lodging, food, and entertainment for travelers. Travel was by foot, on horseback, or by palanquin. There was little vehicular traffic. The Tōkaidō was celebrated in Tokugawa-period literature (Jippensha Ikku's *Shanks' Mare*) and art (Andō Hiroshige's famous woodblock print series *Fifty-three Stages of the Tōkaidō*). Today, major vehicular and rail arteries, including the "bullet train" lines, parallel the Tokugawa-era road.

[*See also* Sekisho.]

Englebert Kaempfer, *The History of Japan, Together with a Description of the Kingdom of Siam, 1690–1692*, 3 vols. (1906). Ichitaro Kondo, *The Fifty-three Stages of the Tōkaidō by Hiroshige*, translated by C. Terry (1960). Robert Hall, "Tokaido: Road and Region," *The Geographical Review* 27 (July 1937) 353–377.

RONALD J. DiCENZO

TOKUDA KYŪICHI

TOKUDA KYŪICHI (1894–1953), prominent member of the Japan Communist Party (JCP) until his death in Beijing. He became involved in the socialist movement in the early 1920s and in 1922 represented Japanese socialists at a conference in Moscow. After returning to Japan he joined the JCP. He was arrested in 1923 during the government's first attempt to suppress the Communist Party and again in 1928 in response to the March Fifteenth Incident, during which leftists were interned for alleged violation of the 1925 Peace Preservation Law. Following his arrest in 1928, Tokuda spent seventeen years in jail, finally being released by American Occupation authorities. He became the general secretary of the JCP in 1945, and in 1946 he was elected to Japan's House of Representatives. After 1950 he became a strong advocate of political extremism in response to the suppression of leftist activities precipitated by American involvement in the Korean War.

[*See also* Communism: Communism in Japan.]

George M. Beckmann and Okubo Genji, *The Japanese Communist Party, 1922–1945* (1969). Robert A. Scalapino, *The Japanese Communist Movement, 1920–1966* (1967).   THOMAS R. SCHALOW

TOKUGAWA HIDETADA

TOKUGAWA HIDETADA (1579–1632), the second shogun, or military governor of Japan, of the Tokugawa lineage. Undoubtedly the achievements of Tokugawa Hidetada suffer by comparison with those of his father, Ieyasu, and his son, Iemitsu, both of whom contributed more decisively to the stability of the Tokugawa regime. Although appointed shogun in 1605, Hidetada came to wield full authority only after his father's death in 1616. On the whole he used this authority to continue Ieyasu's initiatives, but he displayed a far greater concern with social issues, reforming the system of indentured labor and attempting vainly to prohibit the cultivation and sale of tobacco. Edo's water supply system was one of the more enduring monuments to his initiatives.   HAROLD BOLITHO

TOKUGAWA IEMITSU (1604–1651), the third shogun, or military governor of Japan, of the Tokugawa lineage. Tokugawa Iemitsu was the real architect of Tokugawa supremacy. His grandfather Ieyasu and his father Hidetada had attained a certain degree of military security, but it was left to Iemitsu to consolidate their achievements. During his reign, which began in 1623, all the major elements of Tokugawa control were devised. For the first time the *bakufu* was given a coherent structure, with a regular tribunal and councils to deal with routine administrative matters. Through surveillance, impositions (the *sankin kōtai*, or alternate attendance system, among them), and fief transfers and confiscations, the daimyo were made more subservient to Tokugawa rule than they had ever been. So was the imperial court, as the indignant abdication of Emperor Go-Mizunoo attested. In diplomacy, too, Iemitsu, styling himself a monarch, unilaterally restricted Japan's foreign contacts. His impact was therefore profound, but it should be recognized that his reign marked the high point of Tokugawa power. None of his successors, inheritors of a treasury depleted by his spending, was ever to rival his degree of control.   HAROLD BOLITHO

TOKUGAWA IEYASU (1542–1616), Japanese warlord and founder of the Tokugawa shogunate. Tokugawa Ieyasu was born the son of a minor lord in the province of Mikawa (present Aichi Prefecture) and spent most of his career in war or preparations for war. His schooling began at the age of four, when his father sent him as hostage to the neighboring house of Imagawa, only to have him intercepted and held for two years by a hostile family, the Oda. Two years later he was released and redirected to Imagawa control as hostage, in which condition he remained for twelve years. By the time of his release his father had died, and after Oda Nobunaga routed Imagawa forces at the Battle of Okehazama in 1560 Ieyasu shifted his allegiance from Imagawa to Oda. He changed his family name

from Matsudaira (later conferred on favored vassals) to Tokugawa, and his given name from Motoyasu to Ieyasu.

Ieyasu profited from his alliance with Oda Nobunaga by enlarging his domains at the expense of neighboring houses like the Imagawa and Takeda, and by the time of Nobunaga's murder in 1582 Ieyasu was close to having full control of five provinces. After an inconclusive test of strength with Toyotomi Hideyoshi, Ieyasu allied with the new hegemon, sending him a son as hostage.

In 1590 Ieyasu provided the principal military force for the campaign that reduced the Hōjō domain at Odawara, a victory that completed Hideyoshi's control of northern Japan and left him free to plan the conquest of Korea and China. Ieyasu took little or no part in those futile operations but was fully occupied fulfilling Hideyoshi's orders to move from Mikawa to the Kantō (Tokyo plain) provinces that had been Hōjō territory. This development, undoubtedly unwelcome at first, proved to have long-term benefits. The next eight years were spent establishing his vassals and armies in new and unfamiliar country, and the dispositions achieved served as practice for the exercise of national hegemony that came after the death of Hideyoshi. As his capital Ieyasu chose the town of Edo, on a swampy site on Tokyo Bay. His major vassals were assigned realms of strategic importance at the extremes of the Kantō provinces, and the system of canals laid out to drain the swamps around Edo provided transportation for the materials needed to erect the immense castle grounds that would house future shoguns and, after 1868, emperors.

At the time of his death in 1598 Hideyoshi installed his five chief generals as guardians for his young son Hideyori, and, as the most powerful of the guardians, Ieyasu took up residence at Fushimi and turned his attention to national affairs. It was soon evident to the other generals that he was bent on self-aggrandizement, and they challenged him. The resulting great battle at Sekigahara in 1600 left Ieyasu's armies in control of the field. In 1603 he secured the appointment of shogun from the court, a title he transferred to his son Hidetada in 1605, retiring to Sumpu in Shizuoka in order to free himself from administrative routine while remaining, as *ōgosho*, very much in control of matters of major importance.

The Osaka Campaigns of 1614 and 1615 secured Tokugawa dominance by exterminating the Toyotomi line and cause. Meanwhile, regulations for court nobles and the court ruled out warrior contacts with Kyoto and court interference with the military houses, and ordinances for the feudal lords (Buke Shohatto), issued in 1615, laid down the pattern of authoritarian and watchful controls that were to regulate daimyo behavior.

Ieyasu died in 1616. Most of his life had been spent in war, but the system he established brought Japan such order that the Tokugawa period became referred to as "The Great Peace." His times required the ruthlessness he displayed, but he was also deliberate and patient in the execution of his plans. He was also fortunate in outliving his principal competitors and being able to undo their plans, as well as in having sons (five of his nine survived him) ready to take up their tasks at his death without having to depend on the loyalty of lieutenants, as had been the case at the passings of Nobunaga and Hideyoshi.

[See also Oda Nobunaga; Toyotomi Hideyoshi; Sekigahara, Battle of; Osaka Campaigns; and Tokugawa Period.]

Harold Bolitho, "Tokugawa Ieyasu," in *Encyclopedia of Japan*, vol. 8 (1983). A. L. Sadler, *The Maker of Modern Japan: The Life of Tokugawa Ieyasu* (1937).

MARIUS B. JANSEN

TOKUGAWA MITSUKUNI (1628–1700), one of Tokugawa Japan's most outstanding daimyo (feudal lords). Tokugawa Mitsukuni's reputation may be a tribute more to his ideological purity than to any tangible achievement. His intellectual orientation became plain after he succeeded his father as daimyo of Mito in 1661, for one of his first actions was to launch an investigation into religious observance, which resulted in the destruction of 713 of his domain's Buddhist temples and the closure of nearly 400 more. In the process, large numbers of Buddhist priests were forced to revert to lay status. At the same time, however, he offered every encouragement to Shinto shrines and their functionaries, thus demonstrating an abiding preference for the native over the foreign. A similar impulse lay behind his foundation of the Shōkōkan, the historical institute from which issued a number of works (chief among them the *Dai Nihon shi*) emphasizing loyalty to the Japanese imperial house. As testimony to his own sympathies he erected a monument to Kusunoki Masashige, the fourteenth-century loyalist. Mitsukuni's attitude was to be resurrected in Mito in the nineteenth century by zealots and pragmatists alike, for whom its twin strands of chauvinism and ostentatious reverence for the imperial institution proved both palatable and politic. [See also Tokugawa Period.]   HAROLD BOLITHO

TOKUGAWA NARIAKI (1800–1860), Japanese politician of the late Tokugawa period. On becoming daimyo of Mito in 1829, Tokugawa Nariaki set out to reform both his domain and the Tokugawa *bakufu* (military governorship), but without success. In Mito his military, fiscal, economic, and religious reorganizations alienated many, and he won few friends in Edo with his strident interference in *bakufu* affairs. Nevertheless, Nariaki became the spokesman for several influential malcontents, articulating their anxiety over national security and hinting broadly that devotion to the emperor could justify opposition to the *bakufu* if such opposition seemed necessary. He was sentenced to house arrest in 1844, but his national prestige was great enough to secure him a prompt release and an appointment, at first informal but after 1853 official as consultant to the *bakufu* on foreign affairs and defense. From this position, which he held until 1857, Nariaki constantly tried to reverse the government's acquiescence to foreign demands, intriguing to that end with junior officials, daimyo, and Kyoto nobles. He failed in these designs, succeeding only in further destabilizing an already tottering institution and in heightening political polarization between the *bakufu* and the samurai class.   HAROLD BOLITHO

TOKUGAWA PERIOD, the years between 1600 and 1868, during which time political power in Japan was concentrated in the Tokugawa clan.

The home islands of Japan during the Tokugawa period were Honshu, Kyushu, and Shikoku, which had a combined population of about twenty million in 1600 and twenty-six million in 1720. The outlying islands, which served as frontier or buffer areas, were Ezo (also Yezo, i.e., Hokkaido) in the north, the Ryūkyū archipelago in the south, and Tsushima and Iki islands, situated between southeastern Korea and northwestern Kyushu. Ezo was defended by the lord of Matsumae against Russian encroachments; the Sō family of Tsushima served as intermediary between Korea and Japan; and the Ryūkyū kingdom was Japan's indirect contact with China, for it had come under the domination of the southwestern domain of Satsuma in 1609.

The office of shogun, which was held by the Tokugawa for over two and a half centuries, exercized power delegated by the emperor. Located in Edo (Tokyo) was the shogun's administrative organ, the *bakufu*, which administered territories directly controlled by the Tokugawa (about 23 percent of the total arable land of the country) and exercised general supervision over some 265 semiautonomous domains. [See Bakufu and Han.] The number of domains fluctuated with political exigencies. The "Great Peace," a term used appreciatively by contemporary writers, was perhaps the most notable achievement of the Tokugawa government. The long period of political stability enabled people to channel their energies toward economic and social developments and toward remarkable cultural achievements.

The Consolidation of Control. The founder of the dynasty was Tokugawa Ieyasu (1540–1616). With the Battle of Sekigahara in 1600 he emerged as undisputed leader of the country. In 1603 he received the title of shogun, and though he soon transferred the office to his son in order to provide for its continuity within the family, he ruled until his death and was the principal architect of the long-lasting political system. By the end of the reign of Iemitsu (1623–1651), the third shogun, all the basic institutions and policies of Tokugawa administration were in place. [See Sekigahara, Battle of; Tokugawa Ieyasu; and Tokugawa Iemitsu.]

Until the mid-nineteenth century there were only two serious military actions. In 1615 Ieyasu captured Osaka Castle, more by clever strategem than by force, in order to forestall a possible challenge by the son of the previous hegemon, Toyotomi Hideyoshi (1536–1598). In 1637 the peasants of Shimabara revolted to protest economic conditions. The rebellion took on religious overtones as samurai retainers of dispossessed Roman Catholic daimyo in the region joined in, and its suppression required a major military effort in which the Tokugawa went so far as to request artillery assistance from the Protestant Dutch. In the latter half of the period there were innumerable peasant disturbances, but these were usually directed against local lords, corrupt local officials, moneylenders, or others who caused peasant misery. The Ōshio Heihachirō Rebellion of 1837, however, was of some consequence, in that it was led by a former bakufu official and revealed the serious nature of contemporary economic problems. It remained for the arrival of Commodore Matthew C. Perry in 1853 to expose the fact that the political structure of the preceding centuries had become greatly weakened, and this revelation led to the collapse of the regime fifteen years later.

A major policy of the Tokugawa, which contributed to domestic stability and enabled Japan to develop some of her unique qualities, was the decision to "close the nation" (sakoku), to prevent foreigners from coming into the country and Japanese from going out. The measure derived from fear that Spain and Portugal were using Christianity to facilitate the colonization of the country. Although the first of many anti-Christian decrees had been issued by Hideyoshi in 1587, it was the Shimabara Rebellion that provoked the drastic decision for Japan's seclusion policy. In 1640, the last Westerners except the Dutch were expelled from Japan. Moreover, Japanese Christians were forced to recant or were persecuted. From 1640 until 1853 Japan was in semi-isolation from the rest of the world. [See Seclusion and Shimabara.]

However, Japan was not totally isolated. Through the Ryūkyū kingdom, which sent occasional missions to Edo, indirect contact was maintained with China, and the king of Korea also sent missions to Japan, the Sō daimyo serving as escort. More important, Dutch and Chinese merchants were permitted restricted residence in Nagasaki, a port city administered by the bakufu. The Dutch were confined to the tiny man-made island of Deshima, while the Chinese were segregated in another section of the city. Through these limited contacts the shogun and his officials obtained what information they could about events in the outside world. [See Deshima.]

The shoguns also isolated the emperor and court nobility from the military class. Once appointed to office by the emperor, Ieyasu saw to it that competing military houses would not have independent access to the throne, its awards, and its prestige. A high Tokugawa official was stationed in Kyoto and other lords were kept out. The court nobility (kuge) consisted of 137 major houses whose residences clustered around the imperial palace. The greatest of these provided appointees to a court bureaucracy that continued to serve even though deprived of function. Except for one marriage early in the period (of Ieyasu's granddaughter to Emperor Go Mizunoo), the two successional lines of the imperial family remained distinct until the shogun, in the days after Perry, looked for support at court.

The major objective of Ieyasu was to establish permanent control over the many feudal lords, called daimyo, and thus consolidate Tokugawa authority. These daimyo possessed their own domains, or han, complete with local government, taxes, and army, but the shogun had the power to give, take away, reduce, or confirm the daimyo's right to his territory. Three categories of daimyo were established. Those who were related to the shogun were shimpan ("related han") daimyo; those who were Tokugawa allies at Sekigahara were fudai ("hereditary vassal") daimyo; and those who fought against the Tokugawa or did not participate in the conflict were tozama ("outside lord") daimyo. The shimpan

TOKUGAWA–PERIOD DOMAINS IN THE LATE EIGHTEENTH CENTURY

132°   136°   140°

40°

Sea of

Japan

TSUGARU

SATAKE

NAMBU

SADO

SAKAI

DATE   •Sendai

UESUGI

NIWA

Yonezawa   •Wakamatsu

MATSUDAIRA

SAKAKIBARA

MAEDA

ABE

Kanazawa

SANADA

•Mito

MITO-TOKUGAWA

MAEDA

Fukui

MATSUDAIRA

OKUBO

HOTTA

Edo (Tokyo)•

MATSUDAIRA

TODA

OKI

SAKAI   II

Tottori

Hikone

OWARI

IKEDA

Kyoto•   •Nagoya

MATSUDAIRA

SAKAI

Kuwana

TOKUGAWA

Himeji

INABA   MATSUDAIRA

IKEDA

Ōsaka

TŌDŌ

ABE

Okayama

MATSUDAIRA

ASANO

Wakayama

Hiroshima

MATSUDAIRA

MŌRI

HISAMATSU   HACHISUKA   KII-TOKUGAWA

Yamaguchi

Shimonoseki•

YAMAUCHI

KURODA

DATE   •Kochi

OGASAWARA

Fukuoka

Karatsu

ARIMA   Uwajima

NABESHIMA   Saga

TACHIBANA

Nagasaki•   •Kumamoto

HOSOKAWA

SHIMAZU

Kagoshima

EZO (HOKKAIDO)   •Hakodate

•Matsumae

TSUSHIMA

SŌ

Pacific

Ocean

NAMBU   Tozama domains

SAKAI   Shimpan and Fudai domains

■   Major castle town

•   Other cities and towns

0   80   160   240 km
0   40   80   120 miles

132°   136°

held strategic territory guarding the approaches to Edo; the *fudai* were granted relatively small territories scattered about in proximity to the *tozama*; and the *tozama* were the powerful erstwhile enemy who occupied the outer areas of Japan, and, in the wisdom of Ieyasu, were better left with most of their territory than with thoughts of revenge. [*See* Tozama Daimyo.]

The *fudai*, who had the least independent power, were given the most political authority, while the territorially large domain holders, the *shimpan* and *tozama*, were excluded from the decision-making process in national affairs. *Fudai* daimyo monopolized the most important posts of the *bakufu*, namely membership in the Rōjū ("council of elders") and in the Wakadoshiyori ("junior council"). The Rōjū and Wakadoshiyori each arrived at decisions collectively, and their leadership rotated frequently. Each of the councils supervised several lower administrators, many of whom were liege vassals and bannermen of the Tokugawa.

The *shimpan* daimyo enjoyed great prestige as relatives of the shogun without commensurate political responsibilities. They did provide counsel to the main shogunal house in family matters, such as marriage and succession issues. Owari, Kii, and Mito, the major branch families *(gosanke)*, were eligible to provide candidates to the shogunate should there be no suitable heir within the main house.

The *tozama*, among the most powerful and dangerous of lords, were accorded great respect and ceremonial status in the protocol of the shogun's court. They were also the most frequently and heavily burdened by the *bakufu* with costly projects, designed to drain their economic resources, such as flood control work or the maintenance of Tokugawa fortifications. The *tozama* lords did enjoy greater autonomy within their *han* than the *fudai* lords, who were more vulnerable to the shogun's wrath. Satsuma, a *tozama han*, made special efforts to keep *bakufu* spies out of the realm, and when official inspectors arrived from the capital, elaborate preparations insured that they saw and heard only what the local officials wanted them to. [*See* Satsuma.]

The most effective means for maintaining the political status quo and Tokugawa supremacy was the *sankin kōtai* ("alternate attendance") system. This system required all daimyo, with few exceptions, to reside in Edo on alternate years and give tribute to the shogun on ceremonial occasions. When the daimyo returned to their domains their families remained behind in Edo as hostages of the shogun. The trips between domain and Edo were extremely costly, for, depending upon the wealth and prestige of the lord, several hundred to a few thousand samurai and servants accompanied him. Thus, the lord of Satsuma, the second largest of the *tozama* daimyo, was accompanied by three thousand or more retainers who had to travel for about forty days each way. The maintenance of residential and official establishments at home and at the capital also accounted for a sizable part of the *han* budget. [*See* Sankin Kōtai.]

Daimyo were rated in power and prestige by the assessed productivity, or *kokudaka*, of their domains, expressed in *koku* (approximately five bushels of rice). Maeda of Kanazawa, the largest of the *tozama* daimyo, had a realm rated at over one million *koku*. The same ratings affected ceremonial requirements, permissible numbers of samurai in total and in attendance at Edo, location and size of estates maintained in Edo, and service obligations. Twenty-two lords had territories with populations and *kokudaka* between 250,000 and 800,000. But most daimyo administered small domains, many barely over the 10,000 *koku* threshold of daimyo status.

The warrior ethic of loyalty to one's master and the Confucian emphasis on filial piety to parents and respect for superiors were concepts useful to the Tokugawa for maintaining social order and stability. Each person was to know his place and role in society and to behave accordingly. In a Japanese variation of the Chinese social model of four classes, the Tokugawa divided society into the four classes: samurai, peasants, artisans, and merchants. Everyone belonged to one of these categories, and the categories were hereditary and thus in theory permanent. There was also a hereditary outcaste community, and entertainers and prostitutes were classed as *hinin*, subhuman. The samurai were the privileged ruling class. Approximately 5 percent of the total Japanese population were samurai. Below them were commoners divided into separate groups according to their economic functions. Peasants rated high on the Confucian scale of values because they were indispensable to society as producers of food. As in China, agriculture was considered basic to the national economy. Artisans also were productive and useful. Merchants, on the other hand, were unworthy of esteem, as they were nonproducers who took advantage of both producers and consumers by buying cheaply from one and selling dearly to the other. The hereditary nature of this four-class system inhibited social mobility in Tokugawa Japan both laterally and vertically, although the dynamic nature of the economy gradually blurred this sharp division along class lines.

Social and Economic Developments.

Perhaps the single most dramatic development of Tokugawa Japan was the rather sudden growth of the cities of Edo and Osaka. The enforced residence of all daimyo and their families, along with their numerous servants and samurai retainers, made Edo, with a population of nearly one million in the eighteenth century, a leading city in the world. Although the social tone of the city was set by the ruling samurai class, the stereotype of the Edo denizen was a cocky, self-confident merchant. The providers of goods and services were assigned to different sections of the city according to specialization. One that attracted and impoverished many a samurai who had more time on his hands than money in his purse was the Yoshiwara district, the "gay quarters." [See Edo.]

Osaka also became a direct beneficiary of the *sankin kōtai* obligation, and it quickly expanded to a population of 400,000. To feed and supply the mammoth capital of the shogun, Osaka became "the kitchen of Japan," a collecting point and distribution center for goods from all the *han,* with fleets of ships transporting essential supplies to Edo. Because daimyo were constantly in need of cash, they brought their surplus rice and other local products to this commercial center to exchange for money. Compared to their Edo counterparts, the Osaka *chōnin* ("townsmen") were typically more serious in their pursuit of business and profits.

Although supervised by *bakufu* magistrates, the Osaka merchants organized themselves into monopoly associations of service specialties. These associations, called *nakama,* served a dual purpose: they provided security for members through collective action against the politically potent samurai who might be tempted to intimidate the *chōnin* and, by collectively agreeing to rules and regulations governing business ethics and standards, they made external official intervention in city affairs largely unnecessary. [See Chōnin *and* Nakama and Ton'ya.]

Matching Osaka in population was the neighboring city of Kyoto, the centuries-old imperial capital. Overshadowing the elegant and fragile architecture of the palace compound was Nijō Castle, a massive fortification housing *bakufu* officials and samurai, who guarded the palace and city. In this city of serene and ageless temples aristocratic aesthetes perpetuated the traditional arts such as the *nō* drama, the tea ceremony, and flower arranging. Kyoto also was the fashion center of the country, and its artisans produced the finest silk textiles. Until

the mid-nineteenth century there was little to ruffle the calm of Kyoto, but in the closing decade of the Tokugawa period it was to become the center of a political maelstrom. [See Kyoto.]

These major urban centers, but especially Edo and Osaka, greatly affected the way of life of both merchants and samurai, as did the capital of each domain, its castle town, or *jōkamachi.*

The separation of warriors from farmers and the disarming of the commoners that had been carried out at the end of the sixteenth century meant that daimyo collected their samurai at their headquarters, just as the shogun collected his daimyo at Edo. With the seventeenth century peace, the need to service and provision this ruling class brought on a network of castle towns that usually attracted one tenth the population of the domain. The Tokugawa years produced rapid urbanization; Japan was probably the only non-European country with 10 percent of its population in cities of 10,000 or more in the eighteenth century.

With samurai removed from agricultural production, their livelihood depended on salaries that took the form of rice stipends from the daimyo tax yield; these in turn frequently gave way to money payments. Urban life and needs found samurai hard put to maintain their position on a fixed and often declining income. Samurai salaries were depreciated by currency devaluation and price inflation and further eroded by enforced "loans" to their *han* during hard times. Thus, while their taste for city pleasures developed, their financial situation became precarious, sometimes to the point of compromising their samurai status.

Many merchants, by contrast, acquired considerable wealth by providing for the ruling class. Almost from the beginning of the Tokugawa period, some daimyo found it necessary to borrow funds from Osaka moneylenders, and in the latter part of the period even the *bakufu* resorted to coercing loans from merchants. Politically, the shogun or daimyo could arbitrarily cancel or reduce payments owed to merchants, but they could ill-afford to alienate the merchant associations and thus jeopardize future loans. Instead, many daimyo perceived the advantage of employing able merchants to repair the fiscal situations in their domains. For their services, several specially favored merchants received surnames and the privilege of wearing swords like the samurai.

Urbanization and the emergence of an affluent merchant class produced a new type of culture, full of vitality, color, and movement. In drama, the *chōnin* preferred the lively and colorful *kabuki* over the restrained action and simplicity of the *nō* stage. Chikamatsu Monzaemon (1653–1724) wrote about townsmen's lives and was the premier dramatist of the kabuki and puppet *(jōruri)* stage. Instead of the Zen-influenced monochromatic brush paintings favored by the elite, the townsmen snapped up the colorful woodblock prints by Harunobu, Utamaro, Hokusai, Hiroshige, and others who depicted scenes of the demimonde, favorite actors, commoners at work, or the famous views along the Tōkaidō, one of the national highways. Novels, also, were written for commoners. Ihara Saikaku (1642–1692), a leading writer of fiction, portrayed merchant success and, as frequently, profligacy in the licensed quarters. Poetry became simpler and more direct, especially in the hands of Matsuo Bashō (1644–1694). [*See* Genroku Culture.]

Compared to the wealth being amassed in the cities, the economy in rural Japan was relatively static. Yet while the merchants paid only a business license fee *(goyōkin)* and were occasionally dunned for a forced loan to the government, peasants annually turned over a large part of their crop to their lords, often on the formula of "four (parts) to the lord; six to the cultivator." In some *han,* the proportions were reversed. Ironically, the heavy reliance on the agricultural land tax was based on the esteem agricultural labor enjoyed over mercantile activity in Confucian ideology.

The nature of paddy rice cultivation required close cooperation among villages, since they typically shared water from a common irrigation system. Moreover, to facilitate tax collection, subunits of five or more households were formed within each village. The collective concern of these subunits, called *gonin gumi,* was to ensure that each household did its best to produce the rice tax and to provide the required number of days of labor service to the local administration. The close social relationships fostered by the collective responsibility system benefited the villagers in that they obviated the need for on-site official supervision. Thus, most villages were administered by their own leaders, who served as buffers between peasants and officials.

The fixed rice tax was a heavy burden on peasants, but in times of bad crops the government did provide tax relief. Where possible, peasants were encouraged to reclaim marginal land, which at least in the initial years of cultivation was tax free. If the situation became intolerable, peasants sometimes absconded from their villages or resorted to violent protests. However, overall agricultural productivity kept pace with population growth. (By the mid-eighteenth century the overall population had stabilized, but outlying areas continued to grow while urban growth, natural disasters, and famine brought declines in other areas.) New crops, better seeds, better fertilizer, and improved agricultural implements were introduced. Agricultural specialists employed by the *han* circulated among the villages to instruct peasants in the latest methods of cultivation, and instructive books on agriculture increased as the number of literate peasants grew.

An important development in many areas was the emphasis placed on cash crops, a reflection of the spread of the money economy to the villages. Money was used to purchase fertilizer, tools, and other commodities, and it also enabled the peasant to hire labor as needed. With hired labor the advantages of maintaining the large extended family as a labor pool diminished. Thus, many family members went on to become independent cultivators, tenant cultivators, or wage earners. The more successful peasants invested their wealth in rural industries that provided secondary employment for others.

Cash crops also were used by *han* governments to relieve their fiscal difficulties. Special local crops were made *han* monopolies, which might be administered by licensed merchants. With the commercialization of agriculture, merchants often contracted for the crop by advancing capital to the cultivators. By the nineteenth century, these rural merchants had broken the tight control of markets held by the Osaka merchants. All these developments generally benefited peasants, but inevitably many were reduced in respectability and wealth, and others became enmeshed in a web of loans and high interest rates.

The *bakufu* and *han* governments, however, were not beneficiaries of the new economic growth. Reassessment and higher tax demands were seldom successful. Instead, major reforms in the Kyōhō (1716–1733), Kansei (1787–1793), and Tempō (1841) eras, sponsored respectively by the shogun Yoshimune (r. 1716–1745), the *rōjū* Matsudaira Sadanobu (1787–1793), and the *rōjū* Mizuno Tadakuni (1834–1845), were implemented, but they were based on outmoded assumptions that there was a fixed total of national wealth. These were initiatives to reduce spending, revalue currency, reclaim more land for agriculture, force peasants in the city to return to their villages, and provide relief to samurai by cancelling their debts to merchants. These measures did not address the fact that the Tokugawa economy had essentially changed and could not be forced back into a Confucian mold. [*See* Kyōhō Reforms; Kansei Reforms; *and* Tempō Reforms.]

Only the economic program of the grand chamberlain and *rōjū* Tanuma Okitsugu (1769–1786) adopted the positive approach of creating new sources of revenue. Regarded by his colleagues in the Council of Elders as an upstart, he was able to promulgate a number of reforms only because of the patronage of the tenth shogun, Ieharu (1760–1786). Besides encouraging land reclamation, he explored the possibilities of colonizing Hokkaido, increasing foreign trade, developing mines, setting up more government monopolies, and finding new taxable enterprises. Tanuma, however, was not a model of Confucian circumspection. When his patron shogun died Tanuma was brought down in disgrace and accused of unconscionable corruption, and his reforms came to naught. [*See* Tanuma Okitsugu.]

In the mid-nineteenth century, a period of intense crisis brought on by the aggressive diplomacy of Western powers, the *bakufu* and most *han* were incapable of financial response. However, two *tozama han*, Satsuma and Chōshū, had been singularly successful in their economic reforms of the 1830s and 1840s. Chōshū had turned over monopolies of commercial crops to licensed merchants and had set up a savings office that systematically accumulated capital for emergencies and for key investments. Satsuma had established a *han*-controlled monopoly system over several products, among which sugar was the most valuable commodity. The domain also profited from the Ryūkyū trade and from illicit coastal commerce with Chinese vessels, which conveniently "blew off course" into Satsuma's snug harbors. These two domains built up financial resources commensurate with the anti-*bakufu* leadership roles they were to assume in the closing years of the Tokugawa regime.

Intellectual Developments. In intellectual activity, scholars of the Tokugawa period demonstrated independence and vigor of thought despite the long period of isolation. From an early point the *bakufu* tended to favor Confucianism of the Zhu Xi school as a desirable teaching, and Matsudaira Sadanobu made this preference official in 1790. He did so, however, in response to the popularity of other teachings. The teachings of Wang Yangming, or Ōyōmei as he was known in Japan, also had a wide following. The study of Confucianism and the injunctions of scholars such as Ogyū Sorai (1666–1728) to return to the study of the Chinese classics and of antiquity, led others to investigate Japan's own ancient past. This in turn revived interest in

Shinto and provided the basis for a new ethnic nationalism. [*See* Ogyū Sorai.]

An important contribution to the study of national history was made by Tokugawa Mitsukuni (1628–1700), lord of Mito, a major branch of the shogunal house. Mitsukuni ordered the compilation and publication of the *Dai Nihonshi (History of Great Japan),* a mammoth project that began in 1657 and was completed in 1906. Because of this project the Mito *han* was especially respectful of the imperial family, whose unique and unbroken lineage traced back to the sun goddess Amaterasu according to the ancient literature. The reminder of past political centrality of the imperial family created problems for Tokugawa scholars. How should they explain the relationship of the powerful shogun to the reclusive emperor? What began as an intellectual issue became a highly emotional one in the last decade of Tokugawa rule.

Scholars of the Kokugaku ("national studies") school were impressed by what they perceived as the unique qualities of the Japanese when they analyzed ancient literature such as the *Man'yōshū* (a poetry anthology of the eighth century), the *Kojiki* and the *Nihongi* (official histories of Japan, dated 712 and 720 respectively), and the *Genji monogatari (Tale of Genji,* an eleventh-century novel). While scholars like Yamaga Sokō wrote of the manly virtues of *bushidō* ("way of the samurai"), others, like Motoori Norinaga, were impressed by the sensitivity of Japanese to the fleeting qualities of life and nature. Such introspective intellectual endeavors focused attention on the imperial tradition, the center of Japan's presumed uniqueness. [*See* Kokugaku; Bushidō; *and* Motoori Norinaga.]

A different vein of thought was opened in 1720 when the shogun Yoshimune relaxed the ban on the importation of foreign books. Japanese interest in Western books was primarily pragmatic. The *bakufu* selected a few "interpreters" to study Dutch and translate items of interest for the government, but the communication gap was difficult to bridge. Individual scholars also acquired Western books, and by the early 1770s they had produced a translation of a Western work on anatomy. Thereafter, scholars studied Western works on a variety of subjects, such as mathematics, astronomy, navigation, surveying, mapmaking, and, in the nineteenth century, Western military science and industrial technology, including telegraphy, gas illumination, the casting of cannons, and the construction of steam engines and steamships. By the mid-nineteenth century those involved in Western studies were well aware of the technological and military superiority of the West and were eager to learn. [*See* Rangaku.]

The lively competition of ideas in the Tokugawa period helped Japan adjust to the flood of new concepts, institutions, and technology that came in the nineteenth century. Essential to this intellectual vitality was the spread of education. This began in the seventeenth century with domain efforts to convert the martial and often illiterate samurai into peacetime bureaucrats. *Han* schools, normally restricted to samurai, were supplemented by networks of parish *(terakoya)* and private *(shijuku)* schools that provided basic literacy for growing numbers of commoners. Establishment of schools increased year by year during the last century of Tokugawa rule, with the result that by the end of the period almost half of school-age males and one-tenth of females had received some kind of schooling outside the home. These figures suggest the strong motivation for self-improvement throughout Japanese society.

Collapse of the Tokugawa Shogunate. Between 1792 and 1818 Russian and British vessels intruded into Japanese waters several times at Hokkaido, at Nagasaki, and even at Edo. Alarmed by this challenge to the seclusion policy, in 1825 the *bakufu* ordered that any Western vessel in Japanese coastal waters be driven off by gunfire. Between 1844 and 1846 the British and French competed to establish relations with the Ryūkyū kingdom, but with Satsuma backing the Ryūkyū king refused to depart from past policy. American efforts in 1837 and 1846 to open relations with Japan also failed. Finally, in 1853 a show of naval force by Commodore Matthew C. Perry succeeded in forcing the Japanese officials to accept a letter from the president of the United States to the shogun. A second visit by Perry resulted in the Treaty of Kanagawa (31 March 1854), in which the *bakufu* agreed to open the ports of Hakodate and Shimoda and to treat shipwrecked American sailors humanely. The way was left open for assignment of an American consul to Japan, and Japan agreed that any privileges given other countries would extend to the United States. England, Russia, and Holland signed similar treaties soon after. [*See* Perry, Matthew C. *and* Kanagawa Treaty.]

Townsend Harris arrived in Shimoda as American consul in 1856. He convinced the Japanese that it was wiser to sign a commercial treaty with the United States than to risk the humiliation experienced by China at the hands of the British and French. The treaty signed on 29 July 1858 opened two additional ports, Kanagawa and Nagasaki, with Niigata and Hyōgo to be opened later; the right of Americans to residency at Edo and Osaka was promised; trade between the two countries was to be facilitated by low, fixed tariff rates; and the principle of extraterritoriality was accepted by Japan. The *bakufu* signed similar treaties with the Dutch, Russians, British, and French in the same year. These agreements were little different from the "unequal treaties" that had been signed under duress by China. [*See* Harris, Townsend.]

Perry's first trip to Japan caused Abe Masahiro, the senior *rōjū*, to break with precedence by consulting with the imperial court and the leading daimyo as to the course of action Japan should adopt. Some, like Tokugawa Nariaki of Mito, argued for military action, which even if unsuccessful would serve to arouse the martial spirit of the Japanese. A few believed that commerce with the West was a way of making profits that could pay for the weapons required for national defense. Others suggested that some trade concessions should be made in order to gain time for Japan's defense effort.

The signing of the commercial treaties of 1858 aroused even greater furor in domestic politics than did Perry's appearance. Abe's idea of consultation was totally rejected by the new *bakufu* strongman, Ii Naosuke. Despite the imperial court's opposition, Ii signed the treaties; he also placed the powerful daimyo who disagreed with him under house arrest.

The uncompromising rule of Ii led to his assassination by Mito swordsmen in the spring of 1860. Thereafter, *bakufu* prestige and control deteriorated, and the political center of gravity gradually shifted to Kyoto. In 1862 the *sankin kōtai* system was relaxed, and daimyo families were allowed to return to their domains. The release of the hostages encouraged the more powerful daimyo to play a stronger political role in national affairs, and they turned to the imperial court as their stage. The political instability also enabled *rōnin* ("masterless samurai") to terrorize both foreigners and Japanese who supported the commercial treaties. The assassinations they committed and their cry of "Sonnō jōi" ("Revere the emperor; expel the barbarians") were further embarrassments to the *bakufu*.

Chōshū and Satsuma were two of the most powerful and ambitious of the *tozama* domains, and they competed for influence at the imperial court. Between 1861 and 1864 they competed for court favor, and in the process the politically dormant court became activated and a few aristocrats were radicalized. Under the influence of the Chōshū extremists, the court broke precedence by summoning the shogun to Kyoto and forcing him to sign an order for the expulsion of foreigners by 25 June 1863.

Inspired by this extremist rhetoric, Chōshū, on 25 June, fired on Western ships off its coast. American and French naval vessels retaliated by destroying Chōshū's forts and two gunboats. Moreover, in the summer of 1863 the domains of Aizu and Satsuma combined forces to expel Chōshū samurai from Kyoto. When Chōshū forces tried to regain control of the imperial court in 1864 they were driven off again. Soon after, a Western fleet destroyed all of Chōshū's coastal fortifications and imposed a heavy indemnity on the *bakufu*. Furthermore, the *bakufu* launched an expedition to punish Chōshū for her transgressions in October of 1864.

In the meantime, in September 1862, Satsuma samurai killed an Englishman and wounded his three companions. The following year British naval units set fire to Kagoshima, the Satsuma castle town. These encounters with Western military might sobered both Satsuma and Chōshū extremists, and their leaders reversed course by seeking support from the Westerners in their struggles with the *bakufu*. British minister Harry Parkes, while maintaining an officially neutral position in Japan's domestic politics, tacitly agreed by taking no action against his countrymen who sold ships and weapons to Satsuma.

In the first *bakufu* expedition of 1864 Chōshū faced disaster from an overwhelming force and negotiated a moderate settlement. Within Chōshū, radicals revolted and succeeded in negating that settlement. When the *bakufu* tried a second expedition in 1866 Chōshū's revitalized military units dealt humiliating defeats on *bakufu* units. Between the two expeditions, with the assistance of two *rōnin* from Tosa, Sakamoto Ryōma and Nakaoka Shintarō, a secret alliance against the *bakufu* had been negotiated by Saigō Takamori (1827–1877) of Satsuma and Kido Kōin (1833–1877) of Chōshū. [*See* Saigō Takamori *and* Sakamoto Ryōma.]

After the military fiasco of the second Chōshū expedition, the new shogun, Tokugawa Yoshinobu (Keiki), with the counsel of the French minister, Léon Roches, tried to institute sweeping military, economic, and administrative reforms, but time ran out before these measures could bear results. Saigō and Ōkubo Toshimichi (1830–1878) directed Satsuma strategy from Kyoto to counter Yoshinobu's moves. [*See* Ōkubo Toshimichi.] On 8 November 1867 the shogun was persuaded by the Tosa daimyo, Yamauchi Yōdō (Toyoshige), to resign his office. He did so with the assumption that he would take his place in a council of daimyo in which he

would be first. He was outmaneuvered by a court order that he also surrender his lands, and on 3 January an "imperial restoration" was proclaimed.

A brief battle came at the end of the month when the former shogun tried to advance on Kyoto. Unsuccessful, he retreated by ship to Edo, while an "imperial" army made up of Satsuma, Chōshū, Tosa, and additional troops moved toward Edo. The city was surrendered to the coalition army by Katsu Awa (1823–1899), but the newly created Tokugawa navy escaped to Hokkaido. Northern daimyo, suspicious of the motives of the southern coalition, fought on into the late spring of 1869, when the Tokugawa naval units surrendered. [*See* Satsuma; Chōshū; Tosa; *and* Meiji Restoration.]

The transfer of power from Tokugawa to imperial hands was accomplished with relatively little rancor. Japan's dual government had proven incapable of dealing with the foreign threat, and its stratified society would soon give way to a more rational structure capable of dealing with the needs of a modern state. Yet the Tokugawa years had given Japan the cohesion, the discipline, the education, and the sense of nationality that would contribute to the speed of the changes that followed.

[*Many of the shoguns mentioned above are the subject of independent entries.*]

Ronald P. Dore, *Education in Tokugawa Japan* (1965). C. J. Dunn *Everyday Life in Traditional Japan* (1969). John W. Hall, *Tanuma Okitsugu (1719–1788): Forerunner of Modern Japan* (1955). John W. Hall and Marius B. Jansen, eds., *Studies in the Institutional History of Early Modern Japan* (1968). Susan B. Hanley and Kozo Yamamura, *Economic and Demographic Change in Preindustrial Japan, 1600–1868* (1977). William B. Hauser, *Economic Institutional Change in Tokugawa Japan: Osaka on the Kinai Cotton Trade* (1974). Maruyama Masao, *Studies in the Intellectual History of Tokugawa Japan*, translated by Mikiso Hane (1974). George B. Sansom, *The Western World and Japan* (1951). Thomas C. Smith, *The Agrarian Origins of Modern Japan* (1959). Conrad Totman, *Politics in the Tokugawa Bakufu, 1600–1843* (1967).

ROBERT K. SAKAI

TOKUGAWA YOSHIMUNE

TOKUGAWA YOSHIMUNE (1684–1751), the eighth shogun, or military governor of Japan, of the Tokugawa lineage. Tokugawa Yoshimune has a secure reputation as a reformer that is largely, if not totally, deserved. As daimyo (lord) of the Kii domain from 1705 onward he had already become famous for his administrative skills before the death of the seven-year-old Ietsugu in 1716 left the office of shogun vacant. Yoshimune was the natural successor.

Once in office, he reshaped government policy along lines compatible with his domainal experience and congenial to this temperment, which displayed all the qualities associated with muscular Confucianism. The so-called Kyōhō Reforms were the result. To the extent that these were conceived along Confucian lines—that is, to the extent that they were monetaristic, moralistic, and dedicated to reimposition of the economic and social mores of the seventeenth century—Yoshimune failed, and he generated considerable confusion in the attempt. His more utilitarian initiatives, however, were successful; he imposed order on the processes of Tokugawa law, relaxed the long-standing prohibition on Western learning, and, in 1744, through careful management, gave the Tokugawa *bakufu* the highest annual income it had ever had or was ever to have.

[*See also* Kyōhō Reforms.]

HAROLD BOLITHO

TOKUGAWA YOSHINOBU (1837–1913), last shogun, or military governor of Japan, of the Tokugawa lineage. Born the seventh son of Tokugawa Nariaki, daimyo of Mito, Tokugawa Yoshinobu seemed destined for early greatness. Selected at the age of nine to head the Hitotsubashi branch of the Tokugawa house, Yoshinobu was hailed by his sixteenth year as the perfect candidate to succeed Tokugawa Iesada, the thirteenth shogun. However, when Iesada died in 1858, Yoshinobu's claim was rejected, and he spent the next four years in retirement. In 1862 he reemerged as one of a group of political aspirants dedicated to the proposition that the *bakufu* would function best under their control. In 1866, upon his predecessor Iemochi's death, Yoshinobu became the fifteenth Tokugawa shogun, only to find that the power-sharing arrangements initiated by his party had virtually destroyed the government. He was therefore unable to resist both the invitation to restore power to the emperor in 1867 and his own subsequent disenfranchisement. Freed in 1869 after some months under house arrest, the thirty-one-year-old Yoshinobu spent the remaining forty-four years of his life as one of Meiji Japan's most able nonentities.

[*See also* Meiji Restoration.]

HAROLD BOLITHO

TOKUSEI, the cancellation of debts by government fiat in medieval Japan. Although the term literally means "virtuous governance," it also had more specific connotations. In Confucian theory, a ruler's failure to govern virtuously was an affront to Heaven, and might well produce such portents as the appearance of comets and monsters, or such disasters as floods and famines. The occurrence of such portents thus cast strong doubts on a ruler's fitness to govern and often led him to indulge in such expiratory acts of benevolence as general amnesties or the remission of taxes. Such acts were called *tokusei*, and it is in this sense that the term was applied—with decreasing credibility—to the debt-cancellation decrees of the thirteenth through sixteenth century.

The first such decrees were issued by the Kamakura shogunate as a means of aiding shogunal vassals who had been ruined by debt. The orders provided that any vassal whose debts had obliged him to sell or pawn his lands was to have those lands restored to him without any compensation to his creditor. Under the succeeding Muromachi shogunate, debt cancellations became far more broadly based, more frequent, and more cynically motivated. By the fifteenth century *tokusei* might in fact cancel the debts of any class; they were occasionally issued in response to popular uprisings, and they had even become an instrument of government finance. This last situation arose when debtors were forbidden to take advantage of a *tokusei* unless they paid the government a portion of what they would otherwise have owed their creditors, or when creditors were given exemptions from *tokusei* for paying over a portion of what they hoped to wring from their debtors. With the decline of shogunal authority, *tokusei* were also issued by regional daimyo.   PETER J. ARNESEN

TOKUTOMI SOHŌ (Iichirō; 1863–1957), Japanese journalist. Born and raised in Kumamoto, Tokutomi attended the Kumamoto School for Western Learning, where he became a Christian and one of the signers of the Christian declaration known as the Hanaoka Oath. In 1876 he went to Dōshisha University, but he abandoned the school, and Christianity, in 1880. On his return to Kumamoto he founded the Oe Gijuku, a private academy. In 1885 he wrote *Youth and Their Education in Nineteenth Century Japan (Dai jūkyū seiki Nihon no seinen oyobi sono kyōiku)*, and the following year he published *The Future Japan (Shōrai no Nihon)*. These highly popular works brought him national acclaim, and in 1887 he began to publish Meiji Japan's most widely read journal, *Kokumin no tomo*. Through his journal and its society, the Minyūsha, Tokutomi disseminated the political and economic thought of Manchester liberalism.

In the wake of the Sino-Japanese War (1894–1895), however, Tokutomi exchanged his liberal ideas for a new emphasis on nationalism and a positive foreign policy. In 1911 he became a member of the House of Peers, and in the 1920s and 1930s he remained a staunch conservative and supporter of the throne, while he also turned his attention from public issues to historical writing. A prolific author and publicist, he lived through much of Japan's modern century and came to be known as the "grand old man" of Japanese journalism.

[See also Journalism: Journalism in Japan.]

F. G. NOTEHELFER

TOKYO. The political capital of Japan since 1868, Tokyo is the nation's largest city and the center of its economic, political, and cultural life. Edo, as Tokyo was previously called, served for over two and a half centuries as the political capital of the Tokugawa shogunate. [See Edo.] With the collapse of the old regime in early 1868, a debate ensued over an appropriate location for the capital of the restored Meiji emperor. A compromise was reached whereby the emperor would alternate residence between a "western capital" (saikyō) in Kyoto, the ancient imperial seat, and an "eastern capital" (tōkyō) in Edo. In the end, however, the emperor remained in his "eastern capital," where the former Edo Castle was converted into the new Imperial Palace, and Tōkyō (often pronounced "tōkei" in the early Meiji period) became the new name for Edo.

The collapse of the Tokugawa regime resulted in a great exodus of the samurai from the city that halved the city's population of over one million and left the daimyo estates deserted and in disrepair. These unoccupied areas, concentrated in the higher areas of the city to the east, were of great use to the new regime, providing the sites for government offices, military installations, educational and research facilities, and residences for nobility and for government officials. The centralizing reforms of the early Meiji government insured a rapid recovery for the city, which by the mid-1890s had surpassed its peak population during the Tokugawa period.

Tokyo in the 1870s and 1880s was the center of westernizing influence in Japan. The symbol of the era was the Ginza district, rebuilt in Western-style brick architecture after a fire in 1872 and featuring many shops specializing in Western goods. Wheeled vehicles, which had been prohibited in Edo, were introduced in the form of the jinrikisha (a Japanese invention said to be inspired by a Western baby carriage) and the horse-drawn railway.

It was only near the end of the century, however, that Tokyo began to assume its modern shape. The rebuilding of the Imperial Palace, which had been destroyed by fire in 1873, was completed in 1889, and the government district of Kasumigaseki emerged in the late 1880s. In 1890, the Mitsubishi company purchased a large area of land west of the palace and began construction of what would become Marunouchi, Tokyo's business and financial district.

Tokyo continued to grow rapidly in the early twentieth century as government and industry attracted a constant flow of immigrants. These newcomers came from all over Japan, but the majority were from Tokyo's immediate hinterland, the Kantō, and from the Hokuriku region. The problems of adjustment to metropolitan life were eased by the systematic organization of clubs of those from the same prefecture (kenjinkai).

The swelling population of Tokyo pushed its geographic limits outward beyond the borders of traditional Edo. The low-lying Shitamachi area along both sides of the Sumida River became a densely crowded industrial and lower-class residential district, while the hilly Yamanote area to the west emerged primarily as middle-class suburbs extending along the trolley and rail lines that multiplied in the first decades of the century.

The lifestyle of the residents of Tokyo, most of whom had through the end of the nineteenth century remained in circumstances little changed relative to the Tokugawa era, began to change notably in the late Meiji and Taishō periods. Electric trolleys and trains provided far more rapid movement about the city, electric lights encouraged nighttime activities, and housing and diet began gradually to change along more modern and Western lines.

The process of change was accelerated by the disaster of the Kantō Earthquake of September 1923, which destroyed much of the city, particularly the old Shitamachi, and claimed over seventy thousand lives. [See Kantō Earthquake.] Rebuilding afforded the opportunity of some widening and straightening of the road system, but the basic pattern inherited from Edo was not altered.

By the 1920s Tokyo was a conspicuously modern metropolis, with a population in 1930 of over two million for the fifteen-borough (ku) area of Tokyo City and over twice that for the total metropolitan area, which extended well beyond the city limits.

Administratively, the city was split between Tokyo City and Tokyo Prefecture, creating numerous political and jurisdictional problems.

Tokyo in the 1920s was strongly influenced by Western, particularly American, culture. Jazz was the rage, and the young couples who strolled the fashionable Ginza were dressed in the fashions of the Roaring Twenties. The automobile made its appearance, although it was put mostly to commercial use. Postearthquake Tokyo architecture was increasingly Western in appearance as well, with much more building in steel and concrete, at least in the center of the city.

Tokyo in the 1920s and 1930s began to suffer from many of the problems common to large cities everywhere in the modern world. Housing was in short supply and of generally low quality, while pollution of the air and water became a major concern for the first time. Particularly during the depression years of 1930–1932, social problems were numerous. City authorities worked to establish medical and relief facilities for the indigent, although funds were never adequate.

On the eve of World War II the population of metropolitan Tokyo had swelled to over seven million. The war reversed the pattern of steady growth, culminating in the disastrous fire bombing of the city in the spring of 1945, which left over one hundred thousand dead, a toll considerably higher than that of the 1923 earthquake and comparable to that suffered by Hiroshima in the atomic bombing. Thus, Tokyo was reduced to rubble for the second time in the twentieth century, and by the end of the war its population had dropped to three and one-half million.

The rebuilding of Tokyo was rapid, if haphazard, and economic recovery brought its population back to the prewar level by 1954. The 1960s and 1970s were a era of sustained population growth. A 1943 reform had eliminated the old division between Tokyo City and Tokyo Prefecture, creating a unified "Tokyo metropolis" (Tōkyō-to), which by 1970 had a population of eleven million. In fact, however, Tokyo had already become the center of a much larger conurbation that covers much of the Kantō Plain and includes the port of Yokohama and the industrial city of Kawasaki, a vast urban sprawl with a population between twenty to thirty million people, about one-fifth the total population of Japan.

The constant growth of Tokyo throughout its modern history was paralleled by the increasing concentration of Japan's political, economic, and cultural resources in the capital itself. Tokyo's share of the national population rose from about 3 percent in 1900 to over 10 per cent by 1960, and its share in other respects became even greater. Tokyo as of the late 1970s housed the main offices of 60 percent of the nation's largest corporations, while its financial institutions executed one-third of all loans, its wholesalers and retailers accounted for one-third of all commercial sales, its publishing houses produced 90 per cent of all books, and its universities enrolled almost one-fourth of all college students.

From about 1980, however, the population of Tokyo began to stabilize and even decline, while the percentage of native-born Tokyo residents rose steadily. These trends suggest that the pattern of Tokyo history has undergone a fundmental change, although the consequences remain unclear. Meanwhile, the threat of another great earthquake lurks in the future and strengthens the sense of ephemerality and present-mindedness that has characterized Tokyo throughout its history.

Ronald Dore, *City Life in Japan: A Study of a Tokyo Ward* (1958). Fosco Maraini, *Tokyo* (1976). Edward Seidensticker, *Low City, High City: Tokyo from Edo to the Earthquake* (1983). Henry Smith, "Tokyo and London: Comparative Conceptions of the City," in *Japan: A Comparative View*, edited by A. Craig (1979), pp. 49–99. Takeo Yazaki, *Social Change and the City in Japan* (1968).   HENRY D. SMITH II

TON DUC THANG (1888–1980), veteran Communist Party member and successor to Ho Chi Minh as president of the Democratic Republic of Vietnam from 1969 until his death in 1980. Ton Duc Thang was born in Long Xuyen Province, South Vietnam, in 1888. During World War I he went to France, where he became active in radical causes and allegedly took part in a 1918 uprising by French sailors in the Black Sea. On his return to Saigon in 1920 he founded the first labor organization in French Indochina and in 1930 became a founding member of the Indochinese Communist Party. In 1960 he was elected vice-president of the Democratic Republic of Vietnam. He succeeded to the presidency on the death of Ho Chi Minh but possessed little real power.

[*See also* Vietnam, Democratic Republic of *and* Indochinese Communist Party.]

Danny J. Whitfield, *Historical and Cultural Dictionary of Vietnam* (1976).   WILLIAM J. DUIKER

TONGHAK, Korean religious movement, now known as Ch'ŏndogyo, that originated in 1860 and acquired strong political overtones. Its members staged a rebellion against the ruling Yi dynasty in 1894 and then participated in the independence movement during the Japanese occupation of 1910 to 1945. Tonghak was started in 1860 by Ch'oe Che-u, who claimed to have received a vision from heaven that instructed him to establish a religion based on faith in God and man to alleviate the sufferings of the people. Tonghak, "Eastern learning," was chosen as a name to signify its distinctiveness from and superiority over Sŏhak, "Western learning," as Roman Catholicism was known at the time.

Tonghak doctrine, called *ch'ŏndo* ("heavenly way"), drew inspiration from other religions both indigenous and foreign. Ch'oe emphasized the importance of the five relations, the basic tenets that governed Confucian society; adopted the idea of "cleansing the heart" from Buddhism and the idea of cleansing the body from Daoism; took monotheism and certain rituals from Catholicism; and constructed a theory of portents and magic based on traditional geomancy and omens. A sacred formula of twenty-one characters expressed the fundamental religious principle of the movement, the concept that man is God. Its social philosophy stressed the importance and equality of the individual, whose ability to achieve his potential determined the realization of social freedom and harmony. This utopian vision, called *chisang ch'ŏn'guk* ("nation of Heaven on earth"), in which every person would live in equality, harmony, and freedom, was declared to be the ultimate goal of the Tonghak religion. It would be achieved gradually, through the efforts of individuals. Ch'oe eschewed violence and emphasized loyalty to the king, the first precept of the Confucian five relations. While Tonghak theology, in its scholarly conceptual framework, was designed to appeal to the educated elite, its simple practices, such as the recitation of the short sacred formula, and its egalitarian vision of humanity had a strong mass appeal.

Within a few years, Ch'oe acquired a large loyal following in the southern provinces. In early 1864 he was arrested and imprisoned for refusing to give in to local officials' demands for financial contributions. This was during a period when Catholics were persecuted in Korea. When it was revealed that his writings contained such words as *heavenly lord* and *supreme ruler* to refer to God, the same terms used for God in Catholicism, Ch'oe was accused of being a Catholic and, after months of imprisonment and torture, was executed in April 1864.

Ch'oe Si-hyŏng, a distant relative, was chosen as Ch'oe Che-u's successor; he proved to be an effective organizer. Evading government pursuit, he further refined Tonghak doctrine, instituted requirements for prayer, and reorganized the movement into tighter hierarchical units. Despite increasing pressures on him to take action to clear the founder's name, he also managed to avoid violence. When the government outlawed Tonghak in 1892, Ch'oe petitioned the governors of the southern provinces in hopes of clearing the name of the founder and of persuading them that the movement was harmless and loyal to the government. When this effort failed, the Tonghak leadership decided to petition the king directly. Thousands went to the capital and staged a demonstration. Upon receiving an apparent but inexplicit royal promise of favorable treatment, they dispersed. Several successive petitions met with similar evasive responses.

In February 1894 Chŏn Pong-jun, the head of the southern jurisdiction of the Tonghak movement, staged a rebellion that captured Kobu County in Chŏlla Province; by early June he had taken Chŏnju, the provincial capital. Unable to contain the rebellion, the government requested military assistance from China. China responded by sending troops, notifying the Japanese before they disembarked but after they had been dispatched. As the Tianjin Convention of 1885 required that neither country intervene in Korea without prior notice to the other, this led to the dispatch of Japanese troops and, eventually, to the Sino-Japanese War of 1894 to 1895. [See also Sino-Japanese War.] Meanwhile Korean government forces offered Chŏn a truce, promising that if he disbanded his forces, Tonghak members would be free to practice their religion and be protected from discrimination or persecution. Distressed that the uprising had resulted in the arrival of foreign troops, Chŏn withdrew from Chŏnju for the duration of the war. When the government's promise proved false, Ch'oe Si-hyŏng, who had hitherto taken a stance critical of Chŏn, came to his support. The Tonghak rebels, although briefly successful, were decisively defeated by the forces of the Korean army and the Japanese army, which had triumphed over the Chinese army. Chŏn Pong-jun and many other Tonghak leaders were captured and executed.

The Tonghak rebellion is viewed as the first large-scale uprising in Korea aimed at a reorganization of society based on equality. It is also seen as a direct cause of the Sino-Japanese War. The rebellion decimated the Tonghak leadership and much of its membership. The task of reorganizing and revitalizing the movement fell to Son Pyǒng-hǔi, the third Tonghak leader, who received the mantle from Ch'oe Si-hyǒng just before the latter's arrest in 1898. For a short while the Tonghak leaders, thinking that alliance with Japan would secure the future of the Tonghak religion and that Japan would prevail over Russia (which was coming into increased conflict with Japan over its interests in Korea and Manchuria), supported Japan. The Ilchinhoe, a political association that gave active support to Japan, was run by Tonghak members. [See also Ilchinhoe.]

In 1905, after Japan made Korea a protectorate, Son expelled pro-Japanese elements from the Tonghak organization, changed the name of the religion from Tonghak to Ch'ǒndogyo ("religion of the Heavenly Way"), and incorporated new devotional practices and redefined doctrines. In 1907 an active evangelical campaign was launched to propagate the religion and recruit new believers. Two high schools, Tongdǒk Girls' High School and Posǒng Boys' High School, were founded in 1909. In 1911 a training institute was established that instructed new converts as well as local leaders in the newly articulated doctrine. The organization also gradually changed, disseminating control to local units. By 1922 Ch'ǒndogyo no longer had a single leader but instead was run by a committee of forty-six members. This period of committee leadership ended in 1928 with the election of Ch'oe Rin as leader.

The keen interest the movement displayed in social and political matters was embodied in Son's doctrine of the unity of religion and politics. During the period of Japanese colonial rule (1910–1945), this policy was expressed by the active participation of Ch'ǒndogyo members in the Korean independence movement. Of the thirty-three signers of the declaration of independence in 1919, fifteen were Ch'ǒndogyo followers. Son Pyǒng-hǔi was chairman of the convention of thirty-three signers. He died in prison in 1922, but Ch'ǒndogyo faithful continued their activities. In 1923 the religion established a political party. To stimulate intellectual life, Ch'ǒndogyo also published several magazines devoted to literature, philosophy, and politics. Although their political and intellectual activities were rather curtailed as Japanese took increasingly oppressive measures from the mid-1930s, they continued their effort and emerged as a major force in public life after 1945. The division of Korea also split the membership along ideological and geographical lines. Ch'ǒndogyo now functions mainly as a religion, and has several million adherents in South Korea.

[See also Son Pyǒng-hǔi and Sǒhak.]

Yong Choon Kim, The Chondogyo Concept of Man: An Essence of Korean Thought (1978). Susan Shin, "The Tonghak Movement: From Enlightenment to Revolution," Korean Studies Forum 5 (1978–1979): 1–79. Benjamin Weems, Reform, Rebellion and the Heavenly Way (1964).   JAHYUN KIM HABOUSH

TONKIN. The name Tonkin, as it came to be used by Europeans, designates the area of northern Vietnam down to, but excluding, the province of Thanh Hoa. The common Vietnamese names for this region are Bac Bo and Bac Ky, or "northern region." The word Tonkin derives from Dong Kinh ("eastern capital"), the name given to present-day Hanoi by Emperor Le Thai Tong (r. 1428–1433). During the period of Vietnam's division between the Nguyen and Trinh families, Tonkin was the latter's power base. After the arrival of the French, the 1884 Patenotre Treaty established Tonkin as a protectorate within the colony of Indochina.

[See also Patenotre Treaty and Trinh-Nguyen Wars.]

BRUCE M. LOCKHART

TON THAT THUYET (1835–1913), powerful Vietnamese mandarin and resistance figure. Prominent in the violently "hawkish" anti-French faction in Tu Duc's court, he unsuccessfully attacked French troops on 5 July 1885 and then fled to Quang Tri Province with the young emperor Ham Nghi. From this refuge Ton issued a royal edict launching the Can Vuong movement. As resistance spread through central Vietnam, he departed for China to request aid, leaving his two sons to guard Ham Nghi. Failing in this mission and learning of the emperor's capture, Thuyet remained in China until his death in 1913.

[See also Tu Duc; Ham Nghi: and Can Vuong.]

David Marr, Vietnamese Anticolonialism, 1885–1925 (1971). Nguyen Phut Tan, Modern History of Vietnam 1802–1954 (1964).   BRUCE M. LOCKHART

TOOTH RELIC PALACE, generally known as the Dalada Maligawa, Sri Lanka's most important Buddhist temple. As described in the Dhatuvamsa, a Pali text, Shakyamuni's tooth relic was brought to the island in the fourth century CE. Subsequent kings erected temples to house it, the last situated in central Kandy, where the relic remains today. *Bhikkhus* (monks) worship the relic daily, and each year it is taken out on elephantback as part of the Asala Perahara procession.

[*See also* Buddhism; Kandy; *and* Sri Lanka.]

A. M. Hocart, *The Temple of the Tooth* (1931). H. L. Seneviratne, "The Asala Perahara in Kandy," in *Ceylon Journal of Historical and Social Studies* 6.2 (1963): 169–180.   TODD THORNTON LEWIS

TOSA, a province on the Japanese island of Shikoku, established in the seventh century as one of the six "southern circuit" *(nankaidō)* provinces; present-day Kōchi Prefecture retains its boundaries in most respects. In the Edo period the fan-shaped, mountainous province of Tosa was given in fief to the Yamauchi lineage by Tokugawa Ieyasu after the Battle of Sekigahara, the previous holder (Chōsokabe) having opted for the losing cause. Tosa, or Kōchi, domain was an integrated realm with natural mountain and maritime frontiers. Its assessed productivity, 202,600 *koku* (a *koku* equals about five bushels) of rice, made it nineteenth largest among the Tokugawa period domains, and its population grew to about one half million by late Tokugawa times.

Tosa played a major part in the politics of the Meiji Restoration and Meiji periods. It entered the period under an able daimyo, Yamuchi Toyoshige (Yōdō), who was forced into retirement by the *bakufu* minister Ii Naosuke. The Tosa Loyalist Party, organized by Takechi Zuizan, led the fief's administration into loyalist movements until its suppression by Toyoshige, who continued to dominate matters from retirement. It was Toyoshige who presented the last shogun with a plan for voluntary resignation of his powers that served as springboard to the politics of 1868.

In the Meiji period Tosa leaders parted company with their Satsuma and Chōshū counterparts to petition the throne for a constitution and a legislative assembly, and Kōchi became the birthplace of the People's Rights Movement (Jiyū Minken Undō). Prominent Tosa individuals in modern Japan include Iwasaki Yatarō, founder of the Mitsubishi enterprises, and Yoshida Shigeru, prewar diplomat and postwar prime minister.

[*See also* Meiji Restoration.]

Marius B. Jansen, *Sakamoto Ryōma and the Meiji Restoration* (1961).   MARIUS B. JANSEN

TOUNGOO DYNASTIES, Burmese dynasties (c. 1531–1752) that reunited the Irrawaddy River basin after centuries of fragmentation and founded a system of administration that survived with limited modifications to the eve of British colonial rule.

The Irrawaddy Valley had first experienced a degree of political integration under the northern-based Pagan dynasty (c. 1044–1287), but thereafter it had split into mutually hostile principalities. In the late fifteenth and sixteenth centuries, however, a combination of factors produced an unprecedented regional imbalance favorable to reunification under southern auspices: the north suffered from raids by uplanders and from the unrestricted growth of tax-free religious lands, while the south coast benefited from the expansion of inter-Asian maritime trade and from the appearance of Portuguese firearms. It was the achievement of the First Toungoo dynasty (c. 1531–1599) to exploit the ensuing potential for southern ascendancy. In the 1530s First Toungoo kings moved from the southeastern city of Toungoo to Pegu, the traditional capital of Lower Burma. Skillfully integrating Portuguese firearms with conventional forces, they then launched a program of systematic expansion designed inter alia to dominate rival coastal emporiums, to secure access to northern supplies of export commodities, and to gain control over military levies from the interior.

Between 1540 and 1570 all of modern Burma (save Arakan) and extensive areas in modern Manipur, Yunnan, Laos, and Siam came under loose Toungoo suzerainty. It was probably the largest empire in the history of western mainland Southeast Asia. Yet the vast extent of this domain, the primitive state of internal communciations, the lack of common ethnic traditions, and the personal, non-institutional nature of provincial supervision combined to render the First Toungoo empire exceptionally unstable. Toungoo kings became enmeshed in an endless series of punitive campaigns against outlying principalities, particularly Siam. The limited population around Pegu could not support the incessant demands for rice and military manpower, and in the 1590s the empire disintegrated.

With Lower Burma severely disorganized, the political center of gravity now returned to the interior of the Irrawaddy basin. Nyaungyan Min, a minor son of the penultimate king of the First Toungoo dynasty, founded a new line—the Restored Toungoo (or Nyaungyan) dynasty—which lasted from 1597 to 1752. After subduing Lower Burma and the more accessible upland regions, Nyaungyan Min and his sons (who succeeded him on the throne to 1648) made four changes of prime importance in the First Toungoo system. They relinquished claims to Siam and Laos, which had been a source of endless vexation (thus for the first time dynastic Burma approximated the area of the modern Union of Burma); they retained their capital at Ava in Upper Burma, which was traditionally the most productive and populous sector of the Irrawaddy basin; they increased the concentration of hereditary military specialists around the capital; and they overhauled the system of provincial administration so as to reduce the functional autonomy and sovereign attributes of regional heads.

The net effect of these innovations—possibly reinforced by a long-term decline in religious landholdings—was to centralize imperial institutions and to permit a more efficient integration of interior and coastal resources. Henceforth Toungoo kings could remain in the Upper Burma heartland without jeopardizing access to the firearms and trade revenues of the coast. At the same time there is evidence that the continued expansion of maritime and domestic commerce during the long period of internal peace, and the importation of New World silver via the ports, facilitated economic integration throughout the lowlands. This further eroded regional loyalties, which had begun to weaken in the First Toungoo era, and contributed to the success of the centralizing reforms.

Although the Restored Toungoo dynasty endured for more than twice as long as the First Toungoo and was appreciably more stable, in the late seventeenth and eighteenth centuries the administration came under strain from severe intraelite rivalries and cumulative weaknesses in the system of popular organization. Large numbers of royal soldiers abandoned their assigned units in favor of more sheltered status in the private service of powerful court figures. As the strength and morale of military units declined, outlying principalities, including Manipur and Pegu, exploited Ava's difficulties to launch a series of attacks on Upper Burma. These culminated in Pegu's sack of Ava and the capture of the last Toungoo king in 1752. Nonetheless the Restored Toungoo administrative system itself was quickly revived by the successor Konbaung dynasty, and it apparently continued without major reform until the First Anglo-Burmese War of 1824.

[See also Anaukhpetlun; Bayinnaung; Nandabayin; Pyu; Tabinshweihti; and the map accompanying Ayudhya.]

G. E. Harvey, A History of Burma from the Earliest Times (1925; reprint, 1967). Victor B. Lieberman, Burmese Administrative Cycles: Anarchy and Conquest, c. 1580–1760 (1984). Maung Htin Aung, A History of Burma (1967).
VICTOR B. LIEBERMAN

TOWER OF SILENCE, known as *dakhma* in Persian, an enclosed, amphitheater-like stone structure in which the corpses of Zoroastrians are deposited to be eaten by birds of prey. In keeping with the injunctions of the Avesta to protect earth and water from pollution by corpse matter, which is believed to be demon infested, Zoroastrians shun interment; cremation would pollute the sacred creation of fire. In Sasanid times and earlier, corpses were exposed in open, stony places to birds and wild animals; the clean, dry bones were often then interred in ossuaries. It seems that the enclosed structures (*tower of silence* is a modern and unscholarly term) were made mainly after the Islamic conquest to prevent desecration by nonbelievers. Today, Zoroastrians in the West generally bury their dead in impregnable coffins; but the Parsis of India maintain the old custom, and there are several towers of silence on Malabar, a thickly wooded hill in central Bombay.

[See also Zoroastrianism.]

Mary Boyce, History of Zoroastrianism, vol. 1 (1975). J. J. Modi, Religious Ceremonies and Customs of the Parsees (2d ed., 1936).
JAMES R. RUSSELL

TŌYAMA MITSURU (1855–1944), Fukuoka samurai who played a leading role in ultranationalist and expansionist activities in modern Japan. Fukuoka's proximity to the Asian mainland, its relatively backward and coal-based economy, and its political discontents made it a birthplace of right-wing organizations. Tōyama's early sympathies were with the cause of Saigō Takamori and holdouts for samurai privileges and values; his next involvement was with organizations that mushroomed in connection with the People's Rights Movement (Jiyū Minken Undō). It was with the Genyōsha (named for the straits that separate Kyushu from the continent, 1881) and the Kokuryūkai (Amur River, or Black Dragon, Society, 1901), that he found his proper niche. Tōyama and his friends had contacts at all levels of Japanese society, as agitation for treaty reform, against headlong westernization, and against Russia provided occasions for meetings and pronouncements. In addition he was a prominent "Asia-first" spokesman, calling for the cultivation of anti-imperialist and nationalist movements and leaders in other Asian countries and helping those leaders take refuge in Japan when necessary.

[*See also* Jiyū Minken *and* Kokuryūkai.]

Marius B. Jansen, *The Japanese and Sun Yat-sen* (1954). Richard Storry, *The Double Patriots: A Study of Japanese Nationalism* (1957).   MARIUS B. JANSEN

TOYOTOMI HIDEYOSHI

TOYOTOMI HIDEYOSHI (1536–1598), Japanese military leader and national ruler. The son of a farmer and part-time soldier, Toyotomi Hideyoshi governed all Japan by the time of his death. This unprecedented rise from obscurity to national power, together with the flamboyance that accompanied his achievements, made him a major subject of legend and one of the heroes of traditional Japanese history. Hideyoshi is best known as a master military strategist who, through conquest and conciliation, unified the competing warlords of the sixteenth century and thus brought to a close well over one hundred years of civil war in Japan. Equally important was his role as a peacetime governor who forged a political settlement that would serve as the basis of orderly national rule until the nineteenth century. Sometimes described as a megalomaniac (who twice invaded Korea and envisioned the conquest of China), Hideyoshi was a complex ruler of vaulting ambition and theatrical style.

Hideyoshi began his career, at the age of fifteen, as a minor attendant in the army of Imagawa Yoshimoto of Suruga—one of scores of provincial warlords struggling for regional, and ultimately national, hegemony. By 1558 Hideyoshi had entered the service of Oda Nobunaga, a daimyo from Owari who spearheaded the drive toward national unification by taking the capital of Kyoto in 1568 and conquering one-third of the nation's land before his assassination in 1582. [See Oda Nobunaga.] Hideyoshi rose quickly within the Oda ranks to become both a leading general, conducting Oda campaigns throughout western Honshu, and a consequential fief holder, with castles and large holdings in Harima and Ōmi provinces. He acquired nationwide power in the years following Nobunaga's death first by consolidating his hold over the Oda coalition and then by mounting enormous campaigns of conquest in Shikoku (1585), Kyushu (1587), and the Kantō and the northeastern provinces (1590). Hideyoshi and his deputies led up to 250,000 soldiers, including thousands of infantrymen equipped with muskets.

Essential to Hideyoshi's success were peaceful alliances with potential opponents in the Mōri, Kobayakawa, Maeda, Uesugi, and Date houses. Such alliances, which both swelled his armies and freed Hideyoshi from an additional sequence of possibly crippling offensives, were founded upon Hideyoshi's commitment to a division of power. He established a federal model of rule by vesting virtually full governing authority over local domains in his daimyo allies, in his own deputies of daimyo rank, and even in central major adversaries who had been defeated in battles against the Toyotomi. Departing from the centrist and absolutist tendencies of the Oda regime, Hideyoshi built his settlement upon the sturdy dominal foundation formed during the Sengoku ("warring states") period (1467–1590). Hideyoshi's daimyo numbered approximately two hundred at the time of his death.

As national ruler, Hideyoshi reserved to himself jurisdiction over the public sector—mine resources, large cities and ports, foreign relations and international trade, weights, measures, and coinage. He eradicated piracy and initiated the persecution of Christians. Hideyoshi also exercised ultimate jurisdiction over the daimyo, whom he vested with land, transferred on occasion, and disciplined (normally through attainder) in cases of treason or malfeasance; from whom he exacted hostages, military service, labor, and various forms of tribute and homage; and whose secondary fortifications he dismantled, marriages he monitored, and private alliances he proscribed. Yet it was, finally, in the area of public pacification that Hideyoshi exerted a definitive influence upon the future of his nation. In sweeping edicts issued in a magisterial tone, he ordered the disarmament of all farmers (1588), the separation of the population into farming, townsman, and military classes whose members were forbidden changes either of station or residence, and the withdrawal of all soldiers from agrarian villages (1591). Through these initiatives, and particularly through the transformation of formerly enfeoffed warriors into stipendiaries largely confined to dominal castle towns, Hideyoshi engineered a social revolution, intending to eliminate the sources of endemic disorder.

Vital to the implementation of Hideyoshi's polity were standard, systematic, and nationwide cadastral surveys (the Taikō *kenchi*) that produced registers of cultivators and village holdings defined according to size, type and condition, and value (a statement of total annual productivity made uniformly in terms of a rice equivalence, or *kokudaka*).

Drawing upon the associations of the imperial

court with ultimate and universal authority, Hideyoshi governed not under military but under traditional courtly titles—those of *kampaku* (imperial regent, acquired in 1585), *daijō daijin* (great minister of state, 1586), and *taikō* (retired imperial regent, used after 1591, when Hideyoshi transferred the *kampaku* title to his nephew). He built major castle headquarters in Osaka, Fushimi, and in Kyoto, where he undertook monumental construction and reconstruction projects that ranged from repair of the imperial palace and monasteries that had been destroyed during war to the erection of an outer city rampart, new boulevards, a massive Buddhist icon housed in the temple of Hōkōji, and his own residence, called Jurakutei. Hideyoshi also conducted an elaborate ceremonial life (including a five-day entertainment of the emperor at Jurakutei, a tea party for several thousand members of the public at Kitano shrine, and an enormous gathering of daimyo for cherry blossom viewing at Daigo temple) through which he projected personal power and the ambition of his regime. That regime remained focused, however, upon the person and personality of Hideyoshi himself and saw little development of administrative institutions. Governing through his daimyo at both the domainal and the national level, Hideyoshi never built a central bureaucracy, instituted a national system of taxation, or disbanded the domainal armies of his confederates.

During his last years, Hideyoshi mounted two invasions of Korea in anticipation of conquering China (1592 and 1597), ordered sensational executions of his nephew and the tea master Sen no Rikyū, and condemned twenty-six Christians to die by crucifixion in Nagasaki. [*See* Hideyoshi's Invasion of Korea *and* Sen no Rikyū.] Such actions have raised questions about his sanity late in life but may be interpreted as efforts to extirpate potential threats at home, to widen his dominion abroad, and thus to secure the succession of his child heir. In fact, Tokugawa Ieyasu, a member of the council of elders appointed by Hideyoshi to protect the heir, seized power for himself in the years after 1600. Hideyoshi was deified with the title Hōkoku Daimyōjin ("most bright god of the bountiful country") shortly after his death in 1598.

[*See also* Momoyama Period; Sengoku Period; *and* Tokugawa Ieyasu.]

Mary Elizabeth Berry, *Hideyoshi* (1982). Adriana Boscaro, trans., *101 Letters of Hideyoshi* (1975). Walter Dening, *The Life of Toyotomi Hideyoshi* (1930). George Elison and Bardwell L. Smith, eds., *Warlords, Artists, and Commoners: Japan in the Sixteenth Century* (1981). John W. Hall, *Government and Local Power in Japan, 500 to 1700* (1966). Nagahara Keiji and Kozo Yamamura, eds., *Japan Before Tokugawa: Political Consolidation and Economic Growth, 1500 to 1650* (1981).

MARY ELIZABETH BERRY

TOZAMA DAIMYO ("outer lords"), Tokugawa-period (1600–1868) daimyo (feudal lords) of Japan whose status had been acquired prior to 1600, and who, as a result of their oath of allegiance to Tokugawa Ieyasu (1542–1616) following the decisive Battle of Sekigahara (1600), were viewed with suspicion by the shogunate and excluded from participation in the shogunal bureaucracy.

Geographically, the *tozama* daimyo domains were primarily located on the peripheries of the archipelago (extreme northern and western Honshu, Kyushu, and Shikoku), and were thus among the farthest from the shogunal capital at Edo, a reality institutionalized by much of the post-Sekigahara geopolitical restructuring of the archipelago.

In 1602, of 195 daimyo, 119 were *tozama;* by 1853, the number had shrunk to 96 out of a total of 265 daimyo. In terms of size, the *tozama* domains were among the largest in Japan. (Productivity was assessed by the central bureaucracy in terms of *koku,* a measure of rice equal to about five bushels; see table 1.) By contrast, the largest *shimpan* ("related") daimyo domain was that of the Tokugawa of Nagoya (619,000 *koku*), while the largest *fudai* ("inner") daimyo was the Ii house of Hikone (350,000 *koku*).

Like the *shimpan* and *fudai* daimyo, the *tozama* were also subjected to the control mechanisms generated by the Tokugawa to perpetuate their hegemony, the most onerous of which was the alternate attendance (*sankin kōtai*) system. It required daimyo

TABLE 1. *Tozama Daimyo*

DAIMYO	INCOME (in *koku*)	CASTLE TOWN
Maeda	1,200,000	Kanazawa
Shimazu	770,000	Kagoshima
Date	625,000	Sendai
Hosokawa	540,000	Kumamoto
Kuroda	520,000	Fukuoka
Asano	426,000	Hiroshima
Mori	369,000	Hagi
Nabeshima	357,000	Saga
Todo	323,000	Tsu
Ikeda	305,000	Okayama
Hachisuka	257,000	Tokushima

to spend alternate twelve-month periods in Edo (usually from summer to summer) in attendance on the shogun. For the *tozama* daimyo this attendance was nothing more than a simple ritual conducted in Chiyoda Castle in Edo, in which the *tozama* were assigned seats for ceremonial purposes in the Willow Hall (seventy-six seats in 1853) and in the Great Hall (nineteen seats in 1853). Seating in these halls was reserved for daimyo of little political significance, and the inclusion of the *tozama* reflected their exclusion from national politics because of Tokugawa suspicions concerning their loyalty. [*See* Sankin Kōtai.]

Given their treatment at the hands of the Tokugawa shogunate, it seems only natural that the ranks of the *tozama* daimyo and their retainers would provide much of the leadership of the anti-Tokugawa movement of the 1850s and 1860s that toppled the regime in 1868. Shimazu Hisamitsu (1817–1887) of Satsuma, Yamanouchi Yōdō (1827–1872) of Tosa, and the Mōri of Chōshū were all *tozama* daimyo who played important roles in the Meiji Restoration of 1868, together with such of their retainers as Sakamoto Ryōma (1835–1867) of Tosa, Saigō Takamori (1827–1877) and Ōkubo Toshimichi (1830–1878) of Satsuma, and Yoshida Shōin (1830–1859), Kido Kōin (1833–1877), and Itō Hirobumi (1841–1909) of Chōshū. Indeed, men from Satsuma and Chōshū would continue to dominate Japanese history into the twentieth century.

[*See also* Sekigahara, Battle of; Satsuma; Chōshū; Tosa; *and* Meiji Restoration.]

Albert Craig, *Chōshū in the Meiji Restoration* (1961). H. D. Harootunian, *Toward Restoration: The Growth of Political Consciousness in Tokugawa Japan* (1970). Conrad Totman, *Politics in the Tokugawa Bakufu, 1600–1843* (1967).   RONALD J. DiCENZO

TRAILOK. *See* Borommatrailokanat.

TRAN DYNASTY, rulers of Dai Viet (1225–1400). The Tran were descended from Chinese fishermen who settled on the seacoast of the Red River delta in the eleventh century. Their rise to power began in 1208, when the future emperor Ly Hue Tong married a Tran wife, who in 1217 was made empress. Hue Tong retired to a monastery in 1224, leaving the throne to his seven-year-old daughter, Chieu Hoang. Chief Minister Tran Thu Do, head of the Tran family, then announced the betrothal of the child empress to his nephew Tran Canh. Chieu

Hoang transferred power to her husband the following year, thus initiating the Tran dynasty.

The Tran ruled Dai Viet like a family estate. Their court was made up of close relatives, with the chief posts and top military commands being held by Tran princes, who also held the strategically most important areas of the country as fiefs (*thai ap*).

To guard against the infiltration of the clan by outsiders, the Tran practiced endogamous marriage. The principal wives of the designated heirs were always chosen from among the descendants of Tran Canh's elder brother, Tran Lieu.

Another distinctive practice of the Tran, begun to assure orderly successions, was the abdication of the reigning emperor in favor of his heir when the latter achieved his majority. The retired ruler became *thai thuong hoang* ("senior emperor"), continuing to shape policy but gradually relinquishing power as the new emperor gained experience.

The early Tran were vigorous and able rulers. They were particularly interested in economic development, opening new lands to cultivation and building flood-control works, but they also took care to increase and reorganize the armed forces and to expand the administrative apparatus of the state. As a result of these policies, Dai Viet suffered but one famine before 1285, fought a successful war with Champa (1252), and defeated a Mongol expedition (1257).

Scholars learned in the Chinese classics gained increased prestige at court by their successful handling of relations between Dai Viet and the Mongols from 1258 to 1284. This did not presage a growth of Confucian influence over the Viet rulers, however. One of the distinguishing characteristics of the Tran emperors was their devotion to Buddhism. Both Thai Tong (Tran Canh, r. 1225–1258) and his grandson Nhan Tong (r. 1279–1293) wrote Buddhist texts, and the latter was one of the founders of the Truc Lam sect of Thien (Zen) Buddhism. Tran Minh Tong (r. 1314–1329) and Nghe Tong (r. 1370–1372) specifically rejected petitions from their officials calling for the enactment of more Confucian-style measures.

The events for which the Tran dynasty has most often been remembered are the successful resistances to the Mongol invasions of 1285 and 1287–1288. Under the leadership of Tran Quoc Tuan (Tran Hung Dao), the Viet armies were able to recover from initial defeats, fight protracted campaigns of harassment, and crush the weakened Mongol forces in a series of ambushes, most notably at the Bach Dang River (9 April 1288).

TABLE 1. *Emperors of the Tran Dynasty*

EMPEROR	REIGN DATES
1. Tran Thai Tong (Tran Canh)	1225–1258
2. Tran Thanh Tong	1258–1279
3. Tran Nhan Tong	1279–1293
4. Tran Anh Tong	1293–1314
5. Tran Minh Tong	1314–1329
6. Tran Hien Tong	1329–1341
7. Tran Du Tong	1341–1369
Duong Nhat Le (interregnum)	1369–1370*
8. Tran Nghe Tong	1370–1373
9. Tran Due Tong	1373–1377*
10. Tran Nghien De (Phe De)	1377–1388*
11. Tran Thuan Tong	1388–1398*
12. Tran An Tong (Thieu De)	1398–1400*

*Deposed.

The economic recovery of Dai Viet after the Mongol wars was vitiated by the rapid growth of the Tran family. Princely and monastic estates grew more rapidly than new lands could be brought into cultivation, making peasant landlessness a serious problem by the early fourteenth century. This problem was exacerbated by a series of natural disasters: floods, famines, and epidemics, which by the 1340s led to an unprecedented outbreak of peasant unrest.

In the mid-fourteenth century the Tran were again faced with external attack. Champa, taking advantage of the disorder within Dai Viet, began a series of increasingly damaging raids on Viet territory, first in the contested region north of the Hai Van Pass (which had been ceded to Dai Viet in 1306 in exchange for a short-lived marriage alliance), and later on the Red River delta itself.

The Tran rulers proved incapable of dealing with these crises. After the retirement of Minh Tong in 1329, the court became increasingly corrupt and Tran rule more inefficient, especially during the reign of Du Tong (1341–1369). Nghe Tong brought his ambitious cousin Le (Ho) Quy Ly into the government in 1371. Quy Ly gradually increased his power, married into the Tran family, and deposed the last three Tran rulers, finally proclaiming the Ho dynasty in 1400.

After the overthrow of the Ho by the Chinese in 1407, two Tran descendants mounted an ineffective resistance to the Chinese occupation between 1407 and 1413. This resistance is sometimes referred to as the Later Tran dynasty.

[See also Bach Dang, Battles of; Champa; Chu Van An; Confucianism in Vietnam; Dai Viet; Ho Dynasty; Ly Dynasty; Nam Tien; Tran Hung Dao; Tran Nhan Tong; Tran Thai Tong; Tran Thanh Tong; Tran Thu Do; *and* Vietnam.]

Thomas Hodgkin, *Vietnam: The Revolutionary Path* (1981).

JAMES M. COYLE

TRAN HUNG DAO (Tran Quoc Tuan, c. 1221–1300), Viet general most responsible for the defeat of the massive Mongol invasions of Dai Viet in 1285 and 1287–1288. He was the son of Tran Lieu, the older brother of the first Tran emperor, Thai Tong. The date of his birth is not recorded.

Viet tradition holds that Tran Quoc Tuan demonstrated qualities of leadership at a very early age, but he does not appear in the historical record until 1251, when he compromised his cousin, the Thien Thanh princess, so that she might be given to him in marriage, instead of to the husband chosen for her by her father, the emperor.

In 1257 he was charged with the defense of the borders of Dai Viet against the first Mongol attack. What part he played in the eventual Viet victory is not known. He became commander of all Viet forces in 1283.

Early in 1285, with a second Mongol invasion imminent, he issued an *Appeal to Officers (Hich tuong si)* that Vietnamese historians claim was very important in raising the morale of the army. He was also a major participant in the Dien Hong Conference (January 1285), at which the decision was taken to oppose the Mongols by force.

As a commander, his most important attribute was flexibility. When his initial attempt at a forward defense of the capital was overwhelmed (February–March 1285), he adopted a strategy of protracted resistance and harassment that proved so successful that the northern and southern Mongol invasion forces were defeated before they could unite (battles of Ham Tu, Chuong Duong, and Tay Ket; May 1285). The retreating Mongols fell into repeated ambushes and were utterly routed.

The third Mongol invasion, a combined attack by land and sea, was defeated by the same strategy. The Viet armies withdrew until their harassing tactics and the effects of the climate had weakened the Mongols. The Viet then took the offensive, even as the Mongols were deciding to withdraw. A large Mongol contingent attempting to retreat by water was ambushed and annihilated in the Bach Dang estuary, in a battle personally led by Quoc Tuan. The Mongol land forces, retreating in the direction of Lang Son, were repeatedly attacked and suffered enormous losses. After these defeats, the Mongols attempted no further invasions of Dai Viet.

For his triumph over the Mongol armies Tran Quoc Tuan received the title of Hung Dao Vuong in 1288; he is therefore often called Tran Hung Dao. He retired to his home at Van Kiep after the Mongol wars and died there on 15 August 1300. His intelligence, courage, integrity, and conspicuous loyalty to the Tran dynasty led Viet authors to cite him as the ideal of an imperial subject.

In addition to the *Hich tuong si*, Tran Quoc Tuan was the author of two works on military strategy, the *Binh thu yeu luoc (Essentials of Military Strategy)*, part of which has survived to the present, and the *Van Kiep ton bi truyen thu (Mysterious Tactics of Van Kiep)*, no longer extant.

[*See also* Bach Dang, Battles of; Tran Dynasty; Tran Nhan Tong; Tran Thai Tong; *and* Tran Thu Do.]

Thomas Hodgkin, *Vietnam: The Revolutionary Path* (1981).   JAMES M. COYLE

TRAN NHAN TONG, third Tran emperor of Dai Viet (r. 1278–1293). Most of his reign was spent fighting the Mongols who invaded in 1285 and 1287. After the 1285 Dien Hong Conference confirmed the Viet people's will to resist, Tran Hung Dao led troops against the Mongols, although the emperor was forced temporarily to take refuge in Thanh Hoa. The Mongols were defeated, and in 1287 Nhan Tong sent a peace mission to Beijing. He then turned his attention to the widespread famine caused by the fighting, which he was able to alleviate only partly. In 1293 he abdicated, later to found a Buddhist sect.

[*See also* Tran Dynasties *and* Tran Hung Dao.]

Thomas Hodgkin, *Vietnam: The Revolutionary Path* (1981).   BRUCE M. LOCKHART

TRAN QUOC TUAN. *See* Tran Hung Dao.

TRAN QUY CAP (1870–1908), Vietnamese scholar and enthusiastic advocate of *tan hoc* ("new learning"). Although a holder of the highest traditional degrees, he actively opposed those mandarins who continued to support the program of classical learning (*cuu hoc*). Together with fellow scholar Huynh Thuc Khang, he joined Phan Chu Trinh in calling for institutional reforms, particularly in education, and worked to set up schools using French and *quoc ngu* script. Although less involved with anticolonial activities, he was found to have expressed approval of the 1908 riots in his province of Quang Nam and was executed.

[*See also* Phan Chu Trinh.]

William J. Duiker, *The Rise of Nationalism in Vietnam, 1900–1941* (1976). David Marr, *Vietnamese Anticolonialism 1885–1925* (1971).   BRUCE M. LOCKHART

TRANS-IRANIAN RAILWAY, 850-mile railroad that traverses Iran from the Caspian Sea to the Persian Gulf. The Trans-Iranian Railway was constructed between 1927 and 1938 during the reign of Reza Shah, who regularly inspected its progress and personally supervised some of the work. The railroad was financed by special taxes levied upon tea and sugar. In addition, in 1925 the Majles (parliament) granted a monopoly to the government for the purchase, sale, and distribution of all sugar and tea. The Trans-Iranian Railway is noted for its feats of engineering: in one stretch of only 1.5 miles the railway has 127 tunnels. During World War II the railroad was commandeered by the Allied forces and used for shipments of weapons and provisions from the United States to the Soviet Union.

[*See also* Pahlavi, Reza.]

Peter Avery, *Modern Iran* (1965), pp. 300–303. Amin Banani, *The Modernization of Iran, 1921–1941* (1961), pp. 133–135.   ERIC HOOGLUND

TRAN THAI TONG, first Tran emperor of Dai Viet (r. 1225–1258). Brought to the throne by the machinations of Tran Thu Do (1194–1264) against Ly emperor Hue Tong (1210–1224), Thai Tong later tried to renounce power and become a monk. His reign, with the counsel of Tran Thu Do, saw the implementation of numerous administrative and military reforms, as well as a revamping of the mandarinate examination system. In 1257–1258 he sent Tran Hung Dao to defeat a Mongol invasion and then set a dynastic precedent by abdicating in favor of his chosen heir, Emperor Thanh Tong (1258–1278).

[*See also* Tran Dynasties; Tran Hung Dao; *and* Tran Thanh Tong.]

Thomas Hodgkin, *Vietnam: The Revolutionary Path* (1981).   BRUCE M. LOCKHART

TRAN THANH TONG, second Tran emperor of Dai Viet (r. 1258–1278). He took the throne after the abdication of his father, Thai Tong (1225–

1258). During his reign the nation's army was strengthened and reorganized, principally because of the Mongol threat, although this menace was neutralized by his acknowledgment of Yuan-dynasty suzerainty. He also enacted laws allowing aristocrats to set up large estates and hire the landless to work them. Himself a scholar, Thanh Tong also ordered the compilation of Le Van Huu's great history, *Dai Viet su ky*. In 1278 he abdicated in favor of his son Nhan Tong (1278–1293).

[*See also* Tran Dynasties; Tran Nhan Tong; *and* Tran Thai Tong.]

Thomas Hodgkin, *Vietnam: The Revoultionary Path* (1981).   BRUCE M. LOCKHART

TRAN THU DO (1194–1264), minister and adviser to Tran emperors Thai Tong (1225–1258) and Thanh Tong (1258–1278). As regent to former emperor Ly Hue Tong's young daughter, Tran forced her to marry the future Tran Thai Tong. After establishing the Tran dynasty, he compelled Ly Hue Tong to commit suicide and murdered the rest of the former imperial family. Thai Tong, disgusted by his minister's actions, fled the court but was persuaded by Tran Thu Do to return. A powerful figure under the early Tran, Tran Thu Do directed the restructuring of the mandarinate and the military as well as the promulgation of a new penal code.

[*See also* Tran Thai Tong *and* Tran Dynasty.]

Thomas Hodgkin, *Vietnam: The Revoultionary Path* (1981).   BRUCE M. LOCKHART

TRAN TRONG KIM (1887–1953), prominent Vietnamese historian and prime minister of the Japanese-sponsored state under Emperor Bao Dai (April–August 1945). Tran and his cabinet of intellectuals, although not strictly anti-French, were committed to the survival of an independent Vietnam after the war. However, his government faced many crises, including famine in Annam and Tonkin, and attempts to consolidate its authority "were doomed by circumstances and through Japanese obstruction" (Buttinger, p. 293). Increasingly frustrated in his efforts, and denounced by the Viet Minh as a Japanese puppet, Tran resigned with his cabinet several days before Bao Dai abdicated on 25 August 1945.

[*See also* Bao Dai *and* Viet Minh.]

Joseph Buttinger, *Vietnam: A Dragon Embattled* (1967).   BRUCE M. LOCKHART

TRAVANCORE. Situated on the narrow western coastal plain, Travancore was the southernmost princely state in India. Its rulers traced their descent from the ancient Chera dynasty but the consolidation of modern Travancore occurred in the first half of the eighteenth century under the direction of Raja Marthanada Varma. In 1750 he dedicated his state to Sri Padmanabha, his family deity, and he and his successors claimed to rule as servants of Sri Padmanabha. Another unique feature of the Travancore dynasty was their adherence to the law of inheritance through the female line. A maharaja was succeeded either by his brother or by his sister's eldest son. In 1795 Travancore became an ally of the British during the British wars with Mysore.

Travancore had the highest rate of literacy in India, an early growth of popular political associations, and, since 1905, a legislative assembly. In 1949 it joined the Union of Travancore and Cochin in independent India and in 1956 this union along with the Malabar districts of Madras merged to form Kerala state.

[*See also* Kerala *and* Princely States.]

Robin Jeffrey, *The Decline of Nayar Dominance: Society and Politics in Travancore, 1847–1908* (1976). P. K. K. Menon, *The History of Freedom Movement in Kerala*, 2 vols. (1970).   BARBARA N. RAMUSACK

TREATY PORTS. The term *treaty ports* is almost synonymous with *open ports* (ports open to foreign trade) in China, which in many respects embodied foreign imperialism from 1842 to 1943. The existence of the ports had long-range effects on China and symbolized China's reorientation to the West. Strictly speaking, treaty ports were Chinese port cities that were opened by unequal treaties to foreign residence and trade. In addition, there were many other ports opened by China herself. Thus, *open ports* is a more inclusive term for both types of ports. The Chinese called them "trading marts" (*shangbu*) or "trading ports" (*tongshang kouan*), because some of these open ports are not sea or even river ports, but inland cities.

In all, a total of seventy-three treaty ports were established. By the Treaty of Nanjing in 1842, the five southeast China coastal seaports of Guangzhou (Canton), Xiamen (Amoy), Fuzhou, Ningbo, and Shanghai were first thrown open. Between 1858 and 1861 ten more treaty ports were opened, including places in North China (Tianjin) and Manchuria (Niuzhuang), on Taiwan (Danshui), and up the Yangtze River as far as Hankou. During the last two decades of the nineteenth century southwest China also was brought into contact with the outside commercial world by the opening up of six inland cities in addition to other new ports. The vast territory of Manchuria was next forced to open at the turn of the century. Realizing the benefit of trade and taxation, China from 1898 voluntarily opened thirty-two trade marts, such as Qinhuangdao, Wusong, Yuezhou, Ji'nan, and Nanning. Twenty-five "ports of call," at which foreign steamships were privileged to visit, also were established on the Yangtze River and the West River.

Foreign "concessions" or "settlements" were usually established in open ports by Chinese authorities as residential areas for foreigners. This practice started in the mid-nineteenth century when areas of land in the treaty ports were leased in perpetuity by the foreign governments, which paid modest ground rents annually to the Chinese government. Within these leased areas the foreign consulates in turn granted ninety-nine-year leases to land renters. Under extraterritoriality they also exercised legal jurisdiction over their own nationals. In most concessions the right to set up and maintain local administrative agencies for police purposes, sanitation, road construction, and so forth was given to the foreign government concerned. The administrative organs created for these purposes (e.g., the Shanghai Municipal Council) levied taxes, including taxes on Chinese residents without representation.

Thus, the treaty ports became semiforeign cities run by the local foreign land renters under the protection of their treaty rights of extraterritoriality. Nationals of small countries secured extraterritorial privileges by becoming protégés of powerful consulates. For example, the French consuls, rather than the Chinese government, exercised jurisdiction in China over citizens of Monaco, Persia, and Rumania. What had begun as a legal device mainly to protect Western individuals against the old Chinese legal practice gradually became more a device to protect foreign business from Chinese taxation. Western nationals were subject to their country's consular court and could be sued by Chinese plaintiffs only in that court. The Shanghai Mixed Court, with a Chinese and a foreigner as cojudges, handled cases in which Chinese were the defendants and cases between local Chinese. China's sovereignty was therefore seriously infringed upon in the foreign quarters of the major cities.

The treaty ports were mainly economic centers through which foreign goods flowed to China. Because the aim of the foreign traders from the very beginning was to tap the well-developed Chinese distribution system, the treaty ports were generally located on the coast or on rivers navigable by ocean-going steamers, serving as entrance points into the traditional network of Chinese waterborne communications. In addition, foreign settlements usually arose beside the walls of existing major Chinese trade centers. The treaty ports virtually monopolized China's growing foreign trade and became centers of modern commercial institutions such as banking, finance, and insurance. By the beginning of the twentieth century the treaty ports were also centers of industrial development, including arsenals, factories, steamships, and railroads.

The treaty ports rapidly grew to be China's major urban centers where new groups of people emerged: merchants, compradors, entrepreneurs, and bankers. These nouveau riche Chinese in the treaty ports made up a new type of elite who symbolized the rise of the middle class. With the single exception of Beijing, by the 1930s all of the other largest cities—Shanghai, Tianjin, Wuhan, Nanjing, Chongqing, and Shenyang—were treaty ports where new opportunities and lush wealth were accompanied by poverty and crime.

Politically, from the very beginning of the treaty ports there emerged a new type of "treaty-port mandarin." Such "barbarian experts" as Wu Jianzhang and Ding Richang handled the new foreign relations in the treaty ports and made their careers outside the regular official system. The Chinese revolutionaries found havens in the foreign settlements where Chinese police could not operate. It is not surprising that the Republican Revolution started in Wuhan (1911) and that the Chinese Communist Party was founded in Shanghai (1921).

What had begun in the 1840s as a system to control some 350 foreigners in five ports came eventually, in the twentieth century, to include 105 open ports, 25 "ports of call," and about 300,000 foreign residents. At the height of the Chinese "rights recovery" movement in the 1920s and 1930s, Chinese representatives were added to the Shanghai Municipal Council, the Shanghai Mixed Court was supplanted by a purely Chinese district court, and the number of foreign settlements was reduced from thirty-three to thirteen by 1933. The influence of the treaty ports diminished after 1937, when the large-scale Japanese invasion of China started, and the treaty-port system came to a formal end in 1943 when the unequal treaties were replaced by new, equal treaties.

There are three broad interpretations concerning

the historical significance of the treaty ports. The first is that of the "school of imperialism," which believes that the treaty ports embodied foreign exploitation of China both economically and spiritually, and cites such factors as extraterritoriality, foreign settlements, opium trade, the treaty tariff, the coolie trade, and foreign rights of inland navigation, proselytism, and industrialism. Specifically, the treaty ports invited foreign economic intrusion that drained China's economy of its wealth, stifled Chinese-owned modern enterprises, upset China's traditionally self-sufficient economy, and led to the economic ruin of the peasantry.

The second interpretation is that of the "school of modernization," which stresses the positive role of the treaty ports. The scholars of modernization maintain that the treaty ports performed certain important historical functions in China's long-term development because they created the "external economies" (the modern commercial, financial, and communication networks), provided a training ground for Chinese technical personnel and entrepreneurship, and served as a means for mobilizing savings and channeling them into investment in modern enterprises. China's modernization was helped, too, by the social and intellectual innovations in the treaty ports such as newspapers, schools, libraries, hospitals, the legal concepts of incorporation and limited liability, and, more importantly, nationalism.

The "school of isolation" offers a third interpretation. This thesis holds that the influence of the treaty ports on China was limited because the treaty ports, for all their imperialistic and modernizing effects, remained isolated centers in China. In contrast to the treaty ports, the hinterland was vast in size, self-sufficient, and inaccessible, with traditions of intellectual orthodoxy, civil government, and familism devoted to preserving the ongoing Confucian social order. Because China was never colonized, its traditional system remained vigorous, and it was generally successful in checking the influence of the treaty ports on her interior.

Whatever the influence of the former treaty ports might be, they are highly visible in China today. Shanghai, Guangzhou, Xiamen, and Shantou, for instance, have figured prominently in China's ambitious Four Modernizations project. To attract foreign capital and technology, the People's Republic of China in April 1984 opened fourteen coastal port cities to foreign trade and investment; eleven of these are former treaty ports. China was not remade in the image of the treaty ports, but they did play, and will probably continue to play, an important role in its quest for modernity.

[See also Arrow War; Canton; China Trade; Compradors; Imperialism; Maritime Customs Service; and Qing Dynasty.]

John K. Fairbank, *Trade and Diplomacy on the China Coast: The Opening of the Treaty Ports, 1842–1854* (1953). Hsiao-t'ung Fei, *Peasant Life in China* (1939). Yen-p'ing Hao, *The Commercial Revolution in Nineteenth-Century China: The Rise of Sino-Western Mercantile Capitalism* (1985). Rhoads Murphey, *The Treaty Ports and China's Modernization: What Went Wrong?* (1970).
                                    YEN-P'ING HAO

TRENGGANU, Malaysian state. While it was physically close to areas of strong Thai influence, Trengganu succeeded in maintaining the Malay traditions characteristic of the southern peninsula centers of Melaka and Johor. Its adherence to Malay culture contributed to its success in remaining politically independent of Thailand. Unlike several other Malay polities, Trengganu was not centered on one major river but extended from Besut to Kemaman, encompassing a series of rivers flowing down the east coast of the peninsula to the South China Sea. Thus, the local chiefs at the periphery of the state had considerable autonomy. Trengganu's comparative isolation and underdeveloped export economy resulted in an independence in external alliances unusual on the peninsula.

Although there are references to local trading settlements in thirteenth-century Chinese records, the name Trengganu first appears in the fourteenth century as a tributary of the East Java kingdom of Majapahit, as well as in an inscription, found on the Trengganu River, known as the Trengganu Stone, which exhorts the ruler's subjects to uphold Islam and lists punishments for breaches of certain regulations. Information about the period from the fifteenth to eighteenth century is scarce: no local records are extant, the Dutch never established a permanent settlement there, and British traders only visited for pepper en route to Canton.

The Malay chronicle *Sejarah Melayu* records that during the sixteenth century envoys were sent on missions to pay homage to the court of Melaka. Links were maintained with Johor, Melaka's successor, and early in the eighteenth century a younger brother of Sultan Abdul Jalil of Johor was installed as Sultan Zainal Abidin of Trengganu. His descendants still carry the royal line. In 1741 his son Mansur (died c. 1793) began a long reign that established the future pattern of Trengganu's foreign relations. He married into the royal lines of Kelantan and Riau-Johor, installed the first sultan of Kelantan, and spent long periods at the Malay court of Riau-Johor. He sought Dutch assistance to expel Bugis influence from Riau and Selangor. Close kin and political ties are still maintained between the Malay royals of Trengganu, Singapore, and Riau. It was during Mansur's reign that Rama I (1782–1808) of Siam received the first recorded gift of the gold and silver flowers (bunga mas dan perak) from Trengganu, which he regarded as a token of friendship and respect.

In 1839 Baginda Umar (d. 1876) deposed a cousin to assume the sultanate. He revitalized the state, bringing religious teachers from the Malay court of Lingga, appointing religious judges, and encouraging visits from Middle Eastern scholars. He is largely responsible for Trengganu's reputation as a strong Muslim state. Politically he was involved in the Pahang Civil War of 1857 and with Mahmud, the former sultan of Lingga. Umar's great-nephew, Sultan Zainal Abidin III (r. 1881–1918), maintained Trengganu's independence despite British pressure to accept an adviser. By the late nineteenth century the state had a population of more than one hundred thousand Malays. Under the 1909 Anglo-Siamese Treaty, Britain was able to play a more active role in Trengganu, although an adviser was not accepted until 1919. The traditional economy was left largely intact, but in 1928 there was a populist uprising in rural Ulu Trengganu, a reaction to the increased bureaucratization in the area and the influence of non-Muslims on Trengganu's administration.

After the Japanese occupation, the state joined the Federation of Malaya in 1948. Trengganu's large Malay population, devotion to Islam, and recently discovered offshore oil and gas should ensure an increasingly influential role in the future of Malaysia.

[See also Malaysia; Johor; Majapahit; Mansur Syah; and Bunga Mas.]

Shaharil Talib Robert, "The Trengganu Ruling Class in the Nineteenth Century," *Journal of the Malayan Branch Royal Asiatic Society* 50.2 (1977): 25–47. M. C. ff. Sheppard, "A Short History of Trengganu," *Journal of the Malayan Branch Royal Asiatic Society* 22.3 (1949): 1–74. H. Sutherland, "The Taming of the Trengganu Elite," in *Southeast Asian Transitions*, edited by R. T. McVey (1978), pp. 32–85. J. de Vere Allen, "The Ancien Regime in Trengganu, 1901–1919," *Journal of the Malayan Branch Royal Asiatic Society* 41.1 (1968): 23–53.   VIRGINIA MATHESON

TRIADS, secret societies influential in central and southern China from the eighteenth century until the mid-twentieth century. Known generally as the Hongmen (Vast Gate), they are autocephalous sworn brotherhood groups bearing such individual names as Tiandihui (Heaven and Earth Society), Sanhehui (Three Harmonies Society), and Sandianhui (Three Dots Society). Each shares with the others a common tradition, initiation rites, secret signs and languages, and, during the Qing dynasty, an intense anti-Manchu sentiment. Although ordinarily mutual aid organizations and gangs engaging in gambling, smuggling, and racketeering activities, the Triads also participated in antigovernment rebellions.

[See also Rebellions in China and Secret Societies.]

Jean Chesneaux, ed., *Popular Movements and Secret Societies in China, 1840–1950* (1972). Fei-ling Davis, *Primitive Revolutionaries of China* (1971).

RICHARD SHEK

TRIBES. [*This article deals exclusively with the notion of tribe in North and Central Asia; it does not include those people in other parts of Asia who might also be considered "tribal." For tribes in South Asia, see especially* Adivasis.]

The term *tribe* defies agreement as to its definition, and as a concept it lacks precision. The word nevertheless is widely used by specialists and nonspecialists alike. It is commonly used in reference to any small group that exhibits "primordial" loyalty and identity and seemingly cannot be explained in any other manner, but it is also used to refer to the great confederations that have so affected the history of Asia. Furthermore, associations and assumptions link specific tribes with distinct ethnic groups and regions, describe them in occupational terms as pastoral nomads, join them with ideologies of mobility and freedom, and assign them to politically organized hierarchies. Tribes constitute very complex entities, and all the above associations can be contradicted. The problem of the tribe in Asia is further complicated by the breadth and depth of its geography and history; the range of its economies (most often associated with flocks of sheep and goats or herds of horses, camels, or in more limited instances bovines); its interaction with sedentary agriculturalists, trading and administrative urban centers, and associated cultures, especially religion (including Zoroastrianism, Buddhism, Manichaeism, Nestorian Christianity, shamanism, and Islam); the nature of states and empires; the multiplicity of languages and dialects, essentially the Semitic and Persian, later

Turkic, families in the west and the Turco-Mongol-Tunguz group in the east; and the dynamics of social organization.

At the center of the tribe, however, is the notion of a kin structure that allows for flexibility in redefining itself over a period of time as it extends from the family to herding-camping units, to larger units of clans and subtribes, to tribes, and, possibly and ultimately, to a confederation. As the kin structure changes, all the accompanying economic, social, political, cultural, and symbolic relationships are also redefined. Explicitly central to the tribe in Asia are pastoralism and nomadism, although sedentary agriculturalists, too, can be tribally organized. Finally, the manifestation of the tribe in Asia has usually been seen militarily and politically in the form of the great confederations that themselves became imperial states: the Seljuks, Ghaznavids, Mongols, Khitan, Safavids, and Manchus to mention only some of the most obvious examples. Such confederations represent attempts to centralize and institutionalize power but also carry the risk of a loss of their tribal base of support.

Tribes in Asia, regardless of size, are perceived by their members in terms of kin. They are seen as comprehensive, all-encompassing, and discrete systems despite the ephemeral nature of their political leadership, which in itself is a key defining factor. Tribes regard themselves as distinct from other tribes, from sedentary and urban society, and from the bureaucratic, depersonalized imperial governments of Asia.

The tribe begins with the family, the basic economic and social unit of production, and among the pastoralists it owns the flocks or herds and adjusts to their needs within the ecological limits of available territory. This results in mobility and adaptability on an economic level and instability in group relations on a political one. The family takes on the key and enduring ideological role, forming the basis for everyday activity and providing the conceptual basis for the process of group formation. The further the sociopolitical level of organization moves from the family, the weaker the commitment and the identification with the larger groupings, because they have the potential for restricting adaptability. These larger groupings may serve important roles, but generally only in limited instances: pasture "ownership," ajudication of disputes, defense or expansion, distribution of awards or booty, and administration within a state system.

Confederations especially, but even tribes, organize lesser units for military purposes and can integrate them ideologically into a greater cultural system. On the other hand, confederations may be perceived as exploitative or as a structure whose goals are in basic conflict with the encompassed units. Moreover, tribal and confederation leadership in itself is tenuous. Leaders of the lesser units depend primarily upon internal socioeconomic factors. While confederation leaders start from that internal base, they hold their positions of leadership largely in response to external factors and may draw support from the state, from land holdings and incomes, and from leaders and groups outside the tribal base.

Historically, tribal leaders could act as government agents in their role as administrators in the collection of taxes, conscription, and maintenance of order. Those leaders who sought to form states from their tribal base had to maintain its cohesion, but also had to appeal to nonmembers through acceptable ideologies reinforced by the expectation of meeting both groups' economic, social, and political needs. Finally, confederation and tribal leaders' external support and internal domination could give them power so that they could reward and punish individuals or whole units and, despite potential opposition, award pastures, land, or exemptions to external groups in return for their support. Tribes and confederations were inclusive, and the basis for loyalty and identification depended less on kinship, even though it may have provided the necessary terminology, than on economic, political, and moral expediency. Tribes were capable of significant expansion and contraction, but specific configurations were usually of short duration and reflected immediate self-interest. Instability in internal relations and diffusion of power at all levels characterized tribes, and they lacked a central authority that could effectively monopolize military force and impose its will.

Only under the most effective leadership, or under the most extraordinary circumstances, could unification of the polymorphic tribal structure be brought about to form effective confederations, as, for example, was the case with Genghis Khan in Asia in the early thirteenth century. Successful leaders completed the tribal worldview symbolically: the Mongols institutionalized it in their *jasagh* legal code, and the Manchus and Ottomans created their earliest state formations around such comprehensive worldviews. Once tribal leaders took over a state, they utilized its prevailing traditions, especially bureaucratic but even military ones, and offered no alternate long-term concept of power and administration. This effectively separated the leaders from the tribal political base, while the economic base and sociopolitical organization of the lesser tribal units persisted.

Contributing then to tribal and confederational instability was the very institution of political leadership. Leadership in tribes was primarily personal, with only a weak commitment to the office of khan (chief) or great khan (*khaghan;* usually chief of a confederation) or to the chiefly lineage and family. The absence of primogeniture or agreed upon succession, except for tanistry (struggle or conflict), and the multiplicity of candidates for leadership (given generally plural marriage rules) added to instability and fragmentation. The continuing need to build support politically or militarily through conflict (in order to demonstrate leadership qualities and to ward off challengers) required a commitment that tribesmen could not long afford without significant rewards in the form of booty. Consequently tribes and confederations tended toward either expansion or breakup into subtribes, clans, and herding units tied to the modes of production. Expansion and its booty or incomes from land, dues, and grants, although necessary to reward followers, had the potential to diminish of tribal leadership through bureaucratization, centralization, depersonalization, and possible conflict of interest between the larger tribe and its constituent units. Conquest of agricultural and urban areas and management of incomes, especially external ones, and the concomitant need for a reliable military corps, usually resulted in adaptation to bureaucratic and depersonalized systems. The Manchus under Nurhaci successfully retained an overall tribal ideology even though it was separated from the daily economic, social, and cultural activities of the clans. On the other hand, in the twentieth century when the Pahlavis successfully centralized and formed the contemporary Iranian nation-state, and replaced the Bakhtiari great khans with direct rule, tribal ideology continued as a political framework linked to a pastoral nomadic economic base, with which tribal political systems in Asia seemed to be so closely associated.

Asian pastoral nomadism—which in itself is an adaptive economic response—encompasses the arid zone that extends from the northern frontiers of China across Central Asia and the Iranian and Anatolian plateaus, through Mesopotamia and the Arabian peninsula, and continues across North Africa. This environment had low rainfall, usually restricted to winter, and hot, dry summers. Agriculture was often marginal and existed only in riverine areas, in oases, or where irrigation was possible.

Major exceptions were to be found in high plateaus, higher elevations of mountain fringes, and littorals such as that of the Caspian Sea. Two factors of pastoral nomadism have prevailed: a symbiotic relationship with the environment and sedentary society—pastoral nomads must either raise cereals or obtain them through exchange with agriculturalists—and the exploitation of differing environmental niches necessitating movement between them.

Pastoral nomads and sedentary agriculturalists of the arid zone shared a continuum, with a difference in degree and emphasis, as they practiced some of the same pastoral and agricultural skills and, in some cases, competed for the same habitat or pursued complementary economies. The agricultural villagers, like the nomads, shared corporate interests in community self-defense, sometimes in land usage and herding, and often in water usage. In common with pastoral nomads, some village agriculturalists structured themselves in descent categories around which various sociopolitical alignments may have been formed. Often identical outside groups performed specialized tasks for both. Nomads and agriculturalists, even when they may have shared the same values, could be bound together as hostile units by mutual antagonism that grew out of their competitive economic and, at times, political relationships. Such antagonism may have served an ideological function by reinforcing group loyalties. Political autonomy and the means to extort dues are often cited as characteristic of nomads, who were more apt than agriculturalists to be armed, mounted, and mobile. Agriculturalists also have demonstrated these abilities, but through the mechanism of urban society and the state.

The environment—topography, soil, fertility, water and drainage, animal life, plant cover, and the constant modification of all of these by climatic action, erosion, earthquakes, and other types of geological change—affected nomads and agriculturalists alike. Historical factors of inter- and intranational politics, population density, settlement patterns, and land use also affected both groups, and the Mongol expansion of the thirteenth century provides a striking example. Mongol rule was followed by an increase in pastoral nomadism in regions of East and West Asia. A major problem is the absence of historical references to the process of nomadization, except for the dramatic cases. Shifts from agriculture to nomadism, and vice versa, may have occurred in response to geographic, military, or political factors when the state favored one elite over the other or adopted administrative practices that discriminated against one of them. Similarly, the military and administrative practice of removing whole tribal groups to the frontiers and border areas, usually to ward off nomadic incursions, may have extended areas of nomadism. In border regions, too, tribal groups through their mobility have avoided government with its taxes and conscription, and have resisted the imposition of dynastic control and its inherent interest in concentrating and centralizing power. The Mongols under Genghis Khan and his descendants exhibit the antithesis, an offensive rather than a defensive aspect of mobility, with the imposition of their hegemony over other nomads, over sedentary settlement, and even over states and empires.

The nomads' political, military, and ideological organization as tribes or confederations suggest significant differences between nomads and agriculturalists. Herding and movement of flocks to pasture or assertion of power over neighboring agricultural hamlets may have involved only a family, or a small group, whereas the conquest of other tribes, a city, or a state required larger and better organized units with a degree of centralized leadership. These were historically to be found in the nomadic tribes and confederations, but only within the state's army in the case of the agriculturalists. Once in power, however, tribal leaders identified with the state's interests and subsequently its values to maintain their positions. They then turned to curb their supporting tribes, whose political instability, conflicting interests, and potential for autonomy posed threats to the state's sovereignty and stability. The state, with its greater economic, political, military, bureaucratic, and ideological resources, prevailed when it manipulated the tribal-political structure through divide-and-rule policies, conscription and warfare, grants of land and incomes, forced settlement and relocation, retention of hostages and extermination, and confiscation.

Tribes constituted adaptable sociopolitical entities that in their concrete, historic forms contained the potential for their own fragmentation. The tribal ideology of kin was limited in its appeal to sedentary society. Rapid changes (especially in military technology but also in the nature of the state throughout Asia), colonialism and imperialism, and the general process of modernization ended any major military or political challenge tribes or even confederations could have posed, but they continue their economic roles even though the tribal framework is largely ideological or only exists as an administrative unit.

[*The specific peoples mentioned in this article are the subjects of independent entries. See also* Nomadism.]

Elizabeth Bacon, "Types of Pastoral Nomadism in Central and Southwest Asia," *Southwestern Journal of Anthropology* 10.1 (1954): 44–68. Lois Beck, *The Qashqa'i of Iran* (1986). Wolfram Eberhard, *Conquerors and Rulers: Social Forces in Medieval China* (1952). Robert B. Ekvall, *Fields on the Hoof* (1968). Équipe Écologie et Anthropologie Des Societes Postorales, ed., *Pastoral Production and Society* (1979). Joseph Fletcher, "Turco-Mongolian Monarchic Tradition in the Ottoman Empire," in *Eucharisterion*, edited by Ihor Ševčenko and Frank Sysyn, part 1 (1979–1980), pp. 236–251. Morton H. Fried, *The Notion of Tribe* (1975). Gene R. Garthwaite, *Khans and Shahs: A Documentary Analysis of the Bakhtiyari in Iran* (1983). A. M. Khazanov, *Nomads and the Outside World* (1984). Lawrence Krader, *Social Organization of the Mongol-Turkic Pastoral Nomads* (1963). Owen Lattimore, *Inner Asian Frontiers of China* (1962). Richard Tapper, *Pasture and Politics* (1979). Richard Tapper, ed., *The Conflict of Tribe and State in Iran and Afghanistan* (1983).
                                GENE R. GARTHWAITE

TRIBHUVAN, BIR BIKRAM (1907–1955).

Eighth in the line of Nepal's Shah kings, Tribhuvan is remembered as the father of the modern Nepalese nation. He precipitated the breakup of the century-old Rana oligarchy by seeking asylum in the Indian embassy at Kathmandu on 6 November 1950. This action, and his subsequent flight to New Delhi, was the catalyst for an armed insurrection against the Ranas, masterminded by the leaders of Nepal's National Congress Party. More than revolution, however, it was political pressure from the new Congress government in Delhi that forced the Ranas to restore Nepal's monarchy. On his triumphant return to Nepal in February 1951, the reform-minded Tribhuvan proclaimed the creation of a political system based upon a constitution framed by popularly elected representatives. Ill health prevented Tribhuvan from taking a direct role in his own democratic innovations, which were eventually undermined by political factionalism and economic stagnation. Tribhuvan died in 1955 and was succeeded by Crown Prince Mahendra.

[*See also* Mahendra; Rana; *and* Nepal: History of Nepal.]

B. L. Joshi and L. Rose, *Democratic Innovations in Nepal* (1966).   RICHARD ENGLISH

TRIBUTARY SYSTEM,

traditional Chinese system for managing foreign relations. By establishing the rules and controlling the means and symbolic forms by which foreign countries entered into and conducted their relations with China, the Chinese found in the tributary system an effective mechanism for exacting compliance from neighboring states and peoples on important matters of political, defensive, economic, and diplomatic concern to China.

According to the usual practice, foreign peoples would be granted permission to establish trade and contact with China on the condition that their ruler or the ruler's emissaries demonstrate their subservience to the Chinese emperor by personally bearing him tribute. On presenting the tribute, usually a largely token offering of native products or rare and precious commodities, they were also to perform an act of ritual obeisance, the *ketou* (anglicized as "kowtow"), which consisted of three kneelings and nine prostrations or bows of the head to the floor in the presence of the emperor. In return, the Chinese ruler would formally invest the foreign ruler with the nominal status of a vassal. As proof of this status, the ruler was provided with an imperial letter of patent, a seal of rank, and the Chinese calendar, important symbols of legitimacy and acceptance into the civilized Sinocentric world order. In addition, the emissaries received lavish gifts of cloth, silks, gold, and other luxuries that often far exceeded the value of what they had brought. For as long as this relationship was maintained, the tributaries were awarded legal trading privileges and the right to render tribute in the future. Obviously, the very profitable advantages of tribute-trade, as it came to be called, served as a powerful economic inducement, perhaps the real reason why non-Chinese acquiesced to the otherwise inferior status imposed on them by China.

On the Chinese side, the economic motive provided only a secondary purpose, although it did occasionally serve as a useful, if disguised, expedient for material exchange. To the Chinese, the system served constantly to reaffirm their own ethnocentric worldview that posited the Middle Kingdom (Zhongguo) as the source and center of civilization and the Chinese emperor as the supreme and universal ruler who governed by the will or "mandate of Heaven" *(tianming)*; beyond the bounds of China proper, there existed a vast array of culturally inferior, less civilized barbarians, who were inevitably attracted by the brilliance of China's superior civilization. Consequently, it was only natural to expect barbarians to seek its irresistible benefits, or, put another way, "to come and be transformed" *(lai hua)* by it. Thus, the system explained and accommodated this unequal relationship and erected an artificial separation between China and the outside world. The system was also in large measure an extension of the Confucian social and political order, which was hierarchical, conservative, emphasized ritual and ethical behavior, and cast the emperor as the "son of Heaven" *(tianzi)*, the ultimate exemplar of virtue and patriarch of a China-centered family of nations.

Historically, the idea of exacting tribute appears early in China. Shang rulers (fifteenth–eleventh century BCE) imposed the practice on outlying peoples, tribal nomads to the north and west and aborigines to the east and south, as a way to establish their hegemony. In exchange for offerings of horses, oxen, and slaves, titles and protection were bestowed. In Zhou times (eleventh–third century BCE), when China developed a multistate system and the doctrine of the "mandate of Heaven" was devised, petty Chinese rulers as well as non-Chinese were required to pay regular tribute to the house of Zhou as expressions of their dependent, vassal status.

It was under the imperial order of the Han dynasty (206 BCE–220 CE) that the full, Confucian-based tributary system was developed and functioned in East Asia as the main method of handling foreign affairs. From then on throughout imperial times, the system persisted at least in theory, if not always in practice. It must be stressed, however, that the system worked most successfully at times when China's imperial authority was strong and tended to break down when central power waned. For example, in the late Tang and Song (ninth–fourteenth century), China lacked the military power to impose its system on its neighbors and consequently entered into more equal diplomatic and economic relationships and followed more flexible, pragmatic approaches to foreign affairs during those centuries. It is also to be noted that China tended more often to uphold the system among its near neighbors than among those farther away. Most important were the nomadic tribes beyond the Great Wall and adjacent states like Vietnam, Korea, Liuqiu (Ryūkyū), Burma, and Siam, among others.

The system reached its apogee during the Ming dynasty (1368–1644), when contacts with more than a hundred different tributaries were recorded as a result of the vast overseas expansion at the time of the great maritime expeditions of the early 1400s. Although these maritime ties did not long endure, at their height embassies arrived with regularity from countries in South and Southeast Asia, such as Bengal, Sri Lanka, Sumatra, and Java, and from as far away as Hormuz and the east coast of Africa. Tribute from the latter included zebras and even giraffes. During these years, Japan entered the system for the first time, but only until 1549. In the following years, the Western European trading countries of Portugal, the Netherlands, and England also began to arrive and were gradually fitted into the tributary scheme as well.

It was at this stage that the system reached its fully institutionalized form as described in the collected statutes of the Ming and Qing (1644–1911) dynasties. Explicit regulations set forth how frequently embassies could arrive from each country, the time and place of arrival, how many persons could travel to the capital and the route taken, the quantity and type of goods to be carried for tribute and trade, when and where trade would be permitted, and the length of stay in China. From arrival to departure, envoys were escorted by Chinese officials and meals and lodgings were provided. Once at the capital, officials of the Ministry of Rites carefully instructed them in the elaborate protocol of imperial audiences, presentation of tribute, and performance of the *ketou*. Besides receiving gifts, the foreigners were customarily regaled with one or more sumptuous feasts prior to their return home.

As for the Europeans, however, it was precisely the relegation of all foreigners to inferior, unequal status, the restrictions on movement, time, and conduct, and even such details as the performance of the awkward and humiliating *ketou* that increasingly irritated them. Desirous of more trade and eager to establish Western diplomatic practices such as exchange of envoys and the signing of treaties as equals, they began to press China for change. Thus, the English envoy Lord Macartney in 1795 refused to perform the *ketou*, and although a compromise was reached (he knelt on one knee), China refused to yield to Western demands. In the end, these cultural differences led to the many misunderstandings and conflicts that resulted in the Opium Wars. Afterward, China was forced to abandon its traditional system and to adopt European practices as imposed by the West in the new system of Unequal Treaties. Although the formal tributary system was dismantled at that time, it can be argued that some residual aspects of the traditional system and the Chinese worldview that supported it have persisted even into the present.

[*See also* Canton; China Trade; Ming Dynasty; *and* Qing Dynasty.]

John K. Fairbank, ed., *The Chinese World Order: Traditional China's Foreign Relations* (1968). John K. Fairbank, *Trade and Diplomacy on the China Coast: The Opening of the Treaty Ports, 1842–1854* (1953). K. M. Maitra, trans., *A Persian Embassy to China* (reprint, 1970). Mark Mancall, *China at the Center: 300 Years of Foreign Policy* (1984). Morris Rossabi, ed., *China Among Equals: The Middle Kingdom and its Neighbors, 10th–14th Centuries* (1983). Sarasin Viraphol, *Tribute and Profit: Sino-Siamese Trade, 1652–1853* (1977). Wang Yi-t'ung, *Official Relations between China and Japan, 1368–1549* (1953). Yü Ying-shih, *Trade and Expansion in Han China: A Study in the Structure of Sino-Barbarian Economic Relations* (1967).

ROLAND L. HIGGINS

TRICHINOPOLY. *See* Tiruchchirappalli.

TRIEU DA (Chinese, Zhao Tuo) was born in 257 BCE in Shandong, China. In the 210s BCE he led soldiers in the Qin conquest of southern China. When Qin collapsed, he proclaimed himself king of Nan Yue at Canton (Guangzhou). In the 180s BCE he resisted Han pressure, briefly proclaiming himself emperor. He also conquered northern Vietnam, earning a place in Vietnamese legendary traditions. He died in 136 BCE. In the thirteenth century, Le Van Huu, a Vietnamese court historian, cited Trieu Da as the founder of Vietnam's "southern imperial tradition," separate from China's "northern imperial tradition," in his argument for Vietnam's political equality with China.

Keith W. Taylor, *The Birth of Vietnam* (1983).

KEITH W. TAYLOR

TRIEU DYNASTY (207–111 BCE), founded by Trieu Da (Chinese, Zhao Tuo, d. 136 BCE), a Chinese general who had occupied the Xi River area and established the kingdom of Nam Viet (Chinese, Nan Yue) in 207 BCE. Adopting local customs, he was able to ally himself with the neighboring kingdom of Au Lac against Han encroachment. He later moved against An Duong Vuong and annexed Au Lac, dividing its territory into the prefectures of Jiaozhi and Cuu Chan. After Trieu Da's death, the Han threat became increasingly greater, and China conquered Nam Viet in 111 BCE, bringing the Trieu dynasty to an end.

[*See also* An Duong Vuong; Au Lac; Jiaozhi; Nam Viet; *and* Trieu Da.]

Keith W. Taylor, *The Birth of Vietnam* (1983).

BRUCE M. LOCKHART

TRINCOMALEE is an ancient port of Sri Lanka, situated at the entrance to a bay on its east coast and reputed to be one of the best natural harbors of the Indian Ocean. It dates from the earliest Sinhalese and Tamil settlements of the period before the common era under the names of Gokanna (Sinhalese) and of Koresvaram (Tamil). A Shaivite shrine at this place was a well-known center of pilgrimage from South India.

The strategic location of Trincomalee attracted European naval powers. The Portuguese seized it in 1623 and built a fort at the entrance to the bay. The Dutch captured it in 1664 and the British took it from them in 1796. The British half-heartedly developed it as a base for their East India naval squadron, constructing dockyards and coal bunkers. Its growth as a port was slow because of a sparsely populated hinterland. After independence in 1948 the British continued to have use of the naval base by agreement with the Ceylon government. The Bandaranaike government cancelled the agreement in 1957 and took over the naval base.

[*See also* Sri Lanka *and* Bandaranaike, Solomon West Ridgeway Dias.]

S. ARASARATNAM

TRINH CUONG (d. 1729), seventh Trinh lord (1709–1729) of Dai Viet, whose rule saw the enactment of numerous fiscal and judicial reforms. Of particular concern was the growing social crisis caused by unequal distribution of land, which Trinh Cuong attempted to rectify with legislation limiting private holdings and emphasizing redistribution of communal fields. These measures met with much resistance, however, and had little effect on the problem. Like his predecessors, Trinh Cuong forbade the practice of Christianity (1712). He did not continue their proscription of Buddhism, however, and ordered the construction of numerous pagodas.

[*See also* Trinh Lords.]

BRUCE M. LOCKHART

TRINH KHAI (d. 1786), twelfth Trinh lord (1782–1786) of Dai Viet. Forced to fight for his legitimacy—his father, Trinh Sam (d. 1782), had chosen the son of a favorite concubine as his heir—Trinh Khai successfully defeated his half brother and earned recognition from Le emperor Hien Tong (r. 1740–1786). However, he was soon confronted with a revolt among the imperial guard, as well as popular rebellions caused by rice shortages. In July 1786, Tay Son troops under Nguyen Hue and a Trinh defector, Nguyen Huu Chinh, penetrated the

capital. Trinh Khai fled toward Son Tay but was captured by peasants and committed suicide.

[*See also* Trinh Lords; Trinh Sam; *and* Tay Son Rebellion.]

BRUCE M. LOCKHART

TRINH KIEM (d. 1570), first Trinh lord (1539–1570) of Dai Viet. The son-in-law of Nguyen Kim (d. 1545), he succeeded Kim as commander of the forces fighting the Mac. Although very ambitious, Trinh Kiem was persuaded to give nominal acknowledgement of Le sovereignty and enthroned the Emperor Anh Tong (r. 1557–1573). To remove his brother-in-law Nguyen Hoang from the capital, he granted him the governorship of Than Hoa in 1558. Both men continued the struggle against the Mac while strengthening their respective positions. Trinh Kiem was succeeded by his son Trinh Coi, who was quickly overthrown by his powerful brother Trinh Tong (1570–1623).

[*See also* Trinh Lords; Nguyen Kim; Mac Dynasty; *and* Nguyen Hoang.]

BRUCE M. LOCKHART

TRINH LORDS (also known as Trinh Vuong, and Chua Trinh), leaders of the movement to restore the Le dynasty (1545–1593) and actual rulers of northern Dai Viet (1593–1786/87).

The fortunes of the Trinh clan were founded by Trinh Kiem, an obscure adventurer who by military ability rose to command the Le restoration forces on the death of the previous leader, his father-in-law, Nguyen Kim. The major achievements of Kiem and his son Trinh Tung were the capture of Thang Long and the Red River delta from the Mac dynasty and the institutionalization of the Trinh family as hereditary commanders of the army and supreme administrators of the state. The Le emperor was retained, even after the extinction of the principle line of succession in 1558, but he enjoyed only symbolic significance.

Trinh Trang continued the emphasis on military activity that had characterized the policies of his predecessors. Further attacks were launched against the remnants of the Mac in the northern mountains, and a series of campaigns was initiated against the Nguyen, who had become autonomous governors of the southern provinces of the kingdom in 1558.

Trinh Tac, Can, and Cuong were primarily concerned with civil affairs, especially after the end of the Nguyen wars in 1673. Under their leadership,

TABLE 1. *The Trinh Lords*

LORDS	REIGN DATES
1. Trinh Kiem	1545–1569
2. Trinh Coi	1569–1570*
3. Trinh Tung	1570–1623
4. Trinh Trang	1623–1657
5. Trinh Tac	1657–1672
6. Trinh Can	1672–1709
7. Trinh Cuong	1709–1729
8. Trinh Giang	1729–1740*
9. Trinh Doanh	1740–1767
10. Trinh Sam	1767–1782
11. Trinh Can	1782*
12. Trinh Khai	1782–1786*
13. Trinh Bong	1786–1787*

*Deposed or killed.

reforms were enacted or attempted in almost every sphere of state activity, including administration, judicial procedure, land ownership, taxation, conscription and labor service, and the education, recruitment, and evaluation of officials. These efforts to improve the effectiveness of government actually served to make it a greater burden on the population, and hence increased resentment against it. Added to a series of natural disasters and the wasteful, inept, and callous rule of Trinh Giang, the resentment erupted in a succession of popular revolts, the suppression of which preoccupied the next two Trinh lords, Doanh and Sam.

Trinh Sam succeeded in quelling the uprisings to such an extent that he was able to take advantage of the disorder in Nguyen territories caused by the Tay Son movement to invade and occupy the northernmost Nguyen provinces (1774). Sam's personal foibles, however, led to a succession struggle at his death (1782) that permanently split the Trinh family. Four years later the Tay Son general Nguyen Hue needed less than a month to defeat the Trinh and bring an end to their rule. An attempt by Trinh Bong to restore Trinh authority in 1786–1787 was not successful.

The Trinh lords were, for the most part, intelligent, able, industrious, and long-lived rulers. The unusual dual form of government they developed over two centuries was a creative response to the internal and external obstacles to their rule. They lacked, however, both the power and the moral authority to resolve the contradictions inherent in their system of ruling without reigning.

[See also Dao Duy Tu; Le Dynasties; Mac Dynasty; Nguyen Lords; Rhodes, Alexandre de; Tay Son Rebellion; Trinh Cuong; Trinh Khai; Trinh Kiem; Trinh Sam; Trinh Tac; and Trinh-Nguyen Wars.]

Thomas Hodgkin, *Vietnam: The Revolutionary Path* (1981).
JAMES M. COYLE

TRINH-NGUYEN WARS (1627–1673), a series of conflicts between the Trinh and Nguyen lords of Dai Viet. The major result of these bloody and expensive wars was to confirm the division of Dai Viet into two autonomous principalities.

The Nguyen had governed the southern provinces of Than Hoa and Quang Nam for the Le dynasty during the long campaign against the Mac dynasty. Their conflict with the Trinh originated in the Nguyen's refusal to pay the required tribute (which had been established in lieu of regular taxation) or to submit themselves in person to the Le emperor after 1600. The Nguyen countered the Trinh charge of rebellion with the claim that the Trinh had usurped the powers of the Le emperor. Both sides claimed to be acting on behalf of the emperor.

Open warfare broke out in 1627 (though Nguyen sources contend that a 1620 attack by the Trinh was thwarted by the exposure of a conspiracy). A large Trinh military and naval force attacked Nguyen positions along the Nhat Le River (near Dong Hoi) but withdrew after four months of inconclusive fighting.

The Nguyen then began to construct an extensive series of fortifications anchored on the Nhat Le River and created a buffer zone between themselves and the Trinh by establishing military settlements (don dien) between the Nhat Le and the Song Gianh (just south of the eighteenth parallel). In 1634 and again in 1643 the Trinh attacked these defenses without success. Logistical difficulties prevented them from making amphibious attacks farther south.

The most nearly successful Trinh attack was launched in 1648, when the Trinh army penetrated the Truong Duc (Dong Hoi) wall. A Nguyen counterattack, however, drove them back with heavy losses.

The heaviest fighting took place between 1655 and 1661. A Trinh incursion across the Song Gianh provoked a strong counterattack, during which the Nguyen forces penetrated into Nghe An Province as far as the Song Lam (just south of modern Vihn), about 130 kilometers north of the unofficial boundary between the Trinh and Nguyen territories. There the Nguyen offensive stalled. Sporadic combat ensued until December 1660, when a major Trinh attack threw the Nguyen back to the Song Gianh.

The last two Trinh offensives, in 1661–1662 and 1672–1673, were conducted with smaller forces and pursued with less vigor than the previous campaigns and achieved no greater success. An undeclared truce between the contending parties prevailed for a century thereafter, though the Nguyen continued to maintain their defenses.

[See also Trinh Lords; Nguyen Lords; Le Dynasties; Dao Duy Tu; Rhodes, Alexandre de; and Trinh Tac.]

Thomas Hodgkin, *Vietnam: The Revolutionary Path* (1981).

JAMES M. COYLE

TRINH SAM (d. 1782), tenth Trinh lord (1767–1782). After having successfully defeated the last of several rebel Le princes, Trinh Sam turned his attention to the Nguyen lords. On the pretext of removing a hated Nguyen minister, he invaded and occupied Thuan Hoa in 1774. The Tay Son revolt had already begun, and he was able to come to an agreement with Nguyen Nhac. However, a series of famines and natural disasters led to peasant uprisings in the northern provinces, and Trinh Sam himself provoked a succession crisis that left the Trinh vulnerable to the Tay Son after his death.

[See also Trinh Lords; Nguyen Lords; and Tay Son Rebellion.]

BRUCE M. LOCKHART

TRINH TAC (d. 1682), fifth Trinh lord (1657–1682) of Dai Viet. the son of Trinh Trang (d. 1657), he was active in his father's campaign against the Nguyen lords. Imprisoning his brother to put his own son in command, he attacked the Nguyen in 1660, 1661, and 1672. Only the first of these campaigns brought true victory, however, and in 1673 the Trinh forces withdrew northward. In addition to consolidating Trinh political and military control, in 1677 he inflicted the final defeat on the Mac, who had been holding out in Cao Bang since their expulsion from the capital in 1592.

[See also Trinh Lords; Trinh-Nguyen Wars; and Mac Dynasty.]

BRUCE M. LOCKHART

TRIPARTITE TREATY OF ALLIANCE, treaty concluded in January 1942 between Great Britain, the Soviet Union, and Iran. The three countries signed the treaty during World War II to regulate the presence of British and Soviet troops in Iran following the joint Anglo-Soviet invasion and occupation of Iran the previous August. Great Britain and the Soviet Union agreed to limit the impact of their armed forces on Iran's economy, not require Iranian personnel for the war effort, and not interfere with Iran's internal politics. Great Britain and the Soviet Union also pledged to withdraw all their military forces from Iran within six months of the cessation of war hostilities "in all theaters."

J. C. Hurewitz, *Diplomacy in the Near and Middle East: A Documentary Record, 1914–1956* (1956), pp. 232–234. George Lenczowski, *Russia and the West in Iran* (1949).

ERIC HOOGLUND

TRIPLE INTERVENTION, diplomatic demand made by Russia, Germany, and France that Japan retrocede to China the Liaodong Peninsula, which Japan had acquired as a prize of the Sino-Japanese War of 1894 to 1895. While refraining from direct intervention in the war, the Western powers desired to prevent the sudden demise of China, which would escalate international rivalries in East Asia and destabilize the balance of power in the rest of the world. As the Shimonoseki peace conference approached, the Western powers warned Japan that they would not acquiesce in any Japanese territorial acquisition in southern Manchuria.

Barely a week after the signing of the Treaty of Shimonoseki on 17 April 1895, the three powers in concert "advised" Japan to restore the Liaodong Peninsula to China, arguing that the Japanese occupation of the peninsula threatened Beijing, prevented true Korean independence, and impeded permanent peace in East Asia. The powers intimated that should Japan refuse, they would take joint military action against it. Unable to obtain British or American intercession, the Japanese government under Premier Itō Hirobumi and Foreign Minister Mutsu Munemitsu had no choice but to succumb to the trilateral European pressure and gave up the peninsula as China paid an additional indemnity of 30 million taels of silver.

The Japanese were deeply humiliated and convinced that, in the world of power politics, justice or right without power was of no value. As the people attacked their leaders for cowardice, the government tried to diffuse popular indignation with an imperial edict calling for a renewed effort for arms buildup under the slogan *gashin shōtan* ("suffer present privation for future revenge"). The result was the reinforcement of the Japanese imperialistic ambition to fight for power and to take vengeance to force the Western powers to recognize Japan as their equal. The Japanese rage toward Russia, considered to be the Triple Intervention ringleader, was intensified when, only a few years later, Russia leased from China the very peninsula Japan had been compelled to give up in the name of peace in East Asia. Japan then began earnest preparations for the anticipated war with Russia, which took place from 1904 to 1905.

[See also Sino-Japanese War and Shimonoseki, Treaty of.]

William L. Langer, *The Diplomacy of Imperialism* (1956). Mutsu Munemitsu, *Kenkenroku: A Diplomatic Record of the Sino-Japanese War, 1894–1895*, translated by Gordon M. Berger (1982).   SHUMPEI OKAMOTO

TRIPURA. Jutting into Bangladesh, the hilly and heavily forested Indian district of Tripura is the home of roughly nineteen different ethnic groups who were traditionally ruled by the Tripura tribe. Since the colonial era, however, Bengali migrants have moved into the area, so that tribals now number only 29 percent of the district's population. Local resistance, led first by the Communist Party and later by a broadly based tribal coalition, has focused on restoration of land rights and retention of the tribal form of slash and burn agriculture. Violence has been widespread, and the area remains volatile despite the Indian government's efforts at reconciliation.

[See also Adivasis.]

J. Gan-Chaudhuri, ed., *Tripura* (1980). B. Mukherjee and K. Singh, "Tribal Movements in Tripura," in *Tribal Movements in India*, edited by K. Singh (1982).

CHARLES LINDHOLM

TRUNAJAYA (c. 1649–1680), Madurese prince who led the greatest rebellion of seventeenth-century Java. In 1670 he conspired with the Mataram crown prince (later King Amangkurat II; r. 1677–1703) against the latter's father, Amangkurat I (r. 1646–1677). Trunajaya then took over Madura in 1671; the rebellion spread to Java in 1675. He soon abandoned his alliance with the crown prince and took royal titles. In 1677 he conquered Mataram. The Dutch East India Company (VOC) decided to support Amangkurat II, and eventually VOC forces defeated Trunajaya in 1679. Soon afterward Trunajaya was captured and taken to the king, who killed him in January 1680. [See also Amangkurat I *and* Madura.]

M. C. RICKLEFS

TRUNG SISTERS REBELLION. In 40 CE Trung Trac and Trung Nhi, daughters of the Lac lord of Me Linh (Vinh Phu, Vietnam), led an uprising that drove Han authority out of northern Vietnam and parts of southern China. The Han general Ma Yuan captured and beheaded the sisters in 42–43. This rebellion represented the last effort of the pre-Han Vietnamese ruling class to resist Chinese authority; its suppression meant the beginning of direct Chinese overlordship in Vietnam. Thereafter, Lac lords are no longer mentioned and Dong Son civilization ends. A posthumous cult around the Trung Sisters has flourished into the twentieth century. The political role of women in early Vietnam, though open to interpretation, was significant; many of the clan leaders who followed the Trung Sisters were also women.

[See also Dong Son.]

Keith W. Taylor, *The Birth of Vietnam* (1983).

KEITH W. TAYLOR

TRUONG CHINH, leading member of the Vietnamese Communist Party and former chairman of the State Council of the Socialist Republic of Vietnam. Born Dang Xuan Khu near Hanoi in 1907, he joined the Indochinese Communist Party in the early 1930s and assumed the pseudonym of Truong Chinh (Long March). In the early 1940s he became secretary general of the Party and one of its leading theoreticians. In 1956 he was dismissed from his post as a result of errors committed in the land-reform program in North Vietnam, but he retained his membership in the Politburo, where he reportedly defended the rapid socialization of Vietnamese society. In 1982 he was elected chairman of the Council of State, the new collective presidency created by the 1980 consitution. On 17 December 1986, in the largest shake-up in Party history, Truong Chin was one of the prominent leaders who resigned from the Politburo during the Sixth National Vietnamese Party Congress.

[See also Vietnam *and* Indochinese Communist Party.]

Truong Chinh, *Primer for Revolt* (1963). Douglas Pike, *History of Vietnamese Communism, 1925–1976* (1978).

WILLIAM J. DUIKER

TRUONG CONG DINH (1820–1864), Vietnamese leader active in the early campaigns against the French. Originally from central Vietnam, he grew up around Go Cong in the Mekong Delta. After the French attack in 1858, he commanded troops under Nguyen Tri Phuong in the Gia Dinh area, later working to coordinate resistance forces following Nguyen's defeat in 1861. Truong continued to fight even after the 1862 Patenotre Treaty, despite appeals from the court and Phan Thanh Gian. The next two years brought continual pressure from the French armies, but it was not until August 1864 that Truong was killed, after being betrayed by a former subordinate.

[*See also* Vietnam; Patenotre Treaty; *and* Phan Thanh Gian.]

Nguyen Phut Tan, *Modern History of Vietnam 1802–1954* (1964). Truong Buu Lam, *Patterns of Vietnamese Response to Foreign Intervention, 1858–1900* (1967).

BRUCE M. LOCKHART

TRUONG MINH GIANG (d. 1841), Vietnamese general under Emperor Minh Mang (r. 1820–1840). In 1833, after considerable tension with Hue over Cambodia, Siam sent a large force to invade Vietnam. Truong Minh Giang led troops to retake Vietnamese territory and captured Phnom Penh as well. Having established a protectorate there, Truong was closely involved in the Cambodian court's internal affairs. Although Cambodia was incorporated into Vietnam, there was continued popular resistance to the occupying power, sometimes with Siamese support. After Minh Mang's death in 1840, Thieu Tri decided to withdraw Vietnamese troops from Cambodia. Truong Minh Giang died shortly after returning to Vietnam.

[*See also* Minh Mang.]

Nguyen Phut Tan, *Modern History of Vietnam (1802–1954)* (1964).

BRUCE M. LOCKHART

TRUONG SA ARCHIPELAGO. *See* Spratly Islands.

TRUONG VINH KY (1837–1898), Vietnamese collaborator during the colonial period and author of numerous books on the language, history, and culture of Vietnam. The product of Catholic mission schools in Cochinchina, Petrus Ky worked closely with the French in various capacities, including interpreting, teaching, and administrative work. Convinced that only France could help the Vietnamese to advance politically and culturally, he was a fervent advocate of *quoc ngu* and was involved with the *Gia Dinh Bao* newspaper, which was printed in that script. A close friend of Resident-General Paul Bert, Truong Vinh Ky worked briefly with the Co Mat Council at the Hue court.

[*See also* Quoc Ngu.]

Milton Osborne, *The French Presence in Cochinchina and Cambodia* (1969).

BRUCE M. LOCKHART

TSANGYANG GYATSO (1683–1706), the sixth Dalai Lama, proclaimed Dalai Lama in 1697 at the unusually advanced age of fourteen. A pawn of the temporal ruler of Tibet, he frequented the pleasure quarters of Lhasa, wrote love poetry, and paid little attention to his duties. Under the pretext of his misbehavior, the ruler of the Qosot Mongols deposed him with the approval of the Chinese Kangxi emperor. Tsangyang Gyatso died en route to exile in China; it is possible that he was murdered. This incident provoked the Dzungar Mongol invasion of Tibet, but in 1720 the Chinese dislodged the Dzungars and established a protectorate over Tibet.

[*See also* Dalai Lama *and* Tibet.]

L. Petech, *China and Tibet in the Early 18th Century* (2d rev. ed., 1972). Yu Dawchyuan, *Love-Songs of the Sixth Dalai Lama Tshangs-dbyangs-rgyo-mtso* (1930).

ROBERT ENTENMANN

TSONG KHAPA. *See* Gelugpa.

TSUSHIMA, a small (271 square miles) Pacific island, inhabited by ethnic Japanese in historical times, but closer to the Korean mainland (30 miles) than to Kyushu, Japan (80 miles); the principal link between Japan and Korea until modern times. Mountainous and agriculturally poor, Tsushima's economy was based, until the late nineteenth century, on its position as entrepôt in Japan's trade with Korea and on its use as a pirate base. Tsushima came under the rule of the Sō clan, which took the island from the Abiru family in 1245 and governed until 1871.

In the early Yi period, Korea tried to co-opt Tsushima, in order to control piracy, by grants of rice and other commodities, by a major punitive expedition against the island in 1419, by grants to island inhabitants of residential and trading privileges in three ports in southeastern Korea, and by appointment of the Sō and others in Tsushima to special offices in Korea. Tsushima's trading rights were recognized by the Yi government in the Trade Articles of 1443, permitting the Sō to dispatch up to fifty trade ships annually. Under these articles, and the Articles of 1512, a revision undertaken after the 1510 "Japanese rebellion in the three ports" (samp'o waeran), Tsushima was treated as a Korean tributary state.

After 1551, Tsushima monopolized Japan's trade with Korea. Trade and diplomacy were interrupted by the Japanese invasions of Korea, 1592–1598, but after Japan's withdrawal and establishment of the Tokugawa bakufu, Sō Yoshitoshi in 1607 brokered restoration of Japanese-Korean diplomatic relations. He then negotiated the Articles of 1609, which permitted Tsushima to establish a new trading post at Pusan, known as "Japan house," and to reopen trade with Korea. Trade was more restricted than before the war, however, with only twenty vessels permitted to trade each year. Tsushima's ships under the Articles were treated as tributary envoys, and the tribute trade was sufficient to support the financial needs of the Sō clan. But Tsushima also worked to expand the private trade at Pusan as well, and this trade, at its peak in the late seventeenth century, accounted for the majority of Japan's silk imports and made the Sō one of the wealthiest daimyo. The principal imports from Korea were Chinese silks and Korean ginseng (a prized medicinal root), which Tsushima marketed in Japan; the major exports to Korea were Japanese metals, especially silver and copper.

The Sō handled routine shogunal communications with Korea and accompanied Korean ambassadors on the twelve occasions during the Tokugawa period when they came to Japan. Edo recognized Tsushima's unique economic and diplomatic position by granting the Sō clan a rank equivalent to that of a daimyo of a domain with an income of 100,000 koku (measures of rice). Tsushima also gathered East Asian political and strategic intelligence and repatriated distressed seamen. After the Meiji Restoration of 1868, Tsushima sought Korean recognition of the new Japanese government, but Korea rejected the approach, objecting to unilateral abrogation of 260 years of established protocol, and especially to the use of the Japanese title tennō (emperor). Korea's response led to a crisis in Japanese-Korean relations. With the abolition of the daimyo domains in August 1871, all of Tsushima's diplomatic duties were taken over by Japan's Foreign Ministry.

Hilary Conroy, The Japanese Seizure of Korea, 1868–1919 (1960). "Tsushima-han's Korean Trade, 1684–1710," Acta Asiatica 30 (1976): 85–105, and "Foreign Relations during the Edo Period: Sakoku Reexamined," Journal on Japanese Studies 8.2 (1982): 283–306. Ronald P. Toby, State and Diplomacy in Early Modern Japan: Asia in the Development of the Tokugawa Bakufu (1984).

RONALD P. TOBY

TSUSHIMA STRAITS, BATTLE OF, referred to by the Japanese as the Battle of the Japan Sea, naval engagement at the end of the Russo-Japanese War of 1904–1905 in which the Russian fleet was resoundingly defeated by the Japanese. The Russians held Port Arthur when Admiral Z. P. Rozhdestvenski's Second Pacific Squadron (former Baltic Fleet) left Libau, Latvia (October 1904), on its 18,000-mile voyage. Rozhdestvenski's motley warships were slow, overloaded, unstable, and ill-protected; his guns inferior; his crews ill-trained and debilitated. Port Arthur's fall (January 1905) undercut the expedition, but Rozhdestvenski was redirected to Vladivostok. Three dozen Russian warships entered Tsushima, where Admiral Tōgō Heihachirō awaited, having gambled on their appearance. Tōgō's combined fleet included four battleships, twenty-three cruisers, twenty-one destroyers, and forty-four torpedo boats.

Fighting commenced on 27 May. Brilliantly crossing and recrossing the T-formations, Tōgō (aboard Mikasa) quickly destroyed the Russian flagship, Suvorov, and two other battleships; Rozhdestvenski was critically wounded. Admiral N. Nebogatov, next in command, capitulated on the next day. The Russian losses were catastrophic: sixteen ships (including six battleships) were sunk, six ships (two battleships) were captured, five ships were scuttled, and six were interned. Only three small warships reached Vladivostok. Russian dead totaled 4,830; there also were 6,100 prisoners (including wounded) and 1,862 interned. Even Rozhdestvenski was captured. Although several Japanese warships were savaged, only three torpedo boats went down. Japanese dead numbered 116, with around 600 wounded. The great Russian misfortune had obscured Japanese shortcomings, but the war was nearly over. Tsushima's influence on naval warfare was baneful: for too long a period thereafter, navies visualized annihilative battles like Tōgō's Nelsonian victory.

[*See also* Russo-Japanese War; Portsmouth, Treaty of; *and* Tōgō Heihachirō.]

J. N. Westwood, *Witnesses of Tsushima* (1970).

ALVIN D. COOX

TU DUC, fourth emperor of the Nguyen dynasty of Vietnam (r. 1847–1883). Tu Duc was born 22 September 1829, the second son of Prince Tuyen (Nguyen Phuc Thi, later the Thieu Tri emperor). His personal name was Hong Nham.

The accession of Hong Nham was almost certainly engineered by his mother and a cabal of court officials who forged Thieu Tri's valedictory edict to the detriment of Hong Bao, the late emperor's eldest son. Hong Nham was scholarly, cultured, and even-tempered (in contrast to his notably irascible predecessors) but somewhat diffident as a ruler. His writings reveal a deep strain of pessimism.

The greatest achievements of the Tu Duc reign are to be found in the realm of scholarship. Under the sponsorship of the emperor, court officials and historians produced a compendium of the dynasty's administrative regulations (*Dai Nam hoi dien su le*, 1851), a detailed gazetteer (*Dai Nam nhat thong chi*, 1865–1882), and a complete and systematic history of the country, personally annotated by Tu Duc (*Kham dinh Viet su thong giam cuong muc*, 1856–1884).

Tu Duc's internal policies were essentially a continuation of the conservative practices of preceding reigns. Notable among these were the revival of the use of *don dien* (military colonies) to settle the relatively underpopulated Mekong Delta and the proscription of Christianity. This last policy was the immediate cause of the events for which the period is best known today: the gradual subjugation of Vietnam by France.

The reign of Tu Duc was marked by frequent and severe natural disasters (successive cycles of flood, famine, and epidemic, with occasional infestations of locusts and rodents) and by frequent outbreaks of popular unrest, especially in the north (Tonkin), where loyalty to the defunct Le dynasty was never entirely extinguished. These difficulties, as much as the fatalism of the emperor, vitiated the response of the Vietnamese court to French penetration. The Franco-Vietnamese treaties of 1862 and 1874 were made against a background of civil disorder, which the emperor perceived as a greater threat to the dynasty than French imperialism. Tu Duc actively discouraged popular resistance to the French occupation until his death on 17 July 1883.

A childhood illness had rendered Tu Duc sterile. His death thus brought about a succession crisis, during which the final reduction of independent Vietnam to the status of a colony and two protectorates of France took place.

[*See also* Black Flags; Cao Ba Quat; La Grandière, Pierre-Paul-Marie de; Dupré, Jules-Marie; Dupuis, Jean; Garnier, Francis; Genouilly, Charles Rigault de; Locust Rebellion; Nguyen Dynasty; Phan Thanh Gian; Saigon, Treaty of; *and* Truong Cong Dinh.]

J. F. Cady, *The Roots of French Imperialism in Eastern Asia* (1954). Thomas Hodgkin, *Vietnam: The Revolutionary Path* (1981). Truong Buu Lam, *Patterns of Vietnamese Response to Foreign Intervention: 1858–1900* (1967).

JAMES M. COYLE

TU FU. *See* Du Fu.

TUGHLUQ DYNASTY, a dynasty of the Delhi sultanate, in power from 1320 to 1414. Sultan Ghiyas ud-Din Tughluq (r. 1320–1325), Muhammad bin Tughluq (r. 1325–1351), and Firuz Shah Tughluq (r. 1351–1388) were the most outstanding among its eleven sultans.

The Tughluq sultans made a deep impact on the political, social, and economic developments of the period. Although Ghiyas ud-Din and Muhammad bin Tughluq were greater imperialists than Ala ud-Din Khalji, they softened the militaristic aspect of the state and initiated many measures of public welfare. Ghiyas ud-Din Tughluq brought about reform in agrarian administration; Muhammad bin Tughluq formulated a code for agricultural development and established a department for that purpose; Firuz provided irrigational facilities on an extensive scale.

Muhammad bin Tughluq attempted to achieve the political and administrative unity of India and undertook the Qarachil expedition, seeking to complete fortification of vulnerable areas connecting India with China. He established diplomatic relations with West Asian, Central Asian, and even Southeast Asian countries. The empire of Delhi having grown in dimensions during his time, Muhammad bin Tughluq created a second administrative city in the South and named it Daulatabad. Muslim elite administrators, scholars, and mystics were forced to leave Delhi and settle there. The sultan made an experiment in token currency and introduced copper coin in place of silver. Under the influence of Ibn Taimiya, the renowned fundamentalist scholar of

Damascus, Muhammad bin Tughluq punished some of the mystics who did not fall in line with his policies. However, he was extremely liberal in his dealings with the Hindus whose festivals he celebrated, and gave endowments to shelters for cows.

Firuz Shah was interested in the preservation of old buildings and the founding of new cities. According to the accounts of Arab travelers there were one thousand colleges and two thousand mystic centers in Delhi during the time of Muhammad bin Tughluq. The Firuzi College founded by Firuz was an impressive building where free food was given to the students and both teachers and students were required to wear uniforms.

During the later years of Firuz Shah the empire of Delhi began to decline. After Firuz, Tughluq power began to disintegrate, and centifugal tendencies appeared. The invasion of Timur in 1398 destroyed the empire's economic prosperity. The later Tughluqs were unable to cope with the situation and the Tughluq dynasty was replaced by the Sayyids.

[See also Delhi; Delhi Sultanate; Daulatabad; Sayyid Dynasty; and Khalji Dynasty.]

M. Habib and K. A. Nizami, *Comprehensive History of India*, vol. 5 (1970). A. Mahdi Husain, *Tughluq Dynasty* (1963).   KHALIQ AHMAD NIZAMI

TUGHRIL BEG. *See* Toghril Beg.

TUKARAM (1608–1649) was a major saint-poet in the Hindu devotional tradition of Maharashtra. Born in low-caste poverty, Tukaram followed his father's trade as a grocer, but his life was dedicated to meditation upon God. He was a Vaishnavite follower of the Varkari movement and thus a devotee of the god Vithoba of Pandharpur. It was for this deity that Tukaram composed and sang *abhangs*, or hymns of praise. Nearly five thousand in number, these hymns are among the most widely known and beloved in Marathi literature. Although it is unlikely that he met Shivaji, the renowned Maratha leader, Tukaram is credited with contributions to the growth of Maratha national consciousness.

[See also Bhakti; Indo-Aryan Languages and Literatures; and Maharashtra.]

R. D. Ranade, *Mysticism in Maharashtra* (1933). G. B. Sardar, *The Saint-Poets of Maharashtra* (1969).

FRANK F. CONLON

TULSI DAS (1532?–1623), *bhakti* poet of North India. Very little is known about Tulsi's life. His language suggests that he grew up in the eastern portion of the Hindi-speaking region, and it is certain that he spent some time in Ayodhya, the natal city of the hero Rama, before settling in Varanasi. His *Ramcaritmanas (Spiritual Lake of the Deeds of Rama)*, written in the Awadhi dialect, tells the story of Rama with a devotional flavor that emphasizes the salvific value of the name of Rama. Tulsi shows the apparent influence of the *Adhyatma Ramayana* in presenting the epic, in part, as a conversation between the god Shiva and his consort Parvati, and he takes the novel step of introducing an account of their marriage into the tale. This may reflect an effort to make room for the Shaivite predilections of Varanasi in the worship of Rama. The synthetic thrust of Tulsi's piety is also felt in relation to Krishna, to whom he addresses his *Shrikrishnagitavali* and who provides the model according to which he recasts his picture of the childhood of Rama in several works. Tulsi's catholic sensibility, which is also expressed in an effort to balance the claims of Brahmanical orthodoxy with the freer, even ecstatic spirit of *bhakti*, has contributed substantially to his popularity. The *Ramcaritmanas*, a polished, musical work of great originality, is probably the religious work most frequently read, cited, and recited in the Hindi language family.

[See also Bhakti *and* Indo-Aryan Languages and Literatures.]

W. D. P. Hill, trans., *The Holy Lake of the Acts of Rama* (1952).   JOHN STRATTON HAWLEY

TULUVA DYNASTY, a dynasty of Vijayanagara in South India, in power from 1506 to 1570. The brilliant king Krishnadevaraya (r. 1509–1530), noted for his military campaigns, consolidated Vijayanagara's hold on the crucial Raichur doab and Mysore. He established supremacy in the east as far as the delta of the Godavari River. His immediate successors were weak, however, and the last ruler, Sadashiva, was defeated by an alliance of neighboring Muslim rulers at Talikota (or Krishna-Bannihatti) in 1565. This defeat led ultimately to the disintegration of Vijayanagara.

[See also Vijayanagara.]

M. Rama Rao, *Krishnadeva Raya* (1971). Robert Sewell, *A Forgotten Empire (Vijayanagar): A Contribution to the History of India* (1900).   MEERA ABRAHAM

TUMENGGONG. *See* Temenggong.

TUMULI, burial mounds constructed in Japan from about 300 to 700; for this reason the period is known as the Tomb Age. The giant keyhole-shaped tumuli of the late fourth and fifth centuries, known in Japanese as *kofun,* are found mostly in the Kinai. Longer than a football field and more massive than Egypt's Cheops pyramid, these tombs are often surrounded by two or three moats. The internal structure of the mounds may be divided into two parts: a rock-lined passageway that begins at the bottom of the "keyhole," and a circular burial chamber, also made of stone and containing a stone or wooden sarcophagus and the dead person's belongings. The entire structure is normally covered with several tons of earth.

The great tombs contain bronze and iron mirrors, often of Chinese origin, iron swords, breastplates, helmets, and horse trappings such as saddles, stirrups, and bits. New and more durable forms of pottery (*haji* and *sue* ware) and golden jewelry such as crowns, necklaces, and earrings may also be found. Clay figurines (*haniwa*), which line the outside of many mounds, represent warriors, peasants, shamans, horses, granaries, and other common sights of the period.

There can be little doubt that the tombs and the related culture originated on the Asian continent, specifically Korea. The historian Egami Namio once theorized that Japan had been invaded by Tunguz horsemen, who conquered the islands and became a new ruling caste, but the historical record does not clearly support such a view. Many historians believe that the large tumuli symbolize the creation of a state somewhere in the Kinai by about 400. Only a state would possess the coercive force to have such mammoth mounds built. Chinese dynastic chronicles also report "kings of Wa" (Japan) who claimed suzerainty over western Japan, the Kantō, and southern Korea.

Toward the end of the fifth century, the size of the tumuli diminished markedly. The construction of more numerous and smaller mounds represents the dispersion of tomb-building techniques to new classes and new locations: local magnates had acquired the wealth and beliefs to build tumuli of their own. Also beginning in the 500s, new strides were made in agriculture. The irrigation technology necessary to build the moats of the great tombs of the 400s spread to rice farmers. Oxen, which had reached Japan from the continent in the early tomb era, and iron blades for spades, hoes, and sickles allowed cultivators to clear new and more fertile lands. Population may have increased dramatically in this period.

The social and economic changes of the sixth century laid the foundation for the rule of the Soga in the early 600s. In turn, the adoption of Buddhism spelled the end of tomb making. Buddhism required cremation of the dead, not burial. By the year 700 tombs had fallen out of vogue, as is signified by the cremation of such notables as Ōno Yasumaro.

John W. Hall, *Japan from Prehistory to Modern Times* (1973). J. E. Kidder, *Japan before Buddhism* (1959). Ryusaku Tsunoda, trans., *Japan in the Chinese Dynastic Histories* (1951).   WAYNE FARRIS

TUN MAHMUD, *raja muda* of Johor (1708–1718). The younger brother of Sultan Abdul Jalil Riayat Syah, Tun Mahmud was a highly able and ambitious ruler. His aggressive policy was designed to legitimize the new regime by gaining wealth and power through control of the internal traffic of the straits and by drawing foreign trade to Johor's port-capital, which he reestablished at Riau. His policies antagonized Dutch Melaka and alienated two groups of recent immigrants to the straits area, the Minangkabau of Siak, who resented his interference in their trade with Melaka, and the Bugis of Selangor. These conflicts, combined with the weakness of the new regime, led to his defeat and death in a rebellion in 1718.

[*See also* Abdul Jalil Riayat Syah; Mahmud Syah II; *and* Kecil, Raja.]

Leonard Y. Andaya, *The Kingdom of Johor 1641–1728* (1975). Dianne Lewis, "The Last Malay Raja Muda of Johor," *Journal of Southeast Asia* 13.2 (September 1982): 221–235.   DIANNE LEWIS

TUNTIAN, a Chinese system of settling soldiers as self-supporting farmers, particularly in border areas. From *tun* ("camp") and *tian* ("field"), *tuntian* is usually translated as "military colony" or simply "military farm." *Tuntian* were first used by the Han in an attempt to make their garrisons in the far west self-sufficient. Their example was followed by nearly every succeeding dynasty, for the system promised an escape from the onerous burdens of transport and supply for border defenders. The experience of the Ming, whose military system was in theory based on *tuntian*, but which in fact had to pay professional soldiers and ship grain, demonstrated the practical difficulties of implementing what on paper has always seemed an ideal system. Echoes of the idea may be found in the policies of Wang Zhen at Nanniwan, Shaanxi, in the 1940s, and in the subsequent agricultural practices of the People's Liberation Army.

Ray Huang, *Taxation and Governmental Finance in Sixteenth-Century Ming China* (1974). Michael Loewe, *Records of Han Administration*, 2 vols. (1967). Denis C. Twitchett, "Lands under State Cultivation during the T'ang Dynasty," *Journal of the Economic and Social History of the Orient* 2.2 (1959): 162–203, 2.3 (1959): 335–336.   ARTHUR N. WALDRON

TUOBA. *See* Northern Wei Dynasty.

TURFAN, an oasis town in Xinjiang, China and administrative center of a *xian* (district) of the same name. In modern historiography Turfan is an umbrella name covering several important archaeological and historical sites. The most important are Jiaohe (Uighur, Yarkhoto), Gaochang (Uighur, Kocho or Karakhoja), Bezeklik, and Astana. The originally Indo-European and intermittently China-dominated area lay on important crossroads of the Silk Route: this brought Buddhism, Manichaeism, and Nestorian Christianity, as well as artistic and material culture to Turfan from the south, east, and west, resulting in a remarkable amalgam or convergence that has made Turfan famous in modern archaeology, art history, and linguistics.

An important linguistic transformation occurred in the region between the ninth and thirteenth centuries, when Turfan was the principal capital of the Uighur kingdom of Kocho (the Uighur Turks moved here after their khanate in Mongolia had been destroyed by the Kirghiz in 840), for the population became fully turkicized. In other respects, however, it was the Uighurs who adopted Buddhism and in general aligned themselves with the customs of the autochthonous population. In the thirteenth century these Uighurs provided the Mongols led by Genghis Khan with a scribal class *(bakhshis)* and a writing system.

Islam came to Turfan in the fifteenth century and transformed the area to such an extent that the population forgot its Uighur identity (simply calling themselves Turpanliq, "people of Turfan"), Uighur script, and Buddhist religion. Political, economic, and cultural decline since the sixteenth century may also have been accentuated by the partial demise of the transcontinental Silk Route.

René Grousset, *The Empire of the Steppes,* translated by Naomi Walford (1970). Marc Aurel Stein, *Innermost Asia,* vol. 2 (1928), pp. 566–718; and *On Ancient Central-Asian Tracks* (1964), pp. 224–236.   SVAT SOUCEK

TURKESTAN ("land of the Turks"), an ethnic territory as well as a human community with long historical significance. Turkestan has undergone profound changes in geographical location and in human composition over the centuries. Its naming, therefore, is of particular importance.

Turkestan gained its name after Turkic nomads, the Kok Turks, took control of all Central Asia in the sixth century. It had previously been the realm of Iranian Bactrians, Sogdians, Sakas, and others. These Kok Turks continued their dominance of the region, with some setbacks, until the invading Arabs, intruding from the southwest, consolidated their hold on the western part of Turkestan after 737 CE. This major switch from Turkic to Arab power brought about several long-lasting alterations in the position and makeup of Turkestan. First, it pushed the Turkic nomads eastward, back beyond the Syr Darya (Jaxartes, or Sayhun, River), causing a physical contraction in "the land of the Turks." Then, the Arab incursion and occupation introduced Islam to the part of Turkestan called Transoxiana that lies between the Amu Darya (Oxus, or Jayhun, River) and the Syr Darya. That religious expansion failed to penetrate among the Turkic nomads to any extent at that time; it thus left a large, dynamic population of unconverted herdsmen and plainsmen churning just outside the Muslim ideological and cultural sphere for at least another two hundred years.

As a result, medieval Arab geographers and historians such as Ahmad Ya'qubi (d. 897), writing in 891, and Ibn Jarir al-Tabari (d. 923), writing even later, placed "Turkestan" east of Transoxiana, beyond the Syr Darya but still west of China proper. The anonymous tenth-century Persian geography, *Regions of the World,* specifies the town of Urgench (Kath) in the northwest and the region of Khurasan in the southwest as the western gates to Turkestan; it leaves the exact territory of Turkestan undefined, as do all early sources.

Despite the implication in its name, Turkestan's inhabitants never consisted solely of Turkic people. In the thirteenth century, in the fifteenth, and again in the next hundred years, Mongolians under

Genghis Khan (d. 1227), Toghon Temur (d. 1439), and other leaders pushed mounted troops in large numbers into Turkestan from the direction of Karakorum and Dzungaria. None of these influxes, temporarily devastating to Turkestan political organization, life, and property, imparted enough new ethnic stock to the area to alter the predominant Turkic cast of the population. Nevertheless, Mongolian blood added another ethnic feature to the already intricate mixture of Arab, Indian, Iranian, Slavic, and Turkic present in the population. Central Asia (Turkestan) can rightly define itself by its particular combination of ethnic populations, geography, languages, and culture, a formula in which only language seemed to retain its basic identity and the justification for the ethnonym *Turkestan*.

With the arrival of newcomers to the region in the sixteenth century, a most eloquent tribute to Turkestan's beauty came from *The Book of the Guest of Bukhara*, composed by the Persian Fazl Allah ibn Ruzbihan Isfahani in 1513–1515 in honor of the Uzbek chieftain, Muhammad Shaibani Khan (d. 1510). Writing to honor his royal patron, Ruzbihan called Turkestan the head on the world's body, a blessed place that in spring recalled the gardens of paradise celebrated in the Qur'an (89.6), abundant with flowers, brooks, and meadows. By laying such heavy stress upon Turkestan's luxuriant countryside, Ruzbihan dismisses the area's settlements as inconsequential. Ruzbihan uses an oversimplified term when he says that "Turkestan consists of thirty fortresses strung along the bank of the Sayhun River," starting with Arquq. That string of strongpoints facing Transoxiana on the east bank of the Syr Darya garrisoned few troops and concentrated none of the nomads, but it suggested the power of the town in identifying both the surrounding areas and people. In that same period, Shaibani Khan's unsuccessful Timurid archrival for political supremacy in Central Asia, Zahiruddin Muhammad Babur (d. 1530), saw as Turkestan the lands to which the Syr Darya flowed after it turned northward from Khojand (Leninabad) and Shahrukhiyya; he clearly distinguished the area from Transoxiana but set no eastern limits.

The mass migration of Uzbek nomads to Transoxiana at the very end of the fifteenth century renewed the Turkic layers of the population, greatly augmenting the residual Turkic stock that remained from earlier times. So long as the Shaibanid dynasty ruled (1500–1598) in Transoxiana, a fragile unity prevailed in that part of Central Asia. But a stubborn independence repeatedly extracted Khwarazm (Khiva) from their control, and Kazakhs and Mugh-

als dominated the plains across the Syr Darya as far as China. The Shaibanids and the successor dynasty that succeeded them, the Ashtarkhanids (1599–1753), struggled desperately to hold together the components of Turkestan, but their efforts culminated in fragmentation. With the rise of four tribal dynasties at Bukhara, Khiva, Kabul, and Khokand in the eighteenth century, the overarching conception of Turkestan receded from the foreground. The terms *Kazakh, Kirghiz,* and *Turkmen,* referring to internal tribal divisions among these nomadic Turkic peoples, prevailed over the comprehensive *Turkestan,* which might have bridged those divides.

These small khanates and amirates hostilely drove one another into ever deeper isolation from the changing world, totally losing touch with modernizing technology and the social or political thought of the Middle East or Europe. In this period, *Turkestan* became less a name the region gave to itself than a term used or imposed by outsiders. Thus, the situation that had prevailed at the beginning of the turkicization was repeated. So it was in the nineteenth century that when the most recent invaders of Central Asia, the Russians, conquered the heart of western Central Asia, they once more applied the name *Turkestan* to a part of the region. And for the first time in history, Turkestan acquired precise political boundaries and a fixed location, thanks to tsarist administrators. In 1865, before the June conquest of Tashkent, the Russians organized a Turkestan region stretching eastward from the Aral Sea to Lake Issik Kul, temporarily revalidating much of the fifteenth-century vision of a Turkestan across the Syr Darya. The region gave way in July 1867 to a Governor-Generalship of Turkestan, for years headed by a Russian general, A. P. von Kaufman. Its southwestern boundary ran up the course of the Amu Darya from the Aral Sea to the frontier of the amirate of Bukhara, whose eastern side it skirted all the way to the Indian border. From there, the Governor-Generalship's territory, bordering China, reached almost to Lake Zaisan. Its northern limits, starting from the Aral Sea, paralleled the Syr Darya to the east some distance but included a large section of the plains area that had been regarded by the Shaibanids as Turkestan. Lake Balkhash provided the remaining northern marker for this new imperial version of western Turkestan.

Just as tsarist forces were extending Russian hegemony over independent Kazakhstan and Transoxiana, farther to the east contrary currents were flowing. Eastern Turkestan, united with western Turkestan in the sixth and seventh centuries, and again under the Karakhanids in the late tenth and

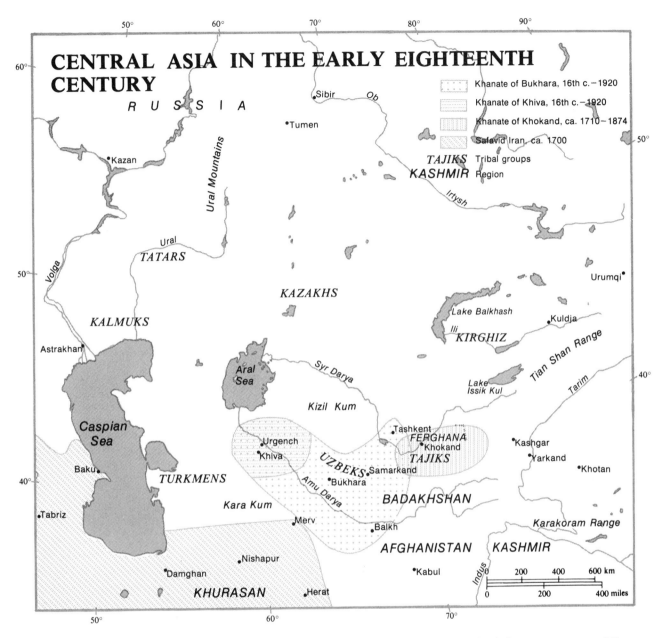

CENTRAL ASIA IN THE EARLY EIGHTEENTH CENTURY

Khanate of Bukhara, 16th c.–1920	
Khanate of Khiva, 16th c.–1920	
Khanate of Khokand, ca. 1710–1874	
Safavid Iran, ca. 1700	
TAJIKS Tribal groups	
KASHMIR Region	

RUSSIA

Sibir · Ob

Tumen ·

· Kazan

Ural Mountains

Irtysh

Urumqi ·

TATARS

Ural

Volga

KAZAKHS

Lake Balkhash

Kuldja ·

KALMUKS

Ili

KIRGHIZ

Tian Shan Range

Astrakhan ·

Aral Sea

Syr Darya

Lake Issik Kul

Tarim

Caspian Sea

Kizil Kum

Tashkent ·

FERGHANA

Khokand ·

Kashgar ·

Baku ·

Urgench ·

Khiva ·

UZBEKS · Samarkand

TAJIKS

Yarkand ·

Khotan ·

TURKMENS

Amu Darya

Bukhara ·

BADAKHSHAN

Tabriz ·

Kara Kum

Merv ·

Balkh ·

Karakoram Range

· Nishapur

AFGHANISTAN   *KASHMIR*

· Damghan

Kabul ·

Indus

0	200	400	600 km
0		200	400 miles

KHURASAN   · Herat

eleventh, slipped from Chinese fingers once more after the mid-nineteenth century. In a typical Turkestani manner, the two parts of the huge region now became linked once again. A strong army commander, pushed out of the center of the khanate of Khokand by intensifying Russian military pressure, came over to Kashgar. Ya'qub Beg (d. 1877) had already demonstrated notable fighting skill against superior Russian arms. He now combined western Turkestani warriors from Khokand and Badakhshan with eastern Dungan, Kazakh, and Kashgar soldiers to destroy Chinese garrisons in the Six Towns (Altishahr) of eastern Turkestan.

Under Khokandian leadership, as it had often functioned, the eastern sector saw a brief period,

from 1865 to 1877, of rule by a native son of Turkestan before Chinese armed forces reinstated foreign government from Beijing. The gap thus opened between eastern and western Turkestan narrowed somewhat in the 1930s and 1940s with the rising cultural and political influence of Russian Turkestan in Kashgar and Urumchi. That rapprochement slackened after the Chinese Communist takeover of eastern Turkestan in 1948–1949. The name *Turkestan* disappeared, and the area it had encompassed became known officially as the Xinjiang-Uighur Autonomous Region.

The days of the name *Turkestan* were also numbered in western Central Asia. From 1870 to 1917 czarist authorities issued an official bulletin in Turkestani languages with the title *Turkistan wilaya-tining gazeti*, and they maintained the Governor-Generalship of Turkestan from 1867 to 1917, although in much reduced size after 1882; the entire portion bordering China was removed into a different tsarist jurisdiction. The tsarist usage and sanction of the name *Turkestan* had begun to popularize it among modern Central Asian intellectuals, who applied *Turkestan* to histories, newspapers, and other writings. This increased after the revolution and coup d'état in 1917, when the Governor-Generalship of Turkestan gave way immediately to a Turkestan republic, soon renamed (1918) the Turkestan Autonomous Soviet Socialist Republic. This heterogeneous unit disintegrated in 1924–1925, when the Communist Party leadership instituted a partition of the Turkestan ASSR into smaller "union" and "autonomous" units, each named for one of the principal Central Asian ethnic communities of the region: Karakalpak, Kirghiz, Tajik, Turkmen, and Uzbek. North of the Turkestan ASSR had lain the great expanse of the Kirghizistan (i.e., Kazakh) Autonomous Soviet Socialist Republic, formed in 1920; its lands were further enlarged by the addition of large portions of the former Turkestan ASSR.

In the process of introducing the unitary ethnic or monoethnic principle of territorial-administrative organization to southern Central Asia, the authorities allowed the Marxist tenet of unifying the working class without regard to ethnic differences to give way to the expediency of an ethnic segregation. They meant, above all, to replace with Russian influence the traditional Kazakh and Uzbek dominance of most areas where the population of other Central Asian nationalities preponderated. At the same time, the new Soviet dictator, Joseph Stalin (d. 1953), relentlessly attacked the very idea of any Turkestan polity through an ideological campaign against what he and other Communist spokesmen labeled pan-Turkism. As the Russian Communists employed ideological and material suasion, they stigmatized the old name *Turkestan* itself.

After 1925, political terror prevented any public mention of the geographical or ethnic name. Turkestan had ceased to exist inside the USSR. After Stalin's death, the term came back into Soviet historical writing and discussion but not into current use for any part of Central Asia other than the Turkestan Military District headquartered in Tashkent. Outside the country, the controversial ethnonym continued to live on in imagination and memory, especially among many thousands of emigrants who fled the region they or their elders had known as

Turkestan. The émigrés persist in their devotion to that supraethnic appellation, using it regularly in headings for books, journals, and newsletters concerned with both the western and eastern, as well as the Afghan, parts of the area. A Turkestan-American Association of several thousand members based in Brooklyn, New York, and similar organizations in Pakistan, Saudi Arabia, and Turkey still actively conduct busy series of cultural, social, and sometimes political events in the last quarter of the twentieth century.

[*See also* Central Asia; Xinjiang; Kazakhs; Kirghizia; Turkmenistan; Uzbekistan; Ferghana; Khwarazm; *and* Shaibanid Dynasty.]

Edward Allworth, ed., *Central Asia: A Century of Russian Rule* (1967). Wilhelm Barthold, "A Short History of Turkistan," in *Four Studies on the History of Central Asia*, translated by V. and T. Minorsky (1956–1962), vol. 1, pp. 1–68, and *Turkestan down to the Mongol Invasion* (2d ed., 1958). Mirza Muhammad Haidar, *A History of the Moghuls of Central Asia, Being the Tarikh-i Rashidi*, translated by E. Denison Ross (1898; reprint, 1970). Edgar Knobloch, *Beyond the Oxus: Archaeology, Art and Architecture of Central Asia* (1972). Owen Lattimore, et al., *Pivot of Asia: Sinkiang and the Inner Asian Frontiers of China and Russia* (1950). Eugene Schuyler, *Turkistan: Notes of a Journey in Russian Turkistan, Khokand, Bukhara, and Kuldja*, 2 vols., (1876–1877). Allen S. Whiting and Sheng Shih-Ts'ai, *Sinkiang: Pawn or Pivot?* (1958).

EDWARD ALLWORTH

TURKIC LANGUAGES. Turkic designates a family of closely related languages that forms a subgroup within the Altaic language group, which also includes Mongolian, Manchu-Tunguz, Korean, and possibly Japanese. The nature of the Altaic relationship is still a matter of controversy. Somewhat less controversial, but nonetheless problematic, is the nature of the relationship of some Turkic languages to each other. At present, Turkic may be divided into two subgroups: Oghuric/Bulgaric/Chuvashic and Common Turkic (Turki, Oghuz, Kipchak, Siberian, and Yakut). These two subgroups are the products of the following historical developments:

1. *Oghuric/Bulgaric/Chuvashic:*
   Ancient Oghuric (sixth–tenth/twelfth? century)
   Middle Bulgaric (thirteenth–fourteenth century)
   Modern Chuvashic

2. *Common Turkic:*
   Ancient Turkic (sixth–tenth century)
   Middle Turkic (tenth–fifteenth century)
   Modern Turkic

Within the two modern subgroups of Modern Chuvashic and Modern Turkic, there are a number of specific languages spoken by a variety of peoples (see figure 1). The following treatment of these languages will take their historical antecedents into account.

Modern Chuvashic. The subgrouping of Modern Chuvashic is so sharply distinguished from the other Turkic languages that some scholars view it as a separate branch of the Altaic group. It is marked by lambdacism *(l* for Turkic *sh)* and rhotacism *(r* for Turkic *z).* Some Turkic languages of early medieval Eurasia were of this type (e.g., Oghur, Onoghur, and Bulgar; the affiliations of Hunnic and Khazar are unclear). It is most closely associated with Danubian and Volga Bulgaric. The former gave way to Slavic (in late ninth-century Bulgaria), which was largely supplanted by Kipchak in the aftermath of the Mongol conquest of the Middle Volga in the thirteenth century. The language survives today only among the 1.7 million speakers of Chuvash in the Chuvash ASSR and adjoining regions of the USSR. Since 1875 Chuvash has been written in the Cyrillic script.

Modern Turkic. There are five groupings within the Modern Turkic subgroup: Oghuz, Kipchak, Siberian Turkic, and Yakut. Each group comprises languages that are closely related historically and/or geographically.

Turki Grouping. The Turki Grouping evolved from the Turk and Uighur (Ancient Turkic) languages recorded in Runic, Uighur, Sogdian, Manichaean, and Brahmi scripts, beginning in the eighth century, if not earlier. These gave way to Karakhanid, Kwarazmian, and Chagatai Turkic (Eastern Middle Turkic, tenth to fifteenth century) in Turkestan. Modern Turki includes Uzbek, Modern Uighur and Khoton, Salar, and Yellow Uighur. There are 12.5 million speakers of Uzbek in the Uzbek SSR and adjacent areas of the USSR. In addition, there are 1.2 million in Afghanistan and between 15,000 and 18,000 in Xinjiang Province, China. Uzbek is now written in the Cyrillic script, but the Arabic script was previously used. There are 5 million speakers of Modern Uighur in Xinjiang Province, 210,000 in the USSR (mostly in the Uzbek, Kazakh, and Kirghiz republics) and a small group speaking the closely related Khoton language in the

FIGURE 1. *Modern Turkic Languages.*

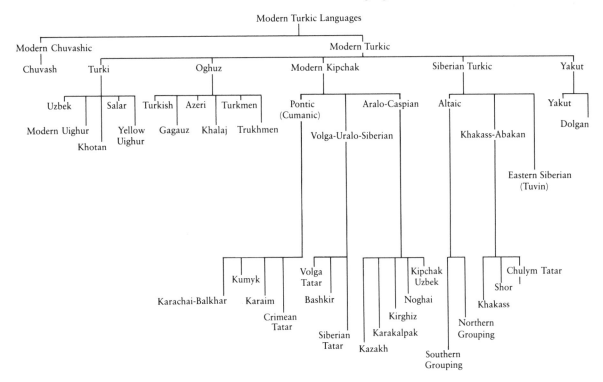

Mongolian People's Republic. Uighurs previously used the Arabic script, but currently use the Latin script in China and the Cyrillic script (since 1947) in the USSR. The Latin script was briefly used in the USSR between 1930 and 1947. There are 30,000 speakers of Salar, which is closely related to Uighur, virtually all of whom live in Gansu Province, China; they use the Arabic script. Speakers of Yellow Uighur number between 4,000 and 10,000; like the Salar, they live in Gansu Province. Other Yellow Uighurs speak Mongol, Tibetan, or Chinese.

Oghuz Grouping. The Oghuz Grouping is most clearly associated with the Syr Darya Oghuz tribal union (late eighth to eleventh century), from which the Seljuk empire emerged. Oghuz words are recorded in Mahmud al-Kashgari's *Diwan lughat al-Turk* (1074). Old Anatolian (Western Middle Turkic), that is, Seljuk and Old Ottoman, texts date back to the thirteenth and fourteenth centuries, respectively. Oghuz dialects are recorded in the fourteenth-century *Rasulid Hexaglot,* and Turkmen words are recorded in the Mamluk Kipchak glossaries (fourteenth–fifteenth century). Modern Oghuz includes Turkish and Gagauz, Azeri, Khalaj, Turkmen, and Trukhmen. Turkish is spoken in Turkey by the majority of its 44 million inhabitants and in parts of the Balkans. Turkish was written in the Arabic script until 1928 and now uses the Latin script. Turkish also includes Gagauz, spoken by some 173,000 Orthodox Christians in the USSR and Bulgaria. Azeri or Azerbaijani Turkic is spoken by 5.4 million people in the Azerbaijan republic and about 5 million in Iran. It is still written in the Arabic script in Iran, but in the USSR it was replaced by the Latin script from 1922 to 1939 and is now written in the Cyrillic script. Khalaj, spoken by 18,000 or 19,000 people in Iran, was formerly considered an Azeri dialect but is now viewed by some Turkologists as distinct. There are 2 million speakers of Turkmen in the Turkmen SSR and adjoining regions of the USSR; in addition, there are 500,000 speakers in Iran and 125,000 in Afghanistan. A small grouping, estimated at only 8,000 in 1970, is the Trukhmen, whose speakers are found in the North Caucasus. Its Arabic script has been replaced by Cyrillic.

Kipchak (or Northwestern) Grouping. The Kipchak Grouping developed out of the Kimek-Kipchak tribal confederation (ninth century) of central Eurasia that, under Cun-Cuman leadership in the eleventh century shifted to the Pontic-Caspian steppes while retaining parts of western Siberian and Kazakhstan. These tribes, later the mainstay of the Golden and White Hordes (thirteenth to sixteenth century), figure prominently in the ethnogenesis of most of the Turkic peoples of Soviet Central Asia and the Urals. Medieval Kipchak (Middle Northwestern Turkic) is known from al-Kashgari, the Mamluk Arabo-Kipchak glossaries (fourteenth to fifteenth century), and the fourteenth-century *Codex Cumanicus.* Modern Kipchak is further separated into three divisions: Pontic or Cumanic, Volga-Uralo-Siberian, and Aralo-Caspian.

1. *Pontic or Cumanic languages.* This group includes Karachai-Balkar, Kumyk, the Karaim language, and Crimean Tatar. Karachai-Balkar is spoken by 131,000 Karachai and 66,000 Balkars in the North Caucasus. Formerly written in the Arabic script, it now uses Cyrillic, as does Kumyk, spoken by 228,400 people who also live in the North Caucasus. The Karaim were a sect of non-Talmudic Jews originally centered in the Crimea and now dispersed in the USSR (3,000–4,000) and Poland (several hundred). Their language, written in Hebrew letters, is moribund. Crimean Tatar derives from the language of the khanate of Crimea (fifteenth to eighteenth century), with strong Oghuz influence. Most of its 500,000 speakers live in Soviet Central Asia, where they were deported by the Soviet government in May 1944. Some 5 million people in Turkey, Rumania, and Poland claim Crimean Tatar descent. The now extinct Byelorussian-Lithuanian Tatar was closely related to Crimean Tatar. Similarly, Krymchak, a form of Crimean Tatar spoken by Talmudic Jews (6,000 in 1926), is virtually extinct.

2. *Volga-Uralo-Siberian Languages.* These languages, all of which formerly used the Arabic script and now use Cyrillic, derive from the Kipchak of the Golden and White Hordes and include Volga Tatar, Bashkir, and Siberian Tatar. There are 6.3 million speakers of Volga Tatar in the Tatar SSR and surrounding regions. Speakers of Bashkir number 1.3 million and live in the Bashkir SSR and adjacent areas. Siberian Tatar designates some 100,000 speakers of dialects deriving from the Kipchak of the White Horde (e.g., Baraba, Tara, etc.). They use Volga Tatar as their literary tongue.

3. *Aralo-Caspian Languages.* The Aralo-Caspian languages evolved from Medieval Eastern Kipchak and comprises Kazakh, Karakalpak, Kirghiz, Noghai, and Kipchak Uzbek. There are 6.5 million speakers of Kazakh in the Kazakh SSR and surrounding areas of the USSR, between 600,000 and 700,000 in China, 40,000 in the Mongolian People's Republic, and 3,000 in Afghanistan. Speakers of Karakalpak number 303,300 in the Karakalpak ASSR and 2,000 in Afghanistan. There are 1.9 mil-

lion speakers of Kirghiz in the Kirghiz, Tajik, and Kazakh republics, 80,000 in China, and 25,000 in Afghanistan. Their ethnogenesis in very complicated. The speakers of Noghai, who number 60,000, live in the North Caucasus and are the descendants of a union of Mongol and Kipchak tribes that formed the horde of Noghai (d. 1300). About 127,000 Kipchak Uzbeks were noted in the Ferghana valley in the early twentieth century; others are in the Khwarazm region with speakers of the Oghuz Uzbek dialect.

Siberian Turkic. Many questions regarding the relationships of the Siberian Turkic languages to each other and to other Turkic groups are unresolved. In the ethnogenesis of these peoples, Samoyed, Ob-Ugrian, and paleosiberian elements played a role in addition to that of the Turkic peoples. There are three divisions within the Siberian Turkic grouping: Altaic, Khakass-Abakan, and Eastern Siberian.

1. *Altaic subgroup.* Its speakers residing in the Gorno-Altai region, this group is further subdivided into the Southern Grouping, of Altai or Oirat, and the Northern Grouping, or Tuva, Cumandu, Lebed', and Khalkhan. The total number of speakers in the subgroup is 60,000.

2. *Khakass-Abakan subgroup.* Centered in the Khakass Autonomous Oblast of the USSR, this group includes the Khakass, the Shor, and the Chulym Tatar. The Khakass, formerly known as the Minusinsk or Abakan Tatars, comprises the Sagai, Beltir, Kacha, Kizil, and Koybal tribal groups totaling 70,700 speakers. There are about 16,000 Shor, formerly known as the Mrastsy or Chernevye Tatars; they reside in the Kuznetskii Alatau region. The Chulym Tatars, whose language is moribund, are included in the figures for the Khakass. They have no written language and were heavily russified in the late nineteenth century.

3. *Eastern Siberian subgroup.* Also called the Tuvin (formerly known as the Soyon or Soyot), the eastern Siberians number about 162,000 in the Tuva ASSR, with small groups in the Mongolian People's Republic. Although they previously used the literary Mongol script, they now use the Cyrillic alphabet.

Yakut. The northernmost of the Turkic peoples, the origins of the Yakuts are unclear but appear to point to an amalgam of Turkic strains coming from the south that mixed with local Siberian peoples. Lexically (more than 50 percent of the vocabulary is non-Turkic), morphologically, and phonetically it diverges considerably from the other Turkic languages. Almost all of the 328,000 speakers of the Yakut language live in the Yakut ASSR. Associated with them are some 5,000 Dolgans.

[*See also* Altaic Languages; Kazakhs; Kirghizia; Kipchaks; Tatars; Uighurs; *and* Uzbekistan.]

S. Akiner, *Islamic Peoples of the Soviet Union* (1983). K. H. Menges, *The Turkic Languages and Peoples* (1968). N. Poppe, *Introduction to Altaic Linguistics* (1965).

PETER B. GOLDEN

TURKMENISTAN. The Turkmen Soviet Socialist Republic is one of fifteen union republics of the Soviet Union. Its territory covers 187,200 square miles, comprising four regions: Ashkhabad, Marv (Merv), Chardzhou (Charjui), and Tashauz. Turkmenistan lies to the east of the Caspian Sea, to the north of Iran, to the west of Afghanistan, and to the south of Kazakhstan and Uzbekistan. The capital city and administrative center is Ashkhabad.

A vast desert called the Kara Kum ("black sand") dominates 90 percent of the republic. The oases on the Amu Darya, Murghab, and Tedzhen rivers, those fed by the alluvial fans of the Kopet Dagh mountains to the south, and the coastal cities on the Caspian are where most of the republic's population resides.

The Turkmen SSR was formed in November 1924 when the Turkestan ASSR was divided along ethnic lines, and all but a very small part of the Soviet Union's Turkmen population lives there. Of the republic's total population of 2,765,000 (1979), the Turkmen represent 68.4 percent, Russians 12.6 percent, Uzbeks 8.5 percent, and Kazakhs 2.9 percent, with the remainder divided among small groups of Tatars, Ukrainians, Armenians, Azerbaijanis, and others. The Turkmens are descendants of the twenty-four tribes of the Oghuz (Ghuzz), an eastern Turkic livestock-herding nomadic people who moved south into present-day Turkmenistan in the eleventh century.

In 1925 an agrarian reform program was begun in Turkmenistan. Despite much resistance among the tribesmen, lands previously communally or tribally owned were expropriated and redistributed. This reorganization was an effective way for the Soviets to increase their power in the territory, since it broke the traditional political and economic relationships based on the availability of water and on control of land for grazing and farming. Eight years later the agricultural lands were reorganized into *kolkhozi* under the collectivization program. Modernization and industrialization during the Soviet period have altered the traditional nomadic ways of the Turkmen. Yet in rural areas a semi-nomadic way of life continues, and clan and tribal awareness persists.

Turkmenistan is the most arid republic in the USSR. Yet, owing to water projects such as the six-hundred-kilometer Kara Kum canal, which brings water from the Amu Darya river, as well as extensive irrigation, farming is one of Turkmenistan's most important economic activities. Crops grown include cotton, wheat, rice, vegetables, grapes, and other fruit. Livestock herding is also important; sheep are most numerous, followed by cattle, goats, horses, and camels.

The Turkmen SSR is the Soviet Union's largest supplier of petroleum resources; it also has large reserves of natural gas. Other natural resources include sulfur, iodine, bromine, natural sodium sulfate, and many nonferrous metals, such as copper, molybdenum, gold, and lead.

[*See also* Ghuzz; Kara Kum; *and* Turkestan.]

Edward Allworth, *Central Asia: A Century of Russian Rule* (1967). A. G. Babaev, *Turkmenistan* (1969). Theodore Shabad, *Basic Industrial Resources of the USSR* (1969). Geoffrey Wheeler, *The Modern History of Soviet Central Asia* (1964).   WILLIAM A. MCCABE

TURKOMANCHAY, TREATY OF.

Signed in 1828, this treaty marked the end of the second war between Iran and Russia (1826–1828), which occurred during the reign of Fath Ali Shah Qajar (1798–1834). Following the 1813 Treaty of Gulistan, which ceded Georgia to Russia, Fath Ali Shah, bent on revenge, started a new war without adequate preparations. Russia annexed the provinces of Erivan and Nakhichevan and thus achieved a more viable border with Iran around the Aras River. The Russians were also given exclusive rights to sail naval vessels on the Caspian Sea, and Iran had to pay a fixed tribute. Iran was also forced to sign a commercial treaty that provided Russian subjects with extraterritorial privileges and thus established a pattern of capitulatory rights for European subjects in Iran under the Qajar dynasty.

[*See also* Qajar Dynasty.]

J. Hurewitz, ed., *The Middle East and North Africa in World Politics,* vol. 1 (1975). R. Ramazani, *The Foreign Policy of Iran: 1500–1941* (1966).   NEGUIN YAVARI

TUYUHUN,

a tribal state in China's far northwest (modern Qinghai Province) that arose as part of the fragmentation of power in North China at the end of the fourth century. Its population was primarily Tibetan, with a ruling class of Xianbei ethnic origin. The loosely organized state endured until its conquest by Emperor Yang of the Sui dynasty in the early years of the seventh century.

Wolfram Eberhard, *A History of China* (3d ed., 1969).

JOHN S. MAJOR

TWELVERS. *See* Ithna Ashari.

TWENTY-ONE DEMANDS.

In January 1915 Japan's government presented the Chinese government with a list of twenty-one items, asking the confirmation, extension, and addition of various Japanese rights and privileges in China. After several months of negotiations the Chinese president, faced with a Japanese ultimatum, acceded to a reduced version of the original demands.

Japanese claims to a special role in China had become more insistent after the Russo-Japanese War (1904–1905), when Japan inherited Russian-leased territory and railway rights in southern Manchuria. The outbreak of war in Europe in 1914 appeared to present an opportunity to advance Japan's position. Immediately siding with the Allies, Japan attacked the German position in Shandong Province and, instead of returning German holdings to the Chinese, kept them under Japanese sovereignty.

Meanwhile, the Japanese foreign minister, Katō Kōmei, put together a package of desiderata that would shore up what was felt to be Japan's unique interest in its large Asian neighbor. The resulting demands, presented to President Yuan Shikai on 18 January 1915, were of different types. Some asked China to extend leases and concessions already held by Japan but due to run out, some as soon as the 1920s, or to confirm positions of uncertain legality, such as the recently acquired holdings in Shandong. Others were new privileges, such as the right to own property and reside as farmers or businessmen in the interior areas of southern Manchuria and eastern Inner Mongolia. Among the new privileges were some so intrusive that they threatened to convert China into a Japanese protectorate.

The more extreme demands were dropped at the insistence of senior statesmen in Japan, when Foreign Minister Katō sought to end Chinese procrastination with an ultimatum. The presentation of the ultimatum on 7 May 1915 was accompanied by Japanese military posturing. Britain recommended to Yuan that he capitulate, and he did so within the two days set by the Japanese. Chinese popular outrage at these events was expressed in a vigorous boycott of Japanese goods. Considered in Japan a bungled effort, the episode left a deep sense of injury in China.

[*See also* China, Republic Period; May Fourth Movement; *and* Yuan Shikai.]

Madeleine Chi, *China Diplomacy, 1914–1918* (1970). Marius B. Jansen, *The Japanese and Sun Yat-sen* (1954). Ian H. Nish, *Alliance in Decline: A Study in Anglo-Japanese Relations, 1908–1923* (1972). James Reed, *The Missionary Mind and American East Asian Policy, 1911–1915* (1983).   ERNEST P. YOUNG

TYABJI, BADRUDDIN (1844–1906), Indian lawyer, politician, and jurist. An adherent of the Sulaimani Bohras, a small Isma'ili sect, Tyabji was the most prominent of the many members of the Tyabji-Fyzee clan who distinguished themselves at the Bombay Bar. The Tyabjis were socially and religiously "liberal" and deeply involved in the civic associations of nineteenth-century Bombay. Before his appointment as a justice of the Bombay High Court in 1895 ended his public political career, Tyabji was one of the few Muslim leaders to involve himself seriously in the Indian National Congress, serving as its president from 1887 to 1888. He engaged in a lengthy debate with Sayyid Ahmad Khan and Amir Ali over whether Muslims should stay out of the Congress. His support of the organization was, however, qualified. He believed that its role should be limited to the discussion of topics on which Hindus and Muslims completely agreed.

[*See also* Bombay; Indian National Congress; Ahmad Khan, Sir Sayyid; *and* Amir Ali.]

Muslim Judges (1932). Peter Hardy, *Muslims of British India* (1972).   GREGORY C. KOZLOWSKI

TYDINGS-McDUFFIE ACT, 1934 act by which the United States granted independence to the Philippines. It was a slightly revised version of the Hare-Hawes-Cutting Act of 1933, which had been passed by Congress over President Hoover's veto but had been rejected by a plebiscite of the Filipino people. The world economic depression, American isolationist sentiment, opposition to Philippine competition from domestic beet sugar, cordage, cotton, and dairy interests as well as from organized labor combined with long-standing anti-imperialist guilt feelings to foster Philippine freedom. The Tydings-McDuffie Act provided for a ten-year transition period from American colonial rule to complete independence on 4 July 1946. During that time the Filipinos wrote a constitution and assumed numerous self-governing functions, while the Americans retained responsibility for defense and foreign affairs. The economic provisions of the Tydings-McDuffie Act were subsequently modified since the Philippines could not be suddenly cut loose from the preferential trade relationships that four decades of American colonial rule had engendered.

[*See also* Philippines.]

Theodore Friend, *Between Two Empires* (1965). Joseph R. Hayden, *The Philippines: A Study in National Development* (1942).   GRANT K. GOODMAN

U

UCHIDA RYŌHEI (1874–1973), ultranationalist activist in Japan. Uchida was born in Fukuoka Prefecture and became a disciple of Tōyama Mitsuru. In 1894 he went to Korea to help the Tonghak rebels. In 1901 he established, with Tōyama's blessing, the Kokuryūkai (Amur River Society) to combat Russian expansion in East Asia, and he remained the leader of that society until the end of his life.

Uchida advocated war against Russia, and when it broke out in 1904 his men helped the Japanese army in Manchuria as agents and translators. In 1905 he helped lead rallies against the Portsmouth Peace Treaty. Uchida assisted leaders of liberation movements in Asia, like Sun Yat-sen in China and Emilio Aguinaldo in the Philippines, hoping thereby to gain their support for Japan's leadership in Asia. He was particularly active in agitation for the annexation of Korea. After the annexation, in 1921, he established the Dōkōkai, an organization dedicated to improving relations between Japanese and Koreans.

Uchida opposed liberalism and universal suffrage. In 1925 he was arrested for complicity in the attempt on the life of the liberal prime minister Katō Takaaki but was released the following month. In 1931 Uchida sponsored the Dai Nihon Seisantō, a fascistic organization of industrialists and workers, and became its first president. In 1934 he joined the religious organization Shōwa Shinseikai of Deguchi Wanisaburō and became its vice president. Although he never held an official post, he maintained close relations with many military and civilian leaders and served as their link to the right wing of Japanese politics and society.

[See also Kokuryūkai and Tōyama Mitsuru.]

Delmer M. Brown, *Nationalism in Japan* (1955). Marius B. Jansen, *The Japanese and the Sun Yat-sen* (1954).

BEN-AMI SHILLONY

UCHIMURA KANZŌ (1861–1930), Japanese essayist and Christian leader. Uchimura's voluminous works became modern classics. They describe the experience of a scrupulous man when he adopts a worldview different from that of his countrymen. Uchimura's life reflected the strains that Meiji westernization imposed upon individuals. Readers turned to him when they also felt themselves unable to live simultaneously as good Japanese and good world citizens.

Uchimura's divided allegiance developed out of his upbringing. His samurai-administrator father lost everything when the Tokugawa government fell. Uchimura aimed to restore family status through academic excellence. Under American teachers he became Christian. When he finished college, he could work freely in English. His ambition and ability led him to attend Amherst College in Massachusetts. An autobiography, *How I Became a Christian* (or, alternatively, *The Diary of a Japanese Convert*), recounts his experiences in Japan and America and reflects both great respect for the United States and perplexity at its pretensions. Back in Japan in 1888, Uchimura found himself unable to work either with American missionaries or Japanese. The missionaries disliked his respect for Japanese traditions. When he hesitated to bow before the signature of the emperor, nationalists accused him of treason. Numerous essays about the problem of divided loyalty made him famous.

Later works dealt with the individual's relation to the state and to the Christian God. As a Christian, Uchimura felt he should object to mistaken government policy. The Treaty of Shimonoseki (1895) convinced him that the government planned to plunder China rather than help it modernize as spokesmen had claimed. At the approach of the Russo-Japanese War in 1903, he advocated pacifism and thenceforth shunned official contacts. Readers after the Pacific

War have considered these acts prophetic. Uchimura seems to shine as a beacon of integrity over a sea of opportunism.

When Uchimura became a pacifist he resigned his post as one of Japan's leading newspaper editors. For the rest of his life he published a small Bible-study magazine. It interpreted the Bible as a work of history, rich in myth and allegory. Uchimura indicated how individuals could live as Christians through studying the Bible and through prayer. The church, he felt, embodied Western Christian experience, which provided the Japanese believer with a distorted view of Christ's legacy. Christianity without the church suited Japanese needs. Uchimura's followers molded these ideas into an independent Christian movement.

Uchimura resembled many educated Asians who feared Western expansion. He accepted Christianity and judged his government by it. He simultaneously insisted that traditional Japanese ethics held much of value. He thus forecast the indigenous theologies that characterizes the young churches of Asia and Africa.

[*See also* Christianity: Christianity in Japan.]

John F. Howes, "Uchimura Kanzō," in *Philosophers and Kings: Studies in Leadership*, edited by Dankwart A. Rustow (1970). Ray Moore, *Culture and Religion in Japanese-American Relations: Essays on Uchimura Kanzō, 1861–1930* (1981). Uchimura Kanzo, *The Diary of a Japanese Convert* (1895).

JOHN F. HOWES

UDAIPUR, town in Rajasthan, India. Udaipur was founded by the Sisodiya Rajput ruler of Mewar, Rana Udai Singh (c. 1537–1572), sometime after the fall of Chitor to the Mughals in 1568 and Udai Singh's death in 1572. It remained little more than a village until the reigns of Rana Jagat Singh (1628–1652) and Rana Raj Singh (1652–1680). These rulers benefited greatly from the alliance with the Mughals worked out in 1614 by their ancestor, Rana Amar Singh (1597–1620), and they used the wealth to which their rank in the Mughal service entitled them to construct many exquisite buildings within their capital. Udaipur grew to be a considerable town by 1660, with a population of some twenty thousand households according to one contemporary estimate. In the British period, Udaipur was the capital of the Udaipur, or Mewar, princely state.

[*See also* Mewar; Rajput; Rajasthan; *and* Chitor.]

RICHARD DAVIS SARAN

UEKI EMORI (1857–1892), Japanese political thinker and Popular Rights activist of the Meiji period. Born a Tosa samurai, Ueki was originally trained in the *han* academy in Edo. Subsequently he lived with Itagaki Taisuke and was much impressed with Itagaki's ideas on popular rights, as well with as those of Fukuzawa Yukichi. As with many other former samurai, Ueki's interest in political thought led him to journalism. In 1876 he published an article titled "A Government that Makes Monkeys out of Men" that led to a confrontation with the authorities. The following year he started a newspaper and magazine with Itagaki, was active in the Risshisha, and lectured throughout the country on behalf of the Popular Rights (Jiyū Minken) Movement. In 1881 he helped organize the national conference of sake brewers out of which the Liberal Party (Jiyūtō) was formed. Known as one of the most important theoreticians of the Popular Rights Movement, Ueki favored a constitutional monarchy with the state organized along federal lines, a unicameral assembly elected by universal suffrage, extensive civil rights (including the right to resist an autocratic state), the reform of the family system, and the liberation of the individual from the fetters of tradition. Elected to the first Diet as a representative from Kōchi Prefecture in 1890, Ueki died at the age of thirty-five in 1892.

[*See also* Jiyū Minken *and* Risshisha.]

F. G. NOTEHELFER

UEMURA MASAHISA (1858–1925), Japanese Christian minister. The eldest son of a high feudal family (*hatamoto*) in Edo, Uemura studied English with the missionaries James Ballagh and S. R. Brown in Yokohama in the early 1870s. In 1873 he was baptized and decided to devote his life to the Christian ministry. In 1880 he teamed up with Kozaki Hiromichi to publish the *Rikugō zasshi*, which became one of the major journals of opinion and ideas in Meiji Japan. Subsequently he took an active role in publishing and editing a variety of Christian papers and magazines. Founder of the Fujimichō church, he was a formidable preacher and evangelist and the acknowledged leader of the "Yokohama band" of Christians. A gifted writer and translator, he helped to translate the Old Testament into Japanese. A strong advocate of Christian individualism, Uemura asserted that conscience could not become subject to the state and resisted government efforts to control the church. In a major debate with Ebina Danjō and the "Kumamoto band," carried out between 1901 and 1902, Uemura defended the conservative position of the church against Ebina's mixture of traditional Japanese thought, nationalism, and Unitarian-Universalist ideas.

[See also Ebina Danjō and Christianity: Christianity in Japan.]

F. G. NOTEHELFER

UESUGI KENSHIN (1530–1578), a powerful daimyo of northern Japan during the late Sengoku period. The Uesugi family had a distinguished lineage and had served as the deputy shoguns of eastern Japan (Kantō Kanrei) from the fourteenth century. In the chaos following the Ōnin War, the branches of the family fell upon each other in internecine warfare. [See Ōnin War.] By the middle of the sixteenth century only Norimasa remained, clinging to the family name and the memory of the family's former military and political prowess. In the late 1550s Norimasa was driven out of the Kantō by Hōjō Ujiyasu and fled to Echigo, where he put himself under the protection of a powerful local warrior, Nagao Kagetora.

Kagetora was a son of the Echigo shugo-dai and had fought his own brothers during the 1540s, winning the family headship and home castle at Kasugayama early in 1548. He continued to achieve battlefield successes, fought the powerful Takeda Shingen to a standstill at Kawanakajima in Shinano in 1553 and again in 1555, and by the end of that decade emerged as one of several powerful daimyo in the northwest, with control over the province of Echigo. When Uesugi Norimasa asked for protection, Kagetora quickly acceded, and even had himself adopted as Norimasa's son so that he could enjoy the benefits of the more illustrious Uesugi name, including appointment to the position of deputy shogun of the Kantō and theoretical claim to the former Uesugi holdings in the Kantō. Nearly two decades later, Kagetora took the tonsure and the name Kenshin, thus assuming the appellation that historians use most often, Uesugi Kenshin.

Shortly after he had had himself adopted by Norimasa, Uesugi Kenshin began to play out his pretensions for greater regional, and even national, power. In 1560 he drove into the Kantō and besieged Odawara castle, the stronghold of Hōjō Ujiyasu. A Hōjō counterattack threw Uesugi back, first to Kamakura and then to the home base in Echigo. Uesugi launched a second abortive attack against the Hōjō the next spring and fought several major,

if indecisive, battles against his old nemesis Takeda Shingen during the 1560s. Indeed, it was only after Shingen died in 1573 that Uesugi was able to secure control over Etchū. That success stimulated greater dreams, and in 1577 Uesugi advanced into Noto, capturing Nanso castle and even defeating the forces of Oda Nobunaga at the Tedori River in Kaga before settling into winter bivouac. But Uesugi died suddenly of a hemorrhage the next spring, just before breaking camp for the campaign that he hoped would take him toward Kyoto and national glory.

Kenshin was succeeded by his adopted son Kagekatsu, who allied himself with Toyotomi Hideyoshi and secured Uesugi domination over Sado, Etchū, and Noto. In 1597 Kagekatsu was appointed one of the five regents (go-tairō) and the next year was transferred to Aizu-Wakamatsu, his total holdings having an assessed productivity of 1,200,000 koku (measures of rice). Kagekatsu fought against Tokugawa Ieyasu at the Battle of Sekigahara, however, and afterward the victorious Ieyasu stripped Kagekatsu of his holdings and transferred the Uesugi family to a much smaller domain in Dewa, rated at just 300,000 koku, a holding that was later reduced by half.

[See also Takeda Shingen; Sengoku Period; and Sekigahara, Battle of.]

Inoue Tesuo, Uesugi Kenshin (1977).

JAMES L. MCCLAIN

UGAKI KAZUSHIGE (1868–1956), Japanese army minister known for arms reduction and his China policy. An Okayama farmer's son, Ugaki graduated from the Army Academy and War College. In 1902 he went to Germany to study military affairs. He served in Manchuria during the Russo-Japanese War. In 1911 he became chief of the Army Ministry's military section. Recognized by General Tanaka Giichi, Ugaki took part in the planning of the Siberian Intervention. Beginning in 1923 he served as army minister in several cabinets.

In 1925, as army minister in the cabinet of Katō Takaaki, he executed the so-called Ugaki arms reduction, which aimed to modernize, as much as to reduce, the army. His action angered many of his military colleagues but was acclaimed in political circles. The young officers who plotted the March 1931 coup d'état slated Ugaki for premiership. It is generally believed that his last minute change of mind aborted the plot. In June 1931 Ugaki became governor-general of Korea. In January 1937 the emperor ordered Ugaki to form a cabinet. Opposed by military leaders, he was unable to carry out the imperial command. In May 1938 he became foreign minister in the cabinet of Konoe Fumimaro and aspired for a negotiated settlement of the war with China. Unhappy with military interference in China diplomacy, he soon resigned. Although purged by the Occupation after the Pacific War, Ugaki was elected to the House of Councillors in 1953.

Masaru Ikei, "Ugaki Kazushige's View of China and His China Policy, 1915–1930," in *The Chinese and the Japanese: Essays on Political and Cultural Interactions,* edited by Akira Iriye (1980), pp. 199–219.

SHUMPEI OKAMOTO

UIGHURS. The Uighurs are a Sunni Muslim Turkic-speaking people inhabiting northwestern China in Xinjiang, the largest province in the People's Republic of China. Population in the early 1980s numbered approximately seven million, with another 211,000 living in the Uzbek, Kazakh, and Kirghiz Soviet Socialist Republics. Xinjiang's major cities are Kashgar and Urumqi, the capital.

The Uighurs rate among the four most important Turkic populations in the world. They are the largest non-Chinese nationality existing within China's borders. The Uighurs have a long tradition of scholarship and high culture that continues to this day. In the past they have served as a bridge between East and West; in modern times they have been a cultural mediator between the cultures of South Asia and Europe and Russia.

The first mention of Uighurs in written sources occurs in the third century CE, when they were one of the many nomadic tribes to migrate from northern Mongolia to Inner Asia. With the founding of an empire in 744, the Uighurs consolidated their ethnic identity. The second emperor, Moyanchuo, built a capital city and an imperial palace beside the Orkhon River.

Prior to the establishment of their empire the Uighurs practiced their autochthonous religion. After Sogdian traders became influential at the Uighur court, the official religion of the Uighurs became Manichaeism, although many were Buddhists. In the tenth century a Uighur prince, Sadiq Burhan al-Din, converted to Islam, but not until the fourteenth century did Islam become the primary Uighur religion.

During their imperial period the Uighurs developed their own language and script by adapting the Sogdian alphabet. At this time the Uighurs abandoned the entirely nomadic existence of their ances-

tors for a more sedentary urban life in which commerce and agriculture were important. When the Mongol khans ruled Central Asia, they borrowed the Uighur alphabet and adapted it to Mongolian phonetics. In the eleventh and twelfth centuries the Uighur script was gradually replaced with the Arabic alphabet.

Before the consolidation of their empire, the Uighurs already had a traditional alliance with the Chinese. Uighur emperors sent horsemen and archers to help the Chinese put down several rebellions as well as an invasion by Tibetan nomads. Since the Chinese treated their Uighur allies as barbarians, and since the Uighurs exploited their power over the Chinese by looting and pillaging rebel-held Chinese cities after battle, the relationship between the two peoples was full of resentment. The trade of Chinese silk for Uighur horses was the basis of their commercial relationship.

After the empire fell to the Kirghiz in 840, the Uighurs migrated to the southern part of the Tarim Basin and settled in the Turfan Oasis. Here they established the Kocho kingdom, which became a vassal state of the Karakhanids in the twelfth century. The Karakhanids were ousted by Genghis (Chinggis) Khan and the Mongols in the thirteenth century. In the fifteenth century Uighuristan made up a part of Mogulistan. In 1566 one of the first in a series of Khoja khans took over the area. These Muslim prelates, who came out of Bukhara and Samarkand, claimed direct descent from the Prophet Muhammad.

In 1760 the Chinese claimed the Uighur state as a part of China and named the area Xinjiang, or New Dominion. As a result of the oppression of their Chinese rulers, Muslim warlords were able to lead several rebellions, yet all were crushed by China's armies.

Not only the Chinese wanted to control Eastern Turkestan, as it was called by the Europeans. At the end of the nineteenth century Germany, England, Russia, and even the United States were seeking to establish their power in the area. The Russians and the British were the most aggressive, spurred on by the reports of gold in the cities of Yarkand and Khotan as well as the strategic importance of Xinjiang. After the Russian Revolution, the Soviets sought to extend their revolutionary ideals into Central Asia. In the early 1930s Uighur nationalists, with Soviet backing, founded the independent Eastern Turkestan Republic. This was quickly taken over by Chinese warlords. Since most Western publications available to Uighurs at the time came out of

Russia, the Russians also had a great cultural influence. Mao's armies defeated the Guomindang (Kuomintang) troops stationed in Xinjiang in 1949, and the Xinjiang-Uighur Autonomous Region was formed in 1955.

Today most Uighurs live in the Xinjiang-Uighur Autonomous Region. Since the Soviet Union, Afghanistan, the People's Republic of Mongolia, Pakistan, and India share Xinjiang's modern borders, and as the province is China's main site for oil and mineral production, it is a sensitive area for China.

In Xinjiang, China has greatly improved the irrigation systems and created a transportation network of railroad and air travel. As of 1985 Xinjiang operated its own airline. A thriving commerce based on agriculture, animal husbandry, and the extraction and refinement of oil and minerals has increased the standard of living of the average Uighur. In the early 1980s the Chinese opened the area to tourists.

The Chinese government has reformed many of the restrictions on the Uighur people that grew out of the Cultural Revolution. The rich literary and musical heritage of the Uighur people continues today. Uighurs publish books in their own language, from ancient historical epics to modern comedies. Urumqi houses the Uighur National Opera. Traditional Uighur musicians and dancers travel to Europe and the United States.

In late 1985 Uighur students staged demonstrations in Beijing, Shanghai, and Urumqi, calling for an end to nuclear testing in Xinjiang, the relaxation of family planning regulations, and increased minority rights.

[See also Xinjiang.]

Jack Chen, *The Sinkiang Story* (1977). Wen-Djang Chu, *The Muslim Rebellion in Northwest China 1862–1877* (1966). Owen Lattimore, *Pivot of Asia* (1950). Colin Mackerras, *The Uighur Empire According to the T'ang Dynastic Histories* (1972). Donald H. McMillen, *Chinese Communist Power and Policy in Xinjiang, 1949–1977* (1979). C. P. Skrine, *Chinese Central Asia* (1926).

ELIZABETH BRIGHT

UJI, early Japanese form of elite political organization. It was based on kinship and predominated from the mid-fifth to the late eighth century. The term is related to Korean *(ul)* and other Tunguz words for blood relative but should not be thought of as a family or clan.

The focus of every *uji* was the chief *(uji no kami)*, who served as the organization's representative at court. He (the chief was always male) received a title *(kabane)* emblematic of his status and was responsible for the delivery of his *uji*'s tribute to the Yamato king *(ōkimi,* later the emperor). The chief also performed ceremonies for the god *(ujigami),* which united the *uji.*

Uji membership included the chief's relatives—his offspring, collaterals, and their families—and several unrelated persons and their kin. Other male members usually bore the title granted to the chief and were thus also qualified to serve at court. Most *uji* were based in the Kinai, although not all members lived in the same locale.

Each *uji* was sustained by slaves, which were the private possessions of individuals, and *be.* Slaves could be bought and sold or inherited and were employed most as personal servants. It was not unusual for women to bring slaves with them as dowry when they married. *Be* were the property of the entire *uji.* They were under the chief's control, yet had their own economic base, often outside the Kinai. Each *be* presented tribute (cloth, labor, fish, grain, etc.) to the *uji,* or directly to the king on behalf of the *uji.*

Uji were created after 450 as clearly defined roles evolved at court. Some early examples are Moitori (helmsman) and Kashiwade (cook); later more well known *uji,* such as the Mononobe (army) and Nakatomi (priest), were set up. Eventually functional surnames fell into disuse and *uji* were based on place names (Heguri, Kose).

In 645, after the Soga had been eliminated in the Taika coup, the court, led by Prince Naka (later Emperor Tenji, r. 668–671), began to adopt a Chinese-style bureaucratic organization. The new system required government control of resources previously held by the *uji,* such as *be.* Advancement at court depended on individual merit. Thus, several attempts were made to restrict or abolish the *uji.* The first effort may have occurred after the coup, when the Emperor Kōtoku proclaimed the Taika Reform edict. Later enactments by the emperors Tenji and Temmu were more successful in undercutting *uji* privilege, yet they continued to be the predominant form of court organization throughout the eighth century. The economic bases of the *uji* were reorganized, but not abolished, and all important posts continued to be controlled by *uji.* The system began to decline in the 800s when the Fujiwara destroyed their rivals. Even then the ceremonial aspects of *uji* organization, such as the chieftainship *(uji no chōja),* were retained.

[See also Be and Taika Reforms.]

W. G. Aston, trans., *Nihongi* (1896). John W. Hall, *Government and Local Power in Japan, 500 to 1700* (1966).   WAYNE FARRIS

UJJAIN, ancient Ujjayini, capital of ancient Avanti, city in present-day Madhya Pradesh, India. A center of political power, commerce, and religious activity, Ujjain was controlled by most of the ruling dynasties of northern India. In the fifth century CE it was the base from which King Vikramaditya (Chandragupta II) defeated the Sakas; he made the city a center of culture, wherein the dramatist Kalidasa resided. Its religious monuments included Buddhist monasteries and important Shiva temples, notably the Mahakala; the city also became a center for the Lingayat sect.

[*See also* Lingayats *and* Madhya Pradesh.]

B. C. Law, *Historical Geography of Ancient India* (reprint, 1976).   GERI HOCKFIELD MALANDRA

UKIYO-E, "floating world pictures," term used primarily to describe the Japanese woodblock prints of beautiful women and actors whose lives exemplified the transient, hedonistic world of pleasure implicit in the word *ukiyo*. In its broader sense, however, *ukiyo-e* may designate all Japanese woodblock prints. For some scholars, the term also embraces paintings of the everyday life of commoners during the Edo period (1600–1868). The history of *ukiyo-e* is generally divided into three periods: the primitives, 1660 to 1765; the brocade print, or *nishiki-e*, 1765 to 1810; and the landscape print, 1810 to 1880.

The seventeenth century saw the rise of the popular culture that was to support and shape *ukiyo-e*. The painter Iwasa Matabei (1578–1650), who was born and raised in Kyoto, is traditionally regarded as the founder of *ukiyo-e,* but Hishikawa Moronobu (d. 1694), who was active in Edo (modern Tokyo), has been shown to have played the decisive role in consolidating the styles that led to the flowering of *ukiyo-e*.

The period between 1660 and 1765 saw the perfection of the techniques necessary for high-quality woodblock printing. *Ukiyo-e* from the second half of the seventeenth century primarily consists of illustrated books and series of independent prints of erotic subject matter. Later, prints featuring large, dramatically posturing actors and courtesans in fashionable attire became popular. Color printing was not widely used at this stage, but occasionally prints were hand colored. By the opening years of the eighteenth century, this painstaking practice was replaced by a method of printing using different blocks for each color. Hishikawa Moronobu, who designed striking black-and-white prints of erotica; Torii Kiyomasu (fl. 1690–1720), founder of an artistic dynasty that was to maintain a near monopoly on the production of prints of costumed Kabuki actors; and Kaigetsudō Andō (fl. early eighteenth century), whose provocative yet refined beauties reflect the feminine ideal of his day, are the leading figures in the first period.

The age of the brocade print, so-called because of its full range of sumptuous colors, was heralded in the work of Suzuki Harunobu (c. 1725–1770). Harunobu first achieved renown through cleverly designed New Year's cards printed for wealthy connoisseurs using the finest papers, colors, and techniques. Full-scale prints from his maturity are noted for their idealistic treatment of daily life and their frail, girlish beauties.

Toshusai Sharaku is believed to have made prints only for a brief ten months between 1794 and 1795. Although he appears not to have been much admired during his lifetime, since the nineteenth century his realistic, psychologically penetrating portraits of Kabuki actors have been much in demand. Kitagawa Utamaro (1753–1806) also specialized in prints revealing the psychological states of his subjects, primarily women. These include frank, sensual portrayals of famed courtesans as well as middle-class women, mothers and their children, and women at work. Unlike his contemporary Sharaku, Utamaro had a long career and his output was prolific.

Katsushita Hokusai (1760–1849) is one of the last great figures in the development of *ukiyo-e*. A multifaceted talent, he sketched, painted, and illustrated books and pioneered the landscape print for which he ultimately became most famous. His series showing views of Mount Fuji at various seasons and times of day immortalized this national landmark. Later, the *Fifty-three Stages of the Tōkaidō*, by Andō Hiroshige (1797–1858), did much the same for the main route linking Kyoto with the Edo capital. Hokusai and Hiroshige's strikingly original designs incorporating experiments in Western perspective had a profound influence on French Impressionist painters.

[*See also* Woodblock Prints, Japanese.]

Richard Lane, *Images from the Floating World* (1978). Muneshige Narazaki, *The Japanese Print: Its Evolution and Essence* (1966). Seiichiro Takahashi, *Traditional Wood-block Prints of Japan* (1972).

CHRISTINE M. E. GUTH

UKKALAPA. *See* Rangoon.

ŬLCHI MUNDŎK, a general of the Korean state of Koguryŏ who lived in the early seventh century. His origins are unknown, but some scholars contend he was of northern Chinese ancestry. According to ancient records, at an early age he demonstrated both literary and military talent, and his intelligent use of resources catapulted him into the highest positions of authority in Koguryŏ. Ŭlchi Mundŏk epitomizes the officials possessed of intelligence and vision who enabled Koguryŏ to dominate the Korean peninsula during much of the sixth and early seventh centuries.

Ŭlchi Mundŏk's most renowned victory came in Koguryŏ's struggle against the Sui Chinese forces. Sui Yangdi (r. 604–618), intent on subjugating Koguryŏ, sent a force, described in Chinese sources as more than one million men, against Koguryŏ in 612. Stymied at Liaodong Fortress, a Koguryŏ outpost, Yangdi dispatched some three hundred thousand men directly toward P'yŏngyang, the Koguryŏ capital. Ŭlchi Mundŏk reconnoitered the Sui positions under the pretense of surrendering; on his successful return, he led the Chinese forces deeper and deeper into Koguryŏ territory. One source claims Mundŏk suffered as many as seven military setbacks in one day, all to make the Sui army feel victorious. Ten miles north of P'yŏngyang the Sui army rested and Mundŏk, again pretending an overwhelming defeat, asked to surrender once more. The Sui generals, wearied by their chase and anxious to return to China, accepted. As the Chinese forces started to withdraw, Koguryŏ forces attacked. Throughout the following weeks, the Koguryŏ army chased the battle-worn Chinese, forcing them in one day and night to flee some 150 miles. When the Sui army finally returned to Liaodong, only 2,700 of the soldiers who had set out to subjugate Koguryŏ survived. This military defeat checked Sui hopes of conquering northern Korea; it also seriously weakened Sui rule, contributing to the demise of that dynasty in 618.

Ŭlchi Mundŏk's strategy, which relied heavily on defensive guerrilla tactics, has earned him recognition as one of East Asian history's greatest generals. His defense of Koguryŏ enabled the Korean civilization to survive military challenges from the Chinese and allowed the Korean people to retain independent control over the Korean peninsula.

[*See also* Koguryŏ.]

EDWARD J. SHULTZ

ULUG BEG (1394–1449), the eldest son of the Timurid ruler Shahrukh and a grandson of Timur (Tamerlane); ruler of Transoxiana as his father's vice-regent from 1409 until Shahrukh's death in 1447, after which Ulug Beg succeeded Shahrukh as ruler of the Timurid realm. Ulug Beg was a cultivated and scholarly man; his capital, Samarkand, became a great center of Islamic culture under his patronage. He embellished the city with numerous architectural monuments, among them a *madrasa* bearing his name and an astronomical observatory regarded by contemporaries as one of the wonders of the world. Keenly interested in mathematics and astronomy, he assembled around him the best astronomers of his day and compiled a new set of astronomical tables in which he sought to correct Ptolemy's computations and which became famous in Europe. His rule, however, saw the growth of religious reaction led by a faction of the Naqshbandi order, as well as the encroachment of the nomadic Uzbeks. His death in 1449 at the hands of his son, Abd al-Latif, ushered in a new period of internecine struggles within the Timurid dynasty.

V. V. Barthold, *Four Studies on the History of Central Asia*, vol. 2 (1958).   MARIA E. SUBTELNY

UMARA, plural of *amir* ("noble"), a term used for the governing class of the two main political entities of medieval India, the Delhi sultanate (1206–1526) and the Mughal empire (1526–1857). The character and composition of the nobility changed over time, in response either to political pressures or to the personal predilections of rulers. The early Turkish sultans recruited the *umara* mainly from the Turks, and Iltutmish consolidated them into "forty families." The Khaljis, however, admitted non-Turks and Muslim converts to the nobility. Under Muhammad bin Tughluq scions of religious families and Alai nobles, converts, Afghans, and Hindus were inducted into the nobility. The land assignments (*iqta*) held by the nobles during the sultanate period were more in the nature of a bureaucratic institution than a feudal fief.

With the advent of the Mughals the nobility underwent further changes. Akbar organized the nobles on the basis of *mansab* (rank), which determined their status, fixed their pay, and laid a concomitant duty of maintaining a certain number of troopers with horses. All *mansabdars* were directly subordinate to the emperor. The *mansab* was represented by two numbers; one indicated *zat* (personal pay) and the other *sawar* (cavalry). Toward the end of Akbar's reign *zat* was used to designate a *mansabdar*'s position in the official hierarchy and helped to determine his pay; the *sawar* rank indicated the number of troopers the *mansabdar* was required to maintain. During Akbar's time *mansabdars* having commands of two hundred or more were entitled to be called *umara;* under Shah Jahan the limit was raised to five hundred.

The Mughal nobility was composed of Turks, Persians, Afghans, Rajputs, and other native-born Indians. Under Akbar, Rajputs gained in importance. During the later Mughal period Iranis and Turanis became the two main groupings, and during the eighteenth century the two were in constant conflict.

The Mughal nobility was not hereditary, but the sons of deceased nobles were often taken into service. The law of escheat operated and hence the property of the nobles could be confiscated on death.

[*See also* Mansabdari System; Iltutmish; Khalji Dynasty; Delhi Sultanate; Tughluq Dynasty; Mughal Empire; *and* Akbar.]

M. Athar Ali, *The Mughal Nobility under Aurangzeb* (1968). M. Habib and K. A. Nizami, *Comprehensive History of India,* vol. 5 (1970).   FARHAN AHMAD NIZAMI

UMAYYAD DYNASTY.

The Umayyad caliphs (661–750) played only a brief and rather indirect, yet nonetheless critical, role in the history of Iran and Central Asia. Generally, the Umayyad central government was more interested in affairs affecting the western portions of the empire (wars with Byzantium and expansion around the Mediterranean basin) than with the east. After consolidating the eastern areas conquered earlier by the Arabs, the Umayyads tended to entrust matters in Iraq and its Iranian dependencies to governors and subgovernors, often chosen from prominent Arab families settled in the respective provinces, who then followed whatever policy they felt best.

One of the most effective and important of these Umayyad officials in Iran was the governor of Khurasan, Qutaiba ibn Muslim al-Bahili (705–715), a protégé of the powerful Umayyad governor of Iraq, al-Hajjaj ibn Yusuf. Qutaiba effectively suppressed a revolt, led by Nizak (or Tirek) of Badghis, of the semiautonomous princes of Tocharistan (on the eastern borders of Khurasan); conquered the city of Bukhara and its environs; invaded and subdued Sogdiana, taking its most important city, Samarkand; conquered Khwarazm and settled a colony of Arabs there; and mounted expeditions against several remote principalities along the Syr Darya as far as what is now Tashkent. All this military activity served a number of useful functions. It diverted the energies of the Arab tribesmen from factional struggles against each other into the new campaigns, thus encouraging cooperation between the Arab and Iranian military elites; it brought in much-needed booty to bolster the local economy; it provided a vehicle for reorganizing and stabilizing the provincial government; and it checked, at least temporarily, the growing power of the Turkic tribes on the far eastern borders of the Islamic empire. Unfortunately, this energetic governor fell from favor with the central government after the death of al-Hajjaj and was killed by his own former soldiers when he attempted to revolt. (Interestingly, the Sogdians he had conquered remained loyal to him to the very end.)

After Qutaiba's death, the authority of the Umayyads in the east deteriorated steadily. The reasons for this are complex but can be reduced to three main points. First, the Umayyads failed to find a permanent means of containing the rivalries, antagonisms, and competition for political and material rewards among their Arab tribal supporters in the provinces. They were thus ultimately confronted with a bitter intra-Arab civil war in Khurasan. Second, they based their power more and more on a narrow elite of Arab tribal warriors, many of them newcomers to the east, and the indigenous Iranian military aristocracy. This alienated the non-Arab peasantry, their village leaders, and the semiassimilated Arab colonists who had become landowners and resided permanently in the region. Third, as both Arabs and Iranians came to think more of their common Islamic, rather than their separate ethnic, identity, the Umayyads were unable to find any convincing justification for the legitimacy of their rule that could appeal to the religious sentiments of the pious-minded Muslim masses in the cities and countryside. These sources of discontent in Khurasan were shrewdly manipulated by various opponents of Umayyad rule, especially by partisans of the Abbasid family who engineered a revolutionary conspiracy in Khurasan that toppled the authority of their governor in that province and subsequently brought down the dynasty itself.

[*See also* Abbasid Dynasty; Arabs; *and* Khurasan.]

H. A. R. Gibb, *The Arab Conquests in Central Asia* (1923; reprint, 1970). M. A. Shaban, *The Abbasid Revolution* (1970). Julius Wellhausen, *The Arab Kingdom and Its Fall*, translated by Margaret Weir (1927).

E. L. DANIEL

UNFEDERATED MALAY STATES, an association that consisted of Kedah, Perlis, Trengganu, Kelantan, and Johor, all states that were not included in the Federated Malay States (FMS), which was formed in 1895. Except for Johor, they were acquired from Siam as late as 1909, and the term *Unfederated Malay States* became current only then. All, except Johor, were less modernized than the Federated Malay States. None had British residents (as did the FMS) but only advisers, indicating looser British control, and none were linked together in any way. In the 1920s the British tried unsuccessfully to woo them to join the FMS through a policy of decentralization.

[*See also* Kedah; Perlis; Trengganu; Kelantan; Johor; *and* Federated Malay States.]

R. S. MILNE

UNIFIED SILLA. *See* Silla.

UNIONIST PARTY. In India, following the first election in the Punjab under the 1919 reforms, a group of rural Hindus and Muslims worked together to represent agricultural interests against presumed urban and primarily Hindu exploitation of agriculturists. The group centered around Fazli Hussain (1877–1936) and adopted the name National Unionist Party in 1923. Generally predominant during the dyarchy period, the party swept to power in 1937 under provincial autonomy, first under Sikandar Hayat Khan (1892–1942) and later under Khizr Hayat Khan Tiwana (1900–1975). Although defeated in Muslim seats in 1946, it retained the ministry until April 1947 through a coalition with the Congress and the Akali Dal. The party stood for rural interests throughout, including debt reduction and remission and quotas for "backward groups" in government service and education. It sought a constitutional solution for India short of partition. The party dissolved after independence but many individuals reappeared in the Republican Party and Ayub Khan's Pakistan Muslim League.

[*See also* Fazli Hussain, Sir Mian; Akali Dal; *and* All-India Muslim League.]

Azim Hussain, *Fazl-i-Hussain, A Political Biography* (1946). Syed Nur Ahmad, *From Martial Law to Martial Law, Politics in the Punjab, 1919–1958*, edited by Craig Baxter (1985).

CRAIG BAXTER

UNITED FRONT, alliances entered into by the Chinese Communist Party (CCP) with other parties, armies, social classes, and individuals in order to achieve what were proclaimed to be common goals. The CCP always sought to exercise leadership over other participants in these coalitions.

The First United Front occurred early in the history of the CCP (1923–1927), when it was allied with the Guomindang (Kuomintang, KMT, or Nationalist Party). This alliance was directed from Moscow by the Communist International (Comintern); it ended in 1927 when the KMT turned on the CCP and very nearly destroyed it.

The Second United Front was a consequence of Japanese aggression in China during the 1930s, which persuaded domestic rivals reluctantly to join ranks. By 1937, the enmity between the KMT and CCP was submerged in a new alliance. This time, however, the CCP had its own territorial base and military forces, and Mao Zedong, rather than Stalin, made the final decisions. Mao also conceived of the united front as much wider than simply two-party coalition. Indeed, by 1940, Mao stated that the united front, armed struggle, and a disciplined CCP guaranteed the success of the revolution in China: the united front to gain allies and isolate enemies, armed struggle to defeat the isolated and now vulnerable enemy, and the CCP to wield these two weapons. Specific allies might be temporary, but the notion of alliance was permanent. Although the CCP and the KMT were fighting each other by 1939, united front strategy continued unabated.

Since the establishment of the People's Republic of China in 1949, *united front* has become a shibboleth. It expresses the unity of the Chinese people in domestic matters and those nations subscribing to Chinese views internationally.

[*See also* Communism: Chinese Communist Party; Comintern; Guomindang; World War II in China; *and* Xi'an Incident.]

LYMAN P. VAN SLYKE

UNITED MALAYS NATIONAL ORGANIZATION (UMNO), Malaysian political party. Founded in 1946 with Dato Onn bin Ja'afar as president, it gained recognition as the principal defender

of Malay interests by leading the protests against the Malayan Union proposal. Dato Onn's later attempt to turn it into a multiethnic party failed, and he was succeeded by Tunku Abdul Rahman, the great ethnic conciliator and father of Malaysian independence. Subsequent leaders have been Tun Abdul Razak (1970–1976), Tun Hussein Onn (1976–1981), and Dato Seri Mahathir Mohamad (1981 until the present).

UMNO has two main roles. It is the party of the majority of the Malays; its main rival, the Alliance Party, was a close contender for that allegiance only at the 1969 election. In this role the UMNO has fought for Malay rights. However, to overcome competition from the Alliance and fundamentalist Islamic groups, the UMNO has had to be accommodating on Islamic issues, as shown by the creation of the Islamic Bank and the International Islamic University. In its second role, as the leading component of the governing coalition (Alliance National Front), it has had an allocative and mediating function, ethnically and regionally. Party and government operations are actually closely linked; the UMNO president is always the prime minister. Elections for office in the UMNO (mostly triennial) are relatively open, exhibiting a complex mix of deference and democracy.

[See also Malaysia; Onn bin Ja'afar, Dato; Malayan Union; Abdul Rahman Alhaj; Abdul Razak; and Alliance Party.]

John Funston, *Malay Politics in Malaysia: A Study of UMNO and PAS* (1980). Diane K. Mauzy, *Barisan Nasional* (1983). Gordon P. Means, *Malaysian Politics* (2d ed., 1976). R. S. Milne and Diane K. Mauzy, *Politics and Government in Malaysia* (2d ed., 1980).   R. S. MILNE

UNITED NATIONAL PARTY, formed in 1946, the governing party of Sri Lanka from 1947 to 1956, from March to July 1960, from 1965 to 1970, and again since 1977. With its rightist-oriented programs, the party has throughout been the clear alternative to the center-left Sri Lanka Freedom Party and the Marxists. The success of Tamil ethnic parties damaged its "national" political party standing, and the Sri Lanka Freedom Party has keenly contested its bases of support in the rural areas. Nonetheless, even when it has failed to come into power, the United National Party has demonstrated that it has considerable popular support in the country.

[See also Sri Lanka Freedom Party *and* Tamils in Sri Lanka.]

A. Jeyaratnam Wilson, *Politics of Sri Lanka, 1947–1979* (1979).   VIJAYA SAMARAWEERA

UNITED NATIONS COMMISSION FOR THE UNIFICATION AND REHABILITATION OF KOREA. By Resolution 376(v) of 7 October 1950, the United Nations General Assembly established a seven-nation Commission for the Unification and Rehabilitation of Korea (UNCURK) to act for the Assembly in fulfilling the terms of the resolution, which called for realization of a unified and democratic Korea. Australia, Chile, the Netherlands, Pakistan, the Philippines, Thailand, and Turkey each designated a representative; the chairmanship rotated among them. A principal secretary headed a small UN staff resident in Seoul. UNCURK went out of existence, on its own recommendation, by UN General Assembly consensus decision on 28 November 1973. UNCURK is to be distinguished from the separate UN Korea Reconstruction Agency (UNKRA), which from 1951 to 1958 oversaw the UN economic reconstruction program, although UNCURK was given a voice in UNKRA policies.

Continuing the work of prior UN commissions since 1947, UNCURK reported annually to the General Assembly on conditions in South Korea, where its members and staff were able to observe and travel. Like its predecessors, UNCURK was never admitted to North Korea, whose authorities held that the Korean question should be solved "by the Korean people themselves, without outside interference"; thus, half the commission's purpose could not be carried out. It observed and reported on all of the Republic of Korea's major elections from 1951 thorugh 1973, finding most of them (with the conspicuous exception of the 1960 presidential election) reasonably honest, but cautiously indicating their shortcomings.

Led by its able and aggressive Australian chairman, UNCURK endeavored to play a restraining role in President Syngman Rhee's coercion of the legislature to ensure his reelection in 1952, but with very little effect. Thereafter, its role in Korean affairs was a largely passive one. The Korean government tolerated its presence as a continuing symbol of the legitimacy accorded by the United Nations recognition of December 1948. The Chilean, Dutch, and Pakistani representatives, who were not resident in Korea, played a largely nominal role in the commission's activities.

[See also Korean War.]

Leland M. Goodrich, *Korea: A Study of U.S. Policy in the United Nations* (1956). Leon Gordenker, *The United Nations and the Peaceful Unification of Korea* (1959). *United Nations Yearbook* (various years). United States Department of State, *The Record on Korean Unification, 1943–1960* (1960).   DONALD S. MACDONALD

UN KHAM (1811–1895), also known as Oun Kham, last king of Luang Prabang (Laos) before the onset of French colonial rule.

The son of King Mangthaturat (r. 1816–1837), Un Kham was *upahat* (heir presumptive) and general during the reign of his older brother, Chantharat (r. 1852–1870), and succeeded him as king in 1870, though his Siamese suzerain did not enthrone him until 1872. His kingdom was too weak to withstand the Ho raiders from China, who pillaged Laos in the 1870s, and Deo Van Tri's armed bands from Dien Bien Phu, who sacked Luang Prabang in 1887. From the latter, Un Kham barely escaped with the assistance of the French vice-consul, Auguste Pavie. Citing his advanced age and ill health, the Siamese retired him and enthroned his son as King Zakharine (Sakkharin; r. 1887–1904). Un Kham died in 1895; his kingdom had become a French protectorate in 1893.

[*See also* Luang Prabang; Ho; *and* Pavie Mission.]

Hugh Toye, *Laos: Buffer State or Battleground* (1968).   DAVID K. WYATT

UNTOUCHABILITY. In the words of the fourteenth-century Untouchable poet Chokhamela,

> In the beginning, at the end,
> there is nothing but pollution.
> No one knows anyone who is born pure.
> Chokha says, in wonder, who is pure?
> *Abhang* 11

Its origins are obscure, its development difficult to trace, but it is clear that the basis of untouchability and the presence of Untouchable castes in India is the concept of purity and pollution. While all humans are considered impure after a death in the family, and women during menstruation and childbirth, more than four hundred castes came over time to be viewed as irrevocably impure from birth. Protests against the concept of permanent pollution are in evidence from the time of the Buddha, but only in modern India has the government attempted to legislate against the idea of hereditary pollution.

Untouchability and its practice were "abolished" in the constitution of independent India (articles 15 and 17) and such practice made punishable by law in the Untouchability (Offences) Act of 1955. One-seventh of the Indian population (i.e., 105 million in the 1981 census), previously considered Untouchable, now belong to more than four hundred castes on a governmental list (Scheduled Castes) who receive political, educational, and governmental job privileges as compensation for previous disabilities. The current situation finds great strides in education, occupational opportunity, and even the arts, along with a "rising tide of violence" (Hiro, 1982, p. 11) as ex-Untouchables claim their rights and privileges.

The earliest Indian text, the *Rig Veda,* does not mention untouchability. Later Vedic texts refer to the prototype of the Untouchable, the *chandala,* only in such references as *Chandogya Upanishad* 5.10.7: one whose actions are evil will be reborn as a dog, a boar, or a *chandala.* The *Arthashastra* of Kautilya (fourth century BCE?) lists occupations for *chandalas* as work in cremation grounds, the punishment of criminals, and the guarding of new settlements, and enjoins them to live separately and to marry within their own groups (Jha, 1975, p. 17). The concepts of purity and pollution were further developed in the *Manusmriti:* "One becomes pure by bathing if one has touched a *chandala,* a menstruating woman, someone who has been outcast for sin, a woman who has just given birth, a corpse, or one who has touched a corpse." Manu gives three origins for the despised *chandala:* the offspring of a *shudra* father and a brahman mother (10.67), a brahman who begs from a *shudra* in order to perform a sacrifice (11.24), or a slayer of brahmans (11.55). No racial basis or polluting occupation having to do with dead cows is mentioned. Manu's harsh restrictions on *chandalas,* the "basest of men," and the idea of groups having lower status than the *shudra* in the fourfold *varna* classification are repeated and developed in later legal texts, along with the occasional use of the term *asprishya* ("untouchable") for certain low castes and menstruating women. [*See also* Law: Judicial and Legal Systems of India.]

By the fifth century CE many of the stern injunctions of the theoretical legal texts seem to have become a reality. The Chinese traveler Faxian observed *chandalas* dwelling apart from others. Xuanzang (seventh century) listed butchers, fishermen, public performers, executioners, and scavengers as marked castes living outside the city. The eleventh-century

Muslim scholar al-Biruni notes that the *chandala* and three other groups are not members of any caste or guild, perform dirty work, and are considered illegitimate (*Tarikh al-hind* 9.4). Both Jha (1975) and Ambedkar (1948) for different reasons consider the centuries just before the Muslim invasions of the thirteenth century as the final determining period for the status and occupational duties of Untouchables.

A number of nonlegal sources from Buddhist times on, however, indicate more liberal views. The *Theragatha* (32, 33) records the entry of two cremation ground watchmen into the Buddhist orders. The Sanskrit play *Mricchakatka* (third century?) introduces two humorous, articulate executioners who declare that the true low-born are those who do violence to a decent man. In the *bhakti* (devotional religion) movement that swept India south to north from the eighth to the eighteenth century, Untouchables are honored as saints and poets: Nandnar (c. 700–900), a Shaivite saint from Tamil Nadu, and his contemporary Tiruppan, one of the twelve Vaishnavite Alvars; Chokhamela and his entire family, *mahars* of fourteenth-century Maharashtra; Ravidas, a fifteenth-century *chamar* cobbler in the North. Kabir, a *bhakti* poet in Banaras of Hindu-Muslim background, inveighed against untouchability. [*See* Kabir.] The heterodox Lingayat movement, begun in Karnataka in the eleventh century, the unorthodox Mahanubhav movement that arose in Maharashtra from the thirteenth century on, and the Sikh movement begun in the Punjab in the fifteenth century each attempted to do away with caste. [*See also* Sikhism.] Many Untouchables converted to Islam, and one, Khusru Khan, a *parwari* from Gujarat, was sultan of the Delhi empire for a few brief months in 1320.

European visitors to India in the modern period noted the existence of despised groups, and the Tamil *pariah* caste lent its name to the English vocabulary as a synonym for an outcast from society. Untouchables in India, however, did constitute societal castes, with caste occupations, mythology, and a sense of their place in the social hierarachy. When change came to specific castes in the nineteenth and twentieth centuries, it was mainly related to the hereditary occupations of those castes.

Modern concern for the Untouchables' status began in a threefold way in the nineteenth century. Christian missions admitted Untouchables into their folds and their schools. Higher-caste Hindus began to speak against the practice of untouchability, and Untouchables themselves began to assert themselves. In 1852 the first school for Untouchables was established in Pune by the *mali* (gardener caste) Jotirao Phule. [*See also* Phule, Jotirao Govindrao.] Late in the nineteenth century or early in the twentieth, the *mahars* (village servants) of Maharashtra, the *adi-dravidas* ("original Dravidians") of the Tamil area, the *namashudras* (boatmen and cultivators) of Bengal, and the *ilavas* (toddy tappers) of the Kerala area began to organize to press for rights [*See* Ilava.] The Jatavs of Agra, a caste within the *chamar* grouping, claimed higher status as the shoemaking industry grew. An Ad-Dharm ("original religion") movement was strong in the Punjab and the United Provinces in the 1920s and 1930s.

Hindu reform groups began work among Untouchables around the turn of the century: the Arya Samaj in the North created *shuddhi* (purification) ceremonies; the Brahmo Samaj in Bengal instituted Untouchability conferences and education work; the Depressed Class Mission was begun by V. R. Shinde in 1906 as an offshoot of the Prarthana Samaj in Bombay Province. A fourth force was added to these in the twentieth century with the increased broadening of parliamentary democracy in British India. Hindu reformers and groups of Untouchables, now known as Depressed Classes, pushed for acknowledgment of the status problem and for entrance of Untouchables into governing bodies. Token nominated members from the Depressed Classes began to serve in the provincial and central legislatures in 1921. [*See also* Arya Samaj; Shuddhi; *and* Brahmo Samaj.]

Political opportunity and fragmentary high-caste Hindu support enabled B. R. Ambedkar, a *mahar* Untouchable from a family that had abandoned its village for service in the British army, to enter fully into educational work, internal reform and organization, and legal and legislative efforts. With a Columbia University Ph.D., a London D.Sc., and the title of barrister, Ambedkar succeeded in establishing newspapers, hostels, a reform organization consisting of Untouchables and high-caste Hindus, and secured an acknowledged role as spokesman for Untouchable rights. In 1930 Ambedkar and Rao Bahadur Rettamalle Srinivasan, a member of the Madras Legislative Council, were Depressed Classes delegates to the Round Table Conference in London. At these planning conferences for further parliamentary reform in India, the differing approaches of politically active Untouchables and of Mohandas K. Gandhi, by then chief spokesman among high-caste Hindus against untouchability, resulted in conflict. In 1931 Gandhi fasted against the granting of separate electorates (analogous to those for the minority Muslim and Sikh communities) for Untouchables. Ambedkar capitulated on this demand, settling for specially designated "reserved" seats for Untouchables in all parliamentary bodies. [See also Ambedkar, Bhimrao Ramji and Gandhi, Mohandas Karamchand.]

In the years before independence, Gandhi continued his efforts to change high-caste Hindu hearts through exhortation and through the Harijan Sevak Sangh (Committee for the Service of the Children of God). Ambedkar continued his educational and political work, intending to change the status of Untouchables by legal means, and in 1935, after a series of unsuccessful mass temple-entry attempts, announced that he "would not die a Hindu." Ambedkar's religious conversion was deferred, however, as he entered the Bombay cabinet and was able to found the People's Education Society and to create the Mahar Batallion, which enabled Untouchables to enter the army for the first time in fifty years. Just before independence Ambedkar became a member of the Constituent Assembly, and as chairman of the Drafting Committee for the Constitution he guided that document through its final acceptance. Only after his resignation as law minister in 1951, and shortly before his death on 6 December 1956, did Ambedkar convert to Buddhism. Since then, more than four million ex-Untouchables, chiefly from Maharashtra and the urban areas of India, have converted to the Buddhist religion, most of them accepting Ambedkar's theory (Ambedkar, 1948) that they had been Buddhists, degraded when Brahmanism was reestablished in India more than a thousand years before.

It has been said that "India's system of official discrimination in favor of the most 'backward' sections of her population [is] unique in the world, both in the range of benefits involved and in the magnitude of the groups eligible for them" (Mahar, 1972, p. 165). This development is owing both to the efforts of Ambedkar and other Untouchable leaders and to the changed attitudes brought about by Gandhi and other caste-Hindu reformers. The current range of aid in education and social welfare, together with reserved places in governmental bodies, is based upon a list or schedule of Untouchable castes made in 1935. Specific castes in specific areas that were customarily denied religious rights of entry into temples and civil rights of entry to public places and the use of wells constitute the 429 "Scheduled Castes." A commissioner of scheduled castes and tribes issues an annual report noting progress and

problems, and an occasional select committee, such as the Elayaperumal Committee of 1969, documents current conditions.

The status of ex-Untouchables today is in flux. Reserved seats in government are still the policy, and there is almost always an ex-Untouchable highly placed in the Indian Cabinet; Jagjivan Ram of Bihar served in a number of ministerial posts from 1946 until the 1980s. The school and college system begun by Ambedkar has burgeoned in the state of Maharashtra, producing a high level of awareness and such movements as the Dalit Panthers in 1972, which modeled its militancy and pride after the Black Panthers in the United States, and the Dalit literary movement, which has become important in Marathi literature. Dalit ("downtrodden, oppressed") has come to replace other terms among politicized ex-Untouchables, and Dalit literary movements have also surfaced in the neighboring states of Gujarat and Karnataka.

On the other hand, large-scale violence took place in the Marathwada area of Maharashtra in 1978 over the renaming of a university to honor Ambedkar, and in Ahmedabad, Gujarat, in 1981 over increased reservations for scheduled castes in medical school. Sporadic violence in the villages when scheduled castes refuse to do traditional work or claim civil rights seems to be increasing. In recent years, literature on both the achievements and the continuing problems of ex-Untouchables has become increasingly abundant, and is now produced not only by Westerners and high-caste Indian scholars but by ex-Untouchables themselves.

[See also Slavery and Serfdom: Slavery and Serfdom in South Asia.]

B. R. Ambedkar, The Untouchables (1948). Dilip Hiro, The Untouchables of India (2d ed., 1982). Vivekanand Jha, "Stages in the History of Untouchables," Indian History Review 2.1 (1975): 14–31. Barbara R. Joshi, Democracy in Search of Equality (1982). Mark Juergensmeyer, Religion as Social Vision: The Movement against Untouchability in 20th Century Punjab (1982). Owen M. Lynch, The Politics of Untouchability (1969). J. Michael Mahar, ed., The Untouchables in Contemporary India (1972). Michael Moffatt, An Untouchable Community in South India: Structure and Consensus (1979).

ELEANOR ZELLIOT

UPANISHADS, a group of texts constituting a branch of Hindu canonical literature. The Sanskrit word upanishad (composed of the elements upa + ni + shad) means literally "a close sitting together," as opposed to *parishad,* or an open assembly; the Upanishads were transmitted privately, even secretly. The term *Upanishads* is often used synonymously with *Vedanta,* "the end of the Vedas" (since they constitute the final part of the Veda and its essence, or "end"). Compiled by semimythical authors between roughly 800 BCE and 300 CE, the Upanishads contain philosophical, contemplative, and homogogical speculations and symbolic interpretations of the ritualistic *samhita* literature, but include a very large amount of ritualistic instruction as well, particularly the two oldest and largest, the *Brihadaranyaka* Upanishad and the *Chandogya* Upanishad. While many lines of thought are represented, the main thrust of the texts is absolutistic and monistic, establishing the ultimate identity of the individual soul (*jiva, jivatma*) with the cosmic absolute (*brahman*). They are the canonical base and referential constant for all Hindu meditational systems and yogic techniques. All traditional commentators wrote exegeses of the Upanishads emphasizing or deemphasizing the monistic (abstract) or the theistic elements of the text, depending on their ideational proclivities. With the exception of the *Arya Samaj,* all Hindu schools accept the canonicity of the Upanishads as part of the Veda. [*See also* Arya Samaj.]

Thirteen Upanishads are seen as the minimal, authentic core. A large number of subsequent texts, some highly apocryphal, were written in later centuries and are, in principle, still being "revealed."

[*See also* Vedas; Vedanta; *and* Hinduism.]

S. N. Dasgupta, *A History of Indian Philosophy,* vol. 1 (1922). R. E. Hume, trans., *The Thirteen Principal Upaniṣads* (reprint, 1971). S. Radhakrishnan, *The Principal Upaniṣads* (1969).   AGEHANANDA BHARATI

UPPER BURMA. Following the conclusion of the Second Anglo-Burmese War, sovereign Burma was landlocked, bordering the British Burmese province of Pegu in the south and China in the north. The capital was moved from Ava to Amarapura and finally to Mandalay. Lower Burma, or Pegu, on the Bay of Bengal was controlled by the British. The main contact between the two regions was via the Irrawaddy River. Upper Burma was conquered by the British in 1885. *Upper* may apply to the upper reaches of the Irrawaddy; another ecological distinction is the different practices of rice growing found in the upper dry zone and the lower wet zone.

[*See also* Anglo-Burmese Wars; Ava; Amarapura; Burma; Lower Burma; *and* Mandalay.]

OLIVER B. POLLAK

URAKAMI INCIDENT. During the two years following the Meiji Restoration (1868) in Japan, some four thousand crypto-Christians from the village of Urakami near Nagasaki were forceably relocated to scattered places in Honshu. Their exile (the Urakami *kuzure*), which lasted until 1873, evoked pressures at home and abroad for religious toleration.

The Urakami believers were remnants of the so-called Hidden Christians (*kakure kirishitan*) who had maintained in secret a syncretistic faith from generation to generation since the early seventeenth-century Tokugawa-period persecutions. After foreign priests returned to Nagasaki in 1859, some of the *kakure* began to practice the faith in open defiance of the *bakufu* proscription. This led to a brief imprisonment of sixty-three Christians of Urakami in the waning months of the shogunate (1867). The exile subsequently imposed by the newly established Meiji regime was provoked in part by the refusal of the Christians, recently released from prison, to contribute labor for a new shrine ordered by the government. Some died in detention.

The fledgling Meiji regime, needing to placate antiforeign elements and marshall national unity around the person of the emperor, had reiterated the ban on the Western "evil sect," and had sought to elevate Shinto and separate it from Buddhism (*shinbutsu bunri*). Frustrations attending the promotion of Shinto produced widespread domestic sentiment in favor of more lenient governmental policies toward religion. As Western ideas gained favor in many quarters and as the hegemony of the leadership grew more secure, the government became amenable to a more relaxed posture.

Meanwhile, Christians in Europe and America, shocked by the exile and the maintenance of the anti-Christian notice boards, prevailed upon their governments to protest Japanese intolerance toward the Western faith. In Japan, diplomatic representatives of Catholic and Protestant nations alike criticized the exile as an uncivilized act. Particularly pointed representations were made to the Iwakura Mission, which toured foreign capitals from 1871 to 1873 in search of Western knowledge and favor. [*See* Iwakura Mission.]

In February 1873 the Dajōkan ordered the notice boards removed, and in the following month the Urakami exiles were released. Although the proscription of Christianity for Japanese remained on the lawbooks, these steps marked the beginning of tacit toleration of the foreign religion.

[*See also* Christianity: Christianity in Japan.]

Thomas W. Burkman, "The Urakami Incidents and the Struggle for Religious Toleration in Early Meiji Japan," *Japanese Journal of Religious Studies* 1.2–3 (June–September 1974):143–216. Otis Cary, *History of Christianity in Japan*, vol 2 (1909). THOMAS W. BURKMAN

URUMQI (Chinese, Wulumuqi), Chinese city, capital of Xinjiang Uighur Autonomous Region of China and former entrepôt on the Silk Road linking China with western Asia. Located in the district of Dzungaria, Urumqi was the last important caravan stop in China in the nineteenth and early twentieth centuries. It had approximately 800,000 inhabitants in 1980. RICHARD W. BULLIET

USULI, a school of Shi'ite jurisprudence that asserts the permissibility of recourse to rational methods (*usul*) and exertion (*ijtihad*) in order to deduce legal ordinances (*ahkam*) from the scriptural sources of the law—the Qur'an and the traditions of the Prophet and the twelve imams. The school is said to have originated with Abu Ja'far al-Tusi (d. 1067), who was the first Shi'ite scholar to expound the permissibility of *qiyas* (analogical reasoning). Usulism, however, was in its origin less an organized school than a current of jurisprudential thought that generally enjoyed majority support, with the exception of a period of Akhbari supremacy in the seventeenth and eighteenth centuries.

The Usuli positions were systematized by Agha Muhammad Baqir Bihbahani and definitively elaborated by Shaikh Murtaza Ansari (d. 1864) and Akhund Khurasani (d. 1911). The Usulis hold that the Shi'ite community (in the continuing absence of the twelfth imam) consists of *mujtahids*—those technically qualified to practice *ijtihad*—and *muqallids*—those who, unable to do so, are obliged to follow the rulings of the former. This analysis has bestowed on the Shi'ite religious scholars a claim to loyalty and obedience that has been decisive for the history of Iran.

[*See also* Akhbari; Bihbahani, Muhammad Baqir; *and* Mujtahid.]

HAMID ALGAR

UTILITARIANISM IN INDIA, a reformist movement based on the philosophy of Jeremy Bentham and James Mill. The utilitarians in England had pushed for legal, political, and educational reforms, and their counterparts in India did likewise. Eschewing the veneration of India held by the eighteenth-century Orientalists, the utilitarians believed that they could reform India by bringing it under the force of rational administration. Influential while William Bentinck was governor-general of India, they preferred a legal code based on universal principles of simplicity and order to the complex and intricate indigenous legal system. They moved to reform the government of India along rational lines of centralized authority and pursued a revenue policy based on what they believed to be universal principles of political economy. Their economic policy was naive and proved harmful in Maharashtra, while their administrative and judicial reforms held sway in India well into the twentieth century. [*See also* Bentinck, William Cavendish *and* Mill, James.]

Eric Stokes, *The English Utilitarians and India* (1959).

LYNN ZASTOUPIL

UTTAR PRADESH, with 110,862,013 people in 1981, is the most populous state in India and includes 16.2 percent of its population. Bounded on the north by the Himalayas, on the south by the foothills of the Vindhya Range, on the east by the state of Bihar, and on the west by Haryana and Rajasthan states, Uttar Pradesh has made a disproportionate contribution to the Hindu and Muslim cultural traditions of the subcontinent and to the history of the Indian National Congress.

The postindependence state of Uttar Pradesh (UP) was virtually identical with the British United Provinces. The provinces were created from a variety of late Mughal political units between 1764 and 1856. Having defeated the *nawab vazir* of Awadh (Oudh) in 1764, the English East India Company secured the tribute of the Hindu raja of Banaras, formerly the nawab's subordinate. [*See* East India Company.] When the raja rebelled against excessive British demands for tribute in 1781, his state was directly annexed by them. Despite its considerable commercial and political interests in the rest of Awadh the company held off from further annexations until 1801. By then the nawab's army and administration were in rapid decline owing to continuing British pressure for tribute and to the activities of British private merchants and officials. Turbulence in Awadh was felt to threaten the stability of Bengal and Banaras. Therefore the governor-general, Lord Richard Wellesley, secured the cession of the most valuable parts of Awadh (the Doab), which lay between the rivers Ganges and Jumna and the western territories of Rohilkhand. To this he added lands conquered between 1803 and 1806 from the Maratha chiefs who ruled tracts of the western Ganges Valley. [*See* Wellesley, Richard Colley.]

The territory thus created was known as the Ceded and Conquered Provinces. In 1835 it became the North-Western Provinces and was placed under a lieutenant-governor. In 1856 those tracts of northern Awadh reserved to the indigenous ruler were seized by the company, impatient for its revenues and for "stable" administration. In 1877 the two provinces were put under a unitary government of the North-Western Provinces and Oudh, and in 1901 the territory was designated the United Provinces of Agra and Oudh. [*See also* Agra *and* Awadh.]

In the early colonial period Uttar Pradesh was significant as a laboratory for British systems of revenue collection. Converting the Mughal tax on agricultural product into a tax on "land," the British had first made arrangements with locally powerful agencies, whether large landlords (*zamindars* and *taluqdars*) or bodies of cosharing village proprietors (so-called *bhaiachara* and *pattidari* settlements). Under the influence of Utilitarian ideas and Ricardo's theory of rent, officials in the 1830s disfavored landlord settlements, searching instead for "true" peasant proprietors. Where landowning groups were well established through village control and customary relationships, neither these measures nor the sale of land for revenue arrears had much effect on the dominant landholding groups of Hindu Rajputs, Jats, and brahmans. Little economic growth occurred before 1850 owing to famine and price depression in the 1830s and the instability of export markets for indigo, opium, and cotton. But severe revenue assessment and colonial meddling with Indian schemes of royalty caused increasing resentment. [*See also* Land Tenure and Reform: Land Tenure, Revenue, and Reform in South Asia.]

A major rebellion commenced in May 1857 with a revolt of the high-caste sepoys of the Bengal army who proceeded to Delhi and proclaimed the reestablishment of full Mughal authority. Awadh, whose magnates and court had been dispossessed after annexation in 1856, formed the second seat of rebellion, while various Hindu chiefs, notably the exiled Maratha prince Nana Sahib, later raised armies. Fearing for their patrimony and honor, aristocrats and landholders were joined by groups of peasants (especially the Jats near Delhi and relatives of the mutinous troops in Awadh and Banaras) who were bearing the burden of high land rents. Active as well were nomadic and pastoral people disadvantaged by the expansion on arable lands. British victory was never in doubt, however, since the rebels were too divided to maintain their lines of communication along the rivers Ganges and Jumna. [*See also* Mutiny, Indian.]

In Awadh the rebellion caused the British to retreat toward a more conservative agrarian policy, attempting to shore up the *taluqdars* and other landlords, whom they now saw as an ancient aristocracy. The relative quiescence of the provinces between 1858 and 1914 was also ensured by a slow and inequitable growth of the economy that enabled independent peasants and moneylenders to benefit from the export of cotton, oilseed, and wheat to other parts of India and abroad. Cities such as Agra and Faizabad became processing centers for exports, while Kanpur's leather and cloth industries initiated industrialization in India's interior. [*See also* Taluqdar.]

Professional men, particularly at Allahabad and Lakhnau (Lucknow), along with some businessmen, were active in the Indian National Congress in the 1880s and 1890s. The provinces were not forward in the Swadeshi (home industry) movement of 1906 to 1910; movements of religious revitalization were more important there. The great Hindu religious centers of Banaras, Allahabad, and Hardwar produced a variety of Hindu associations, which sought to protect orthodox religion against the novelty of the modernizing Arya Samaj and Christian missionaries. [*See also* Arya Samaj.] From 1881 to 1895 the provinces were also the scene of a well-organized rural movement in defense of sacred cattle.

Muslim movements flourished among the descendants of the Mughal intelligentsia and gentry. The Islamic modernist Sayyid Ahmad Khan founded the Anglo-Mohamedan Oriental College at Aligarh in 1875. Purist Muslims created the seminary at Deoband in 1859, while the syllabus of the Farangi Mahal seminary at Lakhnau was spread to many parts of India. Uttar Pradesh also supported a flourishing tradition of Urdu prose and poetry based in Lakhnau and, after the 1880s, a growing movement for writing in Hindi, epitomized by the realist novelist Premchand. The rise of Hindi to become the national language of India was advanced by the UP government's decision in 1900 to accord it equal status with Urdu in administration and the courts and by the activities of voluntary associations such as the Nagari Pracharini Sabha of Banaras. [*See* Ahmad Khan, Sir Sayyid.]

Politics in Uttar Pradesh were vitalized by the economic and ideological consequences of World War I. The Muslim population of the UP (14 percent of the total), led by Mohamed and Shaukat Ali, was prominent in the movement in defense of the Ottoman *khalifa* (1916–1924). [*See* Ali Brothers *and* Khilafat Movement.] The Congress movement dominated the towns after 1917, represented by the Hindu conservative wing of Madan Mohan Malaviya and the secular, socialist trend exemplified by Motilal and Jawaharlal Nehru, residents of Allahabad. [*See* Nehru, Motilal *and* Nehru, Jawaharlal.] Tension mounted in rural Awadh as economic conflicts between *taluqdars* and their tenantry increased. Congress politicians and independent lecturers for the peasants' associations were active in Allahabad, Pratapgarh, Rae Bareilly, and Fatehpur districts, although it was not until the Great Depression in the 1930s that the Congress was able to consolidate its hold in the villages.

Nationalist "no rent" campaigns from 1929 to 1934 created a block of rural support for Congress that was manifested by a sweeping victory in the provincial elections of 1937, when it annihilated landlord parties favored by the British. The Quit India Movement of 1942 was also strong in the eastern district, where a radical Congress leadership and wartime dislocation undermined acquiescence in colonial rule.

Muslim opinion, however, had diverged from Congress after the collapse of the Khilafat movement in 1924. The British had set up separate Muslim electorates for the Provincial Legislative Assembly created by the constitutional reforms of 1909. During the 1920s and 1930s a series of Hindu-Muslim riots took place that made reconciliation more difficult. The alienation of the Muslim leadership was completed during the period of Congress rule in the UP (from 1937 to 1939) that followed the British concession of full responsible government in the provinces under the India Act of 1935. The Congress disputed the claim of Muslim League politicians to represent their community in any way. [*See* All-India Muslim League.] Muslim opinion was suspicious of the extreme Hindu leanings of a minority of Congress politicians; Muslim gentry resented the Congress decision to abolish *zamindars*. UP Muslims thus played a prominent part in the Pakistan Movement (1940–1947). In 1946 and 1947 serious Hindu-Muslim rioting occurred in the cities. A large number of Muslim professional people and landlords migrated to Pakistan following the partition of the subcontinent. [*See* Pakistan *and* Partition of India.]

Since independence Uttar Pradesh has been a stronghold of the Congress. The party remains secure with a large rural vote and the support of Muslim and low-caste minorities fearful of the Hindu right wing represented by the Jana Sangh. [*See* Jana Sangh.] Successive Congress leaders, notably Jawaharlal Nehru, Lal Bahadur Shastri, Indira Gandhi, and Rajiv Gandhi, have been returned from UP constituencies. [*See also* Shastri, Lal Bahadur; Gandhi, Indira; *and* Gandhi, Rajiv.] Industrialization has been rapid in Kanpur and in the west around Ghaziabad, but agrarian progress has been patchy, with the state remaining one of the poorest in India. The Zamindari Abolition Act of 1952 has not broken up the concentration of landed power in the hands of high-caste Rajputs and Bhumihar brahmans in the east, although middle-caste Kurmis in the east and Jats in the west have prospered as independent farmers using new seed varieties. The condition of the low castes and Untouchables remains poor. The Persian and Urdu culture of the landed and administrative elites has disappeared rapidly since independence, but Uttar Pradesh remains the home of the Hindi literary tradition.

[*See also* Indian National Congress; India; Hindustan; Indo-Aryan Languages and Literatures; Allahabad; Varanasi; Kanpur; Mathura; *and* Hindustan.]

Richard B. Barnett, *North India between Empires: Awadh, the Mughals and the British 1720–1801* (1980). C. A. Bayly, *Rulers, Townsmen and Bazaars: North Indian Society in the Age of British Expansion, 1770–1870* (1983). Paul R. Brass, *Factional Politics in a North Indian State: The Congress Party in Uttar Pradesh* (1965). Bernard S. Cohn, "Structural Change in Indian Rural Society," in *Land Control and Social Structure in Indian History*, edited by Robert E. Frykenberg (1969). Thomas R. Metcalf, *Land, Landlords and the British Raj* (1979). Gyanendra Pandey, *The Ascendancy of the Congress in Uttar Pradesh, 1926–34* (1978). Francis Robinson, *Separatism among Indian Muslims: The Politics of the United Provinces Muslims, 1860–1923* (1974). Asiya Siddiqui, *Agrarian Change in a North Indian State: Uttar Pradesh, 1818–38* (1973). Eric T. Stokes, *The Peasant and the Raj: Studies in Agrarian Society and Peasant Rebellion in Colonial India* (1978).
                                                    C. A. BAYLY

UZBEKISTAN ("land of the Uzbeks") first acquired its name no later than the fourteenth century from a source or eponym not yet conclusively identified. Notwithstanding the Uzbeks' long history, they are a group that is still in transition.

Nineteenth- and early twentieth-century scholars and travelers followed earlier chroniclers, such as the Khivan ruler Abu al-Ghazi Bahadur Khan (r. 1642–1663) in his *Shajara-i Turk,* in holding the view that the Uzbeks took their group name from the last powerful Golden Horde potentate, Uzbek (or Ozbeg) Khan (r. 1312–1340), the Islamic proselytizer. Logically, the domain of that khan became the realm of the Uzbek and, it was thought, thereby acquired the designation *Uzbekistan.* Arabic and Persian sources referred to the Uzbeks as the followers of the ruler of the Golden Horde as well as to an Uzbek land located astride the Volga River with its capital at Sarai. These sources thus placed the center of the Uzbek territory near the prominent westernmost bend in the lower reaches of the Volga.

For modern historians, placing the Uzbek lands so far south and west in the Dasht-i Kipchak (Kipchak steppe) created interpretive tension, because the large tribal confederation of medieval Uzbeks was elsewhere, according to early manuscripts, and remained some sixteen hundred kilometers distant to the northeast for decades after 1340. This contradiction persuaded several European and Russian researchers to look for an etymological explanation of the name *Uzbek* that would avoid the link to a specific terrain. Pelliot, Vambery, and others accepted the idea that the Turkic reflexive pronoun *öz* ("self") had combined with the noble title *bek* to form a type of name common in various languages in many tribal societies beyond the Uzbek one. That combination would mean, they reasoned, "master of himself," "the man himself," and the like.

As a personal name, *Uzbek* had been known and recorded at least a century before the rise of Uzbek Khan on the Volga. But by the late twentieth century, scholars had lost enthusiasm for the theory of an eponym like him or for the idea that the Uzbek group name must have come from one of their own chieftains—a practice quite well known among Mongol-Turkic people.

The history of the nomadic Uzbeks, in contrast to the record of Uzbek Khan's followers, shows their emergence from the wreckage of the Shaiban *ulus* ("domain"). Shaiban (d. 1249), a grandson of the Mongol conqueror Genghis Khan (d. 1227), held sway in his time in western Siberia north of the Aral Sea and Lake Balkhash, east and southeast of the Ural chain of hills. The Uzbek center, Tura, west of the Tobol River, served as the capital of the earliest known Uzbek confederation of tribes under young Abu al-Khair Khan between 1428/1429 and 1446. In fact, most relevant sources observe that the Uzbek lands remained in northwestern Siberia until almost the middle of the fifteenth century. Some twenty years after Abu al-Khar Khan moved his capital south to the warmer country on the east bank of the middle Sayhun (Syr Darya) River, an onslaught of Kalmuk Mongols pushing westward from Dzungaria devastated the Uzbeks, costing the Uzbeks their khan and their lands in 1469. Only two years earlier, Uzbek tribal unity had suffered a permanent blow when large dissident numbers split away to become what are today Kazakhs.

Although the polity and territory of the Uzbeks once more lost focus, no later than 1488 a new leader appeared to rally what were reputed to be the ninety-two Uzbek tribes around him. This was Abu al-Khair Khan's educated grandson, Muhammad Shaibani Khan (r. 1451–1510). Trained at combat by his grandfather, Muhammad Shaibani Khan gave most of his attention and huge energy to penetrating even farther south into the realm of the Timurid dynasty (1370–1506) southwest of the Syr Darya, which included the historic cities of Khiva, Bukhara, Samarkand, and Herat. By 1499, the Uzbeks had invaded Transoxiana in full force, and they proceeded to drive out or destroy all meaningful Timurid opposition.

This mass migration of Uzbeks from the Kipchak steppe brought with it a great political change and significant alteration of ethnic (Uzbek) and dynastic (Shaibanid) names. It reconstituted the basis for an Uzbekistan on entirely new ground. The new rulers of the area, like their predecessors in Transoxiana, were Muslim, but less tolerant than earlier rulers, who had heterodox and Shi'ite tendencies. The Shaibanids viewed this new territory not as Uzbekistan, however, for they remained indifferent to an ethnic definition of their homeland. Instead, dynastic reach and power held political attention, and Islam, along with Turkic and Persian aesthetics, pervaded cultural life. Uzbek leaders invariably headed the governments, khanates, and amirates that followed one another in the southern part of western Turkestan throughout the next five centuries. These entities, remembered by dynastic names linked either to a human eponym (Shaiban), regions (Astrakhan, Khiva, Bukhara, Khokand), or tribes (Manghit, Ming, Qongrat) never selected the name *Uzbek* for their states throughout that five hundred years.

After 1924 the Russian authorities formed a new political-administrative unit within the USSR called the Uzbekistan Soviet Socialist Republic, a constituent part of the Soviet Union. The 450,000 square kilometers of this modern creation encompass most major cities of the old dynasties but lack a large part of the former territory and inhabitants. Soviet managers allocated large parcels of land to Turkmenistan, Tajikistan, and similar units in a pattern that appears to constitute a sort of negative ethnic gerrymandering intended to disperse and dilute the Soviet Uzbeks beyond and within their unit boundaries. The 1979 Soviet census reports tell the story. Of the 12.5 million Uzbeks then inhabiting the USSR, 15 percent lived outside the Uzbekistan SSR, mainly in Tajikistan, Kirghizia, Kazakhstan, and Turkmenistan. At the same time, well over 1.3 million non-Uzbek Central Asians resided in the Uzbekistan SSR, principally Kazakhs, Tajiks, and Kirghiz.

The motive of this policy of "dilution" is to diminish the influence of Uzbeks throughout Central Asia's southern reaches, an expanse they dominated almost until the twentieth century. The census report also records a persistent rapid growth in the numbers of Soviet Uzbeks inside and outside their assigned eponymous territorial unit. By 1979 Uzbeks had become the third-largest ethnic group as well as the leading Turkic nationality of the USSR. This trend generated between 1959 and 1979 a modest rise (to 68.6 percent) in the proportion of Uzbeks among the population of the Uzbekistan SSR. Russian and Ukrainian colonists settling in the region of Uzbekistan beginning in the nineteenth century and continuing through the twentieth moved mainly to urban centers. They largely account for the low proportion of Uzbeks in the Uzbekistan SSR. Also, the presence of these outsiders reduced Uzbeks to a minority or slight plurality of inhabitants in Tashkent, the capital, and in most other large towns of the constituent republic. As a result, the outsiders also held a significant percentage of industrial and bureaucratic employment, leaving 70 percent of the Uzbeks in Central Asia still residing in the countryside in 1979. This distribution promises to change only slowly, for Uzbeks in Uzbekistan cannot readily find either adequate housing or suitable employment in the city. Moreover, Uzbeks, like other Central Asians, do not choose to migrate in any substantial numbers to colder, culturally alien parts of the Soviet Union. Nevertheless, its growing numbers give the Uzbek group some grounds for confidence in its ultimate physical survival, despite its brief modern

experience as a politically constituted namesake group for the Uzbekistan SSR. But Uzbeks have reason for concern over their corporate identity; Soviet political and cultural leaders continue to manipulate the content and meaning of national identity in the USSR.

One important instance of this management of group identities occurred about 1947, when Russian and Uzbek authors writing official histories of Uzbekistan (no unofficial ones could appear under Soviet censorship) began to treat the ages before the sixteenth century in a special way. Few of the older scholars seem to have participated in this abrupt switch, which was led not by an Uzbek scholar but evidently by the Russian Marxist Orientalist historian Alexsandr Yakubovskii (1886–1953). He and his associates chose the new Uzbek republic as a geographical reference point, declaring all history prior to 1925 on that land and all Turkic people found there at any time before that year to be Uzbek back to deepest antiquity.

Approved Soviet historiography for Central Asia since World War II, therefore, features Timurid dynastic, political, and cultural leaders as Uzbeks but, with noticeable selectivity, ignores the important role of the Shaibanids and their successors in shaping the life and civilization of western Turkestan. This revisionist policy has produced, among other effects, a confusion of historical identities for the main actors in the formative fifteenth and sixteenth centuries. Soviet histories now, without qualification, give the name *Uzbek* to the archenemies of the contemporary Uzbeks: the Timurid rulers Ulug Beg (1394–1449), Timur's grandson; and Zahiruddin Muhammad Babur (1483–1530), whom the Uzbek troops routed from his small realm in Central Asia. These articulate leaders, along with Muhammad Shaibani Khan, expressed themselves clearly in regard to each other. Babur despised the Uzbeks, he said. Ulug Beg was defeated by them in combat against the forces of the predecessors of Abu al-Khair Khan near Saghanak in 1427, a loss that led to disgrace for him and his field commanders.

Both Marxist periodization and Soviet ideology have necessitated this rewriting of Uzbek history in order to permit a highly selective class interpretation of Central Asian history. To downplay the active Uzbek nomadic place in Uzbekistan's history, this new conception substitutes a racial and territorial foundation for Uzbek group identity for the old sense of unity based on group name and tribal legacy. These complex guidelines, followed carefully by subsequent Uzbek historians, have yet to be fully absorbed in the group consciousness of the Uzbeks; since World War II they have remained unchallenged by any new school of Marxist thought studying Central Asian history. Added to these doctrinal treatments of Uzbek history, the lingering imperfections of the 1924–1925 ethnic partition of Central Asia have seemingly blurred the Uzbek consciousness into a feeling of broader Central Asian identity, an attitude consistent with the actual situation of the Uzbeks up to the Russian invasion that began in the 1850s.

[*See also* Central Asia; Turkestan; Timurid Dynasty; Shaibanid Dynasty; Bukhara, Khanate of; Khiva, Khanate of; Kalmuks; Kazakhs; Babur; *and* Ulug Beg.]

Edward Allworth, *Uzbek Literary Politics* (1964). Zahiruddin Muhammad Babur, *The Babur-Nama in English: Memoirs of Babur,* translated by Annette S. Beveridge (1922; reprint, 1969). Arminius Vambery, *History of Bokhara* (1873; reprint, 1973). Geoffrey Wheeler, *The Modern History of Soviet Central Asia* (1964).

EDWARD ALLWORTH

UZUN HASAN (1425–1478; r. 1457–1478), the most important ruler of the Akkoyunlu dynasty. (The nickname *Uzun,* "the Long," referred to his height.) A Turkish tribal conqueror in the mold of Timur, Uzun Hasan extended Akkoyunlu power over most of Persia, excluding Khurasan. He extinguished the rival Karakoyunlu dynasty in 1467 and defeated the Timurid Abu Sa'id in 1469. He played an active role in international politics, allying with Venice against the Ottomans and marrying the Christian princess Theodora Komnene of Trebizond.

The Akkoyunlu arose at a time and in an area of religious heterodoxy. Although Uzun Hasan was a Sunni Muslim who patronized the religious establishment, he also had high regard for popular religious leaders. He formed an alliance, cemented by marriage ties, with the (Shi'ite) Safavid family, partly in opposition to their common enemy, the Karakoyunlu. However, under Shah Isma'il (Uzun Hasan's grandson), the Safavids drove the Akkoyunlu from Persia.

Uzun Hasan promoted a number of state laws to regularize and centralize revenue collection, and instituted more equitable land taxes. He was a great builder who created a magnificent palace complex and *maidan* (now destroyed) in his capital, Tabriz.

Uzun Hasan was decisively defeated by the Ottomans in 1473, a blow from which the Akkoyunlu never recovered. He died at the age of fifty-two and was buried at the Nasriyya mosque in Tabriz.

[*See also* Akkoyunlu; Karakoyunlu; Safavid Dynasty; *and* Tabriz.]

Edward G. Browne, *A Literary History of Persia* (1928), vol. 3. John E. Woods, *The Aqquyunlu: Clan, Confederation, Empire* (1976).   LAWRENCE POTTER

V

VAISHNAVISM, the Hindu tradition of myths, liturgies, and theologies that view Supreme Being as one person, Vishnu. At the center of its obscure development stands the Vedic cult of the fire sacrifice (c. 1000 BCE) that identifies the god Vishnu with sacred power *(brahman)* as it benefits life in society. Possibly stimulated by the rise of the Buddhists and Jains in approximately 500 BCE, Vedic theologians expanded their view of Vishnu to include other cults alongside the fire sacrifice; some of these, such as yoga, temples, and icons, were non-Vedic. By 400 BCE Vaishnavism had spread from the North throughout South Asia and has since remained an alternate or complement to Shaivism and Shaktism.

Vaishnavism is monotheistic in that it recognizes only one person as Supreme Being, but polytheistic in its belief that Vishnu turns himself into various deities who produce the visible and invisible universe and all of its inhabitants. Vishnu emits, sustains, and consumes all things, remaining transcendent all the while. The transcendent Vishnu is likened to a king who dwells with his queen, Lakshmi, in a palace. The universe is his kingdom, whose cosmic and social order *(dharma)* he protects and whose inhabitants he rules through the law of karma and the movement of time. Lakshmi is his power *(shakti)* to protect the universe and its inhabitants, to give prosperity, and to convey love to those who offer him devoted service *(bhakti)*. In response to *bhakti*, which includes upholding *dharma*, learning about Vishnu, and loving him through ritual service and compassion toward all beings, Vishnu gives prosperity, protection, and eventual freedom from the universe of rebirth *(samsara)*. Emancipation *(moksha)* may come after many lives of devotion, or after only one, but is dependent on the lord's grace. Some Vaishnavites seek an unbroken relationship to Vishnu as their goal, whether it be in *samsara* or in *moksha*.

Vishnu himself stimulates *bhakti* by descending into the universe to sustain its *dharma*. Of these protective and dazzling descents (avatars), ten are most notable: Fish, Tortoise, Man-Lion, Dwarf, Parashurama, Rama, Krishna, Balarama, the Buddha, and Kalki. Of these, Rama and Krishna are the most important in Vaishnavite history. The warrior Rama and his wife Sita portray the *dharma* of householders and royalty in the popular epic *Ramayana* (c. 200 BCE–200 CE). Rama's war against the demon Ravana has for centuries been enacted annually in the North, where Rama, Sita, and Rama's monkey ally, Hanuman, are popular deities—a Hindu response, perhaps, to Muslim rule from the twelfth to the nineteenth centuries. [*See also* Ramayana.]

Krishna, too, was born as a warrior to slay incarnate demons, but lived his childhood and adolescence disguised as a cowherd. Using feelings of astonishment, parental affection, and erotic love to generate *bhakti*, stories about the young Krishna appeared (c. 400–1200 CE) in the *Harivamsha, Vishnu Purana, Bhagavata Purana,* and *Gita Govinda*. [*See* Puranas.]

As a king, the incarnate Vishnu participated in the war of the epic *Mahabharata* (c. 400 BCE–400 CE) and "sang" the *Bhagavad Gita*, perhaps the text most common to Vaishnavites. [*See* Mahabharata *and* Bhagavad Gita.] Krishna is popular throughout India, but an intensely emotional yet highly sophisticated Krishna *bhakti* articulated by southern Tamil poets (c. 600–900) stimulated Vaishnavite sects *(sampradayas)* that, from the twelfth century, were shaped by eminent gurus or *acharyas*—most notably Ramanuja, Madhva, Vallabha, and Chaitanya—into distinct "denominations" within Vaishnavism. For one sect at least, the Gaudiya Sampradaya of Chaitanya, Krishna rather than Vishnu is the identity of Supreme Being. [*See* Chaitanya.]

Vaishnavites may worship Vishnu mentally through imaginative visualization (*dhyana*), but most worship him also through icons in temples. Icons of Vishnu usually portray a royal setting in which he or his avatar sits, or reclines, or stands. He may have two, four, eight, or more arms, each holding weapons or flowers or other items that allude to his heroic activities and have esoteric meaning for initiates. Since Lakshmi is his inseparable *shakti,* she is present in some mode. Some Vaishnavites believe the immovable icon in the temple to be an avatar that dwells there permanently to receive worship. Others, however, share with some other Hindus as well as with Sufis and Sikhs the belief that Supreme Being has no representational form. In place of icons they use words or mantras to capture Vishnu's presence, especially his names (e.g., Hari, Rama, Vasudeva, Narayana), of which there are a thousand, each with its own mythic and symbolic connotations. Mohandas K. Gandhi, the "father" of independent India, was such a Vaishnava.

[*See also* Hinduism *and* Bhakti.]

R. G. Bhandarkar, *Vaisnavism, Śaivism and Minor Religious Systems* (reprint, 1965). Alain Danielou, *Hindu Polytheism* (1964). J. Gonda, *Visnuism and Śivaism: A Comparison* (1970). John S. Hawley, and Donna M. Wulff, eds., *The Divine Consort: Rādhā and the Goddesses of India* (1983). Norvin Hein, *The Miracle Plays of Mathura* (1972). Suvira Jaiswal, *The Origin and Development of Vaisnavism* (1967).   DENNIS HUDSON

VAISHYA, one of the four caste (*varna*) categories of the *Rig Veda,* consisting principally of farmers and businessmen. Along with brahmans and *kshatriyas,* they are among the "twice-born" who wear the sacred thread and study sacred texts. A permeable category, *vaishya* status has been claimed by individuals and groups seeking upward mobility. *Vaishyas* are usually ascribed third rank, but this varies, notably in mainland Gujarat, where they rank ahead of *kshatriyas* and almost equal to *brahmans.* The *vaishya* category may include Jains, who are closely related to Hindu merchant groups.

[*See also* Brahman; Kshatriya; Shudra; *and* Caste.]

M. Marriott and R. B. Inden, "Caste Systems," in *Encyclopedia Britannica,* vol. 14 (1974), pp. 982–991. N. A. Thoothi, *The Vaishnavas of Gujarat. Being a Study in Methods of Investigation of Social Phenomena* (1935).

HOWARD SPODEK

VAJIRAVUDH, or Rama VI, early twentieth-century king of Siam, regarded as the father of Thai nationalism.

Vajiravudh was born in Bangkok in 1881, the second son of King Chulalongkorn (r. 1868–1910) by Queen Saowapha. He had already been sent to study in England when his elder brother, Vajirunhis, who had been designated crown prince, died in 1895. Vajiravudh received military training at Sandhurst, then went to Oxford for studies in history and law, returning home only in 1903. Spending his days mainly in literary pursuits, he served as regent during his father's trip to Europe in 1907. On coming to the throne in October 1910, he began his reign inauspiciously, spending about 8 percent of the annual national budget on his coronation; moving quickly to build his own political and military following in the Wild Tiger Corps, a statewide paramilitary movement; and nudging many of the powerful and experienced princes of the previous reign, mainly his uncles, from the government. A military plot to overturn his government was uncovered early in 1912 among junior army officers and foiled with the arrest of ninety-two men.

Vajiravudh is remembered as a popular king, but he was popular in an unusual sense of the word. A prodigious author and playwright, he used the modern essay and stage script to popularize his ideas of patriotism and "modern" social relations. He used the press and mass organizations to urge the population to accept his ideas about the nation, about one's duty to be willing to die for king and country, and about the virtues of hard work and thrift. He encouraged his people to think of Siam as a meritocracy where anyone could rise to the top by talent and hard work. But while much that he said came across as egalitarian nationalism, Vajiravudh insisted upon the absolutism of the monarchy, and throughout his reign he refused to share his power, opposing even the creation of advisory councils.

The combination of the king's political rigidity, a personal life that many found undignified, and profligate royal spending left the kingdom in disarray upon his premature death on 26 November 1925. Uninterested in marriage until late in life, he failed even in his duty to provide an heir to the throne: his queen gave birth to a daughter two days before his death. He was succeeded by his younger full brother, Prajadhipok (r. 1925–1935).

[*See also* Chakri Dynasty; Chulalongkorn; Prajadhipok; Damrong Rajanubhab; Devawongse Varopakar; *and* Wachirayan Warorot.]

Walter F. Vella, *Chaiyo! King Vajiravudh and the Development of Thai Nationalism* (1978). David K. Wyatt, *Thailand: A Short History* (1984).   DAVID K. WYATT

VAKATAKAS. The Vakataka dynasty (c. 255–510) rose to power in the Vidarbha region of Maharashtra, India, with the downfall of the imperial Satavahanas, and thereafter built an empire comprising Deccan and parts of southern and central India under their emperor Pravarasena (c. 275–335). The emperor also achieved a matrimonial alliance with the Nagas, the leading power of north-central India, and his successors divided the empire into four kingdoms. The elder branch ruled from the capital at Nandivardhana and attained political prominence with the marriage of King Rudrasena II to Prabhayatigupta, daughter of the Gupta emperor Chandragupta II. Prabhayatigupta ruled as regent of her minor sons between 390 and 410, making the Vakataka kingdom a virtual Gupta dependency. Various Vakataka realms achieved unity once again under Harishena (r. 475–510), who revived the dynasty's overlordship of southern and central India and patronized the frescoes and cave architecture at Ajanta.

[*See also* Gupta Empire *and* Ajanta.]

R. C. Majundar and A. S. Altekar, *The Vakataka-Gupta Age* (1967). V. V. Mirashi, *Inscriptions of the Vakatakas* (1963). G. Yazdani, ed., *The Early History of the Deccan*, 2 vols. (1960).   SHIVA BAJPAI

VALIGNANO, ALESSANDRO (1539–1606), Italian Jesuit, vicar-general, and visitor for the Society of Jesus in the Indies from 1574 to 1606. Valignano was an administrator, propagandist, and missionary for the society in Goa, Macao, and Japan. A trained lawyer, he entered the society in 1566. In China and Japan, Valignano stressed training in the vernacular languages of the countries where the society was active and adaptation to their customs, so long as church doctrine was not compromised. To this end he established a center in Macao to train missionaries in the Chinese language.

In Japan, Valignano implemented his policy of moving toward ordination of native clergy by founding two seminaries, a novitiate, and a college during his first visit (1579–1582), and in 1590 he imported a printing press to Japan to spread the faith through the written word. The Jesuit press remained active until 1614, publishing theological tracts, translations, grammars and dictionaries of Japanese, and transcriptions of Japanese works of literature. He was notably successful in gaining support from the Japanese ruling class, particularly in gaining the cession of Nagasaki to the society in 1580, and he used the Nagasaki–Macao trade to finance the mission. He died in Macao in 1606.

[*See also* Christianity: Christianity in Japan *and* Jesuits.]

C. R. Boxer, *The Christian Century in Japan, 1549–1650* (1951). George Elison, *Deus Destroyed: The Image of Christianity in Early Modern Japan* (1973).   RONALD P. TOBY

VANG PAO, prominent Hmong leader in Laos during the 1960s and early 1970s. Vang Pao was born about 1926 into one of the smaller Hmong clans in eastern Xieng Khouang Province. The son of a district leader, he joined the French Colonial Army in 1945 and served until 1954, by which time he was a lieutenant commanding the only Hmong commando battalion.

Vang Pao continued his military career under the Royal Lao government, serving in 1955 as commanding officer of the Second Command Group and commander of the Nam Khan region. He was promoted to brigadier general in 1963 and was appointed to command all Hmong forces. In 1964 he was named deputy commander of Military Region II of Laos, and in January 1965 he was appointed its commanding general. Vang Pao's forces bore a significant share of the fighting during the war in Laos and received large amounts of direct military assistance from the United States.

Following the Communist victories in Vietnam and Cambodia, and the collapse of the non-Communist political forces in Laos, Vang Pao fled to Thailand in May 1975. He subsequently settled in the United States.

[*See also* Hmong *and* Indochina War.]

JOSEPH J. ZASLOFF

VAN LANG, kingdom centered in Vietnam's Red River delta between the seventh and third century BCE, considered to be the first centralized Vietnamese state. Associated with the Dong Son civilization, Van Lang was ruled by the Hong Bang dynasty or Hung Vuong ("Hung kings"), whose origins date back to the quasi-legendary figures of Lac Long Quan and Au Co. Its capital was located at Me Linh, in present-day Vinh Phu Province. Van Lang was overthrown by a man from the neighboring state of Thuc (Chinese, Shu) who reigned under the name An Duong Vuong.

[*See also* Dong Son; Hong Bang Dynasty; Hung Vuong; Lac Long Quan; Au Co; *and* An Duong Vuong.]

Keith W. Taylor, *The Birth of Vietnam* (1983).

BRUCE M. LOCKHART

VAN TIEN DUNG, a leading military commander and former top Communist Party official in the Socialist Republic of Vietnam, credited with building the Ho Chi Minh Trail through Laos and Cambodia in the Vietnam War. General Dung was also the strategist of the final assault on South Vietnam in the mid-1970s. Born the son of a peasant in 1917 near Hanoi, he worked in a textile factory as a youth and joined the Indochinese Communist Party sometime in the 1930s. Arrested twice by the French colonial regime, he managed to escape both times and became secretary of the Party's regional committee in Tonkin during World War II. During the Franco–Viet Minh War he rose rapidly in the armed forces and became a member of the Central Committee in 1951. Elected a full member of the Politburo in 1972, he was chosen to command Communist forces in the Ho Chi Minh Campaign, which conquered Saigon in April 1975. In 1980 he became minister of defense of the Socialist Republic of Vietnam, but he lost his Politburo seat in December 1986 during the Sixth National Vietnamese Communist Party Congress, which marked the largest shake-up in the Party's history, and two months later he lost his post as defense minister.

Van Tien Dung, *Our Great Spring Victory* (1977). Frank Snepp, *Decent Interval* (1977).

WILLIAM J. DUIKER

VAN XUAN ("ten thousand springtimes"), name given to the Viet lands by Ly Bi (Ly Bon) in 544 during his attempt to establish a Viet kingdom independent of Chinese control.

[*See also* Former Ly Dynasty *and* Ly Bon.]

Thomas Hodgkin, *Vietnam: The Revolutionary Path* (1981). Keith W. Taylor, *The Birth of Vietnam* (1983).

JAMES M. COYLE

VARANASI (also known as Banaras, Benares, and Kashi), an ancient city in the North Indian state of Uttar Pradesh with a population of 708,647 (1981).

Varanasi is situated on the left bank of the Ganges River and is considered an important site of pilgrimage by Hindus.

The earliest reference to the area occurs in the writings of the late Vedic period (c. ninth century BCE), where one finds mention of the Kashi kingdom, a name also applied by an early Buddhist text in a list of the "sixteen principal states" of India. At the time of the Buddha's first teaching (sixth century BCE) in nearby Sarnath, Varanasi was known as the capital of the Kashi kingdom. Nevertheless, Varanasi (a Sanskrit compound referring to the Varana and Asi rivers, both of which flow into the Ganges near the opposite boundaries of the city) appears to be the more ancient form of designation and has been revived recently as the official name.

The city enjoyed an unparalleled status as a center of Brahmanical and Buddhist learning until the beginning of Muslim domination in 1194. A succession of Muslim raids destroyed numerous temples and leveled entire sections of the city, with the only significant reprieve coming during the reign of Akbar (d. 1605). The Mughal emperor Shah Jahan (d. 1666) is said to have had seventy-six temples destroyed, while his son and successor, Aurangzeb (d. 1717), had mosques erected where the most sacred Hindu temples had stood before being destroyed by his armies. Muslim rule continued until Varanasi was ceded by Warren Hastings to the nawab of Oudh (Awadh) in 1775, remaining under British administration until independence. [*See* Hastings, Warren.] Beginning in the late eighteenth century the city witnessed a revival of temple building, owing largely to Maratha patronage.

The most striking feature about Varanasi is the *ghat*, a series of steep steps leading to the shore of the Ganges. The *ghats* are descended by the faithful in the early hours of the dawn in order to perform their ablutions; there are more than seventy of these "bathing" *ghats*, with varying degrees of sanctity and popularity (see figure 1). Of the many temples found near the *ghats* and within the city, the most important are those dedicated to the great god Shiva (who is said to reside in Kashi), the monkey god Hanuman, and the goddess Durga. All devout Hindus hope to visit the sacred city at least once in a lifetime and, if possible, to die within the bounds of Kashi, believed by Hindus to ensure *moksha,* or liberation from rebirth.

[*See also* Ganges River *and* Hinduism.]

Diana Eck, *Banaras: City of Light* (1982). E. B. Havell, *Benares, the Sacred City* (1905). Vincent A. Smith, "Be-

FIGURE 1. *Ghats on the Ganges River, Varanasi.*

nares," *Encyclopedia of Religion and Ethics,* edited by James Hastings, vol. 2 (1955).   STUART W. SMITHERS

renne and Politics in Indochina, 1925–1926" in *Aspects of Vietnamese History,* edited by Walter F. Vella (1973).

BRUCE M. LOCKHART

VARENNE, ALEXANDRE (1870–?), governor-general of Indochina (1925–1927). The appointment of Varenne, a prominent socialist, initially caused much optimism among moderate Vietnamese nationalists. Leaders such as Bui Quang Chieu, Nguyen Phan Long, and Nguyen An Ninh presented Varenne with requests for needed reforms, including the well-known *Cahier des Voeux Annamites.* Although his first speech hinted at long-term independence for Vietnam, Varenne soon found himself caught between native nationalists and French colonialists, as heightened political unrest in Cochinchina increased tension. While he did carry out certain social and educational reforms, Varenne did not sanction any significant advance in the colony's political status.

William J. Duiker, *The Rise of Nationalism in Vietnam, 1900–1941* (1976). William Frederick, "Alexandre Va-

VARMAN DYNASTY. During the first half of the eighth century in India, Yashovarman sat on the throne of Kanyakubja (Kanauj), probably ruling much of Uttar Pradesh, Bihar, and Bengal. Neither his predecessors nor successors are known, although a detailed chronicle of his reign, the *Gaudavaho* by Vakpati, survives. His reign is also documented by a lengthy inscription discovered at Nalanda.

[*See also* Kanyakubja.]

N. G. Suru, ed. and trans., *Vākpatirāja's Gaüdavaho* (1975). R. S. Tripathi, *History of Kanauj to the Moslem Conquest* (1964).   FREDERICK M. ASHER

VEDANTA (or Uttara Mimamsa), the most important and influential school of the six orthodox Hindu systems of philosophy. All branches of the school are based on the belief that the highest wisdom, the "end" or "epitome" of the Veda (thus, *vedanta*), is revealed only in the philosophical teachings of the Upanishads.

The earliest text of Vedanta is the *Vedanta Sutras* (also known as the *Brahma Sutras*) attributed to Badarayana (first or second century BCE?). The definitive forms of the principal types of Vedanta did not take shape until much later, however, with the commentaries and other writings of Shankara (788–820 CE), Ramanuja (eleventh century), and Madhva (1197–1276). Shankara taught an uncompromising monism and is regarded as the founder and leading exponent of Advaita ("nondualistic") Vedanta. Ultimate reality *(brahman)* is one, characterized by pure being, pure consciousness, and pure bliss, and the phenomenal world of diversity is considered illusory. Liberation, according to the Advaitins, is the direct realization of the full identity of the individual self *(atman)* with the *brahman*. Ramanuja introduced theism into Vedantic thought and formulated a philosophy of "qualified nondualism" (Vishishta Advaita), which posited a fundamental distinction between the individual self and God and emphasized devotion rather than wisdom as the highest path to liberation. Madhva, the architect of "dualistic" (Dvaita) Vedanta, went even further by maintaining an eternal and complete distinction between God, individual selves, and the material world.

[*See also* Hinduism; Vedas; Shankara; *and* Ramanuja.]

John Braisted Carman, *The Theology of Rāmānuja* (1974). Eliot Deutsch, *Advaita Vedānta: A Philosophical Reconstruction* (1969). K. Narain, *An Outline of Madhva Philosophy* (1962).   Brian K. Smith

VEDAS. The term *Veda* is derived from the Sanskrit root *vid* ("to know") and thus means *knowledge* and specifically *sacred knowledge*. In its narrower sense, *Veda* refers to three collections of sacred knowledge known as *samhitas*. They were composed and transmitted orally in an archaic form of Sanskrit (called Vedic Sanskrit) by the Indo-Iranian tribes who invaded India and who became the Vedic Indians. The oldest of these works, the *Rig Veda Samhita,* is a collection of hymns to the gods and was intended primarily for use in the *soma* sacrifice. Conjectures as to the date of the oldest hymns range from 1800 BCE to 1300 BCE. At that time the Vedic tribes occupied territories on both sides of the Indus

River. The verses of the *Sama Veda,* chants to be sung during the *soma* sacrifice, are, with few exceptions, taken from the *Rig Veda*. The *Yajur Veda,* unlike the other Vedas, consists of five *samhitas,* and these contain sacrificial formulas for the entire spectrum of the ritual, not just the *soma* sacrifice. By the time this Veda was composed, the center of Vedic civilization had moved well to the east of the Indus. The *Atharva Veda* provides us with a picture of ordinary life in Vedic India. It consists characteristically of charms to secure the good things of life and spells to drive off the bad. Because of its popular and magical nature, the *Atharva Veda* was slow to be recognized as canonical—to this day, orthodox South Indian brahmans recognize only the first three Vedas.

In its wider sense, the term *Veda* denotes a whole body of literature, each work of which traces its genealogy to one of the schools represented by the *samhitas* just discussed. The Brahmanas are explanations of the ritual that accompanies the hymns, chants, sacrificial formulas, or spells of the Veda to which they belong. In the Brahmanas the sacrifice was thought of as compelling the gods instead of imploring them; therefore, it, rather than the gods, became the focus of attention. The Aranyakas, or "forest books," are so called because they deal with secret material meant to be studied in the privacy of the forest. They emphasize mystical and speculative aspects of the sacrifice. This tendency continued in the Upanishads, composed around 500 BCE, in which the sacrifice recedes into the background and the ultimate identity of the individual soul *(atman)* with the world soul *(brahman)* is paramount. The Upanishads also developed the ideas of transmigration and the illusoriness of this world.

Ancillary to the Veda proper are the Sutras (aphorisms). These are aids for the recitation of the sacred texts or for the performance of the ritual. The aphorisms on ritual, known as the Shrautasutras, Grihyasutras, and Dharmasutras, are the most important. They deal, respectively, with major sacrifices such as the *soma* sacrifice, domestic ritual, and law.

[*See also* Haoma; Hinduism; Hindu Law; *and* Indo-Aryan Languages and Literatures.]

Arthur Berriedale Keith, *The Religion and Philosophy of the Veda and Upanishads* (1925). Arthur A. Macdonell, *A History of Sanskrit Literature* (1899). Louis Renou, *Vedic India,* translated by Philip Spratt (1971). James A. Santucci, *An Outline of Vedic Literature* (1976).

                    Lucianne C. Bulliet

VEDDAS, Sri Lankan aboriginals, descendants of late Stone Age cave dwellers. The very few Veddas who are left are now confined to a narrow strip of forest in the areas east of the central hill country. Increasingly the Veddas are being resettled in agricultural communities and assimilated into the predominant Sinhalese Buddhist culture. Their adjustment to this more settled existence is rendered easier, although by no means without difficulties, by the absence of any perception of caste inferiority of the Veddas among the Sinhalese peasants in the regions in which they live.

[See also Sri Lanka and Adivasis.]

C. F. Seligmann and Brenda S. Seligmann, *The Veddas* (1911).
K. M. DE SILVA

VELLALA. In South India the name *vellala* is borne by cultivators whose fields are plowed usually by hired or socially bonded laborers. The Vellala myths of origin suggest that they are among the oldest Dravidian-speaking groups in Tamil Nadu. Over the centuries they have patronized nonbrahman monastic institutions.

[See also Tamil Nadu and Caste.]

Stephen A. Barnett, "The Process of Withdrawal in a South Indian Caste," in *Entrepreneurship and Modernization in Occupational Cultures in South Asia*, edited by Milton B. Singer (1973), pp. 179–204. Edgar Thurston, *The Castes and Tribes of Southern India* (1909).
CAROL APPADURAI BRECKENRIDGE

VELOSO, DIOGO (c. 1560–1599), Portuguese soldier of fortune, noted for his intrigues at the Cambodian court. Dispatched to Manila by the king to seek military aid against the Thai on Cambodia's behalf, Veloso returned to Cambodia in time to be captured by a Thai invasion force in 1594. After adventures in Thailand and the Philippines, he returned with a handful of soldiers in 1598 and overthrew a Cambodian usurper-king, replacing him on the throne with the son of his former patron. With the self-confidence of so many colonial adventurers, Veloso sought to place Cambodia under Spanish protection. He failed, and Cham and Malay minorities in Cambodia overthrew the king and massacred his Spanish guardians, including Veloso, in 1599.
DAVID P. CHANDLER

VERBIEST, FERDINAND (known to the Chinese as Nan Huairen; 1623–1688), one of the outstanding Christian missionaries to serve in China. Verbiest attained particular eminence as an astronomer-mandarin. The son of a steward of the marquis of Tarragona, Verbiest was born at Pittem (between Bruges and Kortrijk) in the Spanish Netherlands (now Belgium); he studied at Bruges, Kortrijk, and Leuven (Louvain). Verbiest began almost half a century of service with the Society of Jesus (the Jesuits) in 1641, teaching humanities and rhetoric for five years before completing his own studies in the Spanish Netherlands, Rome, and Spain. He twice traveled from Bruges to Spain in order to obtain a missionary post in South America, but was unsuccessful. Instead, he was sent to China, arriving at Macao in 1658.

Verbiest began his twenty-nine years in the China Mission serving at Xi'an in Shaanxi Province, but after six months was called to Beijing in order to assist the elderly Johann Adam Schall von Bell in his duties as vice president of the Bureau of Astronomy. In 1664 the persecution led by the literatus Yang Guangxian caused the Jesuits and their Chinese assistants in the Bureau of Astronomy to be indicted on criminal charges and imprisoned in chains. After six months the Chinese assistants were executed and the Jesuits were released. Under the Kangxi emperor's rehabilitation, Verbiest was made vice president of the Bureau of Astronomy in 1669. The emperor had such confidence in him that he was allowed to reform the calendar by deleting an intercalary month from the calendar in spite of vehement opposition.

The year 1671 marked the start of a high point in Verbiest's relationship with the Kangxi emperor, as he secured permission for the missionaries to return from exile in Canton (Guangzhou) to their churches in the provinces. Over a five-month period during this time he was called into the emperor's presence on a daily basis for the purpose of tutoring, primarily in European mathematics and astronomy. In 1675 he was appointed as a second president to the Board of Public Works. While interpreting for the Russian ambassador, N. G. Spafary, during important negotiations in 1676, Verbiest conceived of a plan for opening a new route between China and Europe by way of Moscow. During this period he was honored not only by the Chinese but also by his Jesuit superiors in Europe, who appointed him vice-provincial of China in 1676. With this sort of eminence, he was able to act as a protective force for the missionaries in the provinces against constant attacks from unfriendly quarters.

Verbiest's greatest scholarly achievements were in the natural and technical sciences. He built six new instruments for the imperial observatory from 1670 to 1673. He sent astronomical tables to Rome and in 1674 composed a map of the world. To assist the throne in putting down the rebellion of Wu Sangui, Verbiest cast lighter artillery that could be transported through the mountainous regions of southwest China. During his lifetime Verbiest composed a large number of works in Chinese and Latin on the subjects of astronomy, calendrical science, geography, cartography, physics, and medicine, as well as religious works and large number of letters. Most of these writings are extant.

[*See also* Jesuits: Jesuits in China *and* Kangxi Emperor.]

Joseph Needham, *Science and Civilisation in China*, vol. 3, *Mathematics and the Sciences of the Heavens and the Earth* (1959). Jonathan Spence, *The China Helpers: Western Advisers in China, 1620–1960* (1969).

DAVID E. MUNGELLO

VERSAILLES TREATY OF 1918. As a belligerent since 1917 against Germany, China hoped to recover Germany's special concessions in Shandong when the peace treaty ending World War I was drafted. Japan had captured these concessions in 1915 and had immediately begun administering them as her own. Japan obtained various promises from Western governments, and even from the warlord-dominated regime in Beijing, in support of its claims in Shandong. The Chinese delegation at the Paris Peace Conference, which included many progressive nationalistic figures, looked to the United States to support China's case for the return of Shandong. They connected China's claims with President Woodrow Wilson's call for a just and equitable new world order based on national self-determination. In the end, however, President Wilson endorsed Japanese claims and the Treaty of Versailles confirmed Japan's position in Shandong. A Chinese student protest followed, starting in Beijing on 4 May 1919 and leading to what is now known as the May Fourth Movement. The treaty is thus remembered in China as proof of the Great Powers' unfairness toward China and as the spark that started mass movements to overcome China's national humiliation. The Chinese delegation never signed the treaty, thus leaving the so-called Shandong Question between China and Japan unsettled.

[*See also* May Fourth Movement; Shandong Question; *and* World War I in China.]

T. T. Chow, *The May Fourth Movement* (1960), pp. 84–116.

DAVID D. BUCK

VERSAILLES TREATY OF 1787. Signed on 28 November 1787 at the initiative of Bishop Pierre Pigneau de Béhaine, the treaty was to guarantee French support to Prince Nguyen Anh in his attempt to defeat the Tay Son rebels in Vietnam. In return for military aid, France was to receive the port of Tourane and Pulo Condore Island. The treaty also granted the French special rights and trading privileges in Vietnam and set down the basis for a military alliance between the kings of France and Cochinchina. France was facing more pressing problems, however, and did not fulfill its obligations to Nguyen Anh. The bishop returned to Vietnam on his own.

[*See also* Gia Long; Pigneau de Béhaine, Pierre; *and* Tay Son Rebellion.]

Nguyen Phut Tan, *Modern History of Vietnam (1802–1954)* (1964).

BRUCE M. LOCKHART

VIDEVDAT, or *Vendidad*, Pahlavi for the Avestan *Vidaevodata (Law Against the Demons),* a prose work in Avestan of the law and lore of Zoroastrianism in twenty-two chapters, constituting one of the twenty-one *Nasks*, or divisions, of the Avesta. In its final form the *Videvdat* is one of the latest texts of the Avesta, dated to the Parthian period on the basis of Greek measurements mentioned in it that were probably introduced into Iran by the Seleucids. The text deals primarily with the moral, ritual, and physical means whereby death, disease, pollution, and sin—the assaults of the Evil Spirit, Angra Mainyu—may be banished from the world; it elaborates precautions for the disposal of corpses, prescribes quarantines for women in menses, provides instructions for lengthy ablutions to remove impurity, and lists numerous penalties and penances for diverse sins. The text exemplifies the Zorastrian aim of cleansing both the natural world and the soul of evil; it serves as a virtual encyclopedia of Zoroastrian ethics. There is a complete Pahlavi translation of the *Videvdat,* and the Avestan text is used liturgically.

[*See also* Avesta *and* Zoroastrianism.]

B. T. Anklesaria, ed. and trans., *Pahlavi Vendidād* (1949). J. Darmesteter and L. H. Mills, trans., *The Zend-Avesta* (1974). Ilya Gershevitch, "Old Iranian Literature," in Bertold Spuler, ed., *Handbuch der Orientalistik*, pt. 1, vol. 4, sec. 2, chap. 1 (1968), p. 28.

JAMES R. RUSSELL

VIDYASAGAR, ISVARCHANDRA (1820–1891), Bengali writer, Sanskritist, and social reformer. Born to a poor family in rural Bengal, he was brought on foot to Calcutta by his father, who enrolled him in Sanskrit College on a meager scholarship. A brilliant student, he later became professor and then principal of the college. He was profoundly learned in Sanskrit and worked for popular education using the Bengali language. His Bengali works helped shape modern Bengali prose. He championed the cause of female education and widow remarriage and opposed polygamy. Of uncompromising integrity, rooted in his country's traditions yet open to new ideas, he was perhaps the most respected Bengali of his age.

[*See also* Bengal.]

Amales Tripathi, *Vidyasagar: The Traditional Moderniser* (1974).   WARREN GUNDERSON

VIENTIANE, or Viang Chan, capital of the Lao People's Democratic Republic, former administrative capital of Laos, and site of a premodern kingdom.

The Vientiane Plain was settled in prehistoric times, and towns at or near the site of Vientiane were important centers no later than the ninth century, both in Dvaravati times and during the northward spread of the civilization of Angkor. The city was claimed as a vassal by King Ramkhamhaeng of Sukhothai in the 1290s, but this connection was short lived. Vientiane was among the first targets of Fa Ngum when he forged together the new kingdom of Lan Sang in the 1350s.

During the first two centuries of Lan Sang, there were major movements of Lao population southward down the Mekong Valley to the Vientiane Plain and farther south, to the point where King Phothisarat spent much of his time there. In preparation for warfare with Burma in the 1560s, King Setthathirat moved the capital to Vientiane in 1563 and built the That Luang, its greatest Buddhist shrine and palladium. It was this city that Western visitors described on visiting the region in the 1640s.

On the death of King Surinyavongsa about 1694, the Lan Sang kingdom was thrown into chaos. One of Surinyavongsa's grandsons, Sai Ong Ve, returned

TABLE 1. *Kings of Lan Sang-Vientiane*

KING	REIGN DATES
Sai Ong Ve (Sao Ong Hue)	1700–1735?
Setthathirat II (Sai Ong Long)	1735?–1760
Siribunyasan	1760–1781
Nanthasen	1781–1795
Inthavong	1795–1804
Anuvong	1804–1827

from Vietnam with a military force that helped establish him on the throne. The kingdom split apart, however, and Sai Ong Ve ruled only the kingdom of Vientiane that called itself Lan Sang, while one cousin established another Lan Sang in Luang Prabang, and others established a new kingdom at Champassak. The city was conquered by Siamese forces in 1777 and made a Siamese vassal, and when King Anuvong in 1827 went to war to reestablish Lao independence, he provoked Siamese military reprisals that sacked the city and ended the kingdom. Vientiane was deserted, a ghost town, when French explorers traveled up the Mekong River in the 1860s, and it was sacked by the Ho brigands in the 1870s. It came back to life as the administrative headquarters for French rule in Laos. After World War II, as administrative capital for independent Laos, it became a sprawling metropolis. It remains Laos's only modern city.

[*See also* Laos; Anu; Champassak; Fa Ngum; Khun Borom; Lan Sang; Luang Prabang; Mekong Expedition; Phoui Sananikone; Setthathirat; Siang Khwang; Siribunyasan; That Luang; Ho; *and* Ramkhamhaeng.]

René de Berval, ed., *Kingdom of Laos* (1958). David K. Wyatt, *Thailand: A Short History* (1984).

DAVID K. WYATT

VIENTIANE AGREEMENTS. From 1955 to 1957, negotiations were undertaken to accommodate the conflict among Lao factions, principally the incumbent Royal Lao government (RLG) and the rival left-wing movement, commonly known as the Pathet Lao (PL). In November 1957, Prime Minister Souvannaphouma, representing the RLG, reached an agreement with his half brother, Prince Souphanouvong, representing the PL, which included the return of two contested provinces, Phong Saly and Houa Phan, to RLG-led administration; the integration of 1,500 PL troops into the Royal Lao

Army; the entry of two PL ministers into the RLG; and elections to be held in May 1958 to add twenty-one members to the thirty-eight-man National Assembly. Although initial elements of the agreement were carried out, subsequent disputes over allotment of ranks to PL officers led to a serious schism a year later.

[See also Laos and Pathet Lao.]

JOSEPH J. ZASLOFF

VIET CONG. See Vietnam and Indochina War.

VIET MINH. The Viet Nam Doc Lap Dong Minh Hoi (Vietnamese Independence League), more commonly referred to as the Viet Minh, was founded in May 1941 at the Eighth Plenum of the Indochinese Communist Party (ICP). In the preceding months prominent Vietnamese nationalists, both Communist and non-Communist, had been gathering in the southern Chinese province of Yunnan. Anxious to widen the scope of popular support for their struggle, the ICP established the Viet Minh as an ostensibly diverse political front, although the Party remained the dominant force in the organization. The Viet Minh were part of a broader ICP strategy based on a rural guerrilla movement and appeals to Vietnamese nationalism, particularly the numerous "national salvation associations" (cuu quoc hoi). Throughout World War II, the Viet Minh worked successfully to consolidate its popular base, particularly in the northern border areas and Red River delta. Military forces were recruited and trained under the command of Vo Nguyen Giap (b. 1912). Especially significant was the Viet Minh's effective policy toward traditionally hostile ethnic minority groups.

On 29 August 1945, several days after the occupation of Hanoi by Viet Minh forces, the Provisional Revolutionary Government of the Democratic Republic of Vietnam was proclaimed, to be followed by Ho Chi Minh's Declaration of Independence on 2 September. The Viet Minh and ICP held virtually all key posts in the new government. Obtaining French recognition was another matter, and neither negotiations nor Viet Minh concessions could achieve this goal. In December 1946 the First Indochina War broke out with open fighting in Hanoi and Haiphong, whereupon the Viet Minh again took to the countryside to begin an anti-French struggle which would not end until the 21 July 1954 Geneva Agreements.

In February 1951 the ICP, which had been declared dissolved in August 1945, was reestablished as the Vietnam Workers Party (Dang Lao Dong Viet Nam). Although the Viet Minh was replaced by the Lien Viet front, its name remained as a popular designation for the Communist-led anti-French forces.

[See also Vietnam; Indochinese Communist Party; Vo Nguyen Giap; August Revolution; Vietnam, Democratic Republic of; Ho Chi Minh; and Geneva Conference of 1954.]

William J. Duiker, The Communist Road to Power (1981). Bernard Fall, The Two Viet-Nams (1967). Ellen Hammer, The Struggle for Indochina 1940–1955 (1955). Stanley Karnow, Vietnam: A History (1983).

BRUCE M. LOCKHART

VIETNAM. Present-day Vietnam sees its history extending back four thousand years. Archaeology and myth show a continuity in the culture of the people now known as Vietnamese, who emerged in the northern section of their country. This continuity begins with the Neolithic Phung Nguyen culture of the upper Red River delta (early second millennium BCE), goes through the Dong Dau and Go Mun cultures, and reaches an important turning point in the Bronze Age Dong Son culture (first millennium BCE). [See Dong Son.] Myth tells of the Lac people and their Hung Vuong ("Hung kings"), who rose to power in the seventh century BCE. This local development was cut short by an upheaval to the north when in the third century BCE An Duong invaded and set up his capital at Co Loa. [See Hung Vuong; An Duong Vuong; and Co Loa.] He was also followed by the Qin invasion late in the century and Han Wudi's conquest of 111 BCE.

The Lac people formed an agricultural society with bilateral kinship under local lords. Women held political power, and when the Chinese encroachment built up, the Trung Sisters led a revolt in 40 CE. Ma Yuan crushed this uprising two years later, and for the next nine centuries Chinese power ebbed and flowed over Vietnam. [See Trung Sisters Rebellion.] Local families, many of Chinese descent, sought to gain power and wealth from the growing international trade. Chinese imperial patterns, indigenous beliefs, and international Buddhist influence interacted within the country. The Lac people had become Vietnamese and existed in relation to Chinese power. The great Tang period of the seventh and eighth centuries and the growth of Asian trade both had a great impact on Vietnam. Dai La rose

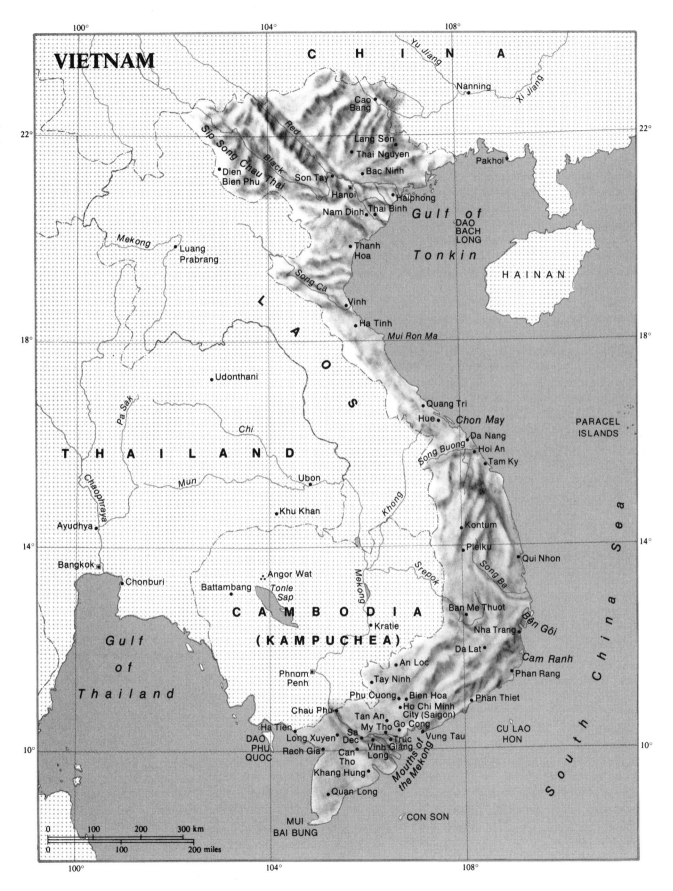

VIETNAM

C H I N A

Yu Jiang

Nanning

Xi Jiang

Cao Bang

22°   22°

Lang Son

Thai Nguyen

Pakhoi

Dien Bien Phu

Son Tay   Bac Ninh

Sip Song Chau Thai

Red

Black

Hanoi   Haiphong

Nam Dinh   Thai Binh   *Gulf of*

Mekong   DAO BACH LONG

Luang Prabrang   Thanh Hoa   *Tonkin*

H A I N A N

Song Ca

Vinh

L   Ha Tinh

18°   A   *Mui Ron Ma*   18°

O

Udonthani   S

Pa Sak   Quang Tri   PARACEL ISLANDS

Hue   *Chon May*

Chi   Da Nang

Song Buong   Hoi An

T H A I L A N D   Tam Ky

Mun   Ubon   *Khong*

Chaophraya   Kontum

Khu Khan

Ayudhya   Pleiku   Qui Nhon

14°   *Song Ba*   14°

Bangkok   *Srepok*

Chonburi   Angor Wat   Ban Me Thuot   *Bien Goi*

Battambang   *Tonle Sap*   Nha Trang

S o u t h   C h i n a   S e a

C A M B O D I A   *Mekong*   Da Lat   *Cam Ranh*

Gulf   (KAMPUCHEA)   Phan Rang

of   Kratie   An Loc

Thailand   Tay Ninh   Phan Thiet

Phnom Penh   Phu Cuong   Bien Hoa

Chau Phu   Ho Chi Minh   CU LAO HON

Ha Tien   Tan An   City (Saigon)

DAO   Long Xuyen   Sa   My Tho Go Cong

PHU   Rach Gia   Dec Truc   Vung Tau

10°   QUOC   Can   Vinh Giang   10°

Tho   Long

Khang Hung   *Mouths of the Mekong*

Quan Long

CON SON

0   100   200   300 km

MUI

BAI BUNG   0   100   200 miles

100°   104°   108°

at the location of Hanoi as a Chinese center. Yet indigenous beliefs continued to be strong in the hinterlands.

An independent Vietnam emerged during the tenth and eleventh centuries. China no longer needed Vietnam's ports, and local leaders vied for overlordship. Ngo Quyen defeated a challenge from Canton at Bach Dang in 939 to rule in Chinese style at Co Loa. [See Ngo Quyen and Bach Dang, Battles of.] In the 960s Ding Bo Ling, followed by Le Hoan, maintained the indigenous values at Hoa Lu. [See Ding Bo Linh; Le Hoan; and Hoa Lu.] Early in the eleventh century Ly Cong Uan, backed by the monk Van Xuan and the Mahayana Buddhist establishment, took the throne and set up the capital of Thang Long (Hanoi). [See Ly Cong Uan; Van Xuan; and Hanoi.]

The Ly state (1009–1225), after 1054 called Dai Viet, is best seen as a classical Southeast Asian polity that adopted various foreign elements—Cham, Chinese, and others—to enhance indigenous royal authority. [See also Ly Dynasty; Dai Viet; Cham; and Champa.] By the 1070s Dai Viet was strong enough both to have a stable succession and to defend itself against China. It achieved this strength through military power, marriages with rival families, and thriving Buddhist institutions and by creating rituals that drew allegiance to the throne (the blood oath) and served a royal cult to De Thich (Indra). Such Chinese intellectual elements as examinations were not of great significance in Vietnam at that time.

The Ly did borrow from China the idea of dynasty, or of a single family passing on power through patrilineal succession. But because the Ly had a bilateral society, succession problems occurred in the twelfth century, particularly in 1127 and 1137. At the same time, from 1128 to 1218, intermittent warfar took place among Dai Viet, Champa, and Angkor for political and economic hegemony in the eastern mainland of Southeast Asia. [See Angkor.]

By 1200 local powers were challenging the Ly hold. In particular, the Tran from Fujian in South China had built up their power in the southern Red River delta on a commercial base (fishing). Now the family became a force in the capital by intermarrying with the Ly, and soon it took the throne for itself. [See Tran Dynasty.]

The Tran dynasty (1225–1400) kept a strong continuity in ritual and ideology, preserving the cult to De Thich, the blood oath, and Buddhism. Structurally, however, it moved to change the Ly weaknesses. Traditionally, primogeniture ruled royal

succession, and marriages were to cousins; the ruler abdicated for his young heir and, as senior ruler, kept power behind the scenes. From the 1230s onward, the Tran began an experiment in bureaucratic administration, placing graduates of a new type of examination in both capital and provincial offices. Two decades later, central power was strong enough to standardize the diking systems of the Red and Ma river systems.

The Mongol threat brought this experiment to an end as a brood of princes, particularly Tran Hung Dao, defeated the invaders (with the final victory at Bach Dang in 1287) and established themselves strongly both in capital and provincial affairs. They, their descendants, and their protégés dominated Vietnamese administration well into the fourteenth century. [See Mongol Empire: Mongol Invasions of Southeast Asia and Tran Hung Dao.]

The Mongol threat had also brought the Vietnamese and Cham together, an amity strengthened by Buddhism, but friction led to two Vietnamese invasions (1312, 1318). In the early fourteenth century, Buddhism was thriving, mythic beliefs were strong, and literati with classical Chinese learning appeared in high administrative positions. Then, in midcentury, dynastic power declined, and two decades of Cham invasions (1370–1390) placed Dai Viet in crisis. Central ideology and resource control failed. From this crisis emerged a powerful minister, Ho Quy Ly of Thanh Hoa, who was linked by marriage to the Tran and whose legitimacy came from classical Chinese allusions. He centralized control over manpower, land, and the money supply, yet his political support failed, and Ho rule (1400–1407) fell before Ming conquest. [See Ho Dynasty.]

The twenty years of Chinese colonial occupation (1407–1427) meant economic exploitation and bureaucratic repression, but it also introduced public schools and Neo-Confucian orthodoxy. Numerous revolts failed before the Lam Son Uprising, which was begun by Le Loi in 1418 in the mountains of Thanh Hoa, drove the Chinese out of Vietnam. The Le dynasty (1428–1527) moved from the hinterland into the void left by a half-century of crisis and foreign threat. [See Lam Son Uprising; Le Loi; and Le Dynasties.] Initially it continued the structure of the Tran and the Ho at the same time that it gained legitimacy from its great victory, but major changes in land tenure and law came quickly. Nguyen Trai helped compile a new code, and village agriculture, under central control, replaced the old apanage/serf system. [See Nguyen Trai.]

The mid-fifteenth century saw an increase in the

influence of modern Ming patterns. By the late 1460s, the young emperor Le Thanh Tong (1460–1497) and his literati supporters had officially established a Chinese-style bureaucracy as the form of administration and Neo-Confucianism as the state orthodoxy. [See Le Thanh Thong.] These changes also affected foreign relations. With moralistic certitude, Dai Viet in 1471 put an end, once and for all, to the Cham threat, annexing their northern territories, and invaded the Lao states in 1479. The next hundred years mark the peak of Ming influence in Vietnam as Confucian elements began to spread among the people. The Le weakened and fell amid feuding between two powerful families from Thanh Hoa, the Nguyen and the Trinh. [See Nguyen Dynasty; Nguyen Lords; Trinh Lords; and Trinh-Nguyen Wars.] In the 1520s, a military man of Confucian family background, Mac Dang Dung, seized power. The Mac dynasty (1528–1592) reestablished Le Thanh Tong's achievements of the Hong Duc period and handled a Chinese threat in the 1540s by diplomacy, not force. [See Mac Dang Dung and Mac Dynasty.]

The Nguyen-Trinh forces joined and maintained themselves in Thanh Hoa, pushing north throughout sixty years to restore the Le (1592–1788) to the throne. The Trinh held power in Thang Long, while the Nguyen split with them and moved to a southern border fief in Thuan Hoa. The Trinh, justifying their domination by the need to crush the Nguyen "rebels," controlled the Le rulers and fought a series of inconclusive campaigns with the south from the 1620s to the 1670s. The Trinh hold was based on military power and old ritual (the blood oath). Literati influence declined with the fall of the Mac, and only in the 1660s did Trinh Tac resurrect the Neo-Confucian ideology and bureaucratic administration. [See Trinh Tac.]

Simultaneously, the Nguyen in the south were expanding their domain in the *nam tien* ("southward advance"). [See Nam Tien.] By the 1690s Vietnamese settlements had appeared in the Saigon area. [See Ho Chi Minh City.] Chinese refugees had already settled at Bien Hoa and My Tho. Through the seventeenth century the Nguyen encouraged links with the growing international trade. As a contact point with the Chinese economy, Hoi An (Faifo), near Da Nang, had thriving markets in which Chinese, Japanese, Europeans, and Southeast Asians traded for silks and metals. The Vietnamese developed plantation crops, especially sugar, for the international markets.

By the eighteenth century major changes were under way that would transform Vietnamese society. The Trinh had frozen the tax base in 1664, but rapid population growth thereafter put pressure on it. The early 1700s saw much population movement and growth of private landholdings in the north. Many people wandered the countryside, joined bandit gangs or the service of local lords, or moved into the bustling cities. Greater concentrations of wealth meant more expenditure on luxuries, and commerce and artisanry grew. Disaffection both in the court and in the countryside led to a number of rebellions through the middle of the century.

The major uprising took place in the south in 1771 at Tay Son in the mountains west of Quinhon. [See Tay Son Rebellion.] The revolt scattered the Nguyen forces, then defeated invading Trinh troops. When the Le ruler called for Chinese intervention, the Tay Son army defeated them at Dong Da in 1789 (the first Tet offensive) and set Nguyen Hue on the throne. Yet the Tay Son (1789–1802) did not wipe out the Nguyen, and a survivor, Nguyen Anh, returned from Bangkok with foreign (including French) support to drive north from the Mekong Delta during the 1790s and defeat them in 1802. [See Gia Long.]

The Nguyen dynasty (1802–1945) ruled Vietnam, by then called Dai Nam, as we know it. [See Nguyen Dynasty and Dai Nam.] The capital, shifted to Hue from Thang Long (Hanoi), ruled from the Chinese border to Cambodia. [See Hue.] Although he adopted Chinese elements, particularly the Qin law code, Anh, the Gia Long emperor, ruled in a personal rather than a bureaucratic fashion. Longtime lieutenants controlled the north and the south. Only in the 1830s was Gia Long's son Ming Mang finally able to displace the old guard with literati officials, bureaucratic procedure, and a strong Neo-Confucian orthodoxy. [See Minh Mang.]

Vietnamese foreign relations shared this orthodoxy, keeping Europeans (and Catholicism) at a distance and attempting to dominate their Southeast Asian neighbors. Vietnam and Thailand fought for control of Cambodia and the Lao states. The Vietnamese took over Cambodia in the 1830s and dominated the Lao mountains, but they weakened under Tu Duc in the middle of the century. [See Tu Duc.] Chinese remnants of the Taiping Rebellion, French adventurers, and growing Thai power challenged the Vietnamese hold outside the central and northern lowlands. As Hue lost its flexibility, the French took control of the south and Cambodia in the 1860s, the north and the center in the 1880s, and the Lao states in the 1890s.

The weakened Nguyen throne had lost the ability to lead. Only Ham Nghi and his officials in 1885 tried, but they were too late. [See Ham Nghi.] The French conquest joined the three *pays* of Vietnam—Cochinchina, Annam, and Tonkin—to Cambodia and Laos to form Indochina and left the Nguyen monarchy in place. [See Indochinese Union.] The Chinese model sunk into acquiesence, encouraged by the French desire for stability. Yet great social and economic change followed, particularly owing to the exploitation and the monopolies (salt, alcohol, opium).

In the first decades of the twentieth century, educated Vietnamese sought a place for Vietnam in the modern world. Some, like Pham Quynh, looked to the French and their ideals for aid. [See Pham Quynh.] Others, like Phan Chu Trinh, sought reform before resistance, while still others followed Phan Boi Chau in seeking violent resistance. [See Phan Chu Trinh *and* Phan Boi Chau.] Yet by the mid-1920s moderate responses met only *colon* intransigence. Chau's capture (1925) and Trinh's death (1926) sparked many among the growing Western-educated intelligentsia to more radical action and the French to harsh repression. The years 1930 and 1931 saw defeat for the nationalists of the Viet Nam Quoc Dan Dang, or the Vietnam Nationalist Party, at Yen Bay and the Communist involvement in the "soviets" of Nghe Tinh. [See Vietnam Nationalist Party; Yen Bay Uprising; *and* Nghe-Tinh Uprising.] Many were executed and thousands jailed. Ho Chi Minh, operating in South China, had helped form the Indochinese Communist Party but had to flee to the Soviet Union. [See Ho Chi Minh *and* Indochinese Communist Party.] Political, religious, and literary activity continued through the 1930s, rising partly to the surface during the Popular Front period of 1936 to 1939.

World War II saw the Japanese control Indochina but leave the French in place. Nationalists and Communists sought links to the Allies in South China, and Ho Chi Minh returned to help establish a united front, the Viet Minh, with an explicit nationalist goal—independence. On 9 March 1945 the Japanese removed the French, leaving a void that was filled by the Viet Minh on the Japanese surrender. This takeover of power is known as the August Revolution, which on 2 September 1945 declared an independent Democratic Republic of Vietnam, ending both colonialism and the monarchy. [See Viet Minh *and* Vietnam, Democratic Republic of.]

But thirty years of war followed. The French attempted to regain their hold, but the Viet Minh fought back with Chinese aid, defeated the French at Dien Bien Phu in 1954, and regained Hanoi. [See Dien Bien Phu.] The Geneva Accords of 1954 and American support led to the development of the Republic of Vietnam (1955–1975) in Saigon under Ngo Dinh Diem and his family. [See Geneva Conference of 1954; Vietnam, Republic of; *and* Ngo Dinh Diem.] Trying to crush opposition and alienating many, the Ngo regime fell as a result of student-and Buddhist political action and a coup in 1963. Twelve years of military rule followed, mainly under Nguyen Cao Ky and Nguyen Van Thieu.

Resistance to the Saigon government rose in the late 1950s. Until 1965 the National Liberation Front (Viet Cong) operated in classic guerrilla style with some help from Hanoi, which concentrated on building socialism in the north. The guerrilla success led to American intervention and greater Hanoi involvement, peaking in the Tet Offensive of 1968. [See Indochina War.] American troop withdrawal and negotiations, backed by bombing, so-called Vietnamization, and the invasions of Cambodia (1970) and Laos (1971), led to the Paris accords of January 1973. [See Paris Peace Conference.] Yet the fighting continued for two years until the sudden fall of the republic in March–April 1975. Hanoi achieved unity through conquest, established socialism as the future of Vietnam, and brought north and south together in the Socialist Republic of Vietnam in July 1976.

William J. Duiker, *The Communist Road to Power in Vietnam* (1981). David G. Marr, *Vietnamese Tradition on Trial, 1920–1945* (1981). Keith W. Taylor, *The Birth of Vietnam* (1983). O. W. Wolters, "Assertions of Cultural Well-Being in Fourteenth Century Vietnam," *Journal of Southeast Asian Studies* 10.2 (1979): 435–450. Alexander B. Woodside, *Vietnam and the Chinese Model* (1971).
                                          JOHN K. WHITMORE

VIETNAM, DEMOCRATIC REPUBLIC OF,

or DRV, established in Hanoi, its capital, on 2 September 1945 under the leadership of Ho Chi Minh (1890–1969). After a long struggle for independence from France, the DRV was given control of territory down to the seventeenth parallel by the July 1954 Geneva accords. Over the next two decades the DRV worked to build a socialist system in the north while maintaining a foreign policy independent of both the USSR and China (PRC). It simultaneously supported and participated in the fight against US-supported regimes in South Vietnam, culminating in the fall of Saigon on 30 April 1975. The two regions were reunified as the Socialist Republic of Vietnam in July 1976.

[*See also* Ho Chi Minh; Geneva Conference of 1954; Vietnam, Republic of; *and* Viet Minh.]

William J. Duiker, *The Communist Road to Power* (1981). Bernard Fall, *The Two Viet-Nams* (1967).

BRUCE M. LOCKHART

VIETNAM, PROVISIONAL REVOLUTIONARY GOVERNMENT OF.

Founded in June 1969, the Provisional Revolutionary Government (PRG) was the political and administrative arm of the National Liberation Front (NLF), established in December 1960 to oppose the Ngo Dinh Diem regime in South Vietnam. Comprising a four-level hierarchy of people's revolutionary councils, the PRG governed the areas of South Vietnam controlled by the NLF. Although a signatory of the 1973 Paris accords, the PRG did not gain official recognition or the chance to hold constructive negotiations with the Nguyen Van Thieu government. It took control of the south after Saigon's fall in April 1975 and was later absorbed into the reunified Socialist Republic of Vietnam in July 1976.

[*See also* Indochina War; Paris Peace Conference; Ngo Dinh Diem; *and* Vietnam.]

William J. Duiker, *The Communist Road to Power* (1981).

BRUCE M. LOCKHART

VIETNAM, REPUBLIC OF,

more commonly known as South Vietnam, was officially founded in 1956 after the dissolution of the State of Vietnam led by Bao Dai. Although the partition along Vietnam's seventeenth parallel stipulated by the 1954 Geneva accords was to have been temporary, the United States upheld President Ngo Dinh Diem's refusal to hold elections for national reunification. Until the fall of the Republic of Vietnam in April 1975, the United States continued to back the successive Saigon regimes against the National Liberation Front and Democratic Republic of Vietnam, despite an increasing lack of popular legitimacy and support. The north and south were reunified as the Socialist Republic of Vietnam in July 1976.

[*See also* Bao Dai; Ngo Dinh Diem; Geneva Conference of 1954; Viet Minh; Indochina War; *and* Vietnam, Democratic Republic of.]

Dennis Duncanson, *Government and Revolution in Vietnam* (1968). Bernard Fall, *The Two Viet-Nams* (1967).

BRUCE M. LOCKHART

VIETNAM, SOCIALIST REPUBLIC OF. See Vietnam *and* Vietnam, Democratic Republic of.

VIET NAM DOC LAP DONG MINH HOI. *See* Viet Minh.

VIETNAM MODERNIZATION ASSOCIATION,

an early political organization promoting the overthrow of French colonial rule in Vietnam. Founded by Phan Boi Chau and other progressive scholar-gentry in 1904, the association (Viet Nam Duy Tan Hoi) aimed at achieving independence through armed insurrection and the creation of a modern state based on constitutional monarchy. The symbolic head of the organization was Prince Cuong De, a descendant of Gia Long's eldest son, Prince Canh. During the next few years it won several hundred adherents, but its efforts to unleash an uprising were abortive, and it was succeeded by the Vietnam Restoration Association in 1912.

[*See also* Phan Boi Chau; Cuong De; *and* Vietnam Restoration Association.]

William J. Duiker, *The Rise of Nationalism in Vietnam, 1900–1941* (1976). David G. Marr, *Vietnamese Anticolonialism, 1885–1925* (1971).

WILLIAM J. DUIKER

VIETNAM NATIONALIST PARTY,

or Viet Nam Quoc Dan Dang (VNQDD), a nationalist organization founded in 1927 by middle-class intellectuals in Hanoi. Violently anti-French, its program focused on preparations for a national revolution to overthrow colonial rule and restore Vietnamese independence. Its ultimate vision of Vietnamese society was less precise. While some VNQDD leaders were interested in socialism, many were anti-Marxist, and the party's program and strategy were fashioned after those of the Chinese revolutionary Sun Yat-sen and his party, the Guomindang (Kuomintang), of which the VNQDD was the namesake.

During the late 1920s the VNQDD's membership swelled to more than one thousand, mostly in Tonkin, and prepared for an armed insurrection against the colonial government. Most of its adherents were townspeople—journalists, students, merchants, and clerks—but the party recruited actively among Vietnamese troops in the colonial armed forces.

As the party grew, French suppression increased. Driven to desperation by official harassment and convinced that popular discontent was rising, party chairman Nguyen Thai Hoc won reluctant approval for an uprising on military posts throughout the Red River delta. Launched on 9–10 February 1930, the so-called Yen Bay uprisings were plagued by poor planning and were easily put down by the authorities. Nguyen Thai Hoc and many other party leaders were arrested, and they were executed in June of that year.

The defeat of the Yen Bay revolt created martyrs of the nationalist cause, but it virtually destroyed the VNQDD. Its remnants split up into reformist and revolutionary factions and attempted to carry on their activities in South China. The party enjoyed a modest revival during World War II and briefly competed with the Communists for power after the August Revolution. After 1954 the VNQDD was active in South Vietnamese politics, but its influence declined during the 1970s.

[*See also* Vietnam; Nguyen Thai Hoc; *and* Yen Bay Uprising.]

William J. Duiker, *The Rise of Nationalism in Vietnam, 1900–1941* (1976). Thomas Hodgkin, *Vietnam: The Revolutionary Path* (1981). Louis Roubaud, *Vietnam* (1935).

WILLIAM J. DUIKER

VIETNAM NATIONAL SALVATION AS-SOCIATIONS, mass organizations formed under the aegis of the Viet Minh during World War II in Vietnam. In the 1930s the Indochinese Communist Party had formed several mass organizations representing peasants, workers, women, students, and other groups in order to extend its popularity in colonial Vietnam. During World War II, such organizations were renamed "national salvation associations" (*cuu quoc hoi*) to appeal to patriotic elements in the struggle against Japanese occupation. Grouped under the overall direction of the Viet Minh Front, they served during the war and the anti-French resistance that followed as vehicles for recruitment into the party's military and civilian organizations and as a conduit for transmitting party directives to the general populace.

[*See also* Viet Minh *and* Indochinese Communist Party.]

John T. McAlister, *Vietnam: The Origins of Revolution* (1969).

WILLIAM J. DUIKER

VIET NAM QUOC DAN DANG. *See* Vietnam Nationalist Party.

VIETNAM RESTORATION ASSOCIATION, revolutionary party established by the Vietnamese patriot Phan Boi Chau. Phan's Vietnam Modernization Association, formed in 1904, had aimed at a constitutional monarchy. In 1912, impressed with the apparent success of the 1911 Revolution in China, he created a new organization, the Vietnam Restoration Association (Viet Nam Quang Phuc Hoi), based on republican principles. The party declined after his arrest in 1914.

[*See also* Phan Boi Chau *and* Vietnam Modernization Association.]

Thomas Hodgkin, *Vietnam: The Revolutionary Path* (1981).

WILLIAM J. DUIKER

VIETNAM RESTORATION LEAGUE (Viet Nam Phuc Quoc Dong Minh Hoi), political organization formed in 1943 by leaders of the Hoa Hao and Cao Dai religious sects in Vietnam. The league sought Japanese help to end French rule in Vietnam. It collapsed with Japan's defeat in 1945.

[*See also* Cao Dai *and* Hoa Hao.].

John T. McAlister, *Vietnam: The Origins of Revolution* (1969).

WILLIAM J. DUIKER

VIETNAM REVOLUTIONARY LEAGUE, an organization of Vietnamese nationalist parties formed under the sponsorship of Chinese authorities in Jiangxi Province in 1942. A rival of the Viet Minh Front, the league (Viet Nam Cach Dong Minh Hoi, or Dong Minh Hoi) attempted, with Chinese support, to play an active role in Vietnamese politics after World War II but was outmaneuvered by the Viet Minh and declined in 1946.

[*See also* Viet Minh.]

William J. Duiker, *The Communist Road to Power in Vietnam* (1981).

WILLIAM J. DUIKER

VIETNAM REVOLUTIONARY YOUTH LEAGUE (Viet Nam Cach Menh Thanh Nien Hoi), the first avowedly Marxist revolutionary organization in Vietnam. Created by Ho Chi Minh in 1925, it won over a thousand adherents and became an influential force in anticolonial circles until it was replaced by a formal Communist Party in 1930.

[*See also* Ho Chi Minh.]

Huynh Kim Khanh, *Vietnamese Communism, 1925–1945* (1982).

WILLIAM J. DUIKER

VIETNAM WAR. *See* Indochina War.

VIJAYA, city in modern Binh Dinh Province (Vietnam), capital of the kingdom of Champa from 1000 to 1471.

Faced with increasing hostility from Vietnam, King Yang Pu Ku Vijaya moved the capital of Champa from Indrapura far south to Vijaya in 1000. Now relatively secure from Vietnamese attacks, Champa increasingly came under attack from Angkorian Cambodia, particularly from the reign of Suryavarman II of Angkor (r. 1113–c. 1150), who seized Vijaya in 1145. Although the Cham took their revenge by sacking Angkor in 1177, Angkor wreaked terrible retaliation in 1190. Long periods of Khmer occupation followed, and by the time Angkor weakened in the course of the thirteenth century, Vietnam again was knocking on Champa's doors. Marco Polo briefly visited Vijaya in 1285. Following repeated defeats at the hands of Vietnam, Vijaya was abandoned in 1471, and the kingdom virtually disappeared.

[*See also* Champa *and* Angkor.]

G. Coedès, *The Indianized States of Southeast Asia,* translated by Susan B. Cowing (1968).

DAVID K. WYATT

VIJAYABAHU I (1055–1100), Sinhalese king. One of the greatest figures in the history of Sri Lanka, Vijayabahu I welded the disparate Sinhalese resistance movements into a cohesive political force in the course of his prolonged campaign to secure the liberation of the island from Chola rule; he achieved this goal by 1070. Although Vijayabahu regained control over the city of Anuradhapura, he followed the Cholas in retaining Polonnaruva as his capital.

During his period of rule the country recovered from the ravages of Chola misrule and long periods of political instability. His achievements in the more prosaic fields of administrative recovery and economic regeneration were no less impressive: he infused fresh energy into the machinery of government; established firm control over the whole island; presided over a rehabilitation of the island's irrigation network; and restored Buddhism to its once-vigorous condition. But Vijayabahu left a disputed succession, and there was another period of civil war that undermined the achievements of Vijayabahu's reign. After this long period, Parakramabahu I became king.

[*See also* Anuradhapura; Polonnaruva; Parakramabahu I; Chola Dynasty; *and* Sri Lanka.]

K. M. de Silva, *A History of Sri Lanka* (1981).

K. M. DE SILVA

VIJAYANAGARA ("city of victory"), situated on the southern bank of the Tungabhadra River in Karnataka, India, was the capital of a Hindu kingdom founded in the middle of the fourteenth century and attaining its greatest extent during the reign of Krishnadevaraya (r. 1509–1529). The city then occupied some twenty-five square miles; this site, now called Hampi, has become one of the major archaeological sites in India. Historians have most often used the name *Vijayanagara* to designate the kingdom as well as the city.

Its location among spectacular outcroppings of granite made the city one of the largest fortified places in the subcontinent, with a series of high, thick, concentric walls providing protection as well as demarcating various internal zones. Descriptions of life in the city during the late fifteenth and early sixteenth centuries have been preserved in chronicles of Muslim and European visitors—mostly merchants—of that time; these record the grandeur and the bustle of the city, its cosmopolitan character, its royal functions and ritual, and finally something of the perils confronting Vijayanagara from Muslim sultanates north of the Tungabhadra who ultimately defeated the kingdom and sacked the city in 1565.

The kingdom of Vijayanagara extended over a major part of peninsular India in the early sixteenth century, from Orissa on the Bay of Bengal to Kanara on the Arabian Sea and south to the tip of the subcontinent at Cape Comorin. According to most historians, Vijayanagara is assumed to have been created to thwart the further expansion of Muslim states after their victories in the Ganges region during the thirteenth and fourteenth centuries. Whether or not this was the intention of the founding warrior family and its learned Hindu counselors, Vijayanagara did close the southern peninsula to Muslim control over the course of its three ruling dynasties and more than two centuries. No previous Hindu kingdom had been so thoroughly militarized as Vijayanagara, which provides one of the earliest examples in India of the importance of European trade in firearms as well as in superior war horses.

The sack of Vijayanagara in 1565 did not end the kingdom. Moving from place to place in South India for another century, the last dynasty of Vijayanagara rulers maintained a continuing royal tradition and, at times, a fair amount of power. Eventually, however, the once-great territory was divided into a set of "*nayaka* kingdoms" whose founders traced their royal authority to Vijayanagar kings on the basis of having served as officers *(nayakas)* of these rulers. [*See* Nayaka.] In each of these smaller kingdoms the Vijayanagara pattern continued, but the apotheosis of the Vijayanagara model of rule came with the seventeenth-century Maratha kingdom, which succeeded Vijayanagara not only in the extent of its territory and duration, but most especially in its regnant ideology and royal rituals.

[*See also* Marathas; Deccan Sultanates; Karnataka; Orissa; *and* Tamil Nadu.]

John M. Fritz, George Michell, and M. S. Nagaraja Rao, *The Royal Centre at Vijaynagara: Preliminary Report* (1985). Burton Stein, *Peasant State and Society in Medieval South India* (1980).   BURTON STEIN

VILAYET-I FAQIH (Persian, "governance of the jurisprudent"), a term used by Ayatollah Ruhollah Khomeini to describe an Islamic state governed by a body of leading scholars or jurists of Islam. Khomeini explained the basis, conditions, and description of the *vilayet-i faqih* while in exile in Najaf, Iraq; these teachings were published in 1971 as *Hukumat-i Islami (Islamic Government)*. The concept of a *vilayet-i faqih* is a radical one for most Shi'ite scholars, owing to its heterodox contention that a just Islamic government may exist in the absence of the twelfth imam, who is in occultation.

[*See also* Khomeini, Ruhollah Musavi.]

Shahrough Akhavi, *Religion and Politics in Contemporary Iran: Clergy-State Relations in the Pahlavi Period* (1980), pp. 163–167. Ruhollah Khomeini, *Islamic Government* (1979).   JAHAN SALEHI

VIRASALINGAM, KANDUKURI (1848–1919), South Indian social reformer. Born in a high-caste brahman family, Virasalingam promoted widow remarriage, female education, monotheism, and the removal of caste restrictions. He was prominent in the Brahmo Samaj and several social reform organizations in Madras. A teacher, writer, and journalist, his direct, contemporary prose style shaped later Telugu literature.

[*See also* Brahmo Samaj.]

V. R. Narla, *Veerasalingam* (1968).

FRANKLIN A. PRESLER

VIVEKANANDA (1863–1902), Indian religious leader and foremost disciple of Ramakrishna. Born Narendranath Dutta to a Calcutta Kayasth family, Vivekananda first had a Western education but then embarked on a search for truth, which was consummated when he became a disciple of Ramakrishna, the spiritually powerful priest of the Dakhineswar Temple, north of Calcutta. After Ramakrishna's death in 1886 Vivekananda traveled around India and then through the West, spreading the teachings of revitalized Hinduism. He made a striking presence at the World Parliament of Religions in Chicago in 1893; he remained in the West until 1897 and returned there again, from 1899 to 1900. After returning to Calcutta in 1897 he established the Ramakrishna Mission in 1897.

Like Keshub Chandra Sen before him, Vivekananda asserted that the West was spiritually deficient and that India had a religious message for humanity. The fundamental truth of Hinduism was the unity of all human and animal life, joined by the immanent *brahman* within each creature. This Hinduism was the faith that could save the world; it was the most scientific and the only moral religion. He believed that spiritual Hinduism could also incorporate Western vitality. Exhorting his listeners to utilize the powers within themselves to build their country, he made remarks that were often taken in a political sense by Indian nationalists.

[*See also* Ramakrishna; Brahmo Samaj; *and* Sen, Keshub Chandra.]

Bhupendranath Dutta, *Swami Vivekananda, Patriot-Prophet* (1954). *The Life of Swami Vivekananda, by His Eastern and Western Disciples* (1912; reprint, 1960). Swami Vivekananda, *Complete Works*, 8 vols. (1926–1936; reprint, 1963).   LEONARD A. GORDON

VOLKSRAAD, or the "People's Council," representative political institution in the Netherlands East Indies (Indonesia) prior to World War II.

Founded in 1917 by the Dutch colonial regime to assist in mobilizing popular support for the government during the difficult conditions of the late years of World War I, the Volksraad at first had only advisory powers. It most usefully functioned to bring together for the first time Indonesians from all parts of the archipelago, who now could begin to express their grievances and aspirations in terms of an all-Indonesian consciousness. The council's powers were expanded in 1927, but as the Dutch governor-general retained a veto power, it never attained much direct influence over colonial policy.

Most prominent nationalist leaders of the period boycotted elections to the Volksraad.

George McT. Kahin, *Government and Revolution in Indonesia* (1952).   DAVID K. WYATT

VO NGUYEN GIAP, a prominent military commander and leading official in the Vietnamese Communist Party. He was born in a poor peasant family in Quang Binh Province in 1910. As a youth, he attended the famous National Academy in Hue and became active in the anticolonialist movement. In the early 1930s he joined the young Indochinese Communist Party and was almost immediately arrested. After his release he earned a college degree at the University of Hanoi and taught history at a French *lycée*. In 1937 he became a journalist and immersed himself in Party activities, coauthoring, with his Party colleague Truong Chinh, a tract entitled *The Peasant Question*.

During World War II he rose rapidly in the Party and was selected by Ho Chi Minh as the commander of the first units of the Vietnamese Liberation Army. When the war of resistance broke out against the French in December 1946 he became minister of defense and a major formulator of Communist military strategy. He was widely identified as one of the proponents of the concept of people's war, and his ideas were incorporated in a short book on strategy entitled *People's War, People's Army*.

After the Geneva Conference of 1954 and the division of Vietnam into two separate states, Vo Nguyen Giap maintained his position as a leading figure in the Democratic Republic of Vietnam and the Party. But he was apparently superseded by others as a leading strategist for the regime, and in 1980 he was replaced as minister of defense by Van Tien Dung. In 1982, reportedly ill, he lost his seat in the Politburo and became increasingly active in promoting science and technology.

[*See also* Vietnam; Indochinese Communist Party; Ho Chi Minh; Geneva Conference of 1954; and Vietnam, Democratic Republic of.]

Archimedes Patti, *Why Viet Nam? Prelude to America's Albatross* (1980). Russell Stettler, ed., *The Military Art of People's War* (1970). Vo Nguyen Giap, *People's War, People's Army* (1962) and *Unforgettable Days* (1975).

WILLIAM J. DUIKER

W

WACHIRAYAN WARAROT (Vajirananava-rorasa), prince-patriarch of Siam, leading Buddhist scholar and ecclesiastic in late nineteenth- and early twentieth-century Thailand.

Wachirayan was born 12 April 1860 to King Mongkut (r. 1851–1868) and Lady Phae, a concubine. As a small boy, he studied first with Thai tutors and then with an Englishman hired by his elder brother King Chulalongkorn (r. 1868–1910). After several aimless years and a period as a royal secretary, he was inspired by two men—Dr. Peter Gowan, a Scottish physician, and Prince Pawaret, a leading Buddhist monk who headed the Thammayutika, the reform order that had been founded by Mongkut—to take ordination as a Buddhist monk in 1879. He embarked seriously upon Pali studies, gaining the fifth rank (of nine) in the royal examinations in 1881, and was given a conferred princely rank by his approving brother the king. He then became deputy patriarch of the reform order and set about modernizing Buddhist education and ecclesiastical organization. A superb administrator, he soon demonstrated himself to be an exceptional intellectual who increasingly was called upon by the king for advice, as in the extension of modern education to the provinces in 1898. In the course of a half century, he completely refashioned the organization and intellectual content of Thai Buddhism. He became patriarch of the reform order in 1893 and supreme patriarch of Buddhism in Siam in 1910. He died on 2 August 1921.

[See also Mongkut; Chulalongkorn; and Thammayutika.]

Craig J. Reynolds, ed. and trans., *Autobiography: The Life of Prince-Patriarch Vajirañana of Siam, 1860–1921* (1979). David K. Wyatt, *The Politics of Reform in Thailand* (1969).   DAVID K. WYATT

WADE-GILES ROMANIZATION. The Wade-Giles system of romanization is based on a transcription created by Thomas Francis Wade for his 1867 work *Yü-yen tzu-erh chi (Yuyan zier ji)*. Wade's system was later modified by Herbert Giles for use in his *Chinese-English Dictionary,* published in 1912. In this modified form, the Wade-Giles system became the standard way of transcribing Chinese in the English-speaking world and was also widely used by the Chinese themselves in their dealings with the West.

Wade-Giles romanization is based on the Beijing dialect. Among its distinguishing features are the use of an apostrophe after stops and affricatives to indicate aspiration and the use of the umlaut (in *ü, üeh*, etc.), the breve (in *ŭ*), and the circumflex accent mark (in *ê, êrh*, etc.) as diacritics for distinguishing different vowel qualities; tone is indicated by the placing of small superscript numerals to the right of syllables. In current practice the breve and circumflex diacritics are generally omitted since their absence does not create any ambiguity.

After the introduction of the Wade-Giles system in the second half of the ninteenth century, it became virtually the only system used in English-language works on China or the Chinese language. *Guoyu,* or National Romanization, developed by a committee of Chinese linguists in the 1920s and adopted officially by the Nationalist government in 1928, never gained wide currency despite its considerable linguistic sophistication. *Latinxua,* a romanization originally created in the Soviet Union, although promoted as a practical writing system within China in the 1930s and 1940s, never seems to have been used extensively abroad. In the 1940s American linguists associated with military language training programs developed a new romanization system that eventually came to be known as the Yale system; it was used for many years as the chief pedagogical system in the United States. All the romanization systems mentioned above have now either been replaced or are in the process of being replaced by *pinyin*, the official romanization of the People's Republic of China. The Wade-Giles system still remains the preferred system of many sinologists, but one can detect an increasing tendency for it to be replaced with *pinyin* in scholarly publications.

[*See also* Pinyin.]

R. H. Mathews, *Mathews' Chinese-English Dictionary*, with an introduction by Yuen-ren Chao (rev. ed., 1943).

JERRY NORMAN

WADIYAR DYNASTY. The Wadiyar dynasty ruled over Mysore, India, from 1399 as a tributary of Vijayanagara until 1610, when Raja Wadiyar (1578–1617) made it an independent kingdom. Kantirava Narasaraja (1638–1659) successfully checked the Bijapur invasions. Chikkadevaraja (1672–1704) was the most celebrated Wadiyar ruler, defeating the Marathas. The Wadiyars maintained the cultural traditions of Vijayanagara.

[*See also* Vijayanagara; Mysore; *and* Marathas.]

C. Hayavadana Rao, *History of Mysore*, 3 vols. (1946). Shama Rao, *Modern Mysore* (1936).   B. SHEIK ALI

WAHHABIS. *See* Ahl-i Hadis.

WALI ULLAH, SHAH (1703–1762). A distinguished Muslim thinker of eighteenth-century North India, Shah Wali Ullah was deeply influenced by a youthful stay in the Hejaz, where he encountered a newly vital commitment to the study of the recorded traditions (*hadith*) of the Prophet as a basis of intellectual renewal and a foundation for social well-being. His subsequent writings deemphasized the teachings of the historic law schools in favor of study of the Qur'an (which he translated into Persian) and the *hadith*. Even more ambitiously, he tried to show the essential unity of the fruits of the epistemologically distinctive Islamic strands of reason (*aql*), tradition (*naql*), and the gnosis (*ma'rifa*) of the Sufis. His work took on urgency in the wake of the decline of the Mughal empire and he sought out Muslim rulers who would work in consultation with scholars like himself in order to create conditions where Muslim law could flourish. Institutionally, he was the head of the Madrasa-i Rahimiyya, a school founded by his renowned father in Delhi;

he was also a revered Sufi elder among the Naqshbandis. Later reformers in the subcontinent looked to him as an exemplar in personality and attainments, a guide to the study of the revealed sciences, a spokesman for an authoritative role for scholars in a properly ruled polity, and an opponent of intellectual and sectarian disunity.

[*See also* Naqshbandi.]

"Al-Dihlawi," *The Encyclopaedia of Islam* (2d ed., 1954–). G. N. Jalbani, *Teachings of Shah Waliullah of Delhi* (2d ed., 1973). John O. Voll, "Hadith Scholars and Tariqahs: An Ulema Group in the Eighteenth Century Haramayn and Their Impact in the Islamic World," *Journal of Asian and African Studies* 15 (1980): 264–273.

BARBARA D. METCALF

WANG ANSHI (1021–1086), leading Northern Song literatus and statesman, responsible for one of the most extensive programs of institutional reform in Chinese history. Before taking office at court in the 1060s Wang served as a highly respected local official and gained a following among idealistic literati through his literary writings. His "Tenthousand Word Memorial" of 1058, regarded as a classic statement of the need for reform, treated antiquity as the model for an integrated social order in the present and made educational reform the basis for institutional renewal.

Between 1069 and his retirement in 1076 Wang's administration adopted a variety of measures collectively known as the "New Policies." These included reforms aimed at improving financial planning and administration, improving and rationalizing tax collection through a national land survey and the rewriting of tax registers, supporting farmers through state loans, stabilizing prices through state marketing organizations, providing for the hiring of local service personnel, establishing collective security networks (the *baojia* system), increasing military supplies, establishing a national system of state schools, and transforming the civil service examination into a test of knowledge of the classics and statecraft. Although an effort was made to abolish the reform from 1085 to 1093, not until Southern Song (1127–1279) did efforts to carry out the program finally cease. Traditional assessments often faulted the New Policies as Legalist measures that ignored the Confucian doctrine of governing through moral example. Wang himself believed his efforts were justified by the classics, in particular the *Rites of Zhou*. In large part the New Policies appear to have been a response to the pressing financial needs of a growing bureaucratic state.

[*See also* Baojia System *and* Song Dynasty.]

James T. C. Liu, *Reform in Sung China: Wang An-shih and His New Policies* (1959). John Meskill, ed., *Wang An-shih: Practical Reformer?* (1963). H. R. Williamson, *Wang An-shih, a Chinese Statesman and Educationalist of the Sung Dynasty* (1935–1937).   PETER K. BOL

WANG CHONG (27–100?), Chinese thinker of the Latter Han period. Wang was a salaried hermit; he chose low bureaucratic positions in order to have time to write. His extant work, the *Lunheng*, translated as *Critical Essays* or *Balanced Inquiries*, reveals the most critical mind of his age. Contrary to accepted opinion of his day, he argued, for example, that Heaven was not purposive and did not send prodigies to warn man. Such events, he said, occurred naturally and were not dependent on human actions. His critical analyses and evidentiary thinking had a profound impact on Chinese thought for many centuries.   JACK L. DULL

WANGCHUK, JIGME DORJE (1928–1972), grandson of Ugyen Wangchuk who succeeded to the throne as third maharaja of Bhutan in 1952. Jigme Dorje shepherded Bhutan into the era of modern political and economic reform, introducing programs for the country's economic development, creating a constitutional monarchy, and establishing Bhutan as a member nation in the nonaligned movement and the UN General Assembly. [*See also* Bhutan.]   RICHARD ENGLISH

WANGCHUK, JIGME SINGYE (b. 1955), the fourth maharaja of Bhutan, succeeded to the throne at the age of seventeen on the death of his father, Jigme Dorje, in 1972. [*See also* Bhutan.]

RICHARD ENGLISH

WANGCHUK, UGYEN (d. 1926), first hereditary monarch of Bhutan. As governor of Bhutan's strategic Tongsa Province, Ugyen Wangchuk rendered valuable assistance to the British Government of India in its attempts to bring Tibet within its sphere of influence early in the twentieth century. In return, Ugyen Wangchuk received British support in his consolidation of regional political power,

which resulted in his being proclaimed Druk Gyalpo, or maharaja of Bhutan, in 1907. [*See also* Bhutan.]

RICHARD ENGLISH

WANG FUZHI (1619–1692), Chinese philosopher and ardent Ming loyalist during the period of the Ming–Qing dynastic transition. His early writings expressed xenophobic sentiments and argued that the segregation of the Chinese and Manchu nationalities was the "Way of Heaven." Wang's patriotic fervor unified moral commitment and political activism in his quest to serve an "enlightened" ruler. In 1650 Wang served briefly in the faction-ridden court of the Yongli emperor (r. 1642–1662), the last of the Ming resistance regimes. Forced to flee for his life, Wang withdrew to his native Hunan Province and spent his remaining days as a reclusive scholar. Although Wang was not well known in his own time, he was "discovered" in the nineteenth and early twentieth centuries as a forerunner of Chinese patriotism.

Feng Yu-lan, *A History of Chinese Philosophy*, vol. 2, translated by Derk Bodde (1953), pp. 641–650. Arthur W. Hummel, ed., *Eminent Chinese of the Ch'ing Period (1644–1912)* (1944), pp. 817–819. Ian McMorran, "The Patriot and the Partisans: Wang Fu-chih's Involvement in the Politics of the Yung-li Court," in *From Ming to Ch'ing: Conquest, Region, and Conformity in 17th-Century China*, edited by Jonathan D. Spence and John Wills, Jr. (1979), pp. 133–166.   ANITA M. ANDREW

WANG GEN (1483–1540), Chinese philosopher; lower-class disciple of Wang Yangming (1472–1529) and founder of the Taizhou branch of the Neo-Confucian School of Mind. Wang was the son of a salt merchant in Taizhou, Jiangsu, and received little formal education. Nevertheless, he became a popular thinker who took to the streets to teach the way of sagehood to the common man. He lectured on the Confucian classics with an evangelistic style and dressed in the manner prescribed by the ancient *Book of Rites*. Wang's philosophy stressed the importance of correct individual conduct as the "measuring square" of the social order and reciprocity as the basis for all social relations.

[*See also* Neo-Confucianism; Taizhou School; *and* Wang Yangming.]

Wm. Theodore de Bary, "Individualism and Humanitarianism in Late Ming Thought," in *Self and Society in Ming Thought*, edited by Wm. Theodore de Bary (1970), pp. 145–247. Fung Yu-lan, *A History of Chinese Philosophy*, vol. 2, translated by Derk Bodde (1953), pp. 623–628.

ANITA M. ANDREW

WANG HONGWEN (b. 1935), Chinese Communist leader and member of the Gang of Four. Born in Jiangsu to a peasant family, Wang served briefly in the military during the Korean War and was then assigned to the Seventeenth Textile Factory in Shanghai as an ordinary worker. As a result of his political activism he was promoted to the position of low-ranking cadre in the Security Department of the factory. During the Cultural Revolution, Wang emerged as the most prominent leader of the Shanghai rebels: he led the attack on the party leadership of the factory in June 1966 and organized the "Shanghai Workers Revolutionary Rebel Headquarters," which directed its attack squarely at the Shanghai Party leaders.

From that time Wang's promotion was rapid; he became a vice-chairman of the Shanghai Revolutionary Committee and a member of the Central Committee of the Ninth Party Congress. After Lin Biao's fall, he moved to Beijing, where he obtained the positions of vice-chairman of the Chinese Communist Party, vice-chairman of the Central Military Affairs Commissions, and member of the Politburo. Representing the new type of leader who emerged from the Cultural Revolution, he was tried as a member of the Gang of Four and sentenced to life imprisonment.

[*See also* Gang of Four *and* Great Proletarian Cultural Revolution.]

HONG YUNG LEE

WANG JINGWEI (1883–1944), leading Guomindang (Kuomintang, KMT, or Nationalist Party) revolutionary in China who ended his life as a puppet politician under the Japanese. After obtaining the *shengyuan* degree by passing the first level of the Qing government's civil service examinations, Wang went to Japan to study law and political theory. While in Japan, he became a member of the Revolutionary Alliance (Tongmenghui), the revolutionary organization headed by Sun Yat-sen. Thereafter, he served as one of Sun's closest collaborators. In 1910, feeling despair because the revolutionary movement was losing momentum, Wang determined to rouse the nation to revolution by assassinating the Qing dynasty's prince-regent, Caifeng, in Beijing. This bold plot was discovered, however, and Wang was arrested. Although he readily confessed his involvement, the government feared that making a martyr of him would rouse the Chinese people against the dynasty; Wang's life was thus spared.

During the 1920s Wang was a leader of the KMT's left wing, and he strongly supported the united front with the Chinese Communists and the Soviet Union. After Sun Yat-sen's death in 1925, Wang was the prime contender to be Sun's successor, but was edged aside in the ensuing struggle for power by the relatively unknown Chiang Kai-shek. Wang thereafter opposed the growing conservatism and militarization of the Nationalist revolutionary movement under Chiang, and he became the leader of a political faction, the Reorganizationist clique, that incorporated many of the young and left-leaning members of the KMT. Following the Japanese invasion of Manchuria (northeastern China) in 1931 and attack on Shanghai in early 1931, Wang made peace with Chiang Kai-shek, and was thereupon named premier of the Nationalist government. As premier, Wang bore the onus of the government's policy of appeasing the Japanese, and in November 1935 a radical critic of the government's policy, posing as a photographer, shot Wang and critically wounded him. After recuperating in Europe, Wang returned to China to become vice-director-general of the KMT under the leadership of Chiang Kai-shek.

A charismatic personality and an enthralling public speaker, Wang was unhappy in his new political role, especially after the war with Japan began in July 1937. He perceived that the continuing fighting with Japan was taking a terrible toll on the nation and the lives of the Chinese people, and he was convinced that the only one to benefit from a protracted war would be the Communist Party, which by now had become Wang's bête noire. Whatever his motives, in December 1938 Wang secretly left the Nationalist capital of Chongqing for Hanoi and thence Shanghai. After prolonged negotiations, in March 1940 Wang became head of a new "National Government" in Nanjing, which was in fact a puppet regime dominated by the Japanese. Although denounced as a traitor, Wang's government did mitigate somewhat the harsher effects of Japanese rule in China. In addition, of course, his prediction that the Communists would be the true beneficiaries of a prolonged war proved accurate. He died in 1944 as a result of complications caused by the bullet wounds sustained in the attempted assassination of 1935.

[*See also* China, Republic of; Guomindang; Chiang Kai-shek; *and* World War II in China.]

LLOYD E. EASTMAN

WANG MANG (45 BCE–23 CE), political figure of the Former Han dynasty in China; founder and only ruler of the Xin dynasty (9–23), a period also known as the Wang Mang interregnum.

Wang Mang was the nephew of Empress Wang, wife of Emperor Yuan (r. 48–33 BCE). Male relatives of Empress Wang had held powerful positions in the central government for more than two decades. Wang Mang thus grew up with important connections in the administration. He had a Confucian education, and was particularly influenced by the ritual texts. In 16 BCE, having been nepotistically promoted to relatively high positions, he was granted a noble title. In 8 BCE he became Grand Minister of War, the equivalent of prime minister. Wang Mang's power was briefly curtailed during the reign of Emperor Ai (r. 6–1 BCE), but when that emperor died Wang's aunt was instrumental in installing his nine-year-old successor, Emperor Ping (r. 1–6 CE), and recalling Wang Mang to the central administration. Wang secured his position by preventing any of the young emperor's consort relatives from participating in the government. His nobility was enhanced when he became the Duke Giving Tranquillity to the Han. After the death of Emperor Ping (some historians have charged that Wang killed him), a two-year-old was installed as heir apparent. Wang now totally dominated the government, serving with the title of acting emperor and finally taking the throne as founder of his Xin ("New") dynasty.

Several factors explain Wang Mang's rise to power. The Han dynasty had long been faced with intractable economic and social problems, and there was a growing belief that it was doomed. Confucianism had become increasingly influenced by ideas concerning omens and prodigies; Wang and his followers manipulated these beliefs so that they predicted Wang's rise. The lengthy domination of the government by Wang's family members meant that he had a huge following in the bureaucracy. Finally, Wang had a superb reputation as a thoroughly committed Confucian who could save China from the manifold difficulties of the time.

As an emperor Wang Mang was a failure. Inspired by Confucian texts, he attempted a series of reforms. He sought to abolish private land ownership and to restore the system of public land ownership of the "well-field" system. This policy, and another intended to abolish slavery, were so unpopular that they had to be eliminated. He abolished the Han coinage system, substituting for it archaic units of exchange that created economic chaos, and alienated the foreigners on China's frontiers, necessitating the mobilization of thousands of Chinese troops. His state monopolies of certain products, instead of increasing state income, disrupted the normal marketing system. His social reforms, including the restoration of the preimperial system of nobility, likewise failed. Toward the latter part of Wang's reign, there was widescale popular and elite discontent with his policies. Hordes of peasants moved into his capital, where he was killed.

In spite of his failures Wang Mang was an important historical figure. He was the first dynastic founder in the imperial era to claim to have received the mandate of Heaven. He was the first historical figure to found a dynasty by having the last ruler of the preceding dynasty abdicate to him; this became the common means of inaugurating dynasties for the next thousand years. Finally, Wang was the last ruler for several centuries to attempt land reform; his land reform failure testifies to the growing power of the landed elite of the time.

[*See also* Han Dynasty.]

Pan Ku (Ban Gu), *The History of the Former Han Dynasty,* translated by Homer H. Dubs, vol. 3 (1955).

JACK L. DULL

WANG MING (originally Chen Shaoyu; 1905?–1974), early Chinese Communist and critic of Mao Zedong. A native of Anhui Province, Chen joined the Chinese Communist Party in 1925. He studied Russian and Marxism-Leninism at Sun Yat-sen University in Moscow from 1925 to 1927. Under his Party name Wang Ming he became known for orthodox Marxist and pro-Moscow policies. In 1931, with the Comintern's support, Wang became secretary general of the Chinese Communist Party for one year. Although he held many posts in the Chinese Communist revolution and government, he often resided in Moscow, where he became an outspoken critic of Mao Zedong. After Beijing's break with the USSR in the 1960s, Wang was castigated by Chinese officials for being both a left and right deviationist.

[*See also* Communism: Chinese Communist Party; Comintern; *and* Mao Zedong.]

RICHARD C. KAGAN

WANG YANGMING (Wang Shouren; 1472–1529), the most famous philosopher and an active official of the Ming dynasty (1368–1644), and the leading thinker of the Neo-Confucian School of Mind (xinxue). The influence of Wang's thought, strong within China for 150 years, also spread to Korea and Japan.

Born to an official family in Zhejiang, Wang grew up in the southern capital of Nanjing. After passing provincial- and national-level civil service examinations Wang began a long period of service to the Ming government. His career was marked by alternate posting in the imperial capitals and isolation in the provinces, as well as an alternation of phases of action and contemplation. From 1499 until 1506 he served in central government ministries. After offending a powerful court eunuch in 1506 Wang Yangming was banished to a remote district in Guizhou. There, at the age of thirty-six, he made his first philosophical breakthrough. In a flash of insight he grasped the true meaning of the Confucian principle of the investigation of things (gewu). After having made himself sick scrutinizing some bamboo for days on end, Wang suddenly realized that the principle of the bamboo was not to be sought externally, but could be found within his own mind.

From 1510 to 1516 Wang held posts in Beijing and Nanjing. Between 1517 and 1519 he served in Jiangxi and Fujian suppressing rebellions, including that of the prince of Ning. It was at this time that Wang developed his techniques for pacification and community reconstruction. He reduced taxes, raised official salaries, opened schools, promoted moral instruction, and organized mutual surveillance groups and community compacts. In recognition of his service he was awarded the title earl of Xinjian. Wang was out of favor at court from 1521 to 1527, during which time he retired to his home district and devoted himself to writing, teaching, and reflection. At the age of forty-nine, after a severe struggle, he formulated his doctrine of the extension of innate knowledge of the good. Between 1527 and 1528 he was again called by the court to suppress rebellion in Jiangxi. His mission accomplished, Wang died en route home on 10 January 1529. Following his death critics at court denounced him and his title and honors were revoked. Only in 1567 was his honorary title restored and an imperial order given that Wang's tablet be placed in the Confucian temple.

The inward-looking quality of Wang's philosophy may be related to his attempt to remain faithful to his ruler and serve him at a time of great governmental corruption and social instability. Wang's philosophy centered around the doctrine of mind. Wang Yangming's view of knowledge, which had some links to the ideas of the Song thinker Lu Jiuyuan (Lu Xiangshan; 1139–1193), differed from the views of the orthodox school of Neo-Confucianism represented by Zhu Xi (1130–1200). Zhu Xi stressed knowledge of principle (li) through the investigation of things; Wang, in contrast, stressed innate knowledge of good and evil within the mind (xin). For Wang, principle was identical with the substance of the mind and did not have to be sought outside the mind. Thus, the study of classical texts and book learning generally became less important, while quiet sitting and meditation more important. Wang's doctrine of the unity of knowledge and action greatly simplified moral calculation. Because moral principle and mind were identified with each other, the mind, if undisturbed, would project knowledge of the good, which would lead directly to action. There was no break between correct moral knowledge and right action.

Wang's detractors criticized his ideas as Buddhism in disguise. While it is true that Wang was influenced by such notions as the Zen (Chinese, Chan) concept of sudden enlightenment, and while he did make use of meditation techniques, his teaching differed fundamentally from Buddhism in the extent to which it was focused on social action in support of Confucian norms. The implications of Wang's doctrines were drawn out by his followers and successors with results that strayed ever further from Confucian orthodoxy. By making the mind the primary source of moral authority Wang opened up the possibility of sagehood to anyone. When Wang Yangming looked within his own mind for moral knowledge, he found there universal Confucian norms. Others, however, found different truths. Wang Gen (1483–1540), He Xinyin (1525–1590), and finally Li Zhi (1527–1602) took Ming thought further and further in the direction of individualism and even selfishness until the core of Confucian commitment was lost.

In addition to his philosophical teachings, Wang Yangming also made a significant contribution to the practice of local control. When serving among the tribal peoples of the southwest he advocated schooling and programs to introduce them to Chinese farming practices. In suppressing rebellions he organized families into groups of ten (baojia) that were responsible for each other's behavior. Wang also utilized the community compact (xiangyue) to get local leaders and wrongdoers to publicly pledge reform with oaths and wine-drinking ceremonies.

[See also Neo-Confucianism; Taizhou School; Baojia System; Lu Xiangshan; Zhu Xi; Wang Gen; and Li Zhi.]

Wing-tsit Chan, *A Source Book in Chinese Philosophy* (1963). Wing-tsit Chan, trans., *Instructions for Practical Living and Other Neo-Confucian Writings by Wang Yang-ming* (1963). Julia Ching, *To Acquire Wisdom: The Way of Wang Yang-ming* (1976). Wm. Theodore de Bary, ed., *Self and Society in Ming Thought* (1970). L. Carrington Goodrich and Chaoying Fang, eds., *Dictionary of Ming Biography* (1976). *Philosophy East and West* 23. 1–2 (1976): *Proceedings of East-West Philosopher's Conference on Wang Yang-ming: A Comparative Study.*

EDWARD L. FARMER

WAQF.

Under Islamic law property may be given as a *waqf* (plural, *awqaf*), or endowment, to provide income and space for the conduct of religiously approved activities such as worship, schooling, and the care of the sick. Such property may no longer be sold, transferred or inherited, but remains under the control of an appointed or hereditary manager (*mutawalli*).

Gregory C. Kozlowski, *Muslim Endowments and Society in British India* (1985).   DAVID S. LELYVELD

WARFARE

WARFARE IN CHINA

The major Chinese dynasties all were founded through warfare. All suffered at least one major mid-dynastic rebellion or foreign invasion, and all ended in violence. During periods of unity China always maintained a military frontier, at least in the North, and often invaded and conquered its neighbors. Every dynasty maintained a large military organization, which typically consumed most of the tax revenues. Despite these facts, China tends to be viewed as a relatively pacific civilization. Members of the Confucian literati class, who wrote the official histories, viewed warfare to unify or defend the empire as legitimate, but were hostile to wars of expansion and to the idea of military glory. Sunzi, the great military strategist of the fourth century BCE, and later Chinese military thinkers shared these cultural values and thus viewed war as a transitory phase to be followed by a normal order in which civil virtues would prevail. The finest general, in this view, is not one who crushes his enemy in a decisive battle but one who forces the enemy to capitulate without fighting.

Under the Western Zhou (1122?–770 BCE) the war chariot carrying an archer of noble birth was the basic military unit. Warfare was stylized and formal, governed by codes of honor, with elaborate challenges before combat. The Zhou king controlled a large standing army and could also summon the troops of his feudal lords through a system of beacon towers. According to later traditions, each chariot was supported by a platoon of twenty-five infantry in five squads; companies of four chariots were then organized by multiples of five into "brigades" (*yu*, 500 men), "divisions" (*shi*, 2,500 men), and finally "armies" (*jun*, 12,500 men). This specific pattern of organization has been repeatedly revived, and the last three terms are now standard in modern Chinese military nomenclature.

During the Spring and Autumn (722–481 BCE) and Warring States (403–221 BCE) periods, chariots and honor both vanished. The state of Zhao created cavalry by introducing saddles and stirrups, and the state of Qin based its military system on conscription and its social system on noble ranks that could be earned only in war or agriculture. These developments (fourth century BCE) led to more than a century of intense violence in which Qin destroyed its rivals, conquered all of China, and soon fell apart owing to rebellions caused by its own policies.

The succeeding Han dynasty (206 BCE–220 CE) brought a more benign spirit but nonetheless continued Qin institutions, including military conscription. Once inducted, soldiers trained for a year and then served for a second year; after they returned to their villages they were subject to recall if needed. They were classified as infantry, cavalry, or sailors, according to the skills they possessed when inducted. Most of them served in the commandery capitals under the commandery governors, who thus had military as well as civil authority. Under the Former Han the governors were assisted by chief commandants. Some of the conscripts served in the imperial capital, which also held a force of professional soldiers, most of whom were cavalry recruited from six commanderies in the northwest. Other conscripts served along the Great Wall, which was carefully maintained as a defended frontier. When a large-scale expedition was planned, one or more leaders would be commissioned as generals (*jiangjun*). In principle the generals gave up their commissions at the end of the campaign, but in practice, especially after the reign of Emperor Wu, certain of the generalships evolved into permanent positions.

Most of the Han soldiers fought as spear-bearing infantry, but in contrast to the Greek phalanx and the Roman legion, Han tactics did not emphasize close order and shock. Rather, the spearmen were to provide a defense behind which archers and crossbowmen were to destroy the enemy by fire. The Han were able to keep the crossbow trigger mechanism a tightly held military secret. Under Huo Qubing and his successors they raised cavalry forces able to compete with the Xiongnu in fighting with the compound bow. Han armies conquered northern Vietnam, central Korea, and Central Asia, and destroyed the Xiongnu as an organized power. While the Latter Han was founded in rebellion and ended in rebellion, China was not menaced by barbarian invasion for a century afterward. The success of Han military institutions was probably a result of the near-universal incidence of the conscription system and the pervasiveness of military skills and values in the governing class.

In the succeeding Three Kingdoms and Northern and Southern Dynasties periods, social disorder and depopulation went along with devolution of central authority to local magnates controlling clan-based military power. Especially in the North, the long-term institutional trend was to rebuild central power by linking title to vacant land with the obligation to perform military service. This led to the *fubing* military system, which the Tang (618–907) inherited from the Sui (581–618). Under this system about 600,000 soldiers (*bing*) were placed under about 600 battalion-level headquarters (*fu*) and given land to farm. They were required to perform active service at the capital for two months out of every eighteen, or more frequently, depending on their distance from the capital. The approximately 50,000 *fubing* soldiers on duty at any one time were under twelve guard (*wei*) headquarters. Like the Han, the Tang capital garrison included a cavalry-heavy professional force, generally known as the Northern Barracks, which figured prominently in the dynasty's many palace coups.

The writings of the Tang general Li Jing show the Tang concept of field organization. Li assumed that from an army of 20,000 some 6,000 would be assigned to guard the baggage trains; the 14,000 effectives would in turn be divided into a center with 2,800 men and six flanking divisions. The center was to have 1,000 cavalry, 400 archers, 400 crossbowmen, 500 skirmishers, and 500 heavy infantry; all five arms were organized in platoons of 50 men each. The other six divisions were smaller, but each included all five arms in comparable proportions. With its large numbers of archers, crossbowmen, and light infantry, Li's army emphasized firepower

and ambush warfare, rather than shock. The idea of dividing an army into smaller forces, each composed of all arms in proportion, was considered a great innovation in the eighteenth-century West but was standard Chinese practice as far back as separate arms can be identified.

Like the contemporary Byzantine theme system that it so strongly resembled, the *fubing* system was best suited to annual campaigns during the agricultural off-season. Unlike the Han system, military obligations rested on a small percentage of the population, and evasion became rampant when *fubing* soldiers were abused in the capital or ordered to spend their duty periods on the distant frontier. In the eighth century the military basis of the Tang state changed to a full-time professional army stationed on the northern frontier. This army reached a strength of 490,000 men (including 80,000 cavalry) by the year 742. Drawn from socially uprooted elements and commanded by generals promoted from within, these troops were alienated from Tang society. The rebellion in 755 of the leading border general, An Lushan, led to warlordism based on these armies. The Tang court raised a new army, the Divine Strategy Army (*shencejun*), composed of the rabble of the capital officered by eunuchs, but could do no more than contain the regional warlords, whose troops had put down strong local roots. The same factors underlay the deeper divisions of the Five Dynasties and Ten Kingdoms period.

The Song founder inherited persistent warlordism in China proper, while the barbarian-ruled Liao and Xixia states threatened the North. He patiently concentrated the warlord armies in and around the Song capital at Kaifeng under his own command. These troops received the designation Imperial Armies (*jinjun*), and came to outnumber the provincial armies (*xiangjun*) found in other areas. These two standing armies were supplemented by a militia. The military effectiveness of the standing armies declined rapidly after the tenth century. They were recruited from the dregs of society and paid subsistence wages, and their officers had low pay and low prestige compared to civil officials. Understandably, the Song emperors valued control above efficiency; to achieve control they frequently shuffled the personnel of individual units, drawing off the best to form new elite units. Garrisons usually included battalions from different regiments, with no common military superior, and an agency run by civil officials, the Bureau of Military Affairs (*shumiyuan*), had the sole authority to order operations. Troop totals rose from 378,000 at the start of the dynasty to around 1,250,000 in the 1040s, without corresponding increases in quality.

The loss of Kaifeng and the North China Plain to the new Jin empire led the Southern Song to emphasize forces to defend its large walled cities, river forces to control the Yangtze Valley, and oceanic naval power. Fortifications were improved and an extensive science of siegecraft developed. Rockets and other weapons employing gunpowder came into use. Song naval forces dominated the East China Sea, keeping open communications with Korea. The Jin attempted to develop similar capabilities, but it was the Mongols who were the first East Asian power to blend the cavalry warfare of the steppe with the advanced technology of South China. Significantly, the Mongols completed their conquest of China by taking Hangzhou by siege (1276) and defeating the last Song emperor in a naval battle (1279).

Genghis Khan, the Mongol founder, had imposed a decimal pattern of organization and strict discipline on his tribesmen, who continued the steppe tradition of cavalry tactics emphasizing the compound bow. As they conquered China the Mongols added infantry and naval units to their forces, but they imposed decimal organization and hereditary recruitment of officers throughout.

The Ming (1368–1644) continued Mongol organizational practices, although they explicitly compared their *weisuo* system to the Tang *fubing* system. Officers' ranks were made hereditary in 1364. Soldiers, whose military obligation also was hereditary, were organized into guards (*wei*, 5,600 men), subdivided into battalions (*suo*, 1,120 men). By 1393 there were 326 guards and 65 independent battalions listed. These units were given lands to farm. Ming armies were able to engage Mongol cavalry successfully through the 1390s, and as late as the 1420s the Yongle emperor was able to lead large armies into Mongolia. The Ming came to power after extensive naval campaigns on the Yangtze River and its tributaries; until the 1430s Ming fleets dominated East Asian waters, reaching as far as the east coast of Africa under the leadership of Zheng He. The Ming made extensive use of cannon and other firearms, and after invading Vietnam set up a department for firearms training in Beijing using Vietnamese instructors.

Later Ming military evolution paralleled that of the Tang. Defending the northern frontier, including the exposed capital at Beijing, was considered to be the major problem. Most of the present Great Wall was built during the Ming, and Chinese superiority in firearms made it generally effective as a defense against the now-divided Mongols. The garrison of the wall became a standing army, even though originally it was conscripted from the *weisuo* soldiers, most of whom became merely an exceptionally disadvantaged sector of the peasantry. However, even in the 1590s Ming armies were effective enough to drive the Japanese armies of Hideyoshi out of Korea. After the 1430s the Ming abandoned all efforts to maintain a seagoing fleet in favor of a much less effective system of small coastal garrisons.

The Manchus were aided in conquering China by the defection of certain units of the Ming standing army. Under the Qing (1644–1911), these troops were designated Green Standard units and distributed in battalion-sized garrisons throughout China, essentially as a constabulary. They were recruited by voluntary enlistment and their officers were promoted from the ranks; the system of military examinations and degrees had little importance for officer selection under either the Ming or the Qing. The Manchus themselves, along with those Chinese and Mongols who had joined them before 1644, were hereditarily enrolled in the Eight Banner system and mostly stationed in Beijing, although a few key provincial cities also had Banner contingents. At the height of Manchu power, Banner forces conquered Central Asia while the Green Standard armies and fleet suppressed the Three Feudatories Rebellion and conquered Taiwan. However, by 1800 both systems were in full decay.

The Taiping Rebellion posed a threat to dynastic survival and led the Qing to sanction the creation of militia armies in response. These—notably the Hunan Army of Zeng Guofan, the Fujian Army of Zuo Zongtang, and the Anhui Army of Li Hongzhang—were organized by the gentry, with units formed whenever possible from men of the same clan or village. Although organized and equipped similarly to the Green Standard units, the militia armies in fact represented the growth of partly autonomous personal power. This was even more the case with the Beiyang Army of Yuan Shikai after 1895, which was organized and uniformed after Western models and trained by Japanese instructors. When the Beiyang Army obeyed Yuan in the Revolution of 1911, it not only destroyed the Qing but also condemned China to a long period of warlordism, in which China was effectively partitioned among a number of armies. Each warlord maintained his local ascendancy by the cultivation of personal loyalties. Overall, the warlord period inhibited the development of modern institutions, including armies, and the brief ascendency of the Guomindang (Kuomintang, KMT) did not transcend these limitations.

The Chinese Communist Party rose to power fighting both the KMT and the Japanese. Making a virtue of the rural exile into which they had been driven, they developed the doctrine of "People's War," a form of guerrilla warfare animated by intense political organization. People's War marked a reversal of the historical traditions of past Chinese civil wars, in that it advocated taking the cities only after the countryside had been secured. This doctrine proved successful in the Chinese civil war of 1945 to 1949. Since then, People's War has been an obstacle to the measures of professionalization and mechanization that are needed if China is to become a military power in the modern sense.

[See also Fubing System; Tuntian; Banners; Warlords; and Warlord Cliques.]

John K. Fairbank and Frank A. Kierman, eds., *Chinese Ways in Warfare* (1974). Ch'i-ch'ing Hsiao, *The Military Establishment of the Yuan Dynasty* (1978). Philip Kuhn, *Rebellion and Its Enemies in Late Imperial China* (1970). Ralph A. Powell, *The Rise of Chinese Military Power* (1955). Edwin G. Pulleyblank, *The Background of the Rebellion of An Lu-shan* (1955). William Whitson, *The Chinese High Command* (1970).   EDWARD L. DREYER

STEPPE WARFARE

With the exception of the Khazar state of Transcaucasia and Transcaspia—which was able, because of its economic importance as a point of commercial exchange at the convergence of the north-south, east-west axes of Asian and international trade, to generate enough surplus wealth for the hiring of mercenary troops to defend its borders—all of the Turco-Mongol states of the Eurasian steppe possessed permanent standing armies. Through subjugation, from earliest times, of tribal and clan interests to the will of a central state authority, steppe societies fielded armies whose disciplinary order, organizational efficiency, and battle prowess became the object of envious respect and even emulation by contemporary states in the Near East and central Europe.

After observing at first hand the effectiveness of Attila's onslaught in the fifth century CE, the Romans closely followed developments in steppe warfare techniques. In later centuries a number of strategical treatises and drill manuals were composed in Europe based on these observations. The Turks arose as a major power in the eastern Eurasian steppe during the sixth through eighth centuries, settling in large numbers on a permanent basis on the fringes of the settled world of Iran and the Byzantine empire toward the end of the eleventh century. With this development, the interest of the West in Central Asian military matters became more than purely academic. As a result of the fear and loathing that the nomadic conquerors from the steppe inspired among settled peoples throughout history, an aura of mythology and exaggerated opinion has dogged them; it persists today more or less intact. Attributions of their military successes to vast superiority in numbers and continued reference to steppe armies as "hordes" is only one part of this mythology, which still stands in need of thorough examination and reassessment.

Among the factors contributing to the specialization in a particular form of warfare among the nomadic populations of Eurasia were two conditions of life in the steppe. The first was the abundance of grasslands for the support of livestock, both sheep and horses, which provided the basis of the steppe economy and also determined patterns of movement and the timing of the periodic forays into areas lying outside the steppe. The availability and abundance of grass permitted the introduction of horse-breeding techniques that are thought to have become widespread in the steppe area sometime between 3000 and 1700 BCE. With time, hearty breeds were developed that were both well suited to the needs of the highly mobile herding populations and, because of their great stamina, ideal for use in battle fronts separated by wide distances. The second factor determining the evolution of warfare in the steppe was the availability of metals, especially iron, and the development of metallurgical techniques. Thus, weaponry and other accoutrements of battle could be developed, and their design evolved and was perfected over long centuries.

Apart from these environmental advantages, the ability of the steppe armies to consistently overcome the armies of their contemporary competitors from settled societies both in China and the West rested primarily on improvements introduced in two further spheres of steppe warfare: (1) the organizational principle of steppe armies and (2) tactics and logistics. In the current scholarship on these questions a great deal of attention has been paid to the significance of technological innovations and improvements during the Middle Ages of specific weapons and items of military equipment, such as the "Scythian" crossbow and the metal stirrup. These inventions, however, are significant only in conjunction with the refinements in organization that governed the most effective use of such equipment. Changes in the administrative organization, unit specialization, and professionalization of military endeavor were, then, the most significant military developments in the steppe and, at the same time, the most characteristic of it.

The introduction of a decimal system for the mobilization and command of troops was the most important institutional innovation in steppe military organization; in its departure from preexisting, purely tribal bases of army organization, the decimal system is a veritable revolution. Through it an unbroken centralized chain of command was constructed; it emanated from the ruler, as commander in chief, to his commanders of ten thousand, and through them to the commanders of subordinate rank organized in regiments of one thousand, battalions of one hundred, and companies of ten. The introduction of the decimal system made possible central coordination and planning of campaigns, rapid communication and transmission of battle orders, and precise timing in the movement and deployment of individual military units; all of these advances greatly contributed to the startling success of steppe armies such as those of Genghis Khan and Timur over the feudal cavalries of their neighbors in China, Iran, and the Byzantine empire.

Drawing on their large herds for fresh mounts on a constantly revolving basis, the steppe armies were composed entirely of mounted forces. Their system of centralized distribution and quick replacement of damaged or lost arms and equipment gave them the advantage over the armies of their more sporadically mobilized competitors. Through a skillful combining of centralized command and superior equipment with tactical maneuvers and battle formations developed through several centuries of experience in warfare, especially with China, the nomadic people of the steppe developed a special type of cavalry warfare known as the "Eastern school." This school reached a peak of technical perfection during the period of the Karakhitai empire (907–1125). It was especially well known for its use of the "Turanian tactic": a sudden and rapid initial attack followed by a feigned retreat and then a gradual encirclement of the pursuing foe. The excellent horsemanship of the steppe warriors, combined with their obedience to centralized command and their split-second execution of orders, enabled them alone to make use of this tactic.

The importation by states outside the steppe, especially in the Islamic world after the ninth century, of Turkish military experts, slave recruits, and mercenaries began a process of Turkish penetration into the Muslim lands. Limited at first to the palace enclosure and royal bodyguards, such as those employed by the Abbasid caliph Mu'tasim at Samarra or the Pecheneg forces in the service of the Roman emperors of Byzantium, this process culminated in the formation of autonomous dynasties and independent states throughout the Islamic Near East in the postclassical age. These states, supported by armies based on the model of the nomadic armies of the steppe, were to play a decisive role in the spread of Islamic civilization. Highly mobile Islamic and Turkic armies served as the medium for not only the spread of political hegemony but also the transfer of agricultural and scientific knowledge and a variety of other cultural and religious influences. Although the invention of the stirrup and the perfection of specialized warfare techniques took place in the steppe, the principal repercussions of these developments were witnessed outside the steppe. The Turco-Islamic armies of the second millennium played a double role, being both conquerors and transmitters of the intellectual inheritance and material culture of the Middle East to the far reaches of Asia and Europe.

[See also Genghis Khan; Khazars; Mines and Metallurgy; Mongol Empire; Pechenegs; Roman Empire; and Timur.]

G. Duby, *The Early Growth of the European Economy: Warrior and Peasants from the Seventh to the Twelfth Century* (1974). H. D. Martin, *The Rise of Chingis Khan and His Conquest of Northern China* (1950), pp. 11–47. J. M. Smith, "Mongol Manpower and Persian Population," *Journal of the Economic and Social History of the Orient* 18 (1975): 271–299. Lynn White, Jr., *Medieval Technology and Social Change* (1962), pp. 14–28. K. A. Wittfogel, et al., *History of Chinese Society: The Liao (907–1125)* (1946), pp. 505–539.

RHOADS MURPHEY, JR.

WARLORD CLIQUES. During the warlord era in early Republican China (1911–1927), militarists tended to form factions or cliques based on personal associations, common interests, and shared ideas and values. The most powerful and best known groups were the Anhui, Zhili, and Fengtian cliques.

The Zhili and Anhui cliques emerged from the Beiyang Army created by Yuan Shikai, the first president of China. During Yuan's presidency, his chief Beiyang officers became accustomed to interfering in national and regional politics to serve Yuan's personal goals. These officers continued such political activities after Yuan's death in 1916, but with Yuan gone there was nobody who could command their obedience and maintain Beiyang unity. [*See also* Yuan Shikai.] During 1916 and 1917 they tried to maintain the group's cohesion, and thus its national influence, through mutual consultations and collective decisions. It proved impossible, however, to maintain unity among Beiyang leaders. Conflict among them arose from the clash of personal ambitions and interests, from personality differences, and from disputes over policy issues, especially the question of how best to re-create a genuine national political unity in the face of secessionist regions.

The chief difference of opinion over the issue of national unity was between a number of militarists led by Duan Qirui, who advocated unification of the country by military force, and those who sought a peaceful solution and looked to Feng Guozhang for leadership. By 1918 these differences had led to the formation of two identifiable groups of militarists. The group led by Feng Guozhang was called the Zhili clique, but not long after the clique clearly emerged, Feng died, and leadership devolved upon Cao Kun and his able subordinate Wu Peifu. Duan Qirui's group was called the Anhui clique. In July 1920 the Zhili group allied with Zhang Zuolin to fight a brief war against the Anhui group. Duan Qirui was defeated, and he subsequently retired. For most practical purposes, the Anhui clique came to an end, although prominent members of the clique continued to be active in national politics, and Duan himself would briefly reappear after a few years. The Zhili and Fengtian cliques dominated Beijing politics until 1922, when Zhili pushed Fengtian forces out of North China. In the fall of 1924 Wu Peifu, then the substantive leader of the Zhili clique militarists, again went to war against Fengtian. Wu lost the war when one of his generals, Feng Yuxiang, turned against him. The reshuffling of alliances that followed this war essentially destroyed the Zhili clique, although individual members of the clique continued to play major roles in Chinese military politics. [*See also* Duan Qirui; Feng Guozhang; Cao Kun; Wu Peifu; *and* Feng Yuxiang.]

The Fengtian Clique was led by Zhang Zuolin, who dominated Manchuria from 1919 until his death in 1928. Because Zhang's chief power base was the province of Fengtian, he and his followers are often called the Fengtian clique or, occasionally, the Manchurian clique. The Fengtian clique supported the Zhili clique against Anhui in 1920. It was in turn defeated by Zhili in 1922, but, with the help of Feng Yuxiang's defection from Zhili, defeated that group in 1924. It was in turn defeated by the Guomindang's Northern Expedition in 1928. [*See also* Zhang Zuolin *and* Northern Expedition.]

The militarists who dominated Guangxi Province beginning in the mid-1920s are often called the Guangxi clique. Its chief members were Li Zongren, generally acknowledged to be the leader of the clique, Bai Chongxi, and Huang Shaohong. Clique leaders were influential in national affairs and also became famous for the reforms and reconstruction work they carried on in Guangxi. [*See also* Guangxi Clique; Li Zongren; *and* Bai Chongxi.] An earlier generation of military men in Guangxi, led by Lu Rongting, is also occasionally called the Guangxi clique.

[*See also* China, Republic Period *and* Warlords.]

Hsi-sheng Ch'i, *Warlord Politics in China, 1916–1928* (1976). Diana Lary, *Region and Nation: The Kwangsi Clique in Chinese Politics, 1925–1937* (1974). Gavan McCormack, *Chang Tso-lin in Northeast China, 1911–1928: Japan and the Manchurian Idea* (1977). Andrew J. Nathan, *Peking Politics 1918–1923: Factionalism and the Failure of Constitutionalism* (1976).

JAMES E. SHERIDAN

WARLORDS, independent militarists in early Republican-period China. The authority of the central government in China was extremely weak from the death of Yuan Shikai in 1916 until the end of the Northern Expedition in 1928. Heads of state followed one another in rapid and impotent succession. Cabinets were formed and re-formed, and parliament went in and out of existence, but none of these agencies of government had much genuinely effective authority. Real power was in the hands of local and regional militarists. Historians often call these men "warlords," although some scholars object to that term because it is pejorative and obscures the diversity of character and views that actually characterized the militarists. The word *warlordism* refers to the general characteristics of political, social, and military activities associated with warlord rule. Features of warlordism, and activities of individual warlords, can be seen before 1916 and after 1928, but those twelve years of extreme political fragmentization are usually called the "warlord period."

The warlords emerged from the militarization and political decentralization that occurred in the late nineteenth and early twentieth centuries. Yuan Shikai was the chief figure in the late Qing military modernization movement, and by the early years of the twentieth century, his Beiyang Army was the strongest military force in the country. When Yuan became president of the newly established republic in 1912, he used his army to maintain national order and unity. After his death in 1916, however, no leader emerged who was strong enough to hold the army together. It began to break up into cliques of militarists, some of whom became prominent warlords. At the same time, the absence of effective national power encouraged ambitious local and regional military men to assert their own independence and seek their own advantage. Soon the country was divided into a host of independent and semi-independent areas.

The essential bases of warlord power were a personal army and control of territory. His army gave the warlord power to tax, to seize resources, to protect himself, and to play a role in local, regional, or national politics. Control of territory was necessary to assure financial and material resources to maintain the army. Some warlords did not always control territory, but none could go for long without a territorial base. Feng Yuxiang, for example, had an excellent and well-trained army, but for years he was vulnerable, and his influence limited, because he could not gain a stable territorial base. The major warlords were military governors of provinces, and in some cases controlled two or three provinces, which allowed them to maintain large armies. Zhang Zuolin controlled all of Manchuria, at that time divided into three provinces. At the height of his career, Wu Peifu similarly headed three provinces, as did other warlords. Petty warlords led small forces and controlled small regions.

Control of territory was a major reason for the many wars that were fought during the warlord era. The major warlords also wanted to control the Beijing government, and the best known wars of North China all had that as one goal. These included the Anhui-Zhili War of 1920, the First Zhili-Fengtian War (1922), the Second Zhili-Fengtian War (1924), and the war between Feng Yuxiang and Zhang Zuolin from 1925 to 1926. In addition to these major wars there was much warfare and generalized violence in all parts of China during the warlord era.

Control of territory involved providing government for that territory, and the character of warlord governments varied with the character of the individual warlords. Wu Peifu had the beginnings of a classical education and had passed the first of the traditional civil service examinations. He held Con-

fucian values—he was sometimes called the "Scholar Warlord"—and his approach to government was conservative. Feng Yuxiang, on the other hand, began his career as an illiterate soldier and worked his way up by dint of study, hard work, and good connections. Feng adopted Christianity, at least partly to further his career at a time when foreigners held much power in China, and he was called the "Christian General." His approach to government was innovative, reformist, and puritanical. Zhang Zongchang started life as a petty thief and gambler, moved on to banditry, and rose to be the ruthless ruler of Shandong Province. His government was harshly exploitative. Even though some had good intentions, few warlords had the time or resources to attempt good government consistently. The constant warfare and political intrigue lent a transient quality to each warlord regime and encouraged exploitative government simply for purposes of survival. It is no accident that the warlord best known for stable government was Yan Xishan, the warlord of Shanxi often called the "Model Governor." Shanxi's relative geographic isolation allowed Yan to stay out of the warlord conflicts until the late 1920s.

So many forces for change were operating in China during the early twentieth century that it is difficult to identify precisely the effects of the warlords. Surely they contributed to the militarization of Chinese politics reflected in Mao Zedong's often-quoted statement that "political power grows out of the barrel of a gun." The threat of the warlords, for example, facilitated the military's gaining control of the Guomindang. The disorder and uncertainty associated with warlord government also precluded the development and implementation of long-range development programs, and thus retarded China's modernization.

[See also Bai Chongxi; Chen Jiongming; China, Republic Period; Feng Yuxiang; Guangxi Clique; Warlord Cliques; Wu Peifu; Yan Xishan; Yuan Shikai; and Zhang Zuolin.]

Hsi-sheng Ch'i, Warlord Politics in China, 1916–1928 (1976). Donald G. Gillin, Warlord: Yen Hsi-shan in Shansi Province, 1911–1949 (1967). Diana Lary, Region and Nation: The Kwangsi Clique in Chinese Politics, 1925–1937 (1974). Gavan McCormack, Chang Tso-lin in Northeast China, 1911–1928: Japan and the Manchurian Idea (1977). Andrew J. Nathan, Peking Politics, 1918–1923: Factionalism and the Failure of Constitutionalism (1976). James E. Sheridan, Chinese Warlord: The Career of Feng Yu-hsiang (1966).

JAMES E. SHERIDAN

WARRING STATES PERIOD, Chinese historical era at the end of the Zhou dynasty (1122?–256 BCE), when various feudal states, completely independent of the Zhou, vied for power. The Warring States period was one of great intellectual and political ferment and is marked by sweeping changes in all aspects of Chinese life. The period ended in 221 BCE, when the state of Qin conquered all of China and initiated an imperial bureaucracy. Scholars, differing over when the period began, have suggested political events as early as 471 BCE and as late as 403 BCE as appropriate dates for its inception.

The political changes of the Warring States period may be seen as fourfold. First, the larger states swallowed up their smaller, weaker neighbors. Although there were brief periods of peace, the period was one of relentless competition, ending in the political unification of China. The second political change occurred within individual states. Powerful ministerial families seized the kingdoms of their rulers and established their own states; thus, elite families tended to replace the old ruling families. The third political change occurred when men of low status rose to prominence; that is, access to political power was more open than it had been. The final change was in the nature of royal power, which became more authoritarian as rulers created bureaucracies that responded to the growing demands that rulers placed on society. By the end of the period a centralized bureaucracy was firmly in place.

Social change occurred at every level in this period. Competitive pressures demanded that the political elite be chosen on the basis of proven skills; consequently, familial relationships and aristocratic values were of diminishing social significance. Merchants became autonomous social and entrepreneurial actors; some gained great wealth, social prestige, and political power. The status of commoners underwent profound changes. Instead of occupying serflike positions they became private landowners. Some, through education, raised their social status; others lost their lands and became tenants or slaves.

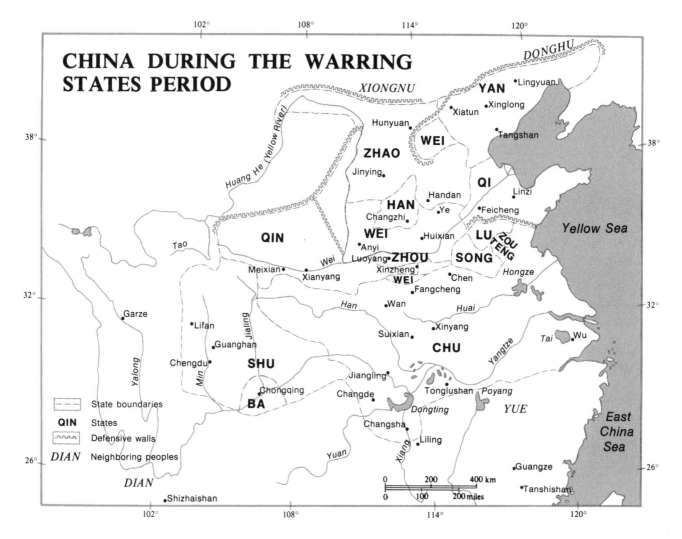

Generally, people of this period were freer of governmental restraints and more dependent upon personal merit than they were in any other period in Chinese history.

The economy of the period flourished in an unprecedented manner. Major changes occurred in agriculture as iron tools came into increasing use after about 500 BCE. Lands were more easily brought under cultivation and acreage increased. Large-scale irrigation systems raised agricultural productivity; the most notable new system was the Zhengguo Canal, which provided Qin with huge grain reserves. The first stages of regional specialization began at this time. Trade was facilitated by the improved transportation systems of the enlarged states and by the common use of coinage.

The period is noted for its great intellectual ferment. Confucius (d. about 479 BCE), the first of the major thinkers, urged benevolence and propriety as means to end the chaos of the period. Later Confucians included Mencius, who asserted that human nature was basically good, and Xunzi, who argued the opposite. The Mohists, the Daoists, and the Legalists constituted the other major schools of the period. The general trend (excluding the Mohists) was toward a highly secular humanism. Late in the period, eclectic trends became dominant: the Legalists borrowed from Daoism to provide a philosophy for their positions and the Confucianists turned to yin-yang and five cosmic forces (*wuxing*) ideas for sanctions. By the end of the Warring States period no single school occupied an exclusive position; the eclectic formulations continued into the Han dynasty.

[*See also* Spring and Autumn Period *and* Zhou Period.]

Cho-yun Hsu, *Ancient China in Transition: An Analysis of Social Mobility, 722–222 B.C.* (1965).

JACK L. DULL

WASSMUSS, WILHELM (1880–1931), German diplomat who served in Iran before, during, and after World War I. During two separate tours as German consular agent in the Persian Gulf, Wassmuss learned to speak Persian fluently and acquired extensive knowledge of southwest Iran. Consequently, he was sent by the German general staff in 1915 to Iran to provoke a general uprising of southern Iranian tribes against the British. His mission was initially successful, forcing Great Britain to divert troops from its campaigns against Ottoman

forces in Iraq. Wassmuss was captured by the British in 1931 and eventually repatriated. He spent the last seven years of his life managing a farm in southwestern Iran.

Christopher Sykes, *Wassmuss: The German Lawrence* (1936).
ERIC HOOGLUND

WATANABE KAZAN AND TAKANO CHŌEI. Watanabe Kazan (1793–1841) and Takano Chōei (1804–1850) were Japanese students of foreign affairs during the late Tokugawa period who were imprisoned in 1839 for criticizing an 1825 *bakufu* edict that ordered the immediate expulsion of all Western ships approaching Japan. Watanabe committed suicide in prison; Takano's suicide took place during his fifth year as a fugitive after breaking out of prison. Their deaths stemmed from personal jealousies within the *bakufu* and official animosity toward Western learning (*rangaku, yōgaku*) in the so-called Bansha Purge of 1839.

Watanbe was a senior official of the Tawara domain who became interested in Western subjects only in his forties. This interest was motivated by desires to strengthen coastal defense and learn about world affairs in order to overcome the threat posed by Western powers. By contrast, Takano was a doctor of Dutch medicine who had studied under Philipp Franz von Siebold in Nagasaki. His interest was in Western medicine and science and was largely devoid of political concerns. Beginning in 1832, Watanabe commissioned Takano to translate and summarize Western treatises. Their working relationship was such that Watanabe paid Takano to supply advanced Western technical knowledge and information on international affairs for application in practical statecraft. Both men joined a discussion group, the Shōshikai, headed by Endō Shōsuke, but it was neither particularly devoted to Western affairs nor connected in any way with the so-called Bansha Purge.

This purge was instigated by Torii Yōzō, a *bakufu* official and orthodox Confucian, who was jealous and resentful of the popularity that Western learning was gaining among government officials and Confucian scholars. Torii and a rival bureaucrat, Egawa Hidetatsu, were ordered to survey the coastline of Edo Bay with a view to setting up defensive fortifications. Egawa sought Kazan's help as an adviser and then outdid Torii by employing advanced Western measuring devices and personnel trained in Western methods. This incensed Torii: he was determined to execute Watanabe and Takano and to prevent Egawa from presenting to the *bakufu* a memorial on defense and foreign affairs drawn up with Watanabe's aid. He also hoped to cause the downfall of Egawa and other officials informed on Western affairs. Torii succeeded in these aims. But after Egawa returned to *bakufu* favor in 1840, following reports of Qing defeats in the Opium War in China, he pushed through many of Watanabe's enlightened proposals on coastal defense and foreign policy. In the end the constructive criticism inspired by Western learning served to strengthen *bakufu* rule.

[*See also* Rangaku.]

BOB TADASHI WAKABAYASHI

WEAVING is the process of forming fabric, usually on a loom, by interlacing threads, yarns, or other strands. Persian and Central Asian artisans mastered a variety of techniques for weaving silk, cotton, and wool clothing, trappings, coverings, and rugs. The burial mounds at Pazyryk (fifth–fourth century BCE) have preserved the oldest examples of Central Asian weaving: a horse's breastband woven of wool, linen, moss, and gold shows how sophisticated the craft was even at this early date.

Flat-woven rugs (as distinct from knotted or pile ones) are produced throughout the area. Almost all are characterized by geometric patterning, but owing to nomadic migration it is often difficult to assign specific locations to motifs or styles. Technique is a safer method of classification: the major types of flat-woven rugs according to this criterion are kilims (tapestry-woven), Sumak rugs (woven with progressive weft-wrapping), brocaded rugs (compound weaves with more than one set of wefts), embroidered rugs (decorated with needlework), compound-weave rugs (woven with supplementary warps and/or wefts), and mixed types. Most pieces are subjected to hard, daily wear; hence, few antique pieces have survived intact. The oldest kilims in existence, for example, are silk pieces woven at Kashan in the sixteenth or seventeenth century; most pieces are far more recent.

[*See also* Carpets.]

Anthony N. Landreau and W. R. Pickering, *From the Bosporus to Samarkand: Flat-Woven Rugs* (1969). S. I. Rudenko, *Frozen Tombs of Siberia*, translated by M. W. Thompson (1970).   SHEILA S. BLAIR

WEI, one of the Warring States in ancient China. Located in present-day southern Shanxi, Wei was formed from part of the state of Jin, which broke

up in 453 BCE. The break was formally recognized by the declining Zhou dynasty in 403 BCE. Wei survived until 230 BCE, when it fell to the state of Qin, which was reunifying China.   EDWARD L. FARMER

WEIHAIWEI, fine natural harbor in China near the Shandong Peninsula's northeastern tip. Weihaiwei was first developed in 1398 by the Ming dynasty as part of a network of defensive forts to protect against Japanese pirates. During the Qing dynasty the port languished under antimaritime policies until the 1880s, when it became a secondary base for the new North Sea (Beiyang) Fleet. The Japanese destroyed the remnants of that fleet at Weihaiwei in February 1895 in the last naval engagement of the Sino-Japanese War and then remained there until 1898, when Great Britain received a lease on the port and its hinterland. Under the British, the Colonial Office administered Weihaiwei and the harbor served as a summer station for the British fleet. In 1930 the British voluntarily returned Weihaiwei to China. The Japanese occupied Weihaiwei from 1938 to 1945 and since 1949 it has served as a Chinese Navy base, but has not greatly developed either as a commercial or industrial port because of its relative isolation and poor overland communications.

DAVID D. BUCK

WEI JINGSHENG (b. 1951), a young activist in the Chinese Democracy Movement of 1978 to 1979. The son of a Communist Party cadre, Wei had first questioned authority as a Red Guard in the Cultural Revolution and had become disillusioned with the socialist system after serving in the People's Liberation Army in northwest China in the early 1970s. After demobilization, he became an electrician in the Beijing zoo rather than serve as a minor official. After posting the article "The Fifth Modernization" on Democracy Wall on 15 December 1978, Wei became editor of the unofficial journal *Exploration (Tansuo)*. Wei and his associates represented the most internationally celebrated and radical of the dissidents, openly calling for human rights and democracy and challenging the leadership of the Communist Party.

After a special issue of 25 March 1979 publicly denounced the "dictatorship" of Deng Xiaoping, Wei and some of his associates were arrested. Six months later he was brought to trial on charges of divulging "official state secrets" and carrying out "counterrevolutionary propaganda and agitation."

An unofficial transcript of his one-day trial, officially open to the public but in fact closed to Wei's friends and to the foreign press, was circulated underground and eventually posted on Democracy Wall. His conviction and sentence to fifteen years in prison on 16 October 1979 brought a brief degree of unity to the Democracy Wall activists, as even "democratic socialist" dissidents came to his defense and denounced the crackdown on the movement. Nevertheless, even though Wei's sentence drew worldwide calls for leniency, including an appeal from Andrei Sakharov, his imprisonment marked the beginning of the decline of the Democracy Movement, which ended by 1981. To date Wei Jingsheng remains in prison, reportedly in solitary confinement.

[*See also* April Fifth Movement; Democracy Wall; *and* Spiritual Pollution.]

Kjeld Erik Brodsgaard, "The Democracy Movement in China, 1978–1979: Opposition Movements, Wall Poster Campaigns, and Underground Journals," *Asian Survey* 21.7 (July 1981): 747–774. Chen Ruoxi, *Democracy Wall and the Unofficial Journals* (1982). Roger Garside, *Coming Alive: China After Mao* (1981). James D. Seymour, ed., *The Fifth Modernization: China's Human Rights Movement, 1978–79* (1980).   JOHN A. RAPP

WEI MAN. *See* Wiman.

WEI YUAN (1794–1856), pathbreaking Chinese political thinker and geographer. Associated with the New Text (Jinwen) school of Confucian scholarship, he probed the classical canon for "ancient subtleties," or fresh moral messages. More demonstrably fruitful were his contributions to the Statecraft, or Practical Learning, school, which stressed government reform and fresh policies to cope with new times. *Collected Writings on Statecraft of the Reigning Dynasty* (1826), which Wei edited, was an influential compendium of essays on administrative topics, and he won additional attention with works on grain transport and Qing dynasty military policy.

Today Wei Yuan is remembered chiefly for his *Illustrated Treatise on the Maritime Kingdoms.* First appearing in the wake of the Opium War in 1844, this book sought to assess the geography, institutions, and strengths of the Western world as an aid toward coping with its aggressiveness. Wei's *Treatise* (or "gazetteer") is often described as China's first serious scholarly work on the West.

Arthur W. Hummel, ed., *Eminent Chinese of the Ch'ing Period* (1943–1944). Susan Mann Jones and Philip A.

Kuhn, "Dynastic Decline and the Roots of Rebellion," in *The Cambridge History of China,* vol. 10, edited by John K. Fairbank (1978), pp. 107–162.

IRWIN T. HYATT, JR.

WEI ZHONGXIAN (1568–1627), Chinese palace eunuch who dominated the Ming government from 1620 to 1627. Wei was probably the most powerful eunuch in Chinese history.

A native of Hebei, Wei became a eunuch at an advanced age and, working in the palace, eventually seized an opportunity to serve the mother of future emperor Zhu Yujiao. Suddenly thrust upon the throne at age fourteen, the young emperor retreated to carpentry, his favorite pastime, and left state affairs to the ambitious eunuch who, together with the boy's nursemaid, had come to dominate the palace. Upright ministers, especially those from the Donglin faction, criticized in vain Wei's overt efforts at self-aggrandizement. Using repression and terror, Wei had many capable officials ruthlessly killed or blacklisted. Thus the bureaucracy became submissive while Wei, at the height of his power, had temples to his own glory constructed throughout the empire and had honors and titles of nobility conferred upon his relatives. When the emperor died suddenly, Wei was banished from the capital and hanged himself rather than face criminal charges. Subsequently, his relatives and followers were all purged, but the government returned to a sounder basis with difficulty.

During Wei's traumatic rule governmental ethics reached a low ebb, administration was paralyzed, and many natural disasters and rebellions occurred. More ominously, all the land east of the Liao River was lost to the Manchus, who were to conquer the Ming within twenty years.

[*See also* Donglin Academy *and* Ming Dynasty.]

Robert B. Crawford, "Eunuch Power in the Ming Dynasty," *T'oung pao* 49.3 (1961): 115–148. Charles O. Hucker, "The Tung-lin Movement of the Late Ming Period," in *Chinese Thought and Institutions,* edited by John K. Fairbank (1957), pp. 132–162.

ROLAND L. HIGGINS

WELD, SIR FREDERICK (1823–1891), British governor of the Straits Settlements (1880–1887). A Catholic aristocrat, Weld spent twenty-five years in New Zealand, where he was premier of the colony in 1864–1865, and was later appointed governor, first of Western Australia (1869–1875) and then of

Tasmania (1875–1880). An imperialist who believed that great nations "must either advance or decay," Weld extended British control in Negri Sembilan and sent a British agent to the court of Pahang. In 1887 he negotiated British supervision of the foreign policies of Brunei, North Borneo, and Sarawak. Weld's vigorous governorship also included the promotion of Malay vernacular education.

A. Lovat, *The Life of Sir Frederick Weld* (1914). E. Sadka, *The Protected Malay States 1874–1895* (1968).

A. C. MILNER

WELLESLEY, ARTHUR (duke of Wellington; 1769–1852), third son of the earl of Mornington and younger brother of Richard, Lord Wellesley, who was governor-general of India. Arthur Wellesley began his rise to fame as an army officer in India (1797–1805) and became the most renowned of all sepoy generals. As commander of the *nizam*'s troops against Tipu Sultan, he was put in charge of Seringapatam after its fall in 1799. There he stopped plundering, restored order, and then governed Mysore territory. In his hunting down Dhoondia Waugh and in his campaign against the Maratha Confederacy, General Wellesley gained experience in guerrilla warfare. In rapid deployment of infantry, artillery, and cavalry, with complexities of logistical and commissariat support over long distances and difficult terrain, he was careful never to allow pillaging or alienating of villages through which his armies passed, preferring if possible to win country people by paying top prices for supplies. These lessons were later to be invaluable in Europe. His two greatest battles in India, Assaye and Argaom (1803), prepared him for his ultimate contests with Napoleon.

[*See also* Seringapatam; Marathas; *and* Sepoy.]

Elizabeth Longford, *Wellington: The Years of the Sword* (1969).   ROBERT E. FRYKENBERG

WELLESLEY, RICHARD COLLEY (earl of Mornington and marquis of Wellesley; 1760–1842), governor-general of India from 1798 to 1805. From impoverished Anglo-Irish gentry (original name, Wesley), Wellesley's ability was apparent long before public life, and titles opened early prospects for his attainment to highest office. As the highest officer in India, a virtually unfettered proconsul of government, he was provided the opportunity to win fame. Reading voraciously and preparing carefully, he cast an imperious eye upon the map of India and decided that the time had come to make the East India Company supreme. Napoleon's presence in Egypt, with grand designs upon India, and Tipu Sultan's "unfriendly" actions were deemed provocations. After destroying the Mysore regime and defeating the Marathas, and with the company's armies numbering some 300,000, he was able to impose his own kind of *Pax Indica*. To each prince, great or small, he gave a choice: either agree to a "permanent treaty," an "ever-lasting" alliance with the company, or face the prospect, at some future time, of being dethroned. Henceforth, so long as a prince let the company handle all relations with other powers; so long as he allowed a company resident at his court (an agent, ambassador, or "watchdog" to see that the regent lived up to treaty terms); so long as he kept a "contingent" of company troops, "camped" (in a cantonment) just outside his capital, for his own "protection"; and so long as he proved himself strong enough to rule his own people, a prince had little to fear. Without much more persuasion, many princely states in India submitted to this system of "subsidiary alliances." While further wars would break out, by the time the Great Proconsul left India in 1805, the East India Company's supremacy over much of India had been achieved. Henceforth, whether directly through hosts of Indian servants or indirectly through a few hundred Indian princes, the Raj would be British.

[*See also* East India Company; Princely States; *and* Governor-General of India.]

Iris Butler, *The Eldest Brother* (1973). Paul E. Roberts, *India under Wellesley* (1929).   ROBERT E. FRYKENBERG

WELLINGTON, DUKE OF. *See* Wellesley, Arthur.

WENG TONGHE (1830–1904), Chinese scholar, tutor to the Guangxu emperor (r. 1875–1898), and promoter of moderate reforms especially in the 1890s. Although he was a highly respected official who held many posts in the Qing court, Weng's reform inclinations angered conservative opponents and he was dismissed as tutor in 1896. Weng remained as an adviser and helped promote the radical reformer Kang Youwei in court circles between 1894 and 1897, but disassociated himself from Kang in May 1898 when the latter's ideas on Confucius as a reformer gained notoriety. In June 1898 Weng was forced to retire, most likely at the emperor's direction and not the empress dowager's, as has long been suspected.

[*See also* Kang Youwei.]

Luke S. K. Kwong, *A Mosaic of the Hundred Days* (1984).   ADRIAN A. BENNETT

WESTERN JIN DYNASTY. *See* Jin Dynasty.

WESTERN LEARNING. *See* Sŏhak.

WHAMPOA MILITARY ACADEMY. In 1924, sensing the fragility of the Guomindang (Kuomintang, Nationalist Party) because it lacked its own army, Sun Yat-sen established the Whampoa Military Academy near Canton (Guangzhou) to train officers for a party-led and controlled National Revolutionary Army. Chiang Kai-shek, the first commandant of the academy, formed close teacher-student relationships with many of the cadets, who fought with legendary courage during the battles of the Northern Expedition (1926–1928). In 1927 the academy was transferred to the new national capital in Nanjing and renamed the Central Military Academy. Many of the Whampoa graduates, especially of the first four classes, were subsequently among Chiang Kai-shek's most loyal supporters, forming what was informally known as the Whampoa clique. [*See also* China, Republic Period.]

LLOYD E. EASTMAN

WHITE LOTUS SOCIETY, Chinese folk sectarian tradition that became a powerful millenarian movement. Under its putative founder, the Southern Song Pure Land and Tiantai master Mao Ziyuan (1086–1166), the White Lotus evolved from its origins in Amidist pietism into a tradition that abandoned priestly celibacy, emphasized lay vegetarianism, and simplified texts and rituals.

By the Mongol Yuan dynasty (1279–1368), however, it had absorbed such cult practices as talismanic magic, prognostication, and exorcism into its belief system. With only one exception, during the period 1313 to 1322, the White Lotus sects were proscribed throughout the Yuan period. The movement underwent a dramatic change in the fourteenth century, when it was combined with Maitreya devotion, Manichaeism, and sectarian Daoism, resulting in the creation of a powerful chiliasm. White Lotus believers increasingly resorted to violence, motivated by an eschatological vision of their im-

minent victory over their evil oppressors. This provided the immediate context for the Red Turban Rebellion in late Yuan times.

With the founding of the Ming dynasty (1368–1644), White Lotus activities persisted despite vigilant proscription. In the sixteenth century White Lotus belief reached its mature form. This involved the worship of the Wusheng Laomu (Eternal Mother) as the progenitor of the human race and the espousal of the three-stage soteriological scheme in which Maitreyan deliverance was considered the imminent and final salvation. The formulation of this mature White Lotus doctrine triggered an intense scripture-writing activity among the sectarians, and numerous *baojuan* (sacred scrolls) were composed during this time.

The White Lotus movement continued to exist during the Qing dynasty. The devastating rebellion of 1796 to 1805 bearing its name was the best manifestation of its tenacity. The tradition lasted well into this century in such groups as the Boxers and the Yiguan Dao.

[*See also* Han Liner; Rebellions in China; Yihetuan; *and* Secret Societies.]

Susan Naquin, *Millenarian Rebellion in China: The Eight Trigrams Uprising of 1813* (1976) and *Shantung Rebellion* (1981). Daniel L. Overmyer, *Folk Buddhist Religion* (1976).   RICHARD SHEK

WICHITWATHAKAN, LUANG (1898–1962), Thai political leader. Born in Uthaithani Province to a business family, Luang Wichitwathakan was educated in temple schools. Leaving a promising career in the monkhood, he joined the Ministry of Foreign Affairs. He studied law in Bangkok and at the University of Paris but never finished. Somewhat of a scholar and a prolific writer, Wichit was appointed director-general of the Fine Arts Department in 1934 and he helped produce nationalistic plays and speeches. Under Luang Phibunsongkhram, Wichit was minister of education and minister of foreign affairs. He was ambassador to Tokyo until the surrender of Japan.

When Phibun returned to power in 1948, Wichit was given the finance and economic affairs portfolios. He later became the political mentor of Sarit Thanarat.

[*See also* Phibunsongkhram, Luang *and* Sarit Thanarat.]

Thak Chaloemtiarana, *Thailand: The Politics of Despotic Paternalism* (1979).   THAK CHALOEMTIARANA

WILLIAM OF RUBRUCK (fl. 1255), Flemish Franciscan missionary sent by King Louis IX of France to the Mongols from 1253 to 1255. His letters, written as a report to Louis IX on William's return to Antioch, added substantially to Europe's knowledge of the Mongol empire and the court of the Grand Khan. This report exists only in four manuscript versions (three at Corpus Christi College, Cambridge, and one in the British Museum). His work lay largely unknown for three centuries until Richard Hakluyt published it in an abbreviated form in his *Principal Navigations* (1598–1600).

Little is known of William's life outside his *Itinerarium,* which modern scholars recognize as an accurate and historically important work. As William's mission was primarily to be apostolic, he gives accounts of many of the religious creeds of Asia in great detail, having debated religious doctrines with various Asian priests. He gives a vivid description of many societies and cultures of Asia, and, although he did not visit China himself, he equates the kingdom of Seres mentioned by the Romans with the empire of Cathay. He relates in detail his audiences with Mongke Khan at the Mongol capital of Karakorum.

C. R. Beazley, *The Texts and Versions of John of Plano Carpini and William of Rubruquis,* in *Works Issued by the Hakluyt Society,* extra series, vol. 13 (1903). William W. Rockhill, ed., *The Journeys of William of Rubruck and John of Pian de Carpine to Tartary in the 13th Century,* in *Works Issued by the Hakluyt Society,* ser. 2, vol. 4 (1900).   THEODORE NICHOLAS FOSS

WILOPO (1909–1981), Indonesian nationalist politician. Wilopo trained as a lawyer and was active in both Taman Siswa and the nationalist Partindo and Gerindo. He helped found the postwar Partai Nasional Indonesia (PNI) and was a leading figure on its liberal-socialist wing. He was minister in the Hatta and Sukiman cabinets and from April 1952 to August 1953 headed a PNI-Masjumi coalition government that introduced austerity measures in the army and bureaucracy, prompting army-sponsored agitation in October 1952 for the dissolution of Parliament. His cabinet fell over its handling of the shooting of squatters being removed by police from Dutch estates in East Sumatra.

[*See also* Taman Siswa; Gerindo; Partai Nasional Indonesia; Hatta, Mohammad; Sukiman Wirjosandjojo; *and* Masjumi.]

Herbert Feith, *The Decline of Constitutional Democracy in Indonesia* (1962). J. Eliseo Rocamora, *National-*

ism in Search of Ideology: The Indonesian Nationalist Party, 1946–1965 (1975).   ROBERT B. CRIBB

WIMAN (Chinese, Wei Man), Chinese military leader who became the ruler of the Korean state of Chosŏn in the second century BCE. During the early years of the Former Han dynasty (206 BCE–8 CE) in China there were a number of unsuccessful risings against the new regime. One of these took place in Yan, in northeastern China; when it was crushed in 195 BCE, Wiman, a lieutenant of the rebels, escaped through the frontier passes to take refuge in northern Korea. This area had been open to Chinese influence for some time, as is suggested by the finds of coins from late Warring States China in the valleys of the Yalu and Taedong rivers. Moreover, Chinese sources of the Han period state that numbers of Chinese refugees fled to northern Korea when the state of Qin unified China and destroyed the ancient kingdom of Yan in 222 BCE and again when the Qin dynasty itself collapsed between 208 and 206 BCE. Wiman apparently made himself leader of these Chinese settlers, and with their support established his own kingdom with its capital at Wanggŏm, near modern P'yŏngyang. [*See also* Yan.]

It is not clear whether any organized state existed in Korea before Wiman's arrival. A third century Chinese text, the *Weilüe,* speaks of a prior kingdom of Chosŏn founded by the ancient Chinese sage Jizi (Korean, Kija), whose descendants are said to have ruled for forty generations before being dispossessed by Wiman, whereupon they migrated to the region inhabited by the Han tribes of southern Korea. No earlier text mentions such a kingdom, however, and it is quite possible that the *Weilüe's* story represents merely the aspirations of sinicized inhabitants of Korea after a long period of Chinese rule. [*See also* Kija Chosŏn.]

Wiman's state endured for three generations—less than a century in all. His grandson Yuqiu (Korean, Ugŏ) annoyed the Han Emperor Wu (r. 141–87 BCE) by harboring political exiles from China and interfering with Chinese contacts with the Han tribes to the south of Chosŏn. The Chinese for their part tried to exploit the tensions that existed between the Chinese ruling house of Chosŏn and the native Korean chieftains. After a series of frontier incidents, two separate armies were dispatched to Korea by land and sea in the autumn of 109 BCE. Operations were prolonged owing to the bitter resistance of Chosŏn and the total inability of the two Chinese generals to cooperate with one another, but in the summer of 108 a group of Chosŏn ministers murdered their king and surrendered. The lands of the former kingdom were annexed to China and divided into four administrative units or commanderies, of which the most important, Lelang, was set up in the heartland of the old Chosŏn kingdom.

[*See also* Commanderies in Korea, Chinese.]

KENNETH H. J. GARDINER

WOMEN

WOMEN IN CHINA

Few societies in history have prescribed for women a more lowly status or treated them in a more routinely brutal way than traditional Confucian China. Belief in the interaction of principles of yin (dark, earth, cold, negative, death, etc.) and yang (light, heaven, warmth, positive, life, etc.) formed the basis of an ancient Chinese cosmology that, it is said, presented an essentially androgynous vision of the universe. However benign the origin of these notions, the confucianization of ancient Chinese cosmology assigned yin to female and yang to male, which froze them in a rigid hierarchy of submission and dominance, passivity and activity, weakness and strength. This hierarchy fundamentally permeated dominant Chinese culture and religion for nearly two thousand years. Few, if any, corners of Chinese life failed to reflect this gender hierarchy, rationalized through cosmological belief and regularized in practice through Confucian ritual.

The classics buried women's personalities and lives under the weight of the "three bonds of obedience": to obey one's father when young, one's husband when married, and one's adult sons when widowed. For centuries, treatises endlessly memorized and recited exhorted females to servility, passivity, and self-effacement. Elite ideals of female propriety encouraged the ultimate act of self-negation—suicide—as an honorable response to violations of chastity. The social position of women was reflected in a practice of female mutilation known as footbinding, a thousand-year-old institution that, among other things, stood as an expression of one of history's most powerful sadomasochistic male fantasies. Throughout their lives, women were supposed to be only slightly more than chattel, routinely bought and sold in marriage, concubinage, or outright slavery.

The life and death consequences of being born female in traditional China can be gleaned from traditional literature, travelers' tales, personal recollections, and scattered statistics, mostly from the nineteenth and twentieth centuries. They include a female suicide profile that exceeded men's at all ages and bulged during the painful years of betrothal and early marriage, relatively high rates of female infanticide in times of economic hardship, and significantly higher mortality rates among the numerous young girls who were "adopted" in childhood for marriage. The unbalanced and sometimes seriously skewed sex-ratios that have been reported among the population (as high as 156 males to 100 females in one Shaanxi county in 1829) reflect in part, at least, these types of horrors.

In the nineteenth and twentieth centuries Chinese began to turn a critical eye upon their own society and a consciousness of the blatant abuses of women began to surface among a segment of the population. Because of the centrality of Confucianism and the heirarchical, male-dominated Confucian family institution to all aspects of traditional society, growing concerns for general political and social reform inevitably led to consideration of issues involving the family and the status of women.

With the decline of the Qing dynasty under the impact of modern imperialism, various types of reformers came to believe that the traditional family and its Confucian values needed to be altered in the effort to revitalize China's national condition. Small but vocal women's rights groups that grew in urban centers called for a broad range of basic rights for women: the right to free choice in marriage, the right to divorce, the right to own and inherit property, the right to receive the same education as their brothers did, the right to vote, and the right to hold political office. The intellectual ferment of the student-based May Fourth Movement in the late 1910s gave further impetus to an increasingly radical critique of Chinese society, including the traditional lowly social and economic status of women.

In the early 1920s an urban-based Chinese Communist Party (CCP) emerged on the heels of the May Fourth Movement and soon embraced the general demands of the urban women's groups. Although suspicious of the reformist, "bourgeois" nature of these groups, the Party nonetheless sought to appeal to activist women students and intellectuals who supported these groups. The Party was even more interested in organizing women workers, who constituted a significant part of China's puny, but volatile, working class. After the mid-1920s the Party also began to look to rural women and youth as sources of support in its efforts to move out from the cities and build a mass peasant base.

Quickly, however, the Party came up against a harsh reality: a major source of Red Army recruits came from families driven off the land, young men aspiring both to regain the land and to restore the traditional familial basis of rural life. It was precisely this marginalized peasantry deprived by poverty and war not only of land but of the prospects of marriage that was traditionally drawn to banditry. If urban youth frequently turned with a vengeance on the traditional Chinese family, many peasant revolutionaries sought to re-create the familial patriarchal, patrilineal structures that poverty denied them. As the party discovered after 1927, when it became fully lodged in the countryside for the duration of the revolutionary struggle, the emancipation of women could be a deeply divisive issue among its primary constituency, the rural (male) poor. As the Party tried to build a rural male army, it increasingly shied away from attempts to propagandize and implement women's rights, especially those that directly challenged traditional masculine rights over women in the family. This tendency has been present in Party policy toward women in most periods of the postrevolutionary era as well.

This is not to assert that the Party abandoned all efforts to change rural women's traditional roles. When central Party priorities have been involved, the Party has moved to enlist women's involvement in revolution and socialist construction in ways that have required changes impinging on the family and traditional female roles, especially economic roles. Through waging a protracted revolutionary guerrilla war, the party came to recognize the important contributions that mobilized rural women could make. Women's labor and support were crucial in recruiting husbands and sons into the army, in replacing men in the agricultural economy, and in performing essential (if "secondary") services for local guerrilla forces and the army (ranging from intelligence gathering to making shoes). The mobilization of women's labor was also key to the success of the labor-intensive "production war" strategy in the early 1940s that saved the Communist-led anti-Japanese base areas during the Yan'an era from economic collapse and strangulation by the enemy. In Yan'an, as in later mobilizations, economic strategies often required that the Party confront certain aspects of traditional taboos and family restrictions on women's time and labor in order to make full use of the resources of women and the family. But the Party has only rarely gone further than necessary to release women's labor.

In emphasizing the mobilization of women's labor as the centerpiece of policy, the dominant Party view has drawn upon the classic, and sorely inadequate, Marxist approach to the liberation of women as derived from the highly influential work of Frederick Engels. According to this view, once women are fully integrated into remunerative social production, interrelated changes in all other areas of family, society, and culture will naturally follow: women's traditional dependence on men will be broken, women will play a larger role in community and family life, and new norms of equality and female worth will reflect the new relationship of women to production. In the late 1950s collectivization and the abolition of private property, which eliminates the family as a basic economic unit and provides the organizational basis for the large-scale participation of women in production outside the home, was supposed to eliminate the remaining bases of patriarchal power and ideology and usher in a society characterized by complete gender equality. Thus, the official view of women has stressed heavily, often exclusively, the economic determinants of the status of women, with the major concern placed on mobilizing women into social production.

The dominant view that changing the relationship of women to production will ineluctably change their family, social, and political status has not, however, been the only perspective advanced since 1949. In the early 1950s, in an atmosphere temporarily more conducive to the promotion of "bourgeois democratic" rights, considerable attention was directed toward the democratic reform of patriarchal family attitudes and customs, even at some risk of creating conflict with male supporters. The proponents of these efforts criticized the overly sanguine views that had dominated "women work" in the 1940s. These reformers stressed that patriarchal structures, customs, and ideology were deeply rooted in popular attitudes and had a tenacity independent of the "feudal" economic and political system that presumably gave rise to and supported them. Such patriarchal structures, beliefs, and customs would not automatically collapse in response to the new political and economic relations being established in the villages.

Thus, reformers urged that the Party carry out a national campaign to implement the new Marriage Law passed in 1950. The law abolished arranged, "buying and selling marriages based on the supremacy of man over woman," and it gave women divorce and child custody rights; equal rights to own, manage, and inherit family property; the right to free participation in work and in social activities;

and the right to retain their own family names after they married.

For a brief period, the Party did in fact respond to those advocating a stronger and more direct approach to women's rights and family reform, organizing a mobilization campaign to popularize and implement the Marriage Law. Through this mobilization campaign, family reformers in the early 1950s sought to challenge directly the patriarchal family system in rural areas. Nevertheless, after years of war and famine, the moral order and security of the ideal traditional family surely retained its appeal for many. The task of marriage reformers was to introduce a new vision of a reformed egalitarian family system at a time when millions who had effectively lost all meaningful family relationships, and millions more who had desperately managed to maintain some semblance of the traditional normative relationships, were attempting to reknit their families.

Not surprisingly, efforts to implement the law stirred resistance in a variety of quarters, including within the ranks of the Party. While some degree of footdragging and avoidance could be found even at the top level of the Party, resistance to the reforms was most noticeable at the bottom of the hierarchy that was dominated by predominantly male rural cadres, many of whom ignored, slighted, or actively subverted the Marriage Law. The reforms also met various forms of resistance, sometimes violent, within the villages. Male resistance to reforms that challenged the normative basis of their traditional family power and privileges was predictable and well documented in newspapers published during the early 1950s. Somewhat less well documented, but clearly evident, was the fact that many women, especially older women, also often resisted the introduction of the new marriage and family practices.

There were a number of hard-headed, self-protecting reasons for older women to resist some of the new family practices. Women who had had no voice in their own marriages, who had already struggled to overcome the traditional lowly status of new stranger-bride and daughter-in-law, expected in their older years to have a strong voice in their children's marriages, especially in the matter of acquiring a daughter-in-law. An obedient, hard-working daughter-in-law who accepted her traditional role could greatly ease the burden on her mother-in-law, while a rebellious, independent, or "modern-minded" young woman (such as the kind who would dare to take a hand in her own marriage) would be far more likely to violate such expectations. Most important, older women sought to use

traditional marriage customs to protect what Margery Wolf has identified as the "uterine family"—an informal mother-centered group that women built within the formal patriarchal, patrilineal family structure.

Women's uterine families were necessarily built around mother-son bonds, for sons remained members of their natal families through life while daughters were "lost" at marriage to another male family group. (Traditionally, marriage was patrilocal, meaning that a woman married into her husband's family and moved to his place of residence. Furthermore, it was often exogamous as well, that is, it was taboo for a woman to marry a man from her native village, so that marriage required that she leave her own kin and native community for the unfamiliar community of her stranger-husband and his kin, a place where she could never fully gain the status of a native.) These uterine families provided women with one of their primary means for overcoming the loneliness of being an outsider in their husbands' families and villages and for circumventing the powerlessness that the formal patriarchal, patrilineal structures and norms sought to impose on them. An arranged blind marriage and the traditional daughter-in-law's lowly status helped older women protect the crucial mother-son bond from the potential threat of a strong husband-wife bond or a strong-willed daughter-in-law striving to establish her own independent uterine family. In this way, the traditional family system pitted women against each other and created generational cleavages that cut across a gender-defined underclass. The Marriage Law threatened not only patriarchal power but, inadvertently, older women's uterine families as well.

Because of the resistance encountered in the villages, marriage reform advocates began to advocate more moderate methods in popularizing the reforms and increasingly emphasized the legal and moral responsibility of adult children to respect and support their parents in old age. At the same time, reform advocates persisted in trying to prod the Party apparatus into more serious implementation efforts.

Finally, the top leadership did increase its organizational and political commitment briefly in late 1952 and early 1953 and the political system responded with some degree of effectiveness. As a result of various educational activities, women and young people in the countryside became more aware of their new rights and larger numbers began to use these rights. In at least some local areas forces favoring reform emerged and appear to have gained in strength. Even before the campaign began, and before the issues had been effectively joined in most areas, however, there were signs of vacillation at the highest levels, where some leaders feared that the campaign would create too much divisive social conflict among peasant activists. Ceremonial activities observing the death of Stalin were allowed to cut short marriage reform activities in early 1953 when these were just getting under way in many rural areas.

After 1953 not even moderate proposals to continue national-level efforts for family and marriage reform commanded the necessary leadership support. Marriage reform never again was accorded sufficiently high priority by the Party to warrant a national campaign. As the state focused on economic construction and cooperative transformation in the countryside, it became increasingly concerned with maintaining family stability and reinforcing the patrilineally shaped traditional bases of community solidarity upon which new cooperative structures could be built. Thus, far from pursuing marriage reform vigorously, it encouraged an increasingly restrictive interpretation of the Marriage Law's divorce clause to reduce the peak divorce levels reached in 1953. Women found it increasingly difficult to exercise their divorce rights and it became increasingly easy for husbands and in-laws to protect bride-price investments that even today remain widespread in many parts of rural China.

The responsibility for overseeing reform and the protection of women's and young people's new family rights fell to unsupervised local male cadres whose political and social orientations in their native villages were heavily shaped by the patrilineal kinship ties and networks of male-defined family groups that have traditionally formed the basis of community in rural China. Collectivization, which the party in the mid- and late 1950s claimed to be the key to fully realizing family reform and women's emancipation, actually reinforced these networks. Policies then froze them in place by prohibiting significant population movement among rural collective units (except, of course, for the movement of women through patrilocal marriage) or from rural units to urban areas. Since the early 1950s with few exceptions issues of gender equality have been raised only when the leadership has felt they bore a direct relation to the success of campaigns and central efforts aimed at other priorities, such as increasing agricultural production and, more recently, controlling population growth.

The major focus of policy toward rural women in most periods has been on the mobilization of their labor. The collectivization drives of the late 1950s were predicated on the notion that there was a reservoir of "underutilized" labor in the countryside that the collectives could productively tap. A major source of this underutilized labor was women. While collectivization, and the state centralization of markets for raw materials, further undermined many cottage handicraft industries that traditionally employed women in some parts of the countryside, women's participation in field labor and collective agricultural sidelines was increased under the collectives. By the late 1970s relatively high and stable rates of female participation in agriculture had been attained.

Efforts to increase these female participation rates over the years were occasionally accompanied by efforts to overcome the nearly universal tendency of the collectives, dominated by male cadres, to discriminate against women in remuneration. While significant improvements were made in many places, many collectives persisted in policies that systematically discriminated against women, such as setting a ceiling of seven work points per day for women while allowing men to earn up to ten work points. In order to facilitate women's higher participation rates, local units were also encouraged to establish day-care services. Such services were set up in increasing numbers of villages in the late 1960s and 1970s, but they remained inadequate to relieve the burdens of more than a minority of working rural mothers. For example, one study of rural Guangdong, where women's participation rates have been among the highest, only slightly less than men's, found that only 19 percent of the production brigades had any kind of year-round day care.

Left with most domestic responsibilities, rural Chinese women have been trapped with the classic double burden of two jobs. The redistribution of domestic work that has occurred has mostly involved a shift from younger to older women within the family. Although women have benefited from expanded economic roles in many respects, they have had to bear a significantly unequal burden for their "liberation through labor."

It is too early to know how the economic reforms of the early 1980s and the current "responsibility system," which decentralizes the management of rural labor to the family, will affect these patterns. Some have argued that the new policies will worsen the position of women. In the mid-1980s it seems unlikely that policies will result in any radical alterations in either direction. In some areas there are indications that women's agricultural labor has decreased under the new system, while women have taken advantage of new opportunities to take up more highly remunerated (and traditionally preferred) handicraft production for local, national, and even international markets. In other areas, such as those close to major urban centers, women seem to be left playing an increasingly dominant role in low-status agricultural labor as men are drawn off to more lucrative nonagrarian work opportunities. With fewer funds available for collective services, it also seems likely that day-care services will diminish, although this will not represent a change for the majority of rural women. Certainly, the double day and double burden are likely to continue for most women as families struggle to take advantage of new income-earning opportunities to improve their still meager standard of living.

In the 1980s the family, and women's relationship to it, has remained one of the most traditional features of a predominantly rural Chinese society. The outcome of nearly a century of upheaval and revolution, born partly of widespread family crises among intellectuals and peasants, has done more to restore the traditional role and structure of the rural family than to fundamentally reform it. The impact of kinship practices and customs of patrilocality and village exogamy on women's subordinate family and community status, the ways in which women were systematically made outsiders to both while men remained rooted natives and life-long members of their parents' families with permanent obligations of loyalty and support, remained unrecognized by Party policy. With respect to "buying and selling" marriages, bride-price practices and the realization of women's property, child custody, and divorce rights, the evidence is that little if any change has occurred in many rural areas.

In the mid-1970s the problems posed by traditional, exclusively patrilineal patterns gained official recognition for the first time. In the context of the 1974 anti-Confucian campaign (the only campaign since the early 1950s to address the impact of traditional male supremacist attitudes on family and society in more than a perfunctory way), matrilocal marriage was proposed as a progressive alternative to exclusive patrilocal patterns. For the first time, it was suggested that the insistence that women always marry into their husbands' families and communities, rather than vice versa, was a manifestation of "feudal" male supremacist attitudes.

Significantly, the issue surfaced not primarily out of concern for gender inequality, but in connection with urgent state efforts to promote rural family planning. As family-planning cadres and top policy makers became more concerned with reducing fertility rates, they had to confront the reasons peasants continued to prefer sons over daughters and therefore resisted pressures to limit the number of children until they had at least one, and preferably two, sons. The fact is that regardless of how much progress is made in expanding women's remunerative economic roles and making women equal breadwinners with men (a goal far from realization), as a result of patrilineal family structures and patrilocal marriage practice, daughters are "lost" at marriage to their husband's family. Even though village exogamous taboos seem to have weakened over the years, they continue to operate in many areas so that daughters usually marry into another village. Embedded in the meaning of marriage for women is the transfer of their labor, filial obligations, and fertility to another patrilineal family groups. Bride-price practices both symbolize and reinforce this transfer of "rights in women" at marriage, while restricting women's own rights to the fruits of their labor, the determination of their personal obligations, and control over their fertility.

Given these traditional practices and structures and given the central importance of traditional corporate forms of family security in dealing with elderly and disabled family members, sons remain crucial to the support of parents in their old age. It was in this context that matrilocal marriage was first suggested. Parents who had no sons might then be able to substitute daughters to fulfill their old-age security needs and younger couples might be more easily convinced that it was not essential to continue to bear children until they produced a son. Since the mid-1970s population limitation has become an increasingly urgent state priority. It is now clear that lack of progress for three decades in formerly "low priority" areas such as women's emancipation had direct and adverse affects on such current priorities as population control and increased living standards for rural people.

Some side effects of family planning are likely to contribute to gender equality by weakening traditional patrilineal family orientations. On the other hand, as the state moves vigorously against behavior rooted in traditional family structures and attitudes, women are sure to be caught in the crossfire. Since the late 1970s women have been pressured to drastically reduce their fertility, in many cases through late abortion, while remaining trapped in unreformed family structures in which their status, personal influence, and security depend on traditional childbearing functions, on the successful development of their own uterine families, and on their personal relationships with sons. The clash between unreformed family structures and attitudes on the one hand, and forcefully implemented government demands for one- (or at most two-) child families on the other, led in the late 1970s and early 1980s to a revival of female infanticide in some areas.

In the long run family planning approaches that seek to overcome attitudes toward fertility rooted in traditional structures exclusively by means of economic incentives, harsh punishments, and political coercion rather than investing in efforts to reform these structures are not only inhumane but may produce a powerful backlash. Current population and family policies are politically and morally costly (far more costly than serious marriage reform efforts ever were); a successful program ultimately requires basic changes in structures and attitudes.

Lucien Bianco, "Birth Control in China: Local Data and their Reliability," *China Quarterly* 85 (March 1981): 85. Deborah Davis-Friedmann, *Long Lives: Chinese Elderly and the Communist Revolution* (1983). Frederick Engels, *The Origin of the Family, Private Property and the State* (1942). Kay Ann Johnson, *Women, the Family and Peasant Revolution in China* (1983). Steven Mosher, *Broken Earth* (1983), chap. 9. William Parish and Martin Whyte, *Village and Family in Contemporary China* (1978). Janet Salaff, "The Emerging Conjugal Relationship in the People's Republic of China," *Journal of Marriage and the Family* (November 1973): 705–717. Margery Wolf, *Women and the Family in Rural Taiwan* (1972). Margery Wolf and Roxane Witke, eds., *Women in Chinese Society* (1975).   KAY ANN JOHNSON

WOMEN IN JAPAN

Japanese women in modern times, as in eras past, reflect the character and spirit of their society. At the same time, they have, since World War II, served as the underlying stabilizing force in their country's dramatic process of social change and economic expansion. Both this role and their conscientious adherence to democracy give them leverage for increased power in national decision making.

Legendary and early historical records point to the important role of women in Japanese society. Mythology holds that the female deity, the sun goddess Amaterasu Ōmikami, founded the imperial line that has reigned more than one thousand years. Early Chinese chronicles describe powerful queens of Yamatai in western Japan who brought order to the land. In the sixth to eighth century, the "epoch of the queens," one-half of the Japanese rulers were

women. Vigorous and intelligent, they set standards of religion and government and encouraged the arts. Imperial enthusiasm for Buddhism, introduced from Korea in the sixth century; for Chinese centralized political organization and Confucianism, introduced a century later; and for the warrior cult that followed slowly modified age-old religious practices and local autonomy and established a hierarchical society. The position of women eroded.

Only in the Heian period of the tenth and eleventh centuries did women again shine forth before the feudal shogunate prevailed. Lady Murasaki, author of the *Tale of Genji,* and other high-born women writers portrayed in their novels, memoirs, and poetry the elegant court life of their time. They created the first—and possibly best—literature in the Japanese language and bequeathed to future Japanese women the influential role of writer as social commentator.

The dictum that characterized women's lives through the middle period of the twelfth to nineteenth century is best summed up in the doctrine of the "three obediences" adjuring them into lifetime obedience, in turn, to father, husband, and son. Japanese Buddhism diminished women, and Neo-Confucian teachings, especially the 1672 book of morals, *Onna daigaku (Greater Learning for Women),* by Kaibara Ekken, admonished them to be subservient and aware of their limited mind and capacity. Legal codes kept pace with these philosophies. While feudal samurai, or warrior-class, women provided examples of physical and moral courage in the many clan power struggles preceding the ascendancy of the Tokugawa, ordinary women drudged at home and in the rice fields. Hōjō Masako, the "general in nun's habit," stands alone for her political impact.

Emergence of modern women since the mid-nineteenth century has involved the contrapuntal balancing of the traditional values and way of life against efforts toward emancipation. The opening of Japan to the West and the Meiji emperor's endorsement of "enlightenment" and industrialization led to universal elementary education and the employment of girls outside the home in the textile industries. Western friends and missionaries helped initiate private middle and higher education and supported overseas training. These unusual intercultural experiences enabled some, including Hiratsuka Raicho, Katō (Ishimoto) Shidzue, and Tsuda Ume, to escape the restraints of the "Confucian box" and to develop the leadership to pioneer in education, early feminism, social freedoms, and economic and political rights. The mainstream pursued the classic role of "good wives and wise mothers." Finally, exigencies of the China and Pacific wars cut short all liberalizing steps until the emancipating constitutional and civil code changes, wrought by the American Occupation of 1945 to 1952, established legal equality.

Contemporary women have quietly implemented a sweeping social revolution. Essentially the *senchūha*, or midwar generation, effected the postwar switchover from the patriarchal "house system" to the nuclear family and coped with the rearing of children under new democratic guidelines. They struggled with new rights of choice about marriage, divorce, or a single existence, and deftly carried out the demographic revolution making the two-child family acceptable. All women now deal with the results of the modernized life cycle: increasing education with more girls than boys graduating from high school and one-third going on to college, smaller families, mechanization in the home, and life expectancy of eighty years, the world's highest. Their success in adjusting the tempo of these traumatic changes has made possible societal stability in the midst of driving economic growth.

Unfinished business in the achievement of equality focuses on the work force and political power—issues of feminist agitation worldwide. Even in these areas, however, women have influenced national trends and policies. Escaping from the time-honored system whereby teenage girls provided cheap, rotating labor, women have pressed their revised life-cycle situation into modifying work-force patterns. The number of working women has risen, doubling from 1961 to 1983. The increase comes from the unprecedented return of married and older women, 60 percent part-time, into the workplace, a phenomenon calling for managerial innovation. Wages have risen, but hover at 53 percent of that of men. Women are concentrated in the service, manufacturing, and retail fields; high tech and computers offer new opportunities. The number of those in the professions has expanded, and some 6 percent are managerial.

Political participation of women has been growing since enfranchisement in 1945, for they take their democratic duties seriously. By the late 1960s more women and a higher percentage than men voted. Not aggressive in party affairs, they hold about 3 percent of Diet seats, but the rate in local and prefectural assemblies continues to grow. They espouse clean politics, for years inspired by Ichikawa Fusae, a political activist since World War I, a Diet member, and a spiritual and political leader for

the young as well as for women. Concerns about community issues of pollution, consumer quality and prices, and social infrastructure have, in the last twenty years, aroused women, organizationally and politically, into citizen action that has compelled national attention and remedies. Women are stalwarts of peace. Their delegate to the United Nations women's conference in 1985 assessed Japanese women's status in the words of the feminist poet Yosano Akiko, "women, who once slept, are everywhere now wide awake and, like the mountains, moving."

Gail Lee Bernstein, *Haruko's World: A Japanese Farm Woman and Her Community* (1983). Alice H. Cook and Hayashi Hiroko, *Working Women in Japan: Discrimination, Resistance, and Reform* (1980). Liza Dalby, *Geisha* (1983). Ishimoto Shidzue, *Facing Two Ways: The Story of My Life* (1984). Susan J. Pharr, *Political Women in Japan: The Search for a Place in Political Life* (1981). Dorothy Robins-Mowry, *The Hidden Sun: Women of Modern Japan* (1983). Sharon L. Sievers, *Flowers in Salt: The Beginnings of Feminist Consciousness in Modern Japan* (1983).   DOROTHY ROBINS-MOWRY

WOMEN IN SOUTH AND SOUTHEAST ASIA

Women in the great span of countries of South Asia and Southeast Asia live in communities diverse in custom and ethnoreligious culture. Broadly speaking, they have been influenced by the major religious traditions of Buddhism, Hinduism, Islam, Christianity, and Confucianism—all of which delineate women's roles and emphasize their obligations. In Hindu India, women's subordination to men was enshrined in religious law and custom, especially through the *Laws of Manu,* which took shape around the second century CE. Women were considered dangerously polluting and were excluded from chief religious rituals. Women's social status in Hinduism was associated with child marriage, the absence of rights to land or property, the prohibition of remarriage for widows, and for divorced women, the loss of access to their children. In Islam, women were granted certain legal rights and theoretical equal status with men, but were socially confined through the practice of *purdah,* or seclusion, which seems to have originated as a custom to enforce standards of feminine modesty.

On the other hand, the Hindu notion of divinity—*shakti* ("power")—is a feminine principle, and the goddesses of the Hindu pantheon were considered far more exemplary than their male counterparts. [*See* Hinduism.] In Buddhist India during the reign of Ashoka, women attained prominence and distinction in the arts and literature. The Mughal court (sixteenth to eighteenth century), in spite of the drawback of *purdah,* could boast of women who excelled in science, philosophy, and literature. Queens throughout the ages wielded political power similar to male rulers.

Women in Southeast Asia historically have enjoyed relatively greater freedom and respect than those in South Asia. Religious and historical mythologies furnished an ethical basis for independent female roles. The predominance of bilateral and matrilineal kinship among Southeast Asian peoples and the abundance of fertile land for cultivation were also responsible factors. The patriarchal practice of dowry gives way to the custom of bride price in Southeast Asia; there is bilateral inheritance and women are able to draw on the support of their families in time of need. Throughout Southeast Asia women control the family budget, purchase and own land, are heavily involved in wet-rice cultivation, and importantly, control local markets and trade. The conjugal relationship tends to be strong, and women's predominance in the family gives them a major sense of responsibility for its survival.

However, women hold low symbolic positions in the religious hierarchy of the Buddhist societies of Burma and Thailand. In Indonesia, *adat,* or customary law associated with high female status, has been modified by Hindu and Islamic influence, and in Malaysia the strong influence of Islam has lowered considerably the status of women. Nevertheless, Burmese and Thai society have egalitarian features similar to those in the largely Islamic Indonesia, the predominantly Catholic Philippines, and the formerly Confucian Vietnam.

Throughout southern Asia women traditionally have labored as cultivators, traders, and family workers. In Southeast Asia women work in paddy cultivation as intensively as men. Female labor outside the family in South India is common, and in many areas of India and Sri Lanka women predominate as landless laborers. Where *purdah* is enforced, as in Islamic Bengal, women tend not to work in the fields or go to the market, working within the confines of the household.

During the epoch of European domination in southern Asia (eighteenth to twentieth century), new economic patterns and roles were introduced. Colonial export economies attracted labor to European estates and coastal cities, undermining women-centered and family-based agriculture in both upland swidden and lowland subsistence agriculture. The migration of immigrant labor, especially Chinese and Indian workers, shifted the balance of ethnic communities, most notably in Malaya. The pressures of population increases and market economies greatly affected family strategies for survival. Beginning in the late nineteenth century, anticolonial movements agitated for political reform, social justice, and women's rights. Indian nationalists—from the nonviolence struggle of Gandhi to the violent activities of revolutionaries—pressed for reform of religious-based rules for women and advocated bringing women into public life. In the 1920s nationalists began pressing for women's suffrage. In Vietnam the anticolonial movement, dominated after 1930 by the Indochina Communist Party, sought radical redefinitions of women's roles in the family and society, leading to their greater social and political participation. Women activists were trained as guerrilla leaders and land reform cadres. In Indonesia there was a proliferation of women's organizations, which helped establish women as part of the struggle for independence against the Dutch. Women were also brought into politics for the first time in Malaya during the anti-British movement.

With independence, the states of southern Asia developed educational opportunities for women and sought to improve their legal and constitutional rights. Women's organizations, such as in Indonesia, Vietnam, and India, continued to press for social reforms and political equality, although mostly under affiliation with male-dominated political parties. Political and economic opportunities have widened for middle- and upper-class women, especially in India and the Philippines. Overall, however, women have failed to achieve full and equal representation in politics and government. Women's participation in the labor force has fluctuated since colonial rule, but some new patterns have emerged. Young women have been drawn into work in factories and industrial centers, as the number of women landless laborers, tourist workers, and migrants—urban and international—continues to expand. At the same time, state-sponsored attempts at religious revival, as in Islamic Pakistan and Malaysia, have challenged westernized norms and values of feminine behavior. In the socialist countries of Indochina, the "feminization" of agriculture has accompanied protracted periods of warfare and military mobilization.

Leela Dube, *Studies on Women in Southeast Asia: A Status Report* (1980). Kok-Sim Fan, *Women in Southeast Asia: A Bibliography* (1982). Rounaq Jahan and Hanna Papanek, *Women and Development: Perspectives from South and Southeast Asia* (1979). Nici Nelson, *Women *in Development: Why Has Development Neglected Rural Women? A Review of the South Asia Literature* (1979). Carol Sakala, *Women of South Asia: A Guide to Resources* (1980). Robert Orr Whyte and Pauline Whyte, *The Women of Rural Asia* (1982).   JAYNE WERNER

WOOD, EDWARD FREDERICK LINDLEY

(Lord Irwin, later Viscount Halifax; 1881–1959), replaced Reading as viceroy of India in 1926. During his vice-royalty (1926–1931), Irwin gained a reputation among members of the Indian nationalist movement as a courteous and willing negotiator. Yet ultimately he neither yielded nor compromised on questions of British sovereignty.

Irwin's tenure began encouragingly. In 1928 he successfully effected a compromise in the Bardoli tax revolt. In the following year, amid agitation sparked by the Simon Commission and the Nehru Report, the Irwin Declaration reaffirmed Britain's pledge to work toward dominion status for India. In 1930, however, the success of M. K. Gandhi's first civil disobedience campaign (the salt *satyagraha*) led Irwin to suppress the nationalists. Gandhi and Motilal Nehru were arrested and the Congress Party was outlawed. In 1931 Irwin initiated discussions with Gandhi on India's future and successfully concluded the Gandhi-Irwin Pact that both lifted the government's repressive measures and suspended the civil disobedience campaign.

[*See also* Government of India; Gandhi, Mohandas Karamchand; Nehru, Motilal; *and* Satyagraha.]

S. Gopal, *The Viceroyalty of Lord Irwin, 1926–1931* (1957).   JAMES A. JAFFE

WOOD, LEONARD

(1860–1927), American soldier, political leader, colonial administrator, medical doctor, and governor-general of the Philippines (October 1921–August 1927). He was also military governor of Moro province (1903–1906), which he governed with empathy for the religious and cultural traditions of the Muslim (Moro) Filipinos and a firm determination that they accept American authority over them.

As commanding general of the Department of the Philippines (1906–1908), Wood worked to build the defenses of the archipelago and develop military training. In March 1921 President Warren G. Harding asked him and former Governor-General William Cameron Forbes to conduct an investigation of the administration of Francis Burton Harrison (1913–1921). While in the Philippines, Wood was appointed governor-general.

Wood's reputation as a conservative but fair-minded individual was tested by a series of challenges from Filipino politicians, who had enjoyed maximum political autonomy under Governor-General Harrison. The most serious threat to Wood's administration was the resignation on 17 July 1923 of the Filipinos in his cabinet. President Harding and his successor, Calvin Coolidge, refused to recall him from Manila, however, and Wood rode out the nationalist storm caused by the resignations. He returned to the United States in June 1927 for the removal of a brain tumor and died on 7 August 1927.

[*See also* Philippines; Moro; Forbes, William Cameron; *and* Harrison, Francis Burton.]

Ronald Fettes Chapman, *Leonard Wood and Leprosy in the Philippines* (1982). Hermann Hagedorn, *Leonard Wood* (1931). Michael Paul Onorato, *Leonard Wood as Governor General* (1969) and *A Brief Review of American Interest in Philippine Development and Other Essays* (1972).   MICHAEL PAUL ONORATO

WOODBLOCK PRINTS, JAPANESE.

Japanese woodblock prints bring the vibrant culture of the Tokugawa period (1600–1868) vividly to life. Americans and Europeans began to collect them avidly as soon as Japan opened its ports to foreign trade, and when the art reached the West it inspired countless artists, including Van Gogh and the Impressionists. The finest collections of early Japanese prints are now in Western museums.

Japanese prints are the most abundant and varied form of Asian art. There are three main reasons that there are so many prints. First, they were multiple originals, not unique. Careful printers could make several thousand impressions by a color print from one set of blocks. Second, they were produced by teamwork. Artists drew designs; professional craftsmen transferred the drawings to woodblocks, cut them, and printed them. This freed the professional artists to create new pictures quickly; it also encouraged talented amateurs to design prints. Hundreds of artists designed a few prints; many designed two or three thousand. Utagawa Kunisada (1786–1864) probably designed more than twenty thousand prints over a period of sixty years. This was nearly ten times the output of Honore Daumier, the most prolific nineteenth-century Western print artist. Third, people from all levels of society liked prints; publishing was a profitable business.

almost effortless acceptance of each moment, sometimes felt like drifting or floating, so, using homophonous graphs, *ukiyo* was rewritten as "the floating world," and the prints and paintings that mirrored this good life were called *ukiyo-e*, "pictures of the floating world."

Many *ukiyo-e* artists specialized in their choice of subject matter. Among the best known are Kitagawa Utamaro (1753–1806), who designed prints of beautiful women, and Toshusai Sharaku (fl. 1794–1795), who drew portraits of *kabuki* actors. Other artists, like Katsushita Hokusai (1760–1849), depicted a wide variety of subjects and used a wide variety of styles. Hokusai remains famous, however, for his views of Mount Fuji, which were done when he was already in his seventies.

Japanese prints present a different way of seeing. Katsukawa Shunsho (1726–1793) shows us two actors whose inner posture is as different as their out-

FIGURE 1. *Beauty Wringing Out a Towel.* By Kitagawa Utamaro (1754–1806). From the series *Fuso Ninsō Juppon (Ten Examples of the Physiognomies of Women),* c. 1790–1800. Woodblock print; ink, color, and mica on paper with printed signature reading *Soken Utamaro ga.* 37.8 cm. × 25 cm.

FIGURE 2. *Two Actors.* By Toshusai Sharaku (active 1794–1795). Woodblock print of Nakamura Konozo as Kanagawaya no Gon and Nakajima Wadaemon as Bodara no Chozaemon; ink, color, and mica on paper with printed signature reading *Toshusai Sharaku ga.* 37.5 cm. × 25.4 cm.

The first European woodblock prints were made in the fourteenth century; by that time the Japanese had been making prints for seven hundred years. Although most of the early prints were religious, in the 1600s a revolution in taste took place in Japan. People suddenly wanted to see pictures and to own them. While wealthy people bought paintings, people with less money bought prints. Prints satisfied a growing taste for the depiction of real people and daily life. Prints showed people enjoying themselves; others provided buyers with pictures of the people who inspired them and seemed larger than life: the great actors and beauties of the period. After centuries of war, Japan was at peace; prints celebrated this.

The old world had been grim; the Buddhists called it *ukiyo*, a world of grief. The new world of the seventeenth century was exciting, pleasant, and safe. People looked forward to change; they gave themselves to life. This pleasant, forward movement, this

ward features, and a woman who is a prostitute and a goddess at the same time. Hiroshige's warm and spacious landscapes are strikingly different from the stark, almost squalid views of the same sites in early photographs. Utamaro shows us a famous young couple meeting shyly for the first time. Although there is nothing in the picture besides their names to tell us, we know that they will die tragically, and this knowledge colors the way we see the picture. Totoya Hokkei (1780–1850) draws a quiet still-life of a butterfly, a radish, and a silver arrowhead, alluding to the story of the young hero Soga no Goro, whose emblem was a butterfly. Sharpening his arrows, he falls asleep, dreams of his brother in terrible distress, wakes and gallops headlong to the coast, whipping his horse with a radish. None of these aspects of the story is in the picture, but the viewer would nevertheless understand. The Japanese print artists had an inclusive view of the world. Their prints give us a chance to share it.

Most woodblock prints were designed by *ukiyo-e* artists, but artists of other schools also designed picture books and prints, particularly artists of the Maruyama, Shijō, and Nanga schools of painting. The last prints in the popular *ukiyo-e* tradition were published during the Russo-Japanese War in 1904, but artists, carvers, and printers continued to collaborate. The members of the New Print (*shin hanga*) movement continued the tradition in the first half of the twentieth century. Even today, Japanese craftsmen are still producing color prints after designs by artists like Richard Diebenkorn, using the same traditional techniques.

Around 1906 a few young Japanese painters broke with tradition and began to make their own prints. This was the beginning of the Creative Print (*sosaku hanga*) movement. Koshiro Onchi (1891–1955) and Shiko Munakata (1903–1975) were two artists whose example initiated a brillant new chapter in the still unfolding history of Japanese woodblock prints.

[*See also* Ukiyo-e.]

Roger Keyes, *Japanese Woodblock Prints* (1984).

ROGER KEYES

WORLD WAR I IN ASIA.

Also known as the European War, World War I was first and foremost a civil war among nations contending for dominance within Europe, where the balance of power established by the Congress of Vienna in 1815 had been knocked askew by the rising strength of Germany.

The European states were further competing for the adjacent spoils of the then-decaying Austro-Hungarian and Ottoman empires. Finally, since the late nineteenth century the Great Powers had increasingly extended their regional rivalries to the more remote horizons of their own empires. In Asia, Britain and Russia played the "great game" of imperialism in Persia, Afghanistan, and Tibet, while France, Germany, and Russia carved themselves pieces of the "Chinese melon." In diplomacy, too, Asia figured in European rivalries, as the French considered offering Indochina to Germany in exchange for Alsace-Lorraine, and Britain concluded its 1902 alliance with Japan to protect British interests in Asia against the Russians and the French.

Thus, World War I began as a European war, which was displaced to Asia and, compared to the ravages in Europe, rather faintly enacted on the soil of lands that Europeans still believed they could dispose of as they wished. In 1914 India was "informed" by the British that it was at war, and Indians—nationalists and Muslims included—rallied to the crown, supplying loans and troops for the Western front. Japan waited only a week in August 1914 before declaring war against Germany on the basis of the Anglo-Japanese alliance, then seized the opportunity to take immediate possession of Germany's slice of China (Shandong) and its Pacific islands in Micronesia. In 1915 Japan served China its Twenty-one Demands, brazenly demonstrating the ambition of the newest imperialist power in Asia, Japan. When China also joined the Allied powers in 1917, it was partly with the expectation of later redress by the West against such Japanese encroachment. At war's end, however, Japan was entrenched in Shandong, its territorial position endorsed by secret treaties with four of those Western powers (Russia, Britain, France, and Italy). In addition to its expansion in China, Japan's huge military presence in the Siberian Expedition gave further witness to the potential power of the Japanese in Asia. [*For the extent of Japan's holdings on the Asian continent, see the map accompanying* Meiji Period.]

For many Asians, the war and the peace settlement at Versailles in 1919 brought first illusion, then disillusion, with the West. Japan's expectation of parity with its Western allies was frustrated at Versailles, as Woodrow Wilson denounced Japanese territorial claims and the racial equality clause was excluded from the covenant of the new League of Nations. China's anticipation of Western protection of its territorial integrity was betrayed, and China refused to sign the treaty. Vietnam's Ho Chi Minh discovered at the peace conference that the proclaimed Wilsonian "right of self-determination" did not apply to Asian colonial peoples. Indian and Burmese nationalists, who had first expected and then in 1917 been promised increased self-government, found that once the victory of "freedom over barbarism" was attained, the British returned to suppression as usual. It was no accident, then, that 1919 saw the March First Movement of Korean nationalism against Japanese colonial rule; the May Fourth Movement of Chinese nationalism against imperialism; Gandhi's call in India for the first nationwide campaign of nonviolent noncooperation (satyagraha) against the British Raj; and a rise of nationalist sentiment throughout much of Asia, sometimes, as with the Indonesians, newly conjoined with a fledgling communist party.

After the war and after the Russian Revolution of 1917, Asian leaders breathed an air reinvigorated with political possibility, from socialism and communism to republicanism and democracy. The road toward power and independence was long, however, and what had been the Great War for Europe was for Asia a small but significant acceleration in claiming its political destiny for its own.

[See also Anglo-Japanese Alliance; Twenty-one Demands; Versailles Treaty of 1918; March First Independence Movement; May Fourth Movement; Satyagraha; and World War I in China.]

CAROL GLUCK

WORLD WAR I IN CHINA. At the outbreak of World War I in Europe, China remained neutral, but some fighting did occur when the Japanese, with the reluctant assistance of the British, invaded the German leasehold at Jiaozhou Bay in 1915. China joined the war officially on the Allied side in August 1917 when the Beijing government was under the dominance of Duan Qirui and the Anfu clique. They used the declaration of war as a means to obtain foreign loans, especially from Japan, for modernizing China's armed forces. There was never any real intent to use these forces in Europe, only to strengthen the Anfu clique's hold on power.

As a belligerent, China's main contribution came through 175,000 supply and construction workers who worked behind Allied lines in Europe, Africa, and the Middle East. Many of the educated Chinese men who went to Europe during these years became active in socialist or communist activities there.

World War I, by both its conduct and its settlement, greatly weakened the authority of Western governments and Western liberal ideas in China, as elsewhere in Asia. The great slaughter of the war, along with the rabid, often blind patriotism of Europeans, undermined the appeal of Europe's pre-1914 political, intellectual, and moral authority. In China the settlement terms of the Treaty of Versailles disillusioned Chinese about Western liberalism and the future of liberal solutions for China. Chinese intellectuals were drawn increasingly to the Bolsheviks in Russia as a model that was still Western, but free from the corrupting taint of those who fought World War I and fashioned the unjust peace.

World War I saw a retreat in Western imperialism as European nations and the United States centered their attention on the conflict. Japan, however, expanded its influence in China, both politically and economically. In a series of endeavors, beginning with the Twenty-one Demands in 1915, Japan tried either to dominate the Chinese central government or bring certain regions of China—particularly the Northeast (Manchuria), Shandong, and Fujian—under her control. Japanese commercial and industrial interests grew rapidly in China after 1914, and the Japanese became the most active foreigners in the economic and cultural spheres.

In spite of Japanese competition, the withdrawal of European interests after 1914 opened up opportunities to Chinese capitalists. Chinese commerce and industry flourished during the war and for a few years afterward in a variety of commercial, banking, and industrial lines previously dominated by foreigners.

[See also World War I in Asia; China, Republic Period; Duan Qirui; Shandong Question; Versailles Treaty of 1918; Twenty-one Demands; and Yuan Shikai.]

Madeline Chi, China Diplomacy, 1914–1918 (1970).

DAVID D. BUCK

WORLD WAR II IN ASIA. From the perspective of Asian and world history, World War II was the first truly global conflict. Not only did the vectors of international warfare cover much of the globe; they also linked points of hostility that had originated separately. Once linked, the different parts of the world would never again escape this newly global dimension. The world itself was also changed. The modern Europocentric "world order" had originated in the fifteenth- and sixteenth-century girdling of the globe and reached a peak in the economic and territorial dominions of the eighteenth and nineteenth centuries. By 1900, however, it had begun to be challenged by developments both outside and beyond the control of Europe. World War II hastened the completion of the process of globalization, leaving a world in which the decline of Europe and the rise of other powers, including those of Asia, would require adjustments in nearly every human sphere.

World War II did not begin globally but in different places and for different reasons, as a survey of the common names for the conflict reveals. The so-called European War (September 1939–May 1945) was fought over the same question of hegemony that World War I had failed to resolve: the place of a strong Germany in a new European balance of power. It was above all a war against Nazism and its allies, waged by Britain, France, Russia, the United States, and others, to save Europe from Hitler's iron grip. Both the Allies and the Axis represented the kind of nation-state alliances traditional in European Great Power politics, with the addition of the United States, whose heritage and interest lay with the Western democracies. During the first two years of Nazi conquest, isolationist sentiment prevented the American government from going to war on behalf of Europe. When the Japanese bombing of Pearl Harbor brought America into the war in December 1941, however, the importance of the European conflict for the United States was underscored by the strategic decision to win the war in Europe first and only then devote full power to the aggressor in the Pacific. The consuming concentration of the Western powers on the fate of Europe had significant consequences for the war as Asia experienced it.

The Sino-Japanese War (July 1937–August 1945) was initiated by Japan to consolidate Japanese hegemony in northeast Asia at a time when it appeared that the warring forces within China—Nationalists, Communists, warlords—might combine to drive the Japanese from their position in North China. This "incident," as the Japanese called the war, was the latest escalation in Japan's efforts to secure its continental empire, the strategic and economic importance of which had long since become an unquestioned premise in Japanese foreign policy. The annexation of Korea in 1910, the establishment of a puppet state in Manchuria in 1932, the subsequent invasion of North China to the Great Wall, and finally, in 1937, all-out aggressive war and a "new order" in East Asia—each step was justified in terms of assuring buffers for empire, as traditional an international form in Asia as alliances were in Europe. This "war," as the Chinese named it, was for them the latest and most heinous depredation of Japanese imperialism, against which they fought for eight desperate years. In 1940 Japan signed the Tripartite Pact with the Axis powers, Germany and Italy, and in 1941, China joined the Western Allies. Yet for both countries, continental East Asia remained the crucial concern. Indeed, the strategic strikes at Pearl Harbor and elsewhere were intended by the Japanese to knock the West quickly out of combat, so that Japan could survive to fulfill its imperial destiny in Asia. [*See also* Manchurian Incident *and the map accompanying* Meiji Period.]

Four days after Pearl Harbor, Japan thus changed the official name of the conflict from the "China incident" to the "Greater East Asia War" (December 1941–August 1945). This was Japan's war for the conquest of Asia, from Manchuria and China in the north through Indochina, Malaya, Burma, and the Dutch East Indies in the south to the Philippines in the Pacific. The war was described as necessary for the "self-preservation and self-defense" of the empire in the face of hostile Western powers that "encircled" it, cutting off trade and oil. It was further legitimated with the rhetoric of "coexistence and coprosperity" among Asian peoples united against white Western imperialism. Both justifications owed much to developments elsewhere, for here occurred one of those links between separate regional hostilities that joined to make "a world at war."

When Japan moved into the Southeast Asian colonies of the Western powers between 1940 and 1942, it did so in the context of a Europe devastated by Hitler. Not only were France and the Netherlands defeated in 1940, but Britain, on whose power the other Asian colonies ultimately depended, was threatened. In 1941 the Soviet Union, the only state with a military presence in Asia capable of meeting the Japanese, had turned all its force to meet the Nazi attack in the West, thus providing more reliable security for the Japanese empire's north Asian borders than the nonaggression pact signed by Tokyo and Moscow a few months before. The United States, more shocked in any case by the fall of France than by the fall of French Indochina, was restrained from overt aid to Europe or its colonies until after Pearl Harbor. Japan was therefore able to take the opportunity, it has been said, in the absence of the imperial mistress to raid the colonial "cookie jar." Also, in this case because of European imperialism itself, Japan was able to rationalize the raid with promises of pan-Asian solidarity and independence

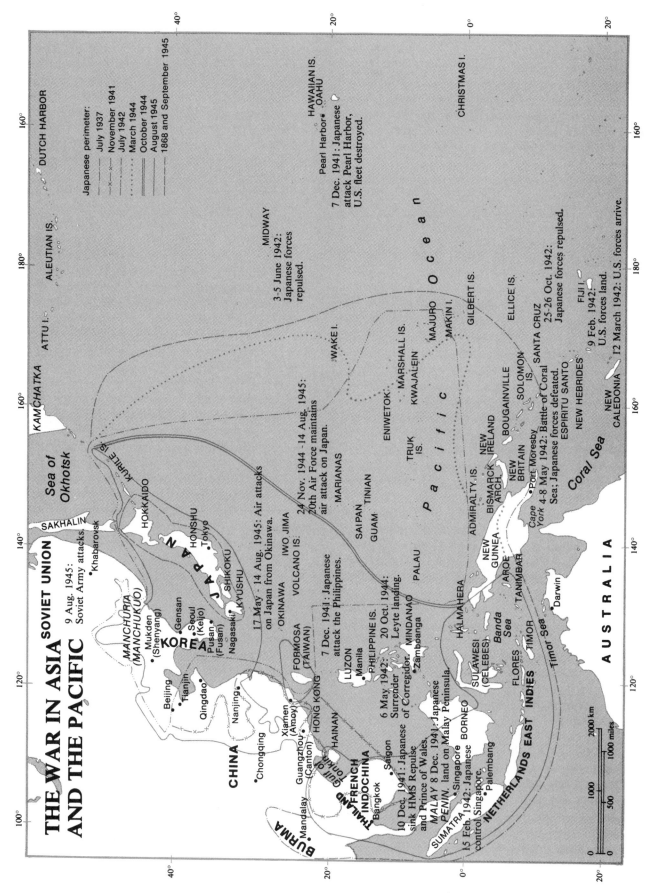

THE WAR IN ASIA AND THE PACIFIC

Japanese perimeter:
- July 1937
- November 1941
- July 1942
- March 1944
- October 1944
- August 1945
- 1868 and September 1945

DUTCH HARBOR

ALEUTIAN IS.

ATTU I.

KAMCHATKA

Sea of Okhotsk

SAKHALIN

SOVIET UNION

9 Aug. 1945: Soviet Army attacks.

Khabarovsk

MANCHURIA (MANCHUKUO)

Mukden (Shenyang)

Beijing

Tianjin

Qingdao

Nanjing

Chongqing

CHINA

Xiamen (Amoy)

Guangzhou (Canton)

HAINAN

HONG KONG

Gulf of Tonkin

FRENCH INDOCHINA

Saigon

Mandalay

BURMA

Bangkok

THAILAND

KURILE IS.

HOKKAIDO

HONSHU

Tokyo

SHIKOKU

KYUSHU

JAPAN

Gensan

Seoul (Keijo)

Pusan (Fusan)

Nagasaki

KOREA

17 May - 14 Aug. 1945: Air attacks on Japan from Okinawa.

OKINAWA

VOLCANO IS.

IWO JIMA

FORMOSA (TAIWAN)

7 Dec. 1941: Japanese attack the Philippines.

LUZON

Manila

PHILIPPINE IS.

20 Oct.1944: Leyte landing.

MINDANAO

Zamboanga

6 May 1942: Surrender of Corregidor.

10 Dec. 1941: Japanese sink HMS Repulse and Prince of Wales.

MALAY 8 Dec. 1941: Japanese PENIN. land on Malay Peninsula.

Singapore

15 Feb. 1942: Japanese control Singapore.

SUMATRA

Palembang

BORNEO

NETHERLANDS EAST INDIES

SULAWESI (CELEBES)

FLORES

TIMOR

Banda Sea

AROE

TANIMBAR

Flores Sea

Timor Sea

Darwin

AUSTRALIA

HALMAHERA

PALAU

24 Nov. 1944 - 14 Aug. 1945: 20th Air Force maintains air attack on Japan.

MARIANAS

SAIPAN

TINIAN

GUAM

TRUK IS.

ENIWETOK

MARSHALL IS.

KWAJALEIN

MAJURO I.

MAKIN I.

GILBERT IS.

ELLICE IS.

WAKE I.

MIDWAY

3-5 June 1942: Japanese forces repulsed.

HAWAIIAN IS.

OAHU

Pearl Harbor

7 Dec. 1941: Japanese attack Pearl Harbor, U.S. fleet destroyed.

CHRISTMAS I.

Pacific Ocean

ADMIRALTY IS.

NEW IRELAND

NEW BRITAIN

BISMARCK ARCH.

NEW GUINEA

Port Moresby

Cape York

4-8 May 1942: Battle of Coral Sea; Japanese forces defeated.

BOUGAINVILLE

SOLOMON IS.

SANTA CRUZ

25-26 Oct. 1942: Japanese forces repulsed.

ESPIRITU SANTO

NEW HEBRIDES

FIJI I.

9 Feb. 1942: U.S. forces land.

NEW CALEDONIA

12 March 1942: U.S. forces arrive.

Coral Sea

2000 km

1000 miles

1000

500

0

0

from the West. And whether Japan meant it or not, for Asia these were later the links that mattered.

After Japan's defeat the United States decreed a change in the name from the Greater East Asian War, with all its aggressive and militaristic overtones, to the Pacific War (December 1941–August 1945), which cast a rather different light on the conflict. Although the term is still widely used in Japan today, there is no doubt that this was the war seen more from Washington than from Tokyo. When the British spoke of the Far Eastern War, they meant the war that took place far to the east of Whitehall but that deeply involved British interests in the area. The sinking of the *Repulse* and the *Prince of Wales* and the fall of Singapore early in the war, later Mountbatten's activities in Burma, and finally the opening of the Burma Road—these were the landmarks of the British war in the Far East. Similarly, the American name stressed the part of the war in which they fought long and hard against the Japanese and in which American interests were considered paramount. The Pacific War, then, was primarily the Japanese-American War, the important participation of other Allies notwithstanding. It began with Pearl Harbor and ended with the atomic bombings of Hiroshima and Nagasaki; in between it covered vast sections of the Pacific, island by island, sea by sea, and also destroyed much of metropolitan Japan.

In the process of mutual destruction, another international link was formed. The United States and Japan, which began the war with their backs to the Pacific—one looking anxiously toward Europe, the other aggressively toward Asia—ended the war face to face with one another. The Allied Occupation of Japan after the war, like the Allied victory in the Pacific, was primarily an American operation. Both the domestic reforms in Japan and the subsequent security alliance with the United States brought the two powers increasingly close together. For Asia, their relationship symbolized both the postwar presence of the United States as a power in Asia and the distancing of Japan from many of the issues that were confronted by other Asian nations in the postwar era.

For the most part, those other Asian nations were not free officially to christen the war as they wished, since their imperial rulers did so for them. In 1939 India was informed that it was, with the crown, once again at war with Germany. In 1942 the Philippines Commonwealth Army fought and lost with MacArthur against Japan; then, under Japanese occupation, the collaborating regime declared war on the United States in 1944. But in the countries subjected to imperialist rule or encroachment—whether by the West, as in India and Ceylon; by Japan, as in China, Korea, and (only ostensibly independent) Thailand; by first the West and then Japan, as in Indonesia, Burma, Malaya, and the Philippines; or by both at the same time, as in Indochina and, historically, China as well—the official name of the war and the global alliances mattered less than the struggle much closer to home. For here was another link that derived from the strange and complicated intermingling of Asian nations involved in a war that was both antifascist and anti-imperialist at the same time. The difficulty, of course, was that the two enemies were not always the same.

For China, so long torn by internal chaos and civil war, the melding of fascism and imperialism in one relentless foe brought a provisional unity of purpose. However nominal the United Front between the Communists and the Nationalists, the fact is that both spent the war years fighting against Japan. The Communists, who had departed on their epochal Long March under the banner of "marching north to resist the Japanese," were more successful in their guerrilla activism than was Chiang Kai-shek in his reliance on Great Power aid. The Communists' success in organizing the peasantry as they fought was a factor in their eventual victory in the revolution of 1949 and the establishment of a fully independent China after a century of travail. [*See also* United Front *and* Long March.]

For India, the situation was more complicated. The Indian Army fought valiantly for the Allies against the Germans and the Japanese, and neither Gandhi nor Nehru could bring himself to side with fascist Japan even against imperialist Britain. Independence lost none of its urgency, however, and wartime British promises ("a post-dated cheque on a bank that was failing," in Gandhi's famous words) were rewarded with the massive Quit India movement of 1942. In the meantime Subhas Bose followed a different route toward independence, joining the Japanese in the cause of a liberated Asia. From his provisional government of Free India in the Andaman Islands, Bose declared war on Britain and the United States in 1943, later leading his Indian National Army from Burma as far as the British garrison at Imphal. For many Asian nationalists, Bose was then, and remained later, a hero. [*See also* Bose, Subhas Chandra *and* Imphal.]

Nationalists like Aung San in Burma, Jose Laurel in the Philippines, and Sukarno in the Dutch East Indies also worked with the Japanese for the sake of independence from hated colonial rule. Such collaboration was often quite sincere, a belief that Japan encouraged by training "independence armies," cultivating Buddhist and Islamic leaders, hosting the Greater East Asian Conference, and, with much fanfare, granting "independence" to Burma and the Philippines in 1943. Two days after Japan lost the war, Sukarno followed through on Japan's promise to Indonesia and declared independence himself. [See also Aung San; Laurel, Jose P.; and Sukarno.]

Others, often within the same country, stood steadfast against their Japanese "liberators." These included underground groups like the Huk guerrillas who formed an Anti-Japanese People's Army in the Philippines, as well as leaders like Vietnam's Ho Chi Minh and Korea's Kim Il Sung (Kim Il-sŏng), who furthered their communist and nationalist movements in resistance to the Japanese. [See also Huk; Ho Chi Minh; and Kim Il Sung.]

These several variations on the theme of belligerence suggest that World War II in Asia was also in part a war of liberation. Japan and Germany had formed but a "hollow alliance," with little mutual respect, even less mutual consultation, and virtually no postwar consequences. On the other side, Roosevelt's Grand Alliance of Britain, America, Russia, and China barely survived the war, as its armies came to rest in spheres of interest that owed little to global partnership and much to traditional geopolitics. The Soviets were in Eastern and Central Europe, the Americans in Japan and the Pacific, the Chinese in continental East Asia. In one respect, however, something had drastically changed: the British (and the French and the Dutch) could not return to Asia again. Those who tried—the Dutch to Indonesia, the French to Vietnam—were in the end violently driven out. Those who submitted more or less peaceably, as the British did in South Asia, had little control over the shape of their former dominions, which in this case meant partition of the Indian subcontinent and repeated Indo-Pakistani wars as its result. For much of Asia, which had already lost millions of civilian lives during the war, not only from enemy action but from famine as well, the struggles did not end with the Japanese surrender but only with the settling of civil war and the shattering of the imperial yoke.

The irony of the outcome between the victor and the vanquished was complete: Britain, France, and the Netherlands had won the war but lost their colonies. Japan had lost the war but Asia won the independence that Japanese propaganda had (falsely) promised it. In fact, of course, neither side

was responsible for the decline of the imperial West in Asia. The process had been long under way, as both the remarkable array of national leadership and the extent of civil strife in the different countries attested. World War II only propelled what Nehru called the "tryst with destiny" to a hastier conclusion.

Decolonization, difficult and momentous as it was, did not, however, destine postwar Asia to be independent of the powers. The Cold War, which began before the hot war had ended, enmeshed Asia in another global struggle and changed both the domestic and international alignments of the Asian countries. The postwar confrontation between the United States and the Soviet Union, like their wartime alliance, arose initially from European concerns, in particular the disposition of territory in Central and Eastern Europe. Again like the war, however, the international links soon extended to Asia and with the same broadening of geopolitical hostilities into full-scale ideological conflict.

In the late 1940s the United States supported Japan as a "bulwark against communism in East Asia" and lamented having "lost" China to the Communists. Korea and Vietnam, each divided into communist North and noncommunist South, suffered calamitous wars with the intervention of the powers. Like the United Nations, the San Francisco Peace Treaty of 1951 bore the marks of global division, for neither the Soviets nor the Chinese were signatories. [See also San Francisco Treaty.] In the postwar decades economic aid was dispensed to Asian governments in exchange for alignment and loyalty, exemplified by the vastly disproportionate sums donated by the superpowers to Pakistan and India in the 1950s. As the new Asian countries made their difficult way toward building the nations they had worked to establish—the road toward independence being always more clearly marked than the road away from it—they faced the additional dilemma of taking sides in a newly divided world. Despite efforts of countries like India toward "nonalignment" of the sort represented by the efforts at the Bandung Conference of 1955, true neutrality in the event proved an almost impossible feat. [See also Bandung Conference.]

The terrible insertion of the nuclear war into the global equation made the postwar legacy for Asian international relations that much more dangerous and complex. The two nuclear powers in Asia, India and China, were also the two most populous nations on earth, each with enormous needs in economic development. Japan, which had claim to America's arsenal, had also become one of the three strongest economies in the world. How each of these nations would link their strategic and economic interests to those of the superpowers remained a conundrum of the postwar years. Such disparities among the Asian nations in wealth and power were accompanied by signal differences in political and economic systems. Such capitalist economies as Japan, South Korea, and Singapore lay in close proximity to peoples' socialist republics like China, North Korea, and Vietnam. Different variants of political autocracy and economic development shared common, and often bloodied, borders. Relations within the region were thus as vexed as those with the wider world.

Although global war did not end in global peace, it nonetheless changed the shape of what is called the "international system." This is in part a wishful appellation, since one of the legacies of World War II was the destruction of the existing order with no clear substitute in sight. The Europocentric order gave way initially to an East-West polarity between two newer powers, Russia and the United States. Then other even "newer" powers like China and Japan—both of them located in the East geographically; one of them, Japan, oriented toward the West politically—added other poles to the international topology. The disadvantaged but collective potential of the Third World divided the globe differently, into North and South, although a number of the countries in the "South" were located in Asia, the traditional "East." Obviously, the cardinal points of the compass no longer sufficed to express the schemata of world order.

World War II was partly responsible for this confusion, and the changes it wrought were decisive for the twentieth century. It may also be, in a now inescapably interdependent globe, that the consequent rise of Asia will prove equally decisive for the world in the twenty-first century.

[See also World War II in China; Pearl Harbor; Yalta Conference; and Occupation of Japan.]

Christopher Thorne, *The Issue of War: States, Societies, and the Far Eastern Conflict of 1941–1945* (1985).
CAROL GLUCK

WORLD WAR II IN CHINA. The Sino-Japanese War, which began with a minor skirmish at the Marco Polo Bridge near Beijing on 7 July 1937, was the true beginning of World War II in Asia. It merged with the global struggle after the Japanese attack on Pearl Harbor (7 December 1941) and lasted until V-J Day in August 1945. This many-sided struggle led to fundamental change within China and in East Asia: the destruction of the Japanese empire, the triumph of the Chinese Communist Party in 1949 and the flight of Chiang Kai-shek's Nationalists to Taiwan, deep involvement of the United States in Asia, and the reemergence of the USSR as a major force on the Pacific rim.

Primarily a struggle between Japanese invaders and Chinese defenders, the war was actually several overlapping conflicts, the many interactions among which created an extraordinarily complex picture. On the Chinese side, the two principal Chinese forces were the Guomindang (Kuomintang, KMT, or Nationalist Party), representing the government of China, and the Chinese Communist Party (CCP), led by Mao Zedong and his colleagues. These two fought quite different wars against Japan. Although nominally allied with one another under a "united front," the Nationalists and Communists also fought one another, more than once approaching the brink of civil war. Another set of struggles involved the puppet forces enlisted by the Japanese all the way from Manchuria to Canton (Guangzhou), especially the Reformed National Government at Nanjing centered around Wang Jingwei, who until his defection to the Japanese in late 1938 had been a sometime colleague and bitter rival of Guomindang leader Chiang Kai-shek. [See also Wang Jingwei.] After Pearl Harbor, as the Pacific War unfolded, the United States came to play an increasingly important role in Chinese affairs, both directly and indirectly. Finally, at the very end of the war, the USSR belatedly entered the struggle, stripped Manchuria of its industrial base, and signed favorable treaties with China.

Few would question that the Sino-Japanese War was the most formative period in the history of the Chinese Communist movement prior to 1949. The Communists entered the war with a party numbering perhaps forty thousand and ended eight years later with 1.2 million members. Spectacular growth also took place in the armed forces and in the population of territories (so-called base areas) controlled by the CCP. The Communists emerged from the War of Resistance (as the war against Japan was called) capable for the first time of contending for power on a regional, perhaps national, scale. Further, by 1945 Party leadership was more unified than ever before, a tight-knit group that, with a few notable exceptions, held together remarkably well until the Cultural Revolution two decades later. The ideology and policies of this period give distinctive cast and coloration to the CCP, both then and later: this was the era of the "thought of Mao Zedong" and the "Yan'an way." [*See also* Yan'an.]

The war might have been an opportunity for the KMT as well, and during its first phase, Chiang Kai-shek and his government were able to gain greater popular acceptance than ever before. In the long run, however, the war did serious harm to the Nationalists, who were unable to mobilize and consolidate popular support. On the contrary, inflation, corruption and inefficiency, and general war weariness took a heavy toll. Even so, the Nationalists ended the war with a much larger armed force than that of the CCP, with a monopoly on international recognition and foreign aid, and with control of the richest areas of the nation.

The eight years of the Sino-Japanese War can be divided into three wavelike phases. Although they are clear enough in general outline, they are hazy in the transition from one to another.

The First Phase: 1937 to Late 1939 or Early 1940. During most of this period, by far the heavier Japanese blows were directed against the Guomindang, as Tokyo sought first to force Chiang Kai-shek into a negotiated settlement, then later to replace his government with a more pliable puppet regime. Japan had no intention of waging a costly, protracted war of attrition in China, but once engaged it proved impossible to extricate itself. Eventually, nearly one million men were assigned to the China theater, exclusive of those in Manchukuo, the Japanese puppet state in Manchuria. China was soon almost entirely isolated from the outside world, and the Nationalist government was forced to retreat from Nanjing to Chongqing in the agriculturally rich but socially backward province of Sichuan. By the end of this period the Japanese advance had lost momentum and the central China front lapsed into stalemate.

For the Communists, the first phase of the war was a period of rapid but rather superficial expansion behind Japanese lines, where they were able to organize or absorb local forces. Territorial bases were established in North China by the Eighth Route Army and began functioning as semipopular political regimes under the control of the CCP, which also initiated such reforms as rent and interest reduction. The situation in central China was more fluid, but by the end of this period, Mao and Liu Shaoqi were urging the New Fourth Army to create similar base areas in Anhui and Jiangsu. [*See also* Eighth Route Army.] During this period, United Front relations between the KMT and the CCP started with apparent cordiality, then began a pro-

gressive decline, as the KMT observed their own reverses so sharply contrasted with rapid growth in Communist influence, which far exceeded what had been authorized. [*See also* United Front.]

The Second Phase: From Late 1940 to Late 1943. During most of this phase the conflict between Japan and KMT forces was relatively low key, with only limited action undertaken by either side. These were the most difficult years of the war for the CCP, however, since both the KMT and the Japanese were now vigorously opposing the Communists. By late 1939 the KMT had thrown a tight blockade around the headquarters base area of Shaanganning (named for Shaanxi, Gansu, and Ningxia provinces), containing the town of Yan'an. Chilly formality at the top covered bloody conflict in areas contested by the armies of the two parties, as the one sought to continue its expansion, the other to halt it. During the summer and fall of 1940 these clashes grew more intense, with the CCP defeating Nationalist forces in Anhui and Jiangsu provinces. The following January, KMT armies took revenge by decimating their rival's headquarters unit in what is known as the New Fourth Army Incident. In the presence of the Japanese threat, both sides pulled back from further large-scale operations, but continued grim tactical operations. Behind Japanese lines, the CCP was generally more successful than the KMT, and by 1943 most Nationalist guerrillas had been cleared from contested areas. [*See also* Shaanganning *and* New Fourth Army Incident.]

Meanwhile, Japanese pressure was an even more critical challenge, as the invaders sought to pacify and economically exploit "occupied" China. Mopping-up campaigns began in the spring of 1940 and were intensified after the CCP's Hundred Regiments Offensive (August 1940) stung the Japanese along the rail and road network of North China. In the two years that followed, CCP-controlled territories and populations were cut nearly in half, and very difficult conditions prevailed elsewhere.

Part of the Communist response to this protracted crisis was a series of interrelated policies: the *zhengfeng*, or ideological and organizational "rectification campaign" of 1942 and 1943; the campaign for "crack troops and simple administration"; the *xiaxiang* ("down to the villages") movement; intensified rent and interest reduction; determined efforts to increase and diversify production; and the cooperative movement. These policies were applied most systematically to the Shaanganning base and much more unevenly in other base areas, but their cumulative effect helped the CCP to survive, to deepen and consolidate its hold on rural society, and to emerge from this period prepared for whatever opportunities might present themselves.

About midway through this period the Sino-Japanese War merged with World War II, following the Japanese attack on Pearl Harbor. Through 1942 into 1943 the United States was in retreat or on the defensive against Japan and could provide little direct assistance to the struggle in China. But the strategic import of US involvement—that Japan would eventually be defeated mainly by the Americans—was understood with increasing clarity by both Chiang Kai-shek and Mao Zedong. Furthermore, the contours of US recognition and support of Chiang and the Nationalists as the permanent legal authority in China were emerging more firmly.

The Third Phase: Early 1944 until the End of the War. During this period the brunt of the war once again fell more heavily on the Nationalists, and the CCP was able to move forward, reaching and then exceeding the high watermarks of expansion early in the conflict. Japan was so increasingly drained by its losing struggle against the US that it could no longer continue costly and ultimately fruitless efforts to eliminate Communist influence. Furthermore, its last great offensive of the war, Operation Ichigo (May–December 1944), was directed once again at the Nationalists, exposing their many weaknesses and rendering effective anti-Communist measures all but impossible. Additionally, CCP action and Japanese mopping-up campaigns had by this time all but obliterated Nationalist forces operating behind Japanese lines.

American involvement in China grew deeper during this period and was increasingly intertwined with plans and hopes for the postwar order in East Asia. By now the flow of US money and matériel was becoming more significant, and all of it was going to the Nationalists. Although KMT shortcomings were further highlighted by the conflict (summer 1944) between General Joseph "Vinegar Joe" Stilwell and Chiang Kai-shek, the US finally recalled Stilwell and remained committed to the Nationalist leader. Thereafter, under the disastrous ambassadorship of Patrick J. Hurley, the US attempted the impossible: to serve as good-faith mediator between the KMT and the CCP while continuing to support one side in the dispute. This set the stage for General George C. Marshall's fruitless peace mission to China and ultimately for the civil war between the Nationalists and the Communists. [*See also* Stilwell, Joseph W.; Hurley, Patrick J.; *and* Marshall, George C.]

Finally, during the last months of the war the USSR reemerged as a significant actor in East Asian power politics. As a result of the agreements outlined at the Yalta Conference (later confirmed in a series of Sino-USSR treaties), and her last-minute entry into the war against Japan, Russia gained a position as advanced as any it had enjoyed under the tsars. [*See also* Yalta Conference.]

At war's end, then, the contest between the Nationalists and Communists hung in fateful balance. Each side sought a combination of diplomatic advantage, political superiority, popular support, and military leverage. Both the United States and the Soviet Union were in positions from which they could influence, but not determine, the outcome.

[*See also* Communism: Chinese Communist Party; Guomindang; Chiang Kai-shek; *and* Mao Zedong.]

Lionel Max Chassin, *The Communist Conquest of China: A History of the Civil War, 1945–1949* (1965). F. F. Liu, *A Military History of Modern China, 1924–1949* (1956). Charles R. Romanus and Riley Sutherland, *The United States Army in World War II: China-India-Burma Theatre*, 3 vols. (1952–1958).   LYMAN P. VAN SLYKE

WRITING SYSTEMS.

Asia is known for its variety and diversity of writing systems. Practically all the known systems of writing in the world, except for Mayan-Aztecan, find their variants or descendants, in one form or another, in the history of Asia.

Origins. This diversity stems from the fact that three out of the four major stocks of writing systems originated in Asia. They are, from west to east, (1) ancient Egyptian, (2) Semitic, and (3) Chinese. No direct descendants of the ancient Egyptian writing system survive, but some unmistakable resemblances are found in the Sinai inscriptions. These similarities show that the birth of the Semitic writing system has as much to do with ancient Egyptian writing as it does with Mesopotamian cuneiform or Cretan hieroglyphic writing. Chinese writing is still very much in use in East Asia, although both North Korea and Vietnam have abandoned it.

Genealogy and Distribution. Descendants of Aramaic, one of the Northern Semitic systems of writing, are distributed in western, northern, South, and Southeast Asia, while East Asia is dominated by the system of Chinese characters and their variants. Aramaic writing gave rise to four major types of writing: (1) Arabic, (2) Kharosthi and Brahmi, (3) Parthian, and (4) Sogdian.

Arabic writing spread to most West Asian Muslim countries and, through India and Malaysia, as far south as Indonesia and part of the Philippines. Kharosthi is found in excavated documents written in some of the dead languages of Central Asia; Brahmi in India developed, in the South, into the Telugu and Tamil writings and, in the North, into Nagari and Pali scripts, from which descended Central Asian Agnean and Kuchean scripts (both now extinct), Tibetan and the now extinct Phags-pa (the unified script for the languages of the thirteenth-century Mongol empire), Southeast Asian Mon and Khmer scripts of Indochina, and Visayan of the Philippines. Burman writing originates from this same Mon, and the Thai and Java scripts from Khmer. Korean writing *(han'gŭl)* seems to be clearly related to Phags-pa, because the phonetic assumptions that underlie the construction and use of both these scripts came from ancient Indian phonetic theory. The two less well known Japanese writings of Tsushima, *hifumi* and *anaichi,* are obviously imitations of *han'gŭl.*

Parthian developed into Kök Turkic, the script of the runes of the Orkhon Inscriptions. The now extinct Khitan, Nüzhi (Jurchen), and Xixia (Tangut) are also related to these runes, although the actual spelling principles for words in these scripts are clearly motivated by the system of graphs from China, the cultural sphere in which all these peoples eventually flourished.

The Sogdian influence spread to North Asia, where the Uighur script was invented. This was later accepted, with some modifications, by the Mongolians and is still in use in Inner Mongolia, although the Outer Mongolians and Soviet Buriats adopted the Cyrillic script. The same Uighur script was also adopted by the Kalmuks and Manchus to write their languages, the Manchu script also being transmitted to the Xibo and now in use in Xinjiang.

Surrounded by these descendants of the Aramaic script and its variants to the north, west, and southeast, East Asia constitutes a unique cultural sphere because of its use of Chinese graphs, which are as conspicuous in the area as is, for example, the traditional use of chopsticks. The earliest forerunners of Chinese characters are found in the oracle-bone inscriptions of the Shang (Yin) dynasty (c. seventeenth to eleventh century BCE). These are followed by various systems of "old characters" in later Chinese history, before the script standardization in the Qin dynasty (221–206 BCE). The linguistic connection between those systems in the oracle-bone inscriptions and later characters is not very clear. However, a certain linguistic continuity in the script is unmistakable, judging from the parallelism in the use of a phonetic component for combination characters (which are composed of signific and phonetic parts).

Recent archaeological excavations have uncovered the mosaic, nonmonolithic nature of ancient Chinese culture. The writing system is reflective of this. Some kind of pre-Chinese writing system was in use even in the very heartland of Chinese civilization—the so-called Guanzhong basin (modern Xi'an and its surrounding area), but records bearing such writing are still too few to allow any systematic decipherment, as are the scriptlike symbols found in the ruins of the legendary Xia dynasty (traditionally c. twenty-second to seventeenth century BCE). This is also true of the recently uncovered Ba-Shu scripts, which spread to most of what is now Sichuan and part of Hunan. Reports on the discovery of the Chu script in Hunan are not yet well documented. Whatever the role of these ancient pre-Chinese and non-Han cultures was, the Chinese characters as first collected, identified, classified, and analyzed by Xu Shen in 100 CE and as known to us to this day must have had a very heterogeneous background. They are also obviously the result of successive standardizations, unifications, and assimilations of numerous local variants of similar writing principles by imperial rescripts as well as by cultural centripetence.

Because of drastic differences in linguistic structures, the three nations that came under direct rule or influence of China in the periphery of the Chinese cultural sphere in East and Southeast Asia—Korea, Japan, and Vietnam—eventually had to abandon the Chinese characters that they had once unanimously accepted as the only possible writing system. The Koreans took the extreme measure of adopting a purely sound-based script *(han'gŭl),* perhaps because of their exposure to Phags-pa script. The Japanese simplified some Chinese characters to create syllabic phonetic graphs *(kana,* both *katakana* and *hiragana),* which they use in conjunction with the Chinese characters. Vietnamese, with the least structural difference from Chinese, compromised and used *chunom,* a large set of combination characters of significs and phonetics, much like Chinese characters but in accordance with Vietnamese syllable structure. Some of the national minorities in southwest China followed the example set by the Vietnamese and created scripts such as Yi (Lolo) and Shui (Sui), which were fashioned on Vietnamese *chunom,* but their use was too limited to consider them full-fledged writing systems. Naxi (Nakhi) pictographs are also very primitive in nature.

Despite these efforts toward cultural (as well as political) independence from China, the official language of these surrounding nations was traditionally Chinese—literary Chinese (commonly called *wenli),* for that matter. Note, in this connection, the widespread Sinophile–Sinophobe ambivalence among the intellectuals in these countries. Because of the large stock of basic ideas and words expressed by Chinese characters and shared by the peoples of these surrounding nations, the East Asian world still maintains its cultural unification despite its heterogeneity of religions.

The adoption of the Latin script in order to substitute for an older one or to create a new one has been witnessed throughout contemporary Asia; in Muslim countries such as Turkey, Malaysia, and Indonesia (in lieu of the former Arabic script); in Vietnam (in lieu of the former Chinese characters and the various *chunom* systems); in the Philippines; and among some of the national minorities of China and the Soviet Union without a long unified cultural history. Countering the trend toward latinization, however, the Soviet Union did change these newly adopted Latin scripts to Cyrillic before World War II in order to promote a cultural homogeneity throughout the Soviet sphere (the very last one of these scripts, that for Dungan, was completed in 1953).

The use of a script is apparently very deeply rooted in a nation's cultural identity and heritage; those that have so far succeeded in the latinization of their old scripts had either a low level of literacy at the outset (Turkish, Uzbek, Dungan, etc.) or were once under direct rule of nations using the Latin alphabet (Vietnam, Indonesia, the Philippines, etc.).

Use and Function. Asian writing systems are also very diverse with regard to their construction, use, and function. Pure pictographs are limited to very primitive writing systems, although even nowadays Chinese graphs like those for "fish" and "horse" are still clearly pictographs. Nonetheless, when the graph for "fish" is called a pictograph, what is referred to is the origin of this character or the principle on which this character was originally created. In actual use, however, it passed the stage of pictographic use in a very early period of its history and has been used since as a symbol for the word for "fish." The use has been commonly misunderstood as pictographical only because the symbol itself is obviously based on the picture of a fish; to make things more confusing, the character could stand for various dialectal forms of the Chinese word for "a fish," thus giving the false impression that it does not stand for any specific linguistic form but remains just a picturelike symbol. In other words, except for the case of some polysyllabic words such as *putao* ("grapes") and *boli* ("glass"), Chinese graphs always stand for a word or at least a meaningful part of longer words. Thus the graph

for "fish" is in fact a logograph for the word meaning "fish" and not an ideograph for the idea of "fish." Chinese graphs are thus best described and classified as "logographs."

Modern experimental psychology has made it clear that recognition of Chinese graphs, even of those that are purely pictographical, can always be achieved by native users through association with the words represented by these graphs. In addition, more than 80 percent of all Chinese characters combine phonetic and "radical" parts (the latter indicating the broad semantic category to which a given graph belongs). Simply put, the majority of Chinese graphs are basically phonetic. With this correct understanding of the nature and function of Chinese graphs, we can classify Asian writing systems into three groups: (1) those utilizing logographs, such as Chinese graphs, *chunom*, the Shui script, and so on; (2) those utilizing syllabic letters, such as Japanese *katakana* and *hiragana;* and (3) those utilizing single-sound letters, such as Korean *han'gŭl,* and the Latin script and its variants, used for languages like Turkish and Indonesian.

The majority of Asian writing systems, however, employ both syllabic and single-sound letters, because they are all descendants of Aramaic script or its modifications. It also happened that the sound shape of the languages for which these scripts were originally invented was such that it was not always necessary to mark the vowels, because they were implied in the representation of consonants. It was not until the Phoenician script was brought to the Hellenic world and gave rise to the Greek and, eventually, Latin scripts that a whole set of symbols for vowels was coined. The Semitic (Aramaic) tradition was maintained, however, long after the writing system was introduced to other parts of Asia, but because the sound shapes in many of these languages were very different from Semitic, there was eventually adopted a system of diacritic marks to indicate the various vowels in one way or another. Usually, for example, the vowel *a* is "implied" after a consonant symbol unless other vowels are specified by a diacritical mark.

Thus the writing systems of Asia are all phonetic, or sound based, in the sense that all of them are designed to record pronounceable words. The word or syllable length, of course, varies. The single Chinese graph for "clock" represents a combination of four single sounds: *b, i, a,* and *o.* The Korean ㄴ stands just for the single sound *n;* the Japanese *kana* come somewhere between and represent a combination of one consonant and one vowel (for example, there is a single *kana* for the syllable made up of the two sounds *k* and *a*). Whereas writing systems like the Chinese require a larger inventory of unit symbols, the known number of which amounts to almost fifty thousand, systems like *han'gŭl* can reduce it to a minimum. Thus the number of *han'gŭl* letters in contemporary use is twenty-four or even fewer (depending upon how diphthongs are counted).

Cultural Connection. Although the use of some writing systems is determined solely by political concerns (the Dungan in Central Asia, for instance, use the Cyrillic writing system, even though their language belongs to the Northern Chinese group of Sino-Tibetan), contemporary Asian writing systems as a whole tend to reflect their cultural-religious background and can be classified according to the following associations: (1) Arabic: Muslim, (2) Brahmi and its variants: Buddhism and Hinduism, (3) Uighur and Tibetan: Lamaism (Tibetan Buddhism), and (4) Chinese characters: Confucianism, Daoism, and Buddhism.

David Diringer, *Writing* (1962). Godfrey R. Driver, *Semitic Writing: From Pictograph to Alphabet* (rev. ed., 1976). I. J. Gelb, *A Study of Writing* (2d ed., 1963).

MANTARO J. HASHIMOTO

WU HAN (1909–1969?), Chinese historian; purged and killed during the Cultural Revolution.

Born in Zhejiang, Wu attended Qinghua University by supporting himself through work. After his graduation, he started a teaching career at the history department of his alma mater, reaching the position of associate professor before the outbreak of the Anti-Japanese War. During the war he moved to Chongqing, teaching at the Southwest United University. There he joined the Chinese Democratic League, which opposed the authoritarian rule of the Nationalist Party. After 1945 he returned to Qinghua University, but continued to be active in pro-Communist academic circles, eventually joining the Communist Party in 1957. In 1952 he became the vice-mayor of Beijing, a position he held until 1966.

As a well-known historian specializing in the Ming period, Wu published several scholarly books. In addition he wrote a historical play, *Hai Rui's Dismissal from Office*, in 1961 when the Chinese Communist Party had somewhat relaxed its control over society and the arts after the failure of the Great Leap Forward. In the play, Wu Han praised Hai Rui, an official of the Ming period (1368–1644) who had been dismissed from office by the emperor after returning to the peasants the land that a corrupt official had seized from them.

The Maoist criticism of the play as a veiled political attack on Mao's 1959 dismissal of Peng Dehuai initiated the Cultural Revolution. As the criticism of his play increased, Wu Han published a self-criticism in January 1966, but it did not save him. He reportedly died from political persecution in 1969; his wife and daughter also died in that year. In 1979 Wu Han was posthumously rehabilitated.

[*See also* Great Proletarian Cultural Revolution.]

HONG YUNG LEE

WU JINGZI (1701–1754), author of China's most famous satirical novel, *Rulin waishi (The Scholars)*. Wu was from a socially and politically prominent family of Quanzhou, Anhui. His own failure to follow in the family traditions of examination success, and particularly to pass the second *boxue hongru* examination of 1736, on which many of his friends were successful, formed the background for his biting indictment of the hypocrisy and insincerity of intellectual and academic life. Critics have differed on the overall significance of the novel, some seeing it as the grumbling of a disaffected eccentric, and others viewing it as a more forceful and coherent attack on the evils of Manchu rule and imperial social structure. However it is characterized, the novel remains one of the high points of early modern Chinese fiction, and is filled with witty and irreverent portraits of Chinese scholars, bureaucrats, and rulers. One of the most memorable characters in the novel, the scholarly and affable Du Shaoqing, who through bumbling and benevolence dissipates his family income, is probably Wu Jingzi's self-portrait.

[*See also* Rulin Waishi.]

Paul S. Ropp, *Dissent in Early Modern China: Ju-lin wai-shih and Ch'ing Social Criticism* (1981). Wu Ching-tzu (Wu Jingzi), *The Scholars*, translated by Yang Hsien-yi and Gladys Yang (1972).   R. KENT GUY

WU PEIFU (1874–1939), the substantive military leader of the Zhili clique of warlords from 1920 to 1924, although his superior, Cao Kun, nominally headed the clique. In 1922 Wu defeated Zhang Zuolin to become the dominant militarist in North China, and launched a campaign to unite the country by military force. In 1924, during the second war against the Fengtian clique, Wu's subordinate Feng Yuxiang turned against him, causing Wu's defeat. Wu rebuilt his forces and cooperated with his former enemy Zhang Zuolin against the Northern Expedition, but retired after defeat in 1927. During the mid-1930s Wu refused Japanese inducements to head a puppet regime in North China.

[*See also* Warlord Cliques; Warlords; Northern Expedition; Cao Kun; Zhang Zuolin; *and* Feng Yuxiang.]

Odoric Y. K. Wou, *Militarism in Modern China: The Career of Wu P'ei-fu, 1916–1939* (1978).

JAMES E. SHERIDAN

WU SANGUI (1612–1678), Chinese general; remembered as the commander in charge of Shanhaiguan (a strategic pass between China and Manchuria) when the Manchus entered China. A native of Liaodong, Wu rose in the Ming military hierarchy, but in 1644 allied with the Manchus to defeat the rebel Li Zicheng, and subsequently campaigned for the Qing, destroying Ming remnants in southern China. Rewarded with a virtually independent jurisdiction in Yunnan, similar to those of two other commanders in Guangdong and Fujian, he revolted in 1673 when the government in Beijing moved to abolish these "Three Feudatories." The Qing met the challenge successfully and crushed the last resistance in 1681.

[*See also* Ming Dynasty; Qing Dynasty; *and* Three Feudatories Rebellion.]

Chaoying Fang, "Wu San-kuei," in *Eminent Chinese of the Ch'ing Period, 1644–1912*, 2 vols., edited by Arthur W. Hummel (1943–1944). Angela N. S. Hsi, "Wu San-kuei in 1644: A Reappraisal," *Journal of Asian Studies* 34.2 (1975): 443–453.   ARTHUR N. WALDRON

WUXI, city in Jiangsu Province, China, located at the northeast corner of Lake Tai directly astride the Grand Canal. Founded more than two thousand years ago, Wuxi remained a small town until the twentieth century, when it became a center for silk and cotton textiles and an important market for agricultural shipments to nearby Shanghai. After 1949 the pace of its industrial development was increased. In addition to its still-dominant textiles

Wuxi is a center of food processing, oil extraction, diesel engine, and machine tool industries, and has grown to a population of nearly 800,000 (1982).

JOHN A. RAPP

WU ZHAO (627?–705), wife of the third Tang emperor, Gaozong (r. 650–683); the only woman in Chinese history to have founded her own dynasty and ruled as an "emperor." From a locally prominent clan in modern Shanxi Province, Wu first entered the palace around 640 to serve the second Tang emperor, Taizong (r. 627–650), as a low-ranking concubine; Gaozong probably fell in love with her at that time. After Taizong's death Wu may not have left the palace, as was the custom for concubines of deceased emperors. By 652 she had borne at least one son to Gaozong and began scheming to displace the emperor's legitimate but childless wife, Empress Wang, in his affections. In 655 he demoted Empress Wang and elevated Wu in her place. Owing to her husband's infirmities and her own political ruthlessness, by 660 Wu had come to dominate the court, where, sitting behind a silken screen, she carried out a harsh, authoritarian rule.

When Gaozong died in 683, Wu retained her position of power. In an unprecedented act for a woman, in 690 she founded her own "Zhou dynasty" and assumed the title of emperor. Thereafter, most members of the Tang dynastic house were systematically liquidated and a cruel reign of terror ensued. It was only in 705, when the empress had become enfeebled, that power was restored to the Tang. As a woman and a usurper, Wu has been excoriated by Confucian historians. Yet she was a remarkably able monarch who gained at least the tacit support of the people. Although Marxists have cited Wu's intensified use of the examination system that brought new blood into the bureaucracy as evidence that she favored a "newly risen landlord class" over the old aristocracy, it is unlikely that she was ever partial to any single social or economic group unless it served her own ends.

[*See also* Tang Dynasty.]

C. P. Fitzgerald, *The Empress Wu* (1955). R. W. L. Guisso, *Wu Tse-t'ien and the Politics of Legitimation in T'ang China* (1978).   HOWARD J. WECHSLER

X

XAVIER, FRANCIS (1506–1552; canonized 1622). A Basque nobleman from Navarre and a brilliant student at the University of Paris, Xavier joined the Society of Jesus on 15 August 1534. His intellectual attainments endeared him to John III of Portugal, who sent him to Goa in 1541 as apostolic nuncio. Xavier left Goa in 1542 to proselytize coastal communities both on the west and east coast of India; he concentrated especially on the Prava fisherman of the Coromandel. He then turned his attention to the conversion of indigenous kings and princes. He used his great influence over the king of Travancore to protect his ever-growing flock of coastal Christians. His missionary endeavors expanded to Ceylon, the Maluku (Moluccas) and in 1549 to Kagoshima, Kyoto, and Yamaguchi in Japan. Hedied on the island of Shangchuan near Canton (Guangzhou) on 2 December 1552 while attempting to carry the faith to China. Xavier was canonized twenty years after his death by Gregory XV. His still-incorrupt body is on display at the Church of Bom Jesu in Goa, where it had been transferred by Portuguese sailors on 15 March 1553. Xavier is considered the founding father of the Ancient Jesuit South Indian Mission.

[*See also* Jesuits *and* Christianity: Christianity in Japan.]

James Brodrick, *St. Francis Xavier, 1506–1552* (1952). George Moraes, *St. Francis Xavier, Apostolic Nuncio, 1542–1552* (1952). P. Rayanna, *St. Francis Xavier and His Shrine* (1954).   PATRICK ROCHE

XERXES (520–465 BCE), Achaemenid king of Persia from 486 to 465 BCE, son of Darius I by Atossa, daughter of Cyrus I ("the Great"). Xerxes (Old Persian, Khshayarsha, "ruling over heroes") was educated by his father to rule a world empire and inherited a major war with Greece. He put down a rebellion in Egypt, reconquered Babylon, and built extensive constructions at Persepolis and other sites.

Despite his reluctance to carry out Darius's plan to invade Greece, his militant advisers, especially his cousin Mardonius, and Athenian exiles induced Xerxes to lead, in the sixth year of his reign, an army of invasion in person. His Greek opponents, in gross exaggeration, claimed that his forces numbered more than five million fighters and servants, but they in fact were composed of some seventy thousand footmen and ten thousand horsemen from Iranian regions (Media, Persis, Elam, Parthia, Aria, Drangiana, Sogdia, Bactria, and Sacaea); most of them were lightly armed and unsystematically marshaled.

Large numbers of Greeks joined Xerxes' expeditionary army as subjects or allies. Under the leadership of Athens and Sparta, the Greek city-states united to form a front against him. First a force under Leonidas, a king of Sparta, and his three hundred heavy-armed infantry (hoplites), blocked Xerxes' way at the Thermopylae Pass, but they were surrounded and destroyed and Athens was taken. Themistocles organized a Greek fleet, drew the Persian navy, which had an equal number of warships but of heavy and slow type, into the narrow strait of Salamis and defeated it. Then Xerxes left Mardonius with a picked army to continue the military operations on land; he himself returned to Sardis, an act misrepresented as cowardly flight. Mardonius was killed and his army vanquished by the Spartan Pausanias at the Battle of Plataea (479), which ended Persia's threat to Greece.

Xerxes spent the rest of his life constructing palaces and administering his vast empire. To him the war and its consequences were far less important than his enemies pictured, and at the end his foes Themistocles and Pausanias both sought refuge from their own citizens at his court. In 465 Xerxes was murdered and entombed in a rock-cut tomb near Persepolis. "Against his one military failure in Europe, not so spectacular to his subjects as it appeared to later generations, must be placed a whole series of victories . . . and his retention of control over the majority of Greeks themselves" (Olmstead, 1948, p. 230). Xerxes has been vilified by many historians as the enemy of culture and freedom, but this is Greek propaganda. Persian sources picture him as a great administrator, builder, and patron of art.

[*See also* Achaemenid Dynasty *and* Darius I.]

Herodotus, *Histories,* translated by Aubrey De Selincourt (1954). C. Hignett, *Xerxes' Invasion of Greece* (1962). R. G. Kent, *Old Persian* (2d ed., 1953), pp. 147ff. A. T. Olmstead, *History of the Persian Empire* (1948). E. F. Schmidt, *Persepolis,* 3 vols. (1953–1969).

A. SHAHPUR SHAHBAZI

XIA DYNASTY

XIA DYNASTY (traditionally dated 2205–1766 BCE), considered by the Chinese to be their first historical state. The most important question that can be asked about the Xia dynasty is whether or not it existed. The historicity of the Xia was firmly implanted in the Chinese cultural tradition until early in the twentieth century, when critical thinkers asserted that the existence of the Xia was only a myth perpetuated by uncritical, premodern historians. The same assertions were made about the succeeding Shang dynasty. Archaeological evidence now confirms that the Shang dynasty existed and, furthermore, that the chronology of the Shang given by Sima Qian (d. about 93 BCE) is remarkably accurate. The reliability of Sima's chronology of the Shang suggests that his record of the Xia is equally reliable.

Sima Qian's history provides us with a skeletal chronicle of the Xia, listing the rulers and, occasionally, providing some anecdotal information about them. If this record reflects Xia reality then one of the major characteristics of the Xia was the difficulty the ruling house had in holding territory under its control, for there are references to lesser rulers in the realm deserting the Xia court, thereby requiring the reassertion of Xia authority. The last Xia ruler, Jie, was an evil man who alienated his people and brought about the downfall of his ruling house. This historical image of the man provided an important cautionary figure for subsequent Chinese statesmen and rulers.

The archaeological record is still not conclusive regarding the existence of this dynasty. There is a growing tendency to identify the early layer of the Erlitou site with the Xia dynasty. But until some written evidence is excavated from a Xia site or perhaps some document from the Shang that refers to the Xia is found, uncertainty about the historical reality of this dynasty, allegedly the first in Chinese history, will remain.

Kwang-chih Chang, *The Archaeology of Ancient China* (1977).

JACK L. DULL

XIAMEN (Amoy), the second largest city of Fujian Province, China. Xiamen is an excellent port located on an island at the mouth of the Jiulong River opposite the Nationalist-held island of Jinmen (Quemoy). With a population of fewer than four hundred thousand, Xiamen mostly handles the trade in sugar, fruits, and tea of the surrounding region. Its industry is limited for the most part to food processing. A military outpost in the Qing dynasty (1644–1911) after its recapture from the Ming loyalist Koxinga (Zheng Chenggong), Xiamen began to thrive as a commercial port following the Qing annexation of Taiwan in 1683. Xiamen was a jumping-off point for emigrants to Taiwan and Southeast Asia beginning in the seventeenth century, and it retains strong connections to Overseas Chinese.

JOHN A. RAPP

XI'AN, Chinese city, capital of Shaanxi Province. Located in the fertile Wei River valley, it is the largest city in northwest China, with a population of 2,180,000 (1982). Xi'an is also one of the most ancient of China's cities. Archaeological evidence reveals that the remains of numerous Neolithic settlements in the environs of Xi'an belong to the so-called Yangshao (painted pottery) culture (c. 6000 BCE). Sites near present-day Xi'an also served as the capital of a number of Chinese dynasties between 1122 BCE and 907 CE. Imperial tombs of these dynasties are found in the hills surrounding Xi'an. In 1974, a subterranean funeral vault of the first emperor of China, Qin Shihuangdi (r. 221–210 BCE) was unearthed near Xi'an. The vault has so far revealed some six thousand life-sized terra-cotta warriors and horses guarding the imperial tomb and is considered one of the great archaeological discoveries of the twentieth century (see figure 1).

Known to the ancient world as Chang'an, the city reached the peak of its development during the Tang dynasty (618–907), when it was the most important center of trade in Asia and had more than one million inhabitants. After the fall of the Tang the city declined until the early fourteenth century. During the Ming dynasty (1368–1644) the city received its present name of Xi'an. It experienced a brief resurgence of its former splendor during the early Qing dynasty (1644–1911), but thereafter lapsed into isolation until the twentieth century.

Xi'an's modern development began with the construction of a railway network linking Xi'an to other industrialized cities in Shaanxi after 1930. Since 1949 Xi'an has emerged as a major administrative, industrial, and cultural center in northwest China. Its local products include coal, mining equipment, iron and steel, heavy machinery, cement, chemicals, paper, textiles, plastics, and electrical instruments.

ANITA M. ANDREW

XIANBEI, a North Asian nomadic tribal confederation, perhaps of Turkic origin. The Xianbei became historically significant in 45 CE when, allied with the Xiongnu, they raided the northern Chinese border. As the Xiongnu confederation dissolved, the Xianbei confederation began to form. By the 160s, under the outstanding leader Tanshihuai, a huge confederation took over the former Xiongnu territory, but it could not be maintained after Tanshihuai's death. In later centuries Xianbei tribes founded seven dynasties in North China; of these dynasties, the Tuoba Wei (386–534) in its heyday ruled the largest empire in the world.

[*See also* Xiongnu *and* Northern Wei Dynasty.]

JACK L. DULL

XIANG YU (232–202 BCE), Chinese general descended from famous military men of the preimperial Chinese state of Chu. When rebels rose against the Qin empire in 209 BCE, Xiang Yu's uncle also rebelled, asserting that he was restoring the Chu state; when his uncle was killed in battle, Xiang Yu took control of the Chu armies. After the Qin dynasty was overthrown, Xiang Yu and Liu Ji fought for five years for control of China. Believing that Liu's forces had conquered his Chu homeland, Xiang Yu committed suicide. Known as an excellent military strategist, Xiang Yu's tearful parting from his concubine and his giving away of his beloved horse are famous Chinese historical scenes. [*See also* Qin Dynasty.]

JACK L. DULL

XI'AN INCIDENT, capture of Chiang Kai-shek by his own forces in Xi'an, December 1936, that led to his agreement to a united policy of resistance to Japanese aggression. In 1936 Chiang was confident that he could completely destroy the Communists with one more campaign. He ordered Zhang Xueliang and his forces, then headquartered in Xi'an, to launch the attack on the remnants of the Communist forces, which had reassembled in northern Shaanxi Province following the Long March. However, Zhang and his officers, who had retreated from their homeland of Manchuria after the Japanese conquest there in 1931–1932, were homesick and convinced that they should fight a war of resistance against the foreign invaders rather than

FIGURE 1. *Horses and Chariot.* Bronze, life-size. Unearthed near Xi'an at the tomb of Qin Shihuangdi (r. 221–210 BCE), unifier of the first Chinese empire.

carry on a civil war against the Communists, who had also proclaimed their wish to fight the Japanese. When Chiang Kai-shek flew into Xi'an on 12 December to enforce his order to commence the attack on the Communists, Zhang and his fellow commanders took him prisoner. Chiang's life was in danger, but after intensive discussions with the Communist representative, Zhou Enlai, Zhang released him on 25 December and flew to Nanjing with him.

Although the matter has long been in dispute, it is now believed that Chiang Kai-shek made only a verbal promise to his captors that he would cease the attacks on the Communists and concentrate on fighting the Japanese. This promise led to the formation of a united front between the Nationalists and the Communists. Chiang's new policy of nonconciliation with the Japanese eventually led to the outbreak of war against Japan in July 1937. Zhang Xueliang, however, was thereafter held under arrest by Chiang Kai-shek and was not released until after Chiang's death in 1975.

[See also Chiang Kai-shek; United Front; and Zhang Xueliang.]

LLOYD E. EASTMAN

XICH QUY QUOC ("country of red devils") was the country ruled by Kinh Duong Vuong in the mythological period of Vietnam's history. Kinh Duong Vuong, himself a descendant of the legendary Chinese monarch Shen Nong, was the ancestor of the eighteen kings known as Hung Vuong ("Hung kings"), whose rule is believed to have begun in the seventh century BCE. His queen was Than Long Nu ("lady dragon spirit"). Their son, Lac Long Quan, and his wife Au Co are revered by the Vietnamese as the progenitors of their race.

[See also Kinh Duong Vuong; Hung Vuong; Lac Long Quan; and Au Co.]

Keith W. Taylor, *The Birth of Vietnam* (1983).

BRUCE M. LOCKHART

XIE FUZHI (1898–1972), early Chinese Communist leader. Xie was born in Hubei, joined the Communist movement in the 1920s, participated in the Long March, and proved himself a remarkably successful political commissar in the Second Field Army under Deng Xiaoping before 1949. In the early 1950s Xie was the ranking Party and military leader in Yunnan Province. From 1959 to the early 1970s Xie was minister of public security and commander of the Public Security Force, and one of the few in charge of China's security apparatus. He sided with Mao against his former superior Deng Xiaoping during the Cultural Revolution, and was rewarded with the membership in the Politburo in 1969. He died in 1972 after sustaining injury in an assassination attempt, and was disgraced posthumously in 1978 after Deng took control of the leadership of China.

PARRIS CHANG

XIENG KHOUANG. *See* Siang Khwang.

XI GUANG. *See* Tich Quang.

XIN DYNASTY. *See* Wang Mang.

XINHAI REVOLUTION. Known in the West as the 1911 Revolution, the Xinhai Revolution overthrew the Manchu Qing dynasty, replacing the centralized bureaucratic monarchy with republican government in China. The name of the revolution refers to the last year of the sixty-year lunar cycle, which corresponds most closely with the Western year 1911.

The revolution began with an uprising of intellectuals and soldiers on 10 October at Wuchang on the middle Yangtze River. As the revolutionary army moved down the Yangtze Valley, coalitions of intellectuals, merchants, gentry, soldiers, and sometimes secret society leaders declared independence from the Qing and established provincial military governments. A provisional national government was established at Nanjing under Sun Yat-sen on 1 January 1912. Because the Qing remained strong in the North, Sun resigned to prevent a long military stalemate. The Manchus then abdicated, and a constitutional republican government was established in Beijing, with the well-known modernizing official Yuan Shikai as president.

Accounts of the 1911 Revolution initially focused on professional revolutionaries, but historians have recognized more complex forces at work. One basic debate has been whether 1911 was a national revolution of elements from all classes against a foreign Manchu dynasty shored up by imperialist powers, or whether it was a bourgeois democratic revolution underlain by capitalist development and imperialist encroachment. Another question has been whether it effectively broke through old patterns of cyclic dynastic change. Numerous subsidiary arguments exist over the roles of different social groups, including students, merchants, secret societies, and the new army. Related issues include the extent to which provincially based movements for a constitutional monarchy contributed to the revolution and the importance of anti-Manchuism in turning opinion against the dynasty.

Although there is no definitive explanation, the 1911 Revolution can be considered a phase in longer nineteenth- and twentieth-century processes. As such, it was a culmination of expanding elite social organization and political aspirations that were most marked in the economically developed regions of China. Among the long-range factors behind the revolution were: (1) commercial expansion during the eighteenth and nineteenth centuries, which did not necessarily result in capitalist modes of production, but tended to fuse the merchant and gentry classes into a vigorous, expansive elite in the economic cores; (2) rapid demographic growth, which contributed to commercial expansion but also fostered social unrest and increased the population beyond the capacity of governmental control; (3) the expansion of both private social organizations (like guilds, religious organizations, or kinship institutions) and elite-run public institutions to meet community needs; and (4) the character of the Qing state, which combined a theoretically autocratic ruler, a sophisticated bureaucratic organization capable of continuing administration when the throne weakened, and a lightly extractive, noninterventionist style of government, which left latitude for expanding social organization and was not, of itself, adequate to meet the crises produced by indigenous secular growth and imperialist encroachment.

Commercial, demographic, and organizational growth were slowly shifting the balance between state and society and attenuating the bonds between the gentry and a government that defined their status through civil examination degrees. Changes leading more directly toward revolution were precipitated by domestic social unrest and foreign imperialism. The mid-nineteenth-century rebellions, particularly the Taiping Rebellion, caused a surge of elite activity outside of bureaucratic control. This was initially military, but elites assumed responsibilities for post-rebellion reconstruction that led to permanent, officially sanctioned increases in public organization. In critical core regions this expansion of the public sphere was connected with growing private organization and commercial expansion fostered by foreign trade and broadened conceptions of a public role in solving national problems.

Imperialism had more unsettling effects. Foreign trade was destabilizing (whether it led to economic growth or decline), leading to social unrest, new patterns of organization and production, and changes in relations between elites and officials. Military invasion or economic encroachment aroused patriotic opposition to officials blamed for failing to defend China. This anger metamorphosed into a patriotic public opinion, encouraged by the press, that called for social mobilization under elite leadership and broader representation in policy-making. Finally, exposure to foreigners not only produced models for economic and military strengthening but also introduced Chinese to institutions that could be used either to strengthen the existing state or to oppose it.

By the end of the Sino-Japanese War (1894–1895), these factors had coalesced to produce the explosion of social organization and nationalistic political activity that led to the 1898 Reform Movement. The turmoil produced power struggles within the capital and the first uprisings against the political system. Extreme political uncertainty fostered wider doubts about governmental leadership.

Historians of the 1911 Revolution have concentrated on the last Qing decade (1902–1911), when republican revolutionary organizations and literature became a major political factor. In a longer perspective, these years were distinguished by sustained competition between state-building and elite social mobilization that had its own dynamics. By then, industrial and educational changes had begun to fragment the old elite into such new components as capitalists, intelligentsia, military officers, and rural oligarchs. Students in new schools, in particular, furnished revolutionary recruits. At the same time, the government embarked on an ambitious program of state-building and national strengthening. Although the throne was weakening, officials had tentatively begun to strengthen the state from the mid-nineteenth century onward, imposing new commercial taxes, promoting industry, and improving the armies. The new policies were a far more sweeping effort to centralize power in Beijing and extend formal state organization, while instituting reforms to strengthen China against foreigners. Official determination to extend control clashed with the determination of already-distrustful social groups to mobilize independently.

The opposition divided into two interacting streams. One consisted of professional revolutionaries and radical intellectuals who sought to establish a democratic republic. They justified revolution with nationalistic and anti-Manchu arguments, attacked Confucian social morality, and expressed usually vague concern over peasant misfortunes. Sun Yat-sen had established the Revive China Society (Xingzhonghui) and had plotted a rising in Canton during the Sino-Japanese War, but the main activity began about 1903. Revolutionaries established societies and front organizations, allied with secret societies, and infiltrated the new army. In 1905 the Revolutionary Alliance (Tongmenghui) was founded in Japan under Sun Yat-sen. The first wave of assassination attempts and uprisings ended in 1908, but the second wave culminated in the Wuchang Uprising.

Although important as catalysts, the revolutionaries were too few, and too weakly organized, to overthrow the dynasty alone. The second stream arose out of a broader organization, mobilization, and politicization of elite society. This mobilization developed through nationalistic, anti-imperialist movements, the provincial constitutionalist movements for representative government, and railway movements. Officially mandated New Policy institutions like chambers of commerce, educational associations, and assemblies, which might have integrated government and elite society, often became oppositionist tools. Unrest among the lower classes, exacerbated by new taxes to support the New Policies, further fostered the impression of governmental inadequacy. Escalating conflicts caused more and more elites to entertain the revolutionary argument that the imperial system was oppressive per se. Anti-Manchuism was useful propaganda, and the unwise determination of Manchu princes to use bureaucratic centralization to increase court authority hastened the break. However, important segments of the elite populace were expanding their political demands more rapidly than the central government could expand its control. Given governmental reluctance to share power, it seems inevitable that the political structure would crack.

Political as well as economic factors contributed to this crucial alienation of elites, but the impetus appears to have come from the cores. In these regions, the 1911 Revolution united elements of old and new elites against a state structure that they considered antithetical to their own interests and the interests of the country and that was not flexible enough to encompass social mobilization. Participation of secret societies, and of urban and rural lower classes, raises the possibility of an all-encompassing union against a foreign dynasty. However, the strongest evidence for prolonged par-

ticipation of a rural "mob" comes from the Canton delta, where villagers had long been affected by foreign trade and emigration. Most rural unrest was more like traditional protests or banditry: it indicated continuing social problems, but in 1911 did more to produce rural elite reaction than to end the imperial system.

The 1911 Revolution (often extended to include the brief flourishing of representational institutions until they were suppressed in 1913) permanently changed political relationships and opened new possibilities for upper-class participation in government. It was not, however, a decisive historical event. Mobilized elites could not dominate the continuing organs of the bureaucratic state, nor were they able to control competing militarists who filled power voids after the Qing. New conflicts and divisions arose within elite society, and elites in and out of the government competed to control social reorganization. Dissident elites eventually made contact with peasants, whose lives were increasingly disrupted during the Republic, and brought rural social discontent into the revolutionary political sphere. The pre-1911 processes of social organization and mobilization changed during the Republic, but the 1911 Revolution had broken through old cyclical patterns, and opened the way for continuing redefinition of polity and society.

[See also Guomindang; Huang Xing; Qiu Jin; Sun Yat-sen; Xuantong Emperor; Yuan Shikai; Qing Dynasty; and China, Republic Period.]

Joseph Esherick, Reform and Revolution in China: The 1911 Revolution in Hunan and Hupeh (1976). John Fincher, Chinese Democracy: The Self-Government Movement in Local, Provincial, and National Politics, 1905–1914 (1983). Michael Gasster, Chinese Intellectuals and the Revolution of 1911 (1969). Winston Hsieh, "Peasant Insurrection and the Marketing Hierarchy in the Canton Delta, 1911," in The Chinese City between Two Worlds, edited by Mark Elvin and G. William Skinner (1974), pp. 119–141. Philip A. Kuhn, "Local Self-Government under the Republic," in Conflict and Control in Late Imperial China, edited by Frederic Wakeman, Jr., and Carolyn Grant (1975), pp. 257–298. Mary Backus Rankin, Early Chinese Revolutionaries: Radical Intellectuals in Shanghai and Chekiang, 1902–1911 (1971). Edward J. M. Rhoads, China's Republican Revolution: The Case of Kwangtung, 1895–1911 (1975). Mary C. Wright, China in Revolution: The First Phase, 1900–1913 (1968).

MARY BACKUS RANKIN

XINING, Chinese city, the provincial capital of Qinghai in northwest China. Xining is an industrial city with a population of fewer than five hundred thousand (1982) located at the eastern end of the province near the border with Gansu. A military garrison and trading center since the sixteenth century, its industrialization began after it was connected to the main Chinese rail network in 1959. Today its industry includes an oil refinery and an iron and steel plant, along with factories producing farm tools, ball bearings, electrical equipment, fertilizers, and chemicals.   JOHN A. RAPP

XINJIANG, formerly known as Turkestan, is China's largest administrative unit, covering about one-sixth of the total area of the country. The Taklamakan, a desert in southern Xinjiang, causes much of the region to be uninhabitable. Another formidable barrier to human habitation is the Tian Shan range, in the center of this vast territory. Directly north of the Tian Shan are the towns of Urumqi (the capital of Xinjiang), Turfan, and Kuldja (Yining), and even farther north are the Dzungarian steppelands. In turn, northern Xinjiang abuts the Soviet Central Asian republics of Kazakhstan, Kirghizia, and Tajikistan. To the south are the oases and towns of the Tarim River basin, including Yarkand, Khotan, and others; the southern boundary is clearly delineated by the Kunlun mountains, which separate Xinjiang from Tibet and Kashmir.

Perhaps Xinjiang's main value to traditional China was its strategic location. Xinjiang was the main gateway to South and West Asia, and such oases as Hami and Turfan in the north and Khotan and Keriya in the south were vital to the operation of the so-called Silk Route. The trade caravans needed these halting places for food, water, and other supplies. The northern routes led to Central Asia and the Middle East while the southern ones wound their way to India. China's interest in Xinjiang was not, however, limited to commerce. The Chinese courts, concerned about defense of their territories, sought buffer zones as a means of protecting their borderlands. Chinese occupation of Xinjiang would keep the non-Chinese inhabitants under control and would protect China's core territories in Gansu and Shaanxi provinces. The more powerful Chinese dynasties thus attempted to control the pastoral nomads, the traders, and the peasants of Xinjiang. The Han (206 BCE–220 CE) and Tang (618–907) dynasties, in particular, overwhelmed the natives and established garrisons in the oases. They could not totally pacify the herdsmen in the steppes and mountains, but they dominated the sedentary population in the towns. China se-

cured its borderlands, and useful side effects were the increase in trade between East and West and the flourishing cultural interchange between China and the rest of Asia. When these great Chinese dynasties declined, however, they lost their holds on Xinjiang, and their garrisons were compelled to withdraw.

The Chinese continued to be influenced by Xinjiang even when they did not occupy this so-called Western Region. As early as the first century CE, Buddhism reached the oases of Xinjiang, and many of the natives converted to the Indian religion. Khotan and Turfan became Buddhist centers. Buddhist patrons supported the building of monasteries, temples, and statues as well as the painting of frescoes and murals. The oases served as intermediaries in the transmission of the new religion to northwest China, leading to the establishment of the great Buddhist artistic and religious center at Dunhuang (in Gansu) and to court patronage of Buddhism in the capitals at Datong, Luoyang, and Chang'an. Islam was also introduced to China through the oases of Xinjiang. Muslim merchants from Central Asia and the Middle East started to arrive in Xinjiang within a few decades after the death of Muhammad in 632. They conducted trade with the Turkic merchants and simultaneously helped to convert some of them to Islam. The Turkic peoples, in turn, transmitted the Islamic teachings to northwest China.

Despite Xinjiang's vital influence on China, it remained independent of the Chinese court until the eighteenth century. The Mongol Yuan dynasty (1279–1368) imposed its authority over the region, but the succeeding Ming dynasty (1368–1644) did not assert its domination over the local people, who enjoyed a satisfactory trade and tribute relationship with the Chinese court. The Qing dynasty (1644–1911), in seeking to secure its borders, overwhelmed the Dzungar Mongols in the 1750s and then occupied Xinjiang. The Manchu rulers wanted to promote the economic recovery of the region rather than exploit its resources. They developed irrigation projects, encouraged commerce, and kept taxes low. The court permitted the natives great leeway in governing themselves and tried not to interfere in local affairs. Yet it could not regulate its own people. Chinese colonists moved into Xinjiang and exploited the non-Chinese. The Chinese and Manchu officials who were dispatched to the newly seized territories discriminated against and oppressed the local populace.

The native response was predictable. A more fundamentalist form of Islam, which stressed the purity of its doctrine and opposed any foreign (i.e., Chinese) influence gained numerous adherents. Economic conflicts between the Chinese and the local peoples erupted and led to bitter animosities. These hostilities repeatedly flared into open warfare. In 1781, 1784, and 1815 minor Muslim insurrections arose and were suppressed. But the Qing forces needed eight years to crush the more organized and more wide-scale rebellion of 1820 led by Jahangir Khoja. The culmination of these hostilities was the devastating conflict of 1862 to 1878. A soldier named Ya'qub Beg eventually became the leader of the Muslim insurgents, and the Qing court assigned Zuo Zongtang to suppress the rebels. The conflict was protracted and destructive but Zuo finally crushed Muslim resistance.

Zuo's success, however, did not end the disturbances in the northwest. To defuse the tensions in the region, in 1884 the Qing court finally changed its status from a tributary territory to the full-fledged province of Xinjiang ("new province"). The province would now be ruled by the civil bureaucracy, not the military. This change in status did not pacify the local people. Disturbances continued throughout the late nineteenth century, with a particularly violent outbreak in 1895.

The fall of the Qing and the resulting lack of a strong central government permitted Xinjiang to be virtually independent from 1911 to 1949. Yang Zengxin, the Chinese governor (or more properly, warlord), seized power in 1912. Although he paid nominal allegiance to the authorities in Beijing, he ruled Xinjiang as an autonomous sovereign. He ingratiated himself with the local people by reducing their tax burden and by punishing Chinese colonists and officials who oppressed them. He crushed the secret societies and the gangs of bandits who had previously harassed the native inhabitants. These policies helped him win the loyalty of many of the non-Chinese, but he was still intent on preventing them from becoming overly powerful. He sought to accentuate the tensions among the Uighurs, Kazakhs, and the various other ethnic groups. Finally, he initiated closer economic and political relations with the USSR, signing a commercial treaty with that relatively new government in 1924. Since the middle of the nineteenth century Russia had attempted to wean Xinjiang away from China. With Yang and with his eventual successor Sheng Shicai, who emerged as the ruler of the region in 1934, the USSR had its opportunity, and it became a partner in the commercial and industrial development of Xinjiang. The Soviet Union's entry into World War II in 1941 and Sheng's fall from power in 1944 created a vacuum that several ethnic leaders tried but failed to fill.

When the Communists assumed the reigns of government in 1949, they were determined to reassert Chinese authority over the natives of Xinjiang. Yet they couched this objective as an effort to promote social justice and to preserve the unique characteristics of the so-called national minorities. In line with this goal, they founded the Xinjiang Uighur Autonomous Region in 1955, implying that the natives had a significant measure of independence. The government's policy has actually been based on the desire to tap the vast oil, uranium, gold, and other mineral resources of the region; the recognition of its potential to absorb a larger population; the awareness that their policy toward the native Muslim peoples would influence China's relations with the Islamic world; and an eagerness to secure this strategic location on the borders of the USSR.

Although the Chinese have acknowledged the economic and political significance of Xinjiang, their policies toward the local peoples have been inconsistent. They have wavered from a stress on consideration of the special characteristics of the national minorities to an attempt to compel these mostly Turkic peoples to acquiesce or assimilate into Chinese culture. The conciliatory approach, which was pursued from 1949 to 1957, 1962 to 1965, and since 1976, permitted the local peoples to use their own languages in the schools and mass media, to practice Islam, to abide by many of their own customs and beliefs, and often to be governed by their own leaders, who were recruited into the Communist Party. The hard-line policy, which was enforced from 1958 to 1961 and during the Cultural Revolution from 1966 to 1976, required the use of the Chinese language in the region, impeded the practice of Islam, replaced the native leaders with Chinese officials, and encouraged Han Chinese colonists to migrate to Xinjiang in order to outnumber the non-Han residents. The ultimate goal of both policies appears to be the assimiliation of the native peoples into Chinese culture. Yet Communist rule has been beneficial in initiating projects to extract the mineral resources, extend the railroad lines, and enlarge the cities in the region. The government has also improved and expanded educational and medical facilities.

The various Turkic peoples of Xinjiang have reacted differently to Communist rule. The Uighurs, the most numerous of the minority nationalities, have traditionally been the town and oasis dwellers. They have generally had fewer difficulties in adapting to the new government. Subsistence agriculture and distribution of goods still remain vital occupations, although some Uighurs are currently joining the industrial labor force. The Kazakhs and the

Kirghiz, who were customarily pastoral nomads, have often resisted Communist policies. The government has encouraged and occasionally demanded that the nomads settle into ranches and limit their annual migrations. The advantages of this policy are that the nomads' animals can be sheltered during the winter and can have better access to food and that the government can more readily control the pastoral peoples. The Kazakhs in particular opposed this effort to make them more sedentary. In 1962 sixty thousand Kazakhs fled from Xinjiang to the USSR. During the early years of the Cultural Revolution Kazakh opposition led to several armed confrontations with government forces. Since 1976 the government's greater sensitivity toward the national minorities has apparently quelled the disruption and chaos in Xinjiang.

M. E. Alonso, ed., *China's Inner Asian Frontier: Photographs of the Wulsin Expedition to Northwest China in 1923,* with historical text by Joseph Fletcher (1979). Chu Wen-djang, *The Moslem Rebellion in Northwest China, 1862–1878* (1966). O. Edmund Clubb, *China and Russia: The "Great Game"* (1971). June Teufel Dreyer, *China's Forty Millions* (1976). Joseph F. Fletcher, Jr., "The Heyday of the Ch'ing Order in Mongolia, Sinkiang and Tibet," in *The Cambridge History of China,* vol. 10, *Late Ch'ing, 1800–1911, Part 1,* edited by John K. Fairbank (1978). Peter Hopkirk, *Foreign Devils on the Silk Road* (1980). Owen Lattimore, *Inner Asian Frontiers of China* (1940). Morris Rossabi, *China and Inner Asia from 1368 to the Present Day* (1975).   MORRIS ROSSABI

XIONGNU, a nomadic people who, led by Maodun (d. 174 BCE), formed the first nomadic empire on the North Asian steppe. The Xiongnu are first mentioned in Chinese records for the year 318 BCE, when they joined with three Chinese states to attack the growing state of Qin. About a century later Qin Shihuangdi, having unified China in 221 BCE, drove the Xiongnu beyond the Yellow River and built the Great Wall to keep them out of China. When the Qin empire crumbled in 209 BCE, however, the Xiongnu moved south again.

In 209 BCE Maodun, the *shanyu* (meaning ruler, a supratribal leader), created a tribal confederacy giving the Xiongnu control of Inner Asia from western Manchuria to Chinese Turkestan. His mounted archers repeatedly raided North China. For more than seventy years the Han dynasty, which had succeeded the Qin, tried to buy off the Xiongnu, but gifts and border trade only reduced but did not end the Xiongnu raids. Around 130 BCE the Chinese began an aggressive policy; huge armies were sent against the Xiongnu, sundering their confederation.

By 51 BCE Huhanxie, one of several competing *shanyu,* turned to the Han for assistance. He was recognized as the legitimate *shanyu,* and he and his followers temporarily moved within the Chinese pale. The Golden Age of the Xiongnu had ended.

Over the next century, Han-Xiongnu relations varied from amicable to antagonistic. Then in 48 CE the Southern Xiongnu, their population and livestock depleted by calamities, surrendered; many of them, turning to Chinese-style agriculture, settled down in North China. Early in the fourth century, descendants of the Southern Xiongnu founded three ephemeral states in North China.

The Northern Xiongnu, under pressure from Han and other armies, migrated westward, disappearing from Chinese records in the first century CE. Some scholars have speculated that the Huns, who appeared in Europe in the fourth century, were the descendants of the Xiongnu.

[*See also* Shanyu *and* Han Dynasty.]

Michael Loewe, *Crisis and Conflict in Han China* (1977).   JACK L. DULL

XISHA ISLANDS. *See* Paracel Islands.

XIXIA. *See* Tanguts.

XIZANG. *See* Tibet.

XUANTONG EMPEROR (Puyi; 1906–1967), last ruler of the Qing dynasty in China, reigning from 1909 to 1912 as a child. Puyi succeeded the Guangxu emperor by order of Empress Dowager Cixi prior to her death in 1908. Upon abdicating in 1912 Puyi remained a pawn in Chinese politics for the rest of his life, manipulated by Chinese warlords and then by the Japanese, who installed him as the puppet emperor of Manchukuo under the reign title Kangde (1934–1945). Held by the Soviets and released to the Chinese in 1950, Puyi spent a decade in reeducation. In 1959 he was allowed to function as a common citizen. He spent the remaining years working on historical materials, including an autobiography.

Aisin-Gioro Puyi, *From Emperor to Citizen: The Autobiography of Aisin-Gioro Puyi* (1964–1965).

ADRIAN A. BENNETT

XUANZANG (600–664), Buddhist monk who ranks as the most famous of the Chinese Buddhist pilgrims who made the difficult journey to India.

Xuanzang is renowned as a prolific translator of Indian Buddhist scriptures into Chinese.

Troubled by lacunae and ambiguities in various scriptures that he was studying, Xuanzang resolved to visit India. In 629 he set out along the northern trade route through Central Asia. Passing westward through Turfan, Karashar, and Tashkent, he arrived in Samarkand. Journeying to the southwest, he passed through the Iron Gates into the region of Bactria. From Bactria he turned to the southeast, crossed the Hindu Kush, and entered northwest India. After visiting various kingdoms there he crossed into Kashmir, where he remained to study for several years. From Kashmir he crossed once again into North India, and by proceeding eastward along the base of the Himalayas and then following the Ganges River he arrived in the central Ganges Plain.

After visiting sites sacred to Buddhism Xuanzang settled at Nalanda Monastery, where he studied scriptures of the Vijnanavada, or "Consciousness Only," school of Buddhism under the patriarch Silabhadra. Leaving Nalanda he proceeded down the eastern coastline to South India with the hopes of visiting Sri Lanka. Unable to reach the island, however, he returned north along the west coast. During the course of his stay in India Xuanzang had developed a reputation as an eminent scholar. When he once again reached North India, the emperor Harsha welcomed him with great honors. Xuanzang left a vivid description of Harsha's character and his reign.

Returning to China along the southern trade route through Central Asia, Xuanzang finally reached Chang'an in 645. Of the numerous materials that he brought back, Xuanzang translated seventy-three works totaling more than one thousand rolls. His translations, renowned for their accuracy, were mainly scriptures associated with the Vijnanavada school. These texts, together with Xuanzang's careful exposition, became the basis of the new Faxiang (Japanese, Hossō) school of Buddhism. Perhaps Xuanzang's most significant contribution, however, is the voluminous record of his travels in India and Central Asia known as *Records of Western Regions*. Although it records the travels of a Buddhist believer, a particular strength of the work lies in the fact that it does not limit itself solely to items of Buddhist interest. Rich in historical and geographical detail, Xuanzang's *Records* is an invaluable source for the study of Central Asian and Indian history.

[*See also* Buddhism: Buddhism in China.]

Samuel Beal, trans., *Buddhist Records of the Western World (Si-yu-ki)* (1884; reprint, 1968). Alan Sponberg, "Hsüan-tsang," in *The Encyclopedia of Religion,* edited by Mircea Eliade (1987), vol. 6, pp. 480–482.

DAN STEVENSON

XU GUANGQI (1562–1633), important Chinese scholar-official of the late Ming dynasty and notable convert to Christianity. Respectfully referred to by the European Jesuit missionaries as one of the "Three Pillars of the Christian faith in China" (along with Li Zhizao and Yang Tingyun), Xu was the first Chinese to translate European books, especially scientific works, into the Chinese language.

A native of Shanghai, Xu received a traditional education, but at the time when he met the Jesuit missionary Lazzaro Cattaneo in Guangdong in 1596, he was having difficulty passing the provincial examinations. Greatly impressed by the famous Jesuit Matteo Ricci, whom he met in Nanjing in 1600, Xu was baptized in that city in 1603 and took the name Paul. Xu received the *jinshi* degree a year later and was assigned to the Hanlin Academy in Beijing, where Ricci was residing. Xu then began a fruitful three-year collaboration with the celebrated Jesuit that resulted in the translation into Chinese of many European works on mathematics (including Euclid's *Elements*), geography, hydraulics, and astronomy. He also wrote original works on trigonometry and agriculture adapting Western ideas.

By the time Ricci died in 1610, Xu had become a loyal supporter of the Jesuit evangelization efforts. He even built a church near his home in Shanghai and held services there. He also gained official respect for the Jesuits by drawing attention to their more advanced scientific knowledge, particularly the accurate prediction of solar eclipses and other calendrical matters of interest to the court. When an anti-Christian persecution erupted in 1616 and again in 1622, Xu protected many of the Jesuits by hiding them in his home and by writing memorials defending and praising them, arguing that Christianity was closer to Confucianism than either Buddhism or Daoism.

In 1629, having successfully demonstrated the superiority of Western astronomy over Chinese and Muslim versions, Xu had several Jesuits (including Adam Schall von Bell) appointed to the new Calendrical Bureau in Beijing. When the Manchus invaded China proper in 1630, Xu used his connections to arrange for Western cannon to be imported from Portuguese Macao for use in defense of the capital. Shortly thereafter, Xu was promoted to grand secretary, but soon fell ill and died in 1633. One of his last acts was the seeking of imperial rewards for the Jesuits' labors in the Calendrical Bureau.

[*See also* Jesuits: Jesuits in China; Cattaneo, Lazzaro; Ricci, Matteo; Schall von Bell, Johann Adam; *and* Xujiahui.]

Arnold H. Rowbotham, *Missionary and Mandarin: The Jesuits at the Court of China* (1966).

ROLAND L. HIGGINS

XUJIAHUI (Shanghai dialect, Zikawei; "Xu family springs"), a site originally located just southwest of Shanghai and a major center of Jesuit activity in China. Initially it contained the village of the Xu family, whose most eminent member was Xu Guangqi (1562–1633), the grand secretary who sponsored the Jesuit missionaries in the late Ming dynasty and who is buried on the site. In addition, Xu's granddaughter Candida Xu (1607–1680) became widely known in Europe as a Chinese patron of Christianity.

Xujiahui was chosen by the Society of Jesus in 1847 as the chief center of missionary work in Jiangnan Province. The library was established in 1847, the museum and observatory were added in 1872, and in 1910 Saint Ignatius Cathedral was built in distinctly European style, with twin spires that were visible throughout Shanghai. Beginning in 1903 an annual calendar was issued by the observatory. In addition, Xujiahui contained Saint Ignatius College (1850), for lower and middle levels of instruction, and the University of Aurora, for more advanced study. The location of Xujiahui in the French Concession of Shanghai caused it to be dominated by French Jesuits, who were often at odds with their Portuguese and Italian counterparts.

Activities at Xujiahui were disrupted with the expulsion of the Jesuits by the Communist government in the early 1950s. In 1966, during the violent antiforeign outbursts of the Cultural Revolution, the Red Guards damaged the spires of the cathedral. By 1977 all of the buildings, except for the observatory, which houses the Shanghai Municipal Meterological Department, were used for other purposes. Since then, the cathedral has been restored and opened for daily religious services. In 1982 the government restored the tomb of Xu Guangqi. Although parts of the library were dispersed during the confusion of civil war from 1945 to 1949, the bulk of the

collection has been preserved and functions as a specialized library in its original building. The collection, which is now administered by the Shanghai Municipal Library, contains more than 100,000 titles, approximately 25,000 of which are European-language works.

[*See also* Xu Guangqi *and* Jesuits: Jesuits in China.]

DAVID E. MUNGELLO

XUNZI (fl. 298–238 BCE), the first major systematic philosopher of the Confucian school of Chinese philosophy. A native of the state of Zhao, he was a member of the Jixia Academy in Qi and held office in Qin, where he died. More prominent than Mencius (Mengzi; 371–289 BCE) through the Han period (206 BCE–220 CE), Xunzi was considered the father of Han Confucianism, although subsequently his influence waned until a revival in recent times. This diminution in his influence stemmed in large part from the reaction to his theory of human nature and his association with Legalism *(fajia)* through his disciples Han Feizi (280?–233 BCE) and Li Si (280?–208 BCE).

Xunzi was not, however, a Legalist, and while his teaching varied from that of Confucius and Mencius, he remained committed to the humanism of Confucianism. Throughout his writings Xunzi stressed the importance of learning: man is declared able to perfect his nature through rigorous learning based upon the classics. Xunzi's opponent was not Mencius, who also stressed learning, but the Daoists, whom the Confucians felt represented a threat to the very preservation of culture itself. Xunzi also emphasized the rectification of names *(zhengming)* as one of the keys to the ordering of society.

Xunzi is said to have described human nature *(xing)* as evil, a radical departure from the position adopted by other Confucians. He argues that all goodness is acquired through learning, specifically, learning that originated with the sages. It is this theory of human nature that cemented his connection with the Legalists in the eyes of later Chinese historians. However a critical reading of the *Xunzi* has led some scholars to suggest the influence of a Legalist redaction. The doctrine of the evil of human nature is discussed in only a single chapter and conflicts with his usual position, a systematic and developed psychology distinguishing nature, emotion, and cognition. Xunzi argues that it is not the root itself that is evil, but what it has been soaked in that creates evil. This would suggest that man's nature is neutral and that environment determines evil.

Whether man's nature was evil or neutral, Xunzi was primarily concerned to see it refined and developed to portray a moral character reflective of the teachings of the sages. For this, learning was essential, but the critical element was ritual *(li)*. For Xunzi, life itself must be based upon ritual. Ritual's origins may be found in the attempt to balance desires and resources. Ritual is the recognition of the need for distinctions in society as well as in the order of the cosmos itself: the triad of Heaven, earth, and man. This was not the reinstatement of early Zhou rites such as Confucius and Mencius desired, but a way of ordering society that at times approximates what the Legalists meant by law—a universal order. In placing man before state and humanism before law, however, Xunzi remained Confucian. Ritual clearly has a profoundity for Xunzi; it is the adumbration of the inner workings of man and Heaven and it is a call for man to focus upon righting the wrongs of the individual and society. Heaven itself stands aloof for Xunzi. It is naturalistic process rather than an active moral agent. Thus, the sages are the architects of human morality and the paradigms of the perfectability of human life. The realism of Xunzi is founded in his assessment of the human condition, but in the end it proved less popular than Mencius's idealistic stance on the inherent goodness of human nature. Even though Xunzi's work remained uncanonized, he left a rich tradition of systematic thought, both in logic and psychology, permanent landmarks in the development of Chinese culture.

[*See also* Confucianism; Confucius; Mencius; Legalism; Han Feizi; *and* Li Si.]

H. H. Dubs, *Hsüntze, the Molder of Ancient Confucianism* (1927). H. H. Dubs, trans., *The Works of Hsüntze* (1928). Fung Yu-lan, *A History of Chinese Philosophy*, vol. 1, translated by Derk Bodde (1952). Edward J. Machle, "Hsün Tzu as a Religious Philosopher," *Philosophy East and West* 26.4 (October 1976): 443–461. Burton Watson, trans., *Hsün Tzu: Basic Writings* (1963).

RODNEY L. TAYLOR

Y

YADAVAS. The Yadavas of Devagiri (modern Daulatabad, India), achieved power under their king Billhama (1175–1193) in the Vidarbha region of Maharashtra state and competed with their southern rivals, the Hoysalas of Dvarasmudra, for control of the disintegrating empire of their overlords, the Chalukyas of Kalyani. Despite the stiff resistance of the Hoysalas, by 1200 the Yadavas consolidated their rule over the region between the Krishna and Godavari rivers, and later dominated the Deccan and central India under their greatest king, Simhana (1210–1246), who had overpowered his northern neighbors, the Paramaras of Malwa and the Chalukyas of Gujarat. In 1296 the Yadava capital of Devagiri was plundered by Ala ud-Din Khalji, who eventually annexed it to his expanding sultanate.

[See also Daulatabad and Khalji Dynasty.]

A. K. Majumdar, *Concise History of Ancient India*, 2 vols. (1977, 1980). G. Yazdani, ed., *The Early History of the Deccan*, 2 vols. (1960).   SHIVA BAJPAI

YAHYA KHAN, AGHA MUHAMMAD (1917–1980), president of Pakistan from 1969 until 1971. Born into a prominent family of the North-West Frontier Province of Pakistan, he received his commission in the army from the Military Academy, Dehra Dun, India, in 1938. During World War II he saw action in the Middle East and Italy. In 1947 he joined the Pakistan Army, becoming a full general and, in 1966, commander in chief. In 1969, when Ayub Khan's government collapsed, Yahya Khan became president of Pakistan under martial law. His rule ended in 1971 with the secession of East Pakistan and the defeat of the Pakistan army in war with India.

[See also Pakistan; Bangladesh; and Ayub Khan, Mohammad.]

G. W. Choudhury, *The Last Days of United Pakistan* (1974). Herbert Feldman, *The End of the Beginning* (1976).   HASSAN N. GARDEZI

YAKUZA, term used to refer to groups (kumi) involved in organized crime in Japan. Also known as *bakutō* or *bōryokudan*, *yakuza* are structured in tight family networks having distinct territories. The name *yakuza* is a gambling term meaning "useless," and points to a favorite pastime of members of *yakuza* familes.

The origin of the *yakuza* is unclear, but most probably they originated in the Tokugawa period (1600–1868). Some historians see modern *yakuza* as reincarnations of urban labor groups that formed in the mid-seventeenth century. Known as *machi yakko,* these groups, led by merchants, protected their interests and the interests of their community from belligerent bands of wandering footmen known as *hatamoto yakko.* The *machi yakko* groups were popularly called *kyōkaku,* "knights of the town," and were viewed as Robin Hood–like protectors of the oppressed. Skirmishes turned into bloody rivalries, and improved shogunal policing led to the disappearance of both the *machi yakko* and the *hatamoto yakko* by the end of the Tokugawa period.

The *yakuza* are also seen to have descended from groups of homeless wanderers and gamblers that formed in post towns along the major roadways. Their sole subsistence being income from gambling, these *kumi* established gambling houses and underground networks, expanding their territories. Such expansion demanded group cohesiveness, which promoted vertical and horizontal ties similar to those that existed among the military class. Occasional gang wars engendered fame and fear among the populace. Twentieth-century *yakuza* groups are involved in typical organized crime activities, such as extortion, blackmail, drug traffic, and insurance fraud.   J. SCOTT MILLER

YALE, ELIHU (1648–1721), traveler to India from England in the service of the East India Company in 1672 who rose to become governor of Madras from 1687 until 1692. Yale later served as a governor of the company in London, and was noted for the fortune he had accumulated while in India. Yale College was named after him because of a gift he gave to aid its foundation.   LYNN ZASTOUPIL

YALTA CONFERENCE, meeting between President Franklin D. Roosevelt, Prime Minister Winston Churchill, and Premier Joseph Stalin held from 4 to 11 February 1945 at the Crimean city of Yalta to make preparations for the coming victory over Germany. The conference also reached important conclusions relating to China and Japan. Stalin assured Roosevelt that the Russians would enter the Pacific War within three months after the German defeat.

The Russians in turn demanded the "return" of lands the Japanese had taken after the Russo-Japanese War in 1905: the southern half of Sakhalin Island, the Kuriles, and the Japanese-held ports in southern Manchuria of Port Arthur and Dairen (Chinese, Dalian; Russian Dalny). Roosevelt may have been inadequately briefed, not realizing that the southernmost Kuriles had never been Russian. Soviet retention of the Shikotan-Habomai-Kunashiri island group has continued to prevent a Japanese-Soviet peace treaty.

With regard to Manchuria, Roosevelt took a firmer line, arguing that the ports should be free ports. In the end Port Arthur was to be leased and Dalny internationalized. In fact, all of Manchuria, including the parts on the Liaodong Peninsula, reverted to Chinese control after the war. Roosevelt also discussed with Stalin cooperation to prevent the return of Western colonialism to East Asia.

In the postwar years Republican leaders in the United States charged that these concessions by Roosevelt had been unwise and unnecessary and contributed to the Communist victory in China, while Roosevelt's defenders have argued that the president could not in any case have prevented Russian power from returning to northeast Asia.

[*See also* World War II in Asia.]

Diane Shaver Clemens, "Yalta Conference," in *Encyclopedia of Japan,* edited by Gen Itasaka (1983), vol. 8, pp. 286–287.   MARIUS B. JANSEN

YAMAGATA ARITOMO (1838–1922), Japanese government and military leader of the Meiji period (1868–1912). Yamagata was born into a samurai family of the lowest rank in Chōshū (Yamaguchi). He was the single most influential military figure in modern Japan, and his descendants still refer to him as *gensui* ("field marshal"). He became adept at spearmanship and in 1863 was a commander of the Chōshū Kiheitai, a military force composed of samurai and commoners. He was wounded in the defense of Shimonoseki against Western warships (1864). He then led forces in pacifying northern Japan for the new Meiji government.

Yamagata was one of the earliest in the government to go abroad, traveling to Europe and the United States from 1869 to 1870 to study Western military systems. He was an architect of the National Conscription Law, enacted in 1873. That year, he was appointed army minister. In 1874 he became *sangi* (state councillor) in recognition of his growing importance. He helped crush a series of minor revolts against the Meiji government in the 1870s and headed the imperial forces that put down Saigō Takamori's Satsuma Rebellion (1877). The following year, he was appointed chief of the Army General Staff.

Like other Meiji leaders, however, Yamagata was not a one-dimensional figure. He served as home minister (1883–1889), and during his tenure he reformed the police system and helped to establish the local government system that helped pave the way for parliamentary government. In late 1888 he took his second trip abroad, again to Europe and the United States, to study local government. When he returned in 1889, he was appointed prime minister and held that office when the first Diet session was convoked. He resigned in 1891 but became justice minister (1892–1893) and president of the Privy Council (1893, a post he held for a total of more than seventeen years, but not consecutively). In 1894, after the outbreak of the Sino-Japanese War, he led the First Army in Korea, only to have illness force his return.

Yamagata was also a diplomat, concluding the Yamagata-Lobanov Agreement (1896) and supporting Katsura Tarō in bringing about the Anglo-Japanese Alliance (1902). In the meantime, he had his second tenure as prime minister (1898–1900). He was chief of the Army General Staff during the Russo-Japanese War (1904–1905), but his main activities after this were in behind-the-scenes political maneuverings. After Itō Hirobumi's assassination (1909), he became the principal organizer of cabinets.

Yamagata was the complete statesman. He was a master garden architect and accomplished in composing poetry, chanting *nō* librettos, and performing the tea ceremony. He was a learner who read avidly and listened attentively, especially to those recently returned from abroad. His accomplishments ranged from military to civil and foreign affairs. He preferred compromise to confrontation and prided himself that he had never dissolved the Diet as prime minister, a point he emphasized by contrasting it with the several dissolutions ordered by his archrival Itō. He was extraordinarily cautious in dealing with the Western powers, recognizing Japan's weakness in the face of any combination of the powers.

[*See also* Meiji Period.]

GEORGE K. AKITA

YAMAMOTO ISOROKU

YAMAMOTO ISOROKU (1884–1943), Japanese admiral, naval aviation proponent, and architect of the Japanese aerial assault on Pearl Harbor. Yamamoto was an early advocate of an integrated air-surface arm for the Japanese navy. He worked with other moderates in the navy, however, to contain the views of extremists and to avoid a confrontation with Western naval powers. Unable to deter the drift to war with the United States, Yamamoto, as commander of the Combined Fleet, directed plans for the surprise attack on the American Pacific Fleet at Pearl Harbor, and it is on the success of that operation that his reputation as a brilliant naval strategist and tactitian largely rests. His subsequent efforts as a wartime commander hardly lived up to that masterstroke. His tactics at the Battle of Midway (1942) led to disaster for the Japanese, and in the long struggle in the Southwest Pacific his strategic plans were repeatedly frustrated by American ability to decode Japanese naval communications. This led directly to Yamamoto's death, which occurred when American fighters shot down his aircraft in the South Pacific in 1943.

Hiroyuki Agawa, *The Reluctant Admiral: Yamamoto and the Imperial Japanese Navy* (1979). Paul Dull, *A Battle History of the Japanese Navy* (1978).

MARK R. PEATTIE

YAMASHITA TOMOYUKI (Hōbun; 1886–1946), Japanese general; conqueror of Malaya early in the Pacific War. Following a number of study and military assignments in Europe in the 1920s, Yamashita held important positions related to military research in the Army Ministry. Yamashita was an influential member of the army's "Imperial Way" faction and as such played an ambiguous role in the Young Officers' Rebellion of 1936. After heading a military observation mission to Germany and Italy in 1940, Yamashita was named commander of the Twenty-fifth Army (1941), the main force that invaded the Malay Peninsula and that forced the surrender of Singapore (February 1942), earning him the nickname "The Tiger of Malaya." Named to command the Fourteenth Area Army two years later, he undertook the unsuccessful Japanese defense of the Philippines against invading American forces (1944–1945) and surrendered in September 1945. After the end of the war Yamashita was tried by an American war crimes commission for atrocities committed by troops technically under his Philippine command. He was found guilty—without sufficient cause, some historians now believe—and hanged.

[*See also* World War II in Asia.]

A. J. Barker, *Yamashita* (1973). A. S. Kenworthy, *The Tiger of Malaya* (1953). John D. Potter, *A Soldier Must Hang* (1963).

MARK R. PEATTIE

YAMATAI (Chinese, Yematai) was a country in the land of Wa (Japan), according to the *History of the Wei Dynasty,* a Chinese court history from the third century CE. The annalists describe Yamatai as having a warm climate and plentiful fish and grain but no horses, cattle, or other large animals. Yamatai officials collected taxes, heard lawsuits, and dispatched tribute missions to the mainland.

The real ruler of Yamatai was alleged to be an old shaman named Himiko (Pimihu), who had come to power after almost a century of warfare. Queen Himiko took no husband but was assisted in her rites by a younger brother. When she died a great mound was constructed, and she was interred with more than one hundred slaves. A man attempted to rule Yamatai after Himiko's demise but was murdered in a rebellion. The country returned to peace only after Himiko's thirteen-year-old sister Iyo (Chinese, Iyu) ascended the throne.

The precise location of Yamatai is uncertain. Some scholars believe that *Yamatai* is the Chinese rendering of the Japanese place-name *Yamato* (modern Nara Prefecture) and that Japan had already been unified under the imperial line by late in the Yayoi period (200 BCE–300 CE). Others argue that many place-names listed in the Wei history describe northern Kyushu, and that Himiko was not related to the imperial line.

[See also Yayoi.]

Ryusaku Tsunoda, trans., *Japan in the Chinese Dynastic Histories* (1951). John Young, *The Location of Yamatai: A Case Study in Japanese Historiography* (1958).   WAYNE FARRIS

YAMATO, originally, the designation for a part of Japan's Nara basin. According to the *Nihon shoki,* Japan's legendary first emperor, Jimmu, entrusted the "land of Yamato" to the supervision of a certain Utsuhiko. The term gradually came to refer to the entire basin. Because Yamato was the cradle of Japanese civilization the word came to symbolize Japan itself. *Yamato* served as a general term for the emperor ("Yamato *neko*"), and is still used to designate the Japanese state of the fifth through the early seventh century. It is often attached as a prefix to denote a uniquely Japanese trait or item (*Yamato tamashii,* the "Japanese spirit"; *Yamato-e,* Japanese-style painting, etc.).

With the formation of a Chinese-style centralized state in the late seventh and early eighth centuries, Yamato's boundaries were fixed more or less at the borders of modern Nara Prefecture, and a provincial office was established. According to early tenth-century sources, Yamato was among the most populous provinces of Japan. It was composed of 15 districts and 89 administrative villages and contained 128 Shinto shrines. However, when the capital was moved from Nara in 784, the province became a backwater under the control of powerful temples. By the early twelfth century aristocrats were avoiding appointment to Yamato.

W. G. Aston, trans., *Nihongi* (1896). John W. Hall, *Japan from Prehistory to Modern Times* (1970).

WAYNE FARRIS

YAMUNA RIVER (Jumna River), a major Indian river some 850 miles long; it rises from the Himalayas near Mount Kamet and flows southeast past Delhi into Uttar Pradesh, where it runs parallel to the Ganges, finally joining it at Allahabad. This confluence, known as Prayag, is a Hindu pilgrimage site of considerable sanctity and great cultural importance. Delhi's Red Fort and the Taj Mahal at Agra are among the many historical sites located on the banks of the Yamuna. [See also Ganges River *and* Allahabad.]

ROBIN JARED LEWIS

YAN, one of the Warring States of ancient China. Yan was the northernmost of the seven major contending states of late Zhou times (403–221). It occupied what is now northern Hebei and western Liaoning provinces and had its capital near the site of present-day Beijing. Yan included many pastoral peoples within its territory and so enjoyed a generous supply of horses. The name Yan is still associated with Beijing, which is sometimes styled Yanjing ("Yan capital"). Yan's rule was ended in 222 BCE, when the state of Qin unified China.

EDWARD L. FARMER

YAN'AN, city in northern Shaanxi Province, China, famous for having been the headquarters of the Chinese Communist Party from 1937 to 1947, a decade that is often referred to as the Yan'an era.

During the Yan'an period Communist Party membership grew from about 20,000 to almost 3 million, the military forces under its command expanded from about 40,000 to more than 1.5 million, and the population in areas under its domination increased from fewer than 1 million people in early 1937 to more than 90 million by the end of the war with Japan in 1945. The Communist movement had been transformed from a desperate struggle for survival to a powerful threat to the established authority.

The Japanese invasion of China in July 1937 had a major effect on the fortunes of the Communists. Earlier in 1937, under the threat of Japanese aggression, the Guomindang (Kuomintang, or Nationalist Party) leadership had been forced by its own generals into a "united front" agreement with its hated Communist rivals. The exhausted Communist remnants of the Long March thereby gained respite from the relentless threat of annihilation. Opportunity for rapid expansion of Communist power was provided by the Japanese, who swept through northern and eastern China, destroying the old governing structure and replacing it only in urban areas and along communications lines. The Communists moved into the rural areas and established ever-expanding bases of operation.

A key to the Communists' success in this period was their talent for politicizing the normally apolitical rural populace and involving them in mass organizations. Through these organizations the Communists recruited their military and administrative personnel and implemented their policies. Militarily, the strategy was to expand areas under Communist control and to harass the Japanese continually, while avoiding main force engagements that could be disastrous. Much of the rural populace was incorporated into one of three types of military organization: the regular army, mobile militia forces of part-time soldiers, and village self-defense forces incorporating virtually everyone else. The idea was not just to repel the Japanese invaders but also to give all of the people a sense of commitment to a cause, the pursuit of which, under Communist leadership, would dramatically alter their lives.

The governmental policy was to involve people in political life through election campaigns in which they would choose their representatives. These campaigns were an excellent vehicle for propagating Communist policies and for identifying and recruiting leadership talent. They also provided an unprecedented opportunity for popular participation in governance; election regulations stipulated that no more than one-third of the elected offices could be held by Party members. Thus, the Communists gained a reputation for democratic reform while never jeopardizing their actual power insofar as they controlled the military and were much better organized and more experienced politically than any potential competitors.

The economic policy was to reduce the burden of the poor and begin to foster institutions to improve production and distribution of goods. Previous Communist policies of direct confiscation and redistribution of land had temporarily ended with the United Front agreements, but stipulations reducing rent and interest payments, in addition to progressive tax policies, won the Communists the gratitude of the rural majority. The government also began to encourage the formation of collective labor exchange teams and cooperatives for production, purchase, and transport, the efficacy of which they hoped to demonstrate. Other important economic measures were to streamline bureaucratic procedures, keeping personnel and paperwork to a minimum, and to reduce taxation to support the army, government offices, schools, and other institutions by having everyone engage in productive labor, making their units as self-reliant as possible.

Under Communist guidance, health and education improved significantly, particularly in areas not devastated by war. The number of schools greatly increased at every level. Mass campaigns to increase literacy and improve hygiene were promoted. Women's organizations began propagating radical ideas about the equality of the sexes, and, more importantly, began changing lives and attitudes by mobilizing women for production and paramilitary activities.

Guiding all of these activities were a set of developing policies that gradually evolved into a coherent ideology. During the Yan'an period the "thought of Mao Zedong" matured to become the building spirit of Chinese Communism for many years to come. The culmination of Mao's rise to ideological leadership was the Rectification (zhengfeng) Campaign that began in 1942. It was a process of thought transformation designed to unify Party members and others in positions of responsibility around a set of common principles, and to eliminate contrary principles. Twenty-two documents, mostly written by Mao, became the standard by which thoughts and actions were judged. Conformity was induced through criticism/self-criticism sessions in which nonconformists were identified and transformed, at least outwardly, or removed from their posts, and in some cases even jailed or killed. The cult of Mao Zedong began in the Yan'an period and techniques to foster it were refined and widely applied following the establishment of the People's Republic.

The Yan'an period was a time of extraordinary success for the Communist Party of China. The loss of Yan'an to Nationalist armies in 1947 was a relatively insignificant setback that officially ended the Yan'an era but only momentarily altered the course of history leading the Communist victory.

There are many who would say that the very success of the "Yan'an way" would turn into its opposite in subsequent years; that Mao Zedong's policies of mass mobilization and political rectification, practiced so successfully in the rural base areas during wartime, were a major cause of unparalleled disaster when dogmatically applied to different circumstances during the Great Leap Forward (1958–1959) and the Great Proletarian Cultural Revolution (1966–1976).

[See also Communism: Chinese Communist Party; World War II in China; and Mao Zedong.]

James P. Harrison, *The Long March to Power: A History of the Chinese Communist Party, 1921–1972* (1972). Chalmers Johnson, *Peasant Nationalism and Communist Power: The Emergence of Revolutionary China, 1937–1945* (1962). Tetsuya Kataoka, *Resistance and Revolution in China: The Communists and the Second United Front* (1974). Warren Kuo, *Analytical History of the*

Chinese Communist Party (1966). Peter Schran, *Guerilla Economy: The Development of the Shensi-Kansu-Ning-hsia Border Region, 1937–1945* (1976). Mark Selden, *The Yenan Way in Revolutionary China* (1971). Ralph Thaxton, *China Turned Rightside Up: Revolutionary Legitimacy in the Peasant World* (1983). Lyman P. Van Slyke, ed., *The Chinese Communist Movement: A Report of the United States War Department, July 1945* (1968).

PETER J. SEYBOLT

YANDABO, TREATY OF, signed 24 February 1826, concluded the First Anglo-Burmese War, which had started in 1826. The Burmese agreed to pay an indemnity of one million pounds. The British held territory as security for the payment. The Burmese also ceded Arakan and Tenasserim, signed a commercial treaty, and agreed to exchange envoys with the British.

The Burmese regarded the treaty as humiliating, and the presence of the British resident in the Burmese capital became increasingly unacceptable. Bagyidaw's (and later Tharawaddy's) actions rendered the residency insecure, and it was withdrawn in 1839, after which the treaty became a virtual dead letter. To save face, King Mindon avoided signing a treaty to conclude the Second Anglo-Burmese War.

[*See also* Anglo-Burmese Wars; Bagyidaw; Tharrawaddy; *and* Mindon.]

Anil Chandra Banerjee, *The Eastern Frontier of British India, 1784–1826* (reprint, 1964). Walter Sadgun Desai, *History of the British Residency in Burma, 1826–1840* (1939).

OLIVER B. POLLAK

YAN FU (1853–1921), China's first translator and interpreter of Western ideas and values into Chinese. Educated in both the traditional Chinese system and in Western ways, Yan was a significant transitional figure in Chinese intellectual circles. By the late 1890s Yan emerged as the leading translator of the time, producing Chinese-language versions of Western classics by Adam Smith, John Stuart Mill, T. H. Huxley, Montesquieu, and Herbert Spencer, interlaced with Yan's own commentaries. Through these works other Chinese discovered ideas of evolution, the principles of sociology, the division of power in government, and ideas of free trade, yet they were all phrased in Classical Chinese. Yan's main point was that Western civilization was action-oriented while China's civilization was stability-oriented, with Western governments promoting rather than stifling individual capabilities.

Benjamin Schwartz, *In Search of Wealth and Strength: Yen Fu and the West* (1964).

ADRIAN A. BENNETT

YANGBAN ("officials of the two orders"), Korean term that denoted those of the ruling class during the Yi dynasty (1392–1910). As initially used during the Koryŏ period (918–1392), *yangban* described military and civil officials. Its meaning later became more general, and referred to the status group, primarily consisting of literati, that dominated the political, cultural, and economic life of the kingdom. Their prestige rested in part on their mastery of literary Chinese and knowledge of the Confucian classics. With their training, they were often able to pass the state examination that enabled them to hold public office. Office holding brought political power and provided economic security, which became an additional source of *yangban* strength. *Yangban* were often landed gentry who could use income from the land to support a refined way of life.

Yangban derived a number of special privileges from their public status. In addition to receiving stipends from the state, they were exempt from paying certain taxes, and because of their work for the government, they were not required to serve in the military. In the major cities and the capital, *yangban* lived in special districts, and in the countryside they often lived apart from the peasantry. *Yangban* tended to marry only *yangban*. To clarify their descent they wrote precise genealogies. *Yangban* were also concerned with fostering Confucian rites and emphasized the veneration of ancestors. Lineages maintained a shrine and members were expected to hold regular services there in honor of a deceased patriarch. *Yangban* adhered to Confucian norms, upholding them as the standard of the kingdom.

There were status differences within the *yangban* themselves. Military officials were regarded with less esteem than their civilian counterparts. Illegitimate children of *yangban* were not accorded *yangban* status and neither were the children of *yangban* concubines and secondary wives. The *yangban* held public office and in that capacity they served as administrators, setting themselves apart from those who held technical posts or served as petty clerks and local functionaries.

It is difficult to define precisely the criteria of *yangban*. Some scholars have sought to determine *yangban* in terms of eligibility for the civil service examination. Using this as the standard, they have concluded that since access to the examination was relatively open, even to men of commoner status, *yangban* status was easily achieved. Other scholars assert that access became more limited in the last centuries of the dynasty. A second group of scholars has defined *yangban* status in terms of economic wealth, primarily landholdings. An upper level of hereditary, landed *yangban* held both degrees and offices. There was also a lower level of *yangban* who did not hold public office. They were local gentry and landlords, and some may have purchased titles.

By the sixteenth century marked social stratification occurred as both upperward and downward mobility decreased. With this change the *yangban* class became more clearly defined and limited. Several centuries later, around the beginning of the eighteenth century, *yangban* status again became blurred. Many former *yangban* families became more and more isolated from power and were commonly referred to as "fallen *yangban*." At the same time rich merchants and landed farmers, enjoying prosperity, were raising their social rank through the purchase of degrees, and frequently were included as *yangban*.

Throughout Korea *yangban* remained at the apex of society and established the cultural, educational, and political norms of the age. Their patronage of Confucian ideology, art, and literature enabled Korea to achieve a sophistication comparable to that of China. *Yangban* standards still dominate much of Korean culture to this day.

[*See also* Korea, Class Structure in *and* Yi Dynasty.]

EDWARD J. SHULTZ

YANGSHAO CULTURE, early Neolithic culture located in North China. According to recent radiocarbon dating, the Yangshao culture lasted from 5000 to 3000 BCE.

Yangshao marks the beginning of the Neolithic period in Chinese prehistory. The Neolithic revolution occurred independently in different parts of the world on the basis of plants that were indigenous to particular areas. In North China, the Neolithic revolution was based upon the native grass millet. Yangshao farmers also grew such crops as mustard greens and Chinese cabbage. Domesticated animals were principally the dog and the pig; hunting and fishing were still essential.

Yangshao dwellings, as indicated by the Banpo site, were semisubterranean, with thatched roofs. The houses all faced toward a larger community building; a moat surrounded the village. Near the typical Yangshao village was one or more kilns for the production of distinctive painted pottery. The pottery, not yet wheel made, was decorated with zoomorphic and geometric designs (see figure 1). Many of the pottery shards contain symbols; although some of the symbols are rather complex, most consist of only one or two strokes. Some schol-

FIGURE 1. *Ceramic Storage Jar.* Yangshao culture, Banshan type; Neolithic period, c. 2200 BCE. Buff earthenware with spiral decoration in read and black slips. Height 39.7 cm., diameter (without handles) 34.9 cm.

ars believe these markings are the direct forerunners of the later Chinese script.

Burial patterns in the Yangshao era are mixed. Children were often buried in urns within the settlements. Adults were buried in well-ordered cemeteries. In some cases there were group burials, perhaps suggesting a family or clan identity. In other sites the bones of the deceased were exhumed in order to rebury them with those of another person.

Kwang-chih Chang, *The Archaeology of Ancient China* (1977).   JACK L. DULL

YANGTZE RIVER, China's most important river and, at 3,900 miles, the third longest in the world (only the Nile and the Amazon are longer). From its source 18,000 feet above sea level on the Tibetan Plateau, the Yangtze—known to the Chinese as the Long River (Changjiang)—flows for almost 2,000 miles through wild, sparsely populated terrain. By Chongqing, 1,500 miles from the sea, the river has fallen to an elevation of only 1,500 feet. As it flows eastward through central China, the Yangtze and its major tributaries drain an area in which nearly 300 million people live. This network of rivers and associated canals carries some 80 percent of China's domestic waterborne traffic. For several years, the Chinese have been engaged in the construction of the massive Gezhouba dam, hydroelectric plant, and navigation complex near Yichang, just east of the Three Gorges. At its mouth, the river discharges nearly a cubic mile of water per day, and carries enough silt to extend its delta by about a mile per century.   LYMAN P. VAN SLYKE

YANTAI (Chefu), Chinese city, a minor local port on the Shandong Peninsula until the arrival of the railway in 1955, which brought with it some minor industry, including a large canning and processing industry and a small steel foundry. Today, Yantai is a major fishing port with a population under two hundred thousand (1982). In 1876 the city was the site of the Chefoo Convention, one of the unequal treaties with the Western powers.   JOHN A. RAPP

YAN XISHAN (1883–1960), warlord in North China in the early twentieth century. Yan became military governor of Shanxi Province in 1912 and retained that position for almost twenty years. He was known as the "Model Governor" because of his stable administration and his social reforms. The relative geographic isolation of Shanxi allowed Yan to stay out of many warlord wars in North China but in 1928 he joined the Guomindang's Northern Expedition against Zhang Zuolin. From 1929 to 1930 he helped Feng Yuxiang resist Chiang Kai-shek's authority and briefly retired from public life when the Yan-Feng coalition was defeated. However, the Nanjing government allowed him to return to his Shanxi post, which he held until he joined the Guomindang's flight to Taiwan in 1949.

[See also Warlords and Feng Yuxiang.]

Donald G. Gillin, *Warlord: Yen Hsi-shan in Shansi Province, 1911–1949* (1967).   JAMES E. SHERIDAN

YAN YUAN (1635–1704), Chinese philosopher; native of the small village of Boye, Hebei, to the southeast of Beijing. The writings of Yan Yuan only became widely read in the early twentieth century. Like others of his generation, Yan opposed the quietistic and metaphysical strains of Song-dynasty Confucianism. His arguments against Buddhism, Daoism, and Zhu Xi's program of mourning rituals and philosophical critique anticipated Dai Zhen's philosophical critique. His advocacy of *shixue* ("real or practical" learning) offered a dynamic, process of education and ritualized daily living.

[See also Dai Zhen; Kaozheng Xue; and Neo-Confucianism.]

Cheng Chung-ying, "Practical Learning in Yen Yuan, Chu Hsi, and Wang Yang-ming," in *Principle and Practicality: Essays in Neo-Confucianism and Practical Learning*, edited by Wm. Theodore de Bary and Irene Bloom (1979), pp. 37–67. Tu Wei-ming, "Yen Yuan: From Inner Experience to Lived Concreteness," in *The Unfolding of Neo-Confucianism*, edited by Wm. Theodore de Bary (1975), pp. 511–541.   JUDITH A. WHITBECK

YAO WENYUAN (b. 1931), radical Chinese leftist and member of the Gang of Four. A native of Zhejiang, Yao's father was a well-known leftist writer and personal friend of Lu Xun, but he withdrew from the Communist Party, condemning it publicly in 1934. Yao started his career as a reporter for Shanghai's *Wenhui bao* in the early 1950s, and published many articles in literary publications. His writings strongly advocated Mao Zedong's radical literary line condemning liberal writers, which earned him the nickname "hitman" in the literary field. He became a national figure when he published an article criticizing Wu Han's play *Hai Rui's Dismissal from Office*. During the Cultural Revolution Yao's political fortune rose rapidly; he became a member of the Politburo in 1969 and thereafter remained one of the leading figures of the Maoist radical group until his purge in 1976. As a member of the Gang of Four he was tried and sentenced to twenty years of imprisonment. [See also Gang of Four; Great Proletarian Cultural Revolution; and Wu Han.]   HONG YUNG LEE

YAP AH LOY (1837–1885), major figure in the early development of Kuala Lumpur. Born in China, Yap emigrated to Malaya in 1854 as a contract laborer. He eventually settled in Selangor, becoming a wealthy businessman, tin-mine owner, and Triad leader. From 1868 to his death he served as *kapitan China* of Kuala Lumpur. As *kapitan*, Yap skillfully handled various Selangor Triad wars and political struggles, improving Kuala Lumpur's position. The major landowner in town, Yap set policies that led to boom conditions in the area's tin industry in the 1870s. The arrival of British control solidified his authority. Yap's leadership and diplomacy laid the groundwork for local Chinese prosperity and the growing political centrality of Kuala Lumpur.

[See also Kuala Lumpur and Kapitan China.]

J. M. Gullick, "Kuala Lumpur, 1880–1895," *Journal of the Malayan Branch of the Royal Asiatic Society* 28 (1955). S. M. Middlebrook, "Yap Ah Loy," *Journal of the Malayan Branch of the Royal Asiatic Society* 24 (1951).   CRAIG A. LOCKARD

YASODHARAPURA, name of the capital city built by Yasovarman (acceded, 889), ruler of the Cambodian kingdom of Angkor. He was the first to site his capital in the area generally known as Angkor, a few miles north of the present-day town of Siem Reap, where major surviving monuments are concentrated. Yasodharapura was planned symmetrically around its ritual center, a shrine built on the summit of a hill, the Phnom Bakheng. The term *Yasodharapura* also refers to the general area of Yasovarman's capital, where subsequent rulers built new or partly new capitals with different ritual centers.

[*See also* Angkor *and* Siem Reap.]

Lawrence P. Briggs, *The Ancient Khmer Empire* (1951).

IAN W. MABBETT

YASOVARMAN II, ruler of the Cambodian kingdom of Angkor (c. 1160–1165). He succeeded Dharanindravarman II, but his relationship to his predecessor is unclear. Inscriptions indicate that he suppressed a revolt led by an individual or individuals called Bharata Rahu. One of his retainers, later honored for his part in defeating the foe, may have been a son of Prince Yasovarman's ally, who later became Jayavarman VII. Yasovarman was assassinated and replaced by a ruler who took the name Tribhuvanaditya.

[*See also* Angkor.]

Lawrence P. Briggs, *The Ancient Khmer Empire* (1951). G. Coedès, *The Indianized States of Southeast Asia*, translated by Susan B. Cowing (1968).   IAN W. MABBETT

YASUDA ZENJIRŌ (1838–1921), founder of the Yasuda *zaibatsu*, the smallest of Japan's "Big Four" *zaibatsu*, or business conglomerates, known for its strength in finance. Yasuda began his career at a young age in money-changing shops, and during the early Meiji years he made a fortune through speculation in currency and samurai bonds. Benefiting from his status as the official handler of funds for the Ministry of Justice, in the 1870s Yasuda set up the Third National Bank and the private Yasuda Bank. He was less successful, however, at diversifying into industry, a setback usually attributed to the exclusive control exercised by the Yasuda family and by its unwillingness to delegate authority to salaried managers in order to develop more effective organization. Instead, Yasuda expanded his influence through his financial institutions. His control of more than twenty banks and numerous insurance

companies gave him substantial indirect interest in many fields of industry. Of special importance were ties he maintained with leading non-banking *zaibatsu* such as Asano and Ōkura. When he was assassinated in 1921 by an anticapitalist extremist, Yasuda was considered the richest man in Japan. His Yasuda Bank was the forerunner of the postwar Fuji Bank.

[*See also* Zaibatsu.]

Kozo Yamamura, *A Study of Samurai Income and Entrepreneurship* (1974).   WILLIAM D. WRAY

YASUKUNI SHRINE, Shinto shrine in Tokyo, Japan, dedicated to the spirits of over 2.4 million servicemen, enshrined by name, rank, and place and date of final action, who have died in Japan's civil and foreign wars since 1853. It was built in 1869 by the Meiji government as a national shrine, named Shōkansha ("spirit-invoking shrine"), to memorialize all those who died to restore imperial rule. From its inception it had close links with the emperor and the military establishment. In 1879 it was renamed Yasukuni Jinja ("shrine for the repose of the nation") and given an annual budget from government funds; it was also assigned priests, who presided at semiannual rites for the nation's war dead. These were accompanied by lavish public festivals. In the 1930s Yasukuni became a major institution fostering military values and patriotic sacrifices for the nation. After Japan's defeat in World War II, Occupation authorities ended government support of the shrine, and it became a private religious institution. Since the 1950s the Liberal Democratic Party, the Bereaved Families Association, and others have advocated legislation restoring government support to the shrine. Socialists, Buddhists, Christians, and others, fearing such support would revive militarism and violate religious freedom, have thus far blocked these efforts.

[*See also* Shinto.]

ROGER F. HACKETT

YAYOI is the name given to Japan's Iron Age (200 BCE–300 CE). The term came to be applied to this era because the first Iron Age pottery shards were excavated from the Yayoi section of Bunkyo Ward in Tokyo. This era saw the advent of wet-rice agriculture, a dramatic increase in population, the formation of social classes, and the development of primitive forms of political organization.

The roots of Yayoi civilization lay in China, where settled agriculture and metallurgy had long been

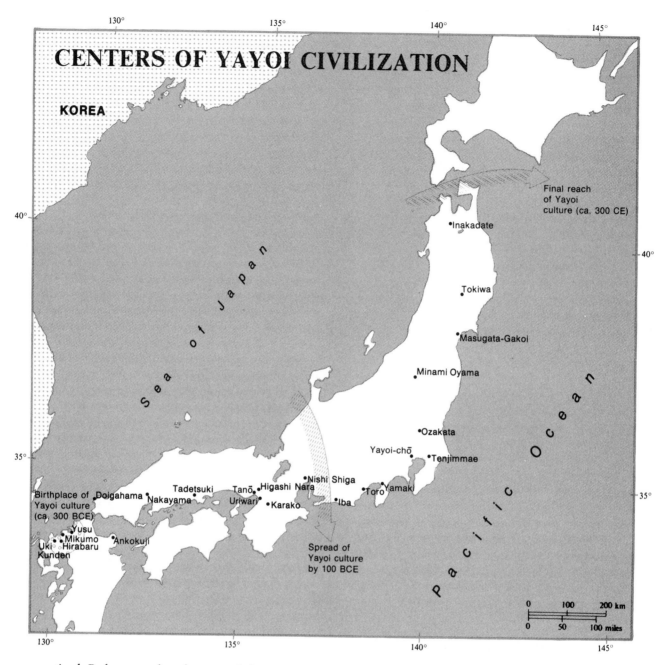

CENTERS OF YAYOI CIVILIZATION

KOREA

Sea of Japan

Pacific Ocean

Final reach
of Yayoi
culture (ca. 300 CE)

•Inakadate

•Tokiwa

•Masugata-Gakoi

•Minami Oyama

•Ozakata

Yayoi-chō•   •Tenjimmae

•Nishi Shiga
Tadetsuki   Tanō• Higashi Nara
Doigahama •   •   •   Iba   •Toro Yamaki
Birthplace of • Nakayama Uriwari• •Karako   •
Yayoi culture
(ca. 300 BCE)
Yusu•
Uki• •Mikumo   •Ankokuji
•Hirabaru
Kunden

Spread of
Yayoi culture
by 100 BCE

0   100   200 km
0   50   100 miles

practiced. Refugees and traders spread the new culture overland through Manchuria and down the Korean peninsula, or across the Yellow Sea from Shandong to southern Korea and on to Japan. Yayoi civilization was adopted early and most completely by the people of northern Kyushu and the Kinai, while eastern and northern Japan and southern Kyushu retained many features of the earlier Jōmon culture.

The Yayoi period saw revolutionary changes in Japan's population. During the long Neolithic (Jōmon) era (10,000–200 BCE), the archipelago contained at most 250,000 people. By the year 300 CE the population totaled ten or fifteen times that figure. The demographic explosion is testimony to the productivity of wet-rice agriculture. Of course, the rice farming of the Yayoi age was extremely primitive: hoes and spades were made of wood and stone knives were employed to clip the rice ear from the stalk at harvest. Most farmland was carved out of easily irrigated low-lying areas.

New patterns of subsistence meant a revolution in daily life for many. Yayoi containers were wheel-thrown and were fired at much higher temperatures and were far more durable than Jōmon pots, which were hand-built. Looms were first used, to make a

FIGURE 1. *Earthenware Jar.* Dated to the Middle Yayoi period, c. first century CE. Height 27.6 cm., diameter 15.9 cm.

rough hemp cloth. New metalworking skills were employed in the production of iron and bronze weapons, mirrors, ceremonial bells *(dōtaku)*, and woodworking tools. Raised granaries and thatched-roof huts became frequent sights in many peasant villages.

Recently, archaeologists have learned much about the social and religious life of the Yayoi period. Burial practices in western Honshu suggest that kinship was bilateral. Comparison of skeletons also indicates that important anatomical differences existed between Japanese living in northern Kyushu and those living in the Kantō. Shamanism and fertility cults were common.

Toward the end of the Yayoi era political organizations developed in several regions. The most famous example is the country of Yamatai described in the *History of the Wei Dynasty,* a Chinese court history of the third century CE. This land was ruled by a shaman named Himiko, and was distinguished by social distinctions and institutionalized political activities, such as tax collection. Many excavated Yayoi villages dating from the second to third century CE were discovered to have been destroyed by fire, possibly the result of a civil war that was the prelude to the unification of western Japan under a single kingship.

[*See also* Jōmon *and* Yamatai.]

John Whitney Hall, *Japan: From Prehistory to Modern Times* (1970). H. Kanaseki and M. Sahara, "The Yayoi Period," *Asian Perspectives* 19 (1979):15-26. J. E. Kidder, *Japan Before Buddhism* (1959).   WAYNE FARRIS

YAZDIGIRD I (399–420), Sasanid ruler of Iran, relaxed the former Sasanid intolerance toward non-Zoroastrians and made peace with the Romans in 409. He is said to have been guardian for Theodosius II and to have married a daughter of the Jewish exilarch; whether or not this was the case, he did permit Jews to settle in Isfahan, and he sponsored a Christian synod at Ctesiphon in 410.

The office of *wuzurg framadar* (prime minister) that appeared during Yazdigird's reign may indicate the increasingly hierarchical administration of the royal domain. Yazdigird I has a reputation as a "sinner" in Zoroastrian tradition.

Ehsan Yarshater, ed., *The Seleucid, Parthian and Sasanian Periods* (1983) and *The Period from the Arab Invasion to the Seljuqs* (1975), vols. 3 and 4 of the *Cambridge History of Iran.*   MICHAEL G. MORONY

YAZDIGIRD III (r. 632–651), grandson of Khusrau II, the last Sasanid ruler of Iran. After his forces were defeated by the Muslims at Qadisiyya in 637 and Nihavand in 642, he fled from Fars to Kerman, Sistan, and Merv, where he was betrayed by the *marzban* and killed by a miller.

[*See also* Sasanid Dynasty.]

Ehsan Yarshater, ed., *The Seleucid, Parthian and Sasanian Periods* (1983) and *The Period from the Arab Invasion to the Seljuqs* (1975), vols. 3 and 4 of the *Cambridge History of Iran.*   MICHAEL G. MORONY

YE JIANYING (1897–1986), Chinese military and political leader. Born to a merchant family in Mei County, Guangdong, Ye was a businessman in Southeast Asia in his youth, a student at the Yunnan Military Academy, and a military officer working for Sun Yat-sen and the Guomindang (Kuomintang, KMT, or Nationalist Party) in South China during the 1920s. In 1927 Ye joined the Chinese Communist Party (CCP), organized the abortive uprisings in Nanchang and Canton (Guangzhou), and fled to Moscow, where he studied military science from 1928 to 1931. Ye was chief of staff of the Communist troops during the Long March and the wars against Japan and the Nationalists. Ye also often represented the CCP to negotiate with the KMT authorities and the United States in the 1940s.

Ye was awarded the rank of marshal in 1955,

together with nine other military leaders, but he achieved political prominence only in the early 1970s. After Marshal Lin Biao's demise in 1971, Ye was named vice-chairman of the CCP Military Commission in charge of China's military affairs and became one of the handful of most influential political figures in the PRC. In October 1976 he engineered the coup that deposed the radical Gang of Four, allowing Hua Guofeng to succeed Mao as CCP chairman. He was CCP vice-chairman (1973–1982) and chairman of the National People's Congress (1978–1983); at the time of his death Ye was still a member of the Politburo Standing Committee and a vice-chairman of both the CCP and the Military Commission.

[See also China, People's Republic of.]

PARRIS CHANG

YELLOW RIVER. Flowing more than 2,700 miles from northwestern China across the North China Plain, the Yellow River (Huang He) empties into the sea on the south side of the Shandong Peninsula. Primitive man of the Paleolithic age, as well as early civilization in the Neolithic era, began in the big bend in the Yellow River in northwestern China. The Huang He constantly builds up its own bed owing to the heavy deposits of yellow-colored loess soil from desert regions to the west. Great water projects to control the river through the centuries have built it up ten to forty feet above the surrounding land in the North China Plain. When flood control projects were left untended under corrupt or incompetent rulers, the catastrophic floods followed by years of famine that often occurred earned the river the nickname "China's Sorrow."

Not only periodic floods but also dramatic shifts in the point at which the Yellow River enters the sea have greatly affected the course of Chinese history, bringing on periods of rebellion and social chaos. Shifting its course for the first time since 1194, the mouth of the river changed from the north to the south of the Shandong Peninsula in 1852, and shifted north again near Tianjin in 1947. Unlike China's other great river to the south, the Yangtze, the Yellow River is for the most part unnavigable. Since 1949 flood control and reforestation projects have begun to conquer its capricious nature.

JOHN A. RAPP

YELLOW TURBANS, Daoist faith-healing sect led by Zhang Jue in rebellion against the Latter Han dynasty (25–220) in 184. In 175 Zhang began to teach the Taipingdao, or Way of Great Peace, a method of faith healing based on earlier Daoist texts. Owing to the severe political and economic oppression and the natural disasters of the late Han, within a few years Zhang had attracted several hundred thousand followers, whom he organized under an elaborate religious and military hierarchy with himself and his two brothers at the top.

After escaping from prison in 184, Zhang led his followers in an uprising that eventually became so widespread (covering over eight entire provinces) that the emperor was forced to call upon regional generals to suppress it. After many campaigns from 184 to 205, the generals finally destroyed the rebel movement, but at a prohibitive cost to the central government, as the generals themselves soon divided the Han empire into rival kingdoms.

Zhang Jue intended to replace the Confucian "Blue Heaven" and the Han (red) fire element of popular cosmology with "Yellow Heaven," symbol of both the (yellow) earth element and the mythical Yellow Emperor (Huangdi), whom the rebels worshiped along with Laozi as the god Huang-Lao. The yellow scarves worn by his followers to symbolize the coming new order gave the movement its popular name. While Zhang probably used religion as a camouflage to build up his movement in the years before open rebellion, setting a precedent for rebels in dynasties to follow, it was as a religious movement that the Yellow Turbans had their greatest influence. They became, along with the contemporaneous Five Bushels of Rice sect in Sichuan, the direct progenitors of modern religious Daoism.

[See also Han Dynasty and Daoism.]

Wilhelm Eichorn, "Description of the Rebellion of Sun En and Earlier Taoist Rebellions," *Mitteilungen* 2.2 (1954). Howard Levy, "Yellow Turban Religion and Rebellion and the End of the Han," *Journal of the American Oriental Society* 76.4 (October–December 1956): 214–227. Anna Seidel, "The Image of the Perfect Ruler in Early Taoist Movements," *History of Religions* 9 (1969–1970). Vincent Shih, "Some Chinese Rebel Ideologies," *T'oung pao* 44 (1956): 150–226. Holmes Welch, *Taoism: The Parting of the Way* (1957).   JOHN A. RAPP

YELÜ CHUCAI (1189–1243), leading Khitan official in the service of the Mongols in China. A descendant of the founder of the Khitan Liao dynasty, a civil official in Jurchen Jin dynasty, and well versed in literati traditions, Yelü survived the capture of Beijing by the Mongols in 1215. He entered Mongol service in 1218 as a secretary-astrologer on the staff of Genghis Khan and continued to serve under Ogedei. In 1229 he became responsible for the taxation of North China and in 1231 was made chief of the Secretariat. Under Ogedei, Yelü led the first attempt to persuade the Mongols to control Chinese territory through traditional Chinese civil institutions. His attempt to establish a tax system staffed by civil officials under central authority, opposed by Mongol aristocrats bent on defending their own power and distrustful of former Jin officials, was soon replaced by a system of tax-farming administered by Central Asians.

[*See also* Khitan; Genghis Khan; Ogedei; *and* Mongol Empire: An Overview.]

Igor de Rachewiltz, "Yeh-lü Ch'u-ts'ai (1189–1243): Buddhist Idealist and Confucian Statesman," in *Confucian Personalities,* edited by Arthur F. Wright and Denis Twitchett (1962), pp. 189–216.   PETER K. BOL

YEN BAY UPRISING, revolt launched by the Vietnam Nationalist Party, or VNQDD, in North Vietnam in 1930. Since the founding of the Party in 1927, its leaders had planned an uprising to overthrow French colonial rule. Native troops in the colonial army had been subverted in preparation for an insurrection at military posts throughout the country. The revolt broke out at Yen Bay and several other French military garrisons in the Red River delta on 9–10 February 1930. But poor planning and betrayal by informers led to disaster, and the revolt was put down with little difficulty.

[*See also* Vietnam Nationalist Party.]

Thomas Hodgkin, *Vietnam: The Revolutionary Path* (1981).   WILLIAM J. DUIKER

YI DYNASTY. The royal Yi family ruled Korea from 1392 to 1910 under the official dynastic name Chosŏn ("morning serenity"). Embracing the Neo-Confucianism of the Chinese philosopher Zhu Xi as its official ideology, the Yi dynasty provided political and social stability for more than five hundred years, but lost its political independence when Japan annexed Korea in 1910.

The dynasty was founded by Yi Sŏng-gye (1335–1408), who had become a prominent general under the preceding Koryŏ dynasty (918–1392) after a series of military successes against the Chinese Red Turban bandit groups and Japanese marauders. In 1388 he staged a successful coup and in 1392, supported by reform-minded Neo-Confucian officials, he proclaimed himself king of the new Chosŏn dynasty. [*See* Yi Sŏng-gye.] The dynastic foundation was solidified under the third king, T'aejong (r.

1400–1418), and his son, Sejong (r. 1418–1450). Renowned for his extraordinary intellect, Sejong was responsible for bringing about Korea's golden age of creativity, during which important achievements were made in many fields, including the invention of the Korean alphabet, known as *han'gŭl.*

The structure and functioning of the government were defined in the *Kyŏngguk taejon,* the national code promulgated in 1471. Although theoretically the king was the sovereign and the source of all legitimacy, in reality he was often restrained by a system of checks and balances within the bureaucratic structure. The State Council was the highest organ of policy deliberation under the king, and its three high state councillors usually sought a consensus. The six ministries—Personnel, Taxation, Rites, Military Affairs, Punishments, and Public Works—performed the duties of executing state policies. One unique feature of the Yi government was the enormous power enjoyed by three censorial organs, namely, the Office of the Inspector-General, the Office of the Censor-General, and the Office of Special Advisers. Administratively, the country was divided into eight provinces, and each province was in turn divided into counties. All provincial governors and county magistrates were centrally appointed.

Most of these officials were recruited through the civil service examinations, which were conducted at two levels. The lower examination awarded the *saengwŏn* degree to classics licentiates and *chinsa* to literary licentiates. These lower degree holders were eligible to compete in the higher examination for the *munkwa* degree, which qualified its holders to become state officials. Legally, these examinations were open to the *yangban* and the commoners. [*See* Korean State Examination System.]

The Yi dynasty maintained a well-structured educational system to promote the Confucian teachings and to prepare qualified individuals for the civil service examinations. In every county, a state-supported county school was established and its students received stipends as well as exemption from military duty. In Seoul, the National Confucian Academy enrolled those who held the licentiate's degree to prepare for the higher civil examination. After 1542 private academies (*sŏwŏn*) began to be organized, and after the seventeenth century they proliferated in the countryside, overshadowing the county schools. [*See* Sŏwŏn.]

The *yangban* was a privileged social class, whose status was largely determined by family lineages and Confucian education. The large majority of the population, however, was commoners. Between the

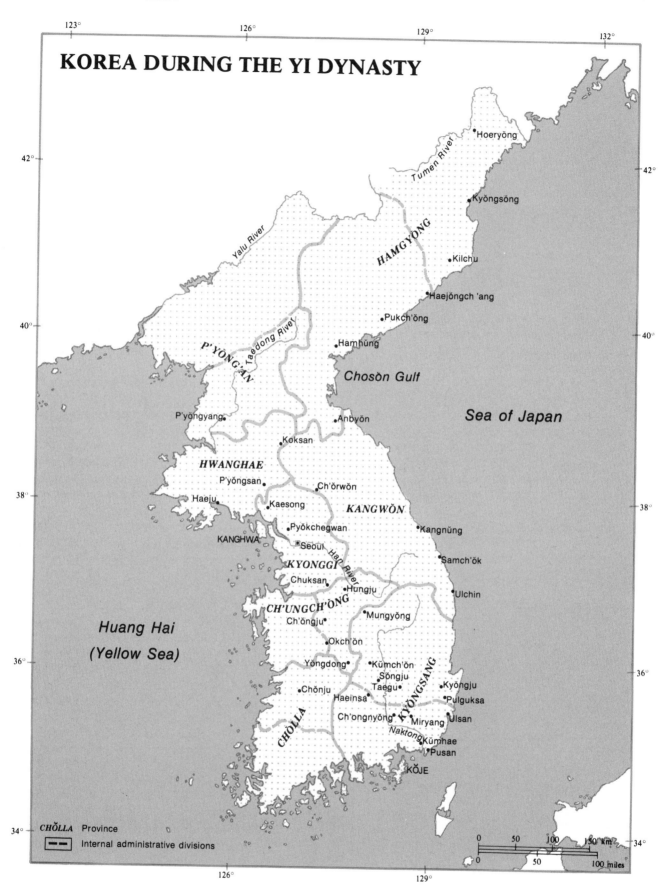

KOREA DURING THE YI DYNASTY

123°   126°   129°   132°

42°   42°

•Hoeryŏng

Tumen River

•Kyŏngsŏng

Yalu River

HAMGYŎNG

•Kilchu

40°   40°

P'YŎNG'AN   Taedong River

Haejŏngch'ang•

•Pukch'ŏng

•Hamhŭng

Choson Gulf

Sea of Japan

P'yŏngyang•   •Anbyŏn

•Koksan

HWANGHAE

P'yŏngsan•   •Ch'ŏrwŏn

38°   38°

Haeju•   •Kaesong   KANGWŎN

•Pyŏkchegwan   •Kangnŭng

KANGHWA   •Seoul

Han River   •Samch'ŏk

KYONGGI

Chuksan•   •Ulchin

•Hŭngju

CH'UNGCH'ŎNG   •Mungyŏng

Ch'ŏngju•

•Okch'ŏn

Huang Hai

(Yellow Sea)

Yŏngdong•   •Kŭmch'ŏn

36°   •Sŏngju   •Kyŏngju   36°

•Chŏnju   Taegu•   •Pulguksa

Haeinsa•   KYŎNGSANG

Ch'ongnyŏng•   •Miryang   •Ulsan

CHŎLLA   Naktong   •Kŭmhae
                                •Pusan

KŎJE

34°   34°

CHŎLLA   Province
─ ─ ─   Internal administrative divisions

0   50   100   150 Km
0   50   100 miles

126°   129°

yangban and the commoners was a small group known as "the middle people" (*chungin*), who filled technical and functionary positions within the government. At the bottom of the society were the low-born, whose status was determined by birth. [*See* Korea, Class Structure in *and* Yangban.]

The Yi-dynasty Confucian branded Buddhism as heresy and generally followed very strict interpretations of Zhu Xi's teachings. Probably the greatest philosopher of Yi-dynasty Korea, Yi Hwang (T'oegye, 1501–1570) set the standard of Zhu Xi orthodoxy with his voluminous commentaries and interpretations of the Confucian sages. The great debate between Yi Hwang and Ki Tae-sŭng (1527–1572) over the roles of principle (*li*) and material force (*qi*) in the functioning of the Four Beginnings and the Seven Emotions led to arguments for more than three hundred years involving virtually every scholar in the country. Yi I (Yulgok; 1536–1584) was another major philosopher-statesman, representing a different school in the debate over *li* and *qi*. [*See* Zhu Xi; Yi Hwang; Yi I; *and* Neo-Confucianism in Korea.]

In politics, four major conflicts known as the "literati purges" flared up, in which a number of government officials were either put to death or sent into banishment. The purges, which occurred in 1498, 1504, 1519, and 1545, have largely been explained in terms of conflict between the meritorious elites (*hungu*), who had long dominated the court, and the new breed of Neo-Confucian literati (*sarim*). Toward the end of the sixteenth century a factional split took place within the bureaucracy, which in turn led to further fragmentations, that impaired the politics of the latter half of the Yi dynasty with bitter factional rivalry. [*See* Literati Purges.]

The peace that Yi Korea had enjoyed for two centuries was abruptly shattered in 1592, when Japan, under Toyotomi Hideyoshi, invaded Korea. For six years, war ravaged the country, decimating the population, destroying innumerable historical and cultural treasures, and leaving long-lasting scars in the minds of the people. With the emergence of the Tokugawa government in Japan, however, peaceful relations between the two countries were restored. [*See* Hideyoshi's Invasion of Korea.] Toward Ming China, the Yi dynasty pursued the friendly policy of *sadae* (respecting the senior state) within the traditional East Asian world order. But the Manchus, invading Korea in 1627 and 1636, forced it to repudiate the Ming dynasty and shift allegiance to their Qing dynasty.

Once peace was restored the Yi government in-troduced several important reforms to regain control over the population and resources and alleviate the people's tax burdens. Perhaps the most important reform was enactment of the Uniform Land Tax Law (*taedongpŏp*) during the seventeenth century. This law commuted the sundry taxes of tribute items and required a uniform payment of rice based on land assessment. This law had a far-reaching impact upon the economy of the mid-Yi dynasty as it gave rise to a new mercantile group known as "tribute men," who in time commanded large sums of commercial capital, and also freed most artisans to become independent manufacturers.

In agriculture, a new technique of transplanting rice seedlings was developed in the early seventeenth century, which resulted in a dramatic increase in crop yields and a marked reduction in labor requirements. This new method also enabled farmers in the southern provinces to harvest two crops, rice in the fall and barley in the spring. In addition, new cash crops, such as ginseng, tobacco, and cotton, made commercial farming popular. Commercial activities also expanded during the seventeenth and eighteenth centuries with the wider circulations of coins and credit certificates (*ŏŭm*), leading to the "commercial equalization" enactment of 1791, which abolished the licensed merchant system, thereby freeing merchants from governmental control.

Using newly gained economic power, an increasing number of people acquired higher social status. As social mobility became more fluid, many *yangban* families tried to distance themselves from these upstarts by publishing genealogies and initiating clan organizations. Economically no longer viable, all the public slaves attached to government offices were freed in 1801 with the dramatic burning of their slave registers.

Beginning in the seventeenth century, the Yi dynasty witnessed the rise of a new intellectual current known as *sirhak* ("practical learning"). Critical of government policies and practices, the *sirhak* scholars wrote voluminously, offering remedies to the outstanding socioeconomic problems. They believed that the foremost priority of the government was to improve the welfare of the people as a whole and their recommendations emphasized pragmatic approach. [*See* Sirhak.]

After the passing of two very capable rulers, Yŏngjo (r. 1724–1776) and Chŏngjo (r. 1776–1800), the royal family was unable to sire kings who reached adulthood. With several boys occupying the throne in succession, the way was opened for domination of the court by the royal in-law families. The government began to lose its hold on the governing process and three important administrations, those for the land tax, military service tax, and grain loan system, fell into disarray, causing extreme hardship for the peasants. Starting with the Hong Kyŏng-nae Rebellion of 1811, popular rebellions broke out in many parts of the country.

This situation allowed new religions to gather momentum. Roman Catholicism was introduced into Korea by Korean scholars who visited China as members of diplomatic missions. Known as "Western learning" (Sŏhak), Catholicism before long gained converts from all classes in spite of government persecution after 1801. Largely to challenge the spread of Catholicism, Ch'oe Cheu (1824–1864) started a new religion called Tonghak ("Eastern learning"). His egalitarian tenets, which included the concept of *in nae ch'ŏn* ("man is God"), were extremely attractive to the oppressed peasants and in time Tonghak became a formidable political and social force. [*See* Christianity: Christianity in Korea; Sŏhak; *and* Tonghak.]

The accession to the throne at the age of twelve by Kojong (r. 1864–1907) enabled his father, the Taewŏn'gun ("grand prince"), to assume the power of government for the next ten years. Dynamic and resolute, the Taewŏn'gun introduced measures to revitalize the dynasty. His rule also coincided with Korea's first clashes with Western powers. In 1866, angry over the execution of nine French missionaries, France sent a punitive expedition to the island of Kanghwa, and in 1871, the United States dispatched a naval squadron to determine the fate of the crews of the lost ship *General Sherman* and negotiate a treaty. These only led to military clashes that resulted in both France and the United States withdrawing. [*See* General Sherman Incident.]

Japan, however, successfully negotiated the Kanghwa Treaty, signed in February 1876. [*See* Kanghwa Treaty.] Before long, a number of Koreans visited Japan to witness the transformation taking place under the Meiji leadership. When they returned to Korea, they became the leaders of the enlightenment movement. Urged on by these men, King Kojong embarked, albeit half-heartedly, on a policy of adopting Western ideas and technologies. Concerned over ascending Japanese influence in Korea, China prevailed upon Korea to sign the Treaty of Amity and Commerce with the United States at Chemulp'o in 1882. Thereafter, Korea signed similar treaties with other Western countries. These developments incurred reactions from conservative

Confucians, who carried out a campaign of total rejection of the West and its supposed surrogate, Japan.

A military mutiny in 1882 brought the anti-foreign Taewŏn'gun back to power, which led China to dispatch troops to Korea, an unprecedented move in the relations of the two countries, and abduct him to China. In 1884, impatient at the slow pace with which Korea was moving toward modern reform, the Enlightenment Party attempted a bloody coup in the hope of instituting Meiji-style reforms. This Kapsin coup, however, failed in three days when the Chinese troops stationed in Seoul intervened. From then until 1894, China dominated Korean affairs, directly intervening in many areas. [*See* 1882 Uprising; Taewŏn'gun; *and* 1884 Coup d'État.]

The government, now under the control of Queen Min and her family, lacked any coherent policy and widespread misgovernment and increasing economic penetration by foreign powers worsened the plight of the peasants. The anger and frustrations of the peasants erupted in the great Tonghak Uprising of 1894, engulfing Chŏlla and Ch'ungch'ŏng provinces. The uprising gave Japan a convenient opportunity to challenge China's supremacy in Korea and its victory in the Sino-Japanese War of 1894 to 1895 eliminated Chinese influence from Korea. Protected by the Japanese, the progressive reformers gained power and introduced a series of drastic measures—known as the Kabo Reforms of 1894—to force Korea to modernize. But Russia's challenge to Japanese influence and court intrigues manipulated by Queen Min soon put an end to these reforms. Repeatedly blocked by the queen, the Japanese minister, Miura Gorō, encouraged a plot that resulted in her assassination in 1895. King Kojong then became fearful for his own safety and sought refuge in the compound of the Russian legation in 1896, where he remained for one year. While Russia and Japan competed over Korea, they and other Western nations scrambled for economic concessions. [*See* Sino-Japanese War; Kabo Reforms; *and* Min, Queen.]

Meanwhile, modern ideas were gaining wider acceptance among Koreans largely through schools organized by the American missionaries, and an increasing number of Koreans became alarmed over the deteriorating domestic conditions and the economic inroads being gained for foreigners. Many of these Koreans joined the Independence Club, organized in 1896 by Sŏ Chae-p'il (Philip Jaisohn). Through the publication of a newspaper, public discussions, and other activities, the Independence

Club desperately attempted to protect Korea's independence and promote Korea's interests. Blinded by selfish interest, however, Kojong forced the club to disband. [*See* Independence Party and Club *and* Jaisohn, Philip.]

The final showdown between Japan and Russia came with the outbreak of the Russo-Japanese War of 1904 to 1905, from which Japan emerged victorious, forcing Russia to renounce all interest in Korea. Japan then moved diplomatically to win the major Western powers' support of her free hand in Korea. In November 1905 Japan compelled Korea to sign the so-called Treaty of Protectorate, under the terms of which Japan was to take charge of Korea's foreign affairs; shortly thereafter, Itō Hirobumi was appointed the resident-general of Korea, thus becoming its virtual ruler. [*See* Russo-Japanese War *and* Itō Hirobumi.]

This growing Japanese control provoked widespread opposition among Koreans, and many of them joined the ranks of guerrilla "righteous armies" and took arms against the Japanese presence. As a last resort, King Kojong secretly dispatched emissaries to the Second Hague Peace Conference to publicize Korea's grievances against Japan. Angered by this move, Japan forced Kojong to abdicate the throne in favor of his son, Sunjong (r. 1907–1910). Japan also disbanded the remnants of the Korean army. [*See* Kojong.]

Having thus removed all effective opposition, Japan proceeded to sign the treaty of annexation in August 1910 in cooperation with a Korean cabinet filled with collaborators. This brought an end to the Yi dynasty, terminated Korea's independent status, and reduced it to a colony of Japan.

[*See also* Korea *and* Korea, Japanese Government-General of.]

Ching Young Choe, *The Rule of the Taewon'gun* (1972). Hilary Conroy, *The Japanese Seizure of Korea 1868–1910* (1960). Martina Deuchler, *Confucian Gentlemen and Barbarian Envoys* (1977). Pyong-choon Hahm, *The Korean Political Tradition and Law* (1967). Woo-keun Han, *The History of Korea*, translated by Kyong-shik Lee (1971). Sang-woon Jeon, *Science and Technology in Korea* (1974). C. I. Eugene Kim and Han-Kyo Kim, *Korea and the Politics of Imperialism* (1967). Key-hiuk Kim, *The Last Phase of the East Asian World Order* (1980). Ki-baik Lee, *A New History of Korea*, translated by Edward W. Wagner (1984). James B. Palais, *Politics and Policy in Traditional Korea* (1975). Edward W. Wagner, *The Literati Purges: Political Conflict in Early Yi Korea* (1974). Benjamin B. Weems, *Reform, Rebellion and the Heavenly Way* (1964).

YŎNG-HO CHʼOE

YI HA-ŬNG. *See* Taewŏn'gun.

YIHETUAN ("righteous and harmonious society"), Chinese sect derived from the Yihequan ("righteous and harmonious fists"), hence the popular term *Boxer*. The Yihetuan was an outgrowth of the Eight Trigrams sect and was associated with the White Lotus Society. It was a mixture of anti-Qing, antiforeign, and anti-Christian elements. In the late 1890s the society engaged in open rebellion, the roots of which lay in natural disasters, disruption of the traditional Chinese economy by the introduction of foreign manufactured goods, and territorial concessions to the Germans, British, and Russians. Foreign railroads and other constructions were blamed for many of the natural disasters because they were said to have disturbed the natural harmony.

An alliance of sorts developed in the autumn of 1899 between antiforeign elements at the Qing court and the rebels, when government troops seized and defeated some of the antidynastic forces in Shandong. After this incident Boxer policies became primarily antiforeign rather than antidynastic. The rebels then laid siege to foreign legations and other foreign buildings in Beijing and Tianjin. Foreign troops fought back and a multinational relief force took Tianjin on 14 July 1900 and advanced toward Beijing on 4 August. The capital fell ten days later and was sacked by the foreign armies. The empress dowager, the emperor, and a small entourage escaped to Xi'an. Li Hongzhang was selected to negotiate a peace settlement, which was formalized in the Boxer Protocol and signed on 7 September 1901. The terms included the execution of ten high officials and the punishment of a hundred others, formal apologies, suspension of examinations in order to punish the gentry, expansion of the legations, destruction of Chinese fortifications, occupation of railway posts by foreigners, an increase in import duties, and a huge indemnity.

[*See also* Empress Dowager; Li Hongzhang; Qing Dynasty; White Lotus Society; *and* Rebellions in China.]

Victor Purcell, *The Boxer Uprising: A Background Study* (1963). Chester Tan, *The Boxer Catastrophe* (1955). JOHN PHILIP NESS

YI HWANG (1501–1570), better known by his honorific name T'oegye, generally regarded as Korea's foremost Neo-Confucian thinker. His father died while T'oegye was in infancy, leaving his mother to raise seven sons and a daughter. Both he and an elder brother passed the civil service examinations and became government officials, a career contrary to T'ogeye's desires but expedient in the family's impoverished circumstances. His extensive intellectual accomplishments as a writer and teacher were achieved mostly after his retirement from office in 1549.

Yi T'oegye was the first Korean thinker to attain a complete and balanced mastery of the complex philosophical and ascetical system welded into a grand synthesis by the great Chinese Neo-Confucian philosopher, Zhu Xi (1130–1200). Neo-Confucianism had been established as the official ideology of the Yi dynasty (1392–1910) at its founding after centuries of Buddhist predominance on the peninsula. During the century that followed attention was devoted mainly to institutional reform and moral cultivation; T'oegye's great contribution was to grasp the entire vision in a way that grounded practice in its necessary theoretical framework. His extensive written works and teaching activity insured an integral grasp of Zhu Xi's vision for future generations, and historians date the coming to full maturity of Korean Neo-Confucianism from him.

T'oegye's most famous contribution was in the area of the Neo-Confucian metaphysically based psychological system, where he explored the implications of the metaphysical dualism of *li* ("principle") and *qi* ("material force") for the active tendencies of the human psyche. His position and its implications were the object of intense debate and set a distinctive intellectual agenda for succeeding generations of Korean Neo-Confucian thinkers.

[*See also* Neo-Confucianism in Korea *and* Yi Dynasty.]

Wm. Theodore de Bary and JaHyun Kim Haboush, eds., *The Rise of Neo-Confucianism in Korea* (1985). Woo-Keun Han, *The History of Korea*, translated by Kyung-shik Lee (1970), Wanne J. Joe, *Traditional Korea: A Cultural History* (1972). Ki-baik Lee, *A New History of Korea*, translated by Edward W. Wagner (1984).

MICHAEL C. KALTON

YI I (1536–1584), better known by his honorific name, Yulgok, commonly paired with Yi Hwang (T'oegye; 1501–1570) as the foremost Neo-Confucian thinkers of Korea. He was educated in his youth by his mother, Sin Saimdang, who is accounted Korea's finest female poet and painter. She died when Yulgok was sixteen, and after a three-year mourning period he entered a Buddhist mon-

astery for several years. Eventually, however, he reaffirmed his committment to the Confucian path and took the civil service examinations, which led to an official career. Before he ever entered office he was already famous, for he took first place in nine consecutive examinations.

Once in office Yulgok was never permitted to retire into the quiet life of study and teaching; although he resigned high positions repeatedly he was always soon recalled. This was the period when the first of what were to become permanent factional divisions split the Korean political world; Yulgok spent much time trying to heal the breach and as a neutral was frequently attacked by both sides. He was among the king's most trusted advisers and his *Collected Works* abound in perceptive and practical counsel for improving the country's administrative, military, and economic life. He is greatly esteemed for this and is often mentioned as the precursor of Korea's school of Practical Learning *(sirhak).*

Philosophically Yulgok is known especially for establishing the counterposition to that of Yi T'oegye in the controversy concerning the role of *li* ("principle") and *qi* ("material force") in the activation of morally correct and incorrect sorts of affective responses. This exploration of the implications of the Chinese Neo-Confucian philosopher Zhu Xi's metaphysical dualism for psychological theory became Korea's distinctive intellectual agenda, and T'oegye and Yulgok became the permanent reference points in a debate that still continues.

[*See also* Neo-Confucianism in Korea; Yi Hwang; *and* Yi Dynasty.]

Wm. Theodore de Bary and JaHyun Kim Haboush, eds., *The Rise of Neo-Confucianism in Korea* (1985). Woo-keun Han, *The History of Korea*, translated by Kyung-shik Lee (1970). Wanne J. Joe, *Traditional Korea: A Cultural History* (1972). Ki-baik Lee, *A New History of Korea*, translated by Edward W. Wagner (1984).

MICHAEL C. KALTON

YI KWANG-SU (1892–1950), Korean writer. Born in Chŏngju, North P'yŏngan Province, the son of a tenant farmer, Yi attended middle school at Meiji Gakuin from 1904 to 1910, at which time he married his first wife. While a student in the philosophy department of Waseda University in Japan (1915–1919), the consumptive Yi was nursed by Hŏ Yŏng-suk, then a medical student in Tokyo, with whom he eloped to Beijing (October 1918).

On his return to Tokyo, Yi drafted a declaration of independence for the Korean Youth Association and escaped to Shanghai to distribute its English version among Korean patriots abroad (1919). He returned to Korea and married Hŏ in May 1921. He served as editor of *Dong-A Daily* (1925–1927 and 1929–1933) and vice president of *Chosŏn Daily* (1933–1934). After serving a six-month prison term for breaking the Japanese security law, Yi was made chairman of the pro-Japanese writers' association (1939). In June 1939 he went with others to Beijing to comfort Japanese soldiers, took a Japanese name (1940), gave speeches in Korea to support the Japanese military (1941), and in Tokyo urged Korean students to volunteer for the Japanese army (December 1942). After the liberation of Korea in 1945 Yi was branded as pro-Japanese but continued to write such works as *My Confession* (1948). On 12 July 1950 Yi, bedridden with high blood pressure, was kidnapped to P'yŏngyang by the North Korean army. He was then sent to Beijing as an instructor of Korean but is said to have died shortly thereafter.

Viewing literature as a political and social means of persuasion and enlightenment, Yi used his characters as instruments to drive home his own authorial interpretations of events. Thus, he leads a story to a conclusion that illustrates his convictions about a social and cultural problem. Yi's reputation was made with *The Heartless* (1917), the first modern Korean novel to preach free love and Western learning, and *The Pioneer* (1914–1918), which was about rural enlightenment. His concept of platonic love, later tinged with Christian love and Buddhist compassion, found expression in *Love* (1938). He voiced his racial consciousness and patriotism in such historical novels as *The Hemp-Clad Prince* (1926–1927), *King Tanjong* (1928–1929), *Yi Sunsin* (1931–1932), *Yich'adon* (1936), *Great Master Wŏnhyo* (1942), and *Love of King Tongmyŏng* (1949). In *Earth* (1932–1933) Yi expressed his Tolstoyan humanism and zeal for agrarian reform. A versatile and prolific writer, he helped create a new literary style that unified the spoken and written languages and developed modern Korean literature. These contributions outweigh his submission to Japanese coercion to cooperate with the Japanese military cause.

Collected Works of Yi Kwangsu, 20 vols. (1963).

PETER H. LEE

YIN AND YANG, Chinese names for two fundamental tendencies, forces, or elements. From ancient times these paired concepts have been used in Chinese philosophy, alchemy, medicine, and other fields to analyze and account for the dynamic qualities of natural systems and processes. Yin has the properties of being female, weak, cold, and dark and is identified with the moon, the northern side of a mountain, the southern bank of a river, and negative ions. By extension, the yin property is associated with that which is private, sinister, or involving the afterlife. Yang, by contrast, is male, strong, warm, and bright. It is identified with the sun, the southern side of a mountain, the northern bank of a river, and positive ions and, by extension, is associated with that which is public, open, or involving the living.

[*See also* Zou Yan.]

Wing-tsit Chan, *A Source Book in Chinese Philosophy* (1973). Wm. Theodore de Bary, Wing-tsit Chan, and Burton Watson, comps., *Sources of Chinese Tradition,* vol. 1 (1960). EDWARD L. FARMER

YINCHUAN, Chinese city, the provincial capital of Ningxia and an important highway center. Its population in 1982 was 360,000. A strategic outpost as early as the Qin dynasty (221–206 BCE), Yinchuan was traditionally an administrative and commercial city specializing in the processing of agricultural products. After the construction of rail links to Beijing and Inner Mongolia in the 1950s, it developed some modern industry, including a linen mill, tanneries, and a farm tool factory.

JOHN A. RAPP

YI SANG-JAE (1850–1927), Korean nationalist and early advocate of modern reforms, especially education for the youth.

Yi, a native of Ch'ungch'ŏng Province, went to Seoul in 1867 and became a protégé of Pak Chŏng-yang, whom he accompanied to Japan in 1881. When Pak went to the United States in 1887 as the first Korean minister, Yi was again in Pak's entourage as a legation secretary and spent more than a year in Washington. Several years later, when a government in favor of reform was installed in Seoul, Yi was appointed, in a rapid succession, to a series of important official positions including the directorship of Educational Administration Bureau. He established a system of modern schools at the primary and secondary levels.

Yi's commitment to westernization and national independence was evident in his active participation in the Independence Club, which he helped Sŏ Chae-p'il, also known as Philip Jaisohn, found in 1896.

Yi gave public lectures, took part in debates, and presided over mass rallies where official corruption was denounced and populist demands were voiced. The Club was disbanded in 1898 and Yi was imprisoned for three years on a fabricated charge.

Yi returned to government service in 1905 but his opposition to the growing Japanese influence in Korea led to his arrest and resignation in 1907. Upon release, he devoted himself to education, especially in his role as director of education at the Seoul YMCA. When Japan formally annexed Korea in 1910 Yi continued his YMCA and other educational work in the belief that education was the key to Korea's eventual salvation. Although he took no active part in the March First Movement protesting Japanese rule in 1919, he agreed in 1924 to head *Chosŏn ilbo*, a Korean language newspaper, and he also lent his prestige to Sin'ganhoe, a thinly veiled anti-Japanese organization, by serving as its first president in 1926, a year before his death.

[*See also* Jaisohn, Philip *and* Independence Party and Club.]

HAN-KYO KIM

YI SŎNG-GYE

YI SŎNG-GYE (1335–1408), the founder of Korea's Yi dynasty (1392–1910). As a military commander in the declining years of the Koryŏ dynasty (918–1392) he attained prominence by curbing the Japanese pirates who preyed on Korea's coastal areas. The dynasty itself, however, was plagued with dire revenue problems, questionable legitimacy in the ruling line, and difficult questions of foreign policy. In 1388 Yi was dispatched north with an army to oppose a move by China's new Ming dynasty (1368–1644) to establish a commandery on the Liaodong Peninsula. Instead, he turned his army and mounted an almost bloodless coup. Among his first measures was a sweeping land reform that broke up the great aristocratic estates and reestablished an economic foundation for the government.

The Neo-Confucian movement had become a powerful force in Song and Yuan China, and in the last eighty years of the Koryŏ dynasty it had been gaining strength in Korea as well. Young Neo-Confucian officials had formed Yi's political power base and engineered his takeover; now they controlled the government. Yi Sŏng-gye was a devout Buddhist, but as part of the new dynasty's program of economic and political reform there was an extensive divestiture of Buddhist landholdings, and limits were placed on the number of temples and monks. In 1398 Yi Sŏng-gye resigned the throne and retired

to a Buddhist monastery, disheartened by a bloody fratricidal struggle for the succession among his sons. During Yi's reign, however, Korea already had begun the transformation that would make it the most thoroughly Neo-Confucian society of East Asia.

[*See also* Koryŏ; Yi Dynasty; *and* Neo-Confucianism in Korea.]

Wm. Theodore de Bary and JaHyun Kim Haboush, eds., *The Rise of Neo-Confucianism in Korea* (1985). Woo-keun Han, *The History of Korea*, translated by Kyung-shik Lee (1970). Ki-baik Lee, *A New History of Korea*, translated by Edward W. Wagner (1984).

MICHAEL C. KALTON

YI SŬNG-MAN

YI SŬNG-MAN. *See* Rhee, Syngman.

YI SUN-SIN

YI SUN-SIN (1545–1598), Korean naval hero during the invasions of Toyotomi Hideyoshi of Japan. Born into a scholar-official family, Yi studied the Confucian classics in his early years but chose a military career by passing the state military examination in 1576. He was first assigned to a frontier garrison on the northern border and thereafter served in minor army and navy posts until 1591, when he was promoted to be naval commander of the Left Chŏlla Province.

Amid rumors of possible Japanese invasion, Yi carried out a program of revitalizing the navy under his command through the development of "turtle ships." Yi covered the decks of ships with iron plate and spikes, like a turtle's back, and equipped them with cannons and guns that could be fired in all directions; posssessed of high maneuverability and speed, a turtle ship could ram enemy ships at will. When Japan invaded Korea in 1592, Yi Sun-sin first engaged the enemy at Okp'o, where he destroyed more than thirty Japanese ships. Thereafter, he defeated the Japanese navy at Sach'ŏn, Tangp'o, Hansan, and Pusan. The victory off Hansan Island was particularly notable, as Yi destroyed more than seventy enemy ships with his famous "crane" formation. These successes gave Korea control of the sea, eliminated any threat from the Japanese navy, and forced the Japanese to carry their supplies the length of the peninsula.

Following the battle of Hansan, Yi was made commander in chief of the Combined Navy of the Three Provinces. In 1597 he was accused of dishonest reporting to the king and of failure to pursue the enemy with sufficient vigor, and was imprisoned briefly for investigation, but in the same year, the defeat of the Korean navy in the second Japanese invasion brought reinstatement to his former post. Once he had rebuilt the shattered navy, Yi engaged the Japanese fleet at the Myŏngnyang Strait and destroyed more than thirty enemy ships. In 1598, as the war was drawing to a close, his fleet, now joined by the Chinese navy, fought a final battle at Noryang and dealt a crushing blow to the Japanese. This was the last battle for Yi Sun-sin, who was killed in action. He was given the posthumous honorary title Ch'ungmu ("loyal and brave"). Universally admired by all Koreans, he is enshrined in Hyŏnch'ung Temple at Yesan, South Ch'ungch'ŏng Province.

[*See also* Hideyoshi's Invasion of Korea.]

Yi Sun-sin, *Nanjung Ilgi: War Diary of Admiral Yi Sun-sin,* translated by Ha Tae-hung and edited by Sohn Pow-key (1977), and *Imjin Changch'o: Admiral Yi Sun-sin's Memorials to Court* (1981). Yune-Hee Park, *Admiral Yi Sun-shin and His Turtleboat Armada* (1978).

YŎNG-HO CH'OE

YITIAOBIANFA, the "Single Whip" system of taxation, was a series of reforms introduced in early sixteenth-century China with the aim of applying a simplified and uniform fiscal policy throughout the empire. The term *single whip* is a pun on the homophones for "combine" and "whip" and refers to the attempt to consolidate the land taxes, service obligations, and miscellaneous fees imposed on the taxpayer into one lump sum that would be payable in silver. The system was applied first in the eastern and southeastern provinces that were the economic center of late Ming China. In such areas, the Single Whip reforms were somewhat effective in increasing the state's revenue, although some scholars contend that the reforms lacked the necessary central coordination to succeed. Ironically, the reforms not only failed to simplify tax collection procedures for officials at the local level of administration but also increased the burden of paperwork for the magistrate and his staff.

The Single Whip system continued to be applied on a piecemeal basis until the early seventeenth century, when military needs of the faltering Ming dynasty became far more important than fiscal reform. The reforms were later revived during the Qing dynasty.

Ray Huang, *Taxation and Governmental Finance in Sixteenth Century Ming China* (1974). Liang Fang-chung, *The Single-whip Method of Taxation in China,* translated by Wang Yu-ch'uan (1956). John R. Watt, *The District Magistrate in Late Imperial China* (1972).

ANITA M. ANDREW

YI T'OEGYE. *See* Yi Hwang.

YI TONG-HWI (1873–1935), Korean leader who advocated armed struggle to defeat Japanese colonialism, occupied key positions in the exile government, and played a pivotal role in the early days of the Korean communist movement.

A native of Hamgyŏng Province in northeast Korea, Yi graduated from a military academy in Seoul and was an army major when Japan disbanded the Korean army in 1907. Yi made an unsuccessful attempt to stage an armed uprising in 1909. Released from Japanese captivity through the intercession of foreign missionaries, Yi crossed the border into the Jiandao region in southeastern Manchuria in 1911 and began organizing the Korean settlers there for political, educational, and military activities.

Pursued by the Japanese, Yi moved to the Russian Maritime Province in 1915 and organized the Han in Sahoedang (Korean People's Socialist Party) in June 1918. This, the first pro-Bolshevik Korean group, was later renamed Koryŏ Kongsandang (Korean Communist Party). At first Yi was probably more interested in securing assistance from the Bolsheviks than in a proletarian revolution. His fame as an anti-Japanese leader carried him to key positions, such as minister of military affairs and later premier, in the Korean Provisional Government created in Shanghai in 1919. Yi's strategy for winning Korean independence through armed campaigns, his communist affiliation, and his monopoly of a sizable fund provided by the Comintern, however, created rivalry with the right-wing nationalists and also with other communist factions such as the "Irkutsk Faction."

Yi resigned from his positions in the government in exile and traveled to Moscow in 1921 to defend himself and his "Shanghai Faction" before the Comintern; he was subsequently appointed by the Comintern to its Korean Bureau, which unsuccessfully tried to unite the feuding factions. Yi retired from politics after 1925 and died in obscurity at a village near Vladivostok. Unlike other anti-Japanese Korean patriots, Yi has not been granted posthumous honors by the South Korean government and he is virtually ignored in the histories published in North Korea and the Soviet Union.

[*See also* Communism: Communism in Korea.]

George L. Paik, *The History of Protestant Missions in Korea, 1832–1910* (3d ed., 1980). Robert A. Scalapino and Chong-sik Lee, *Communism in Korea,* vol. 1, *The Movement* (1972). Dae-sook Suh, *The Korean Communist Movement, 1918–1948* (1967).   HAN-KYO KIM

YI WAN-YONG (1858–1926), pro-Japanese government official in the last years of the Yi dynasty in Korea. As a signer, with four other ministers, of the 1905 Protectorate Agreement with Japan, and for his role in negotiating the subsequent Treaty of Annexation (1910), Yi has become a symbol of collaboration and treachery in Korean nationalist historiography.

Yi was born into a family of the *yangban* ruling class, the son of an important minister of state, Yi Ho-jun. After schooling and success in the civil service examinations in 1882, Yi worked as an editor in the Office of Royal Texts and as an English language student at the new government foreign language school. Yi's first important appointment was as Korean ambassador to the United States between 1888 and 1890. On his return to Korea in 1890, Yi began his rise in Korean government circles. Between 1890 and 1895 he served in a number of offices, most importantly as minister of education and as a member of the State Council. Yi became foreign minister in 1896, a position in which he would preside over Korea's diplomatic relations at a time of tremendous insecurity for the Korean nation.

Between 1905 and 1910 Yi worked closely with the first Japanese resident-general, Itō Hirobumi, and in 1907 became prime minister and head of the Royal Household Office. In 1910 Yi was wounded by Korean patriots and his house was burned during the riots that followed the formal annexation of Korea by Japan. In spite of personal attacks, Yi remained an apologist for Japanese rule; he served as an adviser to the governor-general of Korea, and he was rewarded eventually by being made a count in the Japanese peerage.

[*See also* Yi Dynasty *and* Korea, Japanese Government-General of.]

MICHAEL ROBINSON

YI YULGOK. *See* Yi I.

YOGA. The practice of yoga in one form or another has been one of the distinctive components of Indian religions from the earliest times to the present. De-

rived from the Sanskrit root *yuj* ("to harness") and etymologically related to the English word *yoke,* yoga at its most general refers to a variety of psychophysical disciplines or techniques. Yoga was systematized by Patanjali in his *Yogasutras* (c. second century BCE), and became one of the six orthodox schools of Hindu philosophy closely aligned with Samkhya dualism. Patanjali's yoga (also called raja yoga) entails eight steps: restraint, discipline, physical posture, breath control, withdrawal of the senses, concentration, meditation, and unified consciousness or "enstasis" *(samadhi).* Other yogic systems emphasize physical postures (hatha yoga) or Tantric practices (kundalini yoga), and the *Bhagavad Gita* describes yogas of gnosis *(jnana),* disciplined action *(karman),* and devotion to God *(bhakti).*

[*See also* Hinduism; Samkhya; *and* Bhakti.]

Mircea Eliade, *Yoga: Immortality and Freedom* (1969). Jean Varenne, *Yoga and the Hindu Tradition* (1973).

BRIAN K. SMITH

YOGYAKARTA (also Jogjakarta), name of the court city and kingdom founded by Sultan Hamengkubuwana I (previously Pangeran Mangkubumi; r. 1749–1792) after the partition of Central and East Java at the Treaty of Giyanti (13 February 1755). The name, which reads as Ngayogyakarta Hadiningrat in its full Javanese version, apparently derives from the Sanskrit name Ayodhya (Modern Javanese, Ngayodya), the capital city of the Indian hero Rama in the epic *Ramayana* story. The site of the new *kraton* was close to the erstwhile Mataram court centers of Karta and Plered and was built just to the north of the hunting reserve of the Mataram rulers at Krapyak. The first sultan apparently treasured these connections and saw his state as continuing the regal traditions of Mataram. The Dutch scholar G. P. Rouffaer has even remarked that there was something quintessentially "old-fashioned Javanese" about the Yogyakarta style of administration that was missing in the more outward-looking Surakarta courts.

The fact that Yogyakarta owed its very existence to the successful generalship of the first sultan against the combined forces of the *sunan* of Surakarta and the Dutch also marked the character of the court, imbuing its style with a certain martial austerity and energy. In political affairs it showed itself more willing to take the initiative than its Surakarta counterpart, a propensity that nearly ensured its destruction once the guiding hand of the astute first sultan had been removed. In December 1810 and June 1812 it was invaded twice by European troops. On the last occasion the *kraton* itself was taken by storm when the second sultan (r. 1792–1810, 1811–1812, 1826–1828), a vain and mercurial man, refused to cooperate with the British. Under the terms of the treaties imposed on the courts following this action, large areas of territory were annexed, the rulers were stripped of the bulk of their military forces, and the second sultan was sent into exile.

After 1812, neither Surakarta nor Yogyakarta was able to challenge the European government again, and the creation of the new minor court of the Pakualaman led to a further decline in the sultanate's influence. This reached its nadir during the Java War (1825–1830) when many Yogya officials and members of the royal family made common cause with Dipanagara. In 1830 the court (along with that of Surakarta) lost all its outlying territories, retaining control only over the core regions of Mataram (Sleman and Bantul), Kulon Praga, and the limestone hills of Gunung Kidul. The income available to the court contracted sharply, and many courtiers became increasingly impoverished as their apanage grants and cash stipends were reduced. A growing demoralization of the Yogya aristocracy ensued, but interesting developments took place in the artistic and literary fields, especially during the reign of the fifth sultan (r. 1822–1826, 1828–1855), in which a new style of Yogyakarta dance drama (*wayang wong*) was pioneered.

In the early years of the twentieth century Yogyakarta played an important role in the budding nationalist and Islamic revivalist movements: organizations such as Ki Adjar Dewantara's national-educational Taman Siswa movement (1922) and Haji Ahmad Dahlan's religious and social-oriented Muhammadiyah (1912) were founded locally, and the Budi Utomo held its first congress there in 1908, attracting considerable support from members of the Pakualaman. In 1912 it also served briefly as a focal point for Sarekat Islam activities. During the Great Depression of the 1930s, which hit the Yogyakarta region particularly hard, the Pakempalan Kawula Ngayogyakarta (Organization of the Subjects of Yogyakarta), founded by a half-brother of the eighth sultan (r. 1921–1939), gained an important following among the local peasantry. But Yogyakarta's greatest moment came during the Indonesian Revolution against the Dutch (1945–1949), when the ninth sultan (r. 1939 to present) cooper-

ated closely with the nationalists and invited the government of the nascent republic to reside in his capital from January 1946 onward. In recognition of this action, Yogyakarta was made a "special administrative area" (*daerah istimewa*) after Indonesia finally won its independence from the Dutch in 1949.

[*See also* Mangkubumi; Giyanti, Treaty of; Kraton; Mataram; Pakualaman; Java War; Dipanagara; Taman Siswa; Muhammadiyah; Budi Utomo; Sarekat Islam; *and* Indonesian Revolution.]

Peter Carey, *Pangeran Dipanagara and the Making of the Java War (1825–30): The End of an Old Order in Java* (1986). M. C. Ricklefs, *Jogjakarta under Sultan Mangkubumi 1749–1792: A History of the Division of Java* (1974). Selosoemardjan, *Social Changes in Jogjakarta* (1962).   PETER CAREY

YOKOI SHŌNAN (1809–1869), Japanese Confucian scholar and reformer of the late Tokugawa period. Yokoi Shōnan was born to a samurai family in Kumamoto domain. He traveled to Edo in 1839 and became acquainted with nationally renowned statesmen such as Kawaji Toshiakira and Fujita Tōko. After returning home, he formed the Practical Learning Party and fought unsuccessfully to implement reforms in Kumamoto domain. In 1858 he was invited to Fukui domain to be adviser to Matsudaira Yoshinaga, and here his views were well received. By 1860 he was advocating opening the country to foreign trade and diplomacy, developing commerce and industry, and strengthening the nation's armed forces by adopting Western techniques, all with the aim of overcoming the foreign threat facing Japan. Shōnan also began to envision a new polity—one that united the imperial court and the *bakufu* as well as powerful daimyo hitherto excluded from government. In 1863, a shakeup in Fukui politics caused him to fall from favor and he retired to Kumamoto. But after the Meiji Restoration in 1868, he received a post in the new government, only to be assassinated the following year.

Harry Harootunian, *Toward Restoration* (1970).

BOB TADASHI WAKABAYASHI

YONAOSHI, Japanese term also rendered as *yonaori* or *yonarashi*, literally, "straightening out the world." *Yonaoshi* was a desire for salvation or liberation from oppression displayed by the Japanese masses, and originally stemmed from a messianic belief in the coming of the bodhisattva Maitreya. The earliest evidence of *yonaoshi* dates from the Sengoku (Warring States) period (1467–1568). In the seventeenth and eighteenth centuries it assumed the form of mass prayers or incantations for abundant harvests.

These early manifestations of *yonaoshi* were tied to folk beliefs; they were largely nonviolent, sporadic, and confined to one or a cluster of peasant communities. From the 1830s to the 1870s, however, *yonaoshi* turned violent, became politically organized, broke out in cities, and grew in scale to include whole provinces. In sum, they developed into *yonaoshi* uprisings. Peasants, the rural and urban proletariat, vagabonds, gamblers, and other *lumpen* elements organized violent uprisings against usurers, pawnbrokers, guild merchants, and village headmen. They saw their violence as "straightening out the world," or removing its evils in order to restore it to its original, normal condition in which their sustenance was believed guaranteed by the existing *bakufu* and domain governments. *Yonaoshi* uprisings sought limited political goals, such as debt repudiation, the return of pawned land or goods, or the replacement of evil village headmen with virtuous ones; they did not seek radical, institutional changes in the status quo, only its purification.

[See also Ikki.]

BOB TADASHI WAKABAYASHI

YONGLE EMPEROR. See Zhu Di.

YONGZHENG EMPEROR

(Yinzhen; r. 1722–1735), fourth son of the Kangxi emperor of the Qing dynasty in China. The early part of Yongzheng's reign is noted for his harsh treatment of his opponents and suspicious distrust of his supporters in the succession dispute, of which he has been accused of suppressing the true record. He set the precedent of leaving the name of the imperial heir in a box to be unsealed only after his death.

Yongzheng's "Amplified Instructions," issued in 1724, enlarged on Kangxi's "Sacred Edict" and were universally promulgated. He was interested in Buddhism and Daoism and tolerated some Christian presence in China despite earlier Jesuit involvement in another faction in the succession struggle. His most wide-ranging persecution involved descendants and followers of Lu Liuliang, whose anti-Manchu writings composed fifty years earlier had come to light.

From 1724 to 1727 he suppressed rebellions in Kokonor and in Yunnan. The Treaty of Kiakhta, concluded with Russia in 1727, established the Mongolian-Siberian border; from 1729 to 1732 China sent its first diplomatic mission, to Saint Petersburg.

By 1729 several tax reforms had been implemented. Yongzheng legalized the silver meltage fee, amalgamated the land and poll taxes, and introduced the *yanglian* ("nourishing integrity") supplemental stipend for officials in an attempt to reduce corruption. Meanwhile, he reformed and consolidated the legal code. From 1725 to 1730 he restructured the banner system, establishing banner schools and weakening the princes' power by centralizing control. Under his reign some of those classified as "mean people" were emancipated, and opium was banned. Yongzheng's fiscal and legal reforms provided a sound basis for the splendor of the following reign.

The Grand Council evolved after 1729 into the main organ of state. Gradually it assumed the Grand Secretariat's powers to compose and issue edicts and instructions to the bureaucracy. Its founding members were Zhang Tingyu, Prince Yinxiang, and Jiang Tingxi. [See also Grand Council and Grand Secretariat.]

Yongzheng died in 1736 at the age of fifty-six. He was succeeded by his fourth son, Hongli, who reigned as the Qianlong emperor.

[See also Kangxi Emperor; Qianlong Emperor; and Qing Dynasty.]

Pei Huang, *Autocracy at Work: A Study of the Yung-cheng Period, 1723–1735* (1974). Silas H. L. Wu, *Passage to Power: K'ang-hsi and the Heir Apparent, 1661–1722* (1979). Madeline Zelin, *The Magistrate's Tael: Rationalizing Fiscal Reform in Eighteeth-Century Ching China* (1984).

JOANNA WALEY-COHEN

YŎN KAESOMUN

(d. 666), Korean leader who dominated Koguryŏ's struggle against Tang China and Silla until his death. As a youth Yŏn demonstrated an uncommon intelligence and a mastery over both civil and military matters. He held numerous posts in the Koguryŏ central officialdom and ultimately inherited his father's post of chief minister *(taedaero)*. He built several fortresses that secured Koguryŏ against possible attacks. He also sought to make Koguryŏ spiritually stronger by calling for more Daoist missionaries from China, and he became an active patron of that philosophy. A number of Koguryŏ officials disliked Yŏn's policies, however, and planned to murder him. Yŏn struck back in 642, killing some one hundred antagonists, assassinating King Yŏngnyu (r. 618–642) and placing the dead king's nephew on the throne as King Pojang (r. 642–668).

Yŏn proceeded to dominate Koguryŏ, establishing a tight system of control. He tolerated no domestic opposition and pursued the same strategy in foreign affairs. When Silla turned to Koguryŏ for military aid in its battles with Paekche, he not only spurned the request but demanded that Silla relinquish its control over the Han River basin. China, supporting Silla's entreaties, received a similar rebuke. When China backed up its demands with an invasion, however, the well-prepared Koguryŏ forces inflicted setback upon setback on the Chinese armies, securing Koguryŏ's independence and by some accounts assuring that the people of the Korean peninsula would be saved from Chinese conquest.

Yŏn Kaesomun's military leadership was tested again in 661, when Chinese armies attempted new invasions; as before, the Chinese were forced to withdraw. Nevertheless Koguryŏ resistance slackened as repeated probes from China and Silla took their toll. Moreover, war-weary Koguryŏ lost the will to resist, pushed to its limits by Yŏn's dictatorial policies. When he died, power struggles within his family fractured Koguryŏ's leadership, assuring a victory for China and Silla.

In the end Yŏn Kaesomun's policies helped Silla. His military strategy enabled Koguryŏ to resist Chinese penetration for two decades, but his political control so weakened the country internally that Silla was unable to win the support of disaffected elites and unify much of the peninsula by 675.

[*See also* Koguryŏ *and* Silla.]

EDWARD J. SHULTZ

YOSHIDA SHIGERU (1878–1967), prime minister of Japan five times between 1946 and 1954, and thus the principal architect of postwar Japan's course. His followers Ikeda Hayato, Satō Eisaku, and Ōhira Masayoshi were leading figures of the "Yoshida school" that continued to dominate conservative politics into the 1970s.

Yoshida was the son of Takeuchi Tsuna, a leader of the Popular Rights Movement, or Jiyū Minken Undō, but was subsequently adopted by Yoshida Kenzō, a wealthy merchant who left his fortune to Shigeru upon his death in 1887. Yoshida then pursued the elite track through the Peers' School and Tokyo Imperial University, entered the Foreign Ministry in 1906, and married, in 1909, the daughter of Makino Nobuaki, son of the Meiji statesman Ōkubo Toshimichi and a figure high in court circles. His credentials were thus impressive.

Much of Yoshida's early diplomatic service was in China. He opposed military adventurism there, but he also showed a preference for Japan's early association with England under the Anglo-Japanese Alliance (1902–1921) to the less structured order that followed the Washington Conference of 1922. He was not close to the mainstream of Foreign Ministry thought under Shidehara Kijūrō because of his insistence on maintenance of Japan's rights in China, and, as ambassador to London, the peak of his diplomatic career, he worked for Anglo-Japanese cooperation. His stance, connections, and independence made him unacceptable to the military and he spent the war years in retirement, thus becoming eligible for postwar political service.

In 1945 Yoshida was made foreign minister in the first postsurrender cabinet. As prewar politicians were purged, he rose rapidly. While he was unenthusiastic about many of the Occupation democratizing reforms, his close and careful relations with General Douglas MacArthur made it possible for him to strike a pose at once critical of Occupation bureaucrats and cooperative with larger programs of antimilitarism and economic reconstruction. As the Occupation drew to a close in 1952 Yoshida resisted American pressures for rearmament while agreeing to align Japan's policies closely with those of the United States in the interest of economic recovery. In retirement after 1954 he became a popular figure, serving as symbol of continuity and independence.

[*See also* Occupation of Japan.]

John W. Dower, *Empire and Aftermath: Yoshida Shigeru and the Japanese Experience, 1878–1954* (1979). Shigeru Yoshida, *The Yoshida Memoirs,* translated by Kenichi Yoshida (1962).   MICHIO UMEGAKI

YOSHIDA SHŌIN (1830–1859), Japanese educator, thinker, and reformer of the late Tokugawa period. Born into a samurai family of modest rank in Chōshū *han* (domain), he became an instructor at the *han* academy at an early age and was allowed to study in Edo in 1851. For traveling in northern Japan without permission in 1852 he lost his samurai status, but nevertheless returned to Edo to study with Sakuma Shōzan in 1853. His thirst for learning led him to seek passage to America with

Commodore Matthew C. Perry early in 1854, for which he was imprisoned in Edo and later in Chōshū. Released to house arrest in 1856, he opened a private academy called the Shōka Sonjuku in his own home. His students included future Meiji statesmen Kido Kōin, Itō Hirobumi, and Yamagata Aritomo.

Yoshida's response to the *bakufu*'s Ansei Purge of 1858 was to encourage his students in Kyoto to assassinate Manabe Akikatsu, the *bakufu* police representative there. Yoshida's reformist stance in general and his plans for Manabe led to his execution by the *bakufu* in 1859.

Yoshida is best known for his innovative political writings and for his influence on his students. His followers formed the movement that defeated the *bakufu*, and later acceded to the highest positions in the Meiji state. His writings showed depth of emotion and of scholarship. They created a historico-mythical justification for a new kind of state and advocated new premises for institutional organization. His collected works have been continuously republished.

[*See also* Meiji Restoration.]

Thomas M. Huber, *The Revolutionary Origins of Modern Japan* (1981).   THOMAS M. HUBER

YOSHIHITO (1879–1926), emperor of Japan from 1912 to 1926, known posthumously as the Taishō emperor. During his reign Japan joined the Allies in World War I and was recognized as one of the five leading powers of the world. His reign was a period of immense economic growth and the blossoming of the so-called Taishō Democracy, yet it also witnessed the rice riots (1918), the great Kantō earthquake (1923), and the notorious Peace Preservation Law (1925).

Yoshihito was the third son of Mutsuhito, the Meiji emperor, and an imperial concubine. After his brothers had died, he was designated crown prince. In 1900 he married Kujō Sadako (Empress Teimei), who was then sixteen years old; they had four sons. When the Meiji emperor died on 30 July 1912, Yoshihito ascended the throne and the name of the era was changed to Taishō ("great justice"). Yoshihito was the first crown prince of Japan to receive a Western education: he studied at the Peers' School and later with private tutors. In 1908 he toured Korea, becoming the first crown prince to leave Japan. He was also the first emperor to send his son to the West: his eldest son Hirohito toured Europe in 1921. During his reign the concubinage system in the palace was abolished and monogamy was established. Yoshihito was fond of poetry and composed many poems in Japanese and Chinese. As a constitutional monarch, he rarely interfered in matters of state.

Throughout his life Yoshihito suffered from ill health. When in November 1921 his illness started to affect his mental faculties, Crown Prince Hirohito was appointed regent and Yoshihito was confined to an imperial villa. He died on 25 December 1926 at the age of forty-seven and was succeeded by Hirohito.

[*See also* Taishō Political Change; Rice Riots; Kantō Earthquake; Peace Preservation Law; *and* Hirohito.]

A. M. Young, *Japan under Taishō Tennō* (1929).

BEN-AMI SHILLONY

YOSHINO LINE, a line of Japanese emperors, known also as the Southern Court, that had its seat in the Yoshino region south of Kyoto from 1336 to 1392 and that opposed the so-called Northern Court in Kyoto, the traditional site of emperorship from the late eighth century until modern times (1868). When Japan's first warrior (samurai) government, the Kamakura shogunate (1185–1333), was overthrown in 1333, Emperor Go-Daigo (1288–1339) sought to restore rule by the emperor.

Go-Daigo's restoration government was notably unsuccessful in satisfying the needs of the predominant warrior class of Japanese society, however, and in 1336 Ashikaga Takauji (1305–1358) seized power, forced Go-Daigo to relinquish the emperorship to a member of another branch of the imperial family, and established the Ashikaga, or Muromachi, shogunate (1336–1573). Go-Daigo thereupon fled to Yoshino, where he proclaimed that he was still emperor. Thus began the period of war between the supporters of the Northern and Southern Courts (Nambokuchō), which ended when the Southern Court was extinguished in 1392. This was the only protracted period of dynastic schism in Japanese history, and prompted great debate among later scholars over where the true locus of imperial authority lay in the middle and late fourteenth century.

[*See also* Go-Daigo; Kemmu Restoration; Nambokuchō; *and* Muromachi Period.]

PAUL VARLEY

YOSHINO SAKUZŌ (1878–1933), Japanese scholar, journalist, and advocate of liberal democratic reform in the Taishō era (1912–1926). The eldest son of a small-town merchant from Miyagi Prefecture, Yoshino graduated from Tokyo University's Faculty of Law in 1904. In 1909 he became an assistant professor of the same faculty. His conversion to Christianity as a student brought him into contact with leading Christian liberals and socialists. Extended stays in China (1906–1909) and Europe (1910–1913) deepened his interest in political developments abroad. In a 1916 essay in *Chūō kōron,* Yoshino called for "government based on the people" *(minponshugi).* While affirming that formal sovereignty lay with the emperor, he advocated popular control over the selection of leaders and the setting of policy.

Yoshino's theories legitimized the struggle for universal manhood suffrage and party rule, a struggle opposed by the House of Peers, the Privy Council, and military cliques. He personally inspired a new generation of left-wing students and intellectuals, but the liberal Yoshino rejected the Marxists' belief in class struggle. In 1926 he helped form the moderate Social Democratic Party. He devoted his last years to the study of Japanese history, in an effort to demonstrate the indigenous roots of Japanese democracy.

Peter Duus, "Yoshino Sakuzō: The Christian as Political Critic," *Journal of Japanese Studies* 4 (1978): 301–326. Tetsuo Najita, "Some Reflections on Idealism in the Political Thought of Yoshino Sakuzō," in *Japan in Crisis,* edited by Bernard Silberman and H. D. Harootunian (1974).
SHELDON M. GARON

YOUNGHUSBAND, SIR FRANCIS EDWARD (1863–1942), British explorer. Born in Murree (now Pakistan), Younghusband was educated at Clifton and Sandhurst and entered the army in 1882. In 1886, during a trip from Yarkand to India via the Mustagh Pass of the Karakoram Range, he proved the range to be the watershed between India and Turkestan. In 1890 he was transferred to the Indian Political Department and in 1902 was authorized by Lord Curzon to cross the Tibetan border with a military escort to negotiate trade and frontier issues. When attempts to begin negotiations failed, the escort, under the command of Major General James MacDonald, crossed the border and marched to Lhasa, where Younghusband forced the signing of a trade treaty with the Dalai Lama.

Younghusband was made a KCSI (Knight Com-

mander of the Star of India) in 1917. He wrote several works on philosophy and mysticism and on his travel experiences. These include *India and Tibet* (1910), *Within* (1912), *Life in the Stars* (1927), *Modern Mystics* (1935), and *Wonders of the Himalayas* (1924).
[See also Lhasa.]
WILLIAM F. FISHER

YOUNG MEN'S BUDDHIST ASSOCIATION (YMBA), generally recognized as the first nationalist organization in Burma. The YMBA was founded in 1906 by students at Rangoon College. Its name in Burmese, Buddha Kalya Nayuwa Athin (Society for the Protection of Buddhism), suggests its initial cultural concerns. Its better-known English name indicates that it was modeled organizationally on the idea of the Young Men's Christian Association (YMCA). Although similar organizations had been founded in other towns before 1900, the YMBA was the first to establish branches in other areas. Its first publication, *Buddha Batha Myanma (Burmese Buddhism),* was soon followed by articles and pamphlets of a political nature, published through the YMBA-affiliated *Thuriya (Sun)* Press, Burma's first nationalist newspaper.

In 1917 the YMBA became involved in protests over the wearing of shoes by Europeans in the precincts of pagodas, an affront to Buddhist practice. Following plans to exclude Burma from constitutional reforms intended for the other provinces of British India (of which Burma was then a part), the YMBA sent several delegations to India and London to demand equal treatment. In 1920, with a membership of over two thousand, the YMBA became explicitly political, taking the name General Council of Burmese Associations.

[See also General Council of Burmese Associations.]

Maung Maung, *Burma and General Ne Win* (1969).
ROBERT H. TAYLOR

YUAN DYNASTY (1272/1279–1368), Chinese dynasty that originated as part of the vast Mongol empire that spanned much of the Eurasian continent. During Genghis Khan's own lifetime (1167–1227) the Mongols had already established a secure foothold in North China: the Jurchen Jin dynasty capital of Zhongdu (now Beijing) fell to the Mongols in 1215, and most of modern-day Hebei, Shaanxi,

Shanxi, and Shandong came under Mongol control before Genghis's death. During the decades-long conquest of North China that culminated in the 1234 destruction of the Jin dynasty, the Mongols appointed military-civilian overseers of subjugated cities and territories. These overseers, called *darughachi* in Mongolian and *daluhuaqi* in Chinese, gradually evolved into the top local and regional officials of the Yuan civilian bureaucracy as it took shape in the 1260s.

It was not until Kublai's reign (1260–1294), however, that the conquest of South China was completed (1279) and that the political, social, and economic institutions and policies that set the framework for the Yuan period were devised. By moving the capital from Karakorum to Beijing in 1260, Kublai, the grandson of Genghis, opted for fulfilling the role of a ruler of a conquest dynasty on Chinese territory over the role of a *khaghan* of a greater Mongol empire, which by 1260 was already in the process of fragmenting. In 1272, Kublai, upon the suggestion of Chinese advisers, adopted a Chinese dynastic title, Yuan ("origin," a term derived from the *Book of Changes*), thereby ensuring the Mongols a legitimate place in the succession of Chinese dynasties.

While some of Kublai's reforms incorporated aspects of traditional Chinese bureaucratic practice—setting up ranked, salaried central and local government administrations, for instance—the Mongols rejected other aspects of Chinese tradition. Most notably, during Kublai's reign no civil service

FIGURE 1. *Yuan-dynasty Jar.* Porcelain with blue underglaze decoration, fourteenth century.

examinations were ever held. The Mongols, in keeping with their tribal, preconquest customs, preferred to rely upon hereditary transfer of office, and thus adopted and extensively used the so-called *yin* privilege, whereby high-ranking officials could nominate sons or grandsons for civilian office. It was not until the reign of the emperor Renzong (1311–1320), whose Mongolian name was Ayurbarwada, that examinations were first instituted. While examinations symbolized the continuation of the Confucian tradition, in reality the examinations functioned in a very limited way, with quotas favoring the advancement of Mongols and West and Central Asian peoples over Han Chinese.

Emperor Renzong was the first Mongol emperor of China to achieve the ability to read and write the Chinese language. Even though he and some of his successors were literate in Chinese, however, the official language of government business in Yuan times continued to be Mongolian. Memorials sent to the throne by officials of the fifth rank and above (there were nine ranks in all) were required to use the Mongolian script, although copies of documents were kept in Chinese.

While Kublai's thirty-four-year reign is considered by most historians to be the high point of Mongol political and military consolidation and control in China, the later Yuan imperial reigns are generally portrayed as marred by court factionalism, intense struggles for succession to the throne, and a weakening of the military. The instability at the very apex of the dynasty in the post-Kublai period is indeed reflected in the history of court assassinations and coups d'état. In 1323, for example, the emperor Yingzong (Shidebala) was assassinated; in 1328 civil war between two rival claimants to the throne broke out, ending with the probable assassination of the emperor Mingzong (Khoshila), who had managed to retain the throne for only six months; and in 1332 another struggle for the throne resulted in the last Yuan emperor, Shundi (Toghon Temur), deposing his younger brother Irinjibal, who had ruled for only fifty-three days.

In terms of the post-Kublai weakening of the armed forces, the Mongol military was already on the decline by the turn of the fourteenth century. Factors such as the custom of inheriting military offices, the impoverishment of Mongol military households in China, and the degeneration of the garrison system had incapacitated the Yuan military by the time the White Lotus Rebellion broke out in the Huai River valley in 1351. The White Lotus Rebellion, along with other large-scale rebel movements in South China in the 1350s and 1360s, undermined the Yuan dynasty and enabled Zhu Yuanzhang, a rebel leader of peasant origins, to establish a new dynasty, the Ming, as Emperor Shundi fled Beijing for the steppe in September 1368. [*See also* White Lotus Society *and* Zhu Yuanzhang.]

Social, Economic, and Cultural Policies. The Mongol rulers' policies toward the Chinese population in many ways typify the attitudes of a government of occupation toward a conquered people. The four officially recognized categories of population in Yuan times were based on ethnic and geopolitical background; in descending order of privileged status, those categories were Mongols, West and Central Asian peoples, *hanren* (northern Chinese, Khitan, Jurchen, and other inhabitants of the territory of the former Jin dynasty), and finally the least privileged *nanren* (southern Chinese, or inhabitants of the territory of the former Southern Song dynasty). Thus, for instance, Kublai decreed that the top local government office of *darughachi* be staffed only by Mongols, or in the absence of Mongols, West and Central Asian people, barring Chinese, Khitans, and Jurchens from that office. In theory, the Mongols occupied the top administrative offices throughout China, but in reality, owing to the scarcity of Mongols qualified to act as civilian administrators and the willingness of some Chinese to assume Mongolian names and even to study the Mongolian language, Kublai's repeated decrees limiting the top offices to Mongols were at times ignored.

In spite of opportunities to evade restrictive administrative regulations, many Yuan scholars felt shut out of government with no examination system to provide for upward career mobility. When employing Han Chinese, the Mongols preferred to rely upon nonscholarly clerks who were essentially narrowly trained professional legal experts and whose grounding in Confucian learning was minimal. The response of a segment of the Chinese elite was to withdraw entirely from public life into the posture of recluses living in seclusion. Rather than demand that such scholar-recluses prove their loyalty to the dynasty by taking office, the Mongols tolerated scholarly eremitism. The Mongols displayed a general lack of interest in Chinese culture, rather than an attitude of hostility or scrutiny.

There were exceptions, however, to this lack of interest, most notably the Mongols' fascination with the *Xiaojing (Classic of Filial Piety)*, the precepts of which were consonant with Mongolian notions of proper relations between ruler and subject. None-

theless, there were no literary inquisitions in the Yuan, and, in fact, it has even been suggested that Chinese culture in the thirteenth and fourteenth centuries thrived precisely because of the absence of scrutiny from the very top. Literati were safe to express opinions and even subtle criticism of the dynasty in literature and the arts.

Literature, the Arts, and Religion. The Yuan is known as the golden age of Chinese drama, with 171 extant plays dating from the period. Conflicting opinions exist concerning the nature and degree of Mongol influence upon the development of drama in the thirteenth century. While some scholars stress the continuities between Yuan drama (called *zaju*) and its predecessors in the Song and Jin dynasties, other scholars stress the absence of an examination system in the Yuan and the Mongols' extensive use of clerks in government as crucial factors in forcing unemployed scholars to turn to such pursuits as writing plays to earn a livelihood. Whatever the influence of the Mongols on the development of Yuan drama is judged to be, it is clear that popular drama became a legitimate part of the elite's literary interests in Yuan times.

The Yuan dynasty also witnessed a revolution in painting, as exemplified by the appearance of scholar-amateur artists who superseded the traditional professional artists of Song times. With the disruptions caused by the Mongol conquests and the consequent absence of imperial patronage of painting, professional schools of painting receded in importance, and "amateur" literati styles of painting were developed by scholars who, whether by choice or circumstance, did not serve the Mongol court.

In the paintings of Chinese literati who remained loyal at heart to the defunct Southern Song dynasty and who refused to serve the Yuan, one may find covert symbols of protest against the new Mongol rulers of China. For example, in a handscroll of a Chinese orchid executed by one such Song loyalist, Zheng Sixiao (1241–1318), no earth covers the plant's roots. Asked why he left the roots exposed, Zheng Sixiao supposedly replied that the "barbarians" had stolen the earth, the implication being that the orchid itself symbolized the uncompromising but vulnerable scholar of Yuan times. Similarly, the goat in a painting *Sheep and Goat* by the well-known painter Zhao Mengfu (1254–1322), a descendant of the Song imperial house who did accept high office in the Yuan government, has been interpreted by some art historians as symbolic of the humiliation of those who capitulated to "barbarian" rule.

Given the nomadic origins of the Mongols, it is

not surprising that paintings of horses, for which Zhao Mengfu was famous, were quite numerous in Yuan times. The few Mongol patrons of the arts also favored official portraits, a prime example of which is a painting of Kublai and his attendants hunting by Liu Guandao, one of a small group of court painters in Yuan times.

While the Yuan court was far from exemplary in patronizing the arts, it did display a more active interest in religion, particularly Tibetan Buddhism. Although Tibet remained beyond the reach of Mongol troops throughout the Yuan, in 1253, on the eve of the Mongol invasion of present-day Yunnan, Kublai very wisely invited a leading Tibetan lama, Phags-pa (1235–1280), to visit him in order to establish peaceful relations with the Tibetans. In his long stay at the Yuan court Phags-pa was responsible not only for converting Kublai and much of the imperial clan to Tibetan Buddhism, but also for providing the Mongols with a religious theory of legitimation for their rule, a theory according to which the Yuan rulers were Buddhist universal emperors. Yuan court ritual consisted of an admixture of Buddhist, shamanic, and Confucian ceremonies. [See also Phags-pa.]

Daoism fared less well in Yuan times. Despite Genghis Khan's early interest in Quanzhen Daoism as explicated to him by the Daoist master Qiu Chuji (1148–1227), by Kublai's reign Daoism was perceived by the ruling Mongols as merely a Chinese religion, whereas Buddhism was supranational and thus better suited to the Mongols' worldview. Nonetheless, the Yuan emperors for the most part tolerated Daoism (although in 1281 the court decreed a burning of Daoist texts); in South China religious Daoism flourished with literati encouragement.

Effects of Mongol Rule. The question of how Mongol rule of China affected the lives of commoners in Yuan times involves complex economic and demographic issues. On the one hand, the Mongol conquests of the early thirteenth century devastated areas of North China; it is said that only the arguments of a sinicized Khitan, Yelü Chucai, prevented Ogedei from turning North China's farmland into pasturage. [See also Yelü Chucai.] In terms of demography, the population of China in the thirteenth and fourteenth centuries declined drastically, from a high of more than 100 million to about 60 million. The causes of this enormous decline have yet to be explained satisfactorily.

On the other hand, the Yuan saw the perpetuation of many of the advances in agricultural techniques, commercial activities, and urbanization that had been initiated in Tang and Song times. While the early Mongol rulers initially had to be convinced of the benefits of encouraging agriculture, Kublai established a Bureau of Agriculture in 1270 specifically to promote and reorganize agricultural communities. The printing and reprinting of practical agricultural handbooks, some sponsored by the government, also testifies to the continuation and development of farming technology.

The Yuan dynasty is also renowned for the widespread use of paper money in place of copper, gold, and silver. Inflation appeared as early as the 1270s, however, and continued until the very end of the dynasty, becoming uncontrollable in the 1350s as the costs of suppressing rebellions induced the government to issue huge quantities of paper notes.

Perhaps the greatest cause for dissatisfaction among commoners in Yuan times was the economic hardship resulting from heavy taxation. The unpopularity of Yuan fiscal policy derived not only from the addition of new tax obligations to the traditional Chinese tax and corvée obligations, but also from the Mongols' reliance upon Muslims for their expertise in finance. Central Asian Muslims, many of whom belonged to merchant associations (ortaq), were granted tax-farming privileges to collect taxes throughout China and were employed as financial advisers at the court. Accused of usury and exploitation of the Chinese population, these Muslim financiers, because of their highly visible roles, served as deflectors of hostility that would otherwise have been directed at the Mongol court.

On the whole, the economy of North China was disrupted by Mongol rule far more than that of South China. In North China, the Mongols carved out hereditary land grants for members of the imperial family, Mongol nobles, and meritorious officials; in contrast, patterns of landholding in South China were not greatly affected by the transition from Southern Song to Yuan rule.

The exact nature of the legacy of the Yuan dynasty is a hotly debated issue among historians. Whether thirteenth- and fourteenth-century China was governed by a centralized or decentralized bureaucracy and how the functioning or malfunctioning of that bureaucracy influenced the founder of the Ming dynasty, Zhu Yuanzhang, in his approach to governmental institutions are questions that are still unresolved. Whether the Mongols contributed to the growth of "despotism" in the dual sense of greater imperial control over court ministers and greater dynastic control over the countryside at large is another issue that is being actively debated by historians.

In terms of specific Yuan to Ming continuities,

one may definitively point to the continuation into Ming times of the Yuan practice of a hereditary elite of military officers as well as continuation of Yuan-style census registers that permanently classified the entire population into social and occupational categories. The Ming dynasty also inherited an excellent transport and postal system and administrative provinces. Muslim contributions to astronomy and mapmaking in the Yuan also left an imprint. Finally, the descendants of those Mongols who melted back into the steppe in 1368 and who readjusted with remarkable ease to a nomadic way of life exerted a direct influence upon the seventeenth-century Manchu political-military organization in the decades before the Manchu conquest of China.

[See also Kublai Khan; Mongols; Mongol Empire: An Overview; and Ming Dynasty.]

James Cahill, *Hills beyond a River: Chinese Painting of the Yüan Dynasty, 1279–1368* (1976). Hok-lam Chan and Wm. Theodore de Bary, eds., *Yüan Thought: Chinese Thought and Religion under the Mongols* (1982). Paul Heng-chao Ch'en, *Chinese Legal Tradition under the Mongols: The Code of 1291 as Reconstructed* (1979). John W. Dardess, *Conquerors and Confucians: Aspects of Political Change in Late Yüan China* (1973). Ch'i-ch'ing Hsiao, *The Military Establishment of the Yüan Dynasty* (1978). John D. Langlois, Jr., ed., *China under Mongol Rule* (1981). Frederick W. Mote, "Confucian Eremitism in the Yuan Period," in *The Confucian Persuasion*, edited by Arthur F. Wright (1960). Herbert Franz Schurmann, *Economic Structure of the Yüan Dynasty* (1956).   ELIZABETH ENDICOTT-WEST

YUAN SHIKAI (1859–1916), official of the late Qing dynasty and first president of the Republic of China, was born into a gentry family of Henan Province. Unsuccessful in the civil service examinations, Yuan made use of family connections to enter the staff of one of the regional armies spawned in response to China's mid-century rebellions.

Yuan first achieved prominence in Korea, where his energetic action as acting commander of the Chinese garrison in Seoul forestalled a Japanese-supported coup against the Korean government in 1884. In the aftermath Yuan was appointed Chinese representative in Korea and for a decade worked to increase Qing influence there. The Sino-Japanese War of 1894–1895, however, reversed these achievements.

In the wake of the Qing debacle in that war, Yuan was given the responsibility of fashioning a modern army unit, which after 1900 became the core of the Beiyang Army. His successful experiments in military training on Western models and his evident loyalty to the powerful Empress Dowager Cixi were rewarded by appointment to high civil posts: governor of Shandong (1899–1901), Zhili governor-general (1901–1907), and member of the Grand Council and president of the Ministry of Foreign Affairs (1907–1909). During these years he became preeminent as a leader of official reform.

Soon after the death of the empress dowager in 1908 he was dismissed from office. When the 1911 Revolution broke out, the court recalled him as prime minister. Instead of rescuing the Qing, he negotiated away the dynasty and became president of the new republic.

Yuan's presidency was a frustrating experience for his revolutionary enemies, whom he drove from the country in 1913, and for himself, since his ruthless bureaucratic approach to politics failed to make China strong. Humiliated by Japan's Twenty-one Demands in 1915, he sought rescue in a revived monarchy, but his enthronement only deepened his political isolation. He died in June 1916, his imperial aspirations abandoned and his power dissipated.

[See also Qing Dynasty; Empress Dowager; China, Republic Period; Twenty-one Demands; Li Hongzhang; and Sun Yat-sen.]

Jerome Ch'en, *Yuan Shih-k'ai* (2d ed., 1972). Stephen R. MacKinnon, *Power and Politics in Late Imperial China: Yuan Shikai in Beijing and Tianjin, 1901–1908* (1980). Ernest P. Young, *The Presidency of Yuan Shih-k'ai: Liberalism and Dictatorship in Early Republican China* (1977).   ERNEST P. YOUNG

YU KIL-CHUN (1856–1914), a distinguished Korean civil servant, reformist thinker and writer of the late Yi dynasty (1392–1910). Like his colleague Pak Yŏng-hyo, Yu was influenced by the progressive *sirhak* ("practical learning") school of Korean Confucianism. A visit to Japan in 1881 as an attendant member of the government-sponsored Gentlemen's Observation Mission transformed him into an avid student of modernization. He was one of the first students from Korea at Keiō Gijuku in Japan.

Upon his return to Korea in 1883, Yu served for a time in a junior position in the newly established Foreign Office (to'ngni amun). He also joined the informal circle of progressives called the Independence Party and collaborated with Pak Yŏng-hyo in the founding of Korea's first newspaper. In the same year he also accompanied Korea's first embassy to the United States. Remaining in America, he took private instruction from Edward S. Morse, the distinguished biologist and head of the Peabody Museum in Salem, Massachusetts, and then studied at the Dummer Academy. Yu thus became the first known Korean student in America. After a visit to several European countries in 1885, Yu returned home but was immediately put under house arrest because of his association with the leader of the December 1884 émeute.

During his seven years of detention, Yu wrote many poems and manuscripts on political, social, and economic reform, notably *Sŏyu kyonmun (Observations on the West)*, a book apparently modeled after the Japanese advocate of modernization Fukuzawa Yukichi's *Seiyō jijō (Conditions in the West)*. Yu's work treated the questions regarding reform and modernization that had been raised by the Independence Party and the Independence Club. When published in 1895, his book became a popular text for reformist thinkers in Korea.

In the Japanese-sponsored reform governments of 1894 to 1895 Yu served as chief cabinet secretary and home minister. With the accession to power of a Russian-sponsored cabinet in early 1896, Yu fled to Japan, where he remained until 1907. When he returned to Korea, he spent much of his time organizing various "enlightenment" groups and running a progressive school, as well as in writing on various topics of reform. After its annexation of Korea in 1910, Japan offered him a title of nobility, which he declined. Yu's career substantially parallels those of other Korean reformers who aligned themselves with Japan for bringing modern progress into their country.

[*See also* Pak Yŏng-hyo; 1884 Coup d'État; *and* Independence Party and Club.]

Ki-baik Lee, *A New History of Korea*, translated by Edward W. Wagner (1984).   Vipan Chandra

YUN CH'I-HO (1865–1945), Korean aristocrat, reformer, and Christian leader. Yun was sent to Japan for special training in international languages and returned in 1883 as interpreter for the first American minister to Korea, Lucius Foote. After the uprising of December 1884 he sought safety in Shanghai, enrolling in the Anglo-Chinese College, where in 1887 he became a Christian, the first Korean Methodist, and the first Korean nobleman to become a Protestant.

That same year Yun went to America, where he became an eloquent student champion of foreign missions at Emory College and in the theological course at Vanderbilt University. He returned to China in 1893 and two years later returned to Korea with his Chinese bride. High family connections and

remarkable linguistic ability (he spoke Korean, Chinese, Japanese, English, and French) won him advancement at court as vice-minister of education and Korean representative to the coronation of Tsar Nicholas II of Russia and the jubilee celebrations of Queen Victoria of England. His most important position was as vice-minister of the king's powerful Advisory Council.

In 1896, however, his international experience and ethical convictions led him to risk his career and join the young reformers Philip Jaisohn (Sŏ Chae-p'il) and Syngman Rhee (Yi Sŭng-man) in founding the Independence Club. As president of the club Yi led mass meetings in Seoul in 1898 that wrung from a reluctant officialdom rights of free speech and assembly and certain democratic limitations on royal power. He also edited two early Korean newspapers, one of which, *The Independent*, was bilingual. The official reaction to Yun's activities was swift; he was abruptly sent north as a district magistrate, and the Independence Club collapsed. Yun returned to Seoul in 1904 and served until 1905 as vice-minister of foreign affairs, resigning with the stated goal of devoting himself to educational work when Japan established its protectorate.

Yun founded a successful Anglo-Korean school in Kaesŏng (1907) and was one of two Korean delegates to the World Missionary Conference in Edinburgh (1910). In 1911 he was arrested for alleged conspiracy and sentenced to six years' imprisonment, but was then pardoned in 1913, at which time he accepted the title of baron that the Japanese had conferred on his father. Yun became general-secretary of the YMCA (1915–1920) and during World War II was president of what is now Yonsei University.

[*See also* Independence Party and Club *and* Korea, Japanese Government-General of.]

Donald N. Clark, "Yun Ch'i-Ho (1864–1945): Portrait of a Korean Intellectual in an Era of Transition," in *Occasional Papers on Korea*, no. 4, edited by James B. Palais and M. D. Lang (1975). Yun Ch'i-ho, *Yun Ch'i Ho Ilgi*, 5 vols. (1975), contains an English translation of Yun Ch'i-ho's diaries.   Samuel Hugh Moffett

YUNG WING. *See* Rong Hong.

YUNNAN, province in southwest China with a population of 32,553,817 (1982 census) in an area of 380,000 square kilometers. Only loosely incorporated into the Chinese empire during the Han dynasty (206 BCE–220 CE), Yunnan was the center of the independent Nanzhao and Dali kingdoms from the eighth to the thirteenth century, after which it was reincorporated as a Chinese frontier area under the Yuan dynasty (1279–1368). In the seventeenth and eighteenth centuries Yunnan became an important copper-producing region, although this was exhausted by the nineteenth century, when the area became a producer of opium and a center of Muslim rebellions. After a period of warlordism in the early twentieth century, Yunnan's modernization began with the retreat of the Nationalist government to the southwest during the war with Japan (1937–1945). After 1949 the Communist government continued this development, expanding the railway system begun by the French as part of their sphere of influence in Indochina.

Yunnan is situated on a high plateau divided by river valleys and deep basins, and it contains high mountain ranges on its western borders. With a wet, temperate climate, Yunnan has only 5 percent of its land under cultivation, the rest covered by dense forest. Besides forest products such as timber, tung oil, and tea oil, Yunnan produces rice, wheat, corn, cotton, sugar cane, and tea. Yunnan's most significant industrial production is found in Kunming, the provincial capital, including metal ore smelteries and medium and heavy industry. Yunnan is the homeland of twenty-eight nationalities, the most varied ethnic population in China, including various tribes and subgroups of Yi, Tibeto-Burman, Hui, Hani, Lahu, Turchia, Tai, Mon-Khmer, Miao, and Yao peoples.   JOHN A. RAPP

YURT, the characteristic dwelling of nomads in the Turko-Mongolian steppes. A round structure made of felt mats placed over a framework of poles and latticework, the yurt is portable by pack animal. In earlier times, however, it was occasionally placed entire on a wheeled platform and pulled from place to place. The yurt is one reason for the importance of feltmaking to the nomadic culture. [See also Felt.]   RICHARD W. BULLIET

FIGURE 1. *Yurts, Inner Mongolia.*

Z

ZAFAR, BAHADUR SHAH (1777–1867), poetic pen name of Abu Zafar Siraj ud-Din Muhammad Bahadur Shah, the last Mughal emperor of Delhi. Living only the facade of a royal life, he endured with dignity his helpless position as a British pensioner. His reign began only at the age of sixty; as an old man of eighty he was made the figurehead of the Rebellion of 1857. For this the British exiled him to Rangoon, where he died. He is known as the author of a large number of melancholy and devotional Urdu poems and songs. He is also known for his two brilliant court poets, Zauq and Ghalib.

[See also Delhi; Mutiny, Indian; and Ghalib, Mirza Asadullah Khan.]

Percival Spear, *Twilight of the Mughuls: Studies in Late Mughul Delhi* (2d ed., 1980).   FRANCES W. PRITCHETT

ZAGROS RANGE, the largest mountain range in Iran. It extends roughly 1,400 miles from the northwestern frontier of Iran in Azerbaijan, south and east to the Persian Gulf, then eastward to Baluchistan. The Zagros is actually a series of parallel mountain ranges consisting of foothills and high plains in the northwest and ridges soaring more than 14,000 feet high along Iran's western border; the range tapers to lower elevations in the south and east. The largest mountain ranges are often interspersed with high-altitude plains at between three and five thousand feet above sea level.

JAHAN SALEHI

ZAHIR, MOHAMMAD (b. 1914), king of Afghanistan. Zahir succeeded his father Nadir Khan on the Afghan throne in 1933. His reign lasted until 1973, when he was overthrown in a bloodless coup. He subsequently abdicated the throne. Between 1933 and 1963 the king was dominated by his uncles and his cousin Mohammad Daud. They ruled while he reigned. When he took over the government, he introduced several reforms, including a new constitution allowing greater political competition. After his overthrow he lived in exile in Italy. Three years after the Soviet invasion of December, 1979, the ex-king sought to unify the partisans fighting against the Soviets. While some groups expressed support for the king's initiative, others opposed it.

ZALMAY KHALILZAD

ZAIBATSU, the term designating Japanese business conglomerates as they existed between the Meiji era and 1945. Mitsui, Mitsubishi, Sumitomo, and Yasuda were the "Big Four." More inclusive listings often include Nissan, Asano, Furukawa, Ōkura, Nakajima, Nomura, Shibusawa, Matsushita, Riken, and Nitchitsu. The Big Four were characterized by family ownership, direct control of subsidiaries by holding companies, and a high degree of diversification (covering finance, trading, manufacturing, and mining). Subsidiaries were often required to borrow from the *zaibatsu* bank and to buy and sell through the combine's trading company. By the early 1940s Mitsui and Mitsubishi controlled 300 and 250 companies, respectively.

Although Mitsui and Sumitomo dated back to the Tokugawa era (1600–1868), most *zaibatsu* arose after the Meiji Restoration of 1868. Known as "political merchants," Iwasaki Yatarō (Mitsubishi) and other entrepreneurs expanded their operations through ties to the Meiji government. During World War I and the 1920s, their concerns rapidly diversified and absorbed smaller firms. The *zaibatsu* generously contributed to the established parties, using their political influence to crush trade union legislation in 1931. Such actions aroused widespread

289

anti-*zaibatsu* sentiment among small business owners, farmers, and the public during the early 1930s. Young military officers also denounced the *zaibatsu* for their internationalism and opposition to higher military budgets. In contrast, the "new *zaibatsu*," notably Nissan, supported military expansion because of their greater emphasis on heavy industry and Asian investments. After right-wing officers assassinated Mitsui's Dan Takuma and other leaders in 1932, the *zaibatsu* gave millions of yen to relief projects in an attempt to appear patriotic and socially responsible. While seeking to avoid war with their Anglo-American trading partners before 1941, the combines greatly profited from wartime production when Japan finally went to war.

Following the Japanese defeat, the American Occupation embarked on a program of *zaibatsu* dissolution, believing it would democratize the Japanese economy and remove the economic bases of militarism. The Occupation dissolved the holding companies of the Big Four, ordered family stockholdings sold to the public, and carried out a thorough economic purge of top corporate officers. Cold War concerns and American business opposition, however, prevented the breakup of most other combines after 1947. Critics charge that the subsequent rise of corporate groupings constitutes a revival of the prewar *zaibatsu*, but there are major differences. Postwar groups are structured around banks, rather than family-held holding companies. Moreover, individual companies are no longer compelled to buy, sell, and obtain credit through member companies.

[*See also* Mitsubishi; Mitsui; Sumitomo; *and* Yasuda Zenjirō.]

T. A. Bisson, *Zaibatsu Dissolution in Japan* (1954). Eleanor M. Hadley, *Antitrust in Japan* (1970). Johannes Hirschmeier and Tsunehiko Yui, *The Development of Japanese Business, 1600–1973* (1975). W. W. Lockwood, *The Economic Development of Japan* (1954). John G. Roberts, *Mitsui: Three Centuries of Japanese Business* (1973).   SHELDON M. GARON

ZAKAT, the alms tax, one of the principal religious duties for every Muslim who owns a stipulated minimum of property. The tax (also called *sadaqa*), varying from 2.5 to 10 percent, is levied on certain agricultural products and livestock as well as on gold, silver, and merchandise held unused for longer than one year. The recipients of the *zakat* are specifically named categories of persons in economic need, in keeping with the Qur'an's emphasis on charity and good works. It is the duty of the government to collect and distribute the *zakat*. Muslim modernists envision the revival of the *zakat*, long lapsed in practice except as voluntary alms, as a form of progressive taxation for purposes of social welfare.

Joseph Schacht, *Introduction to Islamic Law* (1964).
JEANETTE A. WAKIN

ZAND, KARIM KHAN (d. 1779), ruler of western Iran from 1751 to 1779. Among the tribal contingents of Nadir Shah Afshar's army that returned to their home ranges after Nadir's assassination in 1747 were the Bakhtiyari, under Ali Mardan Khan, and the Zand, led by Karim Khan. The latter were seminomads of the Lakk people, related to both the Lurs and the Kurds, pasturing between Hamadan and Isfahan.

On the failure of the Afsharids to hold western Iran, these two chiefs in 1750 occupied the former Safavid capital of Isfahan in the name of a minor Safavid protégé styled Isma'il III, with Ali Mardan as *vakil*, or regent, and Karim as commander of the army. While Karim was campaigning in Kurdistan, Ali Mardan staged a coup and plundered the province of Fars; Karim Khan captured Isfahan and defeated his rival in battle. Three other contestants for power occupied all of the Zand leader's energies for three more years; his campaigns ranged from the Persian Gulf to the Caspian coast and the foothills of the Caucasus. The Qajar chief Muhammad Hasan Khan was defeated and killed outside his fortress of Astarabad in 1759. Azad Khan the Afghan was routed by his erstwhile ally, the Afshar leader Fath Ali Khan, in 1760; he surrendered to Karim Khan and spent the rest of his life in Shiraz as a pensioner of the Zands. Fath Ali made a last stand with a tribal coalition in Azerbaijan, but the province fell to the Zands in 1762 and was thereafter administered for them by Najaf Quli Khan Dunbuli, of an eminent local family of turkicized Kurds.

In July 1765, having subdued all the Elburz and Zagros provinces, Karim Khan entered Shiraz and was not to leave for the remaining fourteen years of his life. This strategic southern city had come to be his refuge and capital during his early struggle for power against rivals based in northern Iran, and he now embellished it with a fortress-palace (*arg*), a mosque, a covered bazaar, and other buildings and gardens. During the next decade he sent expeditions led by his relatives to secure the Persian Gulf littoral and its hinterland, the provinces of Lar,

Yazd, and Kerman. He attempted to keep the Qajars in check—with only moderate success—by appointing a son of the late Muhammad Hasan Khan as governor of Damghan and keeping the eldest son, Agha Muhammad Khan, a hostage in Shiraz. Impoverished Khurasan he left in the hands of Nadir Shah's grandson, Shahrukh Shah, as a buffer against the new Afghan monarchy of Ahmad Shah Durrani. North of the Aras River Iran's former vassals, the Georgian kingdom and the Darband khanate, began to drift into the economic and political orbit of Russia.

In the Persian Gulf the commercial center of gravity moved from Bandar Abbas to Bushehr, the natural port of Shiraz, where the East India Company was granted facilities. In 1766 Karim Khan regained Kharg Island from the hands of the colorful pirate Mir Muhanna, who had earlier captured it from the Dutch East India Company; but he was unable to bring Hormuz Island under his control or to intimidate the imam of Oman, his commercial rival in the lower gulf. Repeated expeditions against the Ka'b Arabs of Khuzistan—even with the cooperation of the East India Company and the Ottoman governor of Basra—brought no more than fitful subservience until the death of their strong leader, Shaikh Salman, in 1768. Karim Khan exchanged embassies with Haidar Ali, ruler of the Deccan, and Indian merchants frequented Shiraz and the gulf ports. Armenian and Jewish merchants who had fled during the chaotic interregnum were encouraged to return to Iran, and commerce increased. Agricultural subsidies and rebuilding programs, both in Shiraz and the provinces (e.g., in Isfahan and Kashan, hit by an earthquake in 1778), helped to restore Iran's threadbare economic and social fabric.

Seeking to divert Persian Gulf trade to Bushehr, Karim Khan in 1776 besieged and occupied Basra. His death—probably as a result of tuberculosis—which occurred on 2 March 1779 when he was about eighty years old, prompted an Iranian withdrawal. Ironically, Basra's trade was indeed largely diverted as a result of this war, but to Kuwait, rather than Bushehr. The internecine wars of succession following his death further undermined much of the prosperity he had restored.

Karim Khan's virtues were universally acknowledged, even by his enemies. During his rise to power he displayed prowess in the field, tenacity in adversity, and magnanimity in victory. As ruler he dressed and lived simply (although indulging a taste for wine and women) and never assumed the title *shah:* even

his title *vakil* ("representative") he modified from *vakil al-daula,* "sovereign's regent," to *vakil al-ra'aya,* "people's deputy," which was the designation of a traditional provincial ombudsman appointed by the crown. Apocryphal tales of his justice, kindness, humility, sense of humor, and concern for the safety and prosperity of the common man testify to his continuing place in his countrymen's affection.

[*See also* Afsharid Dynasty; Durranis; Nadir; *and* Zand Dynasty.]

John Malcolm, *History of Persia* (1815; rev. ed., 1829), vol. 2, chap. 16. John R. Perry, *Karim Khan Zand* (1979).

JOHN R. PERRY

ZAND DYNASTY (1751–1794), short-lived Iranian dynasty founded by Karim Khan Zand "the *vakil*" ("regent, deputy"; r. 1751–1779). Between 1750 and 1765 Karim Khan salvaged most of western Iran between Urmia and Bandar Abbas from the wreck of Nadir Shah's empire. With his capital at Shiraz, Karim Khan established a degree of trust and cooperation between tribal armies, urban administrators, and the peasantry, and hence a measure of internal security that encouraged and stimulated trade and agriculture.

On Karim's death in 1779 the internecine power struggle between his relatives destroyed most of what he had achieved. Even before his funeral, his half-brother Zaki slaughtered most of his rivals in Shiraz and ruled in the name of one of Karim's incompetent sons. Ali Murad, of a different branch of the Zand tribe, seized Isfahan in the name of another son of the *vakil.* Zaki was killed by his own men while marching on Isfahan, but an attack by the Qajar chief Agha Muhammad Khan delayed Ali Murad and enabled Karim's brother Sadiq, returning from his occupation of Basra, to seize Shiraz. In 1781 Ali Murad took Shiraz but again had to turn his attention to Qajar attacks from Mazandaran. His half brother Ja'far (son of Sadiq) marched on Isfahan, and Ali Murad died on his way to defending the city in February 1785.

Zand control of the Elburz and upper Zagros mountain ranges was now relinquished to the Qajars. Killed in a palace coup in 1789, Ja'far was succeeded (after a brief reign by Said Murad Khan, a cousin of Ali Murad) by his popular son Lutf Ali Khan, whose energetic campaigns against Qajars and defecting vassals in the south and east briefly staved off the dynasty's impending downfall. But

Haji Ibrahim, the powerful *kalantar* (mayor) of Shiraz, acting out of self-preservation (Lutf Ali had revealed his distrust by taking the son of the *kalantar* hostage) or out of a desire to end the destructive tribal warfare, gained control of the garrison and shut the gates of Shiraz against Lutf Ali's army. Robbed of a base, the young Zand chief retreated to Kerman and finally to the fortress of Bam. Here he was captured by Agha Muhammad Khan Qajar, who blinded, tortured, and finally executed him in November 1794 at Tehran.

The only material monuments of the Zand dynasty are Karim Khan's mosque, fortress, and bazaar in Shiraz, which was sacked by the Qajar ruler before his return to the new capital of Tehran. None of Karim Khan's successors aspired to the title of *shah* (which he had not assumed), or even to Karim's title of *vakil*. The dynasty is remembered chiefly for its founder's unusual humanity and unselfishness, which produced a quarter of a century of comparative peace and prosperity in the middle of Iran's bloodiest century since the Mongol invasions.

[*See also* Afsharid Dynasty; Nadir; Qajar Dynasty; *and* Zand, Karim Khan.]

John Malcolm, *The History of Persia* (1815 and 1829), vol. 2, chaps. 16 and 17. John R. Perry, *Karim Khan Zand* (1979), especially pp. 296–301.   JOHN R. PERRY

ZAYTON (Quanzhou), Chinese city. In the thirteenth century Marco Polo described a bustling city in South China known to the West as Zayton. This city was later identified as Quanzhou, located in southwest Fujian Province. Its name was most likely derived from the Chinese epithet for the type of thorn-bearing *citong* trees that grew around the city walls, and was translated by the Muslim merchant population as "Zayton." An important center of foreign trade during the Southern Song (1127–1279) and Yuan (1279–1368) dynasties, Zayton was known for the production and distribution of satin textiles.   ANITA M. ANDREW

ZEAMI (1363–1443), gifted medieval Japanese playwright, aesthetician, and actor. Zeami, together with his father Kan'ami (1333–1384), transformed Japanese drama from rustic skits and dances into the classic *nō* theater and founded the Kanze school of *nō*. Little is known of Zeami's life, since actors occupied a low position in medieval Japanese society. As a child he acted with his father's troupe, based in Yamato Province (now Nara Prefecture).

The fortunes of the Kanze troupe began to rise in 1374, when Kan'ami and the eleven-year-old Zeami, acting in the play *Okina (Old Man)*, caught the eye of the shogun Ashikaga Yoshimitsu (1358–1408) in Kyoto. Under the patronage of the shogun, who was a devotee of the arts and a perceptive critic, the young Zeami was educated in the literary classics. His training is evident in the plays he was later to write. Works like *Izutsu (The Well-Curb)*, *Atsumori*, *Hanjo (Lady Han)*, and *Kantan* are based on, and quote abundantly from, stories found in Chinese and Japanese literature.

Zeami became head of the Kanze troupe at the age of twenty-one, following Kan'ami's death. He reached the height of his career in 1408, when the troupe appeared before Emperor Gokomatsu. Zeami's patron Yoshimitsu died soon afterward, to be succeeded by shoguns who favored different actors and styles. Zeami wrote many of his best treatises on the art of acting between 1413 and 1423, a period of decline for the Kanze. In 1422 he relinquished the leadership of the troupe to his elder son, Motomasa. But Motomasa died in 1432, Zeami's younger son Motoyoshi became a monk, and the shogun, violently opposed to Zeami, appointed a protégé, On'ami, to head the Kanze troupe. Zeami, by then seventy-one years old, was exiled to the island of Sado, presumably for refusing to initiate On'ami in the secret traditions of his school of *nō*. Zeami's exile probably ended in 1441; he spent the last years of his life in Yamato, dying there in 1443.

[*See also* Nō *and* Muromachi Period.]

Donald Keene, *Nō: The Classical Theatre of Japan* (1966; reprint, 1973). Donald Keene, ed., *Twenty Plays of the Nō Theatre* (1970). J. Thomas Rimer and Yamazaki Masakazu, trans., *On the Art of the Nō Drama: The Major Treatises of Zeami* (1984). Arthur Waley, *The Nō Plays of Japan* (1957).   AILEEN GATTEN

ZEN. The word *Zen*, the Japanese pronunciation of the Chinese *Chan*, designates a school of East Asian Mahayana Buddhism that emphasizes meditation and "seeing into one's own nature and becoming a Buddha." It is from this emphasis on meditation that the school derives its name: *Chan* is the Chinese attempt to represent phonetically the Sanskrit *dhyana*, a technical term for certain types of meditation. Contemporary practitioners, seated in meditation (*zazen*) in the lotus or half-lotus posture, regulating their breathing, and seeking to attain a state of inner awareness of their Buddhahood (*kenshō* or *satori*), belong to a meditative tradition that goes back to the very origins of Buddhism and has as its exemplar the Buddha Shakyamuni. As a separate historical institution and school of thought, however, Zen (Chan) arose in China, not India, and probably not before the sixth or seventh century CE.

Yogic meditative practices were introduced with Buddhism to China from India and Western Asia by the first century CE. There they intermingled with Chinese Daoist ideas and practices and were incorporated as part of the religious practice of most, if not all, Buddhist schools. By the Tang dynasty (618–907), however, groups of Buddhist monks and laymen were emphasizing meditation, *chan*, as the central Buddhist practice, the way to relive most directly the spiritual experience of the Buddha Shakyamuni himself. In stressing the practice of meditation as the best means of attaining a spontaneous intuition of one's own Buddha nature, they deemphasized the textual and ritual aspects of Buddhism. They asserted that the Chan tradition was a "separate transmission outside the sutras, not dependent on words and phrases" but "transmitted from mind to mind."

Chinese Chan practitioners created their own lineage of "separate transmission" proceeding directly from the Buddha himself via his close disciple Kashyapa and a princely Indian monk, Bodhidharma, who was believed to have brought Chan teachings to China, where he transmitted them to Huiko, the first in a line of Chinese patriarchs. After the fifth patriarch, Chan is alleged to have split into a Northern school emphasizing gradual enlightenment and a Southern school stressing sudden enlightenment. In the late Tang and Song dynasties the sudden enlightenment emphasis of the Southern school, descended from the sixth patriarch, Huineng (d. 713), predominated. Southern-school masters like Linji (Japanese, Rinzai, d. 867) developed a very vigorous meditation practice in which students of Chan were encouraged to drive deeper into the emptiness, *shunyata*, of self and to attain a true understanding of their Buddhahood by the use of shouts, blows, and cryptic "cases" (*gong'an*; Japanese, *kōan*). Such major collections of *gong'an* as the *Biyanlu* (Japanese, *Hekiganroku*) and the *Wumenguan* (Japanese, *Mumonkan*) were compiled in the Song dynasty and were incorporated into the practice of Chinese and Japanese Zen.

The meditative practices characteristic of Zen were probably first introduced to Japan by Chinese monks in the Nara period (710–784). Although meditation was practiced within the Tendai and other schools of early Japanese Buddhism, Zen did not begin to take root as an independent branch of Japanese Buddhism until the late twelfth century. Japanese monks like Eisai, Dōgen, and Ennin, who journeyed to China in the late twelfth and early thirteenth centuries, were hoping to draw on a vigorous Chinese Buddhist tradition to reform a faltering Japanese Tendai Buddhism. They found that Chan was the most vital form of Chinese Buddhism. Eisai (1141–1215) is credited with introducing the Rinzai teachings of sudden enlightenment, while Dōgen (1200–1253) brought back the "silent illumination" teachings of the Caodong (Japanese, Sōtō) masters. After initial resistance from Tendai and other established Buddhist schools, Eisai and Dōgen attracted patrons and disciples.

The establishment of Rinzai Zen in Japan was greatly helped by the arrival of Chinese emigré monks fleeing the Mongols in the late thirteenth and early fourteenth centuries. Eisai's Rinzai successors won the patronage of shoguns, members of the imperial court, and powerful provincial warriors. Within the next several centuries hundreds of monasteries were built in Kyoto and Kamakura and throughout the provinces. Five great monasteries in Kyoto and five in Kamakura were designated *gozan* ("five mountains"), and these headed a network of officially sponsored Rinzai monasteries. Other important Rinzai monasteries, like Daitokuji and Myōshinji, remained outside the *gozan* network. The *gozan* monasteries not only provided training in meditation for Buddhist monks but also served as centers for the diffusion of Zen-related Chinese culture and learning. Zen monks like Musō Soseki (1275–1351) and Gidō Shūshin (1325–1388) were familiar with Confucian and Daoist as well as Buddhist learning. They were also poets, painters, and garden designers. Through training in Zen and discussion of these other arts they played a major role in the civilizing of the upper stratum of medieval Japanese warrior society.

The energy of *gozan* Zen was flagging by the sixteenth century. Eventually the *gozan* monasteries were outstripped in influence by Daitokuji and Myōshinji, which traced their traditions from the powerful masters Shūhō Myōchō (1282–1337), Kanzan Egen (1277–1360), and the iconoclastic Ikkyū Sōjun (1394–1481). This tradition was further strengthened in the Edo period by Hakuin Ekaku (1685–1768), who is widely regarded as the founder of modern Japanese Rinzai Zen practice.

Dōgen's Sōtō Zen, based at the monasteries of Eiheiji and Sōjiji, spread widely among warriors and farmers in northern Japan. Although Dōgen had enforced a severe monastic practice that effectively restricted his Zen to monks who were willing to suffer the bitter winter conditions in Eiheiji, his followers introduced prayer ceremonies and funeral rites that gave Sōtō Zen a more popular appeal than Rinzai. Dōgen's writings, especially his monumental collection of treatises on Zen thought and practice, the *Shōbō genzō*, did not become widely known until long after his death. They established his reputation as the most fertile Zen thinker in Japanese religious history.

A third major strain of Zen thought was the Ōbaku teachings imported from China in the seventeenth century. Chinese monks were installed under shogunal patronage in the monastery of Manpukuji, near Kyoto. Ōbaku Zen was strongly influenced by the popular Pure Land Buddhism of Ming-dynasty China.

Zen was first made known to the West in the sixteenth century by Jesuit missionaries, who discovered that Zen monks were redoubtable intellectual opponents. There is no indication that Zen found any adherents in the West at that time. It again came to the attention of Westerners after the reestablishment of close Western contact with Japan in the mid-nineteenth century. But it was only through the prolific writings of Suzuki Daisetsu (known in the West as D. T. Suzuki; 1870–1960) that Zen found a voice really capable of introducing its subtleties to Western readers. Suzuki stressed the importance of the enlightenment experience *(satori)* and the *kōan*. He presented Rinzai Zen as the essence of Japanese religion and culture. Suzuki won a worldwide reputation as an author and lecturer. He stimulated others to read about and practice Zen in the Zen meditation groups that began to spring up in the United States and Europe. Some of these groups were ephemeral. Many, however, guided by Japanese monks or by Westerners trained in Japanese Zen monasteries, have grown into stable communities of lay as well as monastic Zen practitioners.

[*See also* Eisai; Dōgen Kigen; Ennin; *and* Suzuki Daisetsu.]

Martin Collcutt, *Five Mountains, the Rinzai Zen Monastic Institution in Medieval Japan* (1981). Heinrich Dumoulin, *A History of Zen Buddhism* (1963; rev. ed. 1987). Philip Kapleau, *The Three Pillars of Zen: Teaching, Practice, Enlightenment* (1965). Hee-Jin Kim, *Dōgen Kigen, Mystical Realist* (1975). Daisetsu T. Suzuki, *Essays in Zen Buddhism*, 3 vols. (1970) and *The Training of the Zen Buddhist Monk* (1965). Philip B. Yampolsky, *The Platform Sutra of the Sixth Patriarch* (1967) and *The Zen Master Hakuin* (1971).   MARTIN COLLCUTT

ZENG GUOFAN (1811–1872), Confucian scholar and statesman in late imperial China. An ardent Confucian born into a poor Hunan farming family and trained in the school of statecraft, Zeng believed that scholarship must be applied to practical problem solving and that government must be dedicated to the people's welfare.

In 1838 Zeng attained the *jinshi* degree and entered the Hanlin Academy. He also served on the boards of Rites, Punishments, and Civil Appointments, where he proved himself an honest, frugal, and diligent administrator. He gained invaluable experience in practical affairs and wrote many lucid proposals for administrative improvement.

In 1853 the emperor ordered Zeng to organize a temporary militia and a small navy in Hunan to fight the Taiping rebels. In spite of many Taiping victories, Zeng persevered, convinced that the Confucian state must be preserved at all costs. In 1860 he was made governor-general of Guangdong and Guangxi provinces. After the last Taiping rebels were defeated in 1866, Zeng worked hard to restore Confucian orthodoxy by reprinting the classics.

In 1865 Zeng was sent to suppress the Nian rebels in North China. Shortly thereafter, he established the ironworks that became the Jiangnan Arsenal in Shanghai. In 1867 he was made grand secretary and became governor-general of Zhili Province in 1868. In 1870 he was sent to investigate the causes of the Tianjin Massacre. From this experience Zeng became convinced that China must be conciliatory toward the West. He also proposed that Chinese students be sent abroad to study Western science and technology in the effort to achieve "self-strengthening" by linking Confucian ideology with Western material power. This idea was opposed by many of Zeng's tradition-minded colleagues.

It is ironic that Zeng's efforts to build up a local military force to oppose the Taipings and preserve the Confucian dynasty in fact set in motion regionalist forces that fragmented China and contributed to the collapse of the imperial system and its Confucian rationale half a century later.

[*See also* Qing Dynasty *and* Taiping Rebellion.]

William J. Hail, *Tseng Kuo-fan and the Taiping Rebellion* (1927). Kwang-ching Liu, "The Limits of Regional Power in the Late Ch'ing Period: A Reappraisal," *Tsing Hua Journal of Chinese Studies* n.s. 27.2 (July 1974): 176–223. Shen Han-yin Chen, "Tseng Kuo-fan in Peking, 1840–1852: His Ideas on Statecraft and Reform," *Journal of Asian Studies* 27.1 (November 1967): 61–80. Mary C. Wright, *The Last Stand of Chinese Conservatism: The T'ung-chih Restoration, 1862–1874* (1972).

P. RICHARD BOHR

ZHANG BINGLIN (1868–1936), prominent Chinese classical scholar and revolutionary. Trained in traditional philology and textual criticism, Zhang subsequently became famous for his virulent anti-Manchuism. In 1903 he was jailed in Shanghai for ridiculing the Guangxu emperor by calling him a "young clown." After his release in 1906, he went to Japan and joined Sun Yat-sen's Tongmenghui (Revolutionary Alliance). As editor of the Tong-menghui's magazine, *Minbao (People's Journal)*, Zhang launched vitriolic attacks against the Man-chus for their ruthless and corrupt rule. He repeat-edly stressed the racial difference between the Chinese and the Manchus and called for the com-plete extirpation of the Manchu race. He later re-tired from politics and excelled in classical schol-arship and Buddhism.

Howard L. Boorman, ed., *Biographical Dictionary of Republican China* (1967–1971). Michael Gasster, *Chinese Intellectuals and the Revolution of 1911* (1969).

CHANG-TAI HUNG

ZHANG CHUNQIAO (b. 1917), radical Com-munist leader in Shanghai and member of the Gang of Four. Born to a landlord family in Shandong Province, Zhang began his career as a literary critic after graduating from middle school. In the early 1930s he joined the leftist intellectual circle in Shanghai and received national attention by engag-ing in debates with the famous author Lu Xun on the role of literature in the national crisis. When the Japanese occupied Shanghai he went to the Com-munist headquarters at Yan'an, continuing to work in the propaganda field. He returned to Shanghai with the army and stayed there, moving upward in the political hierarchy of the city; he served as the president of Shanghai's *Liberation Daily* and as the director of the Literary Work Department. By 1966 he was the director of the Propaganda Department as well as the secretary of the Secretariat of Shanghai Municipality.

As a result of Zhang's close personal ties with Jiang Qing (the wife of Mao Zedong) and his sup-port of the Maoist radical line, he emerged as the top leader in Shanghai as well as the most important leader in national politics; he became a member of the Politburo in 1969 and was promoted to member of the Politburo Standing Committee, vice-premier, and director of the General Political Department of the People's Liberation Army. As a key member of the Gang of Four he was purged in 1976. He drew the attention of the media by refusing to say even one word throughout the process of his trial.

[*See also* Gang of Four; Great Proletarian Cultural Revolution; *and* China, People's Republic of.]

HONG YUNG LEE

ZHANG FEI (d. 221), Chinese general of the Three Kingdoms period. As young men he and Guan Yu joined Liu Bei against the Yellow Turban rebels. Zhang's fame as a courageous fighter came when he protected Liu Bei as Liu was in flight from Cao Cao in 211. Zhang led Liu's forces in creating a dynastic base for Liu in Sichuan and served as grand administrator of Baxi Commandery—an important post responsible for protecting the Shu Han capital. Two of his daughters were Shu Han empresses. Be-cause of his maltreatment of his troops, Zhang was assassinated by two of his generals. Although in popular lore Zhang is renowned for strictly observ-ing the code of brotherhood toward Liu Bei and Guan Yu, there is no historical evidence for this image of Zhang.

[*See also* Three Kingdoms *and* Liu Bei.]

JACK L. DULL

ZHANG GUOTAO (1897–1979), prominent early Chinese Communist leader. Zhang became ac-tive in labor organization as well as a member of the Party's ruling committee in the early 1920s. He often represented so-called leftist ideas within Party circles. After Party ranks were decimated in 1927, when the United Front with the Guomindang (Kuomintang, or Nationalist Party) collapsed, Zhang went to the Soviet Union. Returning to China in 1931, he became the head of a Communist base area in Hubei Province. In June 1935 his forces joined with those led by Mao Zedong. Zhang was discontented with Mao's leadership, however, and a short while later he unsuccessfully endeavored to establish an independent base area in the extreme southwest. In 1937 he was forced to rejoin Mao; a year later, he left the Party. As one of the few former top Chinese Communist leaders in the West after 1949, he presented Western scholars with a unique insider's view of the revolution.

[*See also* Communism: Chinese Communist Par-ty; Long March; United Front; *and* Mao Zedong.]

Chang Kuo-t'ao (Zhang Guotao), *The Rise of the Chinese Communist Party*, 2 vols. (1971).   LEE FEIGON

ZHANG JUZHENG (1525–1582), chief grand secretary of the Wanli emperor of Ming-dynasty China from 1572 to 1582. Zhang is generally known for his successful attempts to reform and systematize the Ming fiscal administration.

Zhang was a native of Qiangling, a city on the Yangtze River in central China, where his family was registered as a military household. He first took office in 1547. During the 1550s, when the court was under the control of Chief Grand Secretary Yan Song (1480–1565), he withdrew from official life, in part for personal reasons and in part because he could not support Yan's policies. He returned in 1560, rose quickly in rank, and entered the Secretariat in 1567. By 1571 he was shaping imperial policy. He arranged for a treaty with the Mongolian leader Altan Khan (1507–1582), who had been harassing the northern borders of the empire since the 1540s. This negotiated settlement represented a major change in policy and in effect brought an end to hostilities with the Mongols. [See also Altan Khan.]

During the decade from 1572 to 1582 Zhang virtually ran the imperial administration. His most ambitious undertaking, an attempt to resurvey systematically all of the taxable land in the empire, began in 1577. When the preliminary land survey was completed in 1581, Zhang used it as the basis for a new tax accounting system called the single-entry system (popularly known as yitiaobianfa, the "single-whip" system), under which all miscellaneous taxes and labor service obligations were rolled into the land tax and made payable as a single assessment in silver. Although taxes had in fact been collected this way in many areas since the mid-sixteenth century, Zhang tried to regularize the system and to spread it throughout the empire.

Shortly after Zhang's death in 1582 his reputation was attacked by people who had suffered under his policies. He was posthumously disgraced, his property was confiscated, and his family was arrested; those of his sons who survived interrogation were exiled. While many of his bureaucratic reforms were reversed, his fiscal reforms were ultimately accepted in many regions.

[See also Ming Dynasty and Yitiaobianfa.]

Ray Huang, Taxation and Governmental Finance in Sixteenth-Century Ming China (1974) and 1587: A Year of No Significance (1981).
JAMES GEISS

ZHANG SHICHENG (1321–1367), a former salt smuggler from Jiangsu Province, China, who became an important regional leader in the Huai River basin during the anti-Yuan rebellions of the 1350s. His rivals were Chen Youliang and Zhu Yuanzhang,

the latter of whom was the future founder of the Ming dynasty. In 1356 Zhang made his headquarters at Suzhou yet failed to build a secure power base in the surrounding area. Zhang surrendered to the Yuan government in 1358 to strengthen his position against his rivals. In return for his nominal loyalty, Zhang was able to remain the de facto ruler of the lower Yangtze region. In 1363 Zhang established his independent state of Wu and found himself directly in the path of Zhu's drive to control the empire. By 1366 Zhang's stronghold at Suzhou was under siege from Zhu's troops, who finally broke through Zhang's defenses in late 1367. Now a prisoner, Zhang was taken to Zhu's base at Nanjing, where he died by his own hand.

[See also Chen Youliang; Zhu Yuanzhang; and Yuan Dynasty.]

John Dardess, Conquerors and Confucians: Aspects of Political Change in Late Yuan China (1973). L. Carrington Goodrich and Chaoying Fang, eds., Dictionary of Ming Biography (1976), pp. 99–102.
ANITA M. ANDREW

ZHANGUO PERIOD. See Warring States Period.

ZHANG XIANZHONG (1605?–1647), leader of rebel army at the end of the Ming dynasty in China. A native of Shaanxi, Zhang served for a period in the Ming army. By 1630 he had become the leader of a rebel band. After operating in central China for several years, Zhang invaded and conquered Sichuan in 1644. His two-year occupation of the province was marked by violence against the population. Zhang has been traditionally blamed for the depopulation of the province, but military operations, famine, and disease all clearly contributed to the devastation. Zhang was killed by Qing troops in 1647.

Arthur W. Hummel, ed., Eminent Chinese of the Ch'ing Period (1644–1912), 2 vols. (1943–1944). James B. Parsons, The Peasant Rebellions of the Late Ming Dynasty (1970).
ROBERT ENTENMANN

ZHANG XUECHENG (1738–1801), Chinese Confucian scholar of the so-called Eastern Zhejiang school. Zhang was born in Kuaiji, Zhejiang Province, not far from the native home of Huang Zongxi, the progenitor of the tradition of scholarship with which Zhang identified late in life. Like Huang, Zhang approached his subject matter historically and stressed that scholarship be applicable to social and political situations. Zhang's main contribution lay in clarifying the theoretical underpinnings of the historian's craft rather than in the exercise of the craft itself. He stressed the value of private historical writing as opposed to large, state-sponsored projects. Although he passed the metropolitan examination in 1778, Zhang never received an official appointment. His last thirty years were spent teaching, directing academies, compiling bibliographies and local histories, and writing critical essays on history and literature.

[See also Huang Zongxi.]

David Nivison, The Life and Thought of Chang Hsueh-ch'eng (1966). JUDITH A. WHITBECK

ZHANG XUELIANG (b. 1898), key figure in the Xi'an Incident of 1936, which brought about the United Front between the Nationalists and the Communists on the eve of World War II in China. The oldest son of Zhang Zuolin, Zhang, often called the "Young Marshal," inherited power in Manchuria after his father's death in 1928. Despite Japanese opposition, Zhang gave the Nanjing government nominal authority over Manchuria. After Japan's conquest of Manchuria, Zhang came to favor cooperation of Communists and Nationalists against Japan. On 12 December 1936 Zhang and others seized Chiang Kai-shek in Xi'an and forced him to negotiate with the Communists. Chiang was released on 25 December, and subsequent events showed that a united front against Japan had indeed been achieved. For his part in this "Xi'an Incident," Zhang was kept in detention, even after the Nationalists fled to Taiwan.

[See also Zhang Zuolin; Xi'an Incident; and Chiang Kai-shek.]

Wu Tien-wei, The Sian Incident: A Pivotal Point in Modern Chinese History (1976). JAMES E. SHERIDAN

ZHANG ZAI (1020–1077), also known as Zhang Henqu, a cosmological and ethical thinker of the Song dynasty in China who contributed to the rise of Neo-Confucianism. The son of a Song official, Zhang won a degree in the examination system and held a number of minor posts in the Song capital. Zhang is best known for his Western Inscription, in which he extends Confucian ethical values to the entire universe. This work can be seen as part of the Confucian response to Buddhist metaphysics leading up to the synthetic work of Zhu Xi.

[See also Song Dynasty; Neo-Confucianism; and Zhu Xi.]

Wing-tsit Chan, A Source Book in Chinese Philosophy (1963). Wm. Theodore de Bary, Wing-tsit Chan, and Burton Watson, comps., Sources of Chinese Tradition, vol. 1 (1960). EDWARD L. FARMER

ZHANG ZHIDONG (1837–1909), Chinese statesman, a key figure in late Qing dynasty political life and economic development. Highly regarded as a young scholar, Zhang won political prominence as a champion of hard-line resistance in China's 1879 diplomatic crisis with Russia and in the Sino-French War (1884–1885). Won over to reform ideas, he became a leading advocate and practitioner of the Self-Strengthening modernization program. Beginning at Guangzhou (Canton) and continuing for almost two decades at the Wuhan cities (Wuchang, Hankou, and Hanyang) on the Yangtze River, he set up mills, factories, an iron and steel complex, military academies, and technical schools as he strengthened China while building a multifaceted personal power base. Zhang's famous educational slogan, "Chinese learning for fundamental principles, Western learning for practical application," suggests the dilemma of many who sought to preserve Confucian civilization while arming it with foreign technology.

[See also Qing Dynasty.]

William Ayers, Chang Chi-tung and Educational Reform in China (1971). Daniel H. Bays, China Enters the Twentieth Century: Chang Chih-tung and the Issues of a New Age, 1895–1909 (1978). IRWIN T. HYATT, JR.

ZHANG ZUOLIN (1873–1928), often called the "Old Marshal"; one of the most powerful militarists during the era of political fragmentization after the 1911 Revolution in China. By 1919 he controlled all of Manchuria, and he ruled that area essentially as an independent state until his death. During that decade, Zhang also took part in the political and military struggles in North China. Between 1926 and 1928 he dominated Beijing and much of North China, and led the opposition to Nationalist attempts to unify the country. Zhang gave Japan privileges in Manchuria, and in turn Japan supported his rule there but opposed his involvement in North China warlord struggles. After Zhang's death, his oldest son, Zhang Xueliang, succeeded him as warlord in northeast China.

[*See also* China, Republic Period; Warlords; Warlord Cliques; *and* Zhang Xueliang.]

Gavan McCormack, *Chang Tso-lin in Northeast China, 1911–1928: Japan and the Manchurian Idea* (1977).
                                                            JAMES E. SHERIDAN

ZHAO, one of the Warring States of ancient China. Located in present-day northern Shanxi Province, Zhao was formed when the state of Jin broke up in 453 BCE. The declining Zhou dynasty formally recognized Zhao's independence in 403 BCE. Zhao survived until 222 BCE, when it fell victim to the Qin unification of China.   EDWARD L. FARMER

ZHAO RUGUA, thirteenth-century Chinese author of a comprehensive description of China's overseas trade and world geography as known in China. As inspector of foreign trade in Fujian Province, Zhao was in an excellent position to gather information from visiting ships. His *Zhu fan zhi* (c. 1225) briefly describes most of East, Southeast, and South Asia and contains fragments of information about the west coast of Africa, the Middle East, and the Mediterranean. The final third of the treatise describes commodities involved in China's overseas trade and where they could be obtained.

[*See also* Ma Huan.]

F. Hirth and W. W. Rockhill, trans., *Chau Ju-kua: His Work on the Chinese and Arab Trade in the Twelfth and Thirteenth Centuries, entitled Chu-fan-chi* (1911; reprint, 1965).
                                                            DAVID K. WYATT

ZHAO ZIYANG (b. 1919), premier of the People's Republic of China since 1980. Zhao replaced Hua Guofeng, who in 1976 had succeeded both Zhou Enlai as premier and Mao Zedong as chairman of the Chinese Communist Party. Born in Henan Province, Zhao first made a name for himself after 1975, as first secretary of the Sichuan Provincial Party Committee when agricultural production was stimulated by the use of incentive systems. Zhao was elevated to the top government post by his political mentor, Deng Xiaoping, a native of Sichuan. In January 1987, following a wave of student demonstrations calling for greater freedom, Zhao replaced Hu Yaobang, becoming acting general secretary of the Communist Party. It is uncertain what this additional responsibility will mean to Zhao's political future.

[*See also* Communism: Chinese Communist Party; Deng Xiaoping; *and* Responsibility System.]
                                                            EDWARD L. FARMER

ZHEJIANG, Chinese province located on the eastern coast just south of the Yangtze River. Although physically one of China's smallest provinces, with an area of only 102,000 square kilometers, it is densely settled, with a population of approximately 39 million (1982). The provincial capital, Hangzhou, is its largest city, with a population of more than 1 million. Other major cities include Ningbo, for centuries a center of banking and commerce in the region, and Wenzhou, an important port. The northern part of Zhejiang is in a flat alluvial plain and had become a center of highly developed commercial agriculture as early as the Song period (960–1279). Major commodities produced in the province include rice, tea (especially the famous Longjing, or "dragon well," variety), silk, jute, cotton, and fish.

Zhejiang's wealth made it an important cultural and political center in recent centuries. In the Ming period (1368–1644), for instance, Zhejiang produced more scholars who had passed the national-level (*jinshi*) examinations than any other province. In the twentieth century the rise of nearby Shanghai as an industrial, financial, and cultural center has overshadowed the province. The area has not developed a strong industrial base, aside from some light manufacturing and food processing, but does supply important raw materials for Shanghai's industrial plant.

Frederic M. Kaplan and Julian M. Sobin, *Encyclopedia of China Today* (1982). T. R. Treager, *A Geography of China* (1965).
                                                            PARKS M. COBLE, JR.

ZHENG CHENGGONG (1624–1662), known in the West as Koxinga, Ming-dynasty (1368–1644) loyalist who fought against the invading Manchus during the mid-seventeenth century in China. Since he clashed with the European maritime expansion in Chinese waters as well, he has also been viewed as a famous pirate of the time.

Zheng was born in August 1624 in Hirado, Japan; his father was Zheng Zhilong, a former pirate chief from Fujian Province, and his mother was a Japanese woman of the Tagawa family. The Zheng family's power in Fujian was recognized by one of the last Ming princes, who had established his "imperial court" in the area. The young Zheng was given the personal name of Chenggong ("achievement") as well as the title "Lord of the Imperial Surname" (Guoxingye). It was from this title that the Dutch forces on the island of Taiwan came to know of Zheng, and they referred to him as "Koxinga."

In 1646 Zheng Chenggong launched a series of anti-Manchu attacks in the southern provinces of Fujian and Zhejiang. His father had defected to the Qing (1644–1911) that same year, ostensibly to preserve his base in Fujian. Apparently, Zheng Chenggong tried to dissuade his father from this decision but was unsuccessful. Thereafter, Zheng intensified his raids against the Qing forces stationed along the Fujian coast. The Qing attempted to woo Zheng with titles and positions as a way to end his threat to the state, but Zheng remained loyal to the Ming cause.

Zheng's forces met with a crucial defeat at Nanjing in 1659 and he was forced to retreat first to Amoy (Xiamen) and then to Taiwan, where he defeated the Dutch in 1661. From his base in Taiwan, Zheng continued to be a formidable foe of the Qing dynasty until his death on 23 June 1662. Anti-Qing resistance was carried on by his descendants on Taiwan until 1683.

Ralph C. Croizier, *Koxinga and Chinese Nationalism: History, Myth and the Hero* (1977). Arthur W. Hummel, ed., *Eminent Chinese of the Ch'ing Period (1644–1911)* (1943–1944). Donald Keene, *The Battles of Coxinga: Chikamatsu's Play, Its Background and Importance* (1951). John E. Wells, Jr., "Maritime China from Wang Chih to Shih Lang: Themes in Peripheral History," in *From Ming to Ch'ing: Conquest, Region and Continuity in Seventeenth-Century China*, edited by Jonathan D. Spence and John E. Wills, Jr. (1979), pp. 201–238.

ANITA M. ANDREW

ZHENG HE (1371–1433) is best known as the Chinese eunuch who commanded a series of maritime expeditions through Southeast Asia to India and the east coast of Africa for the Yongle emperor (r. 1402–1424) of the Ming dynasty in the first decades of the fifteenth century.

Zheng He was born and raised in a Muslim family in central Yunnan Province in southwestern China. Both his father and his grandfather were known by the title hajji, which was conferred upon Muslims who had made the pilgrimage to Mecca. At least during his early years he was raised as a Muslim and may have acquired some knowledge of Arabic.

In 1381, when his locality was brought under the control of the Ming dynasty, the general in charge of the occupying armies selected Zheng He and a number of other boys for palace service. He was castrated when he was about ten years old, taken to North China, and assigned to serve on the staff of Zhu Di (who later became the Yongle emperor). During this time he gained considerable military experience, because for the most part his duties entailed following Zhu Di on campaign.

Zheng He is described as being very tall and stout (seven feet tall with a girth of five feet by one account) and as having a loud voice and a commanding stare. He was thus physically suited for the rigors of warfare and proved himself capable in battle, first during campaigns against the Mongols between 1393 and 1397 and later during Zhu Di's rebellion of 1399, when he played a key role in the defense of Beijing.

After Zhu Di ascended the throne in 1402, Zheng He became one of his most trusted aides. During the first years of the reign he held important military commissions. In 1405, however, he was put in charge of a large-scale maritime expedition to Southeast Asia, and he continued to supervise such expeditions until his death in 1433.

It is not clear why the Yongle emperor decided to mount these costly maritime expeditions. Several reasons are usually put forth: that he was afraid the Jianwen emperor, whose throne he had usurped, might have escaped to Southeast Asia, and he wanted to find him; that he wanted to suppress piracy in Southeast Asian waters; and that he wanted to extend the hegemony of the Ming empire to the shores of India and Arabia. While there is some truth in each of these reasons, it is likely that it was the last one, the desire to extend the limits of his empire, that kept the expeditions alive for more than two decades.

The Yongle emperor sought to reestablish a universal world empire on the model of the preceding Yuan dynasty. Whereas the Mongols had only had a land-based empire, however, he wanted to establish a maritime empire as well. Zheng He's expeditions were intended to extend the hegemony of the Ming empire throughout Southeast Asia and beyond by demonstrating that the Ming navy was formidable and not easily defeated and that the Ming emperor protected maritime trade and was not hostile toward Islam. It is important to note that Zheng He's expeditions all carried Arabic speakers conscripted from mosques in China who served as translators, for Islamic merchants had by this time come to control most of the trade routes between China and Arabia.

The first expedition, in 1405, carried a crew of

27,000 and comprised a fleet of more than 60 large vessels (440 feet long) and 255 smaller ships. The principal goal of this and the next few expeditions was to make the sea routes between China and India safe for maritime trade. In a major battle near Sumatra, Zheng He destroyed the fleet of a powerful Chinese pirate who had been harassing ships in the Straits of Melaka. During the expedition of 1409 to 1411, which reached the Malabar coast of India, Chinese luxury goods were displayed in Ceylon and other commercial centers to promote trade with China.

The expedition of 1413 to 1415, however, which reached the Arabian Peninsula, had a distinctly diplomatic cast: from this point on the expeditions revolved around carrying tribute missions to and from China. The expedition of 1417 to 1419 returned the envoys who had arrived in 1415. The expedition of 1421 to 1422, which reached the east coast of Africa, returned with even greater numbers of envoys. Yet almost immediately after the Yongle emperor's death in 1424, influential officials at court began to protest that such voyages were too costly to continue, and the expeditions were suspended until 1431. Zheng He, already in his sixties, was unable to visit every country in person during the last expedition, in 1431 to 1433. He may in fact have died en route at Calicut early in 1433, but the details of his death remain obscure.

Although such expeditions were discontinued after Zheng He's death, the hegemony of the Ming emperor throughout Southeast Asia, at least as an arbiter of disputes and successions, remained unchallenged until the Portuguese arrived in the first years of the sixteenth century. In that respect at least, Zheng He did realize the Yongle emperor's ambitions. Furthermore, the expeditions constituted the greatest feat of navigation undertaken in the world until that time. During the first several expeditions all of the major sea routes between China and the Islamic countries of the West were systematically explored and mapped. A vast amount of knowledge was added to the corpus of Chinese geography. Ma Huan (fl. 1413–1451), a Muslim interpreter who went on several of the expeditions, kept a record of about twenty places that he had visited. At least two other accounts were written by other members of the expeditions. Together these works comprise the only major accounts of travel in Asia from the fifteenth century and offer the most accurate and vivid picture of the region prior to the arrival of the Portuguese.

[See also Ming Dynasty; Zhu Di; and Ma Huan.]

J. J. L. Duyvendak, "The True Dates of the Chinese Maritime Expeditions in the Early Fifteenth Century," T'oung pao 34 (1939): 341–412. Ma Huan, Ying-yai sheng-lan: The Overall Survey of the Ocean's Shores, edited and translated by J. V. G. Mills (1970). Joseph Needham, Science and Civilisation in China, vol. 4, part 3, Civil Engineering and Nautics (1971), pp. 479ff.

JAMES GEISS

ZHENG XUAN (Zheng Kangcheng; 127–200), prominent Chinese scholar of the Eastern Han period (25–220) renowned for his voluminous commentaries to the Confucian classics and his contribution to the Old Text (Guwen) school of criticism. A native of Gaomi, Shandong Province, he served as local bailiff before traveling to Luoyang to study at the Imperial Academy. He became a disciple of the Old Text scholar Ma Rong (79–166). Zheng returned to Gaomi, where he shunned political office and devoted himself to teaching and scholarship. His commentaries to the Book of Changes (Yijing), Book of Odes (Shijing), Book of Documents (Shangshu), Book of Rites (Liji), Rites of Zhou (Zhouli), and Book of Ceremonials (Yili) have remained standard until modern times. [See also Guwen and Confucianism.]

M. LAVONNE MARUBBIO

ZHENGZHOU, Chinese city located just south of the Yellow River on the western edge of the North China Plain; capital of Henan Province. Zhengzhou has been continuously settled for more than three thousand years, as it was one of the most populous Shang centers from the sixteenth to the eleventh century BCE. Its modern development began in 1898, when foreign interests began construction of north-south and east-west rail lines with Zhengzhou as the axis.

Owing to Zhengzhou's importance as a rail center, the city was a primary objective of the Japanese push through China in 1937. In a famous incident the Nationalist army breached the Yellow River dikes less than twenty miles northeast of the city in order to prevent capture of the city. Drowning and starvation resulted in great loss of life.

F. F. Liu, A Military History of Modern China, 1929–49 (1956). William Watson, China before the Han Dynasty (1962).

SALLY HART

ZHENLA, name given by the Chinese to a Cambodian state, or states, in the seventh and eighth centuries CE. The Khmer of Zhenla appear to have displaced the previous kingdom or kingdoms known to the Chinese as Funan in the upper reaches of the Mekong River. Chinese sources refer to an eventual division of Zhenla into two parts, Land Zhenla, farther north, and Water Zhenla, extending down to the coast. It is now widely thought, however, that there was never a centralized state corresponding to Zhenla but rather an arena of autonomous Khmer principalities. In the ninth century they were at least partly subordinated to or absorbed by Angkor.

[See also Funan and Angkor.]

Lawrence P. Briggs, *The Ancient Khmer Empire* (1951). G. Coedès, *The Indianized States of Southeast Asia*, translated by Susan B. Cowing (1968).   IAN W. MABBETT

ZHENYAN, or Chinese Tantrism, is an esoteric form of Mahayana Buddhism that enjoyed a high level of popularity, particularly among the upper classes of eighth- and ninth-century China. Certain Tantric practices had been present in China for several centuries before the actual founding of the school. It was during the Tang dynasty (618–906), the cultural period that epitomizes the Chinese fascination with foreign exotica, however, that Tantrism took hold in a more formal way and was established as a separate school.

The founding and flourishing of the Zhenyan school is associated with three major figures. The first, Subhakarasimha (637–735), a native of central India, arrived in Chang'an, the Tang capital, in 716. His teaching focused upon the central teachings of Tantra, the three secrets of the body, speech, and mind. He was responsible for the translation of the *Mahavairocana Sutra*, a text central to the esoteric schools of Buddhism throughout East Asia. Vajrabodhi (663–741), the second of the masters, formally began initiation rites involving the use of the mandala, the diagram of the sacred universe used by the initiate for individual meditation. Amoghavajra (705–774), the third master, arrived in China as a youth and became a disciple of Vajrabodhi. He continued the practice of the mandala initiation ceremony and translated Tantric scripture. Following his death, however, the school declined and was dealt a severe blow by the general suppression of Buddhism in 845. Zhenyan teaching enjoyed brief revivals during the Song and Yuan periods.

Apart from a small continued presence of esoteric Buddhist practice, the influence of the Zhenyan school in China was short lived. That both Subhakarasimha and Amoghavajra were personally close

to several Tang emperors is an indication of the level of influence the school possessed. The principal Zhenyan legacy, however, derives from its teachings and art forms (especially the *mandala*), which were transmitted to Japan in the ninth century, where they flourished as the Shingon school of Japanese Buddhism.

[See also Buddhism: Buddhism in China; Lamaism; Tantra; and Shingon.]

Raoul Birnbaum, *Studies on the Mysteries of Mañjuśrī* (1983). Kenneth Ch'en, *Buddhism in China: A Historical Survey* (1964). Chou I-liang, "Tantrism in China," *Harvard Journal of Asiatic Studies* 8 (1945): 241–332. David L. Snellgrove, *The Hevajra Tantra: A Critical Study* (1959).   RODNEY L. TAYLOR

ZHOU DAGUAN, thirteenth-century Chinese traveler who left an account of the kingdom of Angkor in what is now Cambodia. He left the Chinese coast in 1295 and returned late the following year, accompanying an envoy sent to persuade the ruler of Angkor to offer tribute to the emperor of China, grandson of the Mongol conqueror Kublai Khan. His account of his travels and what he saw and heard was translated into French in 1891 and again in 1902. The latter translation, by Paul Pelliot, was republished in 1951.

Zhou recounts his journey to the Mekong Delta, then up the river and along the tributary connecting it to the Tonle Sap, or Great Lake, north of which was the capital of Angkor. He describes the city, recognizably the Angkor Thom, whose remains still stand; the royal palace, Angkor Wat (which he knew as the "tomb of Lu Ban"); and the great artificial lakes of Angkor. Then he offers a detailed account of the buildings, the clothing worn by the Khmer, and the official religion, customs, festivals, language, and society of the kingdom. He names the ninety provinces, though only a few from his list can be identified. Finally he describes a royal procession in all its pomp and splendor.

The ruler at the time of Zhou's visit was Indravarman III. In his time, the great age of temple building commemorated by Sanskrit inscriptions had already passed. Independent Thai kingdoms were already a threat, and Zhou mentions that there had recently been an exhausting war waged against Thai armies.

He also mentions the intriguing custom whereby the king spent part of each night atop the Phimeanakas monument; reputedly he cohabited there with a serpent spirit appearing in the form of a woman, and the safety of the kingdom depended magically on the rendezvous being kept.

[*See also* Angkor.]

Lawrence P. Briggs, *The Ancient Khmer Empire* (1951). G. Coedès, *The Indianized States of Southeast Asia*, translated by Susan B. Cowing (1968).   IAN W. MABBETT

ZHOU DUNYI (1017–1073), also known by his studio name as Zhou Lianxi, a Song-dynasty thinker recognized as a pioneer of Neo-Confucianism in China. Born in Hunan Province, Zhou had a career as a minor official while pursuing his interests in philosophy. At one point he instructed the brothers Cheng Yi and Cheng Hao, who became major figures in the Song revival of Confucianism. Zhou Dunyi is best known for his essay "An Explanation of the Diagram of the Supreme Ultimate" *(Taiji tushuo)*. Zhou's essay was intended to account systematically for the generation all reality. It begins with a discussion of the supreme ultimate *(taiji)* and goes on to treat the correlative forces of yin and yang and the Five Elements (or agents): water, fire, wood, metal, and earth. Zhou added to Confucian thought by making use of the Daoist idea of nonbeing and by giving a central place to the *Book of Changes (Yijing)*.

[*See also* Song Dynasty; Neo-Confucianism; Zhu Xi; *and* Cheng Brothers.]

Wing-tsit Chan, *A Source Book in Chinese Philosophy* (1963). Wm. Theodore de Bary, Wing-tsit Chan, and Burton Watson, comps., *Sources of Chinese Tradition*, vol. 1 (1960). Rodney L. Taylor, "Chou Tun-i," in *The Encyclopedia of Religion*, edited by Mircea Eliade (1987), vol. 3, pp. 337–339.   EDWARD L. FARMER

ZHOU ENLAI (1898–1976). Until their deaths in 1976, both Mao Zedong and Zhou Enlai were among a handful of leaders of the People's Republic of China (PRC) who wielded immense political influence and did much to shape events in China. Whereas Mao has been publicly criticized for his political and policy errors in recent years, Zhou has become a new Communist saint and remains highly popular with Chinese people.

Zhou was born into a Mandarin family in Huaian, Jiangsu. After he graduated from the Nankai High School in Tianjin in 1917, Zhou went abroad and studied in Japan (1918–1919), in France (1920–1922), and in Germany (1923–1924) and joined the Chinese Communist Party (CCP) in France in 1922. Zhou returned to Canton (Guang-

zhou) in 1924 at a time when the CCP and the Guomindang (Kuomintang, KMT, or Nationalist Party) had forged a united front, and he was appointed director of the Political Department of the Whompoa Military Academy under Commandant Chiang Kai-shek. Zhou received the same assignment in the First Army of the National Revolutionary Army, also under Chiang, when the Northern Expedition was launched in 1926. After the united front collapsed, Zhou organized and led the unsuccessful uprising in Nanchang on 1 August 1927 and quickly emerged as one of the top CCP leaders, engaging simultaneously in armed struggle, underground political work, and mobilization of mass support. Between 1936 and 1945 Zhou also assumed the task of negotiator and was in Nanjing, Wuhan, and Chongqing to deal with the KMT authorities.

After 1949, Zhou was the chief administrator and headed the huge bureaucracy as premier of the Government Administration Council (1949–1954) and of the State Council (1954–1976). He was responsible for running the national economy and implementing other domestic policies. As the chief diplomat of the PRC, he visited many capitals and attended numerous international conferences in the 1950s and 1960s. He was widely acclaimed as a skillful diplomat in the 1955 Afro-Asian Bandung Conference and played a crucial role in the Sino-US and Sino-Japanese rapprochement in the 1970s. Zhou was also a remarkably astute political infighter and survived each and every major leadership purge in the Party for four decades. He was elected to the CCP Politburo in 1927 and held the membership without interruption until his death; he was also a Party vice-chairman (1956–1966, 1973–1976). He was married to Deng Yingchao and had no children.

[*See also* China, People's Republic of; Communism: Chinese Communist Party; Mao Zedong; *and* April Fifth Movement.]

PARRIS CHANG

ZHOU PERIOD. The Zhou displaced the ailing Shang royal house to rule the traditional Chinese heartland for much of the first millennium BCE. The period is traditionally divided into the Western Zhou (c. 1122–770 BCE) and the Eastern Zhou (770–256 BCE). From the divided states of the end of the latter period, a unified Chinese empire emerged.

The Predynastic Period. When the Shang kingdom dominated the loess plain from the "great city of Shang," the Zhou people roamed the highlands north of the Yellow River in the central sections of the present-day provinces of Shanxi and Shaanxi. During the early second millennium they probably lived as Neolithic farmers growing millet in the relatively arid northern land. Their legendary ancestor was even known as Houji, "lord of millet." At some point in their history they abandoned agriculture to take up a "barbarian" livelihood, probably a less settled economy similar to that of the pastoralism of the steppes. After an undetermined period, however, the Zhou once again adopted farming, possibly because they moved to the upper valley of the Jing River, where large numbers of proto-Zhou remains have been found. These archaeological findings suggest that the predynastic Zhou culture absorbed both Shang elements and those of the steppe culture. In that valley the Zhou people formed a state organization based on a foundation of settled agriculture.

Toward the end of the thirteenth century BCE pressures from the nomads forced the Zhou people to move south, finally settling in the Wei River valley. Zhou culture relics supersede those of the Shaanxi Longshan Neolithic cultures. The transition appeared so abruptly that the Zhou culture has been viewed as a late arrival. [See also Longshan Culture.]

Danfu, who led the Zhou to the Wei Valley, built a new capital, established friendly relationships with the Jiang, who then scattered across a wide region near the Wei, and gradually built a Zhou state that even the mighty Shang could not ignore. For three generations after Danfu, the Zhou people continued the effort to enhance the status of Zhou by expanding their territory as well as developing good terms with neighboring states. The relationship between the Shang kingdom and Zhou was alternately peaceful and hostile. Sometimes the Zhou leader yielded to the Shang court as a tributary vassal who policed the west on behalf of the Shang. At other times, Shang sent military expeditions against Zhou. Archaeological evidence verifies that the Zhou culture absorbed many elements from the Shang, while still maintaining their own local characteristics.

King Wen, a grandson of Danfu, finally challenged the hegemony of the Shang kingdom. His desire to conquer Shang was not concluded during his lifetime, for his patient strategy of forming a ring

FIGURE 1. *Gui (Food Vessel)*. Early Western Zhou period, eleventh to tenth century BCE. Bronze; height 21 cm., diameter (of mouth) 22 cm.

of allies around the royal Shang domain took many decades to establish. The final conquest was led by his son, King Wu, who defeated the Shang army at their capital and founded a new dynasty.

The Zhou Conquest. The exact date of the founding of the dynasty is an unsettled issue among scholars because of the great difficulty in reconstructing the chronology of the ancient calendar; nonetheless, a dozen scholars have each offered a precise date based on careful research. The conquest was a cumulative process spanning three generations of Zhou leaders and culminating in a decisive battle at Muye sometime between 1122 and 1027 BCE.

The fact that Zhou could defeat Shang was a surprise to the Zhou people themselves, because the strength of these two contending powers was so greatly mismatched. The Shang probably lost the battle because they were exhausted by foreign wars in the north and in the east. It is also very likely that the Shang kingdom had never been organized into a very effective political system. Nevertheless, the Zhou needed to find justification for their success. They found it useful to propose that the Shang fell because they were immoral and corrupt in their public and private affairs, and that Heaven had selected the morally upright Zhou people to replace the vitiated Shang as the new masters of the world.

For generations after King Wu, the Zhou leaders reminded their own people and the Shang subjects that the heavenly mandate was only bestowed on those who proved themselves worthy. Such a political philosophy might very well have originated for a propagandistic purpose. Moreover, the Zhou also had to argue that Heaven held the same expectation regarding Zhou governance of the world. The result was the formation of the idea that the mandate was given only to a worthy ruler whose performance in governing would be evaluated by Heaven. Throughout Chinese history since the Zhou, this particular notion has remained a significant part of the Chinese worldview.

The Feudal System. After King Wu completely overcame the resistance of the last Shang king, the smaller state of Zhou was not able to occupy the entire conquered territory of the Shang kingdom. The Zhou royal court remained in the Wei Valley, and three brothers of King Wu were entrusted to supervise the people in the former Shang kingdom. One portion was governed by the descendants of the Shang royal house.

King Wu soon passed away; the power of regency went to one of his younger brothers, known as the Duke of Zhou. The entire eastern territory including

the Zhou province rebelled against the Zhou, and it took the Duke of Zhou several years of bloody struggle to regain control of the eastern plain. An eastern capital was then built to control the people of that region. The Zhou, a small nation, had to collaborate with local leaders in the Shang territories as well as in the regions of non-Shang people lying beyond the direct control of the former Shang state. Gradually a network of vassal states evolved, governed either by the Zhou nobles who guarded strategic spots or by chiefs of survivors of old native states where Zhou units or joint forces of the Zhou and the Shang were stationed to guarantee the overlordship of the Zhou.

Kinship ties bonded the Zhou nobles together; matrimonial relations with the Zhou royal clan connected nobles of other groups to the Zhou. Periodic court visits, rituals of ancestor worship in the capital, the exchange of gifts, and the ceremony of investiture constantly renewed the feudal bonds among the members of the ruling class, whether or not they were of the Zhou line.

This Zhou feudal system was not established overnight, nor was it a product of conscientious design. In campaign after campaign, the Zhou stretched its sovereignty over territories far beyond those of the Shang. The Zhou repeatedly adopted a policy of collaboration in an effort to pull the newly subjugated areas into the Zhou orbit. After three or four generations the Zhou kingdom actually embraced much of North China and extended northeast to the Liao River valley and south to the valleys of the Han and Yangtze rivers. The domains under the direct control of the royal court, however, consisted of the homeland in the Wei Valley, the eastern domains in the Luo Valley, and a narrow corridor linking these two capitals. The greater part of China was in the hands of the vassal states within which Zhou kinsmen often occupied the most strategically valuable areas.

The influence of Zhou culture reached beyond its political domain. Archaeological findings serve as evidence that the Zhou culture had reached the eastern and the southern coasts of China. In the vast land south of the Yangtze River, it is possible that there even were Zhou "colonies" among the local culture.

A side effect of Zhou feudalism, however, was the creation of common cultural identity in each vassal state owing to assimilation between the Zhou and the natives. Furthermore, an identity of being "Chinese" was established in the entire Zhou world and cemented by the Zhou feudal network.

From the Western Zhou to the Eastern Zhou.
After eleven kings had reigned for three centuries, the Zhou system began to break down. Institutionally, the Zhou king directly ruled only the royal domain. The vassal states in the east gradually had become localized and their loyalty to the court was replaced by concerns of local interest. Nomadic people to the north and west constantly pressured the Zhou royal domain. The court often had to bear heavy war expenses. The armed forces called in from the eastern vassal states became dependent on the royal court. The Zhou court itself underwent some bureaucratization and developed a complicated organization loaded with courtiers and officials.

In 841 BCE, the first absolute date known in Chinese history, King Li was overthrown by the Zhou people, presumably nobles, because of the tyranny of heavy taxation and harsh rule. The nobles put the crown prince, known as King Xuan, on the throne, but the restoration of the Zhou house did not last long. King You, King Xuan's son, was again a victim of political turmoil. In 722 BCE he was killed by invading nomads who had been invited by some Zhou nobles, because they opposed the king's selection of a successor. The royal domain was forever lost to the pastoral foreigners who had already swarmed into the Wei Valley in large numbers. The crown prince left the old domain to establish a new court in the eastern capital. Thereafter the Zhou was identified in history as the Eastern Zhou.

The Spring and Autumn and Warring States Periods. The first portion of the Eastern Zhou is also known as the Spring and Autumn period (722–481 BCE), named after a chronicle bearing such a title. The original Zhou network was virtually replaced by a multistate system. Since the Zhou king had lost his own home territory, his authority turned to a mere shadow of the former Western Zhou "sons of Heaven." The vassal states struggled among themselves to reach a new balance of power. Some order of hegemony emerged.

At first, the states in the crowded central region of the North China Plain struggled among themselves for superiority. These old states, often small in territory and population, however, had limited resources at their disposal. After the seventh century BCE the major contenders for leadership were the peripheral states that had room to expand. These were Qi in the Shandong Peninsula, Jin in the Shanxi highland, Chu in the Yangtze Valley, and Qin in the Wei Valley. A dozen lesser states were their captured followers.

The states of Jin and Chu were the main contending powers. Although Qi briefly achieved leadership over all of China, the influence of Qi and Qin remained localized. Chu was a large state rising from the South, somewhat beyond the Zhou political sphere. The northern states claimed that their struggle was to defend the civilized world against southern "barbarians" who had already seized some Chinese states. Several wars were fought between these two camps, finally ending in a stalemate.

The second part of the Eastern Zhou is known as the period of Warring States (403–221 BCE). This period developed into a multiparty contest for superiority. Jin had reorganized into three states, Han, Zhao, and Wei, each of which had absorbed numerous minor states and new territories in the northern frontier. Qi expanded by incorporating several eastern states. Qin did the same in the west. Chu had become the largest state in the South and behaved as a Chinese state. Along the southern coast, Wu and Yue rose to challenge the mighty Chu in the South. A few lesser states barely survived. The remnants of the Zhou royal court diminished to a totally insignificant existence.

Each of these states experienced political reform that strengthened their administrative apparatus; finally, all of the major states were governed by strong monarchies. Each of them intended to unify the Chinese world, recognizing that they all shared a common culture. Hence, there was no dispute that China should be politically unified. Wars became more frequent than they had been in the Spring and Autumn period, as each state vied to become China's unifier.

In the early phase of the interstate struggle, Qi and Wei played leading roles. Soon the fast-rising Qin began to manipulate interstate relationships to its advantage. Diplomacy, espionage, and conspiracy affected the battles, in which hundreds of thousands of soldiers participated in combat as part of the game of conquest.

In the fourth century BCE every ruler of a major state claimed the title of king. The Zhou royal court, on the contrary, survived at the mercy of neighboring states. In 367 BCE the tiny domain of eastern Zhou was divided into two parts, each governed by a branch of the royal clan. In 256 and 249 BCE, respectively, these two tiny states were annexed by Qin.

Socioeconomic Developments. The consequences of multistate struggles were manifold. First, the frequent contacts between the Chinese states and the non-Chinese ones finally brought the latter, especially Chu and its allies, into the Chinese cultural sphere. Assimilation took place to such an extent that a common culture was shaped during these two centuries.

Second, the constant struggles among states not only reduced the number of states, but also triggered reorganization of social and political structures within each state. State officials rose to replace the power of feudal lords and the appearance of professionally trained bureaucrats and soldiers. In many major states the government changed hands and adopted the new administrative apparatus, transforming a feudal domain into a territorial state. Throughout the entire period a high degree of social mobility was a visible phenomenon.

Third, the frequent contacts between states, in peace or in war, shaped a segmented economy by creating mutual dependence through use of tributary, exchange of gifts, and state as well as private trade. Use of iron tools and implements became popular. Metal currency was developed as a medium of exchange. Private land ownership spurred an increase of agricultural products. Roads were built to facilitate movement of commodities. Urban centers emerged as a result of concentration of people and resources. In turn, urbanization brought new groups into existence, such as merchants and manufacturers.

The most significant development was the rise of new groups of intellectuals who were aware of their role as carriers of a great heritage and as formulators of new ideologies to answer questions that their contemporaries posed. Confucius was one of these men who served feudal masters as scribes or clerks, eventually rising to the status of advisers and teachers.

The speed of change increased during the Spring and Autumn period and accelerated during the Warring States period. Throughout the entire Eastern Zhou, gradual changes took place in the nature of Chinese society, economy, and political institutions. These changes prepared the way for China's unification into an empire.

The Zhou Legacy. As far as the history of political institutions is concerned, insofar as the royal authority of the Eastern Zhou was shattered long before the formal end of Zhou pretense to rule, the Zhou should not be regarded as a single dynasty. Nevertheless, the entire Zhou period still could, and probably should, be regarded as a long process of continuous evolution through which suzerainty passed to monarchy and monarchy passed to a bureaucratic imperial power, a pattern that was to last in Chinese history for two millennia.

The socioeconomic and ideological changes that took place in the Eastern Zhou period also left a permanent impact on Chinese history, one that was to survive many later dynasties. These factors include the following:

1. *A preference for social mobility.* The process of reorganizing a stratified feudal society into a more open one in the Eastern Zhou period had set a pattern for Qin/Han society in which the commoners were all subjects of the imperial state and were allowed to take part in rather free competition to reach better social status.

2. *An agrarian economy.* The Eastern Zhou farmers had started an intensification of farming that required them to engage in tremendous labor that produced both field crops and some consumer goods from cottage industry. Such a labor-intensive farming system also required a marketing system to redistribute the agricultural products. An incipient mercantile agriculture formed in the Eastern Zhou. Thereafter, Chinese farmers would further the same tradition.

3. *A secular urban network.* In the Eastern Zhou period, cities started to develop administrative and commercial functions rather than purely ceremonial and military ones. There was a differentiation of local towns, regional or state centers, and top-ranked cities at the national level. In later Chinese history an urban network was shaped that covered the whole country with a hierarchy of political and economic links.

4. *A this-worldly humanism.* Ever since the emergence of the concept of the mandate of Heaven and its revelation in the will of man, Zhou political philosophy had undergone a profound humanization of supernatural forces. In early Confucianism there was an ultimate concern with humanism. This attitude was in accord with the socioeconomic changes mentioned above and it was to remain the guiding principle in Chinese minds for many centuries.

Finally, the Zhou legacy should also include the concept that China was not only a nation but also a culture. The territory covered by the Chinese culture was China. It stretched from the edge of the northern steppes to the eastern and southern coasts. The constant struggle between different ancient states led to the formation of a nation of Chinese. Even the then-alien people of Chu, Wu, and Yue were brought into the Chinese nation through a long process of interactions. In the Eastern Zhou period the Chinese cultural sphere was defined. In the subsequent Qin/Han period political consolidation would permanently confirm the extensive domains of Chinese culture. It was in the Zhou period, therefore, that the Chinese culture gradually took on an enduring and distinctive form.

[See also Spring and Autumn Period and Warring States Period.]

Kwang-chih Chang, *The Archaeology of Ancient China* (3d ed., 1977). H. G. Creel, *The Origins of Statecraft in China,* vol. 1 (1970). Cho-yun Hsu, *Ancient China in Transition* (1965) and *Bibliographic Notes on Studies of Early China* (1982). Jaroslav Prušek, *Chinese Statelets and the Northern Barbarians: 1400–300 B.C.* (1971). Richard L. Walker, *The Multi-State System of Ancient China* (1953). William Watson, *Cultural Frontiers in Ancient East Asia* (1971).   CHO-YUN HSU

ZHOU YANG (b. 1908), Chinese leftist literary figure. A native of Yiyang, Hunan Province, Zhou studied in Shanghai's Daxia University (1926–1928) and in Japan (1928–1930). He wrote on literary criticism and translated Russian literature in Shanghai in the 1930s, joined the Chinese Communist Party (CCP), and was secretary-general of the League of Left-wing Writers. He went to the Communist headquarters at Yan'an in 1937, where he became the president of Lu Xun Art Academy.

Between the Communist takeover of China in 1949 and 1966, Zhou was deputy director of the CCP Propaganda Department. In this position, he ruthlessly purged the ranks of China's most creative writers and artists and campaigned against unorthodox thinking. In 1966 China's "cultural czar" suffered the same fate as his victims and was publicly disgraced, only to be rehabilitated in 1978 and appointed chairman of the All-China Federation of Literary and Art Circles.

[See also Hundred Flowers Campaign.]

PARRIS CHANG

ZHUANGZI, or "Master Zhuang," a Daoist philosopher of the late fourth century BCE, probably of the state of Song, one of the Warring States of ancient China. Zhuangzi, named Zhuang Zhou, is traditionally identified as the author of the Daoist classic *Zhuangzi* ([Book of] Master Zhuang). He shares with Laozi and Liezi the distinction of being one of the three creators of classical Daoism.

The present thirty-three-chapter text of the *Zhuangzi* was edited in the fourth century CE by the Neo-Daoist Guo Xiang. (A fifty-five-chapter version, now lost, was recorded in the first century BCE.) Recent scholarship suggests that the first seven chapters are the work of Zhuang Zhou himself; of the rest, some are the work of his own school; some, dated to around 200 BCE, are the work of other more or less similar schools; still others are miscellaneous compilations.

In Zhuang Zhou's time generations of disputation among rival schools had led, probably for the first time in China, to the examination of epistemology and the rules of logic. How do we know what we know, and what constitutes proof? Some thinkers even specialized in the study of such problems. These included Zhuang Zhou's friend and contemporary Hui Shi, the authors of the Mohist canons of around 300 BCE, and Gongsun Long, of the early third century BCE. Zhuang Zhou, as a Daoist, held to intuition as the only access to truth and rejected formal argumentation as necessarily inconclusive. Zhuang Zhou's stature as a thinker is attested by the fact that he used his own mastery of the rules of logic in order to demonstrate their futility.

A central problem for both Zhuang Zhou and Hui Shi was the relation between the plurality of things and the One (the Dao, or Way) that engenders and encompasses them. In one of his arguments, Zhuang Zhou demonstrated the impossibility of verbal definition of the Way by pointing out that the assertion that "the myriad things and I are one" involves a contradiction because the assertion itself is distinct from the "one" that it refers to, and the "one" plus the assertion equals two. In another instance he asserted that the conclusion of any argument was predetermined by the standpoint from which it was made and therefore could not be true in an absolute sense.

Having rejected reason and formal argumentation, Zhuang Zhou held that the Way could only be known directly, that is to say, by submitting to it unreservedly. This in turn required the liberation of the mind from conventional rules and norms and from the very idea of self. To this end he engaged in "quiet sitting" to "empty the mind."

Because liberation of the mind from conventional norms and patterns was prerequisite to direct apprehension of the truth, Zhuang Zhou was necessarily at odds with the followers of Confucius. Confucius is represented in the "Inner Chapters" of the *Zhuangzi* as a well-intentioned busybody who was destined to fall short in his own quest for truth because of his inability to overcome his fundamental dependence upon the traditions of the sage rulers and his beloved ceremonial. Worse, the Confucians' determined efforts to indoctrinate the world with their tradition-bound vision of order could only lead others astray.

While Zhuang Zhou used subtle logical analysis to demonstrate the futility of formal procedures and conventions, he used all the resources of poetry, imagination, myth, and metaphor to convey indirectly his experience of truth. Two of his strategies of exposition are especially noteworthy. One was to illustrate the Way by comparing the incommunicable "knack" of the skilled workman, which accomplishes its end without error and without wasted physical effort, to the laborious and ineffectual book learning of the upper classes. Another was to use death as a central theme, contrasting the Daoist sage's unresisting and even lyrical acceptance of the transforming power of the Way with the fear of death experienced by the unenlightened.

Overshadowed at first by the popularity of Laozi's *Daode jing*, the *Zhuangzi* (portions of which predate the *Daode jing*) began to enjoy great popularity in the third century, when the collapse of the Han dynasty and the attendant decline of Confucianism inspired the Neo-Daoist quest for a new spiritual haven. Since that time it has retained a central place in the Daoist canon.

[*See also* Daoism *and* Laozi.]

Chang Chung-yuan, "The Philosophy of Taoism According to Chuang Tzu," *Philosophy East and West* 27.4 (1977): 409–422. Norman J. Girardot, "Returning to the Beginning and the Arts of Mr. Hun-tun in the *Chuang Tzu*," *Journal of Chinese Philosophy* 5.1 (1978): 21–70. Angus C. Graham, trans., *Chuang-tzu: The Seven Inner Chapters and Other Writings from the Book* (1981). Burton Watson, *The Complete Works of Chuang Tzu* (1968).

ROMEYN TAYLOR

ZHU DE (1886–1976), Chinese revolutionary, the "father" of the Red Army, and a high-ranking leader of the Chinese Communist Party (CCP) and the People's Republic of China (PRC).

Zhu was born to a poor family in Yilong, Sichuan Province. In 1909 he attended the Yunnan Military Academy and joined the Tongmenghui, a revolutionary organization led by Sun Yat-sen. In 1911 Zhu participated in an armed uprising in Yunnan against the Qing dynasty and in subsequent years was an officer in the Yunnan army. In 1922 he gave up his career in Yunnan and went to Germany, where he met Zhou Enlai in Berlin, joined the CCP, and studied political science at the University of Göttingen.

Arrested twice and expelled by the German authorities for political activities in 1925, Zhu went to Russia and, after a short stay, returned to China in 1926 to carry on the revolution. In 1927 Zhu was made commander of the Officer's Training Regiment of the Third Army of the National Revolutionary Army commanded by the Guomindang general Zhu Peide. Concurrently serving as director of the Public Security Bureau of Nanchang, Zhu was an organizer and leader of the unsuccessful Nanchang Uprising on 1 August (the date has been commemorated as the Army Day). In 1928 Zhu, together with Mao Zedong, founded the Red Army; he was its highest officer in the following two decades. Zhu was appointed chairman of the Central Revolutionary Military Commission under the Chinese Soviet Republic; commander of the Eighth Route Army, the reorganized Communist forces (1937); and commander in chief of the People's Liberation Army (1946), on the eve of the civil war between the Communists and the Nationalists.

After the PRC was established in 1949, Zhu was successively vice-chairman of the Central People's Government Council (1949–1954); vice-chairman of the Republic (1954–1959); and chairman of the National People's Congress (1959–1976). He was elected to the CCP Politburo in 1934, and he retained his membership until his death. He was attacked by Red Guard publications and labeled "a big warlord and careerist" during the Cultural Revolution but was not purged. Zhu made major contributions to the Chinese Communist movement before 1949 but held no real power thereafter. He had four marriages; his fourth wife, Kang Keqing, remains a leading political figure in Beijing.

[*See also* China, People's Republic of; Communism: Chinese Communist Party; Chinese People's Liberation Army; *and* Mao Zedong.]

PARRIS CHANG

ZHU DI (1360–1424), third emperor of the Ming dynasty in China, also known by his princely title as the Prince of Yan, by his reign title as the Yongle emperor (r. 1402–1424), and by his posthumous honorific title as Chengzu.

The fourth son of the first Ming emperor, Zhu Yuanzhang, Zhu Di claimed descent as a son of the empress, although it is now generally thought that he was born to a lesser consort and that he later tampered with the records of his birth to enhance his status as a claimant to the throne. He was enfeoffed as the Prince of Yan in 1370 but did not take up residence at his fief, modern Beijing, until 1380. By that time he had been well educated at his father's court and had been trained in military arts by his father's generals. During the 1380s, when he was in his twenties, he served as an aide to one of his father's generals and took part in campaigns against the Mongols. In 1390 he was given his own command and in 1396 drove the Mongols from their pasturelands in the bend of the Yellow River.

Despite these successes, when Zhu Di's eldest brother, the heir apparent, died in 1392, the first Ming emperor designated his grandson the heir apparent. Zhu Di apparently had hoped that he might be named heir instead, but his father insisted on strictly observing the principle of inheritance by primogeniture. Thus, when the first Ming emperor died in 1398, he was succeeded by his twenty-year-old grandson, whose major concern was how to break the power of his uncles, in particular Zhu Di. By 1399 five of Zhu Di's brothers had been deposed, and he rose in rebellion against his nephew. In the summer of 1401, after three years of civil war, Zhu Di entered Nanjing in triumph and declared himself emperor. His young nephew disappeared in the confusion; a charred corpse dragged from the ruins of the imperial palace was alleged to have been his body, but it was also rumored that he had escaped and fled.

For the next two decades Zhu Di, now the Yongle emperor, implemented a number of policies designed to consolidate and expand his father's empire. He was not content simply to guard his patrimony: he wanted to expand it and to create a universal empire on the model of the preceding Mongolian Yuan dynasty. To this end he campaigned on the Mongolian steppe for more than a decade, hoping thereby to bring the Mongol hordes under his hegemony. He dispatched the eunuch Zheng He with a very large navy to Southeast Asia to eradicate piracy and to gain control of the trade routes to India and the Islamic world. He also moved the capital of the Ming empire from Nanjing in the south to Beijing in the north. The relocation of the capital had far-reaching consequences, for it entailed the reorganization of the entire empire. Grain and other supplies had to be transported from the rich lands of the south and southeast to the far north. Eventually the whole Ming fiscal system was restructured to supply the court in Beijing.

Zhu Di died on campaign in Mongolia in 1424. Although efforts were made to reverse or dismantle many of his policies, little came of them. In many ways his policies, more than those of his father, shaped and constrained the course of Ming history for the next two centuries.

[See also Grand Secretariat; Ming Dynasty; Zheng He; and Zhu Yuanzhang.]

Edward L. Dreyer, *Early Ming Government: A Political History, 1355–1435* (1982).   JAMES GEISS

ZHUGE LIANG (181–234), statesman and strategist in China during the late Han and Three Kingdoms period. In 207 he met Liu Bei and began to plan the creation of the Shu Han kingdom. Zhuge helped Liu defeat the well-known general Cao Cao in the famous battle of Chibi. By 221 Liu was able to declare himself emperor. Zhuge, as his chancellor, increased state income by improving silk and salt production and by enlarging the state. Zhuge was a good administrator, but was unsuccessful as a military leader. Zhuge Liang's renown is due on the one hand to two memorials setting forth his Confucian loyalty to the Liu regime and on the other to his Legalistic impartiality in bestowing rewards and punishments. In popular literature he is depicted as a military genius with supernatural powers.

[See also Three Kingdoms *and* Liu Bei.]

JACK L. DULL

ZHU XI (1130–1200), Chinese scholar and philosopher, one of the formulators of Neo-Confucian thought. Zhu was born in Youqi County, Fujian Province, where his father was the subprefectural sheriff.

In 1140 Zhu's father, forced from office because of his outspoken criticism of the Song policy of appeasement toward the Jurchen Jin dynasty, began to instruct Zhu Xi at home. Here Zhu was taught the ideas of Cheng Yi (1032–1107), the Neo-Confucian master of the Northern Song, and the relatively brief canonical texts, *The Great Learning (Daxue)* and *The Doctrine of the Mean (Zhongyong)*. When his father died in 1143, the young Zhu began attending various Daoist and Buddhist schools. According to his own comments, his fascination with Buddhist teachings continued for about ten years, ending when he was twenty-six or twenty-seven. The degree to which his Neo-Confucian teachings may have been directly influenced by Buddhist ideas remains problematic for scholars. There is little doubt, however, that the vigor with which he would later refute Buddhist teachings was affected by what he personally knew their allure to be.

In 1148, his commitment to Confucian teachings still not altogether firm, Zhu Xi passed the *jinshi* civil service examination. That he received the degree at such a young age perhaps helps to explain his prodigious scholarly output. For Zhu could devote those years that most literate Chinese spent preparing for the civil service examinations to independent scholarship. Having passed the examinations, Zhu was appointed subprefectural registrar of Tongan in 1151, a post he took up in 1153 and held until 1158. He conscientiously supervised the local registers there, promoted education, strengthened city defenses, and reported on public morality. He did not hold another important office until 1179 but maintained himself in sinecurial positions.

This period from 1158 to 1179 was an extremely productive one for Zhu the scholar. He wrote and edited about twenty works and at the same time developed close associations with the most prominent scholars and philosophers of the day. For instance, he engaged in discussion of "centrality and harmony" *(zhonghe)* with Zhang Shi (1133–1180), compiled the influential *Jinsi lu (Reflections on Things at Hand)* (1175) with Lü Zuqian (1137–1181), and debated with Lu Xiangshan (Lu Jiuyuan; 1139–1193) at Goose Lake Temple (1175) over the relative importance of "following the path of inquiry and study" *(dao wenxue)* and "honoring the moral nature" *(zun dexing)*. Zhu and Lu would never reconcile the philosophical differences aired at Goose Lake Temple, Zhu insisting on the primacy of inquiry and study, Lu on the primacy of honoring the moral nature. The consequences of these differences were profound; Neo-Confucianism would later split into what has conventionally been characterized as Zhu Xi's School of Principle and Lu Xiangshan's School of Mind.

In 1179 Zhu became the prefect of Nankang (in present Jiangxi Province). There his commitment to education continued, best evidenced by his efforts to revive the White Deer Grotto Academy. His enthusiastic promotion of a private academy in Nankang, an area with its own government school, demonstrates the displeasure Zhu Xi felt at the time toward the learning found in the government schools. According to Zhu, learning for the sake of succeeding in the examinations had come to eclipse what he called "true learning." In restoring the White Deer Grotto Academy, Zhu Xi sought to establish a refuge of learning where students could engage in disinterested study. The *Articles of Learning (Xuegui)* that Zhu Xi wrote for the academy reflect his zealous devotion to learning for the sake of one's own moral improvement, not for the sake of examination success. These articles would have a profound influence not only in China; they served

as model articles for academies in much of East Asia down through the twentieth century.

Zhu Xi's term at Nankang expired in 1181. In 1182 he assumed the duties of Intendant for Ever-normal Granaries, Tea, and Salt for Eastern Liangzhe (present Zhejiang), an area suffering from famine. To alleviate the suffering, he instituted the community granary *(shecang)*, the purpose of which was to provide grain loans to peasants at low rates of interest. It is difficult to know what success Zhu might have had with the community granary system, for he had but brief opportunity to implement it. In 1182, having indicted Tang Zhongyou, the prefect of Taizhou and a relative of the prime minister, for misconduct in office, he found himself an enemy of the most powerful men in the empire. Not only Zhu, but the entire philosophical school with which he was associated, Daoxue ("school of the Way"), now came under attack by high-ranking supporters of Tang. Shortly thereafter Zhu Xi withdrew from office.

Zhu held two other important posts, albeit briefly: he served as prefect of Zhangzhou (Fujian Province) from 1190 to 1191 and prefect of Tanzhou (present Hunan) in 1194. In late 1194 he was invited to become lecturer-in-waiting at court, where he lectured to Emperor Ningzong on the brief classic, *The Great Learning*. This lectureship lasted a mere forty-six days, for Zhu became embroiled in a conflict with the influential imperial relative Han Tuozhou (1151–1207) and returned to Fujian. The attack on Daoxue intensified at this time, and in 1196 it was equated with *weixue*, "false learning," and proscribed by the emperor himself.

During his lifetime Zhu Xi declined many more offices than he accepted; he served in public office for only about nine years, the rest of the time holding temple guardianships. Zhu's apparent unwillingness to serve has been called the defensive reaction of an insecure person. More likely, it is the considered reaction of a person who in his childhood witnessed his father's abrupt and painful dismissal from office over a policy difference with a powerful statesman. Perhaps Zhu also simply wished to avoid what he viewed as the corrupt and unethical politics of the day; to serve when the Way did not prevail might compromise his moral purity. In any case, by avoiding office Zhu Xi was no doubt able to devote more time to teaching and writing. This is not to suggest that Zhu had little interest in the political order. Not only did he acquit himself with distinction in the offices he did hold, but he also submitted sealed memorials to the throne and even went to the capital for personal audiences with the emperor. Certain themes run through these memorials and personal audiences: the emperor, Zhu argued, must rectify his mind and only then might the empire become tranquil (the central message of *The Great Learning*); the military must be made strong so that the central plain, the traditional heartland of Chinese civilization, might be recovered from the Jin; and the emperor must establish sound personnel policies, selecting only worthy and talented men for government service.

Still, it was teaching and writing that were most dear to Zhu. Throughout his life he exhibited an almost missionary zeal to transmit the Confucian Way to others. In his view, the widespread popularity of Buddhist teachings posed a threat to the survival of the Confucian tradition; indeed, the occupation of North China by the Jin "barbarians" served to demonstrate how weak and lifeless the tradition had already become. If the Confucian Way were not made more intelligible and meaningful to the people of his day, it would not survive and China's great cultural tradition would come to an end. The numerous years he spent discussing Confucian teachings with students, the record of which is found in *Zhuzi yulei (The Conversations of Master Zhu in Categories)*, attest strongly to his commitment to transmitting the Way to others; so too do his voluminous writings, particularly his many commentaries on the Confucian classics, which he hoped would help to illuminate the Way embodied in the sacred canon.

Of all Zhu's writings perhaps the most significant were the commentaries on the Four Books *(Sishu jizhu; The Collected Commentaries on the Four Books)*. Zhu Xi spent nearly forty years, from 1163 until three days before his death, writing and revising his commentaries on *The Great Learning, The Analects, The Book of Mencius,* and *The Doctrine of the Mean*. It was in these commentaries that Zhu developed much of his philosophical program.

Convinced that the kernels of Confucian teachings were to be found in the Four Books, Zhu had his students read them before all the other texts in the Confucian tradition, even before the Five Classics—*The Book of Changes (Yijing), The Book of History (Shujing), The Book of Poetry (Shijing), The Book of Rites (Liji),* and *The Spring and Autumn Annals (Chunqiu)*. Hitherto, the Five Classics had been the central texts in the tradition, but from Zhu's time on, the Four Books, together with Zhu Xi's commentaries on them, would serve as the essential works in the Confucian curriculum. Indeed, in 1313, under Yuan rule, they were made the basic texts in the civil service examinations, and they served as such until the abolition of the examination system in the early years of the twentieth century. Few works conditioned the post-Song Chinese intellectual tradition as profoundly as Zhu's exposition of the Four Books.

Indeed, Zhu Xi's greatest achievement, the development of a systematic metaphysics, derived largely from his reading of the Four Books. This reading, in turn, was influenced by ideas advanced by the great thinkers of the Northern Song, men such as Zhou Dunyi (1017–1073), Zhang Zai (1020–1077), Cheng Hao (1032–1085), and Cheng Yi. The concepts of *li* ("principle") and *qi* ("psychophysical stuff") constituted the backbone of his philosophical system. According to Zhu, there was a supreme principle in the universe; each thing—an object, an event, or a relationship—in the universe had its specific principle, which was but a manifestation of the supreme principle. Principle was both the reason why a thing was as it was and the rule to which a thing should conform. *Qi* was the stuff of which the entire universe and all things (including functions and activities of the mind) in it were composed. It was the relative density and purity of each thing's *qi* that gave the thing its peculiar form and individual characteristics. The relationship between principle and *qi* was clearly stated by Zhu: "There has never been any *qi* without principle nor any principle without *qi*." The two entities could not exist independently of each other; without principle the *qi* had no ontological reason for being, and without *qi* principle had nothing to which it might adhere.

Man, like everything else in the universe, was endowed with both principle and *qi*. Principle in man was identical with his human nature. Here Zhu followed the Mencian belief that human nature was originally good and pure, but he gave this early Confucian theory an ontological basis—for him, it was because human nature was principle that it was naturally good. Evil arose in man because his particular allotment of *qi*, the amount and quality of which varied from man to man, was dense or impure and so obscured his nature. The degree of difficulty the individual had in manifesting or realizing his nature depended upon the purity of his *qi*. The aim of the Confucian self-cultivation process was to refine the endowment of *qi* so that the inborn brilliance of one's nature would shine forth without impediment. This was the purpose behind *ge wu*, "apprehending the principle in things." By studying the principle in things external to himself, man could come to know the principle within himself, principle being everywhere the same. Since principle in man was his nature, understanding of principle would lead to the full realization of his nature. Apprehending principle then was nothing other than a means of becoming a fully human, fully moral individual. Thus, in the end, Zhu's metaphysics can be described as a philosophical anthropology, a philosophy concerned primarily with the nature of man and how to realize that nature.

Zhu Xi died on 23 April 1200. Eight years later, after the attacks on Daoxue had run their course, he was honored with the posthumous title Wen. In 1230 he was made state duke of Hui, and in 1241 his tablet was placed in the Confucian temple. In the early fourteenth century Zhu Xi's thought would be declared state orthodoxy.

[See also Song Dynasty; Neo-Confucianism; Lu Xiangshan; Zhou Dunyi; Zhang Zai; and Cheng Brothers.]

Wing-tsit Chan, "Chu Hsi's Completion of Neo-Confucianism," in Études Song: In Memoriam Étienne Balazs, edited by Francoise Aubin, series 2, no. 1 (1973), pp. 69–87. Daniel K. Gardner, Chu Hsi and the Ta-hsüeh: Neo-Confucian Reflection on the Confucian Canon (1985). Conrad M. Schirokauer, "Chu Hsi's Political Career: A Study in Ambivalence," in Confucianism in Action, edited by Arthur Wright and Denis Twitchett (1962), pp. 162–188.   DANIEL K. GARDNER

ZHU YUANZHANG (1328–1398), Chinese military leader who rose from peasant origins to found the Ming dynasty in 1368. He ruled until his death at the age of seventy. His posthumous temple name was Taizu ("great ancestor") and his reign title was Hongwu ("vast martial glory").

It was partly for a lack of leadership in other quarters that the Ming was founded by a peasant. Under the alien rule of the Yuan dynasty, effective military power was monopolized by the Mongol nobility and their foreign associates. Chinese military families were relegated to an auxiliary role. Meanwhile, the literati either entered the service of the Mongols as civil officials or tended their own estates. With few exceptions they either actively supported the regime or stood aside while the military and political initiative passed into the hands of a rabble of small farmers, fishermen, salt workers, artisans, itinerant peddlers, and millenarian preachers.

Zhu Yuanzhang was born into a poor family of the Huai River county of Haozhou. In 1344 a shift in the course of the Yellow River caused floods,

famine, and epidemics. Zhu's family was nearly obliterated. Later in life, Zhu bitterly recalled that the survivors had no land of their own in which to give their dead a decent burial. Zhu, now destitute, presented himself to the local Buddhist monastery as a novice or servant, but he soon was turned out again when the food was gone. His subsequent wanderings took him through a Huai Valley region that had become a hotbed of social unrest. When he was able to return to the monastery in 1348 he may already have made contact with agents of the imminent revolt of the messianic White Lotus Society. After another three years the rebellion had begun and his monastic refuge was burned to the ground by the Yuan militia. Homeless again and afraid for his life, Zhu entered the nearby county seat of Haozhou, which had just been captured by White Lotus rebels. Here he entered the household of their leader as a guardsman, and married the man's adopted daughter, the future Empress Ma.

Dismayed by the chaotic politics of the local rebel leaders, Zhu soon began to distance himself from them, even while formally remaining within the White Lotus regime. He attracted to his service a small band of able soldiers of varied, but always plebeian, social origin. To these he added a few learned men who served him and his generals as advisers and secretaries, and who later became leading administrators in the early years of the Ming.

Military successes, won usually against hastily mobilized and badly led militias, swelled Zhu's army and enabled him to occupy Nanjing in 1356. Acclaimed by his followers as duke of Wu, he proceeded to develop the civil and military organs that were later to be elevated from regional to imperial status. After disposing of his most powerful rivals, Chen Youliang and Zhang Shicheng, Zhu prepared for his assumption of the throne. In 1367 he arranged the assassination of Han Liner, ruler of the White Lotus regime, and began construction of the altars of the imperial cult at Nanjing. [See also Chen Youliang; Zhang Shicheng; Han Liner; and White Lotus Society.]

Buoyed by auspicious signs from Heaven, Zhu was enthroned in January 1368—the only peasant to found a major Chinese dynasty. This fact shaped his despotic rule. His astonishing intellectual vigor allowed him to gain a rough grasp of Neo-Confucian principles and of the classical texts. Thus armed, he held the upper hand over the literati whom he recruited to fill out the thin ranks of his civil administration. The emperor regarded his civil officials with contempt and suspicion, and he feared the unsatisfied ambitions of his old comrades-in-arms. He instituted treason trials that decimated and demoralized the bureaucracy at every level. Inspired by an autocratic ideal that owed more to Daoist than Confucian inspiration, he abolished the highest organs of government, concentrated power in his own hands, and redesigned the imperial sacrifices to Lord of Heaven and Empress Earth in accordance with his view of the cosmic order. The return of native rule to China had become a nightmare to the literati.

Zhu's goals as emperor were marked by a utopian vision of quiet villages, obedient officials, and a modest livelihood for all. To realize this vision, he ordained a system of universal education and flooded the empire with his own exhortatory tracts, but when he was threatened with failure, he resorted to measures of extreme violence. Zhu left an ambiguous legacy that included nearly three hundred years of political unity within secure frontiers, a revitalized agricultural economy, a law code that endured with little change until the twentieth century, a government autocratic in form and harsh in style, and a memory of bloody bureaucratic purges.

[See also Red Turbans; Yuan Dynasty; Hu Wei-yong; Ming Dynasty; and Zhu Di.]

John W. Dardess, *Confucianism and Autocracy: Professional Elites in the Founding of the Ming Dynasty* (1983). Edward L. Dreyer, *Early Ming China* (1982). Edward L. Farmer, *Early Ming Government* (1976). Charles O. Hucker, *The Ming Dynasty: Its Origins and Evolving Institutions* (1978). Romeyn Taylor, trans., *The Basic Annals of Ming T'ai-tsu* (1975).   ROMEYN TAYLOR

ZIA-UL HAQ, MOHAMMAD (b. 1924), military leader and president of Pakistan since 1978. Zia-ul Haq was born in the present Punjab Province of India. He received his army commission from the military academy, Dehra Dun, in 1945. During World War II he saw action in Southeast Asia. In 1947 he joined the Pakistan Army and received additional military training in the United States. Between 1969 and 1971, on loan to Jordan, Zia directed action against Palestinian guerrillas and was decorated by King Hussain. Prime Minister Bhutto made him a full general and chief of staff of the Pakistan Army in 1976.

In 1977, during the agitation of opposition parties against Bhutto's handling of national elections, Zia proclaimed martial law, removed Bhutto from office, and promised to hold fresh elections. These elections were later cancelled and Zia declared the "islamization of Pakistan" as his first priority. In 1978 Zia became president of Pakistan but continued to govern under martial law. Without a popular mandate to rule, he has relied heavily on the external support of his regime by the United States and its Arab allies. In August 1983 the Movement for Restoration of Democracy, an alliance of banned political parties, launched a mass resistance to Zia's regime that was crushed by military action.

[See also Bhutto, Zulfiqar Ali *and* Pakistan.]

Tariq Ali, *Can Pakistan Survive?* (1983). Charles Moritz, ed., *Current Biography, 1980* (1981).

HASSAN N. GARDEZI

ZIKAWEI. See Xujiahui.

ZIYARID DYNASTY. The Ziyarids were one of the many semiautonomous petty dynasties that flourished in northern Iran during the tenth century. The family claimed descent from the pre-Islamic local ruler of Gilan, a small province near the southwestern shores of the Caspian Sea, and was definitely related to the dominant "noble" clan in the Dakhil district near the mouth of the Safid Rud River.

The region from which the Ziyarids came was famous for the military qualities of its inhabitants: the anonymous Persian geographical treatise *Hudud al-alam* noted that in Dakhil and adjacent districts agriculture was left to the women and "the men have no other business but warfare." Their aggressive energy was usually dissipated in constant tribal conflict; however, during the ninth and tenth centuries these warriors tended to enter the armed forces of various Muslim powers and occasionally to succeed in establishing principalities of their own. This was the pattern followed by the founder of the Ziyarid "dynasty," Mardavij ibn Ziyar.

Mardavij first appeared in the service of another Dailamite general, Asfar, who was himself acting as a vassal of the Samanid dynasty of eastern Iran. As the result of some rather murky intrigues, Mardavij was able in 930 to massacre the chiefs of the tribe to which Asfar belonged and then to persuade most of Asfar's remaining troops to defect. Asfar then fled, and Mardavij went on to conquer a sizable territory stretching from Gorgan in northeastern Iran to Hamadan and Dinawar in the west and Ahwaz in the south. After these successes, Mardavij apparently began plans for an assault on Baghdad; supposedly he was scheming to destroy the Abbasid caliphate, to restore the Iranian empire, or even to conquer the whole world. These grandiose plans were abruptly ended in 935 when Mardavij was assassinated by some of his four thousand Turkish slave-troops *(mamluks)*, who were outraged by his abuse of them (and perhaps alarmed by the extent of his ambitions).

Most of Mardavij's conquests were seized after his death by rivals, notably the Buyids, another family of Dailamite soldiers of fortune. However, the Dailamite/Gilani tribal contingents in his army remained loyal to his brother Vushmgir (935–967), who was thus able to salvage control of the Caspian provinces with his principal base of power in Gorgan. Vushmgir and his successors retained some measure of autonomy over this area by voluntarily acting as the vassals of their more powerful neighbors, who included the Buyids but more typically the rulers of eastern Iran: the Samanids, Ghaznavids, and Seljuks, in succession. Of the later Ziyarid rulers only one, Shams al-Ma'ali Qabus (978–1012), enjoyed relative independence and was recognized as a legitimate ruler by the Abbasid caliphate. The Ziyarid dependence on the protection of the eastern Iranian dynasties and the recognition of the caliphs may explain why they, unlike many of the other dynasties of northwestern Iran, were careful to adhere to Sunni Islam in their religious policy.

The Seljuks took direct control of the Caspian provinces toward the middle of the eleventh century, but some petty Ziyarid rulers survived this takeover. The last known member of the dynasty was Gilan Shah (fl. 1080s?).

Politically, the Ziyarids were of little significance. They did make some important contributions to the cultural history of their period. Qabus extended the hospitality of his court to many scholars, notably the scientist and antiquarian Biruni, who dedicated his *Al-athar al-baqiyya (Surviving Monuments)* to Qabus. Qabus's grandson, Kay Ka'us, is especially noteworthy as the author of the *Qabusnama*, one of the finest examples of the Persian *andarz* ("mirror for princes") genre of literature.

[*See also* Abbasid Dynasty *and* Gilan.]

C. E. Bosworth, "On the Chronology of the Later Ziyārids in Gurgān and Tabaristān," *Der Islam* 40 (1964): 24–34. Kay Kā'ūs ibn Iskandar, *A Mirror for Princes: the Qābūs-nāma*, translated by R. Levy (1951).

E. L. DANIEL

ZONGLI YAMEN, subcommittee of the Chinese Grand Council; served as a proto–foreign office at Beijing from 1861 to 1901. China's first major institutional innovation in response to the Western impact, the Zongli Yamen promoted modernization and symbolized China's entrance into the family of nations. To handle diplomatic relations with the West arising from various treaty obligations, the Zongli Yamen (Office for the General Management of Affairs Concerning the Various Countries) was created in March 1861. It was an informal organization, composed of between three and eleven high officials who retained their principal posts elsewhere. It was organized into five bureaus (Russian, British, French, American, and Coastal Defense), with two other offices attached to it: the Maritime Customs Service and the language school called the Tongwenguan.

The Zongli Yamen used international law to protect China's interests in 1864, sponsored the Binchun mission (the first Chinese mission of investigation sent to Europe) in 1866, and secured Anson Burlingame (the retiring American minister to China) as China's first envoy to the Western world in 1868. While the Zongli Yamen marked a forward step, it had weaknesses. All real decisions on foreign policy still had to come from the emperor, and the Yamen was in charge of foreign relations only at Beijing (in the coastal provinces two commissioners for foreign affairs were appointed who reported directly to the emperor).

Although it failed as an effective foreign office, the Yamen, headed by Prince Gong for twenty-seven years (1861–1884 and 1894–1898), succeeded reasonably well as a promoter of modernization projects, such as modern schools, Western science, industry, and communication. The Zongli Yamen's influence diminished after the 1870s, when Prince Gong lost power with Empress Dowager Cixi and the rise of Li Hongzhang in Tianjin overshadowed the Yamen. It was finally replaced by the newly created Ministry of Foreign Affairs in 1901.

[*See also* Gong Yixin; Grand Council; Maritime Customs Service; *and* Qing Dynasty.]

Masataka Banno, *China and the West, 1858–1861: The Origins of the Tsungli Yamen* (1964). Ssu-ming Meng, *The Tsungli Yamen: Its Organization and Functions* (1962).

YEN-P'ING HAO

ZOROASTER (Avestan, Zarathushtra), ancient Iranian prophet and founder of Zoroastrianism. Zoroaster lived probably in the region of Chorasmia, since the eastern Iranian language in which he preached, Avestan, has affinities with the later dialects of that country, but opinions about when he lived vary widely, from about 1500–1200 to about 700–600 BCE. Interpretations of the many obscure passages in Zoroaster's hymns, the *Gathas*, differ accordingly: H. S. Nyberg, (*Die Religionen des Alten Iran,* 1938), accepting an early date, presents Zoroaster as a primitive shaman uttering ecstatic and incoherent verses, while E. Herzfeld (1947) regards the prophet as an astute statesman and finds veiled allusions in the *Gathas* to the policies of the early Achaemenids.

Neither of these two opinions is likely to be correct, but T. Burrow (1973) has demonstrated that Zoroaster's language bears archaic affinities to Old Indian and that only in the later texts of the slowly evolving Avestan tongue can recognizable place names be found, as Zoroaster's religion spread from Central Asia southwest into eastern Iran and Media. Yet still no place names from Pars can be found; Zoroaster must have lived, therefore, long before the Persian Achaemenids; indeed, before 1000 BCE. Most available information about the prophet's life comes from legends, probably very ancient, which were only set down in writing in the Middle Persian (Pahlavi) books composed in the ninth century CE. One of these, the *Selections of Zadspram,* relates various miracles at the time of Zoroaster's birth.

Attacked by evil spirits but protected by the beneficent gods, the prophet was trained in the priestly family of a pastoral tribe; his name means "one who possesses golden camels." He left home at the age of twenty, full of questions about the nature of good and evil, and, presumably, about the true meaning of the elaborate rites of the Indo-Iranian religion. At the end of ten years' wandering in the wilderness he received the revelation coherently proclaimed in the *Gathas.* He married, had children, and at forty-two converted King Vishtaspa to the new faith. At seventy-seven Zoroaster was murdered by a priest of the old religion.

[*See also* Zoroastrianism.]

Mary Boyce, *History of Zoroastrianism,* vol. 1 (1975). T. Burrow, "The Proto-Indoaryans," *Journal of the Royal Asiatic Society* (1973). W. B. Henning, *Zoroaster: Politician or Witch-Doctor* (1951). E. Herzfeld, *Zoroaster and His World,* 2 vols. (1947).   JAMES R. RUSSELL

ZOROASTRIANISM, the religion of pre-Islamic Iran founded by the prophet Zoroaster. Zoroastrianism became the official creed of the Achaemenid, Parthian, and Sasanid empires.

The fundamental tenets of the faith are set forth in the Avesta (meaning something like "authoritative utterance"), a collection of theological and ritual texts in the Old Iranian language of Zoroaster's own hymns, the *Gathas* (which form the core of the Avesta, only a small part of which survives), and in a later dialect called Younger Avestan. Part of the Middle Persian *Zand,* a translation and commentary on the Avestan text, also survives. A number of theological works that reflect ancient traditions survive in Pahlavi. Other sources include the works of Greek and Latin authors, the inscriptions of the Achaemenids and Sasanids, and the writings of later Arab historians.

Zoroaster's tribe practiced a polytheistic religion akin to Vedic Hinduism, in which offerings were made through fire to powerful gods, the *daevas* (Sanskrit, *deva*); a drink made of the intoxicant *haoma* (Sanskrit, *soma*) was prepared ritually (Avestan, *yasna;* Sanskrit, *yajna*); and sacred verses (Avestan, *manthra;* Sanskrit, *mantra*) were composed by priests. In pagan Iran, as in Vedic India, the gods were seen to personify both human characteristics and natural phenomena and to uphold cosmic order (Sanskrit, *rta;* Avestan, *asha;* Old Persian, *arta;* Greek, *arete*). Zoroaster, himself a priest learned in ritual and trained in the composition of religious poetry, was troubled by the often amoral behavior ascribed to the *daevas* and by the violence practiced in their cult and seen in the human and natural world. The answer to his questions came in the revelation of a cosmic dualism proclaimed in all its essentials in the *Gathas* and amplified, though never altered in its ethical character, in all later Zoroastrian literature, notably the Pahlavi *Bundahishn (Creation).*

According to the *Gathas* and other texts, Ahura Mazda, the Wise Lord, and Angra Mainyu, the Destructive Spirit (Pahlavi, Ohrmazd, Ahriman) existed from eternity as wholly separate entities, the first entirely good and all-knowing but not all-powerful, the second evil and implacably hostile. Ahura Mazda, whose desire is increase and beneficence, created the world and invited Angra Mainyu to forsake evil and to partake of the goodness of material being. Angra Mainyu refused, promising instead to corrupt the world, but Ahura Mazda in his omniscience knew that his adversary should be trapped, defeated, and cast from existence in time, lest he invade the material creation. The creator had formed the world through seven lesser divinities, evocations of himself, called the Amesha Spentas ("bounteous immortals"), who guard and personify various of the good creations, while embodying divine attributes. For example, Asha Vahishta ("best righteousness") protects the creation of fire, which with its warmth, light, and energy is said to pervade all the other creations; it remains the living icon of Zoroastrians, who are often mistakenly called fire-worshipers. The cosmic order or rightness Asha Vahishta represents should likewise pervade the moral, spiritual, and temporal worlds. The Amesha Spentas in their turn emanated lesser divinities, the *yazatas* ("beings worthy to be worshiped"), among whom are gods of the pagan pantheon whose moral qualities are consonant with Zoroastrianism, such as Mithra (Sanskrit, Mitra), the lord of covenants.

The *fravashis,* or incorruptible spirits of men, are said to have made a primordial covenant with their creator to assume physical form and to aid Ahura Mazda in the cosmic struggle against evil, but in the present, "mixed" state of the world (Pahlavi, *gumezishn*), in which the good creations have been polluted through the invasion of Ahriman, the souls of men (Pahlavi, *ruwan*) possess free will. They are positively enjoined to procreate, to enjoy in moderation the good things of life, and to further the Good Religion, as Zoroastrianism is called by its adherents, through good thoughts, words, and deeds. Ultimately a savior (Avestan, Saoshyant) will be born of the preserved seed of Zoroaster, the dead will be resurrected and judged, the damned will be annihilated, and the righteous will enjoy eternal earthly bliss.

At about age seven (fifteen in ancient times), the Zoroastrian becomes a full member of the community and assumes moral responsibility for his or her actions with the ceremony of binding the sacred girdle (New Persian, *kusti;* the ceremony is called Navjote, "newborn," among the Parsis). Particular stress is laid upon observance of the laws of purity, as death and disease are regarded as demonic assaults upon the good creation. Accordingly, corpses are exposed in so-called towers of silence to be picked clean by birds rather than being allowed to pollute earth or fire by interment or cremation. After death, the soul rises to heaven to be judged and is sent to await the resurrection, or the renovation of the world (Pahlavi, *frashegird*), and final judgment, in paradise, hell, or limbo (Pahlavi, *hammistagan*). Zoroastrian concepts of heaven, hell, salvation by a good shepherd, resurrection, and the last judgment antedate the appearance of these ideas in Judaism and Christianity, and Islam owes to Zoroastrianism, in addition to the foregoing, the five daily times of prayer, the bridge (Arabic, *sirat*) of judgment, and the idea of the preeternal covenant between God and man (Qur'an 7:172).

All obligatory Zoroastrian rites may be solemnized by priests (the magi, later called *mobads*) be-fore the ritually pure hearth fire, but around the mid-Achaemenid period a temple cult of fire was instituted, probably in response to the establishment of shrines with images of the *yazatas* on the Babylonian model. The holiest grade of temple fire, the *atakhsh i warahran* (Pahlavi, apparently meaning "victorious fire") is elaborately consecrated and must be kept permanently ablaze. Three such fires, Adur Burzen Mihr in Parthia, Adur Gushnasp in Media, and Adur Farnbag in Persia, were particularly famed under the Sasanids; Adur Farnbag still burns in a temple outside Yazd, Iran.

The main feast of the Zoroastrian year is Now Ruz, the vernal new year, which honors fire and anticipates the eternal spring of the renovation; six other seasonal feasts (Pahlavi, *gahambar*) commemorate the creation of the sky, water, earth, plants, animals, and man. In ancient times the feasts of Mithra and Tiri (Mihragan and Tiragan) were also celebrated in royal splendor. The endowments established by individuals for the regular public celebration of feasts are believed to have provided the model for the Islamic *waqf*.

During the Achaemenid period, Zoroastrians came into contact with Mesopotamian civilization: several alien divinities were adapted to Iranian *yazatas;* the myth of the deluge was worked into the Indo-Iranian legend of the primal king, Yima (Sanskrit, Yama; New Persian, Jamshid); and the twelve-thousand-year Babylonian world cycle was fitted to the cosmic drama, with the onslaught of Angra Mainyu dated to the six-thousandth year after creation, and *frashegird* to the twelve-thousandth year. Most significantly, a god of time, Zurvan, was established in priestly doctrine as the single progenitor of Ahura Mazda and Angra Mainyu. This heretical doctrine, expunged from Zoroastrianism after the Sasanid period and never pervasive in the faith, may have evolved as a response to Western monist doctrines.

Although Zurvanism, established in Persia, was the official doctrine of the Sasanids, the ethical dualism of the religion was never altered, and the Zoroastrians retained their unique and separate character among the great religions as adherents of cosmic dualism. There was little proselytism, although the faith had been embraced by various Iranian peoples and by a few other nations with close cultural and dynastic ties to Iran, notably the Armenians, and although Zoroastrian influence on the religions of Iran's neighbors was strong. The stringent requirements of the faith, and the national traditions intertwined with its teachings, may have combined to repel outsiders and to persuade Iranians that their religion was meant for them alone, for the three great dynasties suffered large foreign communities to flourish in Iran and ruled other lands tolerantly, persecuting infidels only when they proselytized among influential Iranians or were seen to favor an external enemy, such as Christian Byzantium. But the authoritative Pahlavi *Denkard (Acts of the Religion)* states uncompromisingly that the religion is meant for all men, of all races; Zoroaster's own *Gathas* likewise envisage a world faith.

Within Iran, two major religious and social movements were born out of Zoroastrianism—Manichaeism and Mazdakism. They were violently suppressed in Iran and left no lasting influence on the faith, although the first became a great and influential religion, from China to Europe, while the second survived the Sasanids to play a role in altered form in early Islam.

Zoroastrianism waned gradually in the three centuries following the Arab conquest of Iran in 651 CE; in the tenth century, a small group of the faithful from the forcibly islamicized province of Khurasan fled to Gujarat in India. At present about ninety thousand Zoroastrians, called Parsis (i.e., Persians), live in India, mainly in the Bombay area. Another twenty thousand remain in Iran, in Tehran, Yazd, and Kerman, survivors of a millennium of systematic persecution and massacre by Islam; and five thousand or more live in other parts of the world, particularly Great Britain and America. The community, which accepts no converts, is dwindling rapidly through intermarriage and a low birthrate. It adheres conservatively to ancient rituals, but theological learning has suffered greatly from the introduction of theosophical, monist, and other doctrines adopted as a defensive response to British Christian proselytism among the Parsis in the nineteenth century.

[*See also* Ahura Mazda; Anahita; Avesta; Bundahishn; Denkard; Fire Temple; Haoma; Manichaeism; Mazdak; Medes; Mithra; Now Ruz; Pahlavi; Parsis; Tower of Silence; *and* Zoroaster.]

Mary Boyce, *A History of Zoroastrianism*, vols. 1 (1975) and 2 (1982) of *Handbuch der Orientalistik*, edited by Bertold Spuler; and *Zoroastrians: Their Religious Beliefs and Practices* (1979). Richard N. Frye, *The Heritage of Persia* (2d ed., 1976). J. R. Hinnells, *Persian Mythology* (1973). A. V. W. Jackson, *Zoroaster, the Prophet of Ancient Iran* (1899). R. C. Zaehner, *The Dawn and Twilight of Zoroastrianism* (1961) and *The Teachings of the Magi, A Compendium of Zoroastrian Beliefs* (1976).

JAMES R. RUSSELL

ZOU RONG (1885–1905), young Chinese revolutionary whose influential and inflammatory tract *Geming jun (The Revolutionary Army)* served as an effective indictment against the declining Qing dynasty. Born in Sichuan Province, Zou came under the influence of revolutionary ideas while studying in Japan in 1902. He published *Geming jun* in Shanghai in 1903. Blaming the Manchus for establishing an oppressive rule in China and for weakening the country, Zou called on the Han race to stage a revolution "to exterminate the five million barbarian Manchus." He was subsequently arrested and sentenced to two years' imprisonment. He died in prison at the age of twenty.

Michael Gasster, *Chinese Intellectuals and the Revolution of 1911* (1969). Mary B. Rankin, *Early Chinese Revolutionaries: Radical Intellectuals in Shanghai and Chekiang, 1902–1911* (1971).   CHANG-TAI HUNG

ZOU YAN (305–240 BCE), Chinese philosopher and official; one of the chief proponents of the Yin-Yang and Five Agents (Chinese, *wuxing*, also called Five Elements) school, also called the School of Naturalists. The Naturalists were chiefly known for their classification of all matter and processes into the categories of yin and yang and the Five Agents. The Naturalists asserted that the alternations of yin-yang and the Five Agents explained not only the movements of nature but also the destinies of men and states. Their theories also influenced the cosmological theories of the Han-dynasty philosopher Dong Zhongshu. There are no extant works of Zou Yan, but Sima Qian, the Han historian, describes Zou's theories of geography, scientific method, and yin-yang proto-physics.

[*See also* Yin and Yang *and* Dong Zhongshu.]

Fung Yu-lan, *A History of Chinese Philsophy*, vol. 1, translated by Derk Bodde (1952). Joseph Needham, "The Fundamental Ideas of Chinese Science," in *Science and Civilisation in China*, vol. 2, *History of Scientific Thought* (1956), pp. 232–278.   VICTORIA B. CASS

ZUNBIL, the dynastic title of certain Hephthalite rulers in Zamindavar (the area of what is now southwestern Afghanistan from Kandahar to Ghazna) from the fifth to ninth century CE. The title may indicate a connection with the cult of the god Zun known to have been practiced in Zamindavar. The Zunbils (sometimes written as *Rutbil*) were independent of Sasanid control and also stoutly resisted Arab attacks from Sistan, thereby blunting and temporarily blocking the Muslim advance toward India. The Saffarid ruler Ya'qub ibn Laith attacked and killed the last known Zunbil in 864; subsequent campaigns until 872 broke the power of the Zunbil's family.

[*See also* Saffarid Dynasty *and the map accompanying* Samanid Dynasty.]

C. E. Bosworth, *Sistan under the Arabs* (1968), pp. 33–35.

E. L. DANIEL

ZUNYI CONFERENCE. *See* Long March.

LIST OF ENTRIES

Kangra
  Richard English
Kang Sheng
  John A. Rapp
Kang Tai
  Ian W. Mabbett
Kangxi Emperor
  Joanna Waley-Cohen
Kang Youwei
  Adrian A. Bennett
Kanishka
  Richard N. Frye
Kanō School
  Christine M. E. Guth
Kanpur
  Ainslie T. Embree
Kansei Reforms
  Herman Ooms
Kantō Earthquake
  Henry D. Smith II
Kan-t'o-li
  Kenneth R. Hall
Kanyakubja
  Shiva Bajpai
Kaozheng Xue
  Judith A. Whitbeck
Kapilavastu
  A. K. Narain
Kapitan China
  Carl A. Trocki
Karachi
  Thomas R. Metcalf
Karakhanid Dynasty
  James M. Kelly
Karakorum
  Arthur N. Waldron
Karakoyunlu
  Lawrence Potter
Kara Kum
  Jahan Salehi
Karen
  Ronald D. Renard
Karen National Defense Organization
  Robert H. Taylor
Karkota Dynasty
  Frederick M. Asher
Karmal, Babrak
  Zalmay Khalilzad
Karnataka
  B. Sheik Ali
Karrami
  Jeanette A. Wakin
Kartasura
  M. C. Ricklefs

Kart Dynasty
  Lawrence Potter
Kartini, Raden Ajeng
  James R. Rush
Kartir
  Richard N. Frye
Karve, Dhondo Keshav
  Frank F. Conlon
Kasa
  Peter H. Lee
Kashgar
  Rhoads Murphey, Jr.
Kashgari, Mahmud al-
  James M. Kelly
Kashmir
  T. N. Madan
Kasravi, Ahmad
  Neguin Yavari
Katayama Sen
  F. G. Notehelfer
Katayama Tetsu
  Michio Umegaki
Kathiawar
  Ainslie T. Embree
Kathmandu
  Prayag Raj Sharma
Katipunan
  Milagros C. Guerrero
Katō Kiyomasa
  James L. McClain
Katō Takaaki
  Sheldon M. Garon
Katsu Kaishu
  Harold Bolitho
Katsura Tarō
  Roger F. Hackett
Kaum Muda—Kaum Tua
  Rajeswary Ampalavanar
Kautilya
  Ludo Rocher
Kavila
  David K. Wyatt
Kayasth
  Karen Leonard
Kaysone Phomvihan
  Joseph J. Zasloff
Kazakhs
  Martha Brill Olcott
Kecil, Raja
  Dianne Lewis
Kedah
  Dianne Lewis
Kediri
  M. C. Hoadley

Keiō Gijuku
  Kimitada Miwa
Kelantan
  Clive S. Kessler
Kemmu Restoration
  Paul Varley
Ken Angrok
  M. C. Hoadley
Kenkokusetsu
  Michio Umegaki
Kerala
  Robin Jeffrey
Kerman
  Vahid Nowshirvani
Kertanagara
  M. C. Hoadley
Khadi
  Mark Juergensmeyer
Khafi Khan, Muhammad Hashim Ali
  Farhan Ahmad Nizami
Khaksar Movement
  S. Razi Wasti
Khalji Dynasty
  Farhan Ahmad Nizami
Khalq
  Zalmay Khalilzad
Khan, Abdul Ghaffar
  Stephen Rittenberg
Khan, Sir Sikandar Hayat
  Stephen Rittenberg
Khan, Tikka
  Stephen Rittenberg
Khandesh
  Catherine B. Asher
Khayyam, Omar
  Mariam Pirnazar
Khazars
  Peter B. Golden
Khieu Samphan
  David P. Chandler
Kilafat Movement
  Gail Minault
Khitan
  Jing-shen Tao
Khiva, Khanate of
  Yuri Bregel
Khmer
  David P. Chandler
Khmer Issarak
  David P. Chandler
Khmer Republic
  David P. Chandler
Khmer Rouge
  David P. Chandler

Madrasa
  Richard W. Bulliet
Ma Duanlin
  Kenneth R. Hall
Madura
  David K. Wyatt
Madurai
  Carol Appadurai Breckenridge
Maeda
  Ronald J. DiCenzo
Magadha
  John S. Strong
Magars
  Prayag Raj Sharma
Magatama
  Wayne Farris
Magellan, Ferdinand
  Bernardita Reyes Churchill
Magsaysay, Ramon
  David K. Wyatt
Mahabalipuram
  Stuart W. Smithers
Mahabandula
  William J. Koenig
Mahabharata
  Barbara Stoler Miller
Mahadammayazadipathi
  David K. Wyatt
Maha-Meghavahana Dynasty
  Frederick M. Asher
Maharashtra
  A. R. Kulkarni
Mahasena
  K. M. de Silva
Mahathammaracha
  David K. Wyatt
Mahathammaracha I
  David K. Wyatt
Mahathammaracha II
  David K. Wyatt
Mahathammaracha III
  David K. Wyatt
Mahathammaracha IV
  David K. Wyatt
Maha Thiha Thura
  William J. Koenig
Mahatthai
  David K. Wyatt
Mahavamsa
  K. M. de Silva
Mahdi
  Abdelaziz Sachedina
Mahendra
  Richard English

Mahinda
  K. M. de Silva
Mahmud of Ghazna
  Russell G. Kempiners, Jr.
Mahmud Riayat Syah III
  Dianne Lewis
Mahmud Syah II
  Dianne Lewis
Ma Huan
  Kenneth R. Hall
Maine, Sir Henry
  Lynn Zastoupil
Maitland, Sir Thomas
  Patrick Peebles
Majapahit
  M. C. Hoadley
Majlisi, Muhammad Baqir
  Hamid Algar
Makassar
  Anthony Reid
Makran
  Ainslie T. Embree
Malabari, Behramji Merwanji
  Usha Sanyal
Malamati
  Jeanette A. Wakin
Malaviya, Madan Mohan
  Judith E. Walsh
Malaya, British Military
  Administration of
  Rajeswary Ampalavanar
Malaya, Federation of
  R. S. Milne
Malayan Chinese Association
  R. S. Milne
Malayan Communist Party
  Stanley Bedlington
Malayan Indian Congress
  Rajeswary Ampalavanar
Malayan People's Anti-Japanese
  Army
  Stanley Bedlington
Malayan Union
  R. S. Milne
Malay Nationalist Party
  A. J. Stockwell
Malays
  Virginia Matheson
Malaysia
  Craig A. Lockard
Malcolm, Sir John
  Lynn Zastoupil
Maldives
  Ainslie T. Embree

Malik, Adam
  Robert B. Cribb
Maliki
  Merlin Swartz
Malkom Khan
  Neguin Yavari
Malla
  Bruce McCoy Owens
Malolos Republic
  Richard E. Welch, Jr.
Maluku
  David K. Wyatt
Malwa
  Frederick M. Asher
Mamluks
  Farhan Ahmad Nizami
Manchu Language
  Jerry Norman
Manchuria
  Arthur N. Waldron
Manchurian Incident
  Mark R. Peattie
Manchus
  Arthur N. Waldron
Mandalay
  Michael Aung-Thwin
Mandokoro
  Wayne Farris
Mandu
  Catherine B. Asher
Mangelun Convention
  Oliver B. Pollak
Mangkubumi
  M. C. Ricklefs
Mangkunagaran
  Peter Carey
Mangrai
  David K. Wyatt
Mani
  Richard N. Frye
Manichaeism
  James R. Russell
Manickavasagam, V.
  Rajeswary Ampalavanar
Manila
  David K. Wyatt
Manila Bay, Battle of
  Richard E. Welch, Jr.
Manila Galleon
  Kenneth R. Hall
Manipur
  Charles Lindholm
Manopakorn Nitithada
  Thak Chaloemtiarana

Mansabdari System
Harbans Mukhia
Man Singh
Harbans Mukhia
Mansur Syah
Dianne Lewis
Manucci, Niccolao
Harbans Mukhia
Man'yōshū
Ian Hideo Levy
Mao Dun
Shan Chou
Mao Zedong
Angus W. McDonald, Jr.
Mappilas
Stephen Frederic Dale
Marathas
A. R. Kulkarni
March First Independence Movement
Marius B. Jansen
March Incident
Mark R. Peattie
Marcos, Ferdinand E.
David A. Rosenberg
Marhaen
Robert B. Cribb
Maritime Customs Service
Yen-p'ing Hao
Marshall, George C.
Stephen R. MacKinnon
Martin, William Alexander Parsons
Irwin T. Hyatt, Jr.
Marwar
Richard Davis Saran
Marwaris
Howard Spodek
Marxism and Socialism: Marxism in
China
Maurice J. Meisner
Marxism and Socialism: Marxism
and Socialism in Southeast Asia
Charles B. McLane
Mashhad
Abdelaziz Sachedina
Masjumi
C. van Dijk
Mataram
Peter Carey
Mathura
John Stratton Hawley
Mat Salleh Rebellion
Craig A. Lockard
Matsu
Richard C. Kagan

Matsudaira Sadanobu
Herman Ooms
Matsukata Masayoshi
George K. Akita
Matsuo Bashō
Aileen Gatten
Matsuoka Yōsuke
Kimitada Miwa
Maududi, Abu'l A'la
Gregory C. Kozlowski
Maukhari Dynasty
Shiva Bajpai
Mauritius
Thomas R. Metcalf
Maurya Empire
John S. Strong
May Fourth Movement
Guy S. Alitto
Ma Yinchu
Parris Chang
May Seventh Cadre Schools
Hong Yung Lee
May Sixteenth Circular
Hong Yung Lee
May Sixteenth Coup d'État
John Kieh-Chiang Oh
May Thirtieth Incident
Lloyd E. Eastman
Mazandaran
Ariel Salzmann
Mazdak
James R. Russell
McMahon Line
Joseph E. Schwartzberg
Medan
Anthony Reid
Medes
James R. Russell
Medicine
Charles Leslie
Megasthenes
John S. Strong
Meghalaya
Charles Lindholm
Meiji Period
George K. Akita
Meiji Restoration
Marius B. Jansen
Meireki Fire
Henry D. Smith II
Mekong Expedition
David K. Wyatt
Melaka
Dianne Lewis

Menander
A. K. Narain
Mencius
Rodney L. Taylor
Merv
Rhoads Murphey, Jr.
Mestizo
Nicholas P. Cushner
Metalwork
Sheila S. Blair
Metcalfe, Sir Charles
Lynn Zastoupil
Mewar
Richard Davis Saran
Miki Takeo
Michio Umegaki
Mill, James
Lynn Zastoupil
Mill, John Stuart
Lynn Zastoupil
Mimana
Wayne Farris
Min, Queen
Michael Robinson
Minami Kikan
Robert H. Taylor
Minamoto
Wayne Farris
Minangkabau
Audrey R. Kahin
Minaret
Jahan Salehi
Mindanao
David K. Wyatt
Mindon
Myo Myint
Mines and Metallurgy
Rhoads Murphey, Jr.
Ming Dynasty
John W. Dardess
Minh Mang
James M. Coyle
Mir, Muhammad Taqi
Frances W. Pritchett
Mir Ja'far
Fritz Lehmann
Mir Jumla
Farhan Ahmad Nizami
Mir Qasim
Fritz Lehmann
Mishima Yukio
Richard Bowring
Mithra
Lucianne C. Bulliet

Senanayake, Dudley Shelton
  Vijaya Samaraweera
Sendai
  Ronald J. DiCenzo
Senggerinchin
  Roland L. Higgins
Sengoku Period
  James L. McClain
Seni Pramoj
  Thak Chaloemtiarana
Sen no Rikyū
  V. Dixon Morris
Seoul
  Shannon McCune
Sepoy
  Thomas R. Metcalf
Seppuku
  Paul Varley
Serendib
  K. M. de Silva
Seringapatam
  B. Sheik Ali
Servants of India Society
  Frank F. Conlon
Sesshū Tōyō
  Yoshiaki Shimizu
Setthathirat
  David K. Wyatt
Seven Sages of the Bamboo Grove
  Anita M. Andrew
Shaanganning
  John A. Rapp
Shaanxi
  John A. Rapp
Shafi'i
  Merlin Swartz
Shahiya Dynasty
  Meera Abraham
Shah Jahan
  Catherine B. Asher
Shahnama
  Mariam Pirnazar
Shahr-i Sukhta
  A. Shahpur Shahbazi
Shahrukh
  Maria E. Subtelny
Shaibanid Dynasty
  Rhoads Murphey, Jr.
Shaikh al-Islam
  Richard W. Bulliet
Shaikhi
  Mangol Bayat
Shaivism
  Stuart W. Smithers

Shamanism
  Peter J. Awn
Shamsher, Bir
  Richard English
Shamsher, Chandra
  Richard English
Shan
  F. K. Lehman
Shandong
  David D. Buck
Shandong Intervention
  Mark R. Peattie
Shandong Question
  David D. Buck
Shang Dynasty
  David N. Keightley
Shanghai
  David D. Buck
Shanghai Communiqué
  John A. Rapp
Shanghai Incident
  Mark R. Peattie
Shang Kexi
  Roland L. Higgins
Shanhaiguan
  Arthur N. Waldron
Shankara
  Stuart W. Smithers
Shan State Independence Army
  Robert H. Taylor
Shantou
  John A. Rapp
Shanxi
  Sally Hart
Shanyu
  John A. Rapp
Shapur I
  Michael G. Morony
Shapur II
  Michael G. Morony
Shari'a
  Jeanette A. Wakin
Shari'ati, Ali
  Jahan Salehi
Shastri, Lal Bahadur
  Marcus Franda
Shato Turks
  John Philip Ness
Shen Buhai
  Rodney L. Taylor
Sheng Xuanhuai
  Chang-tai Hung
Shenyang
  John A. Rapp

Sherpa
  Richard English
Sher Shah
  Catherine B. Asher
Shi'a
  Paul E. Walker
Shiba Kōkan
  Richard Rubinger
Shibli Nu'mani, Muhammad
  David Lelyveld
Shidehara Kijūrō
  Kimitada Miwa
Shiga Naoya
  Richard Bowring
Shigemitsu Mamoru
  Kimitada Miwa
Shijiazhuang
  John A. Rapp
Shi Kefa
  Roland L. Higgins
Shimabara
  Ronald P. Toby
Shimazu Hisamitsu
  Robert K. Sakai
Shimazu Nariakira
  Robert K. Sakai
Shimoda
  W. G. Beasley
Shimonoseki, Treaty of
  Shumpei Okamoto
Shimonoseki Bombardment
  Thomas M. Huber
Shingon
  Martin Collcutt
Shinjinkai
  Henry D. Smith II
Shinran
  Martin Collcutt
Shinshū
  Martin Collcutt
Shinto
  Helen Hardacre
Shiraz
  Richard W. Bulliet
Shivaji
  A. R. Kulkarni
Shōen
  Wayne Farris
Shogun
  Peter J. Arnesen
Shōkyū Incident
  Peter J. Arnesen
Shōtoku Taishi
  Wayne Farris

Thailand
David K. Wyatt

Thammayuttika
David K. Wyatt

Thaneswar
Usha Sanyal

Thanom Kittikachorn
Thak Chaloemtiarana

Than Tun, Thakin
Robert H. Taylor

Thapa, Bhim Sen
Richard English

Tharrawaddy
Oliver B. Pollak

That Luang
David K. Wyatt

Thaton
Michael Aung-Thwin

That Phanom
David K. Wyatt

Thibaw
David K. Wyatt

Thieu Tri
Bruce M. Lockhart

Thiphakorawong Kham Bunnag
Constance M. Wilson

Thirty Comrades
Robert H. Taylor

Thomas
Patrick Roche

Three Feudatories Rebellion
Anita M. Andrew

Three Hans
Edward J. Shultz

Three Kingdoms
Richard Mather

Thuc Dynasty
James M. Coyle

Thunberg, Carl Peter
Marius B. Jansen

Tianjin
Anita M. Andrew

Tian Shan Range
Christopher I. Beckwith

Tibet
Robert A. F. Thurman

Tich Quang
Bruce M. Lockhart

Tilak, Bal Gangadhar
Jim Masselos

Tilework
Sheila S. Blair

Tilokaracha
David K. Wyatt

Timor
Robert B. Cribb

Timur
Beatrice Forbes Manz

Timurid Dynasty
Beatrice Forbes Manz

Tin
Dianne Lewis

Tipu Sultan
B. Sheik Ali

Tirmidh
Robert McChesney

Tirthankara
Randolph M. Thornton

Tiruchchirappalli
Carol Appadurai Breckenridge

Tiwana, Malik Sir Khizr Hayat Khan
Craig Baxter

Tjokroaminoto
C. van Dijk

Tobacco Monopoly
Ian Brown

Tobacco Rebellion
Nikki Keddie

Tōdaiji
Martin Collcutt

Todar Mal
Harbans Mukhia

Todas
Doranne Jacobson

Toghril Beg
Russell G. Kempiners, Jr.

Tōgō Heihachirō
Mark R. Peattie

Tōjō Hideki
Mark R. Peattie

Tōkaidō
Ronald J. DiCenzo

Tokuda Kyūichi
Thomas R. Schalow

Tokugawa Hidetada
Harold Bolitho

Tokugawa Iemitsu
Harold Bolitho

Tokugawa Ieyasu
Marius B. Jansen

Tokugawa Mitsukuni
Harold Bolitho

Tokugawa Nariaki
Harold Bolitho

Tokugawa Period
Robert K. Sakai

Tokugawa Yoshimune
Harold Bolitho

Tokugawa Yoshinobu
Harold Bolitho

Tokusei
Peter J. Arnesen

Tokutomi Soho
F. G. Notehelfer

Tokyo
Henry D. Smith II

Ton Duc Thang
William J. Duiker

Tonghak
JaHyun Kim Haboush

Tonkin
Bruce M. Lockhart

Ton That Thuyet
Bruce M. Lockhart

Tooth Relic Palace
Todd Thornton Lewis

Tosa
Marius B. Jansen

Toungoo Dynasties
Victor B. Lieberman

Tower of Silence
James R. Russell

Tōyama Mitsuru
Marius B. Jansen

Toyotomi Hideyoshi
Mary Elizabeth Berry

Tozama Daimyo
Ronald J. DiCenzo

Tran Dynasty
James M. Coyle

Tran Hung Dao
James M. Coyle

Tran Nhan Tong
Bruce M. Lockhart

Tran Quy Cap
Bruce M. Lockhart

Trans-Iranian Railway
Eric Hooglund

Tran Thai Tong
Bruce M. Lockhart

Tran Thanh Tong
Bruce M. Lockhart

Tran Thu Do
Bruce M. Lockhart

Tran Trong Kim
Bruce M. Lockhart

Travancore
Barbara N. Ramusack

Treaty Ports
Yen-p'ing Hao

Trengganu
Virginia Matheson

DIRECTORY OF CONTRIBUTORS

Susan Abeyasekere
Footscray Institute of Technology, Australia
Jakarta

Meera Abraham
Berne, Switzerland
Chola Dynasty; Kanchipuram; Pallava Dynasty; Pandya Dynasty; Shahiya Dynasty; Tuluva Dynasty

Michael Adas
Rutgers University
Chettiar; Lower Burma; Rangoon

Qeyamuddhin Ahmad
Patna University, India
Ahl-i Hadis; Bihar; Sayyid Ahmad of Rae Bareilly

George K. Akita
University of Hawaii
Hara Takashi; Inoue Kaoru; Inoue Kowashi; Itō Hirobumi; Itō Miyoji; Kuroda Kiyotaka; Matsukata Masayoshi; Meiji Period; Mori Arinori; Ōkubo Toshimichi; Ōkuma Shigenobu; Saionji Kimmochi; Yamagata Aritomo

Meena Alexander
Hunter College, City University of New York
Derozio, Henry Louis Vivian; Naidu, Sarojini

Hamid Algar
University of California, Berkeley
Akhbari; Aqasi, Mirza; Bani Sadr, Abu al-Hasan; Bihbahani, Abd Allah; Bihbahani, Muhammad Baqir; Khomeini, Ruhollah Musavi; Majlisi, Muhammad Baqir; Nuri, Fazl Allah; Tabataba'i, Muhammad; Taleghani, Mahmud; Usuli

B. Sheik Ali
Mangalore University, India
Haidar Ali Khan; Karnataka; Seringapatam; Tipu Sultan; Wadiyar Dynasty

M. Athar Ali
Aligarh Muslim University, India
Aurangzeb; Mughal Empire

Guy S. Alitto
University of Chicago
May Fourth Movement

Thomas T. Allsen
Trenton State College
Mongol Empire: An Overview

Edward Allworth
Columbia University
Turkestan; Uzbekistan

Albert A. Altman
Hebrew University, Jerusalem
Journalism: Journalism in Japan

Abbas Amanat
Yale University
Abbas Mirza; Amir Kabir

Rajeswary Ampalavanar
Hitchin, England
Angkatan Pemuda Insaf; Kaum Muda—Kaum Tua; Malaya, British Military Administration of; Malayan Indian Congress; Manickavasagam, V.; Tan Cheng Lock

Anita M. Andrew
University of Minnesota
Anyang; Baojia System; Bureaucracy in China; Donglin Academy; Empress Dowager; Harbin; Hebei; Heilongjiang; Huhehaote; Jingdezhen; Lijia System; Li Zhi; Luoyang; Qi Baishi; Qin Shihuangdi; Sanyan; Seven Sages of the Bamboo Grove; Suzhou; Tainan; Taipei; Taiyuan; Taizhou School; Tangshan; Three Feudatories Rebellion; Tianjin; Wang Fuzhi; Wang Gen; Xi'an; Yitiaobianfa; Zayton; Zhang Shicheng; Zheng Chenggong

Arjun Appadurai
University of Pennsylvania
Cow; Hinduism

Belinda A. Aquino
University of Hawaii
Aquino, Benigno; New People's Army

S. Arasaratnam
University of New England, Australia
Colombo; Kandy; Queyroz, Fernao de; Rajasinha I; Rajasinha II; Ribeiro, João; Trincomalee

Peter J. Arnesen
University of Michigan
Jitō; Shogun; Shōkyū Incident; Shugo; Tokusei

Catherine B. Asher
Minneapolis, Minnesota
Agra; Ahmad Shahi Dynasty; Fatehpur Sikri; Hindu Shahi Dynasty; Ilyas Shahi Dynasty; Jaunpur; Khandesh; Mandu; Multan; Murshidabad; Red Fort; Shah Jahan; Sher Shah; Suri Dynasty; Taj Mahal

Frederick M. Asher
University of Minnesota
Chandella Dynasty; Gajapati Dynasty; Gurjara-Pratihara Dynasty; Kalachuri Dynasties; Karkota Dynasty; Maha-Meghavahana Dynasty; Malwa; Pala Dynasty; Pushyabhuti Dynasty; Sena Dynasty; Varman Dynasty

Michael Aung-Thwin
Elmira College
Alaungsithu; Anawrahta; Burma; Dhammazedi; Kala; Kyanzittha; Kyaswa; Kyaukse; Kyawswa; Mandalay; Mongmao; Nadaungmya; Narapatisithu; Narathihapade; Padahlin; Pagan; Pegu; Peikthano; Prome; Pyu; Saw, Queen; Thadominbya; Thaton

Robert Austerlitz
Columbia University
Language Families; Siberia

357

Peter J. Awn
Columbia University
Ghazali, al-; Islam; Muhammad; Orientalism; Shamanism; Sufism

Guitty Azarpay
University of California, Berkeley
Sculpture: Iranian and Central Asian Sculpture

David Bachman
Princeton University
Great Leap Forward; People's Communes

Ernst Badian
Harvard University
Alexander III; Antiochus III; Antiochus VII Sidetes; Darius III; Seleucid Dynasty; Seleucus I

Shiva Bajpai
California State University, Northridge
Gahadavalas; Harsha; Indraprastha; Kanyakubja; Maukhari Dynasty; Paramara Dynasty; Pratiharas; Prithviraj Chauhan; Sisodiya Dynasty; Somanath; Vakatakas; Yadavas

David Baker
Delhi University, India
Madhya Pradesh; Nagpur

Marguerite Ross Barnett
University of Missouri
Annadurai, C. N.; Dravidian Movement

Richard B. Barnett
University of Virginia
Asaf ud-Daulah; Awadh; Safdar Jang; Shuja ud-Daulah

John S. Bastin
Chorleywood, England
Crawfurd, John; Farquhar, William; Horsfield, Thomas; Java, British Occupation of; Light, Francis

Susan Neild Basu
Rochester, New York
Madras

Michael L. Bates
American Numismatic Society
Dinar; Dirham; Money: Money in the Islamic World

Craig Baxter
Juniata College
Awami League; Bangladesh; Bangladesh Nationalist Party; Chowdhury, Abu Sayeed; Hindu Mahasabha; Indian Administrative Service; Mujibur Rahman, Sheikh; Patel, Sardar Vallabhbhai; Rahman, Ziaur; Tiwana, Malik Sir Khizr Hayat Khan; Unionist Party

Mangol Bayat
Harvard University
Babi; Baha'i; Shaikhi

C. A. Bayly
Cambridge University
Allahabad; Uttar Pradesh

W. G. Beasley
University of London
Harris, Townsend; Kanagawa Treaty; Perry, Matthew C.; Richardson Incident; Shimoda

Christopher I. Beckwith
Indiana University
Silk Route; Taklamakan; Tarim Basin; Tian Shan Range

Stanley Bedlington
Washington, D.C.
Abdul Rahman Alhaj; Abdul Razak; Alliance Party; Barisan Sosialis; Chin Peng; Independence of Malaya Party; Malayan Communist Party; Malayan People's Anti-Japanese Army; People's Action Party

Adrian A. Bennett
Iowa State University
Kang Youwei; Legge, James; Liang Qichao; Tan Sitong; Weng Tonghe; Xuantong Emperor; Yan Fu

Gordon Bennett
University of Texas
Chinese People's Liberation Army; Chinese People's Political Consultative Conference; Communism: Chinese Communist Party; Revolutionary Committees

Mary Elizabeth Berry
University of California, Berkeley
Kyoto; Momoyama Period; Nijō Castle; Oda Nobunaga; Toyotomi Hideyoshi

Agehananda Bharati
Syracuse University
Tantra; Upanishads

Sheila S. Blair
Cambridge, Massachusetts
Carpets; Felt; Gardens; Metalwork; Painting: Iranian and Central Asian Painting; Tilework; Weaving

P. Richard Bohr
Midwest China Center
Hakka; Hong Ren'gan; Hong Xiuquan; Taiping Rebellion; Zeng Guofan

Peter K. Bol
Harvard University
Cheng Brothers; Fan Zhongyan; Kaifeng; Ouyang Xiu; Sima Guang; Su Dongpo; Wang Anshi; Yelü Chucai

Harold Bolitho
Harvard University
Aizu; Enomoto Takeaki; Katsu Kaishu; Kido Takayoshi; Kōmei; Kyōhō Reforms; Mizuno Tadakuni; Shōya; Tempō Reforms; Tokugawa Hidetada; Tokugawa Iemitsu; Tokugawa Mitsukuni; Tokugawa Nariaki; Tokugawa Yoshimune; Tokugawa Yoshinobu

Michael Bonine
University of Arizona
Altai Mountains; Aral Sea; Caspian Sea; Dasht-i Kavir; Dasht-i Lut; Elburz Mountains; Hindu Kush; Oxus River; Pamirs

Robert Borgen
University of Hawaii
Fujiwara Lineage; Fujiwara Michinaga; Fujiwara Period

Arash Bormanshinov
Lanham, Maryland
Kalmuks

Richard Bowring
Cambridge University
Futabatei Shimei; Genroku Culture; Hearn, Lafcadio; Ihara Saikaku; Mishima Yukio; Mori Ōgai; Murasaki Shikibu; Nagai Kafū; Natsume Sōseki; Nō; Shiga Naoya; Taiheiki; Takizawa Bakin; Tanizaki Jun'ichirō

Carol Appadurai Breckenridge
Philadelphia, Pennsylvania
Coorg; Madurai; Mudaliyar; Nadars; Nayaka; Pillai, Ananda Ranga; Poligar; Tanjore; Tiruchchirappalli; Vellala

Yuri Bregel
Indiana University
Bukhara, Khanate of; Khiva, Khanate of; Khokand, Khanate of

Elizabeth Bright
New York, New York
Uighurs

Delmer M. Brown
Center for Japanese Language Studies, Japan
Heijō; Nara Period; Ritsuryō State; Taika Reforms

Donald E. Brown
University of California, Santa Barbara
Brunei

Ian Brown
University of London
Agency House System; Dutch East India Company; Hall, D. G. E.; Money: Money in Southeast Asia; Spice Trade; Tobacco Monopoly

Judith M. Brown
University of Manchester
Gandhi, Mohandas Karamchand

David D. Buck
University of Wisconsin, Milwaukee
Bai Chongxi; China, Republic of; Guangxi Clique; Ji'nan; Ji'nan Incident; Northern Expedition; Qingdao; Shandong; Shandong Question; Shanghai; Versailles Treaty of 1918; Weihaiwei; World War I in China

Lucianne C. Bulliet
New York, New York
Ahura Mazda; Anahita; Aryans; Haoma; Mithra; Vedas

Richard W. Bulliet
Columbia University
Camel; Caravan; Inju Dynasty; Iran; Jizya; Madrasa; Mosque; Muzaffarid Dynasty; Nishapur; Shaikh al-Islam; Shiraz; Urumqi; Yurt

Thomas W. Burkman
Old Dominion University
Urakami Incident

Robert E. Buswell, Jr.
University of California, Los Angeles
Buddhism: Buddhism in Korea; Koryŏ Tripitaka; Pulguk Temple

Ralph Buultjens
New York, New York
Burghers; Jaffna; Sinhala; Tamils in Sri Lanka

Peter Carey
Oxford University
Daendels, Herman Willem; Dipanagara; Java War; Jayabaya; Kraton; Kyai; Mangkunagaran; Mataram; Pakualaman; Pasisir; Ratu Adil; Regents; Sala; Santri; Yogyakarta

Victoria B. Cass
University of Minnesota
Gongsun Long; Qu Yuan; Zou Yan

Thak Chaloemtiarana
Cornell University
Ananda Mahidol; Bhumibol Adulyadej; Dokmaisot; Franco-Siamese War; Free Thai; Khuang Aphaiwong; Kukrit Pramoj; Manopakorn Nitithada; People's Party of Thailand; Phahon Phonphayuhasena; Phibunsongkhram, Luang; Phot Sarasin; Praphas Charusathian; Preah Vihear; Pridi Phanomyong; Sarit Thanarat; Seni Pramoj; Thanom Kittikachorn; Wichitwathakan, Luang

David P. Chandler
Monash University
Ang Chan; Ang Duang; Ang Eng; Battambang; Cambodia; Coedès, George; Decoux, Jean; Garnier, Francis; Heng Samrin; Kampuchea; Kampuchea, Democratic; Kampuchea, People's Republic of; Khieu Samphan; Khmer; Khmer Issarak; Khmer Republic; Khmer Rouge; Lon Nol; Lovek; Norodom; Norodom Sihanouk; Norodom Suramarit; Oudong; Pavie Missions; Phnom Penh; Pol Pot; Sangkum Reastr Niyum; Siem Reap; Sisowath; Sisowath Monivong; Son Ngoc Thanh; Veloso, Diogo

Vipan Chandra
Wheaton College
Independence Party and Club; Jaisohn, Philip; Pak Yŏng-hyo; Yu Kil-chun

Parris Chang
Pennsylvania State University
Chen Boda; Deng Xiaoping; Li Xiannian; Ma Yinchu; Xie Fuzhi; Ye Jianying; Zhou Enlai; Zhou Yang; Zhu De

K. N. Chaudhuri
University of London
East India Company

Yŏng-ho Ch'oe
University of Hawaii
Ch'oe Ik-hyŏn; Chŏng To-jŏn; Hideyoshi's Invasion of Korea; Yi Dynasty; Yi Sun-sin

Jamsheed K. Choksy
Columbia University
Parsis

Shan Chou
New York, New York
Ba Jin; Bai Juyi; Burning of the Books; Cao Xueqin; Ding Ling; Guo Moruo; Hundred Flowers Campaign; Jinpingmei; Li Bai; Lu Dingyi; Lu Xun; Mao Dun; Pu Songling; Rulin Waishi

Bernardita Reyes Churchill
Washington, D.C.
Anda y Salazar, Simon de; Audiencia; Garcia, Carlos P.; Legazpi, Miguel Lopez de; Magellan, Ferdinand; Romulo, Carlos P.; Silang, Diego

David R. Claussenius
New York, New York
Aquino, Corazon Cojuangco; Macapagal, Diosdado P.; Sulawesi; Surabaya; Tagalog

Parks M. Coble, Jr.
University of Nebraska
Chen Guofu; Chen Lifu; Chen Qimei; Chiang Kai-shek; Guomindang; Li Zong-

ren; Soong, T. V.; Soong, Mei-ling; Zhejiang

Martin Collcutt
Princeton University
Akusō; Amidism; Ashikaga Takauji; Ashikaga Yoshimasa; Ashikaga Yoshimitsu; Dōgen Kigen; Eisai; Ennin; Enryakuji; Go-Daigo; Haibutsu Kishaku; Hōnen; Inoue Enryō; Kamakura Period; Kōyasan; Kūkai; Mongol Empire: Mongol Invasions of Japan; Muromachi Period; Nichiren; Pure Land; Rennyo; Saichō; Shingon; Shinran; Sinshū; Suzuki Daisetsu; Tendai; Todaiji; Zen

Frank F. Conlon
University of Washington
Chitpavan Brahmans; Karve, Dhondo Keshav; Nana Sahib; Prarthana Samaj; Servants of India Society; Tukaram

Alvin D. Coox
San Diego State University
Kwantung Army; Nomonhan, Battle of; Port Arthur; Russo-Japanese War; Tsushima Straits, Battle of

Charles A. Coppel
University of Melbourne
Gestapu; Pancasila; Priyayi

John E. Cort
Washington, D.C.
Jainism

James M. Coyle
Cornell University
An Duong Vuong; Annam; Au Co; Au Lac; Bach Viet; Champa; Co Loa; Confucianism in Vietnam; Dai Co Viet; Dai La Thanh; Dai Nam; Dai Ngu; Dai Viet; Dien Bien Phu; Doumer, Paul; Former Ly Dynasty; French Indochina War; Gia Long; Hanoi; Hoa Lu; Ho Dynasty; Hue; Hung Vuong; Lac Long Quan; Lac Viet; Le Dynasties; Le Loi; Le Thanh Thong; Ly Dynasty; Mac Dynasty; Minh Mang; Nam Viet; Nguyen Dynasty; Nguyen Lords; Tan Vien Mountain; Tay Do; Tay Son Rebellion; Thuc Dynasty; Tran Dynasty; Tran Hung Dao; Trinh Lords; Trinh-Nguyen Wars; Tu Duc; Van Xuan

Robert B. Cribb
Griffith University
Aidit, Dipa Nusantara; Ali Sastroamidjojo; Alimin Prawirodirdjo; Burhanuddin Harahap; Confrontation; Madiun; Malik, Adam; Marhaen; Musso; Partai Komunis Indonesia; Partai Murba; PETA; Subandrio; Suharto; Sukiman Wirjosandjojo; Timor; Wilopo

Michael Cullinane
University of Michigan
Barangay; Barrio; Buencamino, Felipe; Cacique; Calderon, Felipe; Cebu; Ilustrado; Inquilino; Intramuros; Nacionalista Party; Osmeña, Sergio; Parian; Paterno, Pedro; Principalia; Sumulong, Juan

Bruce Cumings
University of Washington
Korean War

Nicholas P. Cushner
Empire State College
Alcalde Mayor; Basco y Vargas, Jose de; Indios; Mestizo; Philippines, British Occupation of; Spain and the Philippines

Norman Cutler
University of Chicago
Dravidian Languages and Literatures

Stephen Frederic Dale
Ohio State University
Indian Ocean; Mappilas; Muslims in Sri Lanka; Nikitin, Afanasi

E. L. Daniel
University of Hawaii
Abbasid Dynasty; Arabs; Babak; Bukhar-Khuda; Buyid Dynasty; Caliphate; Dihqan; Khurasan; Muqanna, al-; Saffarid Dynasty; Samanid Dynasty; Tahirid Dynasty; Umayyad Dynasty; Ziyarid Dynasty; Zunbil

John W. Dardess
University of Kansas
Ming Dynasty

Arun Dasgupta
Calcutta, India
Aceh; Iskandar Muda

Vidya Dehejia
Columbia University
Architecture: South Asian Architecture; Coomaraswamy, Ananda Kentish; Gandhara; Painting: South Asian Painting

Robert J. Del Bontà
San Francisco, California
Chalukya Dynasties; Ganga Dynasties; Hoysala Dynasty; Kakatiya Dynasty

Madhav M. Deshpande
University of Michigan
Indo-Aryan Languages and Literatures

K. M. de Silva
University of Peradeniya, Sri Lanka
Anuradhapura; Dambadeniya; Devanampiya Tissa; Dharmapala, Dom João; Dutthagamani; Elara; Knox, Robert; Kotte; Kurunegala; Mahasena; Mahavamsa; Mahinda; Parakramabahu I;

Parakramabahu II; Peradeniya; Polonnaruva; Rohana; Serendib; Sigiriya; Sri Lanka; Veddas; Vijayabahu I

Martina Deuchler
Zurich, Switzerland
1884 Coup d'Etat; 1882 Uprising; General Sherman Incident; Kanghwa Treaty; Kojong; Moellendorff, Paul Georg von; Taewŏn'gun

Ronald J. DiCenzo
Oberlin College
Bakufu; Daimyo; Echigo; Echizen; Hatamoto; Hizen; Ikeda Mitsumasa; Kii; Maeda; Rōjū; Sankin Kōtai; Sekisho; Sendai; Tanuma Okitsugu; Tōkaidō; Tozama Daimyo

Lowell Dittmer
University of California, Berkeley
China, People's Republic of; Liu Shaoqi

Edward L. Dreyer
Coral Gables, Florida
Fei River, Battle of; Han Liner; Inner Mongolia; Nanjing; Warfare: Warfare in China

William J. Duiker
Pennsylvania State University
August Revolution; Bac Son Uprising; Bao Dai; Black Flags; Dai Viet Party; Dong Du Movement; Dong Kinh Nghia Thuc; Ho Chi Minh; Indochinese Communist Party; Indochinese Union; Klobukowski, Antoni-Wladislas; Le Duan; Le Duc Tho; Nghe-Tinh Uprising; Paracel Islands; Pham Quynh; Pham Van Dong; Phan Boi Chau; Phan Chu Trinh; Sarraut, Albert Pierre; Spratly Islands; Tet Offensive; Ton Duc Thang; Truong Chinh; Van Tien Dung; Vietnam Modernization Association; Vietnam Nationalist Party; Vietnam National Salvation Associations; Vietnam Restoration Association; Vietnam Restoration League; Vietnam Revolutionary League; Vietnam Revolutionary Youth League; Vo Nguyen Giap; Yen Bay Uprising

Jack L. Dull
University of Washington
Sima Qian; Slavery and Serfdom: Slavery in China; Spring and Autumn Period; Wang Chong; Wang Mang; Warring States Period; Xia Dynasty; Xianbei; Xiang Yu; Xiongnu; Yangshao Culture; Zhang Fei; Zhuge Liang

Mary Frances Dunham
New York, New York
Dhaka

Ruth W. Dunnell
Chicago, Illinois
Tanguts

Lloyd E. Eastman
University of Illinois
Chiang Ching-kuo; Communist-Extermination Campaigns; Ding Wenjiang; Hu Hanmin; May Thirtieth Incident; Mukden Incident; Wang Jingwei; Whampoa Military Academy; Xi'an Incident

Richard M. Eaton
University of Arizona
Ahmadnagar; Bahmani Dynasty; Bijapur; Deccan Sultanates; Golconda

Patricia Ebrey
University of Illinois
Song Dynasty

R. Randle Edwards
Columbia University
Law: Law in China

Ainslie T. Embree
Columbia University
Asia; Carey, William; Chaitanya; Cochin; Deb, Radhakanta; Gandhi, Rajiv; Governor-General of India; Grant, Charles; Haryana; Heber, Reginald; India; Jammu; Jats; Jhelum River; Journalism: Journalism in India; Kanpur; Kathiawar; Kulinism; Makran; Maldives; Mutiny, Indian; Naicker, E. V. Ramaswami; Ochterlony, Sir David; Panipat, Battles of; Patiala; Raja; Rajagopalachari, Chakravarti; Rajasthan; Singh, Bhagat; Suraj Mal

Elizabeth Endicott-West
Canton Center, Connecticut
Yuan Dynasty

Richard English
Peshawar, Pakistan
Assam; Bhutan; Birendra; Darjeeling; Everest; Garhwal; Giri, Tulsi; Gurkhas; Hardwar; Himalayas; Hodgson, Brian Houghton; Jung Bahadur Rana; Kangra; Kirata; Koirala, Bishweshwor Prasad; Kot Massacre; Laxmi Devi; Lepcha; Limbu; Mahendra; Namche Bazar; Namgyal, Palden Thondup; Norgay, Tenzing; Rai; Rana; Shamsher, Bir; Shamsher, Chandra; Sherpa; Sikkim; Singh, K. I.; Tamang; Tarai; Tea in India and Sri Lanka; Thapa, Bhim Sen; Tribhuvan, Bir Bikram; Wangchuk, Jigme Dorje; Wangchuk, Jigme Singye; Wangchuk, Ugyen

Robert Entenmann
St. Olaf College
Banners; Chengdu; Guizhou; Qing Dynasty; Sichuan; Tsangyang Gyatso; Zhang Xianzhong

Edward L. Farmer
University of Minnesota
April Fifth Movement; China; Chu; Comintern; Confucius; Dai Zhen; East Asia; Far East; Four Modernizations; Han; Hu Yaobang; Loess; Lu Xiangshan; Northern Liang Kingdom; Qi; Responsibility System; Song Qingling; Ten Kingdoms; Wang Yangming; Wei; Yan; Yin and Yang; Zhang Zai; Zhao; Zhao Ziyang; Zhou Dunyi

Wayne Farris
University of Tennessee
Be; Dajōkan; Dan no Ura; Dazaifu; Hōgen and Heiji Wars; Jimmu; Jōmon; Kojiki; Kuge; Kujō; Magatama; Mandokoro; Mimana; Minamoto; Nihon Shoki; Sakanoue no Tamuramaro; Shōen; Shōtoku Taishi; Soga; Sugawara no Michizane; Taira no Kiyomori; Temmu; Tumuli; Uji; Yamatai; Yamato; Yayoi

Lee Feigon
Colby College
Chen Duxiu; Li Dazhao; Li Lisan; Zhang Guotao

John P. Ferguson
State University of New York Agricultural and Technical College, Cobleskill
Dhammapala; Ledi Sayadaw; Nats; Robe-wrapping Controversy; Shwedagon Pagoda

Michael Fischer
Rice University
Education: Education in Iran and Central Asia; Qom

William F. Fisher
Columbia University
Andaman and Nicobar Islands; Jute; Ladakh; Poonch; Younghusband, Sir Francis Edward

Theodore Nicholas Foss
University of San Francisco
Cathay; Giovanni da Montecorvino; Ibn Battuta; Jesuits: An Overview; Odoric of Pordenone; Polo, Marco; William of Rubruck

Marcus Franda
The Asia Foundation, Thailand
Bhave, Vinoba; Bokaro; Desai, Morarji; Gandhi, Indira; Gandhi, Sanjay; Janata

Morcha; Narayan, Jayaprakash; Prohibition in India; Ram, Jagjivan; Rashtriya Swayamsevak Sangh; Reddy, N. Sanjiva; Shastri, Lal Bahadur

William H. Frederick
Ohio University
Indonesia, Republic of

Morton H. Fried
deceased
Family and Marriage

Richard N. Frye
Harvard University
Aniran; Arachosia; Aria; Bactria; Badakhshan; Behistun; Chionites; Kanishka; Kartir; Khwarna; Mani; Now Ruz; Old Persian; Satrap

Robert E. Frykenberg
University of Wisconsin
Bentinck, William Cavendish; Chait Singh; Clive, Sir Robert; Cornwallis, Charles; Dupleix, Joseph François; Hastings, Warren; Impey, Elijah; Jagat Seth; Macaulay, Thomas Babington; Nabob; Nuncomar; Pitt, Thomas; Ramsay, James Andrew Broun; Wellesley, Arthur; Wellesley, Richard Colley

Marc Galanter
University of Wisconsin
Law: Judicial and Legal Systems of India

Hassan N. Gardezi
Algoma University College, Canada
Ayub Khan, Mohammad; Bhutto, Zulfiqar Ali; Yahya Khan, Agha Muhammad; Zia-ul Haq, Mohammad

Kenneth H. J. Gardiner
Australian National University
Commanderies in Korea, Chinese; Koguryǒ; Later Three Kingdoms; Paekche; Puyǒ; Silla; Wiman

Daniel K. Gardner
Smith College
Zhu Xi

Sheldon M. Garon
Princeton University
Asahi Shimbun; Katō Takaaki; Konoe Fumimaro; Peace Preservation Law; Rice Riots; Seiyūkai; Yoshino Sakuzō; Zaibatsu

Gene R. Garthwaite
Dartmouth College
Qajar Dynasty; Tribes

Aileen Gatten
Ann Arbor, Michigan
Bunraku; Chikamatsu Monzaemon; Chūshingura; Genji Monogatari; Haikai; Kokinshū; Kyōgen; Matsuo Bashō; Saigyō; Zeami

James Geiss
Princeton University
Beijing; Censorate; Hu Weiyong; Zhang Juzheng; Zheng He; Zhu Di

J. Mason Gentzler
Sarah Lawrence College
Confucianism

Lorraine M. Gesick
Elizabeth, Colorado
Ban Chiang; Phra Phutthayotfa Chulalok; Satingpra; Taksin

Ashraf Ghani
Johns Hopkins University
Abdalis; Abd al-Rahman; Afghanistan; Amanullah; Durranis; Ghilzais; Hazarajat; Hazaras; Kabul; Pakhtun

Carol Gluck
Columbia University
World War I in Asia; World War II in Asia

Peter B. Golden
Rutgers University
Khazars; Kipchaks; Pechenegs; Turkic Languages

Barbara Gombach
New York, New York
Money: Money in Pre-Islamic India

Grant K. Goodman
University of Kansas
Davao; Kalibapi; Laurel, Jose P.; Philippines, Commonwealth of; Sakdal; Tydings-McDuffie Act

L. Carrington Goodrich
deceased
Calendars and Eras: Chinese Calendars and Eras; Nestorianism; Paper

Leonard A. Gordon
Brooklyn College
Bose, Subhas Chandra; Communism: Communist Parties in South Asia; Das, Chittaranjan; Fazlul Huq, Abul Kasem; Ghose, Aurobindo; Indian National Army; Naxalites; Ramakrishna; Roy, Manabendra Nath; Suhrawardy, Hussain Shahid; Swadeshi; Vivekananda

Dennis Grafflin
Bates College
Jin Dynasty; Northern Qi Dynasty; Northern Wei Dynasty; Southern and Northern Dynasties

Jerrold D. Green
University of Michigan
Bakhtiar, Shahpur; Bazargan, Mehdi; SAVAK

Paul R. Greenough
University of Iowa
Famine

Milagros C. Guerrero
University of the Philippines
Aguinaldo, Emilio; Katipunan; Samar

Warren Gunderson
The Asia Society
Mitra, Rajendralal; Tagore, Dwarkanath; Vidyasagar, Isvarchandra

Narayani Gupta
New Delhi, India
Delhi

Christine M. E. Guth
Kingston, New Jersey
Hachiman; Ike Taiga; Itō Jakuchū; Kanō School; Sculpture: Japanese Sculpture; Tempyō Era; Ukiyo-e

Pamela Gutman
Red Hill, Australia
Arakan

R. Kent Guy
University of Washington
Education: Education in Imperial China; Literacy: Literacy in China; Wu Jingzi

JaHyun Kim Haboush
University of Illinois
Kabo Reforms; Kim Ok-kyun; Son Pyŏng-hŭi; Tonghak

Roger F. Hackett
University of Michigan
Imperial Rescript to Soldiers; Katsura Tarō; Ōyama Iwao; Taishō Political Change; Tanaka Giichi; Terauchi Masatake; Yasukuni Shrine

Kenneth R. Hall
North Adams State College
Abangan; Airlangga; Albuquerque, Affonso de; Borobudur; Chola Raids; Golden Khersonese; Hacienda; Ho-ling; Ho-lo-tan; Jambi; Kan-t'o-li; Linschoten, Jan Huyghen van; Ma Duanlin; Ma Huan; Manila Galleon; Mongol Empire: Mongol Invasions of Southeast Asia; Palembang; Pararaton; Pires, Tomé; Portuguese: Portuguese in Southeast Asia; Prambanan; Ramannadesa; Sailendra; Sanjaya; Sanskrit in Southeast Asia; Sawah; Srivijaya

Yen-p'ing Hao
University of Tennessee
Arrow War; Compradors; Gong Yixin; Hart, Robert; Maritime Customs Service; Treaty Ports; Zongli Yamen

Helen Hardacre
Princeton University
Ise; Ise Mairi; New Religions in Japan; Shinto; Suika Shinto; Takamagahara

Sally Hart
Saint Paul, Minnesota
Baotou; Changchun; Jiujiang; Nanning; Shanxi; Zhengzhou

Mushirul Hasan
Jamia Millia Islamia, India
All-India Muslim League; Mohamed Ali

Mantaro J. Hashimoto
Institute for Study of Languages and Cultures of Asia and Africa, Tokyo
Writing Systems

Martin Hatch
Cornell University
Music: Music In Southeast Asia

John Stratton Hawley
Barnard College
Bhakti; Mathura; Tulsi Das

Robert M. Hayden
University of Pittsburgh
Law: Judicial and Legal Systems of India

Gregory Henderson
West Medford, Massachusetts
April Nineteenth Student Revolution; Chang Myŏn; Kim Dae Jung; Kim Jong Pil; Park Chung Hee

Linda Hess
University of California, Berkeley
Kabir

Roland L. Higgins
West Lebanon, New Hampshire
Anhui; Chen Youliang; Cohong; Dagu Forts; Fang Guozhen; Fujian; Fuzhou; Hangzhou; Heshen; Li Zicheng; Piracy: Japanese Piracy in China; Senggerinchin; Shang Kexi; Shi Kefa; Tributary System; Wei Zhongxian; Xu Guangqi

Yun-yi Ho
Tacoma, Washington
Chinese Ritual and Sacrifice

M. C. Hoadley
Uppsala University, Sweden
Cirebon; Gajah Mada; Hayam Wuruk; Kediri; Ken Angrok; Kertanagara; Majapahit; Nagarakertagama; Pajajaran; Panataran; Priangan; Singosari; Sugar

Eric Hooglund
Alexandria, Virginia
Pahlavi, Mohammed Reza; Pahlavi, Reza; Persian Cossack Brigade; Qajar, Ahmad; Qajar, Muhammad Ali; Shuster, William Morgan; South Persia Rifles; Sykes, Sir Percy Molesworth; Tehran Conference; Trans-Iranian Railway; Tripartite Treaty of Alliance; Wassmuss, Wilhelm

M. B. Hooker
Eliot College, England
Adat; Law: Law in Southeast Asia

Rose Chan Houston
American Numismatic Society
Money: Money in East Asia

David L. Howell
Princeton University
Ainu

John F. Howes
University of British Columbia
Nitobe Inazō; Uchimura Kanzō

Cho-yun Hsu
University of Pittsburgh
Han Dynasty; Qin Dynasty; Zhou Period

Pei Huang
Youngstown State University
Dorgon; Grand Council; Grand Secretariat; Huang Taiji; Nurhaci

Thomas M. Huber
Leavenworth, Kansas
Chōshū; Kagoshima Bombardment; Mōri; Shimonoseki Bombardment; Yoshida Shōin

Dennis Hudson
Smith College
Vaishnavism

John Huehnergard
Harvard University
Ctesiphon; Cuneiform; Elamites

Franklin E. Huffman
United States Information Agency
Austroasiatic Languages

Chang-tai Hung
Carleton College
Cai Yuanpei; Gu Jiegang; Hu Shi; Liang Shuming; Lin Yutang; Qiu Jin; Sheng Xuanhuai; Zhang Binglin; Zou Rong

G. Cameron Hurst III
University of Kansas
Heian Period

Irwin T. Hyatt, Jr.
Emory University
Li Hongzhang; Lin Zexu; Martin, William Alexander Parsons; Wei Yuan; Zhang Zhidong

Isabella Ibrahimov
Columbia University
Tajikistan

Mehrdad Izady
Columbia University
Gilaki; Gilan; Hamadan; Kurdish; Kurdistan

Doranne Jacobson
Springfield, Illinois
Ahalya Bai; Jajmani; Kshatriya; Lakshmi Bai; Panchayat; Shudra; Todas

James A. Jaffe
New York, New York
Curzon, George Nathaniel; Isaacs, Rufus; Morley-Minto Reforms; Robinson, George Frederick; Wood, Edward Frederick Lindley

Ayesha Jalal
University of Wisconsin
Pakistan

Marius B. Jansen
Princeton University
Amaterasu Ōmikami; Communism: Communism in Japan; Emigration: Japanese Emigration; Hombyakushō; Japan: History of Japan; Kampaku; Kyŏngju; March First Independence Movement; Meiji Restoration; Osadamegaki Hyakkajō; Osaka Campaigns; Rokumeikan; Ryōanji; Sakai Incident; Sakamoto Ryōma; Sorge Incident; Sumo; Thunberg, Carl Peter; Tokugawa Ieyasu; Tosa; Tōyama Mitsuru; Yalta Conference

Robin Jeffrey
Latrobe University, Australia
Ilava; Kerala; Nairs; Namboodripad, E. M. S.

Kay Ann Johnson
Hampshire College
Women: Women in China

Clifford Reis Jones
Santa Rosa, California
Dance; Drama

Kenneth W. Jones
Kansas State University
Arya Samaj; Dayananda Saraswati; Lajpat Rai, Lala; Punjab; Shuddhi

Mark Juergensmeyer
University of California, Berkeley
Amritsar; Gandhi, Kasturbai; Ghadr; Godse, Nathuram; Jallianwala Bagh Massacre; Khadi; Radhasoami Satsang; Satyagraha

Richard C. Kagan
Hamline University
Bethune, Norman; Borodin, Michael; Jinmen; Matsu; Sneevliet, Hendricus J. F. M.; Special Economic Zones; Taiwan; Wang Ming

Audrey R. Kahin
Cornell University
Amir Sjarifuddin; Bandung Conference; Batak; Bengkulu; Minangkabau; Nasu-tion, Abdul Haris; Padang; Padri War; Sjafruddin Prawiranegara; Sumatra; Tan Malaka

Pramod Kale
Westport, Connecticut
Natyashastra; Phalke, Dhundiyaj Govind

Michael C. Kalton
Wichita State University
Chŏng Yag-yong; Hwarang; Korean State Examination System; Literati Purges; Neo-Confucianism in Korea; Sirhak; Sŏhak; Sŏwŏn; Tan'gun; Yi Hwang; Yi I; Yi Sŏng-gye

Hugh W. Kang
University of Hawaii
Koryŏ

Manouchehr Kasheff
Columbia University
Ansari; Firdausi; Hafiz; Jami; Rudaki; Sa'di

Nikki Keddie
University of California, Los Angeles
Afghani, Jamal al-Din al-; Constitutional Revolution; Reuter Concession; Tobacco Rebellion

David N. Keightley
University of California, Berkeley
Shang Dynasty

James M. Kelly
University of Utah
Ghuzz; Karakhanid Dynasty; Kashgari, Mahmud al-; Kutadgu Bilig

Russell G. Kempiners, Jr.
Chicago, Illinois
Ghaznavid Dynasty; Mahmud of Ghazna; Nizam al-Mulk; Seljuk Dynasty; Toghril Beg

Benedict J. Tria Kerkvliet
Australian National University
Huk; Taruc, Luis

Melinda Tria Kerkvliet
Australian National University
Evangelista, Crisanto

Clive S. Kessler
University of New South Wales
Kelantan

Roger Keyes
Center for the Study of Japanese Woodblock Prints
Woodblock Prints, Japanese

Zalmay Khalilzad
Columbia University
Amin, Hafizollah; Daud Beureu'eh, Mohammed; Karmal, Babrak; Khalq; Percham; Taraki, Noor Mohammed; Zahir, Mohammad

Ravindra S. Khare
University of Virginia
Brahman

Han-Kyo Kim
University of Cincinnati
An Chae-hong; An Ch'ang-ho; Korea, Japanese Government-General of; Sin Ch'ae-ho; Yi Sang-jae; Yi Tong-hwi

Kyung-Won Kim
Republic of Korea Mission, United Nations
Chun Doo Hwan

William A. Kinsel
Cornell University
Association of Southeast Asian Nations; Colombo Plan; Southeast Asia Treaty Organization

Stanley A. Kochanek
Pennsylvania State University
Emergency in India, The; Indian National Congress; Jana Sangh; Parliament of India; Swatantra Party

William J. Koenig
Highland, Maryland
Alaunghpaya; Amarapura; Bagyidaw; Baker, George; Bodawhpaya; Burma Road; Cox, Hiram; Glass Palace Chronicle; Hluttaw; Hsinhpyushin; Konbaung Dynasty; Mahabandula; Maha Thiha Thura; Naungdawgyi; Pagan Min; Singu; Symes, Michael

David Kopf
University of Minnesota
Brahmo Samaj; Roy, Rammohan; Sen, Keshub Chandra; Tagore, Debendranath

Gregory C. Kozlowski
De Paul University
Abdullah, Muhammad; Ahmadiyya; Ahrar Party; Ajmer; Amir Ali; Arcot; Azad, Abul Kalam; Chishti Tariqa; Farangi Mahal; Fazli Hussain, Sir Mian; Gilgit; Husain, Zakir; Jamat-i Islami; Kuka Sect; Maududi, Abu'l A'la; Naqshbandi; Pindaris; Rahmat Ali, Chaudhuri; Tabligh Movement; Tyabji, Badruddin

John R. Krueger
Indiana University
Mongolian

A. R. Kulkarni
University of Pune, India
Afzal Khan; Holkars; Maharashtra; Marathas; Peshwa; Pune; Shivaji; Sindhia

Edward J. Lazzerini
University of New Orleans
Gasprinskii, Ismail

Chong-sik Lee
University of Pennsylvania
Communism: Communism in Korea; Korea, Democratic People's Republic of; Korea, Republic of

Hong Yung Lee
Yale University
Deng Tuo; Gang of Four; Great Proletarian Cultural Revolution; Jiang Qing; Liao Mosha; May Seventh Cadre Schools; May Sixteenth Circular; Peng Zhen; Red Guards; Wang Hongwen; Wu Han; Yao Wenyuan; Zhang Chunqiao

Peter H. Lee
University of Hawaii
Ch'oe Nam-sŏn; Hyangga; Kasa; P'ansori; Sijo; Yi Kwang-su

John D. Legge
Monash University
Hatta, Mohammad; Partai Nasional Indonesia; Partai Sosialis Indonesia; Sjahrir, Sutan; Sukarno

F. K. Lehman
University of Illinois
Chin; Kachin; Shan

Fritz Lehmann
University of British Columbia
Alivardi Khan; Baksar, Battle of; Diwani; Mir Ja'far; Mir Qasim; Murshid Quli Khan; Patna

David Lelyveld
Columbia University
Ahmad Khan, Sir Sayyid; Fara'zi Movement; Shibli Nu'mani, Muhammad; Sylhet; Waqf

John G. Leonard
Los Angeles, California
Andhra Pradesh

Karen Leonard
University of California, Irvine
Caste; Kayasth; Salar Jang I

Charles Leslie
University of Delaware
Medicine

Ian Hideo Levy
Tokyo, Japan
Asuka; Gagaku; Jinshin War; Man'yōshū

Dianne Lewis
Arecibo Observatory, Puerto Rico
Abdul Jalil Riayat Syah; Anglo-Dutch Treaty; Bugis; Daeng Parani; Kecil, Raja; Kedah; Laksamana; Mahmud Riayat Syah III; Mahmud Syah II; Mansur Syah; Melaka; Orang Laut; Pepper; Perak; Raffles, Sir Thomas Stamford; Raja; Raja Muda; Riau; Syahbandar; Tin; Tun Mahmud

Robin Jared Lewis
Columbia University
Forster, Edward Morgan; Grand Trunk Road; Imphal; Indus River; Kipling, Joseph Rudyard; Nilgiri Hills; Yamuna River

Todd Thornton Lewis
Columbia University
Ajivika Sect; Nagarjuna; Nalanda; Newar; Nirvana; Sangha; Stupa; Tooth Relic Palace

Chu-tsing Li
University of Kansas
Painting: Chinese Painting

Victor B. Lieberman
University of Michigan
Anaukhpetlun; Ava; Bayinnaung; Nandabayin; Syriam; Tabinshweihti; Toungoo Dynasties

Charles Lindholm
Harvard University
Baluchistan; Garo; Manipur; Meghalaya; Mizo; Nagaland; North East Frontier Agency; North-West Frontier Province; Swat; Tripura

Chun Jo Liu
University of Minnesota
Chinese Literature

Craig A. Lockard
University of Wisconsin, Green Bay
Brooke, Sir Charles; Brooke, Sir Charles Vyner; Brooke, Sir James; Dayak; Gambier; Iban; Kadazan; Kuala Lumpur; Kuching; Labuan; Lim Boon Keng; Malaysia; Mat Salleh Rebellion; Sabah; Sarawak; Yap Ah Loy

Bruce M. Lockhart
Cornell University
Binh Xuyen; Can Lao; Can Vuong; Cao Ba Quat; Cao Dai; Cham; Cho Lon; Chu Nom; Chu Van An; Confucianism in Vietnam; Con Son Islands; Cuong De; Dao Duy Tu; D'Argenlieu, Georges-Thierry; De Tham; Dong Khanh; Dupré, Jules-Marie; Dupuis, Jean; Duy Tan; Fontainebleau Conference; Genouilly, Charles Rigault de; Gia Long Code; Ham Nghi; Harmand, François-Jules; Hoa Hao; Ho Chi Minh City; Hong Bang Dynasty; Hong Duc Code; Huynh Phu So; Indochina; Kinh Duong Vuong; La Grandière, Pierre-Paul-Marie de; Lam Son Uprising; Lattre de Tassigny, Jean de; Le Lai; Le Van Duyet; Le Van Khoi Rebellion; Locust Rebellion; Mac Dang Dung; Muong; Nam Tien; Ngo Dinh Can; Ngo Dinh Diem; Ngo Dinh Nhu; Ngo Dinh Thuc; Ngo Dynasty; Nguyen Du; Nguyen Hoang; Nguyen Kim; Nguyen Thai Hoc; Nguyen Trai; Nung; Oc Eo; Patenotre Treaty; Pham Hong Thai; Phan Dinh Phung; Phan Thanh Gian; Pigneau de Béhaine, Pierre; Quoc Ngu; Rhodes, Alexandre de; Saigon, Treaty of; Thieu Tri; Tich Quang; Tonkin; Ton That Thuyet; Tran Nhan Tong; Tran Quy Cap; Tran Thai Tong; Tran Thanh Tong; Tran Thu Do; Tran Trong Kim; Trieu Dynasty; Trinh Cuong; Trinh Khai; Trinh Kiem; Trinh Sam; Trinh Tac; Truong Cong Dinh; Truong Minh Giang; Truong Vinh Ky; Van Lang; Varenne, Alexandre; Versailles Treaty of 1787; Viet Minh; Vietnam, Democratic Republic of; Vietnam, Provisional Revolutionary Government of; Vietnam, Republic of; Xich Quy Quoc

David Ludden
University of Pennsylvania
Irrigation

Ian W. Mabbett
Monash University
Angkor; Angkor Thom; Angkor Wat; Ba Phnom; Bhavavarman; Chitrasena; Devaraja; Funan; Hariharalaya; Indianization; Ishanapura; Jayavarman I; Jayavarman II; Jayavarman VII; Kambuja; Kang Tai; Suryavarman I; Suryavarman II; Yasodharapura; Yasovarman II; Zhenla; Zhou Daguan

William A. McCabe
New York, New York
Turkmenistan

Robert McChesney
New York University
Balkh; Naw Bahar; Tirmidh

James L. McClain
Brown University
Akechi Mitsuhide; Ashigaru; Kanazawa; Katō Kiyomasa; Konishi Yukinaga; Nagashino, Battle of; Sekigahara, Battle of; Sengoku Period; Takeda Shingen; Tanegashima; Uesugi Kenshin

Shannon McCune
University of Florida
P'yŏngyang; Seoul

Angus W. McDonald, Jr.
Minneapolis, Minnesota
Changsha; Hunan; Mao Zedong

Donald S. Macdonald
Georgetown University
Cho Man-sik; Kim Ku; Kim Kyu-sik; P'anmunjŏm Peace Talks; Rhee, Syngman; United Nations Commission for the Unification and Rehabilitation of Korea

Stephen R. MacKinnon
Arizona State University
Buck, Pearl; Hatem, George; Journalism: Journalism in China; Marshall, George C.; Smedley, Agnes; Snow, Edgar; Stilwell, Joseph W.; Strong, Anna Louise; Stuart, J. Leighton

Charles B. McLane
Dartmouth College
Communism: Communism in Southeast Asia; Marxism and Socialism: Marxism and Socialism in Southeast Asia

W. H. McLeod
University of Otago, New Zealand
Akali Dal; Nanak; Sikhism; Singh, Fateh; Singh, Ranjit; Singh, Tara

T. N. Madan
Institute of Economic Growth, India
Kashmir; Srinagar

Jayanta Mahapatra
Cuttack, India
Orissa

John S. Major
The Asia Society
Dong Zhongshu; Junxian System; Li Si; Liu Bang; Liu Bei; Longshan Culture; Sun Quan; Tuyuhun

John M. Maki
Amherst, Massachusetts
Anglo-Japanese Alliance; Dulles, John Foster; Lansing-Ishii Agreement; MacArthur, Douglas A.; Occupation of Japan; Portsmouth, Treaty of; Rezanov, Nikolai Petrovich; Root-Takahira Agreement; San Francisco Treaty; Taft-Katsura Agreement

Geri Hockfield Malandra
Saint Paul, Minnesota
Ajanta; Amaravati; Aryavarta; Bhubaneswar; Ellora; Nagarjunikonda; Rashtrakuta Dynasty; Sanchi; Sarnath; Ujjain

Wilfred Malenbaum
University of Pennsylvania
Economic Development

Beatrice Forbes Manz
Harvard University
Ghazan; Hulegu; Ilkhanid Dynasty; Mongols; Timur; Timurid Dynasty

M. Lavonne Marubbio
Fargo, North Dakota
An Shigao; Huainanzi; Liezi; Zheng Xuan

Jim Masselos
Sydney University
Bombay; Gokhale, Gopal Krishna; Naoroji, Dadabhai; Phadke, Vasudeo Balwant; Phule, Jotirao Govindrao; Ranade, Mahadev Govind; Savarkar, Vinayak Damodar; Tilak, Bal Gangadhar

Richard Mather
University of Minnesota
Six Dynasties; Three Kingdoms

Virginia Matheson
Australian National University
Malays; Trengganu

Maurice J. Meisner
University of Wisconsin
Marxism and Socialism: Marxism in China

Barbara D. Metcalf
University of California, Davis
Deoband; Wali Ullah, Shah

Thomas R. Metcalf
University of California, Berkeley
Durbar; Karachi; Lutyens, Sir Edwin; Mauritius; Raj; Sepoy; Taluqdar

Barbara Stoler Miller
Columbia University
Bhagavad Gita; Mahabharata; Ramayana

J. Scott Miller
Princeton University
Iwakura Mission; Iwakura Tomomi; Jinrikisha; Kambun; Rakugo; Yakuza

Stuart Creighton Miller
Sausalito, California
Philippine Revolution

R. S. Milne
University of British Columbia
Bumiputra; Emergency in Malaysia, The; Federated Malay States; Lee Kuan Yew; Malaya, Federation of; Malayan Chinese Association; Malayan Union; Pan-Malayan Islamic Party; Straits Settlements; Unfederated Malay States; United Malays National Organization

A. C. Milner
Australian National University
Abdullah bin Abdul Kadir; Ahmad, Ahmuadzam Shah; Clifford, Sir Hugh; Pahang; Pahang War; Weld, Sir Frederick

Gail Minault
University of Texas
Ali Brothers; Hydari, Akbar; Hyderabad; Khilafat Movement

Kimitada Miwa
Sophia University, Japan
Fukuzawa Yukichi; Jiyū Minken; Keiō Gijuku; Matsuoka Yōsuke; Mutsu Munemitsu; Shidehara Kijūrō; Shigemitsu Mamoru

Samuel Hugh Moffett
Princeton Theological Seminary
Allen, Horace Newton; Christianity: An Overview; Christianity: Christianity in Korea; Yun Ch'i-ho

Edwin E. Moise
Clemson University
Agricultural Producers' Cooperatives; Agriculture, Collectivization of; Geneva Conference of 1954; Indochina War; Land Tenure and Reform: Land Reform in Modern China; Paris Peace Conference; Sino-Vietnamese Relations

Michael G. Morony
University of California, Los Angeles
Ardashir I; Bahram Gur; Khusrau Anushirvan; Shapur I; Shapur II; Yazdigird I; Yazdigird III

V. Dixon Morris
University of Hawaii
Sakai; Sen no Rikyū; Tea Ceremony

Larry W. Moses
Indiana University
Mongolian People's Republic

Sharif al-Mujahid
Quaid-e-Azam Academy, Pakistan
Jinnah, Mohammad Ali

Harbans Mukhia
Jawaharlal Nehru University, India
Abu'l Fazl; Akbar; Babur; Badauni, Abdul Qadir; Bernier, François; Birbal; Dara Shikoh; Din-i Ilahi; Humayun; I'timad ud-Daulah; Jagir; Jai Singh; Mansabdari System; Man Singh; Manucci, Niccolao; Nur Jahan; Todar Mal

David E. Mungello
Coe College
Castiglione, Guiseppe; Cattaneo, Lazzaro; Jesuits: Jesuits in China; Macao; Ricci, Matteo; Schall von Bell, Johann Adam; Verbiest, Ferdinand; Xujiahui

J. Kim Munholland
University of Minnesota
Imperialism

Rhoads Murphey
University of Michigan
Agriculture

Rhoads Murphey, Jr.
Columbia University
Bukhara; Ferghana; Jaxartes River; Kashgar; Khwarazm; Khwarazmshah; Merv; Mines and Metallurgy; Orkhon Inscriptions; Samarkand; Shaibanid Dynasty; Tabriz; Tashkent; Warfare: Steppe Warfare

Myo Myint
Cornell University
Letwethondara; Mindon

Moni Nag
Population Council
Population: An Overview

B. R. Nanda
New Delhi, India
Nehru, Jawaharlal; Nehru, Motilal; Pandit, Vijaya Lakshmi

A. K. Narain
University of Wisconsin
Bimbisara; Gondophernes; Greeks; Gupta Empire; Hastinapur; Kalinga; Kapilavastu; Kosala; Kurukshetra; Kushan Dynasty; Menander; Naga; Pataliputra; Poros; Roman Empire; Saka Dynasties; Satavahana Dynasty; Shunga Dynasty; Taxila

Loretta Topalian Nassar
Columbia University
Armenians in South Asia

Walter C. Neale
University of Tennessee
Land Tenure and Reform: Land Tenure, Revenue, and Reform in South Asia

John Philip Ness
University of Minnesota
Longmen; Phags-pa; Shato Turks; Yihetuan

Paula R. Newberg
New York, New York
Refugees

Ng Lun Ngai-ha
Chinese University, Hong Kong
Hong Kong

Farhan Ahmad Nizami
Oxford University
Fatawa-i Alamgiri; Husain Shahi Dynasty; Iltutmish; Jahangir; Khafi Khan, Muhammad Hashim Ali; Khalji Dynasty; Mamluks; Mir Jumla; Muhammad bin Qasim; Rampur; Sirhindhi, Ahmad; Umara

Khaliq Ahmad Nizami
Aligarh Muslim University, India
Amir Khusrau; Balban, Ghiyas ud-Din; Barani, Zia ud-Din; Daulatabad; Delhi Sultanate; Ferishta, Muhammad Qasim; Hemu; Lodi Dynasty; Nizam ud-Din Auliya; Qutb ud-Din Aibak; Raziyya; Sayyid Dynasty; Sebuktigin, Abu Mansur; Tughluq Dynasty

Jerry Norman
University of Washington
Chinese Language; Manchu Language; Pinyin; Sino-Tibetan Languages; Wade-Giles Romanization

Peter Nosco
University of Southern California
Neo-Confucianism

F. G. Notehelfer
University of California, Los Angeles
Ashio Copper Mine; Charter Oath; Ebina Danjō; Hepburn, James Curtis; Itagaki Taisuke; Katayama Sen; Kōtoku Shūsui; Nakae Chōmin; Niijima Jō; Nikolai; Ōi Kentarō; Osugi Sakae; Risshisha; Tokutomi Sohō; Ueki Emori; Uemura Masahisa

Vahid Nowshirvani
Columbia University
Kerman

Stanley J. O'Connor
Cornell University
Ceramics: Southeast Asian Ceramics Trade; Sculpture: Southeast Asian Sculpture

John Kieh-Chiang Oh
Potomac, Maryland
May Sixteenth Coup d'État

Shumpei Okamoto
deceased
Aoki Shūzō; Hibiya Incident; Shimonoseki, Treaty of; Sino-Japanese War; Triple Intervention; Ugaki Kazushige

Martha Brill Olcott
Colgate University
Kazakhs

Veena Talwar Oldenburg
Sarah Lawrence College
Lucknow

Michael Paul Onorato
California State University, Fullerton
Harrison, Francis Burton; Jones Act; Taft, William Howard; Wood, Leonard

Herman Ooms
University of Illinois, Chicago
Kangaku; Kansei Reforms; Matsudaira Sadanobu; Sidotti, Giovanni Battista

Bruce McCoy Owens
Columbia University
Chandigarh; Gelugpa; Himachal Pradesh; Malla; Simla

Michael N. Pearson
University of New South Wales
Calicut; Goa; Portuguese: Portuguese in India; Portuguese: Portuguese in Sri Lanka; Surat

Mark R. Peattie
University of Massachusetts, Boston
Araki Sadao; Manchurian Incident; March Incident; Nogi Maresuke; Nomura Kichisaburō; Pearl Harbor; Saipan; Shandong Intervention; Shanghai Incident; Suzuki Kantarō; Tōgō Heihachirō; Tōjō Hideki; Yamamoto Isoroku; Yamashita Tomoyuki

Patrick Peebles
University of Missouri, Kansas City
Brownrigg, Sir Robert; Ceylon National Congress; Colebrooke-Cameron Reforms; Donoughmore Constitution; D'Oyly, Sir John; Goonetilleke, Sir Oliver Ernest; Gunawardena, Don Philip Rupasinghe; Kotelawala, Sir John Lionel; Maitland, Sir Thomas; Ramanathan, Sir Ponnambalam; Soulbury Commission; Suriya Mal Campaign; Swabhasa Campaign

John R. Perry
University of Chicago
Afsharid Dynasty; Nadir; Zand, Karim Khan; Zand Dynasty

James M. Phillips
Ventnor, New Jersey
Christianity: Christianity in Japan

Rulan Chao Pian
Harvard University
Music: Music in China

Mariam Pirnazar
New York, New York
Khayyam, Omar; Nizami; Persian Literature; Shahnama

Oliver B. Pollak
Omaha, Nebraska
Anglo-Burmese Wars; Lambert, George Robert; Mangelun Convention; Phayre, Sir Arthur P.; Tenasserim; Tharrawaddy; Upper Burma; Yandabo, Treaty of

Robert Poor
University of Minnesota
Architecture: Chinese Architecture; Bronze Age in China; Sculpture: Chinese Sculpture

Gregory L. Possehl
University of Pennsylvania
Indus Valley Civilization

Lawrence Potter
Bellport, New York
Akkoyunlu; Badghis; Herat; Karako-
yunlu; Kart Dynasty; Sarbadarids; Uzun
Hasan

Franklin A. Presler
Kalamazoo College
Five-Year Plans; Justice Party; Krishna
Menon, Vengalil Krishnan; Prasad, Ra-
jendra; Tashkent Agreement; Telengana
Movement; Virasalingam, Kandukuri

Frances W. Pritchett
Columbia University
Dard, Sayyid Khvaja Mir; Ghalib, Mirza
Asadullah Khan; Hali, Altaf Husain;
Iqbal, Sir Muhammad; Mir, Muhammad
Taqi; Zafar, Bahadur Shah

Barbara N. Ramusack
University of Cincinnati
Baroda; Bhopal; Bikaner; Bundi; Gwa-
lior; Indore; Jaipur; Jaisalmer; Mysore;
Princely States; Travancore

Mary Backus Rankin
Washington, D.C.
Huang Xing; Li Yuanhong; Sun Yat-sen;
Xinhai Revolution

John A. Rapp
Beloit College
Amur River; Anarchism; Anshan; Cao
Cao; Chen Yun; Dali; Democracy Wall;
Diaoyutai Islands; Five Bushels of Rice
Sect; Gao Gang; Hefei; Henan; Hubei;
Jiangsu; Jiangxi; Jilin; Kaiping; Kang
Sheng; Kunming; Liaoning; Lin Biao;
Lop Nur; Nanchang; Ningxia; Peng De-
huai; Pescadores; Qingtan; Qiqihar;
Shaanganning; Shaanxi; Shanghai Com-
muniqué; Shantou; Shanyu; Shenyang;
Shijiazhuang; Spiritual Pollution; Wei
Jingsheng; Wuxi; Xiamen; Xining; Yan-
tai; Yellow River; Yellow Turbans; Yin-
chuan; Yunnan

Tapan Raychaudhuri
Oxford University
Bengal

Anthony Reid
Australian National University
Daud Beureu'eh, Muhammad; Demak;
Gerindo; Goa, Kingdom of; Indonesian
Revolution; Lombok; Makassar; Medan;
Pasai; Pedir; Soedirman; Speelman, Cor-
nelis Janszoon

Ronald D. Renard
Chiang Mai, Thailand
Karen

Edward J. M. Rhoads
University of Texas
Canton; China Trade; Country Trade;
Guangdong; Guangxi; Hainan; Rong
Hong

Theodore Riccardi, Jr.
Columbia University
Arunachal Pradesh; Chitral; Drukpa;
Eden Mission; Nepal: Nepalese Archae-
ology, Architecture, and Art

M. C. Ricklefs
Monash University
Agung; Amangkurat I; Babad; Banten;
Giyanti, Treaty of; Hamengkubuwana;
Islamization of Southeast Asia; Java; Ja-
vanese Wars of Succession; Kartasura;
Mangkubumi; Pakubuwana; Trunajaya

Stephen Rittenberg
Columbia University
Khan, Abdul Ghaffar; Khan, Sir Sikandar
Hayat; Khan, Tikka; Khuda'i Khidmat-
gar; Liaqat Ali Khan; Peshawar; Quetta;
Sind

Dorothy Robins-Mowry
Smithsonian Institution
Women: Women in Japan

Michael Robinson
University of Southern California
An Chung-gŭn; Ilchinhoe; Korea; Min,
Queen; Yi Wan-yong

Patrick Roche
Inver Hills Community College
Almeida, Lourenco de; Bharati, Subra-
manya; De Nobili, Roberto; Henriquez,
Henry; Jesuits: Jesuits in India; Schwartz,
Christian Frederick; Thomas; Xavier,
Francis

Ludo Rocher
University of Pennsylvania
Chakravartin; Hindu Law; Kautilya;
Müller, Friedrich Max

Rosane Rocher
University of Pennsylvania
Anquetil-Duperron, A. H.; Asiatic Soci-
ety of Bengal; Jones, Sir WIlliam

Joan G. Roland
New York, New York
Jews

Ayse-Azade Rorlich
University of Southern California
Tatars

Marina Roseman
Tufts University
Orang Asli

David A. Rosenberg
Middlebury College
Marcos, Ferdinand E.; Moro National
Liberation Front; Philippines

Morris Rossabi
The China Institute, New York
Altaic Languages; Altan Khan; Central
Asia; Dzungaria; Galdan; Genghis Khan;
Gobi; Ili; Kublai Khan; Ogedei; Xinjiang

Gilbert Rozman
Princeton University
Cities; Population: Population in China;
Population: Population in Japan

Barry Rubin
Georgetown University
Hostage Crisis; Iran-Iraq War

David Rubin
New York, New York
Devkota, Laxmiprasad; Kalidasa; Kama
Sutra; Premchand

Richard Rubinger
University of Hawaii
Education: Education in Japan; Kaemp-
fer, Engelbert; Ogata Kōan; Ōtsuki Gen-
taku; Rangaku; Shiba Kōkan; Siebold,
Philipp Franz von

James R. Rush
Yale University
Abdul Muis; Amboina Massacre; Coen,
Jan Pieterszoon; Gongsi; Kalimantan;
Kartini, Raden Ajeng; Muhammadiyah;
Natsir, Mohammad; Snouck Hurgronje,
Christian

James R. Russell
Columbia University
Achaemenid Dynasty; Avesta; Bunda-
hishn; Denkard; Fire Temple; Manichae-
ism; Mazdak; Medes; Parthians; Sasanid
Dynasty; Tower of Silence; Videvdat;
Zoroaster; Zoroastrianism

Abdelaziz Sachedina
University of Virginia
Ashura; Ayatollah; Id Fitr; Id Qorban;
Ja'fari; Mahdi; Mashhad; Mujtahid;
Mulla; Sunni

Robert K. Sakai
University of Hawaii
Okinawa; Saigō Takamori; Satsuma;
Shimazu Hisamitsu; Shimazu Nariakira;
Tokugawa Period

Jahan Salehi
Columbia University
Kara Kum; Kizilbash; Kizil Kum; Minaret; Mossadegh, Mohammed; Qajar, Nasir al-Din; Shari'ati, Ali; Vilayet-i Faqih; Zagros Range

George Saliba
Columbia University
Astrology and Astronomy, Islamic; Biruni, al-; Calendars and Eras: Islamic Calendars and Eras; Ibn Sina

Ariel Salzmann
Columbia University
Azerbaijan; Khotan; Khuzistan; Mazandaran; Sistan; Tabaristan

Vijaya Samaraweera
Winchester, Massachusetts
Bandaranaike, Sirimavo Ratwatte Dias; Bandaranaike, Solomon West Ridgeway Dias; Jayawardene, Junius Richard; Johnston, Sir Alexander; Lanka Sama Samaja Party; North, Frederick; Perera, Nanayakkarapathirage Martin; Pilima Talauve; Senanayake, Don Stephen; Senanayake, Dudley Shelton; Sri Lanka Freedom Party; Tennent, Sir James Emerson; United National Party

Usha Sanyal
Columbia University
Age of Consent Act; Ayodhya; Bhabha, Homi Jehangir; Birla Family; Cis-Sutlej States; Danish East India Company; Dayal, Har; Deccan Riots; Fitch, Ralph; French East India Company; Gama, Vasco da; Giri, Varahagiri Venkata; Hawkins, William; Hume, Allan Octavian; Jayakar, Mukund Ramrao; Kisan Sabha; Kitchener, Horatio Herbert; Law, Edward; Lawrence, John Laird Mair; Lawrence, Sir Henry Montgomery; Malabari, Behramji Merwanji; Mleccha; Mulraj, Diwan; Nicholson, John; Radhakrishnan, Sarvepalli; Rathors; Roe, Sir Thomas; Rohillas; Sadhu; Sapru, Tej Bahadur; Strachey, Sir John; Strachey, Sir Richard; Thagi; Thaneswar

Richard Davis Saran
Ann Arbor, Michigan
Chauhan Dynasty; Chitor; Jodhpur; Marwar; Mewar; Rajput; Udaipur

Roger M. Savory
University of Toronto
Abbas I; Isma'il I; Safavi; Safavid Dynasty

Thomas R. Schalow
Princeton University
Burakumin; Hiroshima; Japan: Geographic Regions of Japan; Nagoya; Nihonbashi; Nosaka Sanzō; Ozaki Yukio; Tokuda Kyūichi

John N. Schumacher, S.J.
Loyola School of Theology, Philippines
Bonifacio, Andres; Burgos, Jose; Catholicism in the Philippines; Cavite Mutiny; Friars; Jacinto, Emilio; Liga Filipina; Pilar, Marcelo H. del; Propaganda Movement; Rizal, Jose Mercado

Philip D. Schuyler
Columbia University
Music: Music in Iran, Afghanistan, and Central Asia

Joseph E. Schwartzberg
University of Minnesota
Aksai Chin; Bolan Pass; Deccan; Durand Line; Hindustan; Khyber Pass; McMahon Line; Rann of Kutch; South Asia; Suez Canal

William Henry Scott
Sagada, Philippines
Aglipay y Labayan, Gregorio; Philippine Independent Church; Reyes y Florentino, Isabelo de los

Peter J. Seybolt
University of Vermont
Education: Education in Twentieth-Century China; Eighth Route Army; He Long; Jinggang Shan; Long March; Qu Qiubai; Ruijin; Yan'an

A. Shahpur Shahbazi
La Grande, Oregon
Artaxerxes II; Artaxerxes III; Cyrus II; Darius I; Hasanlu; Huns; Isfahan; Panjikent; Pasargadae; Persepolis; Shahr-i Sukhta; Tepe Hissar; Tepe Yahya; Xerxes

Stephen R. Shalom
William Paterson College
Laurel-Langley Trade Agreement

Prayag Raj Sharma
Tribhuvan University, Nepal
Banepa; Bhaktapur; Gurungs; Kathmandu; Kirkpatrick Mission; Licchavi Dynasty; Lumbini; Magars; Nepal: History of Nepal; Patan; Prithvinarayan Shah

Richard Shek
Carmichael, California
Fang La; Nian Rebellion; Rebellions in China; Red Eyebrows; Red Spears; Red Turbans; Secret Societies; Triads; White Lotus Society

Richard Sherburne
Seattle University
Atisha

James E. Sheridan
Northwestern University
Cao Kun; Chen Jiongming; Duan Qirui; Feng Guozhang; Feng Yuxiang; Warlord Cliques; Warlords; Wu Peifu; Yan Xishan; Zhang Xueliang; Zhang Zuolin

Ben-Ami Shillony
Hebrew University, Jerusalem
Aizawa Incident; Akihito; February Twenty-sixth Incident; Inoue Nisshō; Kita Ikki; Kokuryūkai; Nōhonshugi; Okada Keisuke; Uchida Ryōhei; Yoshihito

Yoshiaki Shimizu
Smithsonian Institution
Okakura Tenshin; Painting: Japanese Painting; Sesshū Tōyō

Donald H. Shively
University of California, Berkeley
Danjurō; Imperial Rescript on Education; Kabuki; Osaka

Edward J. Shultz
West Oahu College
Chang Po-go; Ch'oe Ch'i-wŏn; Ch'oe Ch'ung; Ch'oe Ch'ung-hŏn; Chŏng Mong-ju; Kaesong; Kija Chosŏn; Kim Yu-sin; Kwanggaet'o; Mongol Empire: Mongol Invasions of Korea; Myoch'ŏng; Parhae; Piracy: Japanese Piracy in Korea; Three Hans; Ŭlchi Mundŏk; Yangban; Yŏn Kaesomun

K. S. Singh
Anthropological Survey of India
Adivasis; Gondwana; Jharkand; Munda; Santal

Pradip Sinha
Rabindra Bharati University, India
Calcutta; Charnock, Job; Fort William; Hughly River; Plassey, Battle of; Siraj ud-Daulah; Surman's Embassy

Brian K. Smith
Barnard College
Vedanta; Yoga

Henry D. Smith II
University of California, Santa Barbara
Chōnin; Edo; Kantō Earthquake; Meireki Fire; Shinjinkai; Tokyo

Stuart W. Smithers
Columbia University
Calendars and Eras: Indian Calendars and Eras; Ganges River; Lingayats; Mahabalipuram; Shaivism; Shankara; Varanasi

Clark Sorensen
Vanderbilt University
Korea, Class Structure in

Svat Soucek
New York Public Library
Kirghizia; Turfan

Paul R. Spickard
Bethel College
Coolie Trade; Emigration: Chinese Emigration

Howard Spodek
Temple University
Ahmadabad; Gujarat; Marwaris; Porbandar; Rupee; Sarabhai; Tata Family; Vaishya

Peter W. Stanley
Ford Foundation
Forbes, William Cameron; Philippine Commissions; Quezon, Manuel Luis

Burton Stein
London, England
Slavery and Serfdom: Slavery and Serfdom in South Asia; Tamil Nadu; Vijayanagara

John J. Stephan
University of Hawaii
Hokkaido; Kurile Islands; Shōwa Period

Dan Stevenson
Butler University
Faxian; Fotudeng; Kumarajiva; Xuanzang

A. J. Stockwell
Royal Holloway College, England
Birch, James W. W.; Clementi, Sir Cecil; Idris; Low, Sir Hugh; Malay Nationalist Party; Ord, Sir Harry; Swettenham, Sir Frank; Templer, Sir Gerald

John S. Strong
Bates College
Ashoka; Chandragupta Maurya; Magadha; Maurya Empire; Megasthenes

Maria E. Subtelny
University of Toronto
Baiqara, Husain; Bihzad; Chagatai; Chagatai Literature; Neva'i; Shahrukh; Ulug Beg

Dae Sook Suh
University of Hawaii
Ch'ŏllima Movement; Kim II Sung; Kim Jong Il

Merlin Swartz
Boston University
Ash'ari; Hadith; Hanafi; Hanbali; Maliki; Mu'tazili; Shafi'i

Nina Swidler
Fordham University
Baluchis; Brahui

Jing-shen Tao
University of Arizona
Jurchen; Jurchen Jin Dynasty; Khitan; Liao Dynasty

Keith W. Taylor
National University of Singapore
Bach Dang, Battles of; Cochinchina; Dinh Bo Linh; Dong Son; Jiaozhi; Jiaozhou; Le Hoan; Ly Bon; Ly Cong Uan; Ly Phat Ma; Ly Phat Tu; Ly Thuong Kiet; Ngo Quyen; Si Nhiep; Trieu Da; Trung Sisters Rebellion

Robert H. Taylor
University of London
Anti-Fascist People's Freedom League; Anti-Separation League; Aung San; Ba Maw; Ba Pe; Ba Swe; Bombay-Burmah Trading Corporation; Burma, Socialist Republic of the Union of; Burma, Union of; Burma Defense Army; Burma Socialist Program Party; Burma Workers and Peasants Party; Dobama Asiayon; General Council of Burmese Associations; Karen National Defense Organization; Kodaw Hmaing, Thakin; Kyaw Nyein; Minami Kikan; Ne Win; Nu, U; Ottama; People's Party of Burma; Saw; Shan State Independence Army; Sinyetha Party; Soe, Thakin; Than Tun, Thakin; Thirty Comrades; Young Men's Buddhist Association

Rodney L. Taylor
University of Colorado
Han Feizi; Legalism; Lü Buwei; Lunyu; Mencius; Shen Buhai; Xunzi; Zhenyan

Romeyn Taylor
University of Minnesota
Daoism; Laozi; Zhuangzi; Zhu Yuanzhang

Baas Terwiel
Australian National University
Ahom

Randolph M. Thornton
Columbia University
Krishna; Panini; Puranas; Ramanuja; Rishi; Samkhya; Samskara; Tirthankara

Robert A. F. Thurman
Amherst College
Buddhism: An Overview; Dalai Lama; Lamaism; Lhasa; Panchen Lama; Tibet

Hugh Tinker
Lancaster, England
Cabinet Mission; Cripps Mission; Emigration: South Asian Emigration; Gov-

ernment of India; Government of India Acts; Mountbatten, Louis; Partition of India; Simon Commission

David A. Titus
Wesleyan University
Hirohito; Mutsuhito

Ronald P. Toby
University of Illinois
Adams, William; Amakusa; Deshima; Hirado; Kirishitan; Nagasaki; Namban Bunka; Seclusion; Shimabara; Tsushima; Valignano, Alessandro

Paul M. Toomey
Tufts University
Pilgrimage

Hugh Toye
Oxford, England
Boun Oum; Lao Issara; Phetsarath; Savangvatthana; Sisavangvong; Souphanouvong; Souvannaphouma

Carl A. Trocki
Thomas More College
Abdul Rahman; Abu Bakar; Ali, Sultan of Johor; Bendahara; Bentan Island; Ghi Hin; Hai San Society; Haji, Raja; Hussein, Sultan of Johor and Singapore; Ibrahim; Johor; Kapitan China; Lingga; Onn bin Ja'afar, Dato; Opium; Piracy: Piracy in the Malay World; Singapore; Temenggong

Michio Umegaki
Georgetown University
Etō Shimpei; Fukuda Takeo; Hamaguchi Osachi; Hatoyama Ichirō; Katayama Tetsu; Kenkokusetsu; Kishi Nobusuke; Miki Takeo; Nakasone Yasuhiro; Ohira Masayoshi; Saga Rebellion; Takahashi Korekiyo; Tanaka Kakuei; Yoshida Shigeru

David A. Utz
University of Pennsylvania
Avestan; Dari; Farsi; Pahlavi; Sogdian

C. van Dijk
Leiden, Netherlands
Agus Salim, Haji; Darul Islam; Dewantara, Ki Hadjar; Hizbu'llah and Sabili'llah; Imam Bondjol; Masjumi; Nahdatul Ulama; Pemerintah Revolusioner Republik Indonesia/Perdjuangan Semesta; Sarekat Islam; Semaoen; Teuku Oemar; Tjokroaminoto

Robert Van Niel
University of Hawaii
Bosch, Johannes van den; Douwes Dekker, Eduard; Ethical Colonial Policy; Kultuurstelsel; Netherlands East Indies

Lyman P. Van Slyke
Stanford University
Chongqing; Flying Tigers; Guilin; Guiyang; Hurley, Patrick J.; New Fourth Army Incident; United Front; World War II in China; Yangtze River

Paul Varley
Columbia University
Benkei; Bushido; Hōryūji; Kemmu Restoration; Kusunoki Masashige; Nambokuchō; Ōnin War; Samurai; Seppuku; Yoshino Line

Gauri Viswanathan
Columbia University
Education: Education in South Asia

Bonnie C. Wade
University of California, Berkeley
Music: Music in South Asia

Nancy M. Waggoner
American Numismatic Society
Money: Money in the Ancient Near East

Bob Tadashi Wakabayashi
York University
Aizawa Yasushi; Akō Gishi; Andō Shōeki; Fujita Yūkoku; Hayashi Shihei; Ishida Baigan; Itō Jinsai; Kamo no Mabuchi; Kokugaku; Kumazawa Banzan; Motoori Norinaga; Ninomiya Sontoku; Ogyū Sorai; Rai San'yō; Sakuma Shōzan; Satō Nobuhiro; Sugita Gempaku; Watanabe Kazan and Takano Chōei; Yokoi Shōnan; Yonaoshi

Jeanette A. Wakin
Columbia University
Dhimmi; Husain ibn Ali; Jihad; Karrami; Malamati; Qadi; Qur'an; Ramadan; Salat; Shari'a; Zakat

Arthur N. Waldron
Princeton University
Datong; Dayan Khan; Gansu; Great Wall; Hami; Jiayuguan; Juyongguan; Karakorum; Lanzhou; Manchuria; Manchus; Nomadism; Oirats; Ordos Region; Shanhaiguan; Sogdiana; Tuntian; Wu Sangui

Joanna Waley-Cohen
Guilford, Connecticut
Kangxi Emperor; Qianlong Emperor; Yongzheng Emperor

Paul E. Walker
McGill University
Agha Khan; Alamut; Ali al-Rida; Bohras; Farabi, al-; Imam; Isma'ili; Ithna Ashari; Khojas; Shi'a

Judith E. Walsh
State University of New York, Old Westbury
Anglo-Indians; Bande Mataram; Banerjea, Surendranath; Besant, Annie; Blue Mutiny; Chatterji, Bankim Chandra; Dutt, Michael Madhusudan; Dutt, Romesh Chunder; Hindu Renaissance; Home Rule League; Ilbert Bill; Indigo; Malaviya, Madan Mohan; Sati; Tagore, Rabindranath

Wang Gungwu
Hong Kong University
Five Dynasties

James Francis Warren
Murdoch University, Australia
Balambangan; Jolo; Moro; Moro Wars; Sulu

S. Razi Wasti
Columbia University
Jinnah, Fatima; Khaksar Movement; Lahore; Montagu-Chelmsford Reforms

Howard H. Wechsler
deceased
An Lushan; Chang'an; Du Fu; Dunhuang; Fubing System; Guanzhong; Han Yu; Huang Chao; Sixteen Kingdoms; Sui Dynasty; Tang Dynasty; Wu Zhao

Richard E. Welch, Jr.
Lafayette College
Bell Trade Act; Malolos Republic; Manila Bay, Battle of; Philippine-American War

Jayne Werner
Columbia University
Women: Women in South and Southeast Asia

Judith A. Whitbeck
University of Texas
Feng Guifen; Gong Zizhen; Guwen; Gu Yanwu; Gu Zuyu; Huang Zongxi; Jinwen; Kaozheng Xue; Ruan Yuan; Yan Yuan; Zhang Xuecheng

James W. White
University of North Carolina
Ikki; Osso

John K. Whitmore
University of Michigan
Vietnam

Edgar Wickberg
University of British Columbia
Overseas Chinese

Robert S. Wicks
Miami University, Ohio
Architecture: Southeast Asian Architecture; Painting: Painting in Southeast Asia

Constance M. Wilson
Northern Illinois University
Bodindecha Sing Singhaseni; Bowring, Sir John; Mongkut; Pallegoix, Denis-Jean-Baptiste; Phrakhlang Dit Bunnag; Phra Nang Klao; Phra Phutthaloetla Naphalai; Phra Pin Klao; Sunthon Phu; Thiphakorawong Kham Bunnag

John U. Wolff
Cornell University
Austronesian Languages; Philippine Languages

William D. Wray
University of British Columbia
Iwasaki Yatarō; Mitsubishi; Mitsui; Nakama and Ton'ya; Ōkura Kihachirō; Sumitomo; Yasuda Zenjirō

David K. Wyatt
Cornell University
Anu; Ayudhya; Bali; Bangkok; Borommakot; Borommaracha I; Borommatrailokanat; Budi Utomo; Bunga Mas; Bunnag Family; Burney, Henry; Chakkraphat; Chakri Dynasty; Champassak; Chandrabhanu; Chiang Mai; Chit Phumisak; Chulalongkorn; Damrong Rajanubhab; Devawongse Varopakar; Dvaravati; Education: Education in Southeast Asia; Ekathotsarot; Emerald Buddha; Fa Ngum; Hmong; Ho; Indies Party; Indrapura; Intanon; Kalahom; Kavila; Khun Borom; Kingkitsarat; Kinwun Mingyi; Kra Isthmus; Ku Na; Lamphun; Land Tenure and Reform: Land Tenure, Revenue, and Reform in Southeast Asia; Langkasuka; Lan Na; Lan Sang; Lao; Laos; Literacy: Literacy in Southeast Asia; Lopburi; Lo Thai; Luang Prabang; Madura; Magsaysay, Ramon; Mahadammayazadipathi; Mahathammaracha; Mahathammaracha I; Mahathammaracha II; Mahathammaracha III; Mahathammaracha IV; Mahatthai; Maluku; Mangrai; Manila; Mekong Expedition; Mindanao; Mon; Nakhon Si Thammarat; Narai; Naresuan; Negri Sembilan; Ngam Muang; Paknam Incident; Pangkor Engagement; Patani; Penang; Perlis; Phaulkon, Constantine; Phayao; Phetracha; Phrakhlang; Phra Pathom Chedi; Prajadhipok; Prasat Thong; Province Wellesley; Ramakian; Ramathibodi I; Ramesuan; Ramkhamhaeng; Razadarit; Rolin-Jaequemyns, Gustave; Roxas, Manuel; Sakdi Na; Sam Fang Kaen; Saya San; Selangor; Setthathirat; Siang Khwang; Siribunyasan; Sisuriya-

wong; Slavery and Serfdom: Slavery and Serfdom in Southeast Asia; Soisisamut; Song Tham; Southeast Asia; Sri Indraditya; Sukhothai; Supayalat; Surinyavongsa; Suvarnabhumi; Tai Peoples; Taman Siswa; Tambralinga; Thailand; Thammayuttika; That Luang; That Phanom; Thibaw; Tilokaracha; Un Kham; Vajiravudh; Vientiane; Vijaya; Volksraad; Wachirayan Warorot; Zhao Rugua

Philip Yampolsky
Columbia University
Buddhism: Buddhism in China

Neguin Yavari
Columbia University
Dar al-Fonun; Kasravi, Ahmad; Malkom Khan; Pahlavi, Ashraf; Qavam, Ahmad; Razmara, Ali; Saadabad Pact; Turkomanchay, Treaty of

Ann Yonemura
Smithsonian Institution
Ceramics: Japanese Ceramics

Ernest P. Young
University of Michigan
China, Republic Period; Twenty-one Demands; Yuan Shikai

Joseph J. Zasloff
University of Pittsburgh
Geneva Conference on the Laotian Question; Kaysone Phomvihan; Kong Le; Pathet Lao; Phoui Sananikone; Phoumi Nosavan; Vang Pao; Vientiane Agreements

Lynn Zastoupil
Stanford University
Black Hole; Canning, Charles John; Child, Sir Josiah; Elphinstone, Mountstuart; Haileybury College; Koh-i Nur Diamond; Maine, Sir Henry; Malcolm, Sir John; Metcalfe, Sir Charles; Mill, James; Mill, John Stuart; Munro, Sir Thomas; Napier, Sir Charles; Prinsep, James; Utilitarianism in India; Yale, Elihu

Eleanor Zelliot
Carleton College
Ambedkar, Bhimrao Ramji; Poona Sarvajanik Sabha; Republican Party of India; Untouchability

LIST OF MAPS

WADE-GILES/PINYIN CONVERSION TABLE

WADE-GILES	PINYIN	WADE-GILES	PINYIN	WADE-GILES	PINYIN	WADE-GILES	PINYIN	WADE-GILES	PINYIN
a	a	chou	zhou	hao	hao	jun	run	lan	lan
ai	ai	ch'ou	chou	hei	hei	jung	rong	lang	lang
an	an	chu	zhu	hen	hen			lao	lao
ang	ang	ch'u	chu	heng	heng	ka	ga	le	le
ao	ao	chü	ju	ho	he	k'a	ka	lei	lei
		ch'ü	qu	hou	hou	kai	gai	leng	leng
cha	zha	chua	zhua	hsi	xi	k'ai	kai	li	li
ch'a	cha	ch'ua	chua	hsia	xia	kan	gan	lia	lia
chai	zhai	chuai	zhuai	hsiang	xiang	k'an	kan	liang	liang
chan	zhan	ch'uai	chuai	hsiao	xiao	kang	gang	liao	liao
ch'an	chan	chuan	zhuan	hsieh	xie	k'ang	kang	lieh	lie
chang	zhang	ch'uan	chuan	hsien	xian	kao	gao	lien	lian
ch'ang	chang	chüan	juan	hsin	xin	k'ao	kao	lin	lin
chao	zhao	ch'üan	quan	hsing	xing	kei	gei	ling	ling
ch'ao	chao	chuang	zhuang	hsiu	xiu	k'ei	kei	liu	liu
che	zhe	ch'uang	chuang	hsiung	xiong	ken	gen	lo	luo
ch'e	che	chüeh	jue	hsü	xu	k'en	ken	lou	lou
chen	zhen	ch'üeh	que	hsüan	xuan	keng	geng	lu	lu
ch'en	chen	chui	zhui	hsüeh	xue	k'eng	keng	lü	lü
cheng	zheng	ch'ui	chui	hsün	xun	ko	ge	luan	luan
chi	ji	chun	zhun	hu	hu	k'o	ke	lüan	lüan
ch'i	qi	ch'un	chun	hua	hua	kou	gou	lüeh	lüe
chia	jia	chün	jun	huai	huai	k'ou	kou	lun	lun
ch'ia	qia	chün	qun	huan	huan	ku	gu	lung	long
chiang	jiang	chung	zhong	huang	huang	k'u	ku		
ch'iang	qiang	ch'ung	chong	hui	hui	kua	gua		
chiao	jiao			hun	hun	k'ua	kua	ma	ma
ch'iao	qiao	en	en	hung	hong	kuai	guai	mai	mai
chieh	jie	erh	er	huo	huo	k'uai	kuai	man	man
ch'ieh	qie					kuan	guan	mang	mang
chien	jian	fa	fa	i	yi	k'uan	kuan	mao	mao
ch'ien	qian	fan	fan			kuang	guang	mei	mei
chih	zhi	fang	fang	jan	ran	k'uang	kuang	men	men
ch'ih	chi	fei	fei	jang	rang	kuei	gui	meng	meng
chin	jin	fen	fen	jao	rao	k'uei	kui	mi	mi
ch'in	qin	feng	feng	je	re	kun	gun	miao	miao
ching	jing	fo	fo	jen	ren	k'un	kun	mieh	mie
ch'ing	qing	fou	fou	jeng	reng	kung	gong	mien	mian
chiu	jiu	fu	fu	jih	ri	k'ung	kong	min	min
ch'iu	qiu			jo	ruo	kuo	guo	ming	ming
chiung	jiong	ha	ha	jou	rou	k'uo	kuo	miu	miu
ch'iung	qiong	hai	hai	ju	ru			mo	mo
cho	zhuo	han	han	juan	ruan	la	la	mou	mou
ch'o	chuo	hang	hang	jui	rui	lai	lai	mu	mu

Wade-Giles	Pinyin	Wade-Giles	Pinyin	Wade-Giles	Pinyin	Wade-Giles	Pinyin	Wade-Giles	Pinyin
na	na	pen	ben	shih	shi	tien	dian	ts'ung	cong
nai	nai	p'en	pen	shou	shou	t'ien	tian	tu	du
nan	nan	peng	beng	shu	shu	ting	ding	t'u	tu
nang	nang	p'eng	peng	shua	shua	t'ing	ting	tuan	duan
nao	nao	pi	bi	shuai	shuai	tiu	diu	t'uan	tuan
nei	nei	p'i	pi	shuan	shuan	to	duo	tui	dui
nen	nen	piao	biao	shuang	shuang	t'o	tuo	t'ui	tui
neng	neng	p'iao	piao	shui	shui	tou	dou	tun	dun
ni	ni	pieh	bie	shun	shun	t'ou	tou	t'un	tun
niang	niang	p'ieh	pie	shuo	shuo	tsa	za	tung	dong
niao	niao	pien	bian	so	suo	ts'a	ca	t'ung	tong
nieh	nie	p'ien	pian	sou	sou	tsai	zai	tzu	zi
nien	nian	pin	bin	ssu	si	ts'ai	cai	tz'u	ci
nin	nin	p'in	pin	su	su	tsan	zan		
ning	ning	ping	bing	suan	suan	ts'an	can	wa	wa
niu	niu	p'ing	ping	sui	sui	tsang	zang	wai	wai
no	nuo	po	bo	sun	sun	ts'ang	cang	wan	wan
nou	nou	p'o	po	sung	song	tsao	zao	wang	wang
nu	nu	pou	bou			ts'ao	cao	wei	wei
nü	nü	p'ou	pou	ta	da	tse	ze	wen	wen
nuan	nuan	pu	bu	t'a	ta	ts'e	ce	weng	weng
nüeh	nüe	p'u	pu	tai	dai	tsei	zei	wo	wo
nung	nong			t'ai	tai	tsen	zen	wu	wu
		sa	sa	tan	dan	ts'en	cen		
o	e	sai	sai	t'an	tan	tseng	zeng	ya	ya
ou	ou	san	san	tang	dang	ts'eng	ceng	yai	yai
		sang	sang	t'ang	tang	tso	zuo	yang	yang
pa	ba	sao	sao	tao	dao	ts'o	cuo	yao	yao
p'a	pa	se	se	t'ao	tao	tsou	zou	yeh	ye
pai	bai	sen	sen	te	de	ts'ou	cou	yen	yan
p'ai	pai	seng	seng	t'e	te	tsu	zu	yin	yin
pan	ban	sha	sha	teng	deng	ts'u	cu	ying	ying
p'an	pan	shai	shai	t'eng	teng	tsuan	zuan	yu	you
pang	bang	shan	shan	ti	di	ts'uan	cuan	yü	yu
p'ang	pang	shang	shang	t'i	ti	tsui	zui	yüan	yuan
pao	bao	shao	shao	tiao	diao	ts'ui	cui	yüeh	yue
p'ao	pao	she	she	t'iao	tiao	tsun	zun	yün	yun
pei	bei	shen	shen	tieh	die	ts'un	cun	yung	yong
p'ei	pei	sheng	sheng	t'ieh	tie	tsung	zong		

ACKNOWLEDGMENTS

The publisher gratefully acknowledges permission to publish photographs from the following sources:

VOL. 1, PAGE

36   *Veranda of Rock-cut Temple, Ajanta.*
      Asian Art Archives, University of Michigan.

56   *The Golden Temple, Amritsar.*
      Courtesy Robin Jared Lewis.

67   *Angkor Wat.*
      United Nations.

82   *Pailou.*
      Courtesy Jeffrey P. Edelstein.

82   *Tiantan.*
      Courtesy Jeffrey P. Edelstein.

83   *Palace of Heavenly Purity, Forbidden City.*
      Courtesy Jeffrey P. Edelstein.

84   *Vishvanath Temple, Khajuraho.*
      Asian Art Archives, University of Michigan.

85   *Taj Mahal, Agra.*
      Courtesy Government of India Tourist Office.

86   *High Court, Bangalore.*
      Courtesy Government of India Tourist Office.

86   *High Court, Chandigarh.*
      Courtesy Government of India Tourist Office.

87   *Stone Temple.*
      Asian Art Archives, University of Michigan.

87   *Phimai, near Nakhon Ratchasima.*
      Courtesy Tourism Authority of Thailand.

88   *Shwedagon Stupa, Rangoon, Burma.*
      Asian Art Archives, University of Michigan.

97   *Capital of an Ashokan Pillar.*
      Courtesy Lauraine Schallop.

104   *Astrolabe.*
      The Metropolitan Museum of Art, Bequest of Edward C. Moore, 1891 (91.1.535).

114   *Ayudhya.*
      United Nations.

130 *Ban Chiang Spiral-design Pottery, Udon Thani.*
Courtesy Tourism Authority of Thailand.

132 *Wat Arun (Temple of Dawn), Bangkok.*
United Nations.

145 *Summer Palace.*
Courtesy Jeffrey P. Edelstein.

146 *Tiantan.*
Courtesy Jeffrey P. Edelstein.

147 *Tiananmen Square.*
Courtesy Jeffrey P. Edelstein.

167 *Victoria Terminus.*
Educational Resources Center, New Delhi.

169 *Buddha, Borobudur.*
Asian Art Archives, University of Michigan.

177 *Yu (Ritual Wine Vessel).*
The Asia Society Galleries, Mr. and Mrs. John D. Rockefeller 3d
Collection (1979.100 a, b). Photo: Otto E. Nelson.

180 *Mahabodi Temple, Bodh Gaya, Bihar.*
Courtesy Robin Jared Lewis.

197 *Bunraku Puppets and Operators.*
Courtesy Japan Air Lines. Photo: Morris Simoncelli.

228 *Kazakh Carpet.*
The Metropolitan Museum of Art, the James F. Ballard Collection;
Gift of James F. Ballard, 1922 (22.100.7).

240 *Ceramic Bowl.*
The Asia Society Galleries, Mr. and Mrs. John D. Rockefeller 3d
Collection (1979.252). Photo: Otto E. Nelson.

241 *Covered Jar.*
The Asia Society Galleries, Mr. and Mrs. John D. Rockefeller 3d
Collection (1979.93 a, b). Photo: Charles Uht.

245 *Head of a King or Deity.*
Courtesy Museum of Fine Arts, Boston, Denman Waldo Ross Collection (30.728).

247 *Chandella-period Relief.*
The Asia Society Galleries, Mr. and Mrs. John D. Rockefeller 3d
Collection (1979.32). Photo: Otto E. Nelson.

249 *Little Goose Pagoda.*
Courtesy Jeffrey P. Edelstein.

286 *Porcelain Punch Bowl.*
The Metropolitan Museum of Art, Helena Woolworth Collection;
Gift of the Winfield Foundation, 1951 (51.86.413).

304 *Chola-period Somaskanda-murti.*
The Asia Society Galleries, Mr. and Mrs. John D. Rockefeller 3d
Collection (1979.28). Photo: Otto E. Nelson.

349 *House Tile.*
Joint Expedition of the Metropolitan Museum of Art and the German State Museums to Ctesiphon, 1931–1932; Rogers Fund,
1932 (32.150.151).

349 *Cuneiform Inscription.*
The Metropolitan Museum of Art, Gift of Nazli Heeramaneck,
1950 (50.132).

374   *Qutb Minar.*
        Courtesy Ainslie T. Embree.

390   *Gold Dinar.*
        Courtesy of the American Numismatic Society, New York.

391   *Silver Dirham.*
        Courtesy of the American Numismatic Society, New York.

404   *Buddhist Hanging Scroll.*
        Courtesy Harvard University Art Museums, The Arthur M. Sackler
        Museum; Bequest of Grenville L. Winthrop (1943.57.14).

438   *Elamite-period Statuette of a Woman.*
        The Metropolitan Museum of Art, Rogers Fund, 1951 (51.159).

440   *Kailasa Temple, Ellora.*
        Courtesy Air-India Library.

449   *Enryakuji.*
        Shashinka Photo Library.

463   *Buland Darwaza, Fatehpur Sikri.*
        Courtesy Ainslie T. Embree.

483   *Gagaku Drum.*
        Courtesy The Asia Society.

485   *Buddha.*
        The Asia Society Galleries, Mr. and Mrs. John D. Rockefeller 3d
        Collection (1979.3). Photo: Otto E. Nelson.

499   *Section of a Genji Scroll.*
        Shashinka Photo Library.

508   *Gia Long Code.*
        The Metropolitan Museum of Art, Gift of Samuel P. Avery, 1906
        (06.1025).

511   *Catholic Cathedral, Goa.*
        Courtesy Ainslie T. Embree.

526   *The Great Wall.*
        Courtesy Jeffrey P. Edelstein.

VOL. 2, PAGE

 12   *Shakyamuni Buddha.*
        The Asia Society Galleries, Mr. and Mrs. John D. Rockefeller 3d
        Collection (1979.8). Photo: Otto E. Nelson.

 28   *Early Han Plate.*
        The Asia Society Galleries, Mr. and Mrs. John D. Rockefeller 3d
        Collection (1979.108). Photo: Otto E. Nelson.

 29   *Tomb Figure of a Male Attendant.*
        The Asia Society Galleries, Mr. and Mrs. John D. Rockefeller 3d
        Collection (1979.110). Photo: Otto E. Nelson.

 38   *Jar and Stand.*
        The Metropolitan Museum of Art, Joint Expedition to Hasanlu;
        Rogers Fund, 1960 (60.20.15,16).

 80   *Hōryūji, Nara.*
        Courtesy Japan Air Lines. Photo: Morris Simoncelli.

161   *Ise Shrine.*
        Shashinka Photo Library.

163   *The Shah Mosque, Isfahan.*
        United Nations.

181   *City Wall, Jaisalmer.*
       Courtesy Air-India Library.

222   *Flask.*
       The Asia Society Galleries, Mr. and Mrs. John D. Rockefeller 3d
       Collection (1979.160). Photo: Otto E. Nelson.

229   *Jodhpur Fort.*
       Courtesy Robin Jared Lewis.

231   *Jōmon Figure.*
       The Asia Society Galleries, Mr. and Mrs. John D. Rockefeller 3d
       Collection (1979.198). Photo: Otto E. Nelson.

245   *Kabuki Performance.*
       Courtesy The Asia Society.

257   *Great Amida Buddha of Kamakura.*
       Courtesy Japan Air Lines. Photo: Morris Simoncelli.

268   *The Four Seasons (Detail).*
       The Asia Society Galleries, Mr. and Mrs. John D. Rockefeller 3d
       Collection (1979.216.1). Photo: Otto E. Nelson.

358   *Wine Pot.*
       The Metropolitan Museum of Art, Fletcher Fund, 1927 (27.119.2).

382   *Shakyamuni Buddha.*
       Courtesy Korea National Tourism Office.

384   *Phoenix Hall, Byōdōin, Kyoto.*
       Shashinka Photo Library.

389   *Badhshahi Mosque, Lahore.*
       United Nations.

391   *Wat Phra That Haripunjaya, Lamphun.*
       Courtesy Tourism Authority of Thailand.

439   *Lodi Tomb, Delhi.*
       Courtesy Avinash Pasricha.

442   *Liangzhu Pottery.*
       Courtesy Harvard University Art Museums, The Arthur M. Sackler
       Museum; Purchase of the Dane Fund in Honor of Professor Max
       Loehr (1984.161).

443   *Phra Prang Sam Yot, Lopburi.*
       Courtesy Tourism Authority of Thailand.

446   *Imambara, Lucknow.*
       Educational Resources Center, New Delhi.

459   *View of the Temple Complex, Mahabalipuram.*
       Courtesy Air-India Library.

536   *Incense Burner.*
       The Metropolitan Museum of Art, Rogers Fund, 1951 (51.56).

VOL. 3, PAGE

7   *Ming-dynasty Figurine.*
       Yale University Art Gallery, Gift of Dr. Yale Kneeland, Jr., B.A.
       1922.

16   *Chinese Coins.*
       Courtesy of the American Numismatic Society, New York.

17   *Japanese Coins.*
       Courtesy of the American Numismatic Society, New York.

17   *Korean Coins.*
Courtesy of the American Numismatic Society, New York.

20   *Ancient Near Eastern Coins.*
Courtesy of the American Numismatic Society, New York.

21   *Islamic Coins.*
Courtesy of the American Numismatic Society, New York.

56   *Gilt Bronze Box.*
Courtesy Museum of Fine Arts, Boston, Keith McLeod Fund (70.46).

60   *Moon Lutes.*
The Metropolitan Museum of Art, The Crosby Brown Collection of Musical Instruments, 1889 (89.4.53, 89.4.299).

61   *Tibetan Trumpets.*
The Metropolitan Museum of Art, Rogers Fund, 1908 (184.24–25).

63   *Vina.*
The Metropolitan Museum of Art, Gift of Alice E. Getty, 1946 (46.34.3ab).

64   *Bonang Barung Slendro.*
The Metropolitan Museum of Art, Gift of Carroll C., Beverly, and Garry S. Bratman, 1977 (1977.393.23a–c).

65   *Naggara (Twin Drum).*
The Metropolitan Museum of Art, The Crosby Brown Collection of Musical Instruments, 1889 (89.4.329).

80   *Buddhist Temple.*
Courtesy Tourism Authority of Thailand.

81   *Remains of the Buddhist Monastic University at Nalanda.*
Courtesy Government of India Tourist Office.

87   *Ming Tomb Guardians.*
Courtesy Jeffrey P. Edelstein.

108   *Svayambhunath Stupa, Dome Detail.*
Asian Art Archives, University of Michigan.

109   *Rato Matsyendranath Temple, Ta Bahal, Patan.*
Courtesy Bruce Owens.

110   *Bodhisattva, Probably Avalokiteshvara.*
The Asia Society Galleries, Mr. and Mrs. John D. Rockefeller 3d Collection (1979.49). Photo: Otto E. Nelson.

123   *Nijō Castle.*
Courtesy Japan Air Lines. Photo: Morris Simoncelli.

125   *Ceramic Bowl.*
The Metropolitan Museum of Art, Rogers Fund, 1940 (40.170.15).

128   *Scene from a Nō Play.*
Courtesy the Asia Society.

137   *Yungang Caves, Datong.*
Courtesy Jeffrey P. Edelstein.

138   *Longmen Caves, Luoyang.*
Courtesy Jeffrey P. Edelstein.

159   *Osaka Castle.*
Courtesy Japan Air Lines. Photo: Morris Simoncelli.

178   *Boat with Eight Men (The Golden Image of Chang Gansi).*
       Courtesy Harvard University Art Museums, The Arthur M. Sackler Museum; 1923 Fogg Expedition (1924.41).

179   *Ladies in the Palace.*
       Courtesy Harvard University Art Museums, The Arthur M. Sackler Museum; Purchase of Francis H. Burr Memorial Fund (1945.28).

180   *Bare Willows and Distant Mountains.*
       Courtesy Museum of Fine Arts, Boston, Special Chinese and Japanese Fund (14.61).

181   *Bamboo (Section 3).*
       The Metropolitan Museum of Art, The A. W. Bahr Collection; Fletcher Fund, 1947 (47.18.11).

182   *Marsh Scene with Birds (Section 5).*
       The Metropolitan Museum of Art, The A. W. Bahr Collection; Fletcher Fund, 1947 (47.18.7).

183   *Landscape.*
       The Metropolitan Museum of Art, Kennedy Fund, 1913 (13.100.77).

184   *Ajanta Wall Painting.*
       Asian Art Archives, University of Michigan.

185   *Illuminated Page from the Bhagavata Purana.*
       The Asia Society Galleries, Mr. and Mrs. John D. Rockefeller 3d Collection (1979.55). Photo: Otto E. Nelson.

186   *Abhisarika Nayaka (A Heroine Comes to Her Lover through the Rain).*
       The Asia Society Galleries, Mr. and Mrs. John D. Rockefeller 3d Collection (1979.57). Photo: Otto E. Nelson.

187   *Uji Bridge.*
       Courtesy Museum of Fine Arts, Boston, Special Chinese and Japanese Fund (06.2510).

189   *Landscape.*
       Courtesy Museum of Fine Arts, Boston, Special Chinese and Japanese Fund (05.203).

190   *Poem Scroll with Bamboo.*
       The Asia Society Galleries, Mr. and Mrs. John D. Rockefeller 3d Collection (1979.214). Photo: Otto E. Nelson.

192   *Leaf from Nizami's Khamsa.*
       The Metropolitan Museum of Art, Gift of Alexander Smith Cochran, 1913 (13.228.7).

201   *Pala-period Stele with Khasarpana-Lokeshvara.*
       The Asia Society Galleries, Mr. and Mrs. John D. Rockefeller 3d Collection (1979.39). Photo: Otto E. Nelson.

202   *Pallava-period Sculpture (Seated Queen?).*
       The Asia Society Galleries, Mr. and Mrs. John D. Rockefeller 3d Collection (1979.16). Photo: Otto E. Nelson.

219   *Krishna Mandir, Durbar Square, Patan.*
       Asian Art Archives, University of Michigan.

232   *Tachara Palace Relief, Persepolis.*
       United Nations.

265   *Large Seated Buddha, Polonnaruva.*
       Asian Art Archives, University of Michigan.

285   *Pulguk Temple, Kyŏngju.*
Courtesy Korea National Tourism Office.

306   *Qing-dynasty Porcelain Dish.*
The Asia Society Galleries, Mr. and Mrs. John D. Rockefeller 3d Collection (1979.190). Photo: Charles Uht.

314   *Page of the Qur'an.*
The Metropolitan Museum of Art, Anonymous Gift, 1972 (1972.279).

334   *Red Fort, Delhi.*
Asian Art Archives, University of Michigan.

354   *Rock Garden at Ryōanji.*
Courtesy Jeffrey P. Edelstein.

357   *Leaf from the Bustan of Sa'di.*
The Metropolitan Museum of Art, Louis V. Bell Fund and Astor Foundation Gift, 1974 (1972.294.4).

377   *Samurai Armor.*
The Metropolitan Museum of Art, Fletcher Fund, 1928 (28.60.1).

379   *Gate at the Great Stupa, Sanchi.*
Courtesy R. N. Peters.

388   *Head of a King.*
The Metropolitan Museum of Art, Fletcher Fund, 1965 (65.126).

396   *Jade Bi.*
Courtesy Harvard University Art Museums, The Arthur M. Sackler Museum; Bequest of Grenville L. Winthrop (1941.50.524).

397   *Tomb Figure, Xi'an.*
Courtesy Jeffrey P. Edelstein.

398   *Longmen Caves, Luoyang.*
Courtesy Jeffrey P. Edelstein.

399   *Lion Sculptures, Ming Tombs, Nanjing.*
Courtesy Jeffrey P. Edelstein.

399   *Shaka Triad.*
Shashinka Photo Library.

400   *Sculpture of the Buddhist Monk Ganjin.*
Shashinka Photo Library.

400   *Daibutsu, Tōdaiji, Nara.*
Shashinka Photo Library.

401   *Amida Nyorai, Byōdōin, Kyoto.*
Shashinka Photo Library.

402   *Head of Vishnu.*
The Asia Society Galleries, Mr. and Mrs. John D. Rockefeller 3d Collection (1979.62). Photo: Otto E. Nelson.

402   *Dancing Celestial Figure (Apsara).*
Courtesy Museum of Fine Arts, Boston, Gift of Denman Waldo Ross (22.686).

403   *Seated Buddha.*
Courtesy Museum of Fine Arts, Boston, Frederick L. Jack Fund (57.531).

427   *Yu (Wine Vessel).*
Courtesy Museum of Fine Arts, Boston, Anna Mitchell Richards Fund (34.66).

428   *Shang Ritual Implements.*
      Courtesy Museum of Fine Arts, Boston, General Fund (37.330, 37.331, 37.332).

430   *View along the Bund, Shanghai.*
      Courtesy Ainslie T. Embree.

460   *Shwedagon Pagoda, Rangoon.*
      Asian Art Archives, University of Michigan.

498   *Song-dynasty Meiping Jar.*
      The Asia Society Galleries, Mr. and Mrs. John D. Rockefeller 3d Collection (1979.141). Photo: Otto E. Nelson.

VOL. 4, PAGE

13   *Svayambhunath Stupa, Kathmandu Valley, Nepal.*
      Courtesy Bruce Owens.

23   *Phra Achana.*
      Courtesy Tourism Authority of Thailand.

56   *View of the Taj Mahal, Agra.*
      Courtesy David Sassoon.

65   *Tang-dynasty Horse.*
      The Asia Society Galleries, Mr. and Mrs. John D. Rockefeller 3d Collection (PG 6). Photo: Otto E. Nelson.

73   *Shiva Temple near Tanjore.*
      United Nations.

84   *Ceramic Cup.*
      The Metropolitan Museum of Art, Acquired by Exchange from the Teheran Museum, 1948 (48.98.23).

90   *That Luang, Vientiane.*
      United Nations.

98   *Wall Tiles.*
      The Metropolitan Museum of Art, The H. O. Havemeyer Collection; Gift of Horace Havemeyer, 1941 (41.165.10–39).

106   *Buddha Hall, Tōdaiji, Nara.*
      Courtesy Jeffrey P. Edelstein.

183   *Ghats on the Ganges River, Varanasi.*
      Photo: Samuel Bourne (1865).

228   *Beauty Wringing Out a Towel.*
      The Asia Society Galleries, Mr. and Mrs. John D. Rockefeller 3d Collection (1979.219). Photo: Otto E. Nelson.

228   *Two Actors.*
      The Asia Society Galleries, Mr. and Mrs. John D. Rockefeller 3d Collection (1979.220). Photo: Otto E. Nelson.

245   *Horses and Chariot.*
      Courtesy Beijing Studios.

261   *Ceramic Storage Jar.*
      The Asia Society Galleries, Mr. and Mrs. John D. Rockefeller 3d Collection (1979.125). Photo: Otto E. Nelson.

265   *Earthenware Jar.*
      The Brooklyn Museum, Gift of Carll H. DeSilver (74.26.1).

282   *Yuan-dynasty Jar.*
      The Brooklyn Museum, Gift of the Executors of the Estate of Augustus S. Hutchins (52.87.1).

287 *Yurts, Inner Mongolia.*
Courtesy Jeffrey P. Edelstein.

303 *Gui (Food Vessel).*
Yale University Art Gallery, Hobart and Edward Small Moore Memorial Collection.

SYNOPTIC OUTLINE

The outline below is intended to provide the reader with a guide to the organization and classification of entries in the encyclopedia. It consists of two parts. The *Topical Outline* provides a conceptual overview of the topics treated in this work; the *Outline of Contents* lists the various entries to be found under each of these topics. Because the classifying rubrics employed herein are not always mutually exclusive, multiple listings of certain articles do occur.

Topical Outline

Pan-Asia[1]

China

1. Historical Periods
2. Premodern Civil and Military Administration
3. Rebellions and Millenarian Movements
4. Culture and Society

   A. Religion and Thought
   B. Language and Literature
   C. Arts
   D. Society
   E. Ethnic Groups

5. Encounter with the West
6. Twentieth-Century Political and Military History
7. Economy, Commerce, and Agriculture

   A. Premodern Period
   B. Nineteenth and Twentieth Century

8. Geography

   A. Natural Features
   B. Provinces and Colonies

C. Cities
D. Other

9. Biographies

   A. Premodern Figures
      a. Political and Military Figures
      b. Cultural and Intellectual Figures
      c. Westerners
   B. Twentieth-Century Figures
      a. Political Figures
      b. Military Figures
      c. Cultural and Intellectual Figures
      d. Westerners

Korea

1. Premodern Political and Military History
2. Nineteenth- and Twentieth-Century Political and Military History
3. Culture and Society

   A. Religion and Thought
   B. Literature
   C. Social Organization

4. Geography
5. Biographies

   A. Premodern Figures
      a. Political and Military Figures
      b. Cultural and Intellectual Figures

   B. Nineteenth- and Twentieth-Century Figures

Japan

1. Polities and Eras
2. Premodern Political and Military History
3. Civil and Military Administration
4. Culture and Society

   A. Thought and Religion
   B. Literature
   C. Arts
   D. Society

5. Encounter with the West
6. Meiji and Twentieth-Century Political and Military History
7. Commerce and Industry
8. Geography

   A. Regions
   B. Cities
   C. Other

9. Biographies

   A. Premodern Figures
      a. Political and Military Figures
      b. Cultural Figures
      c. Westerners
   B. Tokugawa Figures
      a. Political and Military Figures
      b. Cultural Figures
      c. Westerners

---

[1]Articles listed in this section treat exclusively topics of general scope discussed in the context of two or more Asian nations, regions, or cultures. For the full range of topics treated in the encyclopedia, see the headings listed for specific nations and cultures below.

C. Meiji and Twentieth-Century Figures
    a. Political and Military Figures
    b. Cultural Figures
    c. Westerners

Tibet

1. History and Geography
2. Religion

South Asia

1. Polities and Eras

    A. Ancient Period (to 1000 CE)
    B. Medieval Period (1000–1700)
    C. Colonial Period
    D. Modern Nation States

2. Culture and Society

    A. Religion and Thought
        a. Hinduism
        b. Buddhism
        c. Islam
        d. Other
    B. Language and Literature
    C. Arts
    D. Society
    E. Social Organization

3. Political and Military History

    A. Civil Administration
    B. Military History and Administration
    C. Nationalist Movements and Organizations
    D. Political Parties and Movements
    E. Reports, Plans, Acts, and Missions

4. Encounter with the West
5. Economy, Commerce, and Agriculture
6. Geography

    A. Natural Features
    B. Countries
    C. Provinces, States, and Regions
    D. Cities
    E. Historical and Archaeological Sites
    F. Other

7. Biographies

    A. Ancient Period (to 1000)
        a. Rulers
        b. Religious Leaders
        c. Literary and Scholarly Figures
    B. Medieval Period (1000–1700)
        a. Rulers
        b. Administrators and Public Figures
        c. Religious Figures
        d. Literary and Scholarly Figures
        e. Westerners
    C. Modern Period (since 1700)
        a. Rulers and Political Figures
        b. Administrators and Public Figures
        c. Nationalist and Political Leaders
        d. Religious Figures
        e. Literary and Scholarly Figures

Southeast Asia

1. Premodern Kingdoms, States, and Civilizations

    A. Burmese
    B. Thai
    C. Lao
    D. Khmer
    E. Viet
    F. Malay and Indonesian

2. Dynasties and Ruling Houses

    A. Burmese
    B. Thai
    C. Viet
    D. Javanese

3. Modern Nations
4. Culture and Society

    A. Religion and Thought
    B. Myth and Legend
    C. Language and Literature
    D. Arts
    E. Society
    F. Ethnic Groups

5. Civil Administration and Foreign Relations

    A. Burmese
    B. Thai
    C. Viet
    D. Malay
    E. Indonesian
    F. Philippine

6. Noncolonial Military History
7. Encounter with the West
    A. General
    B. Burma
    C. Siam
    D. Indochina
    E. Malaya and Singapore
    F. Indonesia
    G. Philippines
        a. Spanish Period
        b. American Period

8. Nationalist and Political Movements and Organizations[2]

    A. General
    B. Burma
    C. Thailand
    D. Laos
    E. Cambodia
    F. Vietnam
    G. Malaya/Malaysia
    H. Singapore
    I. Indonesia
    J. Philippines

9. Postcolonial Conferences and Organizations
10. Indochina War

    A. Organizations, States, and Events
    B. Biographies

11. Economy, Commerce, and Agriculture

    A. General
    B. Burma
    C. Malaysia and Singapore
    D. Indonesia
    E. Philippines

12. Geography

    A. General
    B. Regions, Geopolitical Divisions, and Natural Features
        a. Burma
        b. Thailand
        c. Vietnam
        d. Malaysia
        e. Indonesia
        f. Philippines
    C. Cities
        a. Burma
        b. Thailand
        c. Laos
        d. Cambodia
        e. Vietnam
        f. Malaysia

---

[2]Includes World War II military organizations.

---

[3]This section includes, especially, figures of the colonial period.

Outline of Contents[4]

---

[4]Where appropriate, entries listed under each of the headings below are arranged in approximate chronological order.

Pan-Asia *(cont.)*

Population: An Overview
Refugees
Sculpture
Slavery and Serfdom
Warfare
Women
World War I in Asia
World War II in Asia
Writing Systems

China

1. Historical Periods

Yangshao Culture
Longshan Culture
Bronze Age in China
Xia Dynasty
Shang Dynasty
Zhou Period
Spring and Autumn Period
Warring States Period
  Chu
  Han
  Qi
  Wei
  Yan
  Zhao
Qin Dynasty
Han Dynasty
Three Kingdoms
Six Dynasties
  Jin Dynasty
  Southern and Northern Dynasties
  Fei River, Battle of
  Northern Wei Dynasty
  Northern Qi Dynasty
  Sixteen Kingdoms
  Northern Liang Kingdom
Sui Dynasty
Tang Dynasty
Five Dynasties
Ten Kingdoms
Song Dynasty
Liao Dynasty
Jurchen Jin Dynasty
Yuan Dynasty
Ming Dynasty
Qing Dynasty
China, Republic Period
China, Republic of
China, People's Republic of

2. Premodern Civil and Military Administration

Banners
Baojia System
Bureaucracy in China
Censorate
Fubing System
Grand Council
Grand Secretariat
Junxian System
Law: Law in China
Lijia System
Tributary System
Tuntian
Warfare: Warfare in China
Yitiaobianfa

3. Rebellions and Millenarian Movements

Nian Rebellion
Rebellions in China
Red Eyebrows
Red Turbans
Secret Societies
Taiping Rebellion
Three Feudatories Rebellion
Triads
White Lotus Society
Yellow Turbans

4. Culture and Society

A. Religion and Thought[5]

Buddhism: Buddhism in China
Burning of the Books
Calendars and Eras: Chinese Calendars and Eras
Chinese Ritual and Sacrifice
Confucianism
Daoism
Donglin Academy
Five Bushels of Rice Sect
Guwen
Huainanzi
Jinwen
Kaozheng Xue
Legalism
Lunyu
Neo-Confucianism
Nestorianism
Qingtan
Seven Sages of the Bamboo Grove
Taizhou School
Yin and Yang
Zhenyan

---

[5]In addition to the articles listed here, seminal works attributed to Gongsun Long, Han Feizi, Laozi, Liezi, Mencius, Xunzi, and Zhuangzi are the subject of independent entries.

B. Language and Literature

Chinese Language
Literacy: Literacy in China
Chinese Literature
Jinpingmei
Manchu Language
Paper
Pinyin
Rulin Waishi
Sanyan
Sino-Tibetan Languages
Wade-Giles Romanization

C. Arts

Architecture: Chinese Architecture
Music: Music in China
Painting: Chinese Painting
Sculpture: Chinese Sculpture

D. Society

Education: Education in Imperial China
Education: Education in Twentieth-Century China
Journalism: Journalism in China
Law: Law in China
Nomadism
Population: Population in China
Slavery and Serfdom: Slavery in China
Women: Women in China

E. Ethnic Groups

Hakka
Jurchen
Khitan
Manchus
Mongols
Oirats
Shato Turks
Tanguts
Uighurs
Xianbei
  Tuyuhun
Xiongnu
  Shanyu

5. Encounter with the West

Arrow War
China Trade
Cohong
Compradors
Coolie Trade
Dagu Forts
Emigration: Chinese Emigration
Imperialism
Jesuits: Jesuits in China

C. Cities (cont.)

Port Arthur
Qingdao
Qiqihar
Ruijin
Shanghai
Shantou
Shenyang
Shijiazhuang
Suzhou
Tainan
Taipei
Taiyuan
Tangshan
Tianjin
Turfan
Urumqi
Weihaiwei
Wuxi
Xiamen
Xi'an
Xining
Yan'an
Yantai
Yinchuan
Zayton
Zhengzhou

D. Other

Cathay
Central Asia
China
Dzungaria
East Asia
Far East
Ferghana
Great Wall
Guanzhong
Jiayuguan
Juyongguan
Karakorum
Longmen
Manchuria
Mongolian People's Republic
Samarkand
Shanhaiguan
Silk Route
Sogdiana
Turkestan
Xujiahui

9. Biographies

A. Premodern Figures

a. Political and Military Figures

Altan Khan
An Lushan

Cao Cao
Chen Youliang
Dayan Khan
Dorgon
Empress Dowager
Fang Guozhen
Fang La
Fan Zhongyan
Feng Guifen
Galdan
Genghis Khan
Gong Yixin
Han Liner
Heshen
Hong Ren'gan
Hong Xiuquan
Huang Chao
Huang Taiji
Hu Weiyong
Kangxi Emperor
Kublai Khan
Li Hongzhang
Lin Zexu
Li Zicheng
Liu Bang
Liu Bei
Nurhaci
Ogedei
Ouyang Xiu
Qianlong Emperor
Qin Shihuangdi
Qui Jin
Qu Yuan
Ruan Yuan
Senggerinchin
Shang Kexi
Sheng Xuanhuai
Shi Kefa
Sima Guang
Sun Quan
Wang Anshi
Wang Mang
Wei Zhongxian
Weng Tonghe
Wu Zhao
Wu Sangui
Xiang Yu
Xuantong Emperor
Xu Guangqi
Yelü Chucai
Yongzheng Emperor
Zhang Fei
Zhang Juzheng
Zhang Shicheng
Zhang Xianzhong
Zhang Zhidong
Zheng Chenggong
Zheng He

Zhu Di
Zhuge Liang
Zhu Yuanzhang
Zou Rong

b. Cultural and Intellectual Figures

An Shigao
Bai Juyi
Cao Xueqin
Cheng Brothers
Confucius
Dai Zhen
Dong Zhongshu
Du Fu
Faxian
Fotudeng
Gongsun Long
Gong Zizhen
Gu Yanwu
Gu Zuyu
Han Feizi
Han Yu
Huang Zongxi
Kang Youwei
Kumarajiva
Laozi
Liang Qichao
Li Bai
Liezi
Li Si
Li Zhi
Lü Buwei
Lu Xiangshan
Ma Duanlin
Ma Huan
Mencius
Phags-pa
Pu Songling
Rong Hong
Shen Buhai
Sima Qian
Su Dongpo
Tan Sitong
Wang Chong
Wang Fuzhi
Wang Gen
Wang Yangming
Wei Yuan
Wu Jingzi
Xuanzang
Xunzi
Yan Fu
Yan Yuan
Zhang Binglin
Zhang Xuecheng
Zhang Zai
Zhao Rugua

Zheng Xuan
Zhou Daguan
Zhou Dunyi
Zhuangzi
Zhu Xi
Zou Yan

c. Westerners

Castiglione, Giuseppe
Cattaneo, Lazzaro
Giovanni da Montecorvino
Hart, Robert
Legge, James
Martin, William Alexander Parsons
Odoric of Pordenone
Polo, Marco
Ricci, Matteo
Schall von Bell, Johann Adam
Verbiest, Ferdinand
William of Rubruck

B. Twentieth-Century Figures

a. Political Figures

Chen Boda
Chen Duxiu
Chen Guofu
Chen Jiongming
Chen Lifu
Chen Qimei
Chen Yun
Chiang Ching-kuo
Chiang Kai-shek
Deng Xiaoping
Hu Hanmin
Hu Yaobang
Jiang Qing
Kang Sheng
Li Dazhao
Li Lisan
Liu Shaoqi
Li Xiannian
Lu Dingyi
Mao Zedong
Peng Zhen
Qu Qiubai
Song Qingling
Soong, T. V.
Soong Mei-ling
Sun Yat-sen
Wang Hongwen
Wang Jingwei
Wang Ming
Wei Jingsheng
Xie Fuzhi
Yao Wenyuan
Yuan Shikai
Zeng Guofan

Zhang Chunqiao
Zhang Guotao
Zhao Ziyang
Zhou Enlai
Zhou Yang

b. Military Figures

Bai Chongxi
Cao Kun
Duan Qirui
Feng Guozhang
Feng Yuxiang
Gao Gang
He Long
Huang Xing
Lin Biao
Li Yuanhong
Li Zongren
Peng Dehuai
Wu Peifu
Yan Xishan
Ye Jianying
Zhang Xueliang
Zhang Zuolin
Zhu De

c. Cultural and Intellectual Figures

Ba Jin
Cai Yuanpei
Deng Tuo
Ding Ling
Ding Wenjiang
Gu Jiegang
Guo Moruo
Hu Shi
Liang Shuming
Liao Mosha
Lin Yutang
Lu Xun
Mao Dun
Ma Yinchu
Qi Baishi
Wu Han

d. Westerners

Bethune, Norman
Borodin, Michael
Buck, Pearl
Hatem, George
Hurley, Patrick J.
Marshall, George C.
Smedley, Agnes
Sneevliet, Hendricus J. F. M.
Snow, Edgar
Stilwell, Joseph W.
Strong, Anna Louise
Stuart, J. Leighton

Korea

1. Premodern Political and Military History

Korea
Three Hans
Puyŏ
Commanderies in Korea, Chinese
Koguryŏ
Paekche
Silla
Mimana
Parhae
Later Three Kingdoms
Koryŏ
   Mongol Empire: Mongol Invasions of Korea
Yi Dynasty
   Piracy: Japanese Piracy in Korea
   Hideyoshi's Invasion of Korea

2. Nineteenth- and Twentieth-Century Political and Military History

Korea
General Sherman Incident
Kanghwa Treaty
1882 Uprising
1884 Coup d'État
Kabo Reforms
Independence Party and Club
Ilchinhoe
Korea, Japanese Government-General of
March First Independence Movement
United Nations Commission for the Unification and Rehabilitation of Korea
Communism: Communism in Korea
Korean War
P'anmunjŏm Peace Talks
Korea, Republic of
Korea, Democratic People's Republic of
Ch'ŏllima Movement
April Nineteenth Student Revolution
May Sixteenth Coup d'État

3. Culture and Society

A. Religion and Thought

Buddhism: Buddhism in Korea
Christianity: Christianity in Korea
Korean State Examination System
Koryŏ Tripitaka
Literati Purges
Neo-Confucianism in Korea

B. Cities

Dazaifu
Edo
Heijō
Hiroshima
Kanazawa
Kyoto
Nagasaki
Nagoya
Nihonbashi
Osaka
Sakai
Sendai
Shimoda
Tokyo

C. Other

Enryakuji
Hōryūji
Ise
Kōyasan
Nijō Castle
Ryōanji
Tōdaiji
Tōkaidō
Yasukuni Shrine

9. Biographies

A. Premodern Figures

a. Political and Military Figures

Akechi Mitsuhide
Ashikaga Takauji
Ashikaga Yoshimasa
Ashikaga Yoshimitsu
Fujiwara Lineage
Fujiwara Michinaga
Go-Daigo
Jimmu
Katō Kiyomasa
Konishi Yukinaga
Kujō
Kusunoki Masashige
Minamoto
Sakanoue no Tamuramaro
Shōtoku Taishi
Soga
Sugawara no Michizane
Taira no Kiyomori
Takeda Shingen
Temmu
Uesugi Kenshin

b. Cultural Figures

Benkei
Dōgen Kigen

Eisai
Ennin
Hōnen
Kūkai
Murasaki Shikibu
Nichiren
Rennyo
Saichō
Saigyō
Sen no Rikyū
Sesshū Tōyō
Shinran
Zeami

c. Westerners

Valignano, Alessandro
Xavier, Francis

B. Tokugawa Figures

a. Political and Military Figures

Ikeda Mitsumasa
Katsu Kaishu
Kōmei
Maeda
Mizuno Tadakuni
Mōri
Ninomiya Sontoku
Oda Nobunaga
Satō Nobuhiro
Shimazu Hisamitsu
Shimazu Nariakira
Tanuma Okitsugu
Tokugawa Hidetada
Tokugawa Iemitsu
Tokugawa Ieyasu
Tokugawa Mitsukuni
Tokugawa Nariaki
Tokugawa Yoshimune
Tokugawa Yoshinobu
Toyotomi Hideyoshi

b. Cultural Figures

Aizawa Yasushi
Andō Shōeki
Chikamatsu Monzaemon
Danjūrō
Fujita Yūkoku
Hayashi Shihei
Ihara Saikaku
Ike Taiga
Ishida Baigan
Itō Jakuchū
Itō Jinsai
Kamo no Mabuchi
Kumazawa Banzan
Matsuo Bashō

Motoori Norinaga
Ogata Kōan
Ogyū Sorai
Ōtsuki Gentaku
Rai San'yō
Sakuma Shōzan
Shiba Kōkan
Sugita Gempaku
Takizawa Bakin
Uchimura Kanzō
Watanabe Kazan and Takano
  Chōei
Yokoi Shōnan
Yoshida Shōin

c. Westerners

Adams, William
Harris, Townsend
Kaempfer, Engelbert
Perry, Matthew C.
Rezanov, Nikolai Petrovich
Sidotti, Giovanni Battista
Siebold, Philipp Franz von
Thunberg, Carl Peter

C. Meiji and Twentieth-Century Figures

a. Political and Military Figures

Akihito
Aoki Shūzō
Araki Sadao
Enomoto Takeaki
Etō Shimpei
Fukuda Takeo
Hamaguchi Osachi
Hara Takashi
Hatoyama Ichirō
Hirohito
Inoue Kaoru
Inoue Kowashi
Inoue Nisshō
Itagaki Taisuke
Itō Hirobumi
Itō Miyoji
Iwakura Tomomi
Katayama Sen
Katayama Tetsu
Katō Takaaki
Katsura Tarō
Kido Takayoshi
Kishi Nobusuke
Kita Ikki
Konoe Fumimaro
Kōtoku Shūsui
Kuroda Kiyotaka
Matsudaira Sadanobu

Matsukata Masayoshi
Matsuoka Yōsuke
Miki Takeo
Mori Arinori
Mutsuhito
Mutsu Munemitsu
Nakae Chōmin
Nakasone Yasuhiro
Nogi Maresuke
Nomura Kichisaburo
Nosaka Sanzō
Ohira Masayoshi
Ōi Kentarō
Okada Keisuke
Ōkubo Toshimichi
Ōkuma Shigenobu
Ōsugi Sakae
Ōyama Iwao
Ozaki Yukio
Saigō Takamori
Saionji Kimmochi
Sakamoto Ryōma
Shidehara Kijūrō
Shigemitsu Mamoru
Suzuki Kantarō
Takahashi Korekiyo
Tanaka Giichi
Tanaka Kakuei
Terauchi Masataka
Tōgō Heihachirō
Tōjō Hideki
Tokuda Kyūichi
Tōyama Mitsuru
Uchida Ryōhei
Ueki Emori
Ugaki Kazushige
Yamagata Aritomo
Yamamoto Isoroku
Yamashita Tomoyuki
Yoshida Shigeru
Yoshihito

b. Cultural Figures

Ebina Danjō
Fukuzawa Yukichi
Futabatei Shimei
Inoue Enryō
Iwasaki Yatarō
Mishima Yukio
Mori Ōgai
Nagai Kafū
Natsume Sōseki
Niijima Jō
Nitobe Inazō
Okakura Tenshin
Ōkura Kihachirō
Shiga Naoya

Suzuki Daisetsu
Tanizaki Jun'ichirō
Tokutomi Sohō
Uemura Masahisa
Yasuda Zenjirō
Yoshino Sakuzō

c. Westerners

Dulles, John Foster
Hearn, Lafcadio
Hepburn, James Curtis
MacArthur, Douglas A.
Nikolai

Tibet

1. History and Geography

Tibet
Lhasa

2. Religion

Lamaism
Gelugpa
Drukpa
Dalai Lama
Panchen Lama
Tsangyang Gyatso
Atisha
Phags-pa

South Asia

1. Polities and Eras

A. Ancient Period (to 1000 CE)

Chalukya Dynasties
Chandella Dynasty
Chola Dynasty
Gahadavalas
Gajapati Dynasty
Gandhara
Ganga Dynasties
Gupta Empire
Gurjara-Pratihara Dynasty
Hindu Shahi Dynasty
Kakatiya Dynasty
Kalachuri Dynasties
Kalinga
Kanyakubja
Karkota Dynasty
Kirata
Kosala
Licchavi Dynasty
Magadha
Maha-Meghavahana Dynasty
Malla
Maukhari Dynasty

Maurya Empire
Naga
Pala Dynasty
Pallava Dynasty
Pandya Dynasty
Paramara Dynasty
Pratiharas
Pushyabhuti Dynasty
Rashtrakuta Dynasty
Satavahana Dynasty
Sena Dynasty
Shahiya Dynasty
Shunga Dynasty
Thaneswar
Vakatakas
Varman Dynasty
Yadavas

B. Medieval Period (1000–1700)

Ahmad Shahi Dynasty
Bahmani Dynasty
Chauhan Dynasty
Dambadeniya
Deccan Sultanates
Delhi Sultanate
Golconda
Hoysala Dynasty
Husain Shahi Dynasty
Ilyas Shahi Dynasty
Khalji Dynasty
Lodi Dynasty
Mamluks
Mughal Empire
Sayyid Dynasty
Sisodiya Dynasty
Suri Dynasty
Tughluq Dynasty
Tuluva Dynasty
Vijayanagara
Wadiyar Dynasty

C. Colonial Period

East India Company
Government of India
Governor-General of India
Princely States

D. Modern Nation States

Bangladesh
Bhutan
India
Maldives
Nepal: History of Nepal
Pakistan
Sri Lanka

2. Culture and Society

A. Religion and Thought[6]

a. Hinduism

Ajivika Sect
Arya Samaj
Bhakti
Brahmo Samaj
Chakravartin
Hinduism
Hindu Law
Hindu Mahasabha
Hindu Renaissance
Krishna
Prarthana Samaj
Rishi
Sadhu
Samkhya
Samskara
Sati
Shaivism
Shuddhi
Tantra
Vaishnavism
Vedanta
Yoga

b. Buddhism

Buddhism: An Overview
Drukpa
Gelugpa
Nirvana
Sangha
Stupa

c. Islam

Ahl-i Hadis
Ahmadiyya
Bohras
Chishti Tariqa
Deoband
Din-i Ilahi
Farangi Mahal
Fara'zi Movement
Fatawa-i Alamgiri
Kuka Sect
Naqshbandi
Sufism
Tabligh Movement

d. Other

Jainism
Parsis
Radhasoami Satsang

---

[6]For texts associated with South Asian religious traditions, see section 2B below.

Sikhism
Tirthankara

B. Language and Literature

Bhagavad Gita
Brahui
Dravidian Languages and Literatures
Indo-Aryan Languages and Literatures
Kama Sutra
Mahabharata
Mahavamsa
Natyashastra
Puranas
Ramayana
Sinhala
Upanishads
Vedas

C. Arts

Architecture: South Asian Architecture
Music: Music in South Asia
Nepal: Nepalese Archaeology, Architecture, and Art
Painting: South Asian Painting

D. Society

Calendars and Eras: Indian Calendars and Eras
Education: Education in South Asia
Hindu Law
Journalism: Journalism in India
Law: Judicial and Legal Systems of India
Women: Women in South and Southeast Asia

E. Social Organization

Adivasis
Anglo-Indians
Armenians in South Asia
Aryans
Brahman
Burghers
Caste
Chettiar
Chitpavan Brahmans
Garo
Gurkhas
Gurungs
Ilava
Jajmani
Jats
Kayasth
Kshatriya

Kulinism
Lepcha
Limbu
Lingayats
Magars
Mappilas
Marathas
Marwaris
Mizo
Mleccha
Mudaliyar
Munda
Muslims in Sri Lanka
Nadars
Nairs
Nayaka
Newar
Parsis
Pakhtun
Pindaris
Rai
Rajput
Rathors
Rohillas
Santal
Sepoy
Sherpa
Shudra
Slavery and Serfdom: Slavery and Serfdom in South Asia
Tamang
Tamils in Sri Lanka
Thagi
Todas
Untouchability
Vaishya
Veddas
Vellala

3. Political and Military History

A. Civil Administration

Diwani
Durbar
East India Company
Government of India
Governor-General of India
Indian Administrative Service
  Haileybury College
Jagir
Law: Judicial and Legal Systems of India
Mansabdari System
Nabob
Panchayat
Parliament of India
Peshwa
Poligar

---

[7]Specific events associated with South Asia's encounter with the West are listed in section 3 above.

C. Provinces, States, and Regions
(*cont.*)

Jammu
Jharkand
Jodhpur
Kangra
Karnataka
Kashmir
Kathiawar
Kerala
Khandesh
Ladakh
Madhya Pradesh
Maharashtra
Malwa
Manipur
Marwar
Meghalaya
Mewar
Mysore
Nagaland
North East Frontier Agency
North-West Frontier Province
Orissa
Patiala
Poonch
Punjab
Rajasthan
Rampur
Sikkim
Sind
Swat
Sylhet
Tamil Nadu
Travancore
Tripura
Uttar Pradesh

D. Cities[8]

Agra
Ahmadabad
Ahmadnagar
Ajmer
Allahabad
Amritsar
Anuradhapura
Arcot
Ayodhya
Banepa
Bhaktapur
Bhopal
Bhubaneswar
Bijapur
Bokaro

---

[8]Some cities that are also names of regions are listed in section 6C above and vice versa.

Bombay
Calcutta
Calicut
Chandigarh
Chitor
Colombo
Darjeeling
Daulatabad
Delhi
Dhaka
Goa
Gwalior
Hardwar
Imphal
Indore
Jaffna
Jaunpur
Kanchipuram
Kandy
Kanpur
Karachi
Kathmandu
Kotte
Kurunegala
Lahore
Lucknow
Madras
Madurai
Mathura
Multan
Murshidabad
Nagpur
Namche Bazar
Pataliputra
Patan
Patna
Peradeniya
Peshawar
Polonnaruva
Porbandar
Pune
Quetta
Seringapatam
Simla
Somanath
Srinagar
Surat
Tanjore
Tiruchchirappalli
Trincomalee
Udaipur
Ujjain
Varanasi

E. Historical and Archaeological Sites

Ajanta
Amaravati
Ellora

Fatehpur Sikri
Fort William
Hastinapur
Indraprastha
Indus Valley Civilization
Kapilavastu
Kurukshetra
Lumbini
Mahabalipuram
Mandu
Nagarjunikonda
Nalanda
Red Fort
Sanchi
Sarnath
Sigiriya
Taj Mahal
Taxila
Tooth Relic Palace

F. Other

Aryavarta
Durand Line
Grand Trunk Road
McMahon Line
Mauritius
Rohana
Serendib
South Asia

7. Biographies

A. Ancient Period (to 1000)

a. Rulers

Ashoka
Bimbisara
Chandragupta Maurya
Devanampiya Tissa
Dutthagamani
Elara
Gondophernes
Harsha
Mahasena
Menander
Poros
Prithviraj Chauhan
Rajasinha I
Rajasinha II

b. Religious Leaders

Mahinda
Nagarjuna
Shankara
Thomas

c. Literary and Scholarly Figures

Kalidasa
Kautilya

Megasthenes
Panini

B. Medieval Period (1000–1700)

a. Rulers

Ahalya Bai
Akbar
Aurangzeb
Babur
Balban, Ghiyas ud-din
Dara Shikoh
Dharmapala, Dom João
Hemu
Humayun
Iltutmish
Jahangir
Jai Singh
Man Singh
Nur Jahan
Parakramabahu I
Parakramabahu II
Qutb ud-Din Aibak
Raziyya
Sebuktigin, Abu Mansur
Shah Jahan
Sher Shah
Shivaji
Vijayabahu I

b. Administrators and Public Figures

Afzal Khan
Birbal
I'timad ud-Daulah
Todar Mal

c. Religious Figures

Atisha
Chaitanya
Kabir
Nanak
Nizam ud-Din Auliya
Ramanuja
Sirhindhi, Ahmad
Tukaram
Tulsi Das

d. Literary and Scholarly Figures

Abu'l Fazl
Amir Khusrau
Badauni, Abdul Qadir
Barani, Zia ud-Din
Ferishta, Muhammad Qasim
Khafi Khan, Muhammad Hashim
  Ali

e. Westerners

Albuquerque, Affonso de
Almeida, Lourenco de
Bernier, François
De Nobili, Roberto
Fitch, Ralph
Gama, Vasco da
Hawkins, William
Henriquez, Henry
Knox, Robert
Linschoten, Jan Huyghen van
Manucci, Niccolao
Nikitin, Afanasi
Queyroz, Fernao de
Roe, Sir Thomas

C. Modern Period (from 1700)

a. Rulers and Political Figures

Alivardi Khan
Asaf ud-Daulah
Birendra
Chait Singh
Haidar Ali Khan
Holkars
Jung Bahadur Rana
Laxmi Devi
Mahendra
Mir Ja'far
Mir Jumla
Mir Qasim
Muhammad bin Qasim
Murshid Quli Khan
Namgyal, Palden Thondup
Nana Sahib
Pilima Talauva
Prithvinarayan Shah
Rana
Shamser, Bir
Shamsher, Chandra
Shuja ud-Daulah
Sindhia
Siraj ud-Daulah
Suraj Mal
Thapa, Bhim Sen
Tipu Sultan
Tribhuvan, Bir Bikram
Wangchuk, Jigme Dorje
Wangchuk, Jigme Singye
Wangchuk, Ugyen
Zafar, Bahadur Shah

b. Administrators and Public Figures

Ahmad Khan, Sir Sayyid
Bentinck, William Cavendish
Bhabha, Homi Jehangir
Birla Family

Brownrigg, Sir Robert
Canning, Charles John
Carey, William
Charnock, Job
Child, Sir Josiah
Clive, Sir Robert
Cornwallis, Charles
Curzon, George Nathaniel
Deb, Radhakanta
D'Oyly, Sir John
Dupleix, Joseph François
Elphinstone, Mountstuart
Grant, Charles
Hastings, Warren
Hume, Allan Octavian
Husain, Zakir
Hydari, Akbar
Impey, Elijah
Isaacs, Rufus
Jagat Seth
Johnston, Sir Alexander
Jones, Sir William
Kitchener, Horatio Herbert
Lakshmi Bai
Law, Edward
Lawrence, John Laird Mair
Lawrence, Sir Henry Montgomery
Lutyens, Sir Edwin
Macaulay, Thomas Babington
Maine, Sir Henry
Maitland, Sir Thomas
Malcolm, Sir John
Metcalfe, Sir Charles
Mill, James
Mill, John Stuart
Mulraj, Diwan
Munro, Sir Thomas
Napier, Sir Charles
Nicholson, John
Norgay, Tenzing
North, Frederick
Nuncomar
Ochterloney, Sir David
Pillai, Ananda Ranga
Pitt, Thomas
Prinsep, James
Radhakrishnan, Sarvepalli
Rajagopalachari, Chakravarti
Ramsay, James Andrew Broun
Ribeiro, João
Robinson, George Frederick
Safdar Jang
Salar Jang I
Sarabhai
Strachey, Sir John
Strachey, Sir Richard
Tata Family

b. Administrators and Public Figures (*cont.*)

Tennent, Sir James Emerson
Tyabji, Badruddhin
Wellesley, Arthur
Wellesley, Richard Colley
Wood, Edward Frederick Lindley
Yale, Elihu
Younghusband, Sir Francis Edward

c. Nationalist and Political Leaders

Abdullah, Muhammad
Ali Brothers
Ambedkar, Bhimrao Ramji
Annadurai, C. N.
Ayub Khan, Mohammad
Azad, Abul Kalam
Bandaranaike, Sirimavo Ratwatte Dias
Bandaranaike, Solomon West Ridgeway Dias
Banerjea, Surendranath
Besant, Annie
Bhave, Vinoba
Bhutto, Zulfiqar Ali
Bose, Subhas Chandra
Chowdhury, Abu Sayeed
Das, Chittaranjan
Dayal, Har
Dayananda Saraswati
Desai, Morarji
Fazli Hussain, Sir Mian
Fazlul Huq, Abul Kasem
Gandhi, Indira
Gandhi, Kasturbai
Gandhi, Mohandas Karamchand
Gandhi, Rajiv
Gandhi, Sanjay
Giri, Tulsi
Giri, Varahagiri Venkata
Godse, Nathuram
Gokhale, Gopal Krishna
Goonetilleke, Sir Oliver Ernest
Gunawardena, Don Philip Rupasinghe
Jayakar, Mukund Ramrao
Jayawardene, Junius Richard
Jinnah, Fatima
Jinnah, Mohammad Ali
Khan, Abdul Ghaffar
Khan, Sir Sikandar Hayat
Khan, Tikka
Koirala, Bishweshwor Prasad
Kotelawala, Sir John Lionel
Krishna Menon, Vengalil Krishnan
Lajpat Rai, Lala
Liaqat Ali Khan

Malaviya, Madan Mohan
Maududi, Abu'l A'la
Mohamed Ali
Mujibur Rahman, Sheikh
Naicker, E. V. Ramaswami
Naidu, Sarojini
Namboodripad, E. M. S.
Naoroji, Dadabhai
Narayan, Jayaprakash
Nehru, Jawaharlal
Nehru, Motilal
Pandit, Vijaya Lakshmi
Patel, Sardar Vallabhbhai
Perera, Nanayakkarapathirage Martin
Phule, Jotirao Govindrao
Prasad, Rajendra
Rahman, Ziaur
Rahmat Ali, Chaudhuri
Ramanathan, Sir Ponnambalam
Ram, Jagjivan
Ranade, Mahadev Govind
Reddy, N. Sanjiva
Roy, Manabendra Nath
Sapru, Tej Bahadur
Savarkar, Vinayak Damodar
Senanayake, Don Stephen
Senanayake, Dudley Shelton
Shastri, Lal Bahadur
Singh, Bhagat
Singh, Fateh
Singh, K. I.
Singh, Ranjit
Singh, Tara
Suhrawardy, Hussain Shahid
Tilak, Bal Gangadhar
Tiwana, Malik Sir Khizr Hayat Khan
Yahya Khan, Agha Muhammad
Zia-ul Haq, Mohammad

d. Religious Figures

Agha Khan
Heber, Reginald
Ramakrishna
Sayyid Ahmad of Rae Bareilly
Schwartz, Christian Frederick
Sen, Keshub Chandra
Tagore, Debendranath
Tagore, Dwarkanath
Vivekananda
Wali Ullah, Shah

e. Literary and Scholarly Figures

Amir Ali
Anquetil-Duperron, A. H.
Bharati, Subramanya

Chatterji, Bankim Chandra
Coomaraswamy, Ananda Kentish
Dard, Sayyid Khvaja Mir
Derozio, Henry Louis Vivian
Devkota, Laxmiprasad
Dutt, Michael Madhusudan
Dutt, Romesh Chunder
Forster, Edward Morgan
Ghalib, Mirza Asadullah Khan
Ghose, Aurobindo
Hali, Altaf Husain
Heber, Reginald
Hodgson, Brian Houghton
Iqbal, Sir Muhammad
Karve, Dhondo Keshav
Kipling, Joseph Rudyard
Malabari, Behramji Merwanji
Mir, Muhammad Taqi
Mitra, Rajendralal
Müller, Friedrich Max
Phadke, Vasudeo Balwant
Phalke, Dhundiyaj Govind
Premchand
Roy, Rammohan
Shibli Nu'mani, Muhammad
Tagore, Rabindranath
Vidyasagar, Isvarchandra
Virasalingam, Kandukuri

Southeast Asia

1. Premodern Kingdoms, States, and Civilizations

A. Burmese

Ava
Pagan
Pegu
Pyu
Ramannadesa

B. Thai

Ayudhya
Dvaravati
Lan Na
Lopburi
Nakhon Si Thammarat
Phayao
Sukhothai

C. Lao

Anu
Champassak
Lan Sang
Luang Prabang
Siang Khwang

---

[9]Articles treating economic aspects of Southeast Asia's encounter with the West are listed under Section 11 below.

B. Burma

Anti-Fascist People's Freedom
  League
Anti-Separation League
Burma Defense Army
Burma Socialist Program Party
Burma Workers and Peasants Party
Dobama Asiayon
General Council of Burmese Asso-
  ciations
Karen National Defense Organiza-
  tion
Minami Kikan
People's Party of Burma
Shan State Independence Party
Sinyetha Party
Thirty Comrades

C. Thailand

Free Thai
People's Party of Thailand

D. Laos

Lao Issara
Pathet Lao

E. Cambodia

Khmer Issarak
Khmer Rouge
Sangkum Reastr Niyum

F. Vietnam

August Revolution
Bac Son Uprising
Binh Xuyen
Can Lao
Can Vuong
Cao Dai
Dai Viet Party
Dong Du Movement
Hoa Hao
Indochinese Communist Party
Viet Minh
Vietnam, Provisional Revolution-
  ary Government of
Vietnam Modernization Associa-
  tion
Vietnam Nationalist Party
Vietnam National Salvation Asso-
  ciations
Vietnam Restoration Association
Vietnam Restoration League
Vietnam Revolutionary League
Vietnam Revolutionary Youth
  League
Yen Bay Uprising

G. Malaya/Malaysia

Alliance Party
Angkatan Pemuda Insaf
Emergency in Malaysia, The
Independence of Malaya Party
Malayan Chinese Association
Malayan Communist Party
Malayan Indian Congress
Malayan People's Anti-Japanese
  Army
Malay Nationalist Party
Pan-Malayan Islamic Party
United Malays National Organiza-
  tion

H. Singapore

Barisan Socialis
People's Action Party

I. Indonesia

Budi Utomo
Confrontation
Darul Islam
Gerindo
Gestapu
Hizbu'llah and Sabili'llah
Indies Party
Indonesian Revolution
Masjumi
Nahdatul Ulama
Partai Komunis Indonesia
Partai Murba
Partai Nasional Indonesia
Partai Socialis Indonesia
Pemerintah Revolusioner Republik
  Indonesia/Perdjuangan Semesta
PETA
Sarekat Islam
Taman Siswa

J. Philippines

Huk
Kalibapi
Katipunan
Liga Filipina
Malolos Republic
Moro National Liberation Front
Nacionalista Party
New People's Army
Philippine Revolution
Propaganda Movement
Sakdal

**9. Postcolonial Conferences and
   Organizations**

Association of Southeast Asian Nations

Bandung Conference
Fontainebleau Conference
Geneva Conference of 1954
Geneva Conference on the Laotian
  Question
Paris Peace Conference
Preah Vihear
Southeast Asia Treaty Organiza-
  tion
Vientiane Agreements

10. Indochina War

**A. Organizations, States, and
   Events**

French Indochina War
Indochina War
Dien Bien Phu
Tet Offensive
Geneva Conference of 1954
Paris Peace Conference
Vietnam, Democratic Republic of
Vietnam, Republic of
Vietnam
Laos
Cambodia
Pathet Lao
Khmer Rouge
Viet Minh
Binh Xuyen
Cao Dai
Hoa Hao

B. Biographies

Ho Chin Minh
Le Duan
Le Duc Tho
Ngo Dinh Diem
Pham Van Dong
Vo Nguyen Giap
Lon Nol
Pol Pot
Heng Samrin
Norodom Sihanouk

**11. Economy, Commerce, and Agri-
   culture**

A. General

Ceramics: Southeast Asian Ceramic
  Trade
Gongsi
Land Tenure and Reform: Land
  Tenure, Revenue, and Reform in
  Southeast Asia
Money: Money in Southeast Asia
Pepper
Sawah

d. Vietnam

Co Loa
Dai La Thanh
Hoa Lu
Indrapura
Oc Eo
Tay Do

e. Malay Peninsula

Golden Khersonese
Suvarnabhumi

f. Indonesia

Kartasura
Palembang

13. Biographies

A. Ancient and Medieval Rulers

a. Burmese

Alaungsithu
Anaukhpetlun
Anawrahta
Bayinnaung
Dhammazedi
Kyanzittha
Kyaswa
Kyawswa
Nadaungmya
Nandabayin
Narapatisithu
Narathihapade
Razadarit
Tabinshweihti
Thadominbya

b. Thai

Borommaracha I
Borommatrailokanat
Chakkraphat
Chandrabhanu
Ekathotsarot
Ku Na
Lo Thai
Mahathammaracha
Mahathammaracha I
Mahathammaracha II
Mahathammaracha III
Mahathammaracha IV
Mangrai
Narai
Naresuan
Ngam Muang
Phetracha
Prasat Thong
Ramathibodi I
Ramesuan

Ramkhamhaeng
Sam Fang Kaen
Song Tham
Sri Indraditya
Surinyavongsa
Tilokaracha

c. Lao

Fa Ngum
Setthathirat

d. Khmer

Ang Chan
Bhavavarman
Chitrasena
Jayavarman I
Jayavarman II
Jayavarman VII
Suryavarman I
Suryavarman II
Yasovarman II

e. Viet

An Duong Vuong
Dinh Bo Linh
Hung Vuong
Le Hoan
Le Loi
Le Thanh Tong
Ly Bon
Ly Cong Uan
Ly Phat Ma
Ly Phat Tu
Mac Dang Dung
Ngo Quyen
Nguyen Hoang
Nguyen Kim
Si Nhiep
Tich Quang
Tran Nhan Tong
Tran Thai Tong
Tran Thanh Tong
Trieu Da
Trinh Kiem
Trinh Tac

f. Malay

Abdul Jalil Riayat Syah
Daeng Parani
Iskandar Muda
Mahmud Syah II
Mansur Syah

g. Javanese

Agung
Airlangga
Amangkurat I
Gajah Mada

Hayam Wuruk
Jayabaya
Ken Angrok
Kertanagara
Sanjaya
Trunajaya

B. Modern Rulers (since 1700)

a. Burmese

Alaunghpaya
Bagyidaw
Bodawhpaya
Hsinhpyushin
Mahadammayazadipathi
Mindon
Naungdawgyi
Pagan Min
Saw, Queen
Singu
Supayalat
Tharrawaddy
Thibaw

b. Thai/Siamese

Ananda Mahidol
Bhumibol Adulyadej
Borommakot
Chulalongkorn
Intanon
Kavila
Mongkut
Phra Nang Klao
Phra Phutthaloetla Naphalai
Phra Phutthayotfa Chulalok
Phra Pin Klao
Prajadhipok
Taksin
Vajiravudh

c. Lao

Kingkitsarat
Savangvatthana
Siribunyasan
Sisavangvong
Soisisamut
Un Kham

d. Khmer/Cambodian

Ang Chan
Ang Duang
Ang Eng
Norodom
Norodom Sihanouk
Norodom Suramarit
Sisowath
Sisowath Monivong

e. Viet

Bao Dai
Cuong De
Dong Khanh
Duy Tan
Gia Long
Ham Nghi
Minh Mang
Thieu Tri
Trinh Cuong
Trinh Khai
Trinh Sam
Tu Duc

f. Malay

• Local Rulers

Abdul Rahman
Abu Bakar
Ahmad, Ahmuadzam Shah
Ali, Sultan of Johor
Haji, Raja
Hussein, Sultan of Johor and Singapore
Ibrahim
Idris
Kecil, Raja
Mahmud Riayat Syah III
Tun Mahmud

• White Rajas of Sarawak

Brooke, Sir Charles
Brooke, Sir Charles Vyner
Brooke, Sir James

g. Javanese

Dipanagara
Hamengkubuwana
Mangkubumi
Pakubuwana

C. Administrators and Military Figures

a. Burma

Baker, George
Burney, Henry
Cox, Hiram
Kinwun Mingyi
Lambert, George Robert
Mahabandula
Maha Thiha Thura
Mountbatten, Louis
Phayre, Sir Arthur P.
Symes, Michael

b. Thailand

Bodindecha Sing Singhaseni
Bowring, Sir John

Bunnag Family
Devawongse Varopakar
Phaulkon, Constantine
Phrakhlang Dit Bunnag
Rolin-Jaequemyns, Gustave
Sisuriyawong
Thiphakorawong Kham Bunnag

c. Indochina

Dao Duy Tu
D'Argenlieu, Georges-Thierry
Decoux, Jean
Doumer, Paul
Dupré, Jules-Marie
Dupuis, Jean
Garnier, Francis
Genouilly, Charles Rigault de
Harmand, François-Jules
Klobukowski, Antoni-Wladislas
La Grandière, Pierre-Paul-Marie de
Lattre de Tassigny, Jean de
Le Lai
Le Van Duyet
Ly Thuong Kiet
Phan Thanh Gian
Sarraut, Albert Pierre
Tran Hung Dao
Tran Thu Do
Truong Minh Giang
Varenne, Alexandre
Veloso, Diogo

d. Malaya and Singapore

Albuquerque, Affonso de
Birch, James W. W.
Clementi, Sir Cecil
Clifford, Sir Hugh
Crawfurd, John
Farquhar, William
Light, Francis
Low, Sir Hugh
Ord, Sir Harry
Raffles, Sir Thomas Stamford
Swettenham, Sir Frank
Templer, Sir Gerald
Weld, Sir Frederick
Yap Ah Loy

e. Dutch East Indies

Bosch, Johannes van den
Coen, Jan Pieterszoon
Daendels, Herman Willem
Speelman, Cornelius Janszoon
Teuku Oemar

f. Philippines

• Spaniards

Anda y Salazar, Simon de
Basco y Vargas, Jose de

Legazpi, Miguel Lopez de
Magellan, Ferdinand

• Americans

Forbes, William Cameron
Harrison, Francis Burton
Taft, William Howard
Wood, Leonard

D. Modern Nationalist and Political Leaders

a. Burma

Aung San
Ba Maw
Ba Pe
Ba Swe
Kyaw Nyein
Ne Win
Nu, U
Ottama
Saw
Saya San
Than Tun, Thakin

b. Thailand

Kaysone Phomvihan
Khuang Aphaiwong
Kukrit Pramoj
Manopakorn Nitithada
Phahon Phonphayuhasena
Phibunsongkhram, Luang
Phot Sarasin
Praphas Charusathian
Pridi Phanomyong
Sarit Thanarat
Seni Pramoj
Soe Thakin
Thanom Kittikachorn
Wichitwathakan, Luang

c. Laos

Boun Oum
Kong Le
Phetsarath
Phoui Sananikone
Phoumi Nosavan
Souphanouvong
Souvannaphouma
Vang Pao

d. Cambodia

Heng Samrin
Khieu Samphan
Lon Nol
Norodom Sihanouk
Pol Pot
Son Ngoc Thanh

B. Political and Military Figures
(*cont.*)

Bani Sadr, Abu al-Hasan
Bazargan, Mehdi
Daud Beureu'eh, Mohammed
Gasprinskii, Ismail
Karmal, Babrak
Khomeini, Ruhollah Musavi
Mossadegh, Mohammed
Muqanna, al-
Nizam al-Mulk
Pahlavi, Ashraf
Qavam, Ahmad
Razmara, Ali
Taraki, Noor Mohammed

C. Religious Figures

Ali al-Rida
Ansari
Bihbahani, Abd Allah

Bihbahani, Muhammad Baqir
Ghazali, al-
Husain ibn Ali
Kartir
Khomeini, Ruhollah Musavi
Majlisi, Muhammad Baqir
Mani
Mazdak
Muhammad
Nuri, Fazl Allah
Tabataba'i, Muhammad
Taleghani, Mahmud
Zoroaster

D. Literary, Artistic, and Intellectual Figures

Bihzad
Biruni, al-
Farabi, al-

Firdausi
Hafiz
Ibn Battuta
Ibn Sina
Jami
Kashgari, Mahmud al-
Kasravi, Ahmad
Khayyam, Omar
Malkom Khan
Neva'i
Nizami
Rudaki
Sa'di
Shari'ati, Ali

E. Westerners

Shuster, William Morgan
Sykes, Sir Percy Molesworth
Wassmuss, Wilhelm

INDEX

A

413

C

E

Q

X

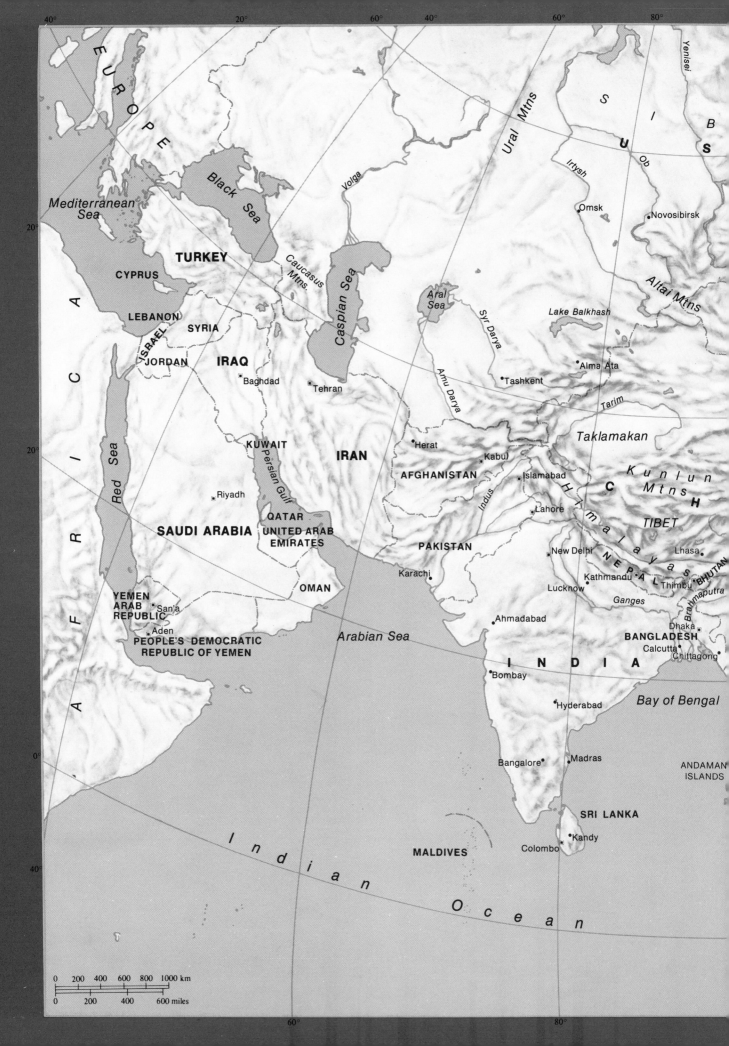